Financial Management
for Decision Makers

Visit the *Financial Management for Decision Makers, fourth edition*, Companion Website at **www.pearsoned.co.uk/atrillmclaney** to find valuable **student** learning material including:

- Multiple choice questions to test your learning
- Learning outcomes for each chapter
- Solutions to end of chapter review questions
- Revision questions to help you check your understanding
- Extensive links to valuable resources on the web
- An online glossary to explain key terms
- Flashcards to test your knowledge of key terms and definitions

4th Edition

Financial Management
for Decision Makers

Peter Atrill

FT Prentice Hall
FINANCIAL TIMES

An imprint of **Pearson Education**
Harlow, England • London • New York • Boston • San Francisco • Toronto
Sydney • Tokyo • Singapore • Hong Kong • Seoul • Taipei • New Delhi
Cape Town • Madrid • Mexico City • Amsterdam • Munich • Paris • Milan

Pearson Education Limited

Edinburgh Gate
Harlow
Essex CM20 2JE
England

and Associated Companies throughout the world

Visit us on the World Wide Web at:
www.pearsoned.co.uk

First published 1997
Second edition published 2000
Third edition published 2003
Fourth edition published 2006

ISBN: 978-0-273-70249-8

British Library Cataloguing-in-Publication Data
A catalogue record for this book is available from the British Library

Library of Congress Cataloging-in-Publication Data
Atrill, Peter.
    Financial management for decision makers / Peter Atrill. – 4th ed.
        p. cm.
    Includes bibliographical references and index.
    ISBN 0-273-70249-1 (pbk.)
    1. Accounting. 2. Decision making. I. Title.
    HF5635.A8846 2005
    658.15–dc22

                                        2005048813

10 9 8 7 6 5 4 3 2
10 09 08 07

Typeset in 9.5/12.5pt Stone Serif by 35
Printed and bound by Graficas Estella, Navarro, Spain

The publisher's policy is to use paper manufactured from sustainable forests.

For Simon and Helen

Contents

Supporting resources

Visit **www.pearsoned.co.uk/atrillmclaney** to find valuable online resources

Companion Website for students
- Multiple choice questions to test your learning
- Learning outcomes for each chapter
- Solutions to end of chapter review questions
- Revision questions to help you check your understanding
- Extensive links to valuable resources on the web
- An online glossary to explain key terms
- Flashcards to test your knowledge of key terms and definitions

For instructors
- Complete, downloadable Instructor's manual
- PowerPoint slides that can be downloaded and used as OHTs
- Progress tests, consisting of various questions and exercise material with solutions
- Tutorial/seminar questions and solutions
- Solutions to individual chapter exercises

Also: The Companion Website provides the following features:

- Search tool to help locate specific items of content
- E-mail results and profile tools to send results of quizzes to instructors
- Online help and support to assist with website usage and troubleshooting

For more information please contact your local Pearson Education sales representative or visit **www.pearsoned.co.uk/atrillmclaney**

Preface

This book has been written for those who wish to achieve a broad understanding of financial management at either undergraduate or postgraduate/post-experience level. It is aimed primarily at students who are not majoring in financial management but who, nevertheless, are studying introductory-level financial management as part of their course in business, management, economics, computing, engineering or some other area. Students who are majoring in financial management should, however, find the book useful as an introduction to the main principles which can serve as a foundation for further study. The book should also be suitable for those who are not following a particular course but nevertheless need an understanding of financial management to help them manage their business.

As there are several excellent books on financial management already in publication, you may wonder why another book is needed in this area. Well, a problem with many books is that they are too detailed and demanding to provide a suitable introduction to the subject. They are often around a thousand pages in length and contain mathematical formulae that many find daunting. This book assumes no previous knowledge of financial management (although a basic understanding of financial statements is required) and is written in an accessible style. Each topic is introduced carefully and there is a gradual building of knowledge. In addition, mathematical formulae have been kept to a minimum.

The book rests on a solid foundation of theory but the main focus throughout is its practical value. It is assumed that readers are primarily concerned with understanding financial management in order to make better financial decisions. The title of the book has been changed for this new edition to reflect this decision-making focus.

The book is written in an 'open learning' style. That is, it tries to involve you in a way not traditionally found in textbooks. Throughout each chapter there are activities and self-assessment questions for you to attempt. The purpose of these is to help check understanding of the points that are being made and to encourage you to think around particular topics. More detail concerning the nature and use of these activities and self-assessment questions is given in the 'How to use this book' section following this preface. The open learning style has been adopted because, I believe, it is more 'user friendly'. Irrespective of whether you are using the book as part of a taught course or for independent study, the interactive approach employed makes it easier for you to learn.

I recognise that most of you will not have studied financial management before and so I have tried to minimise the use of technical jargon. Where technical terminology is unavoidable, I try to provide clear explanations. To help you further, all the key terms are highlighted in the book and then listed at the end of each chapter with a page reference to help you rapidly revise the main concepts. All these key terms are listed alphabetically with a short definition in the glossary, which can be found towards the end of the book.

In writing the fourth edition, I have taken account of helpful comments and suggestions made by lecturers, students and other readers. I have expanded certain parts of the book in order to ensure that key topics, such as financing the business, are given proper coverage. Many areas have been revised to improve the clarity of the writing and I have introduced more diagrams and graphs to aid understanding. The number of real world exhibits has been greatly increased to help illustrate the practical application and importance of the topics discussed. As from January 2005, large businesses in the UK must conform to International Accounting Standards when preparing their financial statements. In this new edition, all the financial statements are based on these standards.

I do hope that you will find the book readable and helpful.

Peter Atrill
2006

Acknowledgements

I would like to thank the Chartered Association of Certified Accountants for permission to include questions from the Certified Diploma in Finance and Accounting at suitable points in the book and for allowing me to use material that I wrote originally for inclusion in the Certified Diploma Magazine.

I also wish to thank my wife Vera Iordanova for helping me to proof-read the draft of the book and for her help in developing the graphs and diagrams.

Publisher's acknowledgements

We are grateful to the following for permission to reproduce copyright material:

Eidos PLC for an extract from their website www.eidos.co.uk; Cadbury Schweppes PLC for an extract from their website www.cadburyschweppes.com; Kingfisher PLC for an extract from their Annual Report 2004; Independent Newspapers for 'Shareholders Take Aim at New Targets in Row Over Directors Pay' by Griffiths and Waugh published in *The Independent*, 21 May 2003; AFX News Limited for 'VW Profit Warning Based on "Worse Case" Scenario of 5.1 Min Unit Sales' published in *AFX Europe (Focus)*, 23 July 2004; Marks and Spencer Group PLC for extracts from their Annual Reports 2003 and 2004; NI Syndication Limited for 'Dirty Laundry: How Companies Fudge the Numbers' published in *The Times, Business*, 22 September 2002 and 'Privatised Stationer "to Float"' published in *The Sunday Times*, 30 June 2002; Blackwell Publishing for 'The Theory Practice Gap in Capital Budgeting: Evidence from the United Kingdom' by Arnold and Hatzopoulos published in *Journal of Business Finance and Accounting*, June/July 2000 and 'How Do CFOs Make Capital Budgeting and Capital Structure Decisions?' by Graham and Harvey published in *The Journal of Applied Corporate Finance* 15, 1, 2002; Hampshire County Council and Portsmouth City Council for extracts from their website www.hants.gov.uk/lrt; VNU Business Publications Limited for an extract from 'Generating Cash Bonds' published in *Accountancy Age*, 17 July 2003; The McGraw Hill Companies for an adapted extract from *Corporate Finance: A Valuation Approach* by Benninga and Sarig; 3i Group PLC for an extract from 3i Venturespeak Glossary of Words and Phrases published at www.3i.com/pdfs/venturespeak.pdf; Tesco Stores Limited for extracts from Tesco PLC Annual Report and Financial Statements 2003; Scottish and Newcastle PLC for extracts from their Annual Report 2003; Guardian Newspapers Limited for 'Irate City Puts PRU Chief Under Pressure: Investors seek explanation for confused signals about dividend policy' published in *The Guardian*, 26 February 2003, © Guardian Newspapers Limited 2003; Cronor Group Limited for an adapted extract from *Accountancy*, April 2000; Hanson PLC for an extract from Hanson PLC Annual Report 2004; Solo Syndication for 'UK's Biggest Merger Generates £100 Million in Advisors' Fees' published in *The Evening Standard*, 26 November 2002; and Mr Warren Buffett for an extract from his 'Letter to Shareholders 1981' published at www.berkshirehathaway.com

We are grateful to the Financial Times Limited for permission to reprint the following material:

Real World 1.2 'Profit without honour', © *Financial Times*, 29/30 June 2002; Real World 1.4 'Ethics', © *Financial Times*, 3 April 2003; Real World 2.1 'Nokia raises sales and profits forecast', © *Financial Times*, 10 September 2004; Real World 3.2 'Sony sets more steps to raise profit margins', FT.com, © *Financial Times*, 6 October 2003; Real World 3.3 'Shell disposals of $4 billion double initial estimate', FT.com, © *Financial Times*, 23 December 2003; Real World 3.4 'Small companies surprise on lending', © *Financial Times*, 25 April 2003; Real World 3.5 'Extracts from FT', © *Financial Times*, 12 October 2004; Real World 4.8 'Satellites need space to earn', FT.com, © *Financial Times*, 14 July 2003; Real World 6.1 'Bulmer warns of breach of covenants', © *Financial Times*, 25 January 2003; Real World 6.2 'New appetite develops for Eurobonds', © *Financial Times*, 18 September 2004; Real World 6.5 'S&P cuts British Airways to "junk" status', FT.com, © *Financial Times*, 1 July 2003; Real World 6.6 'EDS warns of a dividend cut', © *Financial Times*, 11 May 2004; Real World 6.11 'Travelodge to raise £400m via sale and leaseback plan', © *Financial Times*, 12 July 2004; Real World 6.12 'M&B prices largest UK pub securitisation', © *Financial Times*, 7 November 2003; Real World 7.3 'Benfield earmarks almost ten per cent for fees in £100m flotation', © *Financial Times*, 9 June 2003; Real World 7.4 'Climbing aboard the flight from flotation', © *Financial Times*, 6 September 2003; Real World 7.6 'New issues but old problems', © *Financial Times*, 8 August 2003; Real World 7.8 'It does not always pay to follow the stars', © *Financial Times*, 15 May 2004; Real World 7.9 'Laura Ashley to close 35 European stores', FT.com, © *Financial Times*, 23 January 2003; Real World 7.10 'FT Money – Markets week world: Clinton Cards', FT.com, © *Financial Times*, 4 October 2003; Real World 7.11 'Tesco raises £810m in placing as sales rise', © *Financial Times*, 13 January 2004; Real World 7.14 'Survey highlights UK private equity growth', © *Financial Times*, 1 November 2004; Real World 7.17 'Aim markets its appeal around the world', FT.com, © *Financial Times*, 5 October 2004; Real World 8.7 'Water companies' plans threatened by investor reluctance', © *Financial Times*, 7 April 2003; Real World 8.9 'Gearing levels fall amid fears over risks', FT.com, © *Financial Times*, 30 April 2005; Real World 9.3, Figure 9.1, Compiled from data in FT, © *Financial Times*, 2/3 October 2004; Real World 9.5 'Samsung and the joys of middle age: sharing out the cash', FT.com, © *Financial Times*, 27 September 2004; Real World 9.8 'Microsoft $32bn special dividend smashes corporate pay-out records', © *Financial Times*, 21 July 2004; Real World 10.2 'Pallets lost at Brambles', © *Financial Times*, 27 November 2002; Real World 10.3 'Lex Column', © *Financial Times*, 19 February 2003; Real World 10.4 'Small stores keep up with the big boys', FT.com, © *Financial Times*, 5 February 2003; Real World 10.9 'K-Mart's fall is tale of poor governance', © *Financial Times*, 29 January 2003; Real World 11.1 'VW to alter management focus', FT.com, © *Financial Times*, 1 September 2003; Real World 12.2 'Technology key to Abbey takeover', © *Financial Times*, 26 July 2004; Real World 12.4 'The myth of the mega-bank: after the failures of diversification, wary lenders scale back their global ambitions', © *Financial Times*, 6 January 2004; Real World 12.8, Extract from table concerning takeover bids and mergers, FT Money Section, © *Financial Times*, 15/16 January 2005; Real World 12.9 'Safeway directors' £5.5m compensation', © *Financial Times*, 10 June 2003; Real World 12.13 'Toys Я Us mulls spin-off of baby unit', © *Financial Times*, 12 August 2004; Real World 12.14 'Trying to put a price on a promise', © *Financial Times*, 9 March 2004; Figures 3.3 and 3.4, Constructed from data from the FT, © *Financial Times*, 2/3 October 2004.

We are grateful to the following for permission to use copyright material:

Real World 1.1 'Assessing the Rate of Return' from *Financial Times Mastering Management Series*, 1995, Supplement No. 1, © Elroy Dimson.

How to use this book

The contents of the book have been ordered in what I believe is a logical sequence and, for this reason, I suggest that you work through the book in the order in which it is presented. Every effort has been made to ensure that earlier chapters do not refer to concepts or terms that are not explained until a later chapter. If you work through the chapters in the 'wrong' order, you will probably encounter concepts and points that were explained previously but which you have missed.

Irrespective of whether you are using the book as part of a lecture/tutorial-based course or as the basis for a more independent form of study, I recommend you follow broadly the same approach.

Integrated assessment material

Interspersed throughout each chapter are numerous **Activities**. You are strongly advised to attempt all these questions. They are designed to stimulate the sort of 'quick-fire' questions that a good lecturer might throw at you during a lecture or tutorial. Activities seek to serve two purposes:

- To give you the opportunity to check that you understand what has been covered so far.
- To encourage you to think about the topic just covered, either to see a link between that topic and others with which you are already familiar, or to link the topic just covered to the next.

The answer to each Activity is provided immediately after the question. This answer should be covered up until you have deduced your solution, which can then be compared to the one given.

Towards the end of most chapters, there is a **Self-assessment question**. This is rather more demanding and comprehensive than any of the Activities and is designed to give you an opportunity to see whether you understand the core material in the chapter. The solution to each of the Self-assessment questions is provided at the end of the book. As with the Activities, it is very important that you attempt each question thoroughly before referring to the solution. If you have difficulty with a Self-assessment question, you should go over the relevant chapter again.

End-of-chapter assessment material

At the end of each chapter, there are four **Review questions**. These are short questions requiring a narrative answer or discussion within a tutorial group. They are intended to enable you to assess how well you can recall and critically evaluate the core terms and concepts covered in each chapter. Suggested answers to these questions are included at the end of the book. Again, a real attempt should be made to answer these questions before referring to the solutions.

At the end of a chapter, there are normally seven **Exercises**. (However, Chapter 1 has none, Chapter 9 has six, Chapter 10 has seven and Chapter 11 has five.) These are mostly computational and are designed to reinforce your knowledge and understanding. Exercises are of varying complexity, with the more advanced ones clearly identified. Although the less advanced Exercises are fairly straightforward, the more advanced ones can be quite demanding. Nevertheless, they are capable of being successfully completed if you have worked conscientiously through the chapter and have attempted the less advanced Exercises beforehand.

Answers to those Exercises marked with a coloured number are provided at the end of the book. Three out of the seven Exercises normally found in a chapter are marked with a coloured number to enable you to check progress. The marked Exercises will be a mixture of less advanced and more advanced Exercises. Solutions to the Exercises that are not marked with a coloured number are given in a separate lecturer's Solutions Manual. Yet again, a thorough attempt should be made to answer these Exercises before referring to the solutions.

Guided tour of the book

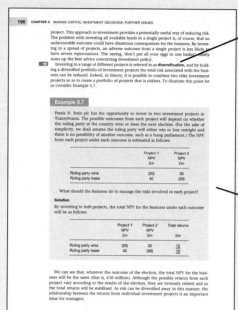

Key terms The key concepts and techniques in each chapter are highlighted in colour where they are first introduced, with an adjacent icon in the margin to help you refer back to the most important points.

Examples At frequent intervals, throughout most chapters, there are numerical examples that give you step-by-step workings to follow through to the solution.

Learning outcomes Bullet points at the start of each chapter show what you can expect to learn from that chapter, and highlight the core coverage.

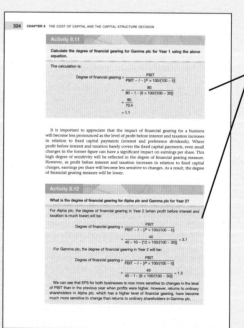

Activities These short questions, integrated throughout each chapter, allow you to check your understanding as you progress through the text. They comprise either a narrative question requiring you to review or critically consider topics, or a numerical problem requiring you to deduce a solution. A suggested answer is given immediately after each activity.

'Real World' illustrations Integrated throughout the text, these illustrative examples highlight the practical application of accounting concepts and techniques by real businesses, including extracts from company reports and financial statements, survey data and other interesting insights from business.

Self-assessment questions   Towards the end of most chapters you will encounter one of these questions, allowing you to attempt a comprehensive question before tackling the end-of-chapter assessment material. To check your understanding and progress, solutions are provided in Appendix C.

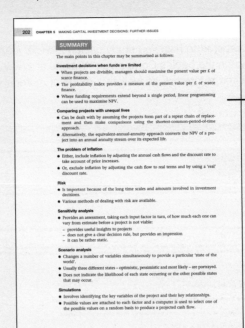

Bullet point chapter summary   Each chapter ends with a 'bullet point' summary. This highlights the material covered in the chapter and can be used as a quick reminder of the main issues.

Key terms summary   At the end of each chapter, there is a listing (with page reference) of all the key terms, allowing you to easily refer back to the most important points.

Review questions
These short questions encourage you to review and/or critically discuss your understanding of the main topics covered in each chapter, either individually or in a group. Solutions to these questions can be found on the Companion Website at **www.pearsoned.co.uk/ atrillmclaney**

Further reading   This section comprises a listing of relevant chapters in other textbooks that you might refer to in order to pursue a topic in more depth or gain an alternative perspective.

References   Provides full details of sources of information referred to in the chapter.

Exercises   These comprehensive questions appear at the end of most chapters. The more advanced questions are separately identified. Solutions to some of the questions (those with coloured numbers) are provided in Appendix D, enabling you to assess your progress. Solutions to the remaining questions are available for lecturers only. Additional exercises can be found on the Companion Website at **www.pearsoned.co.uk/atrillmclaney**

Guided tour of the Companion Website

Extra material has been prepared to help you study using *Financial Management for Decision Makers*. This material can be found on the book's Companion Website at **www.pearsoned.co.uk/atrillmclaney**. You will find links to websites of interest, as well as a range of material including:

Interactive quizzes

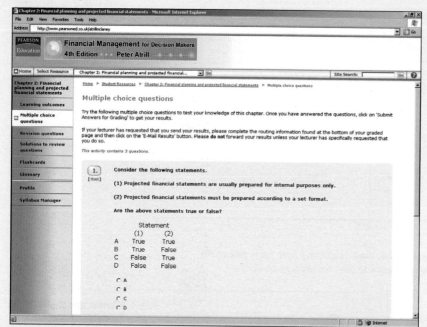

For each chapter there is a set of interactive multiple choice questions, plus a set of fill-in-the blanks questions and an extra exercise. Test your learning and get automatic grading on your answers.

Revision questions

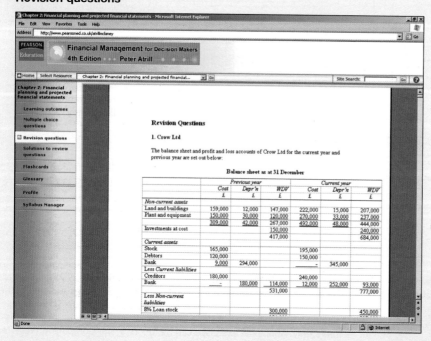

Sets of questions covering the whole book are designed to help you check your overall learning whilst you are revising.

Solutions to review questions

Answers to end-of-chapter review questions that appear in the book are to be found on the website, so you can check your progress.

Glossary and flashcards

Full version of the book's glossary to help you check definitions while you are online. Flashcards help you to learn and test yourself on definitions of key terms. A term is displayed on each card: 'flip over' for the definition, 'shuffle' the cards to randomly test your knowledge.

1

Introduction to financial management

LEARNING OUTCOMES

When you have completed this chapter, you should be able to:

● Discuss the role of the finance function within a business.

● Identify and discuss possible objectives for a business.

● Explain why the wealth maximisation objective is considered to be the primary objective of a business.

● Explain the agency problem faced by owners of a business and discuss how this problem may be either prevented or minimised.

INTRODUCTION

We begin this chapter by considering the role of the finance function within a business. The tasks of the finance function are identified and their relation to the tasks of managers is discussed. We then go on to consider the objectives that a business may have. Modern financial management theory assumes that the primary objective of a business is to maximise the wealth of the owners (shareholders). We examine this and other possible objectives for a business and discuss reasons why the wealth maximisation objective is considered to be the most appropriate. Finally, we consider the potential conflict between the interests of managers and the shareholders that they represent. The source of this conflict is examined and ways in which it may be minimised are discussed.

The role of the finance function

Put simply, the finance function within a business exists to help managers to manage. To understand how the finance function can do this, we must first be clear about what managers do. One way of describing the role of managers is to classify their activities into the following categories:

● *Strategic management.*   This refers to their role in developing overall objectives for the business and then formulating long-term plans to achieve those objectives. When formulating long-term plans, possible courses of action (strategies) must be identified and evaluated. A particular course of action will then be chosen from the options available according to which has the greatest potential for achieving the objectives specified.
● *Operations management.*   This refers to the day-to-day decision making and control that managers undertake. Managers must ensure that events conform to the plans that have been made and take appropriate actions to see that this occurs.
● *Risk management.*   This refers to the way in which risks faced by the business are controlled or managed. Risks may arise from the nature of the business operations and/or the way in which the business is financed.

As we can see from Figure 1.1, these three categories do not represent separate and distinct areas. They are interrelated and overlaps arise between each category. When considering a particular strategy, for example, managers must also make a careful assessment of the risks involved and how these risks may be managed. Similarly, when making operational decisions, managers must try to ensure they fit within the strategic plans that have been formulated.

Figure 1.1	**The role of managers**

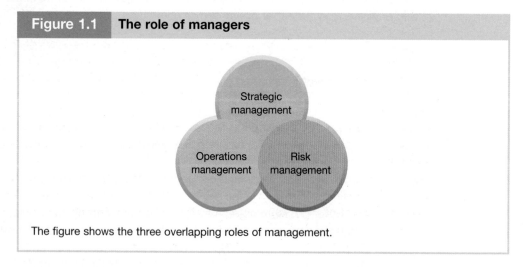

The figure shows the three overlapping roles of management.

The finance function is concerned with helping managers in each of the three areas identified. The key tasks undertaken by the finance function are set out in Figure 1.2 and described below.

● *Financial planning.*   The likely effect of proposals on the financial performance and position of the business is a vitally important input to the overall planning process. By developing projected financial statements (such as cash flow statements and profit statements), as well as other financial estimates, the viability of proposed courses of action can be evaluated.

Figure 1.2	The tasks of the finance function

The figure shows the four main tasks of the finance function and their key relationships.

- *Investment project appraisal.* Assessing the profitability and riskiness of proposed investment projects is another important input to the overall planning process. By appraising projects in this way, managers can make more informed decisions concerning either their acceptance or rejection, or their prioritisation.
- *Financing decisions.* Future strategies and investment projects have to be financed. It is important, therefore, to be able to identify and assess possible sources of finance available. When choosing among different financing options, consideration must be given to the overall financial structure of the business. This involves achieving the appropriate balance between long-term and short-term finance and between the financing contribution of shareholders and that of lenders. Not all financing requirements are derived from external sources: some funds may be internally generated. An important source of internally generated funds is profits, and the extent to which the business reinvests profits rather than distributing them in the form of dividend is another important issue.
- *Capital market operations.* The business may try to raise funds from the capital markets and so finance staff should understand how these markets work. There must be an appreciation of how finance can be raised through the markets, how securities (shares and loan capital) are priced and how the markets are likely to react to proposed investment and financing plans.
- *Financial control.* Once plans are put into action, managers must ensure that things stay on course. Finance staff can provide information on matters such as the profitability of investment projects, levels of working capital and cash flows, which can be relayed to managers as a basis for evaluating performance and, where necessary, taking corrective action.

The links between the tasks of managers and the tasks of the finance function are many and varied. Strategic management decisions, for example, may require an input from the finance function on issues relating to financial planning, investment project appraisal, financing and capital market operations. Operations management may require an input on issues relating to financial planning, investment project appraisal, financing and financial control. Risk management may require an input from the finance function on issues relating to all of the tasks identified above.

Structure and organisation of the book

In this book, each of the tasks of the finance function described above are considered. We begin, in Chapter 2, by examining the way in which financial plans are prepared and the role of projected financial statements in helping managers to assess likely future outcomes.

In Chapter 3 we go on to consider how financial statements can be analysed and interpreted. The financial techniques examined in this chapter are important both for the evaluation of projected financial statements and for other areas such as financing decisions and the control of working capital, which are discussed later in the book.

Chapters 4 and 5 are concerned with investment decision making. In these two chapters we look at the various methods that can be used to assess investment proposals, the way in which investment projects are monitored and how we can deal with the problem of risk when evaluating investment proposals.

Chapters 6 to 9 are concerned with various aspects of the financing decision. First we consider the various sources of finance available and then go on to consider the role and efficiency of capital markets. We then examine the issues surrounding the appropriate mix of finance that a business should have within its capital structure. Finally, we consider the dividend decision and the factors that must be taken into account when deciding between the retention and distribution of profits.

In Chapter 10, we look at the ways in which the managers can exert financial control over the working capital of the business. We examine each element of working capital (stocks, debtors, cash and creditors) and discuss various techniques of control that are available.

In Chapter 11, we examine methods for measuring and managing shareholder wealth. We shall evaluate their effectiveness and explore their links to the strategic objectives and plans of the business.

Finally, in Chapter 12, we look at mergers and takeovers. When examining this area we draw on our understanding of a number of topics that were covered earlier, particularly those relating to investment appraisal, financing and capital market operations. We consider the effect of mergers on shareholder wealth and the ways in which merger proposals may be evaluated. We also discuss the ways in which shares may be valued for mergers or for other purposes.

The essential features of financial management

In the early years of its development, financial management was really an offshoot of accounting. Much of the early work was descriptive, and arguments were based on casual observation rather than any clear theoretical framework. However, over the years, financial management has been increasingly influenced by economic theories and the reasoning applied to particular issues has become more rigorous and analytical. Indeed, such is the influence of economic theory that modern financial management is often viewed as a branch of applied economics.

Economic theories concerning the efficient allocation of scarce resources have been taken and developed into decision making tools for management. This development of economic theories for practical business use has usually involved taking account of both the time dimension and the risks associated with management decision making. An investment decision, for example, must look at both the time period over which the investment extends and the degree of risk associated with the investment. This fact has led to financial management being described as the *economics of time and risk*. Certainly time and risk will be recurring themes throughout this text.

 Economic theories have also helped us to understand the importance of **capital markets**, such as stock markets and banks, to a business. Capital markets have a vital role to play in bringing together borrowers and lenders, in allowing investors to select the type of investment that best meets their risk requirements and in helping to evaluate the performance of businesses through the prices assigned to their shares.

Real World 1.1 is an extract from an article by Professor Dimson of London Business School. It neatly sums up the essence of modern financial management.

REAL WORLD 1.1

Finance on the back of a postage stamp   FT

The leading textbooks in finance are nearly 1,000 pages long. Many students learn by making notes on each topic. They then summarise their notes. Here is one student's summary of his Finance course . . . Time is money . . . Don't put all your eggs in one basket . . . You can't fool all the people all of the time.

● The idea that time is money refers to the fact that a sum of money received now is worth more than the same sum paid in the future. This gives rise to the principle that future cash flows should be discounted, in order to calculate their present value.
● You can reduce the risk of an investment if you don't put all your eggs in one basket. In other words, a diversified portfolio of investments is less risky than putting all your money in a single asset. Risks that cannot be diversified away should be accepted only if they are offset by a higher expected return.
● The idea that you can't fool all of the people all of the time refers to the efficiency of financial markets. An efficient market is one in which information is widely and cheaply available to everyone and relevant information is therefore incorporated into security prices. Because new information is reflected in prices immediately, investors should expect to receive only a normal rate of return. Possession of information about a company will not enable an investor to outperform. The only way to expect a higher expected return is to be exposed to greater risk.

These three themes of discounted cash flow, risk and diversification, and market efficiency lie at the very heart of most introductory finance courses.

Each of these themes will be considered in this book.

Source: Assessing the Rate of Return, E. Dimson, Financial Times Mastering Management Series, supplement issue, no. 1, 1995, p. 13.

The objectives of a business

A key idea underpinning modern financial management is that the primary objective
 of a business is **shareholder wealth maximisation**. In a market economy, the shareholders will provide funds to a business in the expectation that they will receive the

maximum possible increase in wealth for the level of risk that must be faced. When we use the term 'wealth' in this context, we are referring to the *market value of the ordinary shares*. The market value of the shares will, in turn, reflect the future returns the shareholders will expect to receive *over time* from the shares and the level of risk involved. Note that we are concerned not with maximising shareholders' returns over the short term, but rather with providing the highest possible returns over the long term.

Wealth maximisation or profit maximisation?

Wealth maximisation is not the only financial objective that a business can pursue. Profit maximisation is often suggested as an alternative objective for a business. Profit maximisation is different from wealth maximisation in a number of important respects, as we shall see. However, before we consider these differences, we must first decide what we mean by the term 'profit'.

There are various measures of profit that could be maximised, including the following:

- operating profit (that is, net profit before interest and taxation)
- net profit before tax
- net profit after tax
- net profit available to ordinary shareholders
- net profit per ordinary share, and so on.

These different possible measures of profit may pose problems as the evaluation of a particular opportunity can vary according to the choice of profit measure used. This point is illustrated in Activity 1.1 below.

Activity 1.1

Pointon Ltd has the following long-term capital and annual profits:

Capital invested (£1 ordinary shares)	£100,000
Net profits after tax	£ 15,000

It is considering the issue of 20,000 new £1 ordinary shares and investing the amount raised in an opportunity that provides a profit after tax of £2,000.
What should the managers do if the objective of the business is:

(a) To maximise total profits available to ordinary shareholders?
(b) To maximise profit per ordinary share?

Although the total profits available to ordinary shareholders will be increased by the investment, the profit per share will be decreased. (The current rate of return per share is 15 per cent (£15,000/£100,000) whereas the expected rate of return on the investment is 10 per cent (£2,000/£20,000).) An objective of maximising net profit available to shareholders would therefore lead to a decision to invest, whereas an objective of maximising net profit per ordinary share would lead to a decision to reject the opportunity.

Profit maximisation is usually seen as a short-term objective whereas wealth maximisation is a long-term objective. There can be a conflict between short-term and long-term performance. It would be quite possible, for example, to maximise short-term profits at the expense of long-term profits.

Activity 1.2

How might the managers of a business increase short-term profits at the expense of long-term profits?

The managers may reduce operating expenses by:

- cutting research and development expenditure
- cutting staff training and development
- buying lower quality materials
- cutting quality control mechanisms.

These policies may all have a beneficial effect on short-term profits but may undermine the long-term competitiveness and performance of a business.

In recent years, many businesses have been criticised for failing to consider the long-term implications of their policies on the wealth of the owners. **Real World 1.2** gives some examples of how an emphasis of short-term profits can have a damaging effect.

REAL WORLD 1.2

Short-term gains, long-term problems   **FT**

John Kay argues that some businesses have achieved growth in short-term increases in profits by sacrificing their longer-term prosperity. He points out that:

> The business of Marks and Spencer, the retailer, was unparalleled in reputation but mature. To achieve earnings growth consistent with a glamour rating the company squeezed suppliers, gave less value for money, spent less on stores. In 1998, it achieved the highest (profit) margin in sales in the history of the business. It had also compromised its position to the point where sales and profits plummeted.
>
> Banks and insurance companies have taken staff out of branches and retrained those that remain as sales people. The pharmaceuticals industry has taken advantage of mergers to consolidate its research and development facilities. Energy companies have cut back on exploration.
>
> We know that these actions increased corporate earnings. We do not know what effect they have on the long-run strength of the business – and this is the key point – do the companies themselves know? Some rationalisations will genuinely lead to more productive businesses. Other companies will suffer the fate of Marks and Spencer.

Source: 'Profit without honour', John Kay, *Financial Times*, Weekend section, 29–30 June 2002.

A final problem with the use of profit maximisation as an objective is that it fails to take account of risk. As we discuss in some detail later, the higher the level of risk, the higher the expected return required by investors for a particular investment. This means that, logically, a profit maximisation policy should lead managers to invest in high-risk projects. Such a policy, however, may not reflect the needs of the shareholders. When considering an investment, shareholders are concerned with both *risk* and the *long-run returns* that they expect to receive. Only a wealth maximisation objective takes both of these factors into account. Managers who pursue this objective will choose investments that provide the highest returns in relation to the risks involved.

To maximise or to satisfy?

Even if we reject the use of profit and accept shareholder wealth as an appropriate financial objective, we may still question whether the *maximisation* of shareholder wealth is appropriate. Accepting this objective implies that the needs of the shareholders are paramount. Shareholders are not the only ones, however, that have a financial interest in a business. A business can be viewed as a coalition of various interest groups, with each group having a 'stake' in the business.

Activity 1.3

What other 'stakeholder' groups may have a financial interest in a business?

The following groups may be seen as stakeholders:

- shareholders
- employees
- managers
- suppliers
- customers
- the community.

This is not an exhaustive list. You may have thought of others.

If we take a broader view of the business, shareholders simply become one of a number of stakeholder groups whose needs have to be satisfied. It can be argued that, instead of seeking to maximise the returns to shareholders, the managers should try to provide each stakeholder group with a *satisfactory return*. The term **satisficing** has been used to describe this particular business objective. Although this objective may sound appealing, there are practical problems associated with its use.

Within a market economy there are strong competitive forces at work that ensure that failure to maximise shareholder wealth will not be tolerated for long. Competition for the funds provided by shareholders and competition for managers' jobs should ensure that the interests of the shareholders prevail. If the managers of a business do not provide the expected increase in shareholder wealth, the shareholders have the power to replace the existing management team with a new team that is more responsive to shareholder needs. Alternatively, the shareholders may decide to sell their shares in the business (and reinvest in other businesses that provide better returns in relation to the risks involved). The sale of shares in the business is likely to depress the market price of the shares, which management will have to rectify in order to avoid the risk of takeover. This can only be done by pursuing policies that are consistent with the needs of shareholders.

Do the above arguments mean that the interests of shareholders are all that managers must consider and that the interests of other stakeholders are irrelevant? The answer is almost certainly no. Satisfying the needs of the other stakeholder groups will often be consistent with the need to maximise shareholder wealth. A dissatisfied workforce, for example, may result in low productivity, strikes and so forth, which will in turn have an adverse effect on the shareholders' investment in the business. This kind of interdependence has led to the argument that the needs of other stakeholder groups must be viewed as constraints within which shareholder wealth should be maximised.

Viewing the needs of the other stakeholders as constraints that must be satisfied is a rather neat way of reconciling the shareholder wealth maximisation objective with the interests of other stakeholders. It assumes, however, that a business should *maximise* the wealth of shareholders but provide only a *satisfactory return* to other stakeholders. Whether or not this assumption is considered valid will involve a value judgement being made. It is important to recognise, however, the implications of ignoring the needs of shareholders in a competitive market economy. It is likely that all other stakeholder groups will suffer if the share price performance of the business falls below the expectations of the shareholders.

A final argument made in support of the wealth maximisation objective is that, even if we accept the view that wealth maximisation is not necessarily appropriate, the models that are based on this objective may still be useful for management decision making. By employing these models, managers can identify the most appropriate course of action from the shareholders' viewpoint and can see the costs borne by shareholders if a different (that is, non-wealth maximising) course of action is decided upon. The managers would then have to account to shareholders for their decision.

Wealth maximisation and mission statements

A business will often express its ultimate purpose in the form of a **mission statement**. These statements are widely published and frequently adorn the annual reports and websites of businesses. Mission statements are usually concise and try to convey the essence of the business. Real World 1.3 provides examples of businesses that proclaim a commitment to maximising shareholder wealth in their mission statement.

REAL WORLD 1.3

On a mission   FT

The mission statement of Dana Petroleum plc states:

> Dana Petroleum plc is a leading British independent oil company, committed to maximising shareholder value through the creation and execution of high impact opportunities.

Source: www.dana-petroleum.com

Another business, United Drug plc, states:

> Our mission is to be a leading healthcare services provider, dedicated to maximising shareholder value.

Source: Annual Report 2002.

Wealth maximisation and ethical behaviour

The importance of maximising shareholder wealth has been given added impetus in recent years. One of the effects of the global deregulation of markets and of technological change has been to provide investors with greater opportunities to increase their returns. They are now able to move their funds around the world with comparative ease. This has increased competition among businesses for investment funds and has put managers under greater pressure to produce returns that are attractive in international, rather than merely national, terms.

Given these pressures, there is a risk that shareholder wealth maximisation may be pursued by managers using methods that are not acceptable to the community. Examples may include paying bribes to government officials to secure contracts, employing child labour in developing countries to minimise production costs, polluting the environment to avoid the cost of emission controls, and so on. Some managers may feel such behaviour is acceptable because 'all is fair in business'. However, Professor Rose argues that the responsibility 'to maximise the wealth of shareholders does not mean that managers are being asked to act in a manner which absolves them from the considerations of morality and simple decency that they would readily acknowledge in other walks of life' (see reference 2 at the end of the chapter).

Thus, when considering a particular course of action, managers should ask themselves whether it conforms to accepted moral standards, whether it treats people unfairly and whether it has the potential for harm. It can be argued that wealth maximisation and ethical behaviour need not conflict; indeed, high ethical standards may be a necessary condition for wealth maximisation. A business that treats customers, suppliers and employees fairly and with integrity is more likely to flourish over the longer term. Some support for this view is set out in **Real World 1.4**.

REAL WORLD 1.4

Profiting from ethics   **FT**

The following article appeared in the *Financial Times*.

'Blessed are the ethical companies for their shareholders shall inherit the earth.' This sort of argument – that ethical companies are likely to outperform less morally aware ones – has long been popular among advocates of socially responsible investing. But until now, the statistical evidence to support their arguments has not been easy to come by.

Today the Institute of Business Ethics publishes a survey suggesting there is a link. It compared a group of companies in the FTSE 250 index over a period of four years, divided into those that had codes of ethics for five years or more and those that explicitly said they did not.

It found that on three measures – economic value added, market value added and stability of price/earnings ratios – the ethical companies outperformed, though on a fourth measure – return on capital employed – the figures were more mixed.*

Some caveats are perhaps in order. The time period for the study is not that long. And taking the existence of ethical codes as a proxy for ethical behaviour could be stretching reality. After all, even Enron had a code of ethical behaviour.

So while indicative, this is not likely to be the last word. As the study admits, it is not clear why an ethical stance should mean better results. Maybe it is simply that good managers, who produce good results, tend to view ethical codes as part of good business.

* Each of these measure is discussed later in the book.
Source: 'Ethics', Martin Dickson, *Financial Times*, 3 April 2003.

Businesses often proclaim their commitment to high standards of ethics and social responsibility in their dealings and develop appropriate policies to guide managers and employees in carrying out their work. **Real World 1.5** provides an example of one such business and offers an insight to the sort of policies that may be adopted.

REAL WORLD 1.5

Playing the game

Eidos plc is one of the world's leading developers and publishers of entertainment, with a portfolio of game titles for PC, PlayStation, GameCube, Xbox and N-Gage. Its website sets out in some detail, the business's attitude to ethical standards and social responsibility. An extract from this website is set out below:

> Eidos has a strong commitment to its customers, shareholders, employees and, in a wider context, to local communities and the environment generally. We recognise that in today's business world, corporate social responsibility (CSR) and the maximisation of long-term shareholder value are not incompatible but increasingly interdependent. Accordingly, and in taking ultimate responsibility for enhancing its good corporate citizenship status with all stakeholders, Eidos is committed to developing and implementing CSR policies and best conduct practices which are targeted at:
>
> ● complying with local laws and regulations;
> ● providing safe and healthy working conditions;
> ● promoting equality, fairness and ethical behaviour;
> ● maintaining corporate integrity and reputation;
> ● caring for the environment and participating in the community; and
> ● requiring similar commitments from third parties.
>
> *Source*: www.eidos.co.uk

Ethics and the finance function

Integrity and ethical behaviour are particularly important within the finance function where many opportunities for sharp practice exist. Although there may be rules in place to try to prevent such practice, these will only provide a partial answer. The finance staff themselves must appreciate the importance of fair play in building long-term relationships for the benefit of all those connected with the business. It is, perhaps, not surprising that a survey of senior finance officers of large UK businesses revealed that they regarded integrity as the most valued attribute of finance staff, as Figure 1.3 shows.

To demonstrate their commitment to integrity and ethical behaviour, some businesses provide a code of standards for their finance staff. **Real World 1.6** provides an example of one such code.

REAL WORLD 1.6

Cadbury's ethical code

Cadbury Schweppes plc, the confectionery and soft drinks business, has a code of ethics for its senior financial officers and its chief executive officer. The key elements of this code are that these individuals should:

● act with honesty and integrity, including the ethical handling of actual or apparent conflicts of interest between personal and professional relationships;
● comply, and cause the business to comply, with all governmental laws, rules and regulations;

→

Real World 1.6 continued

- report any matter that may affect the disclosure of full, fair, timely, accurate and under-standable disclosure that the business communicates to the public or publicly files;
- report any violation of the code which has either occurred or could be expected to occur.

Source: www.cadburyschweppes.com

| Figure 1.3 | **Key attributes of finance staff** |

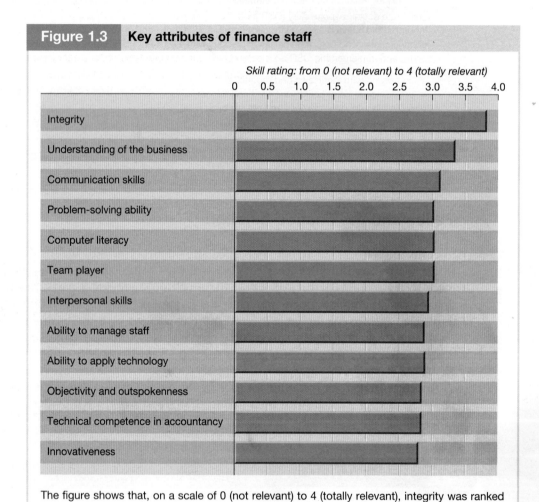

The figure shows that, on a scale of 0 (not relevant) to 4 (totally relevant), integrity was ranked highest of the key attributes by senior finance staff.

Source: Adapted from Phillips and Ross (1996), p. 31 (see reference 3 at the end of the chapter). Reprinted with the kind permission of Elsevier/CIMA.

Corporate governance and the agency problem

In recent years, the issue of **corporate governance** has generated much debate. The term is used to describe the ways in which companies are directed and controlled. The issue of corporate governance is important because, in companies of any size, those who own the company (that is, the shareholders) are usually divorced from the day-to-day control of the business. The shareholders employ professional managers (known as directors) to manage the company for them. These directors may, therefore, be viewed as *agents* of the shareholders (who are the *principals*).

Given this agent–principal relationship, it may seem reasonable to assume that the best interests of shareholders will guide the directors' decisions. However, in practice this does not always occur. The directors may be more concerned with pursuing their own interests, such as increasing their pay and perks (such as expensive cars, overseas visits and so on) and improving their job security and status. As a result, a conflict can occur between the interests of shareholders and the interests of directors.

It can be argued that in a competitive market economy, this **agency problem**, as it is termed, should not persist over time. The competition for the funds provided by shareholders and competition for directors' jobs referred to earlier, should ensure that the interests of the shareholders will prevail. However, if competitive forces are weak, or if information concerning the directors' activities is not available to shareholders, the risk of agency problems will be increased. Shareholders must be alert to such risks and should take steps to ensure that the directors operate the business in a manner that is consistent with shareholder needs.

Activity 1.4

What kinds of actions might be taken to ensure the directors act in accordance with the shareholders' interests?

Two types of action are employed in practice:

- The shareholders may insist on monitoring closely the actions of the directors and the way in which the resources of the business are used.
- The shareholders may introduce incentive plans for directors that link their remuneration to the share performance of the business. In this way, the interests of directors and shareholders will become more closely aligned.

Whilst both types of action identified in Activity 1.4 are widely used, they do not provide a perfect solution. The first option is fine in theory, but can be both difficult to implement and costly. Many businesses are now extremely large and their shareholders, who may individually own only a very small proportion of the shares of the business, may find it difficult to act collectively with other shareholders. However, if they try to monitor manager behaviour on an individual basis, the costs will be high in relation to the benefits. In such a situation, doing nothing may be a better option for a shareholder.

The second option available to shareholders (that is, incentive plans) can also be difficult to implement and costly. A common form of incentive plan is to give managers **share options**. These options give managers the right, but not the obligation, to purchase shares in the business at an agreed price at some future date. If the current market value exceeds the agreed price at that due date, the managers will make a gain by taking up the options.

Activity 1.5

What problems may arise with this form of management incentive? Are share prices influenced solely by managers' actions?

Movements in the price of the shares of the business may be influenced by a variety of factors such as interest rates, inflation and taxation policy, over which the managers have no control. These factors can, however, have a significant effect on the rewards that managers receive where share options are used.

Corporate governance and economic performance

Where directors pursue their own interests at the expense of the shareholders, it is clearly a problem for the shareholders. However, it may also be a problem for society as a whole. If shareholders feel their funds are likely to be mismanaged, they will be reluctant to invest. A shortage of funds will mean fewer investments can be made and the costs of funds will increase as businesses compete for what funds are available. Thus, a lack of concern for shareholders can have a profound effect on the performance of the economy. To avoid these problems, most competitive market economies have a framework of rules to help monitor and control the behaviour of directors.

These rules are usually based around three guiding principles:

- *Disclosure.* This lies at the heart of good corporate governance. An OECD report (see reference 4 at the end of the chapter for details) summed up the benefits of disclosure as follows:

  > Adequate and timely information about corporate performance enables investors to make informed buy-and-sell decisions and thereby helps the market reflect the value of a corporation under present management. If the market determines that present management is not performing, a decrease in stock (share) price will sanction management's failure and open the way to management change.

- *Accountability.* This involves defining the roles and duties of the directors and establishing an adequate monitoring process. In the UK, company law requires that directors of a business act in the best interests of shareholders. This means, among other things, that they must not try to use their position and knowledge to make gains at the expense of the shareholders. The law also requires larger businesses to have their annual financial statements independently audited. The purpose of an independent audit is to lend credibility to the financial statements prepared by the directors.

- *Fairness.*   Directors should not be able to benefit from access to 'inside' information that is not available to shareholders. As a result, both the law and the London Stock Exchange place restrictions on the ability of directors to deal in the shares of the business. One example of these restrictions is that the directors cannot buy or sell shares immediately before the announcement of the final results of the business for a year or before the announcement of a significant event such as a planned merger or the loss of the chief executive.

Strengthening the framework of rules

The number of rules designed to safeguard shareholders has increased considerably over the years. This has been in response to weaknesses in corporate governance procedures, which have been exposed through well-publicised business failures and frauds, excessive pay increases to directors and evidence that some financial reports were being 'massaged' so as to mislead shareholders.

The codes of practice

During the 1990s there was a real effort by the accountancy profession and the London Stock Exchange to address the problems mentioned above. A code of Best Practice on Corporate Governance emerged in 1992. This was concerned with accountability and financial reporting. In 1995, a separate code of practice emerged. This dealt with directors pay and conditions. These two codes were revised, 'fine tuned' and amalgamated to produce the **Combined Code**, which was issued in 1998.

The Combined Code was revised in 2003, following the recommendations of the Higgs Report. These recommendations were mainly concerned with the roles of the company chairman (senior director) and the other directors. They were particularly concerned with the role of 'non-executive' directors. These are directors who do not work full time in the company, but act solely in the role of director. This contrasts with 'executive' directors who are salaried employees. For example, the finance director of most large companies is a full-time employee. This person is a member of the board of directors and, as such, takes part in the decision making at board level. At the same time, he or she is responsible for managing the departments of the company that act on those board decisions as far as finance is concerned.

The view reflected in the 2003 Combined Code is that executive directors can become too embroiled in the day-to-day management of the company to be able to take the broad view. It also reflects the view that, for executive directors, conflicts can arise between their own interests and those of the shareholders. The advantage of non-executive directors can be that they are much more independent of the company than their executive colleagues. Non-executive directors are remunerated by the company for their work, but this would normally form only a small proportion of their total income. This gives them an independence that the executive directors may not have. Non-executive directors are often senior managers in other businesses or people who have had good experience of such roles.

The Combined Code embodies the ideas of fairness, disclosure and accountability that were discussed earlier. It also aims to ensure that the power and responsibilities of directors are clearly delineated and that appropriate checks and balances are in place. **Real World 1.7** outlines some of the more important elements of the Code.

REAL WORLD 1.7

The Combined Code

Some of the key elements of the Combined Code are as follows:

- Every listed company should have a board of directors to lead and control the company.
- There should be a clear division of responsibilities between the chairman and the chief executive officer of the company to ensure that a single person does not have un-bridled power.
- There should be a balance between executive and non-executive (who are often part-time and independent) members of the board, to ensure that small groups of individuals cannot dominate proceedings.
- The board should receive timely information that is of sufficient quality to enable them to carry out their duties.
- Appointments to the board should be the subject of rigorous, formal and transparent procedures. All directors should submit themselves for re-election by the shareholders within a maximum period of three years.
- Boards should use the annual general meeting to communicate with private investors and to encourage their participation.
- The board should publish a balanced and understandable assessment of the company's position and performance.
- Internal controls should be in place to protect the shareholders' wealth.
- The board should set up an audit committee of non-executive directors to oversee the internal controls and financial reporting principles that are being applied, and to liaise with the external auditors.

Both the 1998 and 2003 Combined Codes received the backing of the London Stock Exchange. This means that companies listed on the London Stock Exchange are expected to comply with the requirements of the Code or must give their shareholders good reason why they do not. Failure to do one or other of these can lead to the company's shares being suspended from the listing. This is an important sanction against non-compliant directors.

Strengthening the framework of rules has improved the quality of information available to shareholders, resulted in better checks on the powers of directors and provided greater transparency in corporate affairs. However, rules can only be a partial answer. A balance must be struck between the need to protect shareholders and the need to encourage the entrepreneurial spirit of directors – which could be stifled under a welter of rules. This implies that rules should not be too tight, and so unscrupulous directors may still find ways around them.

Real World 1.8 shows an extract from the statement on corporate governance made by the directors of Kingfisher plc, the retail business that owns B&Q and Comet, in the UK, and a number of other chains in various European countries, particularly in France. Note how much emphasis is placed on the distinction between executive and non-executive directors in the membership of the various committees. The committees operated by Kingfisher are broadly as recommended by the Combined Code. The last committee mentioned by Kingfisher, the Share Option Committee, arises because many senior managers and directors are awarded bonuses in the form of share options. This is an area where directors of some companies have been criticised for being over-generous to themselves.

REAL WORLD 1.8

Corporate governance at Kingfisher

The following extract from the 2004 annual report of Kingfisher plc starts with a general statement that the directors have complied with the Combined Code during the year in question. It then goes on to detail how they complied in the specific context of board meetings and the establishment of committees to deal with sensitive issues.

Corporate governance – Combined Code statement

Kingfisher recognises the importance of, and is committed to, high standards of corporate governance. During the year to 31 January 2004, it complied with the requirements of the Combined Code as it then applied, including the reduction in the notice period for directors' service contracts to 12 months for all directors from August 2003.

The principles of good governance adopted by Kingfisher have been applied in the following way:

Board of directors

Kingfisher's Board currently comprises the Chairman, the Deputy Chairman, five other non-executive directors, the Chief Executive and three other executive directors.

Their biographies and details of Committee memberships . . . illustrate the directors' range of experience, which is intended to ensure an effective Board to lead and control the Group. Non-executive directors are appointed for an initial term of three years. The company has identified a Senior Independent Director, namely John Nelson, the Deputy Chairman. Each director receives appropriate training.

The Board has adopted a schedule of matters reserved for its decision and is collectively responsible for the strategic direction of the Group. All directors are provided with, and have full and timely access to, information that enables them to make informed decisions on corporate and business issues discussed. The Board has completed a further independent review of its performance by the Institute of Chartered Secretaries and Administrators. These reviews examine the operation of the Board in practice, including its corporate governance and the operation and content of its meetings.

During the year to 31 January 2004, the Board met 11 times to deal with regular business and a further 14 times principally to approve periodic trading statements or in connection with the demerger . . . The Board has a schedule of matters reserved for itself, which has been reviewed and updated during the year. In addition, the Board has established the following six standing committees with defined terms of reference: . . .

Audit Committee – comprises Phil Bentley (Chairman), plus two other independent non-executive directors and the Chairman of the Board. This committee provides an independent oversight of the effectiveness of the Group's internal control systems and financial reporting processes. It receives and considers reports from both the internal and external auditors and approves the annual report and financial statements and the half-year results announcement. The Committee and the Board reviewed membership against the Combined Code as it will apply for the financial year ending 29 January 2005 (the 'new Combined Code') and concluded that it was essential for proper control and in the interests of the shareholders for the Chairman (non-executive) of the Board to be a member of the Committee. Each major operating business has its own audit committee, meetings of which are attended by both Kingfisher's Director of Risk and Audit and the external auditors.

Nomination Committee – comprises Sir Francis Mackay (Chairman), plus two independent non-executive directors and the Chief Executive. The committee considers and recommends appointments of new directors as and when necessary.

Remuneration Committee – comprises John Nelson (Chairman), plus two other independent non-executive directors and the Chairman of the Board. The committee advises the Board on the Company's executive remuneration policy and its costs, and is responsible for its application. The Board and the Committee considered the question of the Company Chairman's membership of the Committee and concluded that it is in the shareholders' best interests that, as a Non-Executive

---

Real World 1.8 continued

Chairman and with three independent Non-Executive directors as members, it remained appropriate for him to be a member. The Chairman will not be present when his own remuneration will be discussed . . .

Social Responsibility Committee – comprises Margaret Salmon (Chairman), plus the Chief Executive, two other executive directors and representatives of the operating companies. This Committee is responsible for discussing and developing a general policy relating to environmental, community and equal opportunities matters. The Board director with overall responsibility for environmental matters is the Chief Executive.

The Finance Committee – comprises the Chairman of the Board, the Chief Executive, the Group Finance Director and any one other director. The Committee is responsible for the treasury operations of the Group, the approval and authorisation of financing documents and signature authorities on bank accounts within its terms of reference and the authority limits laid down by the Board. It reviews borrowing arrangements and other financial transactions, and makes appropriate recommendations. It also allots new shares in the Company to Group employees following the exercise of share options.

The Share Option Committee comprises any two directors or any one director and the Company Secretary. Its role is to consider the Group's share funding policy in respect of share incentive awards and to decide upon the level of contributions of ESOP and QUEST in respect of the dilution cost when new shares are issued. This Committee also considers the making of loans to the ESOP in respect of grants that are hedged with existing shares. It has no authority in respect of the making of awards which is a matter reserved to the Remuneration Committee.

The rise of shareholder activism

Although a framework of rules is important to good corporate governance, it is equally important for shareholders to play their part by actively monitoring and controlling the behaviour of directors. In the past, shareholders have been criticised for being too passive and for allowing the directors too much independence; however, there is evidence that shareholders are beginning to play a more active role. This has coincided with the growing power of financial institutions, such as insurance businesses, pension funds, investment trusts and banks. These institutions now own, or manage on behalf of individual shareholders, the majority of shares listed on the London Stock Exchange.

Financial institutions are often committed to the long-term success of the businesses in which they invest, even though this may not be through choice. This is because selling the shares of a poorly managed business may not always be a realistic option. There are at least two reasons for this. First, where the financial institution invests on behalf of individuals, such as an investment trust, there may be an obligation to 'track' a stock market index by investing in the businesses that go to make up the index. In such a situation, it may not be possible to sell the shares of a particular business without deviating from the index. Second, the number of shares that a financial institution holds in a particular business can be very large indeed and it may not be possible to sell such a large investment in the business without incurring heavy losses. In both cases, therefore, it may be better to try to influence the actions and decisions of managers by exercising (or threatening to exercise) the voting rights attached to the shares rather than selling the shares.

While financial institutions may intervene publicly to curb blatant mismanagement or excesses, they often exert their power in less public, more subtle, ways. For example, they may improve corporate governance procedures within a business by ensuring that non-executive directors are appointed who can be relied upon to ensure that necessary changes are made (see reference 5 at the end of the chapter).

A particularly rich source of contention between shareholders and directors concerns directors' remuneration. In recent years there have been some very public spats over one particular aspect of directors' remuneration: compensation payments available to directors who lose their jobs. **Real World 1.9** mentions the problems experienced by some well-known businesses over this issue.

REAL WORLD 1.9

Shareholders take aim at new targets in row over directors' pay

HSBC, ICI and Tesco are the next of Britain's biggest companies to face a showdown with shareholders in the controversy over payments for failure in boardrooms.

The companies are bracing themselves for revolts at their annual meetings after investors in GlaxoSmithKline voted down a pay packet for its chief executive on Monday which could have seen him walk away with up to £22m if sacked from the drugs giant.

At HSBC, William Aldinger, head of its newly acquired US business, is in line for £24m over three years. He would receive a substantial proportion of the cash even if he were fired. He has access to the company's jet for his private use and is entitled to private health care for him and his wife for life, courtesy of HSBC.

The outcry at lavish rewards for directors and so-called golden goodbyes has been fuelled this year by the Government's decision to change company law to allow shareholders to participate in an advisory vote on directors' pay.

Patricia Hewitt, the Trade and Industry Secretary, has praised Glaxo shareholders for taking action against the remuneration of Jean-Pierre Garnier. Ms Hewitt said yesterday that it was not the job of politicians to set corporate pay levels and responsibility lay primarily with boards and shareholders . . .

'We have no problem with big rewards for big success but I do have an issue with rewards for failure,' she said. 'When directors walk away from failing companies with huge pay-offs it's bad for shareholders, bad for employees, and bad for the UK corporate governance image.'

Shareholders in HSBC have been urged to reject its pay report at its meeting a week on Friday, while ICI is set for a rough ride tomorrow over a pay-off for its ousted chief, Brendan O'Neill. Sir Terry Leahy, chief executive of Tesco, is heading for a bruising encounter at the shareholder meeting in June.

Source: Katherine Griffiths and Paul Waugh, *The Independent*, 21 May 2003.

SUMMARY

The main points in this chapter may be summarised as follows:

The finance function

- Helps managers in carrying out their tasks of strategic management, operations management and risk management.
- Helps managers in each of these tasks through financial planning, investment appraisal, financing decisions, capital market operations and financial control.

Modern finance

- Is influenced by economic theory.
- Has been described as the economics of time and risk.

Shareholder wealth maximisation

- Is assumed to be the primary objective of a business.
- Is a long-term rather than a short-term objective.
- Takes account of both risk and the long-run returns that investors expect to receive.
- Must take account of the needs of other stakeholders.
- Is often proclaimed in the mission statements of businesses.

Ethical behaviour

- Need not conflict with the maximisation of shareholder wealth objective.
- May be set out in policies and codes.
- Is particularly important in the finance function.

Agency problems

- May exist between shareholders and managers.
- May be overcome or minimised by monitoring the activities of directors and/or aligning directors' interests to those of shareholders.
- Have led to rules, set out in the Combined Code, to help monitor and control the behaviour of directors.

Shareholder activism

- Has coincided with the growing importance of financial institutions as investors in the London Stock Exchange.
- Has provided some curb on directors' excesses.

 Key terms

Capital markets p. 5	**Corporate governance** p. 13
Shareholder wealth maximisation p. 5	**Agency problem** p. 13
Satisficing p. 8	**Share options** p. 14
Mission statement p. 9	**Combined Code** p. 15

For definitions of these terms see the Glossary, pp. 562–571.

Further reading

If you wish to explore the topics discussed in this chapter in more depth, try the following books:

Boards at Work, *Stiles, P. and Taylor, B.*, Oxford University Press, 2001, chapter 1.

Corporate Finance and Investment, *Pike, R. and Neale, B.*, 4th edn, Financial Times Prentice Hall, 2003, chapters 1 and 2.

Corporate Financial Management, *Arnold, G.*, 2nd edn, Financial Times Prentice Hall, 2002, chapter 1.

Corporate Governance, *Monks, R. and Minnow, N.*, 2nd edn, Blackwell, 2001, chapters 1–3.

Reading the *Financial Times* and *Investors' Chronicle* on a regular basis can help to keep up to date on financial management topics.

References

1 **Assessing the Rate of Return**, *Dimson, E.*, Financial Times Mastering Management Series, supplement issue no. 1, 1995, p. 13.

2 **Tasks of the Finance Function**, *Rose, H.*, Financial Times Mastering Management Series, supplement issue no. 1, 1995, p. 11.

3 'The future structure of the finance function, 2', *Phillips, G. and Ross, J.*, **Management Accounting**, September 1996, p. 31.

4 **Corporate Governance: Improving competitiveness and access to capital in global markets**, OECD Report by Business Sector Advisory Group on Corporate Governance, Organisation for Economic Co-operation and Development, 1998.

5 **Boards at Work**, *Stiles, P. and Taylor, B.*, Oxford University Press, 2001, p. 7.

REVIEW QUESTIONS

Answers to these questions can be found in Appendix D at the back of the book.

1.1 What are the main functions of the finance department within a business?

1.2 Why is the maximisation of wealth viewed as superior to profit maximisation as a business objective?

1.3 Some managers, if asked what the main objective of their business is, may simply state 'To survive!' What do you think of this as a primary objective?

1.4 Some businesses try to overcome the agency problem referred to in the chapter by using an incentive scheme that is based on the growth of profits over a period. What are the drawbacks of this type of scheme?

2

Financial planning and projected financial statements

LEARNING OUTCOMES

When you have completed this chapter, you should be able to:

- Explain the role of projected financial statements in the planning process.

- Prepare projected financial statements for a business and explain their usefulness for decision-making purposes.

- Discuss the strengths and weaknesses of the per-cent-of-sales method as an alternative method of preparing forecast financial statements.

- Explain the ways in which projected financial statements may take into account the problems of risk and uncertainty.

INTRODUCTION

In this chapter, we take a look at projected financial statements. These statements play an important role in the planning process and, in particular, in assessing the impact of management decisions on the performance and position of a business. We shall see how these statements are prepared and what issues are involved in their preparation.

This chapter and the following one assume that you have some understanding of three major financial statements: the cash flow statement, the profit and loss account and the balance sheet. If you need to brush up on these statements, please take a look at Chapters 1–5 of *Financial Accounting for Decision Makers* by Atrill and McLaney (4th edn, Financial Times Prentice Hall, 2005).

Planning for the future

It is vitally important that a business develops plans for the future. Whatever a business is trying to achieve, it is unlikely to be successful unless its managers have clear in their minds what the future direction of the business is going to be. Finance lies at the very heart of the planning process. A business has limited financial resources – which must be used carefully and in a way that enhances shareholder wealth. It is, therefore, important to evaluate the financial implications of pursuing each proposed course of action. In this section we briefly examine the planning process within a business and then, in later sections, go on to consider the ways in which those plans are expressed in financial terms.

Developing plans for a business involves the following key steps:

1 *Setting the aims and objectives of the business.*   The starting point in the planning process is to establish the aims and objectives of the business. These will set out what the business is basically trying to achieve and should provide a clear sense of direction.
2 *Identifying the options available.*   To achieve the aims and objectives set for the business, a number of possible options (strategies) may be available to the business. These options must be identified and this will involve collecting information, which can be extremely time consuming, particularly when the business is considering entering new markets or investing in new technology.
3 *Evaluating the options and making a selection.*   When deciding on the most appropriate option(s) to choose, there must be an examination of each option to see whether it fits with the objectives that have been set and to assess whether it is feasible to provide the resources required. The effect of pursuing each option on the future financial performance and position of the business must also be considered. It is in this final part – the financial evaluation of the various options – that projected financial statements have a valuable role to play.

Figure 2.1 sets out this process diagrammatically.

Figure 2.1	Steps in the planning process

The figure shows that there are three main steps in the planning process as described in the chapter.

The role of projected financial statements

Projected financial statements reveal the predicted financial outcomes of pursuing a particular course of action. By showing the financial implications of certain decisions, managers should be able to allocate resources in a more efficient and effective manner. The projected financial statements will normally comprise:

● a projected profit and loss account (income statement)
● a projected balance sheet
● a projected cash flow statement.

When taken together, these will provide a comprehensive picture of likely future performance and position.

Where there are competing options, projected statements can be prepared for each of the options being considered. They will reveal the impact of each option on the future profitability, liquidity and financial position of the business so that comparisons can be made. Where managers are considering only one course of action, projected financial statements can still be extremely useful. The preparation of projected statements will provide a valuable insight to the effect of the particular course of action on the future financial performance and position of the business. Where, for example, a business is considering a move to increase market share, managers will need to know the likely effect on profits and whether the resources are adequate to sustain the planned growth in sales.

When managers are developing plans for the future, a forecast horizon of three to five years is typically employed and projected financial statements for each year of the forecast period can be prepared for each option being considered. When we examine the preparation of these statements later in the chapter, however, we shall deal with a shorter time period for the sake of simplicity. The main principles of preparation are not affected by the particular forecast horizon.

Projected financial statements are prepared for management purposes and only on rare occasions, such as seeking new finance, will external parties see these statements. The reasons for keeping the statements within the business are often that publication may damage the competitive position of the business or that they may be misunderstood by investors. Some large businesses, however, do publish key figures based on projections that have been made. These figures are usually forecast sales and profit figures for the forthcoming three, six or twelve months. **Real World 2.1** discusses the sales and profit forecast figures for a major mobile phone operator.

REAL WORLD 2.1

Nokia raises sales and profits forecasts   **FT**

Nokia, the world's largest supplier of mobile phones, raised its third quarter sales and profit forecasts yesterday as the company benefited from 'prudent cost control' and a buoyant global handset market.

The Finnish group, which has issued a series of profit warnings this year, also said it was winning back market share helped by price cuts and the success of new products.

The upbeat statement follows comments last week by Gartner, the research group, which said the overall global handset market could exceed 650m units this year, up from 520m in 2003.

Overall demand was now so strong that Nokia indicated there was an 'industry-wide tightness in some components'.

The announcement caught investors by surprise and Nokia's shares jumped 9 per cent in Helsinki, before falling back to close about 6 per cent higher at €11.15. Shares in Motorola, the world's second largest supplier, rose 3 per cent to $15.54 in early New York trading.

Real World 2.1 continued

Nokia said that after looking at its performance in July and August, it now expected earnings a share in the three months to September 30 to be €0.11–€0.13, compared with the previous guidance range of €0.08–€0.10.

Sales are expected to reach €6.8bn–€6.9bn ($8.3bn–$8.4bn) compared with previous guidance of €6.6bn–€6.8bn.

The company said the handset market 'continued its strong volume growth in the third quarter, and Nokia expects healthy sequential volume growth in its mobile device sales . . . The company has been able to deliver mobile devices in higher volumes.'

In the first six months of 2004, weakness in Nokia's product line – most notably a lack of clamshell models and mid-market camera phones – allowed rivals such as Samsung, Motorola and SonyEricsson to close the gap on the Finnish group.

Nokia's market share fell from 38 per cent in 2003 to 31 per cent in the second quarter, and many analysts believe it is now below 30 per cent.

Rick Simonson, chief financial officer, said he expected 'market share to be up sequentially due to some uptick in Europe, the Middle East and Africa' but the company did face 'some challenges in North America'.

He said the group had launched 23 models so far in 2004, in line with plans to launch 35 models during the full year.

Analysts said Nokia had been able to use its size to take advantage of the economies of scale the higher volumes offered.

Source: 'Nokia raises sales and profits forecasts', *Financial Times*, 10 September 2004.

Preparing projected financial statements

In the sections that follow, we look at some of the issues involved in developing projected financial statements. As the main purpose of this chapter is to discuss the preparation of projected statements and their usefulness, we shall deal fairly briefly with the forecasting issues.

Preparing projected financial statements involves four major steps, which are as follows.

Step 1: Identify the factors that provide a framework for the projected statements

These factors can be divided into two broad categories: external and internal. Factors from the external environment are considered first.

External factors

Changes in government policy and in key economic factors can have a significant effect on future performance and position. In particular, expected changes to the following must be identified:

● the rate of corporation tax
● interest rates for borrowings
● the rate of inflation.

There is usually a great deal of published information available to help identify expected changes. Care must be taken, however, to ensure that the particular impact on the business of any changes is properly taken into account. When estimating the likely rate of inflation, for example, each major category of item affected by inflation should be considered separately. Using an average rate of inflation for all items is usually inappropriate as levels of inflation can vary significantly between items.

Internal factors

Internal factors cover policies and agreements to which the business is committed. Examples include:

- capital expenditure commitments
- financing agreements
- stockholding policies
- credit period allowed to customers
- creditor payment policies
- accounting policies (for example, depreciation rates and methods)
- dividend policy.

The last item listed may require some clarification. For large businesses at least, a target level of dividends is often established and managers are usually reluctant to deviate from this target. The target may be linked to the level of profits for the particular year and/or to dividends paid in previous years. (This issue is discussed in more detail in Chapter 9.)

Step 2: Forecast the sales for the period

Once the framework has been assembled, it is possible to begin the process of forecasting the particular elements that go to make up the projected financial statements. We have to make a start somewhere and the usual starting point is to forecast sales for the period. Sales are regarded as a key element within the financial statements because the level of sales will normally determine the level of operating activity for the period. This means that other elements of the financial statements, such as materials, stocks debtors and so on are influenced by the level of sales.

Producing a reliable sales forecast involves an understanding of the likely competitive environment and deciding upon a particular approach to forecasting. Each of these is considered below.

The competitive environment

To understand the likely competitive environment, there must be an appreciation of general economic conditions, the industry within which the business operates and the potential threat posed by major competitors.

General economic conditions   Most businesses are affected by economic cycles. During an upturn in a cycle, sales and profits will increase and businesses will increase their scale of operations. During a downturn in a cycle, the reverse will happen. Sales and profits will decrease and businesses will decrease their scale of operations. The particular phase of the economic cycle can, therefore, exert a significant influence on sales.

The industry   A careful examination of industry factors that can influence sales should be carried out. These factors include:

- market size and growth prospects
- level of competition within the industry
- bargaining power of customers
- threat of substitute products or services.

Competitor analysis An appreciation of the threat posed by major competitors can be achieved through **competitor profiling**. This involves developing a profile of each major competitor by gathering information about its:

- goals and strategies
- resources, including financial, technological and human resources
- products and/or services being developed
- alliances and joint ventures with other businesses that affect market power
- cost structures, profits and sales.

This information can help assess the capacity of a major competitor to upset sales plans and initiatives.

Competitor information is not always easy to obtain as businesses are reluctant to release information that may damage their competitive position. Nevertheless, there are sources of information that can be used to help build a picture of competitors, such as their published accounts (which are obligatory for limited companies) press reports, industry reports, physical observation, information gathered from customers and suppliers and so on.

Forecasting approaches

Once an understanding of the competitive environment is gained, an approach to forecasting sales must be selected. Two main approaches can be found in practice: the subjective approach and the objective approach.

Subjective approach This approach normally relies on the views of the salesforce or sales managers. It is a 'bottom-up' approach which involves aggregating forecasts from those with specialist knowledge of particular products, services or market segments. It is often useful for fairly short forecasting horizons; however, care must be taken to ensure that there is no bias, particularly towards optimism, in the forecasts developed.

Objective approach This approach relies on statistical techniques or, in the case of very large businesses, such as multinational motor-car manufacturers, econometric models. These techniques and models can range from simple extrapolation of past trends to extremely sophisticated models which incorporate a large number of variables with complex interrelationships.

There are no hard and fast rules concerning the most appropriate approach to use. Each business must assess the benefits of the various approaches in terms of reliability, and then weigh these benefits against the associated costs. It may be useful to use more than one approach. By using sales managers' forecasts and statistical analysis a cross-check on the accuracy of the forecast figures may be achieved.

The sales forecast, however derived, may be modified if senior managers believe that proper account has not been taken of the competitive environment.

Step 3: Forecast remaining elements of financial statements

Having forecast the level of sales, all items appearing in the cash flow statement, profit and loss account and balance sheet will then be forecast.

Forecasting operating costs

Let us begin by considering how operating costs can be forecast. It was mentioned earlier that the level of sales will have an influence on many other items in the financial statements, including certain costs. However, not all costs relating to a business will vary with the level of sales. Although some costs vary in direct proportion to the level of sales, other costs are unaffected by the level of sales during a period.

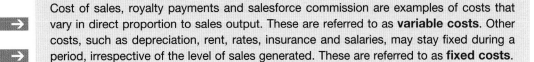

Activity 2.1

Try to identify two costs that are likely to vary in direct proportion to the level of sales and two costs that are likely to stay constant irrespective of the level of sales.

Cost of sales, royalty payments and salesforce commission are examples of costs that vary in direct proportion to sales output. These are referred to as **variable costs**. Other costs, such as depreciation, rent, rates, insurance and salaries, may stay fixed during a period, irrespective of the level of sales generated. These are referred to as **fixed costs**.

Some costs have both a variable and a fixed element and so may vary partially with sales output. These are referred to as **semi-variable** (or semi-fixed) **costs**. These costs may be identified by examining past records of the business. Heat and light costs may be an example of a semi-variable cost. A certain amount of heating and lighting will be incurred irrespective of the level of sales. If, however, overtime is being worked due to heavy demand, this cost will increase. Semi-variable costs can be broken down into their fixed and variable elements (perhaps using a statistical technique such as regression analysis). Once this has been done, the total variable costs and total fixed costs can be established. By splitting costs into their fixed and variable elements it is possible to forecast the likely impact of a particular level of sales output much more reliably.

As the total costs of a business have both a variable and a fixed element, they will rise directly, but not proportionately, with the level of output. The behaviour of total costs in relation to the level of activity is shown in Figure 2.2.

Figure 2.2   Graph of total cost against the level of activity

The bottom part of the graph represents the fixed cost element. To this is added the wedge-shaped top portion, which represents the variable costs. The two parts together represent total costs. At zero level of output, the variable costs are zero so total costs equal fixed costs. As activity increases so do the total costs, but only because variable costs increase.

The forecast of sales and operating costs along with forecasts of corporation tax rates, interest rates and dividend policy, will provide the basis for preparing the forecast profit and loss account for the period.

Forecasting assets, liabilities and capital

The level of sales will have an effect on the level of certain assets and liabilities held. When sales increase, there will be a 'spontaneous' increase in some items.

Activity 2.2

Can you think of two items (either assets or liabilities) that will increase 'spontaneously' as a result of an increase in the level of sales?

An increase in the level of sales is likely to lead to:

● an increase in trade debtors, and
● an increase in stock to meet the increase in demand.

An increase in the level of sales should also lead to:

● an increase in trade creditors as a result of increased purchases, and
● an increase in accrued expenses as a result of increased overhead costs.

The particular policies adopted by the business (for example, to offer customers a one-month credit period or to hold stock equivalent to two months' sales) can help determine the amounts of 'spontaneous' assets and liabilities held at the end of the forecast period. These amounts are needed to prepare the forecast balance sheet.

An increase in sales may also lead to an increase in non-current (fixed) assets if they are already being operated at full capacity. If this is not the case, an increase in sales may simply absorb excess capacity. A temporary decrease in sales will probably have no effect on the level of non-current assets.

Loan capital and share capital will not increase spontaneously with increases in sales. The amount of long-term finance invested at the beginning of the period, which can be gleaned from the opening balance sheet, will remain unchanged unless management decides otherwise. Retained profits will change as a result of any profits (losses) for the period. This item, therefore, has an indirect relationship to sales.

Forecasting cash flow items

Once the sales, costs and changes to the assets and liabilities have been forecast, all the information needed to forecast the cash flow items for the period is available. It is a relatively simple matter to identify cash received from customers, payments to suppliers, payments for operating costs and the cash flow effects of changes in assets and liabilities.

Example 2.1 below provides a simple example of how this may be done. The amount of cash that is forecast to be received from customers is calculated to illustrate the process.

Example 2.1

Assume that:

1 The opening balance of debtors (receivables) is £200,000 (representing the previous month's sales).
2 Sales for the month are forecast to be £300,000, of which 80 per cent are on credit.
3 The business allows one month's credit to its credit customers.

What is the cash received from sales during the month?

Solution

The cash received from customers during the month will be:

	£
Opening debtors	200,000
Sales for the month	300,000
Total amount due	500,000
Less Closing debtors (80% × £300,000)	240,000
Cash received from customers	260,000

A broadly similar approach can be taken for other cash flow items mentioned.

Step 4: Prepare the projected financial statements

Having prepared forecasts for the various elements of the financial statements, the final step is to include them in the projected financial statements. The way in which we prepare these statements will be considered in some detail in the following section.

Figure 2.3 illustrates the steps in the planning process just described.

Figure 2.3   Steps in preparing projected financial statements

Step 1   Identify factors that provide a framework for the projected statements

Step 2   Prepare sales forecasts

Step 3   Prepare forecasts for remaining elements of financial statements

Step 4   Prepare projected financial statements

The figure sets out the steps that must be taken to prepare financial statements that have been described in the chapter.

Preparing the projected statements: a worked example

Having discussed the issues surrounding the development of appropriate forecasts, we can now turn our attention to the preparation of the projected financial statements. It was mentioned earlier that these are:

- the projected cash flow statement
- the projected profit and loss account (income statement)
- the projected balance sheet.

If you already have some background in accounting, the following sections should pose few problems. This is because the methods and principles employed for projected financial statements are the same as those employed for historic financial statements. The only real difference lies in the fact that the statements are prepared using *forecast* information rather than *actual* information.

To illustrate the preparation of projected financial statements let us consider the following example.

Example 2.2

Designer Dresses Limited is a small business to be formed by James and William Clark to sell an exclusive range of dresses from a boutique in a fashionable suburb of London. On 1 January, they plan to invest £50,000 cash to acquire 25,000 £1 shares each in the business. Of this, £30,000 is to be invested in new fittings in January. These fittings are to be depreciated over three years on the straight-line basis (their scrap value is assumed to be zero at the end of their lives). The straight-line basis of depreciation allocates the total amount to be depreciated evenly over the life of the asset. In this case, a half-year's depreciation is to be charged in the first six months. The sales and purchases projections for the business are as follows:

	Jan	Feb	Mar	Apr	May	June	Total
Sales (£000)	10.2	30.6	30.6	40.8	40.8	51.0	204.0
Purchases (£000)	20.0	30.0	25.0	25.0	30.0	30.0	160.0
Other costs* (£000)	9.0	9.0	9.0	9.0	9.0	9.0	54.0

* 'Other costs' includes wages but excludes depreciation.

The sales will all be made by credit card. The credit card business will take one month to pay and will deduct its fee of 2 per cent of gross sales before paying amounts due to Designer Dresses. One month's credit is allowed by suppliers. Other costs shown above do not include rent and rates of £10,000 per quarter, payable on 1 January and 1 April. All other costs will be paid in cash. Closing stock at the end of June is expected to be £58,000.

You should ignore taxation. For your convenience you are advised to work to the nearest £000.

Required:
(a) Prepare a cash flow projection for the six months to 30 June.
(b) Prepare a projected profit and loss account for the same period.
(c) Prepare a projected balance sheet at 30 June.

(Note that, for the sake of simplicity, the example considers only one course of action and all the forecast figures are provided for use in preparing the projected financial statements. This should help in getting to grips with the main principles of preparation.)

Projected cash flow statement

A projected cash flow statement is useful because it helps to identify changes in the liquidity of a business over time. Cash has been described as the 'life-blood' of a business. It is vital for a business to have sufficient liquid resources to meet its maturing obligations. Failure to maintain an adequate level of liquidity can have disastrous consequences for the business. The projected cash flow statement helps to assess the impact of expected future events on the cash balance. It will identify periods where there are cash surpluses and cash deficits and will allow managers to plan for these occurrences. Where there is a cash surplus, managers should consider the profitable investment of the cash. Where there is a cash deficit, managers should consider the ways in which this can be financed.

The cash flow statement is fairly easy to prepare. It simply records the cash inflows and outflows of the business. The main sources of cash inflows and outflows are set out in Figure 2.4.

When preparing the cash flow statement for a fairly short period, such as six months, it is often useful to provide a monthly breakdown of the cash inflows and outflows. This helps managers to monitor closely changes in the cash position of the

Figure 2.4   The main sources of cash inflows and outflows

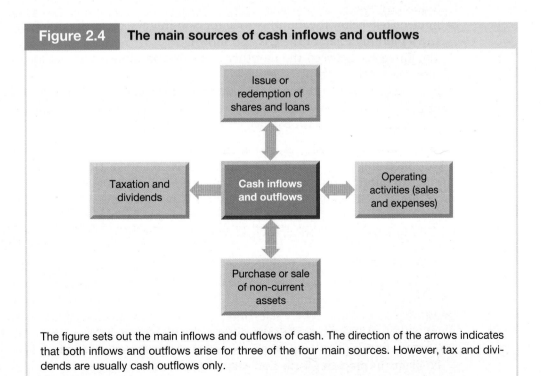

The figure sets out the main inflows and outflows of cash. The direction of the arrows indicates that both inflows and outflows arise for three of the four main sources. However, tax and dividends are usually cash outflows only.

business. The further the business projects its cash flow statements into the future, however, the more difficult it becomes to provide a monthly breakdown.

There is no set format for the projected cash flow statement as it is normally used for internal purposes only. Managers are free to decide on the form of presentation that best suits their needs. Set out below is an outline projected cash flow statement for Designer Dresses Ltd for the six months to 30 June. This format seems to be widely used and is as good as any format proposed. It is recommended, therefore, that this format be used when preparing projected cash flow statements.

	Jan £000	Feb £000	Mar £000	Apr £000	May £000	June £000
Cash inflows						
Issue of shares						
Credit sales						
	____	____	____	____	____	____
	____	____	____	____	____	____
Cash outflows						
Credit purchases						
Other costs						
Rent and rates						
	____	____	____	____	____	____
	____	____	____	____	____	____
Net cash flow						
Opening balance	____	____	____	____	____	____
Closing balance	____	____	____	____	____	____

We can see from this outline that:

● Each column represents a monthly period.
● At the top of each column the cash inflows are set out and a total for each month's inflows is shown.
● Immediately below the monthly total for cash inflows, the cash outflows are set out and a monthly total for these is also shown.
● The difference between the monthly totals of cash inflows and outflows is the *net cash flow* for the month.
● If we add this net cash flow to the opening cash balance, which has been brought forward from the previous month, we derive the closing cash balance. (This will become the opening cash balance in the next month.)

When preparing a cash flow statement, there are really two questions that must be asked concerning each item of information that is presented. The first question is: does the item of information concern a cash transaction (that is, does it involve cash inflows or outflows)? If the answer to this question is no, then the information should be ignored when preparing this statement. There are various items of information relating to a particular period, such as depreciation charges, that do not involve cash movements.

If the answer to the question above is yes, then a second question must be asked, which is: when did the cash transaction take place? When providing a monthly break-down of cash flows, it is important to identify the particular month in which the cash movement takes place. Where sales and purchases are made on credit, the cash move-ment will often take place after the month in which the sale or purchase takes place. (We return to this point later when discussing the projected profit and loss account.)

Problems in preparing cash flow statements usually arise because these two ques-tions above have not been properly addressed.

Activity 2.3

Fill in the outline cash flow statement for Designer Dresses Ltd for the six months to 30 June using the information contained in Example 2.2 above.

The projected cash flow statement for the six months to 30 June is:

	Jan £000	Feb £000	Mar £000	Apr £000	May £000	June £000
Cash inflows						
Issue of shares	50					
Credit sales	–	10	30	30	40	40
	50	10	30	30	40	40
Cash outflows						
Credit purchases	–	20	30	25	25	30
Other costs	9	9	9	9	9	9
Rent and rates	10			10		
Fittings	30					
	49	29	39	44	34	39
Net cash flow	1	(19)	(9)	(14)	6	1
Opening balance	–	1	(18)	(27)	(41)	(35)
Closing balance	1	(18)	(27)	(41)	(35)	(34)

Notes

1 The receipts from credit sales will arise one month after the sale has taken place. Hence, January's sales will be received in February, and so on. Similarly, trade creditors are paid one month after the goods have been purchased.
2 The closing cash balance for each month is deduced by adding to (or subtracting from) the opening balance, the cash flow for the month.

It is worth emphasising that the format used above is for internal reporting purposes only. When a (historic) cash flow statement is prepared for external reporting purposes, a summary of the cash flows for the year rather than a monthly breakdown of cash flows is provided. Furthermore, a particular format for presenting the information must be followed.

Projected profit and loss account (income statement)

A projected profit and loss account provides an insight to the anticipated level of future profits (losses), which can be defined as the difference between the anticipated level of sales and expenses. When preparing this statement, sales made on credit will normally be recognised *before* the cash is actually received. An accounting convention asserts that revenue should normally be recognised when goods have been passed to, and accepted by, the customer. Expenses must be matched to the relevant sales so that they are included in the same profit and loss account. The purpose of the profit and loss account is to show the wealth generated during the period, which may bear little relation to the cash generated. The timing of the cash inflows from credit sales and cash outflows for expenses is, therefore, irrelevant for this statement.

The format of the projected profit and loss account for Designer Dresses Ltd for the six months to 30 June will be as follows:

	£000	£000
Credit sales		
Less Cost of sales		
Opening stock		
Add Purchases		
Less Closing stock	____	____
Gross profit		
Credit card discounts		
Rent and rates		
Other costs		
Depreciation of fittings	____	____
Net profit		____

Activity 2.4

Fill in the outline profit and loss account for Designer Dresses Ltd for the six months to 30 June, using the information contained in Example 2.2 above.

The projected profit and loss account for the six months to 30 June is:

	£000	£000
Credit sales		204
Less Cost of sales		
Purchases	160	
Less Closing stock	58	102
Gross profit		102
Credit card discounts	4	
Rent and rates	20	
Other costs	54	
Depreciation of fittings	5	83
Net profit		19

Notes
1 There was no opening stock in this case.
2 The credit card discount is shown as a separate expense and not deducted from the sales figure. This approach is more informative than simply netting off the amount of the discount against sales.

Projected balance sheet

The projected balance sheet reveals the end-of-period balances for assets, liabilities and capital and should normally be the last of the three statements to be prepared. This is because the other statements will produce information to be used when preparing the projected balance sheet. The projected cash flow statement reveals the end-of-period cash balance for inclusion under 'current assets' (or where there is a negative balance, for inclusion under 'current liabilities'). The projected profit and loss account reveals the projected profit (loss) for the period for inclusion under the 'equity' section of the balance sheet. It is important to remember that the depreciation charge for the period, which appears in the projected profit and loss account, must also be taken into account when preparing the 'non-current assets' section of the projected balance sheet. The format of the projected balance sheet for Designer Dresses Ltd as at 30 June will be as follows:

	£000	£000	£000
Non-current assets			
Fittings at cost			
Less Accumulated depreciation			____
Current assets			
Stock (inventory)			
Debtors (receivables)		____	
Less **Current liabilities**			
Trade creditors (payables)			
Bank overdraft	____	____	____
Net assets			____
Equity			
Share capital			
Retained profit			____

Activity 2.5

Fill in the outline balance sheet for Designer Dresses Ltd as at 30 June using the information contained in Example 2.2 and in the projected cash flow statement and profit and loss account for the period to 30 June.

The projected balance sheet as at 30 June is:

	£000	£000	£000
Non-current assets			
Fittings at cost			30
Less Accumulated depreciation			5
			25
Current assets			
Stock		58	
Debtors (£51,000 less 2%)		50	
		108	
Less **Current liabilities**			
Trade creditors	30		
Bank overdraft	34	64	44
Net assets			69
Equity			
Share capital			50
Retained profit			19
			69

Note: The debtors figure represents June credit sales (less the credit card discount). Similarly, the creditors figure represents June purchases.

Projected financial statements and decision making

The finished projected financial statements should be examined with a critical eye. There is a danger that the figures will be too readily accepted. Forecast figures are unlikely to be completely accurate and it is important to form an opinion as to how much they can be relied upon. Thus, managers should ask such questions as:

● How were the projections developed?
● What underlying assumptions have been made and are they valid?
● Have all relevant items been included?

Only when the managers have received satisfactory answers to these questions should they use the statements for decision-making purposes.

Unfortunately, projected financial statements do not come with clear decision rules indicating whether a proposed course of action should go ahead. Managers must rely on their judgement. To help form this judgement, they may examine the statements for answers to the following questions:

● Are the cash flows satisfactory? Can they be improved by changing policies or plans (for example, delaying capital expenditure decisions, requiring debtors to pay more quickly and so on)?
● Is there a need for additional financing? Is it feasible to obtain the amount required?
● Can any surplus funds be profitably reinvested?
● Is the level of projected profit satisfactory in relation to the risks involved? If not, what could be done to improve matters?
● Are the sales and individual expense items at a satisfactory level?
● Is the financial position at the end of the period acceptable?
● Is the level of borrowing acceptable? Is the business too dependent on borrowing?

Activity 2.6

Evaluate the projected financial statements of Designer Dresses Ltd. Pay particular attention to the projected profitability and liquidity of the business.

The projected cash flow statement reveals that the business will have a bank overdraft throughout most of the period under review. The maximum overdraft requirement will be £41,000 in April. Although the business will be heavily dependent on bank finance in the early months, this situation should not last for too long provided the business achieves, and then maintains, the level of projected profit and providing it does not invest heavily in further assets.

The business is expected to generate a profit of 9.3p for every £1 of sales. The profit of £19,000 on the original outlay of £50,000 by the owners seems high. However, the business may be of a high-risk nature and therefore the owners will be looking to make high returns. As this is a new business, it may be very difficult to project into the future with any accuracy. Thus, the basis on which the projections have been made requires careful investigation.

Some further points regarding profitability can be made. It is not clear from the question whether the wages (under 'other costs' in the profit and loss account) include any remuneration for James and William Clark. If no remuneration for their efforts has been included, the level of profit shown may be overstated. It may not be possible to extrapolate the projected revenues and expenses for the six-month period in order to obtain a projected profit for the year. It is likely that the business is seasonal in nature and, therefore, the following six-month period may be quite different.

Activity 2.7

Dalgleish Ltd is a wholesale supplier of stationery. In recent months, the business has experienced liquidity problems. The business has an overdraft at the end of November 2005 and the bank has been pressing for a reduction in this overdraft over the next six months. The business is owned by the Dalgleish family who are unwilling to raise finance through long-term borrowing. The balance sheet of the business as at 30 November 2005 is as follows:

	£000	£000	£000
Non-current assets			
Freehold land and premises at cost		250	
Less Accumulated depreciation		24	226
Fixtures and fittings at cost		130	
Less Accumulated depreciation		38	92
			318
Current assets			
Stock at cost		142	
Debtors		120	
		262	
Less Current liabilities			
Trade creditors	145		
Bank overdraft	126	271	(9)
			309
Equity			
£1 ordinary shares			200
Profit and loss account			109
			309

The following projections for the six months ended 31 May 2006 are available concerning the business:

1 Sales and purchases for the six months ended 31 May 2006 will be as follows:

	Sales £000	Purchases £000
December	160	150
January	220	140
February	240	170
March	150	110
April	160	120
May	200	160

2 Seventy per cent of sales are on credit and 30 per cent are cash sales. Credit sales are received in the following month. All purchases are on one month's credit.

Activity 2.7 continued

3 Wages are £40,000 for each of the first three months. However, this will increase by 10 per cent as from March 2006. All wages are paid in the month they are incurred.
4 The gross profit percentage on goods sold is 30 per cent.
5 Administration expenses are expected to be £12,000 in each of the first four months and £14,000 in subsequent months. These figures include a monthly charge of £4,000 in respect of depreciation of non-current assets. Administration expenses are paid in the month they are incurred.
6 Selling expenses are expected to be £8,000 per month except for May 2006 when an advertising campaign costing £12,000 will be paid for. The advertising campaign will commence at the beginning of June 2006. Selling expenses are paid for in the month they are incurred.
7 A dividend of £20,000 will be proposed and paid in December 2005.
8 The business intends to purchase, and pay for, new fixtures and fittings at the end of April 2006 for £28,000. These will be delivered in June 2006.

Required:
(a) Prepare a cash flow projection for Dalgleish Ltd for each of the six months to 31 May 2006.
(b) Prepare a projected profit and loss account for the six months to 31 May 2006.
(c) Briefly discuss ways in which the business might reduce the bank overdraft as required by the bank.

(a) The cash flow projection for the six months to 31 May 2006 is:

	Dec £000	Jan £000	Feb £000	Mar £000	April £000	May £000
Cash inflows						
Credit sales	120	112	154	168	105	112
Cash sales	48	66	72	45	48	60
	168	178	226	213	153	172
Cash outflows						
Purchases	145	150	140	170	110	120
Admin. expenses	8	8	8	8	10	10
Wages	40	40	40	44	44	44
Selling expenses	8	8	8	8	8	20
Fixtures					28	
Dividend	20					
	221	206	196	230	200	194
Cash flow	(53)	(28)	30	(17)	(47)	(22)
Opening balance	(126)	(179)	(207)	(177)	(194)	(241)
Closing balance	(179)	(207)	(177)	(194)	(241)	(263)

(b) The projected profit and loss account for the six months to 31 May 2006 is:

	£000	£000
Sales		1,130
Less Cost of sales (balancing figure)		791
Gross profit (30% of sales)		339
Wages	252	
Selling expenses (exc. ad. campaign)	48	
Administration expenses (inc. depreciation)	76	376
Net loss		(37)

Note: The advertising campaign relates to the next financial period and will therefore be charged to the profit and loss account of that period.

(c) You may have thought of a number of possible options. The following (or perhaps some combination of these) might be feasible:

- an injection of new share capital by the Dalgleish family or others
- reduce stock levels
- delay purchase/payment of fixtures
- sell non-current assets
- increase the proportion of cash sales
- delay payment of trade creditors.

(Note that the Dalgleish family has ruled out the possibility of raising a loan.) Each of the above options has advantages and disadvantages and these must be carefully assessed before a final decision is made.

Per-cent-of-sales method

An alternative approach to preparing a forecast profit and loss account and balance sheet is the **per-cent-of-sales method**. This is a less thorough approach to forecasting than the approach discussed earlier. It assumes that most items appearing in the profit and loss account and balance sheet vary according to the level of sales. As a result, these financial statements can be prepared by expressing most items as a percentage of the sales for the forecast period.

To use this method, an examination of past records needs to be undertaken to see by how much items vary with sales. It may be found, for example, that stock levels have been around 30 per cent of sales in previous periods. If the sales for the forecast period are, say, £10 million, the level of stocks will be forecast as £3 million (that is, 30% × £10 million). The same approach will be used for other items.

Shown below is a brief summary of how key items appearing in the profit and loss account and balance sheet are derived.

Profit and loss account

The per-cent-of-sales method assumes that the following profit and loss account items can be expressed as a percentage of sales:

- all operating expenses
- the net profit figure, which is the difference between sales and expenses.

However:

- corporation tax and dividends are assumed to vary with the level of net profit and so are expressed as a percentage of the net profit figure.

Balance sheet

The per-cent-of-sales method assumes that the following balance sheet items can be expressed as a percentage of sales:

- current assets that increase spontaneously with sales, such as stock and debtors;
- current liabilities that increase spontaneously with sales, such as trade creditors and accrued expenses;
- cash (as a projected cash flow statement is not prepared to provide a more accurate measure of cash).

However:

- non-current assets will only be expressed as a percentage of sales if they are already operating at full capacity – otherwise they will not usually change;
- non-current liabilities and share capital will not be expressed as a percentage of sales but will be based on figures at the beginning of the forecast period (unless changes are made as a result of management decisions).

Identifying the financing gap

When there is an increase in sales, there is a risk that a business will outgrow the finance that has been committed. The forecast increase in assets may exceed the forecast increase in liabilities and the retained profits and so a financing gap may arise. This gap is easily identified under the per-cent-of-sales method because the balance sheet will not balance. The additional finance required by the business will be the amount necessary to make the balance sheet balance.

The way in which a business decides to fill the financing gap is referred to as the **plug**. There are various forms of finance that may be used as a plug, including loan capital and share capital. We shall, however, leave a discussion of the different forms of finance available until Chapter 5.

A worked example

Let us go through a simple example to show how the per-cent-of-sales method works.

Example 2.3

The financial statements of Burrator plc for the year that has just ended are as follows:

Profit and loss account (income statement) for the year ended 31 December Year 8

	£000	£000
Credit sales		800
Less Cost of sales		600
Gross profit		200
Selling expenses	80	
Distribution expenses	20	
Other expenses	20	120
Net profit		80
Corporation tax (25%)		20
Net profit after tax		60
Dividends proposed and paid (50%)		30
		30

Balance sheet at 31 December Year 8

	£000	£000
Non-current assets		160
Current assets		
Stock (inventory)	320	
Trade debtors (receivables)	200	
Cash	20	
	540	
Current liabilities		
Trade creditors (payables)	240	
Taxation	20	
	260	
Net current assets		280
Total assets less current liabilities		440
Equity		
Share capital – 25p ordinary shares		60
Profit and loss account		380
		440

The following information is relevant for Year 9:

1 Sales are expected to be 10 per cent higher than in Year 8.
2 The non-current assets of the business are currently operating at full capacity.
3 The corporation tax rate will be the same as in Year 8 and 50% of the tax due will be outstanding at the year end.
4 The business intends to maintain the same dividend policy as for Year 8.
5 Half of the tax relating to Year 9 will be outstanding at the year end. Tax due at the end of Year 8 will be paid during Year 9.
6 Any financing gap will be filled by an issue of loan capital.

Required:

Prepare a forecast profit and loss account and balance sheet using the per-cent-of-sales method. (Assume that Year 8 provides a useful guide to past experience.)

Solution

To prepare the forecast profit and loss account we calculate each expense as a per-centage of sales for Year 8 and then use this percentage to forecast the equivalent expense in Year 9. Tax and dividends are calculated as a percentage of the profit for Year 9, using percentages from Year 8.

The forecast profit and loss account is therefore as follows:

Forecast profit and loss account (income statement)
for the year ended 31 December Year 9

	£000	£000
Credit sales [800 + (10% × 800)]		880
Less Cost of sales (75% sales)		660
Gross profit (25% sales)		220
Selling expenses (10% sales)	88	
Distribution expenses (5% sales)	22	
Other expenses (5% sales)	22	132
Net profit (10% sales)		88
Corporation tax (25% of net profit)		22
Net profit after tax		66
Dividends proposed and paid (50% of net profit after tax)		33
		33

We apply the same broad principles when preparing the forecast balance sheet for Year 9.

Activity 2.8

Prepare the forecast balance sheet of Burrator plc for Year 9.

Balance sheet at 31 December Year 9

	£000	£000
Non-current assets (20% sales)		176
Current assets		
Stock (40% sales)	352	
Trade debtors (25% sales)	220	
Cash ($2\frac{1}{2}$% sales)	22	
	594	
Current liabilities		
Trade creditors (30% sales)	264	
Taxation (50% tax due)	11	
	275	
Net current assets		319
Total assets less current liabilities		495
Non-current liabilities		
Loan capital (balancing figure)		22
		473
Equity		
Share capital – 25p ordinary shares		60
Profit and loss account (380 + 33)		413
		473

The advantage of the per-cent-of-sales method is that the task of preparing the projected financial statements becomes much more manageable. It can provide an approximate figure for the finance required without having to prepare a projected cash flow statement. It can also help reduce the time and cost of forecasting every single item appearing in the projected profit and loss account and balance sheet. These can be of real benefit, particularly for large businesses.

The problem with this method, however, is that it takes the relationships between particular items and sales as being fixed. The forecasts prepared are based on relationships that have existed in the past. These relationships may change over time because of changes in strategic direction (for example, launching completely new products) or because of changes in management policies (for example, liberalising credit facilities to customers).

Projected financial statements and risk

When making estimates concerning the future, there is always a chance that things will not turn out as expected. The likelihood that what is estimated to occur will not actually occur is referred to as **risk** and this will be considered in some detail in Chapter 5. However, it is worth taking a little time at this point to consider the ways in which managers may deal with the problem of risk in the context of projected financial statements. In practice, there are various methods available to help managers deal with uncertainty concerning the figures contained within the projected financial statements. Below we consider three possible methods.

Sensitivity analysis

→ **Sensitivity analysis** is a useful technique to employ when evaluating the contents of projected financial statements. This involves taking a single variable (for example, volume of sales) and examining the effect of changes in the chosen variable on the likely performance and position of the business. By examining the shifts that occur, it is possible to arrive at some assessment of how sensitive changes are for the projected outcomes. Although only one variable is examined at a time, a number of variables, which are considered to be important to the performance of a business, may be examined consecutively.

One form of sensitivity analysis is to pose a series of 'what if?' questions. If we take sales as an example, the following 'what if?' questions may be asked:

● What if sales volume is 5 per cent higher than expected?
● What if sales volume is 10 per cent lower than expected?
● What if sales price is reduced by 15 per cent?
● What if sales price could be increased by 20 per cent?

In answering these questions, it is possible to develop a better 'feel' for the effect of forecast inaccuracies on the final outcomes. However, this technique does not assign probabilities to each possible change nor does it consider the effect on projected outcomes of more than one variable at a time.

Scenario analysis

Another approach to helping managers gain a feel for the effect of forecast inaccuracies is to prepare projected financial statements according to different possible 'states of the world'. For example, managers may wish to examine projected financial statements prepared on the following bases:

● an optimistic view of likely future events
● a pessimistic view of likely future events
● a 'most likely' view of future events.

→ This approach is referred to as **scenario analysis** and, unlike sensitivity analysis, it will involve changing a number of variables simultaneously in order to portray a possible state of the world. To help in assessing the level of risk involved, knowing the likelihood of each state of the world occurring, however, would also be useful.

The most pessimistic scenario is usually referred to as the 'worst case scenario'. **Real World 2.2** reveals the worst case scenario for sales of a major car maker.

REAL WORLD 2.2

Worst case scenario

Volkswagen AG has slashed its forecast full year operating profit before one-offs this year to only 1.9 bln euros based on a 'worst case' scenario that it only sells 5.1 mln cars, management board chairman Bernd Pischetsrieder said in a telephone conference call.

'In the worst case scenario, it would be 1.9 bln eur before the 400 mln eur one-offs based on a volume of 5.1 mln car sales this year,' he said.

'If we sell more it would obviously improve the situation . . . If the volume is above 5.1 mln cars, from an operational point of view, then everything else is under control,' he added.

Earlier today, the company announced first half deliveries to customers totalled 2.516 mln, up 1.7 pct, while vehicle sales rose 5.2 pct to 2.646 mln.

VW sold 5.015 mln cars in 2003, up by 0.6 pct from the year-earlier level.

Also earlier today, VW cut its full year forecast for operating profit before one-offs to 1.9 bln euros from the previous target of 2.5 bln after weak markets and unfavourable exchange rates pushed the first half figure 19.8 pct lower to 979 mln euros.

In the same conference call, VW brand sales and marketing chief Detlef Wittig said VW expects its sales volume in China to grow by 5–7 pct in 2004 compared with last year.

Wittig said January–May sales in China were higher but fell in June after price cuts were made by competitors.

He said VW has 'realigned' its prices so that in July, it was 'back to last year's level'.

Pischetsrider said VW does not intend to confront competitors in China by matching its price cuts because the company's priority is profitability and not gaining market share.

Source: 'VW profit warning based on "worst case" scenario of 5.1 mln unit sales', *AFX Europe (Focus)*, 23 July 2004.

Simulations

The **simulation** approach is really a development of sensitivity analysis that we discussed earlier. The approach creates a distribution of possible values to key variables in the projected financial statements and a probability of occurrence is attached to each value. A computer is used to select one of the possible values from each distribution on a random basis. It then generates projected statements on the basis of the selected values for each variable. This process represents a single trial. The process is then repeated using other values for each variable until many possible combinations of values for the key variables have been considered. This may, in practice, mean that thousands of trials are carried out.

From the huge amount of information produced, a range of likely outcomes may be deduced and the probability of each outcome identified. For example, a business may carry out 4,000 trials based on key variables in the projected profit and loss account. These trials may indicate that the expected profit for the following period will fall within the range £100,000–£500,000. There may be 20 per cent of the trials producing an expected profit between £100,000 and £200,000; 30 per cent of the trials producing a profit between £200,001 and £300,000; 35 per cent of the trials producing an expected profit between £300,001 and £400,000; and 15 per cent of the trials producing a profit between £400,001 and £500,000. This information may help managers decide whether the expected level of performance is satisfactory.

This approach is claimed to make managers think carefully about the relationships between the key variables in the projected statements. In practice, however, there is a danger that carrying out simulations will lead to a rather mechanical approach to dealing with risk. Undue emphasis may be placed on carrying out trials and producing their results, and insufficient emphasis may be given to a more critical evaluation of the underlying assumptions and issues.

Projected financial statements and spreadsheets

Preparing projected financial statements is facilitated by the use of spreadsheet packages. In essence, a spreadsheet package is simply a matrix of rows and columns that can be loaded on to a computer and viewed on the computer screen. The intersection of a row and a column is referred to as a cell. In each cell it is possible to insert numbers, equations or descriptions. A simple model can be built using this matrix. For example, the projected cash flow statement for Dalgleish Ltd dealt with in Activity 2.7 may be prepared using the rows and columns of a spreadsheet package as follows:

	A	B	C	D	E	F	G
		Dec	Jan	Feb	Mar	April	May
1		£000	£000	£000	£000	£000	£000
2							
3	Cash inflows						
4	Credit sales	120	112	154	168	105	112
5	Cash sales	48	66	72	45	48	60
6		168	178	226	213	153	172
7							
8	Cash outflows						
9	Purchases	145	150	140	170	110	120
10	Admin. expenses	8	8	8	8	10	10
11	Wages	40	40	40	44	44	44
12	Selling expenses	8	8	8	8	8	20
13	Fixtures					28	
14	Dividend	20					
15		221	206	196	230	200	194
16							
17	Cash flow	(53)	(28)	30	(17)	(47)	(22)
18	Opening balance	(126)	(179)	(207)	(177)	(194)	(241)
19	Closing balance	(179)	(207)	(177)	(194)	(241)	(263)

Cell B6 can be made equal to the sum of cells B4 and B5, cell C6 can be made equal to the sum of C4 and C5, and so on, so that all calculations are carried out by the package. The spreadsheet package is particularly useful if managers wish to carry out sensitivity analysis on the projected statements. One variable may be altered and the spreadsheet will quickly recalculate the totals to show the effect of the change.

Not only can figures be linked through formulae within a particular statement but different financial statements can also be linked. This means, for example, that the final cash balance shown in G19 can be inserted in another cell in the spreadsheet dealing with the balance sheet. Similar links can be made between many of the figures that appear in the various projected statements. This means that the statements can be produced with the minimum of entry information and no calculation at all, yet can be produced very quickly and accurately.

In practice, the spreadsheet can have all manner of refinements and user-friendly features incorporated, which can reduce further the amount of data entry by the preparer. It can be so designed that data can all be entered in one corner of the spreadsheet, in a data entry area, to save the preparer scrolling up and down the spreadsheet to enter them. The spreadsheet model would automatically pick up an item of data from where it had been entered and use it, as appropriate, to produce the projected financial statements.

Self-assessment question 2.1

Quardis Ltd is an importer of high quality laser printers, which can be used with a range of microcomputers. The balance sheet of Quardis Ltd as at 31 May 2005 is as follows:

	£000	£000	£000
Non-current assets			
Freehold premises at cost		460	
Less Accumulated depreciation		30	430
Fixtures and fittings at cost		35	
Less Accumulated depreciation		10	25
			455
Current assets			
Stock (inventory)		24	
Debtors (receivables)		34	
Cash at bank		2	
		60	
Less **Current liabilities**			
Trade creditors (payables)	22		
Taxation	24	46	14
			469
Less **Non-current liabilities**			
Loan – Highland Bank			125
			344
Equity			
£1 ordinary shares			200
Retained profit			144
			344

The following forecast information is available for the year ended 31 May 2006:

1 Sales are expected to be £280,000 for the year. Sixty per cent of sales are on credit and it is expected that, at the year end, three months' credit sales will be outstanding. Sales revenues accrue evenly over the year.

2 Purchases of stock during the year will be £186,000 and will accrue evenly over the year. All purchases are on credit and at the year end it is expected that two months' purchases will remain unpaid.

3 Fixtures and fittings costing £25,000 will be purchased and paid for during the year. Depreciation is charged at 10 per cent on the cost of fixtures and fittings held at the year end.

4 Depreciation is charged on freehold premises at 2 per cent on cost.

5 On 1 June 2005, £30,000 of the loan from the Highland Bank is to be repaid. Interest is at the rate of 13 per cent per annum and all interest accrued to 31 May 2006 will be paid on that day.

6 Stock-in-trade at the year end is expected to be 25 per cent higher than at the beginning of the year.

7 Wages for the year will be £34,000. It is estimated that £4,000 of this total will remain unpaid at the year end.

8 Other overhead expenses for the year (excluding those mentioned above) are expected to be £21,000. It is expected that £3,000 of this total will still be unpaid at the year end.

9 A dividend of 5p per share will be announced and paid during the year.

10 Corporation tax is payable at the rate of 35 per cent. Corporation tax outstanding at the beginning of the year will be paid during the year. Half of the corporation tax relating to the year will also be paid during the year.

All workings should be shown to the nearest £000.

Required:

(a) Prepare a projected profit and loss account (income statement)for the year ended 31 May 2006.

(b) Prepare a projected balance sheet as at 31 May 2006.

(c) Comment on the significant features revealed by these statements.

Note: A projected cash flow statement is not required. The cash figure in the projected balance sheet will be a balancing figure.

SUMMARY

The main points in this chapter may be summarised as follows:

Planning for the future

- Developing plans involves:
  - setting aims and objectives
  - identifying the options available
  - evaluating the options and making a selection.
- Projected financial statements help in evaluating the options available;

Preparing financial statements

- Involves a four-stage process:
  - identifying the external and internal factors that provide a framework for the forecast statements
  - forecasting sales for the period by analysing the competitive environment and using an appropriate forecasting method
  - forecasting the remaining elements of the financial statements
  - preparing the projected financial statements.
- The projected financial statements normally prepared are:
  - the projected cash flow statement
  - the projected profit and loss account (income statement)
  - the projected balance sheet.
- The projected cash flow statement is usually broken down into monthly periods.

Projected financial statements and decision making

● The projected statements should be checked for reliability before using them for decision-making purposes.

● They do not provide clear decision rules for managers, who must employ judgement.

Per-cent-of-sales method

● Provides a less rigourous approach to forecasting.

● Assumes that most items on the profit and loss account and balance sheet vary with sales.

● Calculates any financing gap by reference to the amount required to make the balance sheet balance.

● The form of finance used to fill any financing gap is referred to as the plug.

● This method makes the preparation of forecast statements easier and less costly but assumes that relationships between individual items and sales that held in the past will also hold in the future.

Projected financial statements and risk

● Three methods of dealing with risk are:
   – sensitivity analysis
   – scenario analysis
   – simulations.

● Spreadsheets are ideal for preparing projected statements and for calculating sensitivities.

→ Key terms

Projected financial statements p. 24	**Per-cent-of-sales method** p. 41
Competitor profiling p. 28	**Plug** p. 42
Variable costs p. 29	**Risk** p. 44
Fixed costs p. 29	**Sensitivity analysis** p. 45
Semi-variable costs p. 29	**Scenario analysis** p. 45
	Simulation p. 46

For definitions of these terms see the Glossary, pp. 562–571.

Further reading

If you wish to explore the topics discussed in this chapter in more depth, try the following books:

Financial Management, *Brigham, E. and Ehrhardt, M.*, 10th edn, Harcourt, 2002, chapter 4.

How to Forecast, *Morrell, J.*, Gower, 2001.

Principles of Corporate Finance, *Brealey, R. and Myers, S.*, 7th edn, McGraw-Hill, 2002, chapter 29.

Prospective Financial Statement Analysis, *Kopczynski, F.*, Wiley, 1996.

REVIEW QUESTIONS

Answers to these questions can be found in Appendix D at the back of the book.

2.1 In what ways might projected financial statements help a business that is growing fast?

2.2 'The future is uncertain and so projected financial statements will almost certainly prove to be inaccurate. It is, therefore, a waste of time to prepare them.' Comment.

2.3 Why would it normally be easier to prepare projected financial statements for an existing business than for a new one?

2.4 Why is the sales forecast normally of critical importance to the preparation of projected financial statements?

EXERCISES

Exercises 2.5 to 2.7 are more advanced than 2.1 to 2.4. Those with coloured numbers have answers at the back of the book.

 If you wish to try more exercises, visit the students' side of the Companion Website.

2.1 Choice Designs Ltd operates a small group of wholesale/retail carpet stores in the north of England. The balance sheet of the business as at 31 May 2005 is as follows:

	£000	£000	£000
Non-current assets			
Freehold premises at cost		600	
Less Accumulated depreciation		100	500
Fixtures and fittings at cost		140	
Less Accumulated depreciation		80	60
			560
Current assets			
Stock (inventory)		240	
Debtors (receivables)		220	
Bank		165	
		625	
Less **Current liabilities**			
Trade creditors (payables)	268		
Taxation	166	434	191
			751
Equity			
£1 ordinary shares			500
Retained profit			251
			751

As a result of falling profits the directors of the business would like to completely refurbish each store during June 2005 at a total cost of £300,000. However, before making such a large capital expenditure commitment, they require projections of performance and position for the forthcoming year.

The following information is available concerning the year to 31 May 2006:

- The forecast sales for the year are £1,400,000 and the gross profit is expected to be 30 per cent of sales. Eighty per cent of all sales are on credit. At present the average credit period is six weeks but it is likely that this will change to eight weeks in the forthcoming year.
- At the year end stocks are expected to be 25 per cent higher than at the beginning of the year.
- During the year the directors intend to pay £40,000 for a fleet of delivery vans.
- Administration expenses for the year are expected to be £225,000 (including £12,000 for depreciation of premises and £38,000 depreciation of fixtures and fittings). Selling expenses are expected to be £85,000 (including £10,000 for depreciation of motor vans).
- All purchases are on credit. It has been estimated that the average credit period taken will be 12 weeks during the forthcoming year.
- Taxation for the year is expected to be £34,000. Half of this will be paid during the year and the remaining half will be outstanding at the year end.
- Dividends proposed and paid for the year are expected to be 6.0p per share.

All workings should be made to the nearest £000.

Required:
(a) Prepare a projected profit and loss account for the year ended 31 May 2006.
(b) Prepare a projected balance sheet as at 31 May 2006.

Note: The cash balance will be the balancing figure.

2.2 Prolog Ltd is a small wholesaler of powerful microcomputers. It has in recent months been selling 50 machines a month at a price of £2,000 each. These machines cost £1,600 each. A new model has just been launched and this is expected to offer greatly enhanced performance. Its selling price and cost will be the same as for the old model. From the beginning of January Year 6, sales are expected to increase at a rate of 20 machines each month until the end of June Year 6 when sales will amount to 170 units per month. They are expected to continue at that level thereafter. Operating costs including depreciation of £2,000 a month, are forecast as follows:

	Jan	Feb	Mar	Apr	May	June
Operating costs (£000)	6	8	10	12	12	12

Prolog expects to receive no credit for operating costs. Additional shelving for storage will be bought, installed and paid for in April costing £12,000. Corporation tax of £25,000 is due at the end of March. Prolog expects that debtors will take two months to pay. To give its customers a good level of service, Prolog plans to hold enough stock at the end of each period to fulfil anticipated demand from customers in the following month. The computer manufacturer, however, grants one month's credit to Prolog. Prolog Ltd's balance sheet appears below.

Balance sheet at 31 December Year 5

	£000	£000
Non-current assets		80
Current assets		
Stock	112	
Debtors	200	
Cash	–	
	312	

	£000	£000
Current liabilities		
Trade creditors	112	
Taxation	25	
Overdraft	<u>68</u>	
	<u>205</u>	
Net current assets		<u>107</u>
Total assets less current liabilities		<u>187</u>
Equity		
Share capital – 25p ordinary shares		10
Profit and loss account		<u>177</u>
		<u>187</u>

Required:

(a) Prepare a projected cash flow statement for Prolog Ltd showing the cash balance or required overdraft for flow statement the six months ending 30 June Year 6.

(b) State briefly what further information a banker would require from Prolog before granting additional overdraft facilities for the anticipated expansion of sales.

2.3 Davis Travel Ltd specialises in the provision of winter sports holidays but it also organises outdoor activity holidays in the summer. You are given the following information:

Abbreviated balance sheet as at 30 September 2005

	£000
Non-current assets	560
Current assets	
Cash	<u>30</u>
	590
Current liabilities	
Trade creditors (payables)	<u>180</u>
Total assets less current liabilities	410
Non-current liabilities	
Loans	<u>110</u>
	<u>300</u>
Equity	
Share capital	100
Reserves	<u>200</u>
	<u>300</u>

Its sales estimates for the next six months are:

	Number of bookings received	Number of holidays taken	Promotion expenditure (£000)
October	1,000		100
November	3,000		150
December	3,000	1,000	150
January	3,000	4,000	50
February		3,000	
March		<u>2,000</u>	
Total	<u>10,000</u>	<u>10,000</u>	<u>450</u>

1 Holidays sell for £300 each. Ten per cent is payable when the holiday is booked, and the remainder after two months.
2 Travel agents are paid a commission of 10 per cent of the price of the holiday one month after the booking is made.
3 The cost of a flight is £50 per holiday and a hotel £100 per holiday. Flights and hotels must be paid for in the month when the holidays are taken.
4 Other variable costs are £20 per holiday and are paid in the month of the holiday.
5 Administration costs, including depreciation of non-current assets of £42,000, amount to £402,000 for the six months. Administration costs can be spread evenly over the period.
6 Loan interest of £10,000 is payable on 31 March 2006 and a loan repayment of £20,000 is due on that date. For your calculations you should ignore any interest on the overdraft.
7 The creditors of £180,000 at 30 September are to be paid in October.
8 A payment of £50,000 for non-current assets is to be made in March 2006.
9 The airline and the hotel chain base their charges on Davis Travel's forecast requirements and hold capacity to meet those requirements. If Davis is unable to fill this reserved capacity a charge of 50 per cent of those published above is made.

Required:
(a) Prepare:
  (i) A projected cash flow statement for the six months to 31 March 2006.
  (ii) A projected profit and loss account for the six months ended on that date.
  (iii) A projected balance sheet at 31 March 2006.
(b) Discuss the main financial problems confronting Davis Travel Ltd.

Ignore taxation in your calculations.

2.4 Changes Ltd owns a chain of eight shops selling fashion goods. In the past the business maintained a healthy cash balance. However, this has fallen in recent months and at the end of September 2005 the company had an overdraft of £70,000. In view of this, Changes Ltd's managing director has asked you to prepare a cash forecast for the next six months. You have collected the following data:

	Oct £000	Nov £000	Dec £000	Jan £000	Feb £000	Mar £000
Sales forecast	140	180	260	60	100	120
Purchases	160	180	140	50	50	50
Wages and salaries	30	30	40	30	30	32
Rent			60			
Rates						40
Other expenses	20	20	20	20	20	20
Refurbishing shops				80		

Stock at 1 October amounted to £170,000 and creditors were £70,000. The purchases in October, November and December are contractually committed, and those in January, February and March are the minimum necessary to restock with spring fashions. Cost of sales is 50 per cent of sales and suppliers allow one month's credit on purchases. Taxation of £90,000 is due on 1 January. The rates payment is a charge for a whole year and other expenses include depreciation of £10,000 per month.

Required:
(a) Compute the projected cash balance at the end of each month, for the six months to 31 March 2006.
(b) Compute the projected stock levels at the end of each month for the six months to 31 March 2006.
(c) Prepare a projected profit and loss account for the six months ended 31 March 2006.
(d) What problems might Changes Ltd face in the next six months and how would you attempt to overcome them?

(*Hint*: A forecast of stock flows is required to answer part (b). This will be based on the same principles as a cash flow statement, that is, inflows and outflows with opening and closing balances.)

2.5 Kwaysar Ltd sells television satellite dishes both to retail outlets and direct to the public. The balance sheet of the business as at 31 May 2005 is as follows:

	£000	£000	£000
Non-current assets			
Freehold premises at cost		350	
Less Accumulated depreciation		60	290
Fixtures and fittings at cost		80	
Less Accumulated depreciation		42	38
			328
Current assets			
Stock (inventory) at cost		44	
Debtors (receivables)		52	
Cash at bank		120	
		216	
Current liabilities			
Trade creditors (payables)	32		
Accrued overheads	12	44	172
			500
Non-current liabilities			
Loan			48
			452
Equity			
£1 ordinary shares			200
Share premium account			80
General reserve			40
Retained profit			132
			452

In the second half of the financial year to 31 May 2005, the business generated a net profit of £62,400 and sales of £525,000. It is believed that this level of performance will be repeated in the forthcoming six-month period provided the business does not implement any changes to its marketing strategy. The business, however, is determined to increase its market share and is considering the adoption of a new marketing strategy that has been developed by the marketing department. The main elements of the new strategy are as follows:

1 The selling price of each satellite dish will be reduced to £90. At present each dish is sold for £120.
2 There will be an increase in the amount of advertising costs incurred by the business. Advertising costs will increase from £6,500 per month to £12,000 per month.
3 Retail outlets will be allowed to pay for satellite dishes three months after delivery. At present, trade debtors are allowed one month's credit. Those retail outlets that continue to pay within one month will, for future sales, be given a 2 per cent discount.

The marketing department believes that, by adopting the new strategy, sales in each of the first three months to retail outlets will rise to 1,000 units and sales to the public will rise to 300 units. Thereafter, sales each month will be 1,200 units and 400 units respectively.

Assuming the strategy is adopted, the following forecast information is available:

1 The purchase of satellite dishes will be made at the beginning of each month and will be sufficient to meet that month's sales. Each satellite dish costs £50. Trade creditors are paid one month after the month of purchase.
2 Depreciation will be charged on freehold premises at 2 per cent per year on cost and for fixtures and fittings at 15 per cent per year on cost.

3 Motor vans costing £80,000 will be acquired and paid for immediately. These are required to implement the new strategy and will be depreciated at 30 per cent per year on cost.

4 Wages will be £18,000 per month and will be paid in the month in which they are incurred.

5 Advertising costs will be paid for in the month incurred.

6 Other overheads (excluding those mentioned above) will be £14,000 per month and will continue to be paid for one month after the month in which they are incurred.

7 The loan of £48,000 will be repaid in July 2005.

8 Sales direct to the public will continue to be paid for in cash. No credit will be allowed.

9 It is estimated that 50 per cent of retail sales will continue to be on one month's credit and 50 per cent will be on three months' credit.

Ignore taxation.

Required:

Assuming that the new marketing strategy is adopted:

(a) Prepare a projected profit and loss account for the six-month period to 30 November 2005. (A monthly breakdown of profit is not required.)

(b) Prepare a projected cash flow statement for the six-month period to 30 November 2005. (A monthly breakdown of cash flows is not required.)

(c) Comment on the financial results of Kwaysar Ltd for the six-month period to 30 November 2005.

2.6   Newtake Records Ltd owns a chain of 14 shops selling CDs and DVDs. At the beginning of June, the business had an overdraft of £35,000 and the bank has asked for this to be eliminated by the end of November of the same year. As a result, the directors of the business have recently decided to review their plans for the next six months in order to comply with this requirement.

The following forecast information was prepared for the business some months earlier:

	May £000	June £000	July £000	Aug £000	Sept £000	Oct £000	Nov £000
Expected sales	180	230	320	250	140	120	110
Purchases	135	180	142	94	75	66	57
Admin. expenses	52	55	56	53	48	46	45
Selling expenses	22	24	28	26	21	19	18
Taxation payment				22			
Finance payments	5	5	5	5	5	5	5
Shop refurbishment	–	–	14	18	6	–	–

Notes

1 Stock held at 1 June was £112,000. The business believes it is necessary to maintain a minimum stock level of £40,000 over the period to 30 November of the same year.

2 Suppliers allow one month's credit. The first three months' purchases are subject to a contractual agreement that must be honoured.

3 The gross profit margin is 40 per cent.

4 All sales income is received in the month of sale. However, 50 per cent of customers pay with a credit card. The charge made by the credit card business to Newtake Records Ltd is 3 per cent of the sales value. These charges are in addition to the selling expenses identified above. The credit card business pays Newtake Records Ltd in the month of sale.

5 The business has a bank loan that it is paying off in monthly instalments of £5,000 per month. The interest element represents 20 per cent of each instalment.

6 Administration expenses are paid when incurred. This item includes a charge of £15,000 each month in respect of depreciation.

7 Selling expenses are payable in the following month.

Required:

(a) Prepare a projected cash flow statement for the six months ended 30 November that shows the cash balance at the end of each month.

(b) Compute the projected stock levels at the end of each month for the six months to 30 November.

(c) Prepare a projected profit and loss account for the six months ended 30 November. (A monthly breakdown of profit is not required.)

(d) What problems is Newtake Records Ltd likely to face in the next six months? Can you suggest how the business might deal with these problems?

2.7 Goya Music Direct Ltd operates a mail order business offering classical music CDs to the general public. The balance sheet of the business for the year ended 31 May 2005 is as follows:

	£	£	£
Non-current assets			
Fixtures and fittings at cost		72,000	
Less Accumulated depreciation		24,000	48,000
Motor vehicles at cost		46,000	
Less Accumulated depreciation		28,000	18,000
			66,000
Current assets			
Stock (inventory) at cost		80,000	
Trade debtors (receivables)		107,000	
Cash at bank		27,000	
		214,000	
Current liabilities			
Trade creditors (payables)	93,000		
Accrued overheads	17,000	110,000	104,000
			170,000
Non-current liabilities			
10% debentures 2007/2008			60,000
			110,000
Equity			
£1 ordinary shares			10,000
General reserve			60,000
Retained profit			40,000
			110,000

The following forecast information for the six months ended 30 November 2005 is available:

1 Sales and purchases for the six months ended 30 November 2005 are estimated as follows:

	Sales £	Purchases £
June	130,000	102,000
July	140,000	118,000
August	150,000	115,000
September	110,000	88,000
October	90,000	67,000
November	105,000	110,000

2 The gross profit margin on goods sold is 40 per cent.

3 Customers are allowed one month's credit.

4 Salaries and wages are expected to be £30,000 each month. In addition, an annual staff bonus of £12,000 is due for payment in October 2005. All salaries and wages are paid in the month incurred.

5 Selling and administration expenses are expected to be £20,000 per month, which is payable one month in arrears. This figure includes a monthly charge of £3,000 per month in respect of depreciation of non-current assets. In addition to these expenses, the business is committed to a large advertising campaign. This is not due to commence until December 2005 although advance payments of £60,000 must be made to newspapers and magazines in November 2005.

6 The only finance expense incurred by the business is debenture interest which is not payable until the year end.

7 £10,000 of the debenture loan will be repaid in August 2005.

The business has agreed with the bank an overdraft limit of £100,000 to cover the next 12 months, which both parties are anxious should not be exceeded.
Ignore taxation.

Required:

(a) Prepare a projected cash flow statement for each of the six months to 30 November 2005.

(b) Prepare a projected profit and loss account for the six months to 30 November 2005. (A monthly breakdown is not required.)

(c) Discuss the problems, if any, the business is likely to face in the next six months and how these might be resolved.

3

Analysing and interpreting financial statements

LEARNING OUTCOMES

When you have completed this chapter, you should be able to:

- Identify the major categories of ratios that can be used for analysis purposes.

- Calculate important ratios for assessing the financial performance and position of a business, and explain the significance of the ratios calculated.

- Discuss the limitations of ratios as a tool of financial analysis.

- Discuss the use of ratios in helping to predict financial failure.

INTRODUCTION

In this chapter we consider the analysis and interpretation of the financial statements. We shall see how financial (or accounting) ratios can help in assessing the financial health of a business. We shall also discuss the problems that are encountered when applying this technique.

Financial ratios can be used to examine various aspects of financial position and performance and are widely used for planning and control purposes. As we shall see in later chapters, they can be very helpful to managers in a wide variety of decision areas, such as profit planning, working capital management, financial structure and dividend policy.

Financial ratios

Financial ratios provide a quick and relatively simple means of assessing the financial health of a business. A ratio simply relates one figure appearing in the financial statements to some other figure appearing there (for example, net profit in relation to capital employed) or, perhaps, to some resource of the business (for example, net profit per employee, sales revenue per square metre of counter space, and so on).

Ratios can be very helpful when comparing the financial health of different businesses. Differences may exist between businesses in the scale of operations, and so a direct comparison of, say, the profits generated by each business may be misleading. By expressing profit in relation to some other measure (for example, sales revenue), the problem of scale is eliminated. A business with a profit of, say, £10,000 and sales revenue of £100,000 can be compared with a much larger business with a profit of, say, £80,000 and sales revenue of £1,000,000 by the use of a simple ratio. The net profit to sales revenue ratio for the smaller business is 10 per cent [(10,000/100,000) × 100%] and the same ratio for the larger business is 8 per cent [(80,000/1,000,000) × 100%]. These ratios can be directly compared whereas comparison of the absolute profit figures would be less meaningful. The need to eliminate differences in scale through the use of ratios can also apply when comparing the performance of the same business over time.

By calculating a small number of ratios, it is often possible to build up a good picture of the position and performance of a business. They can highlight financial strengths and weaknesses and so it is not surprising that ratios are widely used by those who have an interest in businesses and business performance. However, ratios provide only the starting point for further analysis. Changes in a particular ratio may be due to a variety of factors and a ratio cannot, by itself, explain why certain strengths or weaknesses exist, or why certain changes have occurred. Only a detailed investigation will reveal these underlying reasons.

Ratios can be expressed in various forms, for example as a percentage or as a proportion. The way that a particular ratio is presented will depend on the needs of those who will use the information. Although it is possible to calculate a large number of ratios, only a few, based on key relationships, tend to be helpful to a particular user. Many ratios that could be calculated from the financial statements (for example, rent payable in relation to current assets) may not be considered because there is no clear or meaningful relationship between the two items.

There is no generally accepted list of ratios that can be applied to the financial statements, nor is there a standard method of calculating many ratios. Variations in both the choice of ratios and their calculation will be found in practice. However, it is important to be consistent in the way in which ratios are calculated for comparison purposes. The ratios discussed below are those that are widely used because many consider them to be among the more important for decision-making purposes.

Financial ratio classification

Ratios can be grouped into categories, each of which relates to a particular aspect of financial performance or position. The following broad categories provide a useful basis for explaining the nature of the financial ratios to be dealt with. There are five of them:

● *Profitability.* Businesses generally exist with the primary purpose of creating wealth for their owners. Profitability ratios provide an insight to the degree of success in achieving this purpose. They express the profits made (or figures bearing on profit, such as overheads) in relation to other key figures in the financial statements or to some business resource.

- *Efficiency.* Ratios may be used to measure the efficiency with which particular resources have been used within the business. These ratios are also referred to as *activity* ratios.
- *Liquidity.* It is vital to the survival of a business for there to be sufficient liquid resources available to meet maturing obligations (that is, debts that must be paid in the near future). Some liquidity ratios examine the relationship between liquid resources held and creditors (payables) due for payment in the near future.
- *Financial gearing.* This is the relationship between the contribution to financing the business made by the owners of the business and the amount contributed by others in the form of loans. The level of gearing has an important effect on the degree of risk associated with a business, as we shall see. Gearing is, therefore, something that managers must consider when making financing decisions. Gearing ratios tend to highlight the extent to which the business uses loan finance.
- *Investment.* Certain ratios are concerned with assessing the returns and performance of shares held in a particular business from the perspective of shareholders who are not involved with the management of the business.

The analyst must be clear *who* the target users are and *why* they need the information. Different users of financial information are likely to have different information needs, which will in turn determine the ratios that they find useful. For example, shareholders are likely to be interested in their returns in relation to the level of risk associated with their investment. Thus profitability, investment and gearing ratios will be of particular interest. Long-term lenders are concerned with the long-term viability of the business, and to help them to assess this the profitability and gearing ratios of the business are also likely to be of particular interest. Short-term lenders, such as suppliers of goods and services on credit, may be interested in the ability of the business to repay the amounts owing in the short term. As a result, the liquidity ratios should be of interest.

We shall consider ratios falling into each of the five categories (profitability, efficiency, liquidity, gearing and investment) a little later in the chapter.

The need for comparison

Merely calculating a ratio will not tell us very much about the position or performance of a business. For example, if a ratio revealed that the business was generating £100 in sales revenue per square metre of counter space, it would not be possible to deduce from this information alone whether this particular level of performance was good, bad or indifferent. It is only when we compare this ratio with some 'benchmark' that the information can be interpreted and evaluated.

Activity 3.1

Can you think of any bases that could be used to compare a ratio you have calculated from the financial statements of a particular period?

In answering this activity you may have thought of the following bases:

- *Past periods.* By comparing the ratio we have calculated with the same ratio, but for a previous period, it is possible to detect whether there has been an improvement or

Activity 3.1 continued

deterioration in performance. Indeed, it is often useful to track particular ratios over time (say, five or ten years) to see whether it is possible to detect trends. The comparison of ratios from different time periods brings certain problems, however. In particular, there is always the possibility that trading conditions may have been quite different in the periods being compared. There is the further problem that, when comparing the performance of a single business over time, operating inefficiencies may not be clearly exposed. For example, the fact that net profit per employee has risen by 10 per cent over the previous period may at first sight appear to be satisfactory. This may not be the case, however, if similar businesses have shown an improvement of 50 per cent for the same period. Finally, there is the problem that inflation may have distorted the figures on which the ratios are based. Inflation can lead to an overstatement of profit and an understatement of asset values.

● *Similar businesses.*   In a competitive environment, a business must consider its performance in relation to that of other businesses operating in the same industry. Survival may depend on the ability to achieve comparable levels of performance. Thus a very useful basis for comparing a particular ratio is the ratio achieved by similar businesses during the same period. This basis is not, however, without its problems. Competitors may have different year ends, and therefore trading conditions may not be identical. They may also have different accounting policies, which can have a significant effect on reported profits and asset values (for example, different methods of calculating depreciation or valuing stock (inventory)). Finally, it may be difficult to obtain the financial statements of competitor businesses. Sole proprietorships and partnerships, for example, are not obliged to make their financial statements available to the public. In the case of limited companies, there is a legal obligation to do so. However, a diversified business may not provide a breakdown of activities that is sufficiently detailed for analysts to compare them with the activities of other businesses.

● *Planned performance.*   Ratios may be compared with the targets that management developed before the start of the period under review. The comparison of planned performance with actual performance may therefore be a useful way of revealing the level of achievement attained. However, the planned levels of performance must be based on realistic assumptions if they are to be useful for comparison purposes.

Planned performance is likely to be the most valuable benchmark for the managers to assess their own business. Businesses tend to develop planned ratios for each aspect of their activities. When formulating its plans, a business may usefully take account of its own past performance and that of other businesses. There is no reason, however, why a particular business should seek to achieve either its own previous performance or that of other businesses. Neither of these may be seen as an appropriate target.

Analysts outside the business do not normally have access to the business's plans. For these people, past performance and the performances of other, similar, businesses may be the only practical benchmarks.

Key steps in financial ratio analysis

When undertaking ratio analysis, analysts follow a sequence of steps. The first step involves identifying the key indicators and relationships that require examination. In carrying out this step, the analyst must be clear *who* the target users are and *why*

they need the information. We saw earlier that different types of users of financial information are likely to have different information needs that will, in turn, determine the ratios that they find useful.

The next step in the process is to calculate ratios that are considered appropriate for the particular users and the purpose for which they require the information.

The final step is interpretation and evaluation of the ratios. Interpretation involves examining the ratios in conjunction with an appropriate basis for comparison and any other information that may be relevant. The significance of the ratios calculated can then be established. Evaluation involves forming a judgement concerning the value of the information uncovered in the calculation and interpretation of the ratios. Whereas calculation is usually straightforward, and can be easily carried out by computer, the interpretation and evaluation are more difficult and often require high levels of skill. This skill can only really be acquired through much practice. The three steps described are shown in Figure 3.1.

Figure 3.1	The key steps of financial ratio analysis

The three steps involve: firstly, identifying for whom and for what purpose the analysis and interpretation is required; secondly, selecting appropriate ratios and calculating them; and, finally, forming a judgement on the information produced.

Calculating the ratios

Probably the best way to explain financial ratios is through an example. Example 3.1 provides a set of financial statements from which we can calculate important ratios.

Example 3.1

The following financial statements relate to Alexis plc, which operates a wholesale carpet business:

Balance sheets as at 31 March				
	2005		*2006*	
	£m	*£m*	*£m*	*£m*
Non-current assets				
Property, plant and equipment (at cost less depreciation)				
Freehold land and buildings	381		427	
Fixtures and fittings	129		160	
		510		587

→

Example 3.1 continued

	2005 £m	2005 £m	2006 £m	2006 £m
Current assets				
Stock (inventory) at cost	300		406	
Trade debtors (receivables)	240		273	
Bank	4		–	
	544		679	
Current liabilities				
Trade creditors (payables)	(221)		(314)	
Dividends approved, but unpaid	(40)		(40)	
Corporation tax due	(30)		(2)	
Bank overdraft	–		(76)	
	(291)	253	(432)	247
		763		834
Non-current liabilities				
9% debentures (secured)		(200)		(300)
		563		534
Equity				
£0.50 ordinary shares (Note 1)		300		300
Retained profit		263		234
		563		534

Profit and loss accounts (income statements) for the year ended 31 March

	2005 £m	2006 £m
Revenue (Note 2)	2,240	2,681
Less Cost of sales (Note 3)	1,745	2,272
Gross profit	495	409
Less Operating costs	252	362
Net profit before interest and tax	243	47
Less Interest payable	18	32
Net profit before tax	225	15
Less Corporation tax	60	4
Net profit after tax	165	11
Add Retained profit brought forward	138	263
	303	274
Less Dividends approved, but unpaid (Note 4)	40	40
Retained profit carried forward	263	234

Notes
1 The market value of the shares of the business at the end of the year was £2.50 for 2005 and £1.50 for 2006.
2 All sales and purchases are made on credit.
3 The cost of sales figure can be analysed as follows:

	2005 £m	2006 £m
Opening stock	241	300
Purchases (Note 2)	1,804	2,378
	2,045	2,678
Less Closing stock	300	406
Cost of sales	1,745	2,272

4 The dividend had been approved by the shareholders before the end of the accounting year (in both years), but not paid until after then.
5 The business employed 13,995 staff at 31 March 2005 and 18,623 at 31 March 2006.
6 The business expanded its capacity during the year ended 31 March 2006 by setting up a new warehouse and distribution centre in the north of England.
7 At 1 April 2004, the total of equity stood at £438m and the total of equity and non-current liabilities stood at £638m.

A brief overview

Before we start our detailed look at the ratios for Alexis plc (in Example 3.1), it is helpful to take a quick look at what information is obvious from the financial statements. This will usually pick up some issues that the ratios may not be able to identify. It may also highlight some points that could help us in our interpretation of the ratios. Starting at the top of the balance sheet, the following points can be noted:

● *Expansion of non-current assets.* These have increased by about 15 per cent (from £510m to £587m) over the year. However, as the closing figure reflects the position after depreciation for the year has been deducted, the amount actually invested in non-current assets during the year will be higher than the difference between the opening and closing figures. Note 5 mentions a new warehouse and distribution centre, which may account for much of the additional investment in non-current assets. We are not told when this new facility was established, but it is quite possible that it was well into the year. This could mean that not much benefit was reflected in terms of additional sales revenue or cost saving during 2006. Sales revenue, in fact, expanded by about 20 per cent (from £2,240m to £2,681m), greater than the expansion in non-current assets.

● *Major expansion in the elements of working capital.* Stock (inventory) increased by about 35 per cent, trade debtors (receivables) by about 14 per cent and trade creditors (payables) by about 33 per cent between 2005 and 2006. These are major increases, particularly in stock and creditors (which are linked because the stock is all bought on credit – see Note 2).

● *Reduction in the cash balance.* The cash balance fell from £4m (in funds) to a £76m overdraft, between 2005 and 2006. The bank may be putting the business under pressure to reverse this, which could raise difficulties.

● *Apparent debt capacity.* Comparing either the non-current assets or the net assets with the long-term borrowings implies that the business may well be able to offer security on further borrowing. This is because potential lenders usually look at the value of assets that can be offered as security, when assessing loan requests. Lenders seem particularly attracted to freeholds as security. For example, at 31 March 2006, non-current assets had a balance sheet value of £587m, but long-term borrowing was only £300m (though there was also an overdraft of £76m). Balance sheet values are not normally, of course, market values. On the other hand, freeholds tend to have a market value higher than their balance sheet value owing to inflation in land values.

● *Lower profit.* Although sales revenue expanded by 20 per cent between 2005 and 2006, both cost of sales and operating costs rose by a greater percentage, leaving both gross profit and, particularly, net profit significantly reduced. The level of staffing, which increased by about 33 per cent (from 13,995 to 18,623), may have greatly affected the operating costs. (Without knowing when during 2006 the additional employees were recruited, we cannot be sure of the effect on operating costs.) Increasing staffing by 33 per cent must put an enormous strain on management, at least in the short term. It is not surprising, therefore, that 2006 was not successful for the business.

Having had a quick look at what is fairly obvious without calculating the normal ratios, we shall now go on to do so.

Profitability

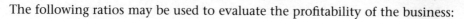

The following ratios may be used to evaluate the profitability of the business:

- return on ordinary shareholders' funds
- return on capital employed
- net profit margin
- gross profit margin.

We now look at each of these in turn.

Return on ordinary shareholders' funds (ROSF)

The **return on ordinary shareholders' funds** compares the amount of profit for the period available to the owners, with the owners' average stake in the business during that same period. The ratio (which is normally expressed in percentage terms) is as follows:

$$\text{ROSF} = \frac{\text{Net profit after taxation and preference dividend (if any)}}{\text{Ordinary share capital plus reserves}} \times 100\%$$

The net profit after taxation and any preference dividend is used in calculating the ratio, as this figure represents the amount of profit that is left for the owners.

In the case of Alexis plc, the ratio for the year ended 31 March 2005 is:

$$\text{ROSF} = \frac{165}{(438 + 563)/2} \times 100\% = 33.0\%$$

Note that, in calculating the ROSF, the average of the figures for ordinary shareholders' funds as at the beginning and at the end of the year has been used. It is preferable to use an average figure, as this might be more representative. This is because the shareholders' funds did not have the same total throughout the year, yet we want to compare it with the profit earned during the whole period. We know, from Note 7, that the total of the shareholders' funds at 1 April 2004 was £438m. By a year later, however, it had risen to £563m, according to the balance sheet as at 31 March 2005.

The easiest approach to calculating the average amount of shareholders' funds is to take a simple average based on the opening and closing figures for the year. This is often the only information available, as is the case with Example 3.1. Where not even the beginning-of-year figure is available, it is usually acceptable to use just the year-end figure, provided that this approach is adopted consistently. This is generally valid for all ratios that combine a figure for a period (such as net profit) with one taken at a point in time (such as shareholders' funds).

Activity 3.2

Calculate the ROSF for Alexis plc for the year to 31 March 2006.

The ROSF for 2006 is:

$$\text{ROSF} = \frac{11}{(563 + 534)/2} \times 100\% = 2.0\%$$

Broadly, businesses seek to generate as high as possible a value for this ratio, provided that it is not achieved at the expense of potential future returns by, for example, taking on more risky activities. In view of this, the 2006 ratio is very poor by any standards; a bank deposit account will yield a better return than this. We need to try to find out why things went so badly wrong in 2006. As we look at other ratios, we should find some clues.

Return on capital employed (ROCE)

→ The **return on capital employed** is a fundamental measure of business performance. This ratio expresses the relationship between the net profit generated during a period and the average long-term capital invested in the business during that period.

The ratio is expressed in percentage terms and is as follows:

$$\text{ROCE} = \frac{\textbf{Net profit before interest and taxation}}{\textbf{Share capital + Reserves + Long-term loans}} \times 100\%$$

Note, in this case, that the profit figure used is the net profit *before* interest and taxation. This is because the ratio attempts to measure the returns to all suppliers of long-term finance before any deductions for interest payable to lenders or payments of dividends to shareholders are made.

For the year to 31 March 2005, the ratio for Alexis plc is:

$$\text{ROCE} = \frac{243}{(638 + 763)/2} \times 100\% = 34.7\%$$

ROCE is considered by many to be a primary measure of profitability. It compares inputs (capital invested) with outputs (profit). This comparison is vital in assessing the effectiveness with which funds have been deployed. Once again, an average figure for capital employed may be used where the information is available.

Activity 3.3

Calculate the ROCE for Alexis plc for the year to 31 March 2006.

For 2006, the ratio is:

$$\text{ROCE} = \frac{47}{(763 + 834)/2} \times 100\% = 5.9\%$$

This ratio tells much the same story as ROSF: namely a poor performance, with the return on capital employed, or net assets, being less than the rate that the business has to pay for most of its borrowed funds (that is, 9 per cent for the debentures).

Real World 3.1 shows how financial ratios are used by businesses as a basis for setting profitability targets.

REAL WORLD 3.1

Setting profitability targets

The ROSF and ROCE ratios are widely used by businesses when establishing targets for profitability. These targets are sometimes made public and here are a few examples:

- Volkswagen, Europe's largest car maker, announced in 2003 that it aims to achieve a 9 per cent return on ordinary shareholders' funds by 2006.
- Deutsche Bank, one of Europe's largest banks, announced in 2004 that it aims to increase its pretax return on ordinary shareholders' funds from 13 per cent to 25 per cent in the following two years.
- Imperial Chemical Industries plc, a major UK chemical company, announced in 2003 that it aimed to increase ROCE to 10 per cent from between 7.0 and 7.8 per cent, which had been achieved over the previous five years.

Sources: 'VW's Poetsch sees 9pct return on equity by 2006', *AFX UK (Focus)*, 2 December 2003; 'Deutsche Bank aims for 25pct pretax return on equity in next two years', *AFX UK (Focus)*, 25 March 2004; 'Ambitions go hand in hand with targets at ICI. A positive chemical reaction', www.FT.Com, 31 October 2003.

Net profit margin

The **net profit margin ratio** relates the net profit for the period to the sales revenue during that period. The ratio is expressed as follows:

$$\text{Net profit margin} = \frac{\text{Net profit before interest and taxation}}{\text{Sales revenue}} \times 100\%$$

The net profit before interest and taxation is used in this ratio as it represents the profit from trading operations before the interest costs are taken into account. This is often regarded as the most appropriate measure of operational performance, when used as a basis of comparison, because differences arising from the way in which the business is financed will not influence the measure.

For the year ended 31 March 2005, Alexis plc's net profit margin ratio is:

$$\text{Net profit margin} = \frac{243}{2,240} \times 100\% = 10.8\%$$

This ratio compares one output of the business (profit) with another output (sales revenue). The ratio can vary considerably between types of business. For example, supermarkets tend to operate on low prices and, therefore, low profit margins in order to stimulate sales and thereby increase the total amount of profit generated. Jewellers, on the other hand, tend to have high net profit margins but have much lower levels of sales volume. Factors such as the degree of competition, the type of customer, the economic climate and industry characteristics (such as the level of risk) will influence the net profit margin of a business.

Activity 3.4

Calculate the net profit margin for Alexis plc for the year to 31 March 2006.

The net profit margin for 2006 is:

$$\text{Net profit margin} = \frac{47}{2,681} \times 100\% = 1.8\%$$

Once again a very weak performance compared with that of 2005. Whereas in 2005 for every £1 of sales revenue an average of 10.8p (that is, 10.8%) was left as profit, after paying the cost of the carpets sold and other expenses of operating the business, for 2006 this had fallen to only 1.8p for every £1. Thus the reason for the poor ROSF and ROCE ratios was partially, perhaps wholly, a high level of expenses relative to sales revenue. The next ratio should provide us with a clue as to how the sharp decline in this ratio occurred.

Real World 3.2 describes how one well-known business intends to increase its net profit margin over time.

REAL WORLD 3.2

Increasing the net profit margin   **FT**

Sony has vowed to increase net profit margins from 2.5 per cent in 2002 to 10 per cent in three years. This is expected to be achieved by cutting costs and increasing competitiveness. As part of its strategy, Sony plans to reduce the number of parts it uses in its consumer electronics division from 840,000 to 100,000 by the end of 2005. A Sony representative explained that 'In order to differentiate our products and raise their competitiveness, it is becoming necessary to even differentiate the parts that go into those products'. By reducing the number of parts it uses, Sony hopes to also free up product developers' time, so that they can concentrate more on the design of the product itself. The reduction in parts is expected to affect Sony's 4,700 parts suppliers, whose number Sony wants to reduce to 1,000. In a further effort to cut costs and increase competitiveness, Sony decided to broaden its voluntary redundancy programme for staff.

Source: Adapted from 'Sony sets more steps to raise profit margins', www.FT.com, 6 October 2003.

Gross profit margin

 The **gross profit margin ratio** relates the gross profit of the business to the sales revenue generated for the same period. Gross profit represents the difference between sales revenue and the cost of sales. The ratio is therefore a measure of profitability in buying (or producing) and selling goods before any other expenses are taken into account. As cost of sales represents a major expense for many businesses, a change in this ratio can have a significant effect on the 'bottom line' (that is, the net profit for the year). The gross profit margin ratio is calculated as follows:

$$\text{Gross profit margin} = \frac{\text{Gross profit}}{\text{Sales revenue}} \times 100\%$$

For the year to 31 March 2005, the ratio for Alexis plc is:

$$\text{Gross profit margin} = \frac{495}{2,240} \times 100\% = 22.1\%$$

Activity 3.5

Calculate the gross profit margin for Alexis plc for the year to 31 March 2006.

The gross profit margin for 2006 is:

$$\text{Gross profit margin} = \frac{409}{2,681} \times 100\% = 15.3\%$$

The decline in this ratio means that gross profit was lower *relative* to sales revenue in 2006 than it had been in 2005. Bearing in mind that:

Gross profit = Sales revenue – Cost of sales (or cost of goods sold)

this means that cost of sales was higher *relative* to sales revenue in 2006, than in 2005. This could mean that sales prices were lower and/or that the purchase cost of goods sold had increased. It is possible that both sales prices and goods sold prices had reduced, but the former at a greater rate than the latter. Similarly, they may both have increased, but with sales prices having increased at a lesser rate than costs of the goods sold.

Clearly, part of the decline in the net profit margin ratio is linked to the dramatic decline in the gross profit margin ratio. Whereas, after paying for the carpets sold, for each £1 of sales revenue 22.1p was left to cover other operating expenses and leave a profit in 2005, this was only 15.3p in 2006.

The profitability ratios for the business over the two years can be set out as follows:

	2005	2006
	%	%
ROSF	33.0	2.0
ROCE	34.7	5.9
Net profit margin	10.8	1.8
Gross profit margin	22.1	15.3

Activity 3.6

What do you deduce from a comparison of the declines in the net profit and gross profit margin ratios?

We can see that the decline in the net profit margin was 9 per cent (that is, from 10.8 per cent to 1.8 per cent), whereas the decline in the gross profit margin was only 6.8 per cent (that is, from 22.1 per cent to 15.3 per cent). This can only mean that operating expenses were greater, compared with sales revenue in 2006, than they had been in 2005. Thus, the declines in both ROSF and ROCE were caused partly by the business incurring higher stock purchasing costs relative to sales revenue and partly through higher operating expenses to sales revenue. We should need to compare these ratios with the planned levels for them before we could usefully assess the business's success.

The analyst must now carry out some investigation to discover what caused the increases in both cost of sales and operating costs, relative to sales revenue, from 2005 to 2006. This will involve checking on what has happened with sales and stock prices over the two years. Similarly, it will involve looking at each of the individual expenses that make up operating costs to discover which ones were responsible for the increase, relative to sales revenue. Here further ratios, for example staff costs (wages and salaries) to sales revenue, could be calculated in an attempt to isolate the cause of the change from 2005 to 2006. In fact, as we discussed when we took an overview of the financial statements, the increase in staffing may well account for most of the increase in operating costs.

Real World 3.3 shows how one well-known international business is seeking to improve its ROCE.

REAL WORLD 3.3

Lazy assets raise the ROCE at Shell

During 2003 Shell, the oil business (The 'Shell' Transport and Trading Company plc) disposed of $4 billion of, what it called, 'lazy assets'. These are assets that the business felt were not earning their keep and were holding down ROCE below the target range of 13 to 15%. The business had also identified a further $3 billion of assets that could be 'improved', so that they could also boost the business's ROCE.

Source: 'Shell disposals of $4 billion double initial estimate', Toby Shelley, www.FT.com, 22 December 2003.

Efficiency

Efficiency ratios examine the ways in which various resources of the business are managed. The following ratios consider some of the more important aspects of resource management:

● average stock (inventory) turnover period
● average settlement period for debtors (receivables)

- average settlement period for creditors (payables)
- sales revenue to capital employed
- sales revenue per employee.

We now look at each of these in turn.

Average stock (inventory) turnover period

Stocks often represent a significant investment for a business. For some types of business (for example, manufacturers), stocks may account for a substantial proportion of the total assets held (see Real World 10.1, p. 388). The **average stock turnover period** measures the average period for which stocks are being held. The ratio is calculated as follows:

$$\text{Average stock turnover period} = \frac{\text{Average stock held}}{\text{Cost of sales}} \times 365$$

The average stock for the period can be calculated as a simple average of the opening and closing stock levels for the year. However, in the case of a highly seasonal business, where stock levels may vary considerably over the year, a monthly average may be more appropriate.

In the case of Alexis plc, the stock turnover period for the year ended 31 March 2005 is:

$$\text{Average stock turnover period} = \frac{(241 + 300)/2}{1,745} \times 365 = 56.6 \text{ days}$$

This means that, on average, the stock held is being 'turned over' every 56.6 days. So, a carpet bought by the business on a particular day would, on average, have been sold about eight weeks' later. A business will normally prefer a short stock turnover period to a long one, as funds tied up in stocks cannot be used for other purposes. In judging the amount of stock to carry, the business must consider such things as the likely demand for the stock, the possibility of supply shortages, the likelihood of price rises, the amount of storage space available and the perishability of the stock. The management of stocks is considered in more detail in Chapter 10.

This ratio is sometimes expressed in terms of months rather than days. Multiplying by 12 rather than 365 will achieve this.

Activity 3.7

Calculate the average stock turnover period for Alexis plc for the year ended 31 March 2006.

The average stock turnover period for 2006 is:

$$\text{Average stock turnover period} = \frac{(300 + 406)/2}{2,272} \times 365 = 56.7 \text{ days}$$

Thus the average stock turnover period is virtually the same in both years.

Average settlement period for debtors

A business will usually be concerned with how long it takes for customers to pay the amounts owing. The speed of payment can have a significant effect on the business's cash flow. The **average settlement period for debtors** calculates how long, on average, credit customers take to pay the amounts that they owe to the business. The ratio is as follows:

$$\text{Average settlement period for debtors} = \frac{\text{Trade debtors}}{\text{Credit sales revenue}} \times 365$$

A business will normally prefer a shorter average settlement period to a longer one as, once again, funds are being tied up that may be used for more profitable purposes. Though this ratio can be useful, it is important to remember that it produces an *average* figure for the number of days for which debts are outstanding. This average may be badly distorted by, for example, a few large customers who are very slow or very fast payers.

Since all sales made by Alexis plc are on credit, the average settlement period for debtors for the year ended 31 March 2005 is:

$$\text{Average settlement period for debtors} = \frac{240}{2{,}240} \times 365 = 39.1 \text{ days}$$

As no figures for opening debtors are available, the year-end debtors figure only is used. This is common practice.

Activity 3.8

Calculate the average settlement period for Alexis plc's debtors for the year ended 31 March 2006. (In the interests of consistency, use the year-end debtors figure rather than an average figure.)

The average settlement period for 2006 is:

$$\text{Average settlement period for debtors} = \frac{273}{2{,}681} \times 365 = 37.2 \text{ days}$$

On the face of it, this reduction in the average settlement period is welcome. It means that less cash was tied up in debtors for each £1 of sales revenue in 2006 than in 2005. Only if the reduction were achieved at the expense of customer goodwill or a high direct financial cost, might the desirability of the reduction be questioned. For example, the reduction may have been due to chasing customers too vigorously or as a result of incurring higher costs, such as discounts allowed to customers who pay quickly.

Average settlement period for creditors

The **average settlement period for creditors** measures how long, on average, the business takes to pay its trade creditors. The ratio is calculated as follows:

$$\text{Average settlement period for creditors} = \frac{\text{Trade creditors}}{\text{Credit purchases}} \times 365$$

This ratio provides an average figure, which, like the average settlement period for debtors ratio, can be distorted by the payment period for one or two large suppliers.

As trade creditors provide a free source of finance for the business, it is perhaps not surprising that some businesses attempt to increase their average settlement period for trade creditors. However, such a policy can be taken too far and result in a loss of goodwill of suppliers. We return to the issues concerning the management of trade debtors and trade creditors in Chapter 10.

For the year ended 31 March 2005, Alexis plc's average creditors' settlement period is:

$$\text{Average settlement period for creditors} = \frac{221}{1,804} \times 365 = 44.7 \text{ days}$$

Once again, the year-end figure rather than an average figure for creditors has been used in the calculations.

Activity 3.9

Calculate the average settlement period for creditors for Alexis plc for the year ended 31 March 2006. (For the sake of consistency, use a year-end figure for creditors.)

The average settlement period for creditors is:

$$\text{Average settlement period for creditors} = \frac{314}{2,378} \times 365 = 48.2 \text{ days}$$

There was an increase, between 2005 and 2006, in the average length of time that elapsed between buying stock and paying for it. On the face of it, this is beneficial because the business is using free finance provided by suppliers. If, however, this is leading to a loss of supplier goodwill that could have adverse consequences for Alexis plc, it is not necessarily advantageous.

Sales revenue to capital employed

The **sales revenue to capital employed** ratio (or net asset turnover ratio) examines how effectively the assets of the business are being used to generate sales revenue. It is calculated as follows:

$$\frac{\text{Sales revenue to}}{\text{capital employed}} = \frac{\text{Sales revenue}}{\text{Share capital} + \text{Reserves} + \text{Long-term (non-current) loans}}$$

Generally speaking, a higher sales revenue to capital employed (net asset turnover) ratio is preferred to a lower one. A higher ratio will normally suggest that the long-term capital invested in assets is being used more productively in the generation of revenue. However, a very high ratio may suggest that the business is 'overtrading on its assets', that is, it has insufficient capital (net assets) to sustain the level of sales revenue achieved. (Overtrading is discussed in more detail later in the chapter.) When comparing this ratio for different businesses, such factors as the age and condition of assets held, the valuation bases for assets and whether assets are rented or purchased outright can complicate interpretation.

A variation of this formula is to use the total assets less current liabilities (which is equivalent to long-term capital employed) in the denominator (lower part of the fraction) – the identical result is obtained.

For the year ended 31 March 2005 this ratio for Alexis plc is as follows:

$$\text{Sales revenue to capital employed} = \frac{2{,}240}{(638 + 763)/2} = 3.19 \text{ times}$$

Calculate the sales revenue to capital employed ratio for Alexis plc for the year ended 31 March 2006.

The sales revenue to capital employed ratio for 2006 is:

$$\text{Sales revenue to capital employed} = \frac{2{,}681}{(763 + 834)/2} = 3.36 \text{ times}$$

This seems to be an improvement, since in 2006 more sales revenue was being generated for each £1 of capital employed (£3.36) than was the case in 2005 (£3.19). Provided that overtrading is not an issue, this is to be welcomed.

Sales revenue per employee

The **sales revenue per employee** ratio relates sales revenue generated to a particular business resource, that is, labour. It provides a measure of the productivity of the workforce. The ratio is:

$$\text{Sales revenue per employee} = \frac{\textbf{Sales revenue}}{\textbf{Number of employees}}$$

Generally, businesses would prefer to have a high value for this ratio, implying that they are using their staff efficiently.

For the year ended 31 March 2005, the ratio for Alexis plc is:

$$\text{Sales revenue per employee} = \frac{£2{,}240m}{13{,}995} = £160{,}057$$

Calculate the sales revenue per employee for Alexis plc for the year ended 31 March 2006.

The ratio for 2006 is:

$$\text{Sales revenue per employee} = \frac{£2{,}681m}{18{,}623} = £143{,}962$$

This represents a fairly significant decline and probably one that merits further investigation. As we discussed previously, the number of employees had increased quite notably (by about 33 per cent) during 2006 and the analyst will probably try to discover why this had not generated sufficient additional sales revenue to maintain the ratio at its 2005 level. It could be that the additional employees were not appointed until late in the year ended 31 March 2006.

The efficiency, or activity, ratios may be summarised as follows:

	2005	2006
Average stock turnover period	56.6 days	56.7 days
Average settlement period for debtors	39.1 days	37.2 days
Average settlement period for creditors	44.7 days	48.2 days
Sales revenue to capital employed (net asset turnover)	3.19 times	3.36 times
Sales revenue per employee	£160,057	£143,962

Activity 3.12

What do you deduce from a comparison of the efficiency ratios over the two years?

Maintaining the stock turnover period at the 2005 level seems reasonable, though whether this represents a satisfactory period can probably only be assessed by looking at the business's planned stock period. The stockholding period for other businesses operating in carpet retailing, particularly those regarded as the market leaders, may have been help- ful in formulating the plans. On the face of things, a shorter debtor collection period and a longer creditor payment period are both desirable. On the other hand, these may have been achieved at the cost of a loss of the goodwill of customers and suppliers, respec- tively. The increased asset turnover ratio seems beneficial, provided that the business can manage this increase. The decline in the sales revenue per employee ratio is undesirable but, as we have already seen, is probably related to the dramatic increase in the level of staffing. As with the stock turnover period, these other ratios need to be compared with the planned standard of efficiency.

The relationship between profitability and efficiency

In our earlier discussions concerning profitability ratios on page 66, we saw that return on capital employed (ROCE) is regarded as a key ratio by many businesses. The ratio is:

$$\text{ROCE} = \frac{\text{Net profit before interest and taxation}}{\text{Long-term capital employed}} \times 100$$

where long-term capital comprises share capital plus reserves plus long-term loans. This ratio can be broken down into two elements, as shown in Figure 3.2. The first ratio is the net profit margin ratio, and the second is the sales revenue to capital employed (net asset turnover) ratio, which we discussed earlier.

Figure 3.2	The main elements comprising the ROCE ratio

The ROCE ratio can be divided into two elements: net profit to sales and sales to capital employed. By analysing ROCE in this way, we can see the influence of both profitability and efficiency on this important ratio.

By breaking down the ROCE ratio in this manner, we highlight the fact that the overall return on funds employed within the business will be determined both by the profitability of sales and by efficiency in the use of capital.

Example 3.2

Consider the following information concerning two different businesses operating in the same industry:

	Antler plc	Baker plc
Profit before interest and tax	£20m	£15m
Long-term capital employed	£100m	£75m
Sales revenue	£200m	£300m

The ROCE for each business is identical (20 per cent). However, the manner in which the return was achieved by each business was quite different. In the case of Antler plc, the net profit margin is 10 per cent and the sales revenue to capital employed ratio is 2 times (so, ROCE = 10% × 2 = 20%). In the case of Baker plc, the net profit margin is 5 per cent and the sales revenue to capital employed ratio is 4 times (and so, ROCE = 5% × 4 = 20%).

Example 3.2 demonstrates that a relatively low net profit margin can be compensated for by a relatively high sales revenue to capital employed ratio, and a relatively low sales revenue to capital employed ratio can be compensated for by a relatively high net profit margin. In many areas of retail and distribution (for example, supermarkets and delivery services) the net profit margins are quite low but the ROCE can be high, provided that the assets are used productively.

Activity 3.13

Show how the ROCE ratio for Alexis plc can be analysed into the two elements for each of the years 2005 and 2006.
   What conclusions can we draw from your figures?

	ROCE	=	Net profit margin	×	Sales revenue to capital employed
2005	34.7%		10.8%		3.19
2006	5.9%		1.8%		3.36

Thus the relationship between the three ratios holds for Alexis plc, for both years. The small apparent differences arise because the three ratios are stated above only to one or two decimal places.

Though the business was more effective at generating sales (sales revenue to capital employed ratio increased) from 2005 to 2006, it fell well below the level necessary to compensate for the sharp decline in the effectiveness of each sale (net profit margin). As a result, the 2006 ROCE was well below the 2005 value.

Liquidity

Liquidity ratios are concerned with the ability of the business to meet its short-term financial obligations. The following ratios are widely used:

- current ratio
- acid test ratio.

We now consider each of these.

Current ratio

The **current ratio** compares the 'liquid' assets (that is, cash and those assets held that will soon be turned into cash) of the business with the current liabilities. The ratio is calculated as follows:

$$\text{Current ratio} = \frac{\text{Current assets}}{\text{Current liabilities}}$$

Some people seem to suggest that there is an 'ideal' current ratio (usually 2 times, or 2:1) for all businesses. However, this fails to take into account the fact that different types of business require different current ratios. For example, a manufacturing business will often have a relatively high current ratio because it is necessary to hold stocks of finished goods, raw materials and work in progress. It will also normally sell goods on credit, thereby incurring debtors. A supermarket chain, on the other hand, will have a relatively low ratio, as it will hold only fast-moving stocks of finished goods and will generate mostly cash sales revenue. (See Real World 10.1 on p. 388.)

The higher the ratio, the more liquid the business is considered to be. As liquidity is vital to the survival of a business, a higher current ratio might be thought to be preferable to a lower one. If a business has a very high ratio, however, it may be that funds are tied up in cash or other liquid assets and are not, therefore, being used as productively as they might otherwise be.

As at 31 March 2005, the current ratio of Alexis plc is:

$$\text{Current ratio} = \frac{544}{291} = 1.9 \text{ times (or 1.9:1)}$$

Activity 3.14

Calculate the current ratio for Alexis plc as at 31 March 2006.

The current ratio as at 31 March 2006 is:

$$\text{Current ratio} = \frac{679}{432} = 1.6 \text{ times (or 1.6:1)}$$

Though this is a decline from 2005 to 2006, it is not necessarily a matter of concern. The next ratio may provide a clue as to whether there seems to be a problem.

Acid test ratio

The **acid test ratio** is very similar to the current ratio but it represents a more stringent test of liquidity. It can be argued that, for many businesses, stock cannot be converted into cash quickly. (Note that, in the case of Alexis plc, the stock turnover period was about 57 days in both years (see p. 72).) As a result, it may be better to exclude this particular asset from any measure of liquidity. The acid test ratio is a variation of the current ratio, but excluding stock.

The minimum level for this ratio is often stated as 1.0 times (or 1:1, that is, current assets (excluding stock) equals current liabilities). In many highly successful businesses that are regarded as having adequate liquidity, however, it is not unusual for the acid test ratio to be below 1.0 without causing particular liquidity problems. (See Real World 10.1 on p. 388.)

The acid test ratio is calculated as follows:

$$\text{Acid test ratio} = \frac{\text{Current assets (excluding stock)}}{\text{Current liabilities}}$$

The acid test ratio for Alexis plc as at 31 March 2005 is:

$$\text{Acid test ratio} = \frac{544 - 300}{291} = 0.8 \text{ times (or 0.8:1)}$$

We can see that the 'liquid' current assets do not quite cover the current liabilities, and so the business may be experiencing some liquidity problems.

Activity 3.15

Calculate the acid test ratio for Alexis plc as at 31 March 2006.

The acid test ratio as at 31 March 2006 is:

$$\text{Acid test ratio} = \frac{679 - 406}{432} = 0.6 \text{ times}$$

The 2006 ratio is significantly below that for 2005. The 2006 level may well be a cause for concern. The rapid decline in this ratio should lead to steps being taken, at least, to stop further decline.

The liquidity ratios for the two-year period may be summarised as follows:

	2005	2006
Current ratio	1.9	1.6
Acid test ratio	0.8	0.6

Activity 3.16

What do you deduce from the liquidity ratios set out above?

Though it is probably not really possible to make a totally valid judgement without knowing the planned ratios, there appears to have been an alarming decline in liquidity. This is indicated by both of these ratios. The apparent liquidity problem may, however, be planned, short term and linked to the expansion in non-current assets and staffing. It may be that when the benefits of the expansion come on stream, liquidity will improve. On the other hand, short-term creditors may become anxious when they see signs of weak liquidity. This anxiety could lead to steps being taken to press for payment and this could cause problems for Alexis plc.

Gearing

Financial gearing occurs when a business is financed, at least in part, by borrowing, instead of by finance provided by the owners (the shareholders). A business's level of gearing (that is, the extent to which it is financed from sources that require a fixed return) is an important factor in assessing risk. Where a business borrows heavily, it takes on a commitment to pay interest charges and make capital repayments. This can be a significant financial burden; it can increase the risk of the business becoming insolvent. Nevertheless, most businesses are geared to some extent.

Given the risks involved, we may wonder why a business would want to take on gearing (that is, to borrow). One reason may be that the owners have insufficient funds and therefore the only way to finance the business adequately is to borrow from others. Another reason is that gearing can be used to increase the returns to owners. This is possible provided the returns generated from borrowed funds exceed the cost of paying interest. The issue of gearing is important and we leave a detailed discussion of this topic until Chapter 8.

There are two ratios that are widely used to assess gearing:

- gearing ratio
- interest cover ratio.

Gearing ratio

The **gearing ratio** measures the contribution of long-term lenders to the long-term capital structure of a business. It may be calculated as follows:

$$\text{Gearing ratio} = \frac{\text{Long-term (non-current) loans}}{\text{Share capital + Reserves + Long-term (non-current) loans}} \times 100\%$$

The gearing ratio for Alexis plc, as at 31 March 2005, is:

$$\text{Gearing ratio} = \frac{200}{(563 + 200)} \times 100\% = 26.2\%$$

This ratio reveals a level of gearing that would not normally be considered to be very high.

Activity 3.17

Calculate the gearing ratio of Alexis plc as at 31 March 2006.

The gearing ratio as at 31 March 2006 is:

$$\text{Gearing ratio} = \frac{300}{(534 + 300)} \times 100\% = 36.0\%$$

This ratio reveals a substantial increase in the level of gearing over the year.

Interest cover ratio

The **interest cover ratio** measures the amount of profit available to cover interest payable. The ratio may be calculated as follows:

$$\text{Interest cover ratio} = \frac{\text{Profit before interest and taxation}}{\text{Interest payable}}$$

The ratio for Alexis plc for the year ended 31 March 2005 is:

$$\text{Interest cover ratio} = \frac{243}{18} = 13.5 \text{ times}$$

This ratio shows that the level of profit is considerably higher than the level of interest payable. Thus a significant fall in profits could occur before profit levels failed to cover interest payable. The lower the level of profit coverage, the greater the risk to lenders that interest payments will not be met, and the greater the risk to the shareholders that the lenders will take action against the business to recover the interest due.

Activity 3.18

Calculate the interest cover ratio of Alexis plc for the year ended 31 March 2006.

The interest cover ratio for 2006 is:

$$\text{Interest cover ratio} = \frac{47}{32} = 1.5 \text{ times}$$

Alexis plc's gearing ratios are:

	2005	2006
Gearing ratio	26.2%	36.0%
Interest cover ratio	13.5 times	1.5 times

Activity 3.19

What do you deduce from a comparison of the gearing ratios over the two years?

The gearing ratio altered significantly. This is mainly due to the substantial increase in the long-term loan during 2006, which has had the effect of increasing the relative contribution of long-term lenders to the financing of the business.

The interest cover ratio has declined dramatically from a position where profit covered interest 13.5 times in 2005, to one where profit covered interest only 1.5 times in 2006. This was partly caused by the increase in borrowings in 2006, but mainly caused by the dramatic decline in profitability in that year. The later situation looks hazardous; only a small decline in future profitability in 2006 would leave the business with insufficient profit to cover the interest payments. The gearing ratio at 31 March 2006 would not necessarily be considered to be very high for a business that was trading successfully. It is the low profitability that is the problem.

Without knowing what the business planned these ratios to be, it is not possible to reach a totally valid conclusion on Alexis plc's gearing.

Real World 3.4 below provides some evidence concerning the gearing of listed businesses.

REAL WORLD 3.4

The gearing of listed businesses   **FT**

Larger listed businesses tend to have higher levels of gearing than smaller ones. A Bank of England report on the financing of small businesses found that the average level of gearing among smaller listed businesses was 27 per cent compared with 37 per cent for the top 350 listed businesses. Over recent years the level of borrowing by larger listed businesses has risen steadily whereas the level of borrowing for smaller listed businesses has remained fairly stable. This difference in gearing levels between larger and smaller businesses flies in the face of conventional wisdom.

Recent government investigations have found that smaller listed businesses often find it hard to attract the interest of investors. Many large institutional investors, who dominate the stock market, are disinterested in the shares of smaller listed businesses because the amount of investment required is too small. As a result, shares in smaller businesses are less marketable. In such circumstances, it may be imagined that smaller businesses would become more reliant on loan financing and so would have higher levels of gearing than larger businesses. However, this is clearly not the case.

Although smaller businesses increase the level of shareholder funds by issuing relatively low dividends and therefore retaining more profits, they tend to be less profitable than larger businesses. Thus, higher retained profits do not seem to explain this phenomenon satisfactorily.

The only obvious factors that could explain this difference between smaller and larger businesses are the level of tax relief on loan interest, and borrowing capacity. Broadly, larger businesses pay tax at a higher rate than their smaller counterparts. This means that the tax benefits of borrowing tend to be greater per £ of interest paid for larger businesses than for smaller ones. It may well be that larger businesses can borrow at lower interest rates than smaller ones, if only because they tend to borrow larger sums and so the economies of scale may apply. Also, larger businesses tend to be less likely to get into financial difficulties than smaller ones, so they may be able to borrow at lower interest rates.

Source: Adapted from 'Small companies surprise on lending', *Financial Times*, 25 April 2003.

Investment ratios

There are various ratios available that are designed to help investors assess the returns on their investment. The following are widely used:

- dividend payout ratio
- dividend yield ratio
- earnings per share
- price/earnings ratio.

Dividend payout ratio

The **dividend payout ratio** measures the proportion of earnings that a business pays out to shareholders in the form of dividends. The ratio is calculated as follows:

$$\text{Dividend payout ratio} = \frac{\text{Dividends announced for the year}}{\text{Earnings for the year available for dividends}} \times 100\%$$

In the case of ordinary shares, the earnings available for dividend will normally be the net profit after taxation and after any preference dividends announced during the period. This ratio is normally expressed as a percentage.

The dividend payout ratio for Alexis plc for the year ended 31 March 2005 is:

$$\text{Dividend payout ratio} = \frac{40}{165} \times 100\% = 24.2\%$$

The information provided by this ratio is often expressed slightly differently as the **dividend cover ratio**. Here the calculation is:

$$\text{Dividend cover ratio} = \frac{\text{Earnings for the year available for dividend}}{\text{Dividend announced for the year}}$$

In the case of Alexis plc, for 2005 the dividend cover ratio would be 165/40 = 4.1 times. That is to say, the earnings available for dividend cover the actual dividend by just over four times.

Activity 3.20

Calculate the dividend payout ratio of Alexis plc for the year ended 31 March 2006.

The ratio for 2006 is:

$$\text{Dividend payout ratio} = \frac{40}{11} \times 100\% = 363.6\%$$

This would normally be considered to be a very alarming decline in the ratio over the two years. Paying a dividend of £40m in 2006 would probably be regarded as very imprudent.

Dividend yield ratio

→ The **dividend yield ratio** relates the cash return from a share to its current market value. This can help investors to assess the cash return on their investment in the business. The ratio is:

$$\text{Dividend yield} = \frac{\text{Dividend per share}/(1 - t)}{\text{Market value per share}} \times 100\%$$

where t is the 'lower' rate of income tax. The dividend yield ratio is also expressed as a percentage.

The numerator (the top part) of this ratio requires some explanation. In the UK, investors who receive a dividend from a business also receive a tax credit. This tax credit is equal to the amount of tax that would be payable on the dividends received by a lower-rate taxpayer. As this tax credit can be offset against any tax liability arising from the dividends received, the dividends are in effect issued net of tax to lower-rate income tax payers.

Investors may wish to compare the returns from shares with the returns from other forms of investment. As these other forms of investment are often quoted on a 'gross' (that is, pre-tax) basis it is useful to 'gross up' the dividend to make comparison easier.
→ We can achieve this by dividing the **dividend per share** by $(1 - t)$, where t is the 'lower' rate of income tax.

Assuming a lower rate of income tax of 10 per cent, the dividend yield for Alexis plc for the year ended 31 March 2005 is:

$$\text{Dividend yield} = \frac{0.067^*/(1 - 0.10)}{2.50} \times 100\% = 3.0\%$$

* Dividend proposed/number of shares = 40/(300 × 2) = £0.067 dividend per share (the 300 is multiplied by 2 because they are £0.50 shares).

Activity 3.21

Calculate the dividend yield for Alexis plc for the year ended 31 March 2006.

Your answer should be as follows:

$$\text{Dividend yield} = \frac{0.067^*/(1 - 0.10)}{1.50} \times 100\% = 5.0\%$$

* $40/(300 \times 2) = £0.067$

Earnings per share

→ The **earnings per share** (EPS) ratio relates the earnings generated by the business, and available to shareholders, during a period to the number of shares in issue. For equity (ordinary) shareholders, the amount available will be represented by the net profit after tax (less any preference dividend, where applicable). The ratio for equity shareholders is calculated as follows:

$$\text{Earnings per share} = \frac{\text{Earnings available to ordinary shareholders}}{\text{Number of ordinary shares in issue}}$$

In the case of Alexis plc, the earnings per share for the year ended 31 March 2005 is as follows:

$$\text{EPS} = \frac{£165}{600} = 27.5\text{p}$$

Many investment analysts regard the EPS ratio as a fundamental measure of share performance. The trend in earnings per share over time is used to help assess the investment potential of a business's shares. Though it is possible to make total profits rise through ordinary shareholders investing more in the business, this will not necessarily mean that the profitability *per share* will rise as a result.

It is not usually very helpful to compare the earnings per share of one business with those of another. Differences in capital structure (level of gearing) can render any such comparison meaningless. However, it can be very useful to monitor the changes that occur in this ratio for a particular business over time.

Activity 3.22

Calculate the earnings per share of Alexis plc for the year ended 31 March 2006.

The earnings per share for 2006 is:

$$\text{EPS} = \frac{£11}{600} = 1.8\text{p}$$

Price/earnings (P/E) ratio

→ The **price/earnings ratio** relates the market value of a share to the earnings per share. This ratio can be calculated as follows:

$$\text{P/E ratio} = \frac{\text{Market value per share}}{\text{Earnings per share}}$$

The P/E ratio for Alexis plc as at 31 March 2005 is:

$$\text{P/E ratio} = \frac{£2.50}{27.5\text{p}^*} = 9.1 \text{ times}$$

* The EPS figure (27.5p) was calculated on p. 85.

This ratio reveals that the capital value of the share is 9.1 times higher than its current level of earnings. The ratio is a measure of market confidence in the future of a business. The higher the P/E ratio, the greater the confidence in the future earning power of the business and, consequently, the more investors are prepared to pay in relation to the earnings stream of the business.

P/E ratios provide a useful guide to market confidence concerning the future and they can, therefore, be helpful when comparing different businesses. However, differences in accounting policies between businesses can lead to different profit and earnings per share figures, and this can distort comparisons.

Activity 3.23

Calculate the P/E ratio of Alexis plc as at 31 March 2006.

Your answer to this activity should be as follows:

$$\text{P/E ratio} = \frac{£1.50}{1.8\text{p}} = 83.3 \text{ times}$$

The investment ratios for Alexis plc over the two-year period are as follows:

	2005	2006
Dividend payout ratio	24.2%	363.6%
Dividend yield ratio	3.0%	5.0%
Earnings per share	27.5p	1.8p
P/E ratio	9.1 times	83.3 times

Activity 3.24

What do you deduce from the investment ratios set out above?

Can you offer an explanation why the share price has not fallen as much as it might have done, bearing in mind the very poor (relative to 2005) trading performance in 2006?

We thought that, although:

- the EPS has fallen dramatically, and
- the dividend payment for 2006 seems very imprudent

the share price seems to have held up remarkably well (fallen from £2.50 to £1.50, see p. 64). This means that dividend yield and P/E value for 2006 look better than those for 2005. This is an anomaly of these two ratios, which stems from using a forward-looking value (the share price) in conjunction with historic data (dividends and earnings). Share prices are based on investors' assessments of the business's future. It seems with Alexis plc that at the end of 2006 the 'market' was not happy with the business, relative to 2005, evidenced by the fact that the share price had fallen by £1 a share. On the other hand, the share price has not fallen as much as profits. It appears that investors believe that the business will perform better in the future than it did in 2006. This may well be because they believe that the large expansion in assets and employee numbers that occurred in 2006 will yield benefits in the future: benefits that the business was not able to generate during 2006.

Real World 3.5 gives some information about the shares of several large, well-known UK businesses. This type of information is provided on a daily basis by several newspapers, notably the *Financial Times*.

REAL WORLD 3.5

Market statistics for some well-known businesses   **FT**

The following information was extracted from the *Financial Times* of 12 October 2004, relating to the previous day's trading of the shares of some well-known businesses on the London Stock Exchange.

Share	Price	(+/–)	52 week High	Low	Y'ld Gr's	P/E	Volume 000s
BP	549¹/₂	–2	556¹/₂	402	2.8	18.5	60,033
JD Wetherspoon	250¹/₄	+1³/₄	324	240	1.6	14.1	64
BSkyB	506¹/₂	–¹/₂	786	465¹/₂	1.2	26.6	10,700
Marks and Spencer	343	–1³/₄	368¹/₄	264	3.4	14.7	13,049
Rolls-Royce	253	–1	265³/₄	165	3.3	20.6	16,802
Vodafone	136¹/₄	–1¹/₄	150¹/₄	114	1.5	14.7	165,681

The column headings are as follows:

Price	Mid-market price (that is, the price midway between buying and selling price) of the shares at the end of 11 October 2004.
(+/–)	Gain or loss (usually stated in pence) from the previous day's mid-market price.
High/Low	Highest and lowest prices reached by the share during the year (stated in pence).
Y'ld gr's	Gross dividend yield, based on the most recent year's dividend and the current share price.
P/E	Price/earnings ratio, based on the most recent year's after-tax profit and the current share price.
Volume	The number of shares (in thousands) that were bought and sold on 11 October 2004.

Real World 3.6 shows how investment ratios can vary between different industry sectors.

REAL WORLD 3.6

How investment ratios vary between industries   **FT**

Investment ratios can vary significantly between businesses and between industries. To give some indication of the range of variations that occur, the average dividend yield ratios and average P/E ratios for listed businesses in 12 different industries are shown in Figures 3.3 and 3.4 respectively.

These ratios are calculated from the current market value of the shares and the most recent year's dividend paid (dividend yield) or earnings per share (P/E).

Some industries tend to pay out lower dividends than others, leading to lower dividend yield ratios. Pharmaceutical businesses tend to invest heavily in developing new drugs, hence their tendency to pay low dividends compared with their share prices. Electricity businesses probably tend to invest less heavily than pharmaceuticals, hence their rather higher level of dividend yields. Some of the inter-industry differences in the dividend yield ratio can be explained by the nature of the calculation of the ratio. The prices of shares at any given moment are based on expectations of their economic futures; dividends are actual past events. A business that had a good trading year recently may have paid a dividend that, in the light of investors' assessment on the business's economic future, may be high (a high dividend yield).

Figure 3.3	Average dividend yield ratios for businesses in a range of industries

Times (y-axis, 0 to 6)

Industry	Value
Oil and gas	2.82
Construction and building materials	3.21
Chemicals	3.65
Engineering and machinery	3.37
Pharmaceuticals and biotechnology	2.86
Tobacco	4.43
Transport	3.23
Leisure and hotels	2.37
Food and drug retailers	2.69
Electricity	4.23
Real estate	2.55
Banks	4.12

Average levels of dividend yield tend to vary from one industry to the next.

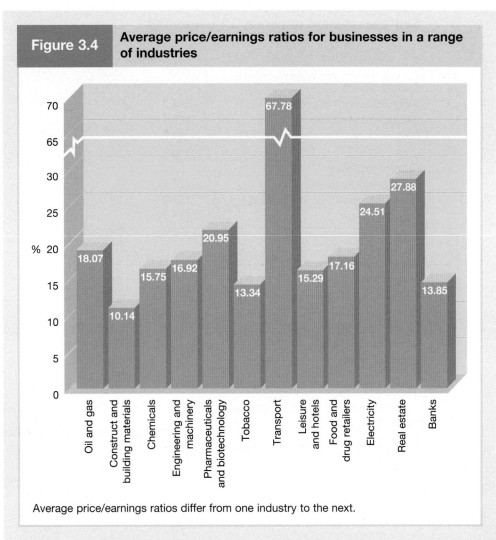

Figure 3.4   **Average price/earnings ratios for businesses in a range of industries**

Average price/earnings ratios differ from one industry to the next.

Businesses that have a high share price relative to their recent historic earnings have high P/E ratios. This may be because their future is regarded as economically bright, which may be as a result of investing heavily in the future at the expense of current profits (earnings).

Source: Graphs constructed from data appearing in the *Financial Times*, 2–3 October 2004.

Self-assessment question 3.1

Both Ali plc and Bhaskar plc operate electrical stores throughout the UK. The financial statements of each business for the year ended 30 June 2006 are as follows:

Balance sheets as at 30 June 2006

	Ali plc		Bhaskar plc	
Non-current assets	£000	£000	£000	£000
Property, plant and equipment (cost less depreciation)				
Freehold land and buildings		360.0		510.0
Fixtures and fittings		87.0		91.2
		447.0		601.2

Self-assessment question 3.1 continued

	Ali plc		Bhaskar plc	
	£000	£000	£000	£000
Current assets				
Stock (inventory) at cost	592.0		403.0	
Debtors (receivables)	176.4		321.9	
Cash at bank	84.6		91.6	
	853.0		816.5	
Current liabilities				
Trade creditors (payables)	(271.4)		(180.7)	
Dividends (approved, but unpaid)	(135.0)		(95.0)	
Corporation tax	(16.0)		(17.4)	
	(422.4)	430.6	(293.1)	523.4
		877.6		1,124.6
Non-current liabilities				
Debentures		(190.0)		(250.0)
		687.6		874.6
Equity				
£1 ordinary shares		320.0		250.0
General reserves		355.9		289.4
Retained profit		11.7		335.2
		687.6		874.6

Profit and loss accounts (income statements) for the year ended 30 June 2006

	Ali plc		Bhaskar plc	
	£000	£000	£000	£000
Revenue		1,478.1		1,790.4
Less Cost of sales				
Opening stock	480.8		372.6	
Purchases	1,129.5		1,245.3	
	1,610.3		1,617.9	
Less Closing stock	592.0	1,018.3	403.0	1,214.9
Gross profit		459.8		575.5
Less Operating expenses		308.5		408.6
Net profit before interest and tax		151.3		166.9
Less Interest payable		19.4		27.5
Net profit before tax		131.9		139.4
Less Corporation tax		32.0		34.8
Net profit after taxation		99.9		104.6
Add Retained profit brought forward		46.8		325.6
		146.7		430.2
Less Dividends approved, but unpaid		135.0		95.0
Retained profit carried forward		11.7		335.2

All purchases and sales were on credit. The dividends for both years had been approved by the shareholders before the respective year ends, but were paid after those times. The market values of a share in each business at the end of the year were £6.50 and £8.20 respectively.

Required:
For each business, calculate two ratios that are concerned with liquidity, gearing and investment (six ratios in total). What can you conclude from the ratios that you have calculated?

Financial ratios and the problem of overtrading

→ **Overtrading** occurs where a business is operating at a level of activity that cannot be supported by the amount of finance that has been committed. For example, the business has inadequate finance to fund the level of debtors and stocks necessary for the level of sales revenue that it is achieving. This situation usually reflects a poor level of financial control over the business. The reasons for overtrading are varied. It may occur in young, expanding businesses that fail to prepare adequately for the rapid increase in demand for its goods or services. It may also occur in businesses where the managers may have miscalculated the level of expected sales demand or have failed to control escalating project costs. It may occur as a result of a fall in the value of money (inflation), causing more finance to be committed to stock in trade and debtors, even where there is no expansion in the real volume of trade. It may occur where the owners are unable both to inject further funds into the business and to persuade others to invest in the business. Whatever the reason for overtrading, the problems that it brings must be dealt with if the business is to survive over the longer term.

Overtrading results in liquidity problems such as exceeding borrowing limits, or slow repayment of lenders and creditors. It can also result in suppliers withholding supplies, thereby making it difficult to meet customer demand. The managers of the business might be forced to direct all their efforts to dealing with immediate and pressing problems, such as finding cash to meet interest charges due or paying wages. Longer-term planning becomes difficult and managers may spend their time going from crisis to crisis. At the extreme, a business may fail because it cannot meet its maturing obligations.

To deal with the overtrading problem, a business must ensure that the finance available is commensurate with the level of operations. Thus, if a business that is overtrading is unable to raise new finance, it should cut back its level of operations in line with the finance available. Although this may mean lost sales and lost profits in the short term, it may be necessary to ensure survival over the longer term.

Activity 3.25

If a business is overtrading, do you think the following ratios would be higher or lower than normally expected?

(a) Current ratio
(b) Average stock turnover period
(c) Average settlement period for debtors
(d) Average settlement period for creditors.

Your answer should be as follows:

(a) The current ratio would be lower than normally expected. This is a measure of liquidity, and lack of liquidity is an important symptom of overtrading.
(b) The average stock turnover period would be lower than normally expected. Where a business is overtrading, the level of stocks held will be low because of the problems of financing stocks. In the short term, sales revenue may not be badly affected by the low stock levels and therefore stocks will be turned over more quickly.
(c) The average settlement period for debtors may be lower than normally expected. Where a business is suffering from liquidity problems it may chase debtors more vigorously in order to improve cash flows.
(d) The average settlement period for creditors may be higher than normally expected. The business may try to delay payments to creditors because of the liquidity problems arising.

Trend analysis

It is often helpful to see whether ratios are indicating trends. Key ratios can be plotted on a graph to provide a simple visual display of changes occurring over time. The trends occurring within a business may, for example, be plotted against trends for rival businesses or for the industry as a whole for comparison purposes. An example of trend analysis is shown in **Real World 3.7**.

REAL WORLD 3.7

Trend setting

In Figure 3.5 below, the current ratio of Tesco plc is plotted against the same ratio for two other businesses within the same industry – J. Sainsbury plc and Wm Morrison plc – over a five-year period. We can see that the current ratio of Tesco plc has risen slightly over the period but it is, nevertheless, consistently lower than that of its main rivals.

| Figure 3.5 | Graph plotting current ratio against time |

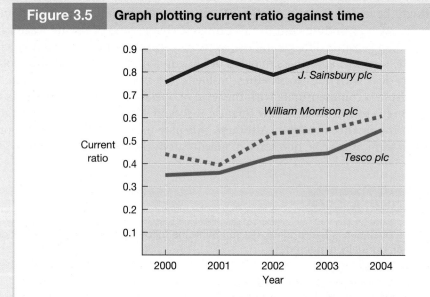

The current ratio for Tesco plc is plotted for the financial years ending 2000–2004. On the same graph the current ratio for J. Sainsbury plc and Wm Morrison plc is plotted for the same financial years, enabling comparison to be made between the ratio for Tesco plc and those of its rivals.

Source: Compiled using information in the annual reports of Tesco plc, J. Sainsbury plc and Wm Morrison plc.

Many larger businesses publish certain key financial ratios as part of their annual reports to help users identify significant trends. These ratios typically cover several years' activities. **Real World 3.8** is based on extracts from tables of 'key performance measures' of Marks and Spencer plc (M&S), the well-known UK high street store that were published in its annual reports of 2003 and 2004. After many years of profitable growth, M&S suffered a decline in its fortunes during the late 1990s. This was seen by the directors, and by many independent commentators, as arising from the business allowing itself to be drawn away from its traditional areas of strength into such activities as operating overseas businesses. Steps were taken to deal with the problem and the business seemed to have 'turned the corner'. M&S seems to have reached its low point in the year ended March 2001 when it incurred a significant overall loss, with a trading profit only about 40 per cent of what had been achieved in 1998. We can see from the table that the gross (profit) margin seemed not to be the cause of the problem. In fact turnover was down in 2001 and expenses were up. The improvements in 2003 and 2004 are very clear. The return to equity (return on ordinary shareholders funds) in 2004 is significantly better than for any others in the previous five years. Also in 2004, both the gross (profit) and net (profit) margins are better than in the previous five years.

REAL WORLD 3.8

Key performance measures of Marks and Spencer Group plc

	2004	2003	2002	2001	2000	1999
	53 weeks	52 weeks	52 weeks	52 weeks	53 weeks	52 weeks
Gross profit margin	36.6%	36.2%	35.8%	34.3%	31.8%	31.1%
Net profit margin	9.9%	9.1%	8.3%	6.2%	6.6%	8.0%
Earnings per share	24.2p	21.8p	5.4p	(0.2)p	9.6p	13.0p
Dividend per share	11.5p	10.5p	9.5p	9.0p	9.0p	14.4p
Dividend cover	2.1×	2.1×	2.2×	n/a	1.1×	0.9×
Return on equity	25.2%	22.4%	11.5%	(0.1)%	5.7%	7.8%

Source: Marks & Spencer Group plc Annual Reports 2003 and 2004. Reproduced by kind permission of Marks & Spencer Group plc.

Using ratios to predict financial failure

Financial ratios, based on current or past performance, are often used to help predict the future. However, both the choice of ratios and the interpretation of results are normally dependent on the judgement and opinion of the analyst. In recent years, however, attempts have been made to develop a more rigorous and systematic approach to the use of ratios for prediction purposes. In particular, researchers have shown an interest in the ability of ratios to predict the financial failure of a business.

By financial failure, we mean a business either going out of business or being severely adversely affected by its inability to meet its financial obligations. It is often referred to as 'going bust' or 'going bankrupt'. This, of course, is an area with which all those connected with the business are likely to be concerned.

Using single ratios

Many methods and models employing ratios have now been developed that claim to predict future financial failure. Early research focused on the examination of ratios on an individual basis to see whether they were good or bad predictors of financial failure. Here a particular ratio (for example, the current ratio), for a business that had failed, was tracked over several years leading up to the date of the failure. This was to see whether it was possible to say that the ratio had showed a trend that could have been taken as a warning sign.

Beaver (see reference 1 at the end of the chapter) carried out the first research in this area. He calculated the average (mean) of various ratios for 79 businesses that had actually failed, over the ten-year period leading up to their failure. Beaver then compared these average ratios with similarly derived ratios for a sample of 79 businesses that did not fail over this period. (The research used a matched-pair design, where each failed business was matched with a non-failed business of similar size and industry type.) Beaver found that some ratios exhibited a marked difference between the failed and non-failed businesses for up to five years prior to failure. This is shown in Figure 3.6.

To explain Figure 3.6, let us take a closer look at graph (a). This plots the ratio, cash flow (presumably the operating cash flow figure, taken from the cash flow statement) divided by total debt. For the non-failed businesses this stayed fairly steady at about +0.45 over the period. For the failed businesses, however, this was already well below the non-failed businesses at about +0.15 even five years before those businesses eventually failed. It then declined steadily until, by one year before the failure, it was less than −0.15. Note that the scale of the horizontal axis shows the most recent year (Year 1) on the left and the earliest one (Year 5) on the right. The other graphs ((b) to (f)) show a similar picture for five other ratios. In each case there is a deteriorating average ratio for the failed businesses, as the time of failure approaches.

What is shown in Figure 3.6 implied that failure could be predicted by careful assessment of the trend shown by particular key ratios.

Research by Zmijewski (see reference 2 at the end of the chapter), using a sample of 72 failed and 3,573 non-failed businesses over a six-year period, found that failed businesses were characterised by lower rates of return, higher levels of gearing, lower levels of coverage for their fixed interest payments and more variable returns on shares. While we may not find these results very surprising, it is interesting to note that Zmijewski, like a number of other researchers in this area, did not find liquidity ratios particularly useful in predicting financial failure. Intuition might have led us (wrongly it seems) to believe that the liquidity ratios would have been particularly helpful in this context.

The approach adopted by Beaver and Zmijewski is referred to as **univariate analysis** because it looks at one ratio at a time. Although this approach can produce interesting results, there are practical problems associated with its use. Let us say, for example, that past research has identified two ratios as being good predictors of financial failure. When applied to a particular business, however, it may be found that one ratio predicts financial failure whereas the other does not. Given these conflicting signals, how should the decision maker interpret the results?

Using combinations of ratios

The weaknesses of univariate analysis have led researchers to develop models that combine ratios in such a way as to produce a single index that can be interpreted more clearly. One approach to model development, much favoured by researchers, applies **multiple discriminate analysis (MDA)**. This is, in essence, a statistical technique that is similar to regression analysis and which can be used to draw a boundary between those businesses that fail and those businesses that do not. This boundary is referred to as the

Figure 3.6   Average (mean) ratios of failed and non-failed businesses

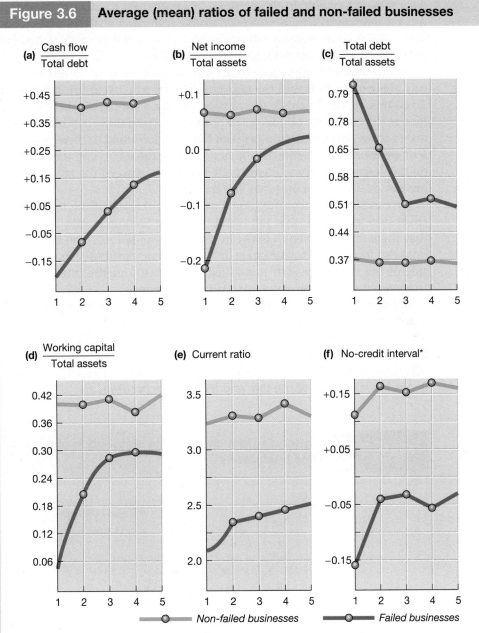

Each of the ratios (a) to (f) above indicates a marked difference in the average ratio between the sample of failed businesses and a matched sample of non-failed businesses. The vertical scale of each graph is the average value of the particular ratio for each group of businesses (failed and non-failed). The horizontal axis is the number of years before failure. Thus Year 1 is the most recent year and Year 5 the earliest of the years. For each of the six ratios, the difference between the average for the failed and the non-failed businesses can be detected five years prior to the failure of the former group.

Source: 'Financial ratios as predictors of failure', W. H. Beaver *Empirical Research in Accounting: Selected Studies*, supplement to *Journal of Accounting Research*, Autumn, 1966, pp. 71–111.

discriminate function. In this context, MDA attempts to identify those factors likely to influence financial failure. However, unlike regression analysis, MDA assumes that the observations come from two different populations (for example, failed and non-failed businesses) rather than from a single population.

To illustrate this approach, let us assume that we wish to test whether two ratios (say, the current ratio and the return on capital employed) can help to predict failure. To do this, we can calculate these ratios, first for a sample of failed businesses and then for a matched sample of non-failed businesses. From these two sets of data we can produce a scatter diagram that plots each business according to these two ratios to produce a single coordinate. Figure 3.7 illustrates this approach. Using the observations plotted on the diagram, we try to identify the boundary between the failed and the non-failed businesses. This is the diagonal line in Figure 3.7.

We can see that those businesses that fall to the left of the line are predominantly failed ones and those that fall to the right are predominantly non-failed ones. Note that there is some overlap between the two populations. The boundary produced is unlikely, in practice, to eliminate all errors. Some businesses that fail may fall on the side of the boundary with non-failed businesses, and the other way round as well. However, it will *minimise* the misclassification errors.

The boundary shown in Figure 3.7 can be expressed in the form:

$$Z = a + (b \times \text{Current ratio}) + (c \times \text{ROCE})$$

where a is a constant and b and c are weights to be attached to each ratio. A weighted average or total score (Z) is then derived. The weights given to the two ratios will depend on the slope of the line and its absolute position.

Figure 3.7   **Scatter diagram showing the distribution of failed and non-failed businesses**

The distribution of failed and non-failed businesses is based on two ratios. The line represents a boundary between the samples of failed and non-failed businesses. Although there is some crossing of the boundary, the boundary represents the line that minimises the problem of misclassifying particular businesses.

Source: After Atrill (2003), p.

Z score models

Altman (see reference 3 at the end of the chapter) was the first to develop a model using financial ratios that was able to predict financial failure. His model, the Z score model, is based on five financial ratios and is as follows:

$$Z = 1.2a + 1.4b + 3.3c + 0.6d + 1.0e$$

where: a = Working capital/Total assets
  b = Accumulated retained profits/Total assets
  c = Profit before interest and taxation/Total assets
  d = Market value of ordinary and preference shares/Total liabilities at book value
  e = Sales revenue/Total assets.

In developing this model, Altman carried out experiments using a paired sample of failed businesses and non-failed businesses and collected relevant data for each business for five years prior to failure. He found that the model represented by the formula above was able to predict failure for up to two years before it occurred. However, the predictive accuracy of the model became weaker the further the period from failure.

The ratios used in this model were identified by Altman through a process of trial and error, as there is no underlying theory of financial failure to help guide researchers in their selection of appropriate ratios. According to Altman, those businesses with a Z score of less than 1.81 tend to fail, and the lower the score the greater the probability of failure. Those with a Z score greater than 2.99 tended not to fail. Those businesses with a Z score between 1.81 and 2.99 occupied a 'zone of ignorance' and were difficult to classify. However, the model was able overall to classify 95 per cent of the businesses correctly. Altman based his model on US businesses.

In recent years, this model has been updated and other models, using a similar approach, have been developed throughout the world. In the UK, Taffler (see reference 4 at the end of the chapter) has developed separate Z score models for different types of business.

The prediction of financial failure is not the only area where research into the predictive ability of ratios has taken place. Researchers have also developed ratio-based models that claim to assess the vulnerability of a business to takeover by another. This is another area that is of vital importance to all those connected with the business.

Limitations of ratio analysis

Although ratios offer a quick and useful method of analysing the position and performance of a business, they are not without their problems and limitations. Some of the more important limitations are as follows:

- *Accounting conventions.* It must always be remembered that ratios are based on financial statements, and the results of ratio analysis are dependent on the quality of these underlying statements. Ratios will inherit the limitations of the financial statements on which they are based. A significant example of this arises from the application of the prudence convention to internally generated intangible non-current assets (as compared with purchased ones). This convention tends to lead to assets of considerable value, such as goodwill and brand names, being excluded from the balance sheet. This can mean that ratios, like ROSF, ROCE and the gearing ratio, fail to take account of these assets.

● *Creative accounting.*   Despite the proliferation of accounting rules and the independent checks that are imposed, there is evidence that the directors of some companies
have employed particular accounting policies or structured particular transactions in
such a way that portrays a picture of financial health that is in line with what they
would like users to see rather than what is a true and fair view of financial position
and performance. This practice is referred to as **creative accounting** and it can pose
a major problem for those seeking to gain an impression of the financial health of
a business.

Activity 3.26

Why might the directors of a business engage in creative accounting?

There are many reasons and these include:

● to get around restrictions (for example, to report sufficient profit to pay a dividend);
● to avoid government action (for example, the taxation of excessive profits);
● to hide poor management decisions;
● to achieve sales or profit targets, thereby ensuring that performance bonuses are paid
to the directors;
● to attract new share capital or loan capital by showing a healthy financial position; and
● to satisfy the demands of major investors concerning levels of return.

The particular methods that unscrupulous directors use to manipulate the financial
statements are many and varied. They can involve overstatement of revenues, manipulation of expenses, concealing losses and liabilities, and overstating asset values.

Overstating revenues has been a particularly popular target for creative accounting.
The methods used often involve the early recognition of sales income or the reporting
of sales transactions that have no real substance. **Real World 3.9** is an extract from an
article in *The Times*, which provides examples of both types of revenue manipulation.

REAL WORLD 3.9

Overstating revenue

Hollow swaps: telecoms companies sell useless fibre optic capacity to each other in order to generate revenues on their income statements. Example: Global Crossing.

Channel stuffing: a company floods the market with more products than its distributors can sell,
artificially boosting its sales. SSL, the condom maker, shifted £60 million in excess stock on to
trade customers. Also known as 'trade loading'.

Round tripping: also known as 'in-and-out trading'. Used to notorious effect by Enron. Two or
more traders buy and sell energy among themselves for the same price and at the same time. Inflates
trading volumes and makes participants appear to be doing more business than they really are.

Pre-dispatching: goods such as carpets are marked as 'sold' as soon as an order is placed . . .
This inflates sales and profits.

Note that some of the techniques used, such as round tripping, may inflate the sales for
a period but do not inflate reported profits. Nevertheless, this may still benefit the company. Sales growth has become an important yardstick of performance for some investors
and can affect the value they place on the company.

Source: 'Dirty laundry: how companies fudge the numbers', *The Times*, Business Section, 22 September 2002.

When examining the financial statements of a business, a number of checks may be carried out to help gain a 'feel' for their reliability. These can include checks to see whether:

- the reported profits are significantly higher than the operating cash flows for the period, which may suggest that profits have been overstated;
- the corporation tax charge is low in relation to reported profits, which may suggest, again, that profits are overstated, although there may be other, more innocent, explanations;
- the valuation methods used for assets held are based on historic cost or current values, and if the latter approach has been used why and how the current values were determined;
- there have been any changes in accounting policies over the period, particularly in key areas such as revenue recognition, stock valuation and depreciation;
- the accounting policies adopted are in line with those adopted by the rest of the industry;
- the auditors' report gives a 'clean bill of health' to the financial statements; and
- the 'small print', that is, the notes to the financial statements, is, not being used to hide significant events or changes.

Although such checks are useful, they are not guaranteed to identify creative accounting practices, some of which may be very deeply seated.

- *Inflation.* A persistent, though recently less severe, problem, in most western countries is that the financial results of businesses can be distorted as a result of inflation. One effect of inflation is that the values of assets held for any length of time may bear little relation to current values. Generally speaking, the value of assets will be understated in current terms during a period of inflation as they are usually recorded at their original cost (less any amounts written off for depreciation). This means that comparisons, either between businesses or between periods, will be hindered. A difference in, say, return on capital employed may simply be owing to the fact that assets in one of the balance sheets being compared were acquired more recently (ignoring the effect of depreciation on the asset values). Another effect of inflation is to distort the measurement of profit. Sales revenue for a period is often matched against costs from an earlier period. This is because there is often a time lag between acquiring a particular resource and using it in the business. For example, stocks may be acquired in one period and sold in a later period. During a period of inflation, this will mean that the costs do not reflect current prices. The cost of goods sold figure is usually based on the historic cost of the stock concerned. As a result, costs will be understated in the current profit and loss account and this, in turn, means that profit will be overstated. One effect of this will be to distort the profitability ratios discussed earlier.
- *The restricted vision of ratios.* It is important not to rely exclusively on ratios, thereby losing sight of information contained in the underlying financial statements. As we saw earlier in the chapter, some items reported in these statements can be vital in assessing position and performance. For example, the total sales revenue, capital employed and profit figures may be useful in assessing changes in absolute size that occur over time, or differences in scale between businesses. Ratios do not provide such information. In comparing one figure with another, ratios measure *relative* performance and position, and therefore provide only part of the picture. Thus, when comparing two businesses, it will often be useful to assess the absolute size of profits, as well as the relative profitability of each business. For example, Business

A may generate £1 million profit and have a ROCE of 15 per cent, and Business B may generate £100,000 profit and have a ROCE of 20 per cent. Although Business B has a higher level of *profitability*, as measured by ROCE, it generates lower total profits.

- *The basis for comparison.* We saw earlier that for ratios to be useful they require a basis for comparison. Moreover, it is important that the analyst compares like with like. When comparing businesses, however, no two businesses will be identical, and the greater the differences between the businesses being compared, the greater the limitations of ratio analysis. Also, when comparing businesses, differences in such matters as accounting policies, financing methods (gearing levels) and financial year ends will add to the problems of evaluation.

- *Balance sheet ratios.* Because the balance sheet is only a 'snapshot' of the business at a particular moment in time, any ratios based on balance sheet figures, such as the liquidity ratios above, may not be representative of the financial position of the business for the year as a whole. For example, it is common for a seasonal business to have a financial year end that coincides with a low point in business activity. Thus stocks and debtors may be low at the balance sheet date, and the liquidity ratios may also be low as a result. A more representative picture of liquidity can only really be gained by taking additional measurements at other points in the year.

Real World 3.10 points out another way in which ratios are limited.

REAL WORLD 3.10

Remember it's people that really count . . .

Lord Weinstock (1924–2002) was an influential industrialist whose management style and philosophy helped to shape management practice in many UK businesses. During his long and successful reign at GEC plc, a major engineering business, Lord Weinstock relied heavily on financial ratios to assess performance and to exercise control. In particular, he relied on ratios relating to sales revenue, costs, debtors, profit margins and stock turnover. However, he was keenly aware of the limitations of ratios and recognised that, ultimately, people produce profits.

In a memo written to GEC managers he pointed out that ratios are an aid to good management, rather than a substitute for it. He wrote:

> The operating ratios are of great value as measures of efficiency but they are only the measures and not efficiency itself. Statistics will not design a product better, make it for a lower cost or increase sales. If ill-used, they may so guide action as to diminish resources for the sake of apparent but false signs of improvement.
>
> Management remains a matter of judgement, of knowledge of products and processes and of understanding and skill in dealing with people. The ratios will indicate how well all these things are being done and will show comparison with how they are done elsewhere. But they will tell us nothing about how to do them. That is what you are meant to do.

Source: Extract from *Arnold Weinstock and the Making of GEC* by S. Aris (Aurum Press, 1998), published in *The Sunday Times*, 22 February 1998, p. 3.

SUMMARY

The main points in this chapter may be summarised as follows:

Ratio analysis

- Ratios compare two related figures, usually both from the same set of financial statements.
- Ratios are an aid to understanding what the financial statements portray.
- Ratio analysis is an inexact science and so results must be interpreted cautiously.
- Past periods, the performance of similar businesses and planned performance are often used to provide benchmark ratios.
- A brief overview of the financial statements can often provide insights that may not be revealed by ratios and/or may help in the interpretation of them.

Profitability ratios – concerned with effectiveness at generating profit

- Return on ordinary shareholders' funds (ROSF).
- Return on capital employed (ROCE).
- Net profit margin.
- Gross profit margin.

Efficiency ratios – concerned with efficiency of using assets/resources

- Average stock turnover period.
- Average settlement period for debtors.
- Average settlement period for creditors.
- Sales revenue to capital employed.
- Sales revenue per employee.

Liquidity ratios – concerned with the ability to meet short-term obligations

- Current ratio.
- Acid test ratio.

Gearing ratios – concerned with relationship between equity and loan financing

- Gearing ratio.
- Interest cover ratio.

Investment ratios – concerned with returns to shareholders

- Dividend payout ratio.
- Dividend yield ratio.
- Earnings per share.
- Price/earnings ratio.

Overtrading occurs when a business operates at a level of activity that it is insufficiently funded to sustain.

Individual ratios can be tracked (for example, plotted on a graph) to detect trends.

Ratios can be used to predict financial failure.

● Univariate analysis – involves looking at just one ratio over time in an attempt to predict financial failure.

● Multiple discriminate analysis – involves looking at several ratios, put together in a model, over time in an attempt to predict financial failure – *Z* scores.

Limitations of ratio analysis

● Ratios are only as reliable as the financial statements from which they derive.

● Creative accounting can distort the portrayal of financial health.

● Inflation can also distort the information.

● Ratios have restricted vision.

● It can be difficult to find a suitable benchmark (for example, another business) to compare with.

● Some ratios could mislead due to the 'snapshot' nature of the balance sheet.

→ Key terms

Return on ordinary shareholders' funds (ROSF) p. 66	Acid test ratio p. 79
Return on capital employed (ROCE) p. 67	Financial gearing p. 80
	Gearing ratio p. 81
Net profit margin ratio p. 68	Interest cover ratio p. 81
Gross profit margin ratio p. 70	Dividend payout ratio p. 83
Average stock turnover period p. 72	Dividend cover ratio p. 83
	Dividend yield ratio p. 84
Average settlement period for debtors p. 73	Dividend per share p. 84
	Earnings per share p. 85
Average settlement period for creditors p. 73	Price/earnings ratio p. 86
	Overtrading p. 91
Sales revenue to capital employed p. 74	Univariate analysis p. 94
	Multiple discriminate analysis p. 94
Sales revenue per employee p. 75	Discriminate function p. 96
Current ratio p. 78	Creative accounting p. 98

For definitions of these terms see the Glossary, pp. 562–571.

Further reading

If you wish to explore the topics discussed in this chapter in more depth, try the following books:

Financial Accounting and Reporting, *Elliott, B. and Elliott, J.*, 7th edn, Financial Times Prentice Hall, 2003, chapters 25 and 26.

Financial Analysis, *Rees, B.*, 2nd edn, Prentice Hall International, 1995, chapters 1–3.

International Financial Reporting and Analysis, *Alexander, D., Britton, A. and Jorissen, A.,* Prentice Hall, 2003, chapters 26 and 27.

The Analysis and Use of Financial Statements, *White, G., Sondhi, A. and Fried, D.,* 3rd edn, Wiley, 2003, chapter 4.

References

1 'Financial ratios as predictors of failure', *Beaver, W. H.,* **Empirical Research in Accounting: Selected studies,** supplement to **Journal of Accounting Research,** Autumn 1966, pp. 71–111.

2 **Predicting Corporate Bankruptcy: An empirical comparison of the extent of financial distress models,** *Zmijewski, M. E.,* Research Paper, State University of New York, 1983.

3 'Financial ratios, discriminant analysis and the prediction of corporate bankruptcy', *Altman, E. I.,* **Journal of Finance,** September 1968, pp. 589–609.

4 'The assessment of company solvency and performance using a statistical model: a comparative UK-based study', *Taffler, R.,* **Accounting and Business Research,** Autumn 1983, pp. 295–307.

5 **Arnold Weinstock and the Making of GEC,** *Aris, S.,* Aurum Press, 1998, reprinted in *Sunday Times,* 22 February 1998, p. 3.

REVIEW QUESTIONS

Answers to these questions can be found in Appendix D at the back of the book.

3.1 Some businesses operate on a low net profit margin (for example, a supermarket chain). Does this mean that the return on capital employed from the business will also be low?

3.2 What potential problems arise for the external analyst from the use of balance sheet figures in the calculation of financial ratios?

3.3 Is it responsible to publish Z-scores of businesses that are in financial difficulties? What are the potential problems of doing this?

3.4 Identify and discuss three reasons why the P/E ratio of two businesses operating within the same industry may differ.

EXERCISES

Exercises 3.5 to 3.7 are more advanced than 3.1 to 3.4. Those with coloured numbers have answers at the back of the book.

 If you wish to try more exercises, visit the students' side of the Companion Website.

3.1 Set out below are ratios relating to three different businesses. Each business operates within a different industrial sector.

Ratio	A plc	B plc	C plc
Net profit margin	3.6%	9.7%	6.8%
Sales to capital employed	2.4 times	3.1 times	1.7 times
Stock turnover period	18 days	n/a	44 days
Settlement period for debtors	2 days	12 days	26 days
Current ratio	0.8 times	0.6 times	1.5 times

Required:
State, with reasons, which of the above is:

(a) A holiday tour operator
(b) A supermarket chain
(c) A food manufacturer.

3.2 Amsterdam Ltd and Berlin Ltd are both engaged in retailing, but they seem to take a different approach to it according to the following information:

Ratio	Amsterdam Ltd	Berlin Ltd
Return on capital employed (ROCE)	20%	17%
Return on ordinary shareholders' funds (ROSF)	30%	18%
Average settlement period for debtors	63 days	21 days
Average settlement period for creditors	50 days	45 days
Gross profit margin	40%	15%
Net profit margin	10%	10%
Stock turnover period	52 days	25 days

Required:

Describe what this information indicates about the differences in approach between the two businesses. If one of them prides itself on personal service and one of them on competitive prices, which do you think is which and why?

3.3 Conday and Co. Ltd has been in operation for three years and produces antique reproduction furniture for the export market. The most recent set of financial statements for the business is set out as follows:

Balance sheet as at 30 November Year 8

	£000	£000	£000
Non-current assets			
Property, plant and equipment			
Freehold land and buildings at cost			228
Plant and machinery at cost		942	
Less Accumulated depreciation		180	762
			990
Current assets			
Stocks (inventories)		600	
Trade debtors (receivables)		820	
		1,420	
Less **Current liabilities**			
Trade creditors (payables)	665		
Taxation	48		
Bank overdraft	432	1,145	275
			1,265
Less **Non-current liabilities**			
9% debentures (Note 1)			200
			1,065
Equity			
Ordinary shares of £1 each			700
Retained profits			365
			1,065

Profit and loss account (income statement) for the year ended 30 November Year 8

	£000	£000
Revenue		2,600
Less Cost of sales		1,620
Gross profit		980
Less Selling and distribution expenses (Note 2)	408	
Administration expenses	194	
Finance expenses	58	660
Net profit before taxation		320
Less Corporation tax		95
Net profit after taxation		225
Less Dividend paid		160
Retained profit for the year		65

Notes

1 The debentures are secured on the freehold land and buildings.

2 Selling and distribution expenses include £170,000 in respect of bad debts.

The directors have invited an investor to take up a new issue of ordinary shares in the business at £6.40 each making a total investment of £200,000. The directors wish to use the funds to finance a programme of further expansion.

Required:

(a) Analyse the financial position and performance of the business and comment on any features that you consider to be significant.

(b) State, with reasons, whether or not the investor should invest in the business on the terms outlined.

3.4 The directors of Helena Beauty Products Ltd have been presented with the following abridged financial statements:

Helena Beauty Products Ltd
Profit and loss account for the year ended 30 September

	2005		2006	
	£000	£000	£000	£000
Revenue		3,600		3,840
Less Cost of sales				
Opening stock	320		400	
Purchases	2,240		2,350	
	2,560		2,750	
Less Closing stock	400	2,160	500	2,250
Gross profit		1,440		1,590
Less Expenses		1,360		1,500
Net profit		80		90

Balance sheet as at 30 September

	2005		2006	
	£000	£000	£000	£000
Non-current assets		1,900		1,860
Current assets				
Stock	400		500	
Debtors	750		960	
Bank	8		4	
	1,158		1,464	
Less Current liabilities	390	768	450	1,014
		2,668		2,874
Equity				
£1 ordinary shares		1,650		1,766
Reserves		1,018		1,108
		2,668		2,874

Required:
Using six ratios, comment on the profitability (three ratios) and efficiency (three ratios) of the business as revealed by the statements shown above.

3.5 Threads Limited manufactures nuts and bolts, which are sold to industrial users. The abbreviated financial statements for 2005 and 2006 are as follows:

Profit and loss account for the year ended 30 June

	2005		2006	
	£000	£000	£000	£000
Revenue		1,180		1,200
Cost of sales		(680)		(750)
Gross profit		500		450
Operating expenses	(200)		(208)	
Depreciation	(66)		(75)	
Interest	(–)		(8)	
		(266)		(291)
Profit before tax		234		159
Tax		(80)		(48)
Profit after tax		154		111
Dividend – paid		(70)		(72)
Retained profit for year		84		39

Balance sheet as at 30 June

	2005		2006	
	£000	£000	£000	£000
Non-current assets		702		687
Current assets				
Stocks	148		236	
Debtors	102		156	
Cash	3		4	
	253		396	
Current liabilities				
Trade creditors	(60)		(76)	
Other creditors and accruals	(18)		(16)	
Tax	(40)		(24)	
Bank overdraft	(81)		(122)	
	(199)		(238)	
Net current assets		54		158
Non-current liabilities				
Bank loan		–		(50)
		756		795
Equity				
Ordinary share capital of £1 (fully paid)		500		500
Retained profits		256		295
		756		795

Required:

(a) Calculate the following financial ratios for *both* 2005 and 2006 (using year-end figures for balance sheet items):
  (i)   Return on capital employed
  (ii)   Net profit margin
  (iii) Gross profit margin
  (iv)   Current ratio
  (v)   Acid test ratio
  (vi)   Settlement period for debtors
  (vii) Settlement period for creditors
  (viii) Stock turnover period.

(b) Comment on the performance of Threads Limited from the viewpoint of a business considering supplying a substantial amount of goods to Threads Limited on usual trade credit terms.

3.6   The financial statements for Harridges Limited are given below for the two years ended 30 June 2005 and 2006. Harridges Limited operates a retail and wholesale store in the centre of a small town.

Harridges Limited
Profit and loss account for the years ended 30 June

	2005	2005	2006	2006
	£000	£000	£000	£000
Revenue		2,600		3,500
Cost of sales		(1,560)		(2,350)
Gross profit		1,040		1,150
Expenses: Wages and salaries	(320)		(350)	
Overheads	(260)		(200)	
Depreciation	(150)		(250)	
		(730)		(800)
Operating profit		310		350
Interest payable		(50)		(50)
Profit before taxation		260		300
Taxation		(105)		(125)
Profit after taxation		155		175
Dividend (approved, but unpaid at the year end)		(65)		(75)
Profit retained for the year		90		100

Balance sheet as at 30 June

	2005	2005	2006	2006
	£000	£000	£000	£000
Non-current assets		1,265		1,525
Current assets				
Stocks	250		400	
Debtors	105		145	
Cash at bank	380		115	
	735		660	
Current liabilities				
Trade creditors	(235)		(300)	
Dividend (approved, but unpaid)	(65)		(75)	
Other	(100)		(110)	
	(400)		(485)	
Net current assets		335		175
Total assets less current liabilities		1,600		1,700
Non-current liabilities				
10% loan stock		(500)		(500)
		1,100		1,200
Equity				
Share capital: £1 shares fully paid		490		490
Share premium		260		260
Profit and loss account		350		450
		1,100		1,200

Required:

(a) Choose and calculate eight ratios that would be helpful in assessing the performance of Harridges Limited. Use end-of-year values and calculate ratios for both 2005 and 2006.

(b) Using the ratios calculated in (a) and any others you consider helpful, comment on the business's performance from the viewpoint of a prospective purchaser of a majority of shares.

3.7   Genesis Ltd was incorporated in 2002 and has grown rapidly over the past three years. The rapid rate of growth has created problems for the business, which the directors have found difficult to deal with. Recently, a firm of management consultants has been asked to help the directors to overcome these problems.

In a preliminary report to the board of directors, the management consultants state: 'Most of the difficulties faced by the business are symptoms of an underlying problem of overtrading.'

The most recent financial statements of the business are set out below:

Balance sheet as at 31 October 2005

	£000	£000	£000
Non-current assets			
Property, plant and equipment			
Freehold land and buildings at cost		530	
Less Accumulated depreciation		88	442
Fixtures and fittings at cost		168	
Less Accumulated depreciation		52	116
Motor vans at cost		118	
Less Accumulated depreciation		54	64
			622
Current assets			
Stock in trade		128	
Trade debtors		104	
		232	
Less **Current liabilities**			
Trade creditors	184		
Taxation	8		
Bank overdraft	358	550	(318)
			304
Less **Non-current liabilities**			
10% debentures (secured)			(120)
			184
Equity			
Ordinary £0.50 shares			60
General reserve			50
Retained profit			74
			184

(continued over)

Profit and loss account for the year ended 31 October 2005

	£000	£000
Revenue		1,640
Less Cost of sales		
Opening stock	116	
Purchases	1,260	
	1,376	
Less Closing stock	128	(1,248)
Gross profit		392
Less Selling and distribution expenses	204	
Administration expenses	92	
Interest expenses	44	(340)
Net profit before taxation		52
Corporation tax		(16)
Net profit after taxation		36
Dividends paid		(4)
Retained profit for the year		32

All purchases and sales were on credit.

Required:

(a) Explain the term 'overtrading' and state how overtrading might arise for a business.
(b) Discuss the kinds of problem that overtrading can create for a business.
(c) Calculate and discuss *five* financial ratios that might be used to establish whether or not the business is overtrading.
(d) State the ways in which a business may overcome the problem of overtrading.

4

Making capital investment decisions

LEARNING OUTCOMES

When you have completed this chapter, you should be able to:

- Explain the nature and importance of investment decision making.

- Identify and discuss the characteristics of the four main investment appraisal methods used in practice.

- Use each method to reach a decision on a particular practical investment opportunity.

- Explain the methods used to monitor and control investment projects.

INTRODUCTION

In this chapter we look at how businesses can make decisions involving investments in new plant, machinery, buildings and similar non-current assets. The general principles that apply to assessing investments in these types of assets can also, equally well be applied to investments in the shares of businesses, irrespective of whether the investment is being considered by a business or by a private individual. We examine four major investment appraisal methods and consider evidence relating to the use of these methods in practice.

Once a decision has been made to implement a particular capital investment proposal, proper review and control procedures must be in place. We therefore discuss the ways in which managers can oversee capital investment projects and how control may be exercised throughout the life of the project.

The nature of investment decisions

The essential feature of investment decisions is *time*. Investment involves making an outlay of something of economic value, usually cash, at one point in time, which is expected to yield economic benefits to the investor at some other point in time. Usually, the outlay precedes the benefits. Also, the outlay is typically one large amount and the benefits arrive as a series of smaller amounts over a fairly protracted period.

Investment decisions tend to be of crucial importance to the business because:

- *Large amounts of resources are often involved.*   Many investments made by businesses involve laying out a significant proportion of their total resources (see Real World 4.2 below). If mistakes are made with the decision, the effects on the businesses could be significant, if not catastrophic.
- *It is often difficult and/or expensive to 'bail out' of an investment once it has been undertaken.*   It is often the case that investments made by a business are specific to its needs. For example, a hotel business may invest in a new, purposely designed hotel complex. The specialist nature of this complex will probably lead to it having a rather limited second-hand value to another potential user with different needs. If the business found, after having made the investment, that room occupancy rates were not as buoyant as planned, the only possible course of action might be to close down and sell the complex. This would probably mean that much less could be recouped from the investment than it had originally cost, particularly if the costs of design are included as part of the cost, as logically they should be.

Real World 4.1 gives an illustration of a major investment by a well-known business operating in the UK.

REAL WORLD 4.1

Brittany Ferries launches an investment

In the spring of 2004, Brittany Ferries, the cross-Channel ferry operator, launched a new ship. The ship had cost the business about £100 million. Although Brittany Ferries is a substantial business, this level of expenditure is significant. Clearly, the business believes that acquisition of the new ship will be profitable for it, but how would it have reached this conclusion? Presumably the anticipated future cash flows from passengers and freight operators will have been major inputs to the decision. The ship was specifically designed for Brittany Ferries, so it would be difficult for the business to recoup a large proportion of its £100 million, should these projected cash flows not materialise.

Source: Publicity material published by Brittany Ferries.

The issues raised by Brittany Ferries' investment are the main subject of this chapter.

Real World 4.2 indicates the level of annual investment for a number of randomly selected, well-known UK businesses. It can be seen that the scale of investment varies from one business to another. (It also tends to vary from one year to the next for a particular business.) In nearly all of these businesses the scale of investment is very significant.

REAL WORLD 4.2

The scale of investment by UK businesses

	Expenditure on additional non-current (fixed) assets as a percentage of:	
	Annual sales	Start of year non-current assets
JD Wetherspoon plc	9.5	9.6
Astra-Zeneca plc	8.7	17.3
Bristol Water plc	23.2	15.2
Royal Dutch/Shell Group	6.1	11.7
Chloride plc	5.5	15.2
Yates Group plc	9.6	6.2
United Utilities	49.4	14.1
Tesco plc	7.3	15.9
J. Sainsbury plc	5.7	12.5

Source: Annual reports of the businesses concerned for the accounting years ending in 2003 or 2004.

Real World 4.2 is limited to considering the non-current (fixed) asset investment, but most non-current asset investment also requires a level of current asset investment to support it (additional stock in trade (inventories), for example), meaning that the real scale of investment is even greater than indicated above.

Activity 4.1

When managers are making decisions involving capital investments, what should the decision seek to achieve?

Investment decisions must be consistent with the objectives of the particular business. For a private sector business, maximising the wealth of the shareholders is usually assumed to be the key objective.

Methods of investment appraisal

Given the importance of investment decisions to investors, it is essential that proper screening of investment proposals takes place. An important part of this screening process is to ensure that the business uses appropriate methods of evaluation.

Research shows that there are basically four methods used in practice by businesses throughout the world to evaluate investment opportunities. They are:

● accounting rate of return (ARR)
● payback period (PP)
● net present value (NPV)
● internal rate of return (IRR).

It is possible to find businesses that use variants of these four methods. It is also possible to find businesses, particularly smaller ones, which do not use any formal appraisal method, but rely more on the 'gut feeling' of their managers. Most businesses, however, seem to use one (or more) of the four methods listed above and that we shall now review.

We are going to assess the effectiveness of each of these methods and we shall see that only one of them (NPV) is not flawed to some extent. We shall also see how popular these four methods seem to be in practice.

To help us to examine each of the methods, it might be useful to consider how each of them would cope with a particular investment opportunity. Let us consider the following example.

Example 4.1

Billingsgate Battery Company has carried out some research that shows that the business could provide a standard service that it has recently developed.

Provision of the service would require investment in a machine that would cost £100,000, payable immediately. Sales of the service would take place throughout the next five years. At the end of that time, it is estimated that the machine could be sold for £20,000.

Sales of the service would be expected to occur as follows:

	Number of units
Next year	5,000
Second year	10,000
Third year	15,000
Fourth year	15,000
Fifth year	5,000

It is estimated that the new service can be sold for £12 a unit, and that the relevant (variable) costs will total £8 a unit.

To simplify matters, we assume that the cash from sales and for the costs of providing the service are paid and received, respectively, at the end of each year. (This is clearly unlikely to be true in real life. Money will have to be paid to employees (for salaries and wages) on a weekly or a monthly basis. Customers will pay within a month or two of buying the service. On the other hand, making the assumption probably does not lead to a serious distortion. It is a simplifying assumption that is often made in real life, and it will make things more straightforward for us now. We should be clear, however, that there is nothing about any of the four approaches that *demands* this assumption being made.)

Bearing in mind that each unit of the service sold will give rise to a net cash inflow of £4 (that is, £12 − £8), the total net cash flows (receipts less payments) for each year will be as follows:

Time		£000
Immediately	Cost of machine	(100)
1 year's time	Net profit before depreciation (£4 × 5,000)	20
2 years' time	Net profit before depreciation (£4 × 10,000)	40
3 years' time	Net profit before depreciation (£4 × 15,000)	60
4 years' time	Net profit before depreciation (£4 × 15,000)	60
5 years' time	Net profit before depreciation (£4 × 5,000)	20
5 years' time	Disposal proceeds from the machine	20

Note that, broadly speaking, the net profit before deducting depreciation (that is, before non-cash items) equals the net amount of cash flowing into the business. Apart from depreciation, all of this business's expenses cause cash to flow out of the business. Sales revenues lead to cash flowing in.

Having set up the example, we now go on to consider how each of the appraisal methods works.

Accounting rate of return (ARR)

→ The **accounting rate of return (ARR)** method takes the average accounting profit that the investment will generate and expresses it as a percentage of the average investment made over the life of the project. Thus:

$$\text{ARR} = \frac{\text{Average annual profit}}{\text{Average investment to earn that profit}} \times 100\%$$

We can see from the equation that, to calculate the ARR, we need to deduce two pieces of information:

● the average annual profit
● the average investment for the particular project.

In our example, the average annual profit *before depreciation* over the five years is £40,000 [that is, £(20 + 40 + 60 + 60 + 20)/5]. Assuming 'straight-line' depreciation (that is, equal annual amounts), the annual depreciation charge will be £16,000 [that is, £(100,000 – 20,000)/5]. Thus the average annual profit *after depreciation* is £24,000 (that is, £40,000 – £16,000).

The average investment over the five years can be calculated as follows:

$$\text{Average investment} = \frac{\text{Cost of machine + disposal value}}{2}$$

$$= \frac{£100,000 + £20,000}{2}$$

$$= £60,000$$

Thus, the ARR of the investment is:

$$\text{ARR} = \frac{£24,000}{£60,000} \times 100\%$$

$$= 40\%$$

To decide whether the 40 per cent return is acceptable, we need to compare this percentage return with the minimum rate required by the business.

Activity 4.2

Chaotic Industries is considering an investment in a fleet of ten delivery vans to take its products to customers. The vans will cost £15,000 each to buy, payable immediately. The annual running costs are expected to total £20,000 for each van (including the driver's salary). The vans are expected to operate successfully for six years, at the end of which period they will all have to be sold, with disposal proceeds expected to be about £3,000 a van. At present, the business uses a commercial carrier for all of its deliveries. It is expected that this carrier will charge a total of £230,000 each year for the next five years to undertake the deliveries.

What is the ARR of buying the vans? (Note that cost savings are as relevant a benefit from an investment as are net cash inflows.)

The vans will save the business £30,000 a year [that is, £230,000 – (£20,000 × 10)], before depreciation, in total.

Thus, the inflows and outflows will be:

Time		£000
Immediately	Cost of vans	(150)
1 year's time	Net saving before depreciation	30
2 years' time	Net saving before depreciation	30
3 years' time	Net saving before depreciation	30
4 years' time	Net saving before depreciation	30
5 years' time	Net saving before depreciation	30
6 years' time	Net saving before depreciation	30
6 years' time	Disposal proceeds from the vans (10 × 3)	30

The total annual depreciation expense (assuming a straight-line approach) will be £20,000 [that is, (£150,000 – £30,000)/6]. Thus, the average annual saving, after depreciation, is £10,000 (that is, £30,000 – £20,000).

The average investment will be:

$$\text{Average investment} = \frac{£150,000 + £30,000}{2}$$

$$= £90,000$$

Thus, the ARR of the investment is:

$$\text{ARR} = \frac{£10,000}{£90,000} \times 100\% = 11.1\%$$

ARR and ROCE

We should note that ARR and the return on capital employed (ROCE) ratio take the same approach to performance measurement, in that they both relate accounting profit to the cost of the assets invested to generate that profit. We saw in Chapter 3 that ROCE is a popular means of assessing the performance of a business, as a whole, *after* it has performed. ARR is an approach that assesses the potential performance of a particular investment, taking the same approach as ROCE, *before* it has performed.

Managers using the ARR method must have a minimum target ARR in mind. The decision rule should be:

- For any project to be acceptable, it must achieve the target ARR.
- If competing projects (for example, the business can choose only one of several viable projects) achieve the target ARR, the project with the highest ARR should be selected.

Perhaps the minimum target would be based on the rate that previous investments had actually achieved (as measured by ROCE). Perhaps it would be the industry-average ROCE.

Since private sector businesses are normally seeking to increase the wealth of their owners, ARR may seem to be a sound method of appraising investment opportunities. Profit can be seen as a net increase in wealth over a period, and relating it to the size of investment made to achieve it seems a logical approach.

ARR is said to have a number of advantages as a method of investment appraisal. It was mentioned earlier that ROCE seems to be a widely used measure of business performance. Shareholders seem to use this ratio to evaluate management perform-ance, and sometimes the financial objective of a business will be expressed in terms of a target ROCE. It therefore seems sensible to use a method of investment appraisal that is consistent with this overall approach to measuring business performance. It also gives the result expressed as a percentage. It seems that some managers feel com-fortable with using measures expressed in percentage terms.

Problems with ARR

Activity 4.3

ARR suffers from a very major defect as a means of assessing investment opportunit-ies. Can you reason out what this is? Consider the three competing projects, A, B and C, whose cash flows are shown below. All three of these involve investment in a machine that is expected to have no residual value at the end of the five years. Note that all of the projects have the same total net profits over the five years.

Time		A £000	B £000	C £000
Immediately	Cost of machine	(160)	(160)	(160)
1 year's time	Net profit after depreciation	20	10	160
2 years' time	Net profit after depreciation	40	10	10
3 years' time	Net profit after depreciation	60	10	10
4 years' time	Net profit after depreciation	60	10	10
5 years' time	Net profit after depreciation	20	160	10

(*Hint*: The defect is not concerned with the ability of the decision maker to forecast future events, although this too can be a problem. Try to remember the essential fea-ture of investment decisions, which we identified at the beginning of this chapter.)

The problem with ARR is that it almost completely ignores the time factor. In this exam-ple, exactly the same ARR would have been computed for each of the three projects.

Since the same total profit over the five years arises in all three of these projects (that is, £200,000) and the average investment in each project is £80,000 (that is, £160,000/2), this means that each case will give rise to the same ARR of 50 per cent (that is, £40,000/ £80,000).

Given a financial objective of increasing the wealth of the owners of the business, any rational decision maker faced with a choice between the three projects set out in Activity 4.3 would strongly prefer Project C. This is because most of the benefits from the investment arise within 12 months of investing the £160,000 to establish the project. Project A would rank second, and Project B would come a poor third in the rankings. Any appraisal technique that is not capable of distinguishing between these three situations is seriously flawed. We shall look in more detail at the reason for timing being so important later in the chapter.

There are further problems associated with the use of ARR. (Un)Real World 4.3 illustrates a paradox that may arise when using this method. This paradox results from the approach taken to derive the average investment in a project.

 (UN)REAL WORLD 4.3

How to increase ARR by throwing away money!

To illustrate the daft results that ARR can produce, let us assume that we have put forward an investment proposal to our superior based on the following information:

Cost of equipment	£200,000
Estimated residual value of equipment	£40,000
Average annual profit before depreciation	£48,000
Estimated life of project	10 years
Annual straight-line depreciation charge	£16,000 [(£200,000 − £40,000)/10]

The ARR of the project will be:

$$ARR = \frac{(48,000 - 16,000)}{[(200,000 + 40,000)/2]} \times 100\%$$

$$= 26.7\%$$

We are told by our superior, however, that the minimum ARR for investment projects of this nature is 27 per cent. Although we are disappointed, we realise that there is still hope. In fact, all that we have to do is to agree to give away the piece of equipment at the end of its useful life rather than to sell it. The residual value of the equipment will then be zero and the annual depreciation charge will become [(£200,000 − £0)/10] = £20,000 a year. Our revised ARR calculation will then be as follows:

$$ARR = \frac{(48,000 - 20,000)}{[(200,000 + 0)/2]} \times 100\%$$

$$= 28\%$$

ARR is based on the use of accounting profit. When measuring performance over the whole life of a project, however, it is cash flows rather than accounting profits that are important. Cash is the ultimate measure of the economic wealth generated by an investment. This is because it is cash that is used to acquire resources and for distribution to shareholders. Accounting profit, on the other hand, is more appropriate for reporting achievement on a periodic basis. It is a useful measure of productive effort for a relatively short period, such as a year or half-year. Thus, it is really a question of 'horses for courses'. Accounting profit is fine for measuring profit over a short period but cash is the appropriate measure when considering the performance over the life of a project.

The ARR method can also create problems when considering competing investments of different size.

Activity 4.4

Sinclair Wholesalers plc is currently considering opening a new sales outlet in Coventry. Two possible sites have been identified for the new outlet. Site A has a capacity of 30,000 sq. metres. It will require an average investment of £6 million, and will produce an average profit of £600,000 a year. Site B has a capacity of 20,000 sq. metres. It will require an average investment of £4 million, and will produce an average profit of £500,000 a year.

What is the ARR of each investment opportunity? Which site would you select, and why?

The ARR of Site A is £600,000/£6 million = 10 per cent. The ARR of Site B is £500,000/£4 million = 12.5 per cent. Thus, Site B has the higher ARR. However, in terms of the absolute profit generated, Site A is the more attractive. If the ultimate objective is to maximise the wealth of the shareholders of Sinclair Wholesalers plc, it might be better to choose Site A even though the percentage return is lower. It is the absolute size of the return rather than the relative (percentage) size that is important. This is a general problem of using comparative measures, like percentages, when the objective is measured in absolute ones. If businesses were seeking through their investments to generate a percentage rate of return on investment, ARR would be more helpful. The problem is that most businesses seek to achieve increases in their absolute wealth (measured in pounds, euros, dollars and so on), through their investment decisions.

Real World 4.4 illustrates how using percentage measures can lead to confusion.

REAL WORLD 4.4

Increasing road capacity by sleight of hand

During the 1970s, the Mexican government wanted to increase the capacity of a major four-lane road. It came up with the idea of repainting the lane markings so that there were six narrower lanes occupying the same space as four wider ones had previously done. This increased the capacity of the road by 50% [that is, $(6 - 4)/4 \times 100\%$]. A tragic outcome of the narrower lanes was an increase in deaths from road accidents. A year later the Mexican government had the six narrower lanes changed back to the original four wider ones. This reduced the capacity of the road by 33% [that is, $(6 - 4)/6 \times 100\%$]. The Mexican government reported that it had increased the capacity of the road by 17% (that is 50% − 33%), despite the fact that its real capacity was identical to that which it had been originally. The confusion arose because each of the two percentages (50% and 33%) is based on different bases (four and six).

Source: G. Gigerenzer, 'Reckoning with risk' *Penguin Books* (2002).

Payback period (PP)

→ The **payback period (PP)** is the length of time it takes for an initial investment to be repaid out of the net cash inflows from a project. Since it takes time into account, the PP method seems to go some way to overcoming the timing problem of ARR – or at least at first glance it does.

It might be useful to consider PP in the context of the Billingsgate Battery example. We should recall that in essence the project's costs and benefits can be summarised as:

Time		£000
Immediately	Cost of machine	(100)
1 year's time	Net profit before depreciation	20
2 years' time	Net profit before depreciation	40
3 years' time	Net profit before depreciation	60
4 years' time	Net profit before depreciation	60
5 years' time	Net profit before depreciation	20
5 years' time	Disposal proceeds	20

Note that all of these figures are amounts of cash to be paid or received (we saw earlier that net profit before depreciation is a rough measure of the cash flows from the project).

As the payback period is the length of time it takes for the initial investment to be repaid out of the net cash inflows, it will be three years before the £100,000 outlay is covered by the inflows. This is still assuming that the cash flows occur at year ends. The payback period can be derived by calculating the cumulative cash flows as follows:

Time		Net cash flows £000	Cumulative cash flows £000	
Immediately	Cost of machine	(100)	(100)	
1 year's time	Net profit before depreciation	20	(80)	(−100 + 20)
2 years' time	Net profit before depreciation	40	(40)	(−80 + 40)
3 years' time	Net profit before depreciation	60	20	(−40 + 60)
4 years' time	Net profit before depreciation	60	80	(20 + 60)
5 years' time	Net profit before depreciation	20	100	(80 + 20)
5 years' time	Disposal proceeds	20	120	(100 + 20)

We can see that the cumulative cash flows become positive at the end of the third year. Had we assumed that the cash flows arise evenly over the year, the precise payback period would be:

$$2 \text{ years} + (40/60) = 2\tfrac{2}{3} \text{ years}$$

where 40 represents the cash flow still required at the beginning of the third year to repay the initial outlay, and 60 is the projected cash flow during the third year. Again we must ask how to decide whether $2\tfrac{2}{3}$ years is acceptable. A manager using PP would need to have a minimum payback period in mind. The decision rule to be used is:

● For any project to be acceptable, it must fall within the maximum payback period.
● Where there are competing projects that meet the maximum payback period requirement, the project with the shortest payback period should be selected.

Thus if, for example, Billingsgate Battery had a maximum payback period of three years, the project would be acceptable. If there were two competing projects that both met the minimum payback period requirement, the decision maker should select the project with the shorter payback period.

Activity 4.5

What is the payback period of the Chaotic Industries project from Activity 4.2?

The inflows and outflows are expected to be:

Time		Net cash flows £000	Cumulative net cash flows £000	
Immediately	Cost of vans	(150)	(150)	
1 year's time	Net saving before depreciation	30	(120)	(−150 + 30)
2 years' time	Net saving before depreciation	30	(90)	(−120 + 30)
3 years' time	Net saving before depreciation	30	(60)	(−90 + 30)
4 years' time	Net saving before depreciation	30	(30)	(−60 + 30)
5 years' time	Net saving before depreciation	30	0	(−30 + 30)
6 years' time	Net saving before depreciation	30	30	(0 + 30)
6 years' time	Disposal proceeds from the machine	30	60	(30 + 30)

The payback period here is five years, that is, it is not until the end of the fifth year that the vans will pay for themselves out of the savings that they are expected to generate.

The PP approach has certain advantages. It is quick and easy to calculate, and can be easily understood by managers. The logic of using PP is that projects that can recoup their cost quickly are economically more attractive than those with longer payback periods, that is, it emphasises liquidity. PP is probably an improvement on ARR in respect of the timing of the cash flows. PP is not, however, the whole answer to the problem.

Problems with PP

Activity 4.6

In what respect, is PP not the whole answer as a means of assessing investment opportunities? Consider the cash flows arising from three competing projects:

Time		Project 1 £000	Project 2 £000	Project 3 £000
Immediately	Cost of machine	(200)	(200)	(200)
1 year's time	Net profit before depreciation	40	10	80
2 years' time	Net profit before depreciation	80	20	100
3 years' time	Net profit before depreciation	80	170	20
4 years' time	Net profit before depreciation	60	20	200
5 years' time	Net profit before depreciation	40	10	500
5 years' time	Disposal proceeds	40	10	20

(*Hint*: Again, the defect is not concerned with the ability of the manager to forecast future events. This is a problem, but it is a problem whatever approach we take.)

Activity 4.6 continued

The PP for each project is three years and so the PP method would regard the projects as being equally acceptable. It cannot distinguish between those projects that pay back a significant amount early in the three-year payback period and those that do not.

In addition, this method ignores cash flows after the payback period. A decision maker concerned with maximising shareholder wealth would prefer Project 3 in the table above because the cash flows come in earlier (most of the cost of the machine has been repaid by the end of the second year) and they are greater in total.

The cumulative cash flows of each project in Activity 4.6 are set out in Figure 4.1.

Figure 4.1 **The cumulative cash flows of each project in Activity 4.6**

The payback method of investment appraisal would view Projects 1, 2 and 3 as being equally attractive. In doing so, the method completely ignores the fact that Project 3 provides the payback cash earlier in the three-year period and goes on to generate large benefits in later years.

We can see that the PP method is not concerned with the profitability of projects; it is concerned simply with their payback period. Thus cash flows arising beyond the payback period are ignored. While this neatly avoids the practical problems of forecasting cash flows over a long period, it means that relevant information may be ignored.

You may feel that, by favouring projects with a short payback period, the PP approach does at least provide a means of dealing with the problems of risk and uncertainty. However, this is a fairly crude approach to the problem. It only looks at the risk that the project will end earlier than expected. However, this is only one of many risk areas. What about, for example, the risk that the demand for the product may be less than expected? There are more systematic approaches to dealing with risk that can be used and we shall look at these later in the chapter.

PP takes some note of the timing of the costs and benefits from the project. Its key deficiency, however, is that it is not linked to promoting increases in the wealth of the business. PP will tend to recommend undertaking projects that pay for themselves quickly. As we saw earlier, ARR ignores timing to a great extent, but it does take account of all benefits and costs.

Net present value (NPV)

To make sensible investment decisions, we need a method of appraisal that:

● considers *all* of the costs and benefits of each investment opportunity; and
● makes a logical allowance for the *timing* of those costs and benefits.

The **net present value (NPV)** method provides us with this.

Consider the Billingsgate Battery example, which we should recall can be summarised as follows:

Time		£000
Immediately	Cost of machine	(100)
1 year's time	Net profit before depreciation	20
2 years' time	Net profit before depreciation	40
3 years' time	Net profit before depreciation	60
4 years' time	Net profit before depreciation	60
5 years' time	Net profit before depreciation	20
5 years' time	Disposal proceeds	20

Given that the principal financial objective of the business is to maximise shareholder wealth, it would be very easy to assess this investment if all of the cash inflows and outflows were to occur now (all at the same time). All that we should need to do would be to add up the cash inflows (total £220,000) and compare them with the cash outflows (£100,000). This would lead us to the conclusion that the project should go ahead, because the business would be better off by £120,000. Of course, it is not as easy as this, because time is involved. The cash outflow (payment) will occur immediately if the project is undertaken. The inflows (receipts) will arise at a range of later times.

The time factor is an important issue because people do not normally see £100 paid out now as equivalent in value to £100 receivable in a year's time. If we were to be offered £100 in 12 months, provided that we paid £100 now, we should not be prepared to do so, unless we wished to do someone (perhaps a friend or relation) a favour.

Activity 4.7

Why would you see £100 to be received in a year's time as unequal in value to £100 to be paid immediately? (There are basically three reasons.)

The reasons are:

● interest lost
● risk
● effects of inflation.

We now take a closer look at these three reasons in turn.

Interest lost

If we are to be deprived of the opportunity to spend our money for a year, we could equally well be deprived of its use by placing it on deposit in a bank or building society.

In this case, at the end of the year we could have our money back and have interest as well. Thus, unless the opportunity to invest will offer similar returns, we shall be incurring an *opportunity cost*. An opportunity cost occurs where one course of action, for example making an investment in, say, a computer, deprives us of the opportunity to derive some benefit from an alternative action, for example putting the money in the bank.

From this we can see that any investment opportunity must, if it is to maximise our wealth, do better than the returns that are available from the next best opportunity. Thus, if Billingsgate Battery Company sees putting the money in the bank on deposit as the alternative to investment in the machine, the return from investing in the machine must be better than that from investing in the bank. If the bank offered a better return, the business would become wealthier by putting the money on deposit.

Risk

Buying a machine to manufacture a product, or to provide a service, to be sold in the market, on the strength of various estimates made in advance of buying the machine, exposes the business to **risk**. Things may not turn out as expected.

Activity 4.8

Can you suggest some areas where things could go other than according to plan in the Billingsgate Battery Company example?

We have come up with the following:

● The machine might not work as well as expected; it might break down, leading to loss of the service.
● Sales of the product or service may not be as buoyant as expected.
● Labour costs may prove to be higher than was expected.
● The sale proceeds of the machine could prove to be less than was estimated.

It is important to remember that the decision as to whether or not to invest in the machine must be taken *before* any of these things are known. It is only after the machine has been purchased that we could discover that the level of sales, which had been estimated before the event, is not going to be achieved. It is not possible to wait until we know for certain whether the market will behave as we expected before we buy the machine. We can study reports and analyses of the market. We can commission sophisticated market surveys, and these may give us more confidence in the likely outcome. We can advertise strongly and try to promote sales. Ultimately, however, we have to decide whether or not to leap into the dark and accept the risk if we want the opportunity to make profitable investments.

Normally, people expect to receive greater returns where they perceive risk to be a factor. Examples of this in real life are not difficult to find. One such example is that banks tend to charge higher rates of interest to borrowers whom the bank perceives as more risky. Those who can offer good security for a loan, and who can point to a regular source of income, tend to be charged fairly low rates of interest.

Going back to Billingsgate Battery Company's investment opportunity, it is not enough to say that we should not advise making the investment unless the returns from it are higher than those from investing in a bank deposit. Clearly, we should want returns above the level of bank deposit interest rates, because the logical equivalent to investing in the machine is not putting the money on deposit but making an alternative investment that is risky.

In practice, we tend to expect a higher rate of return from investment projects where the risk is perceived as being higher. How risky a particular project is, and therefore how large this **risk premium** should be, are matters that are difficult to handle. It is usually necessary to make some judgement on these questions and we consider this point in more detail in the following chapter.

Inflation

If we are to be deprived of £100 for a year, when we come to spend that money it will not buy as many goods and services as it would have done a year earlier. Generally, we shall not be able to buy as many tins of baked beans or loaves of bread or bus tickets as we could have done a year earlier. This is because of the loss in the purchasing power of money, or **inflation**, that occurs over time. Clearly, the investor needs this loss of purchasing power to be compensated for if the investment is to be made. This is on top of a return that takes account of what could have been gained from an alternative investment of similar risk.

In practice, interest rates observable in the market tend to take inflation into account. Rates that are offered to potential building society and bank depositors include an allowance for the rate of inflation that is expected in the future.

Actions of a logical investor

To summarise, we can say that the logical investor, who is seeking to increase his or her wealth, will only be prepared to make investments that will compensate for the loss of interest and purchasing power of the money invested and for the fact that the returns expected may not materialise (risk). This is usually assessed by seeing whether the proposed investment will yield a return that is greater than the basic rate of interest (which would include an allowance for inflation) plus a risk premium.

These three factors (interest lost, risk and inflation) are set out in Figure 4.2.

Figure 4.1   The factors influencing the required returns from investors

The figure shows the three factors influencing the required return from investors which were discussed earlier.

Naturally, investors need at least the minimum returns before they are prepared to invest. However, it is in terms of the effect on their wealth that they should logically assess an investment project. Usually it is the investment with the highest percentage return that will make the investor most wealthy, but we shall see later in this chapter that this is not always the case. For the time being, therefore, we shall concentrate on wealth.

Let us now return to the Billingsgate Battery Company example. We should recall that the cash flows expected from this investment are:

Time		£000
Immediately	Cost of machine	(100)
1 year's time	Net profit before depreciation	20
2 years' time	Net profit before depreciation	40
3 years' time	Net profit before depreciation	60
4 years' time	Net profit before depreciation	60
5 years' time	Net profit before depreciation	20
5 years' time	Disposal proceeds	20

Let us assume that, instead of making this investment, the business could make an alternative investment with similar risk and obtain a return of 20 per cent a year.

We have already seen that it is not sufficient just to compare the basic cash inflows and outflows for the investment. It would be useful if we could express each of these cash flows in similar terms, so that we could make a direct comparison between the sum of the inflows over time and the immediate £100,000 investment. Fortunately, we can do this.

Activity 4.9

We know that Billingsgate Battery Company could alternatively invest its money at a rate of 20 per cent a year. How much do you judge the present (immediate) value of the expected first year receipt of £20,000 to be? In other words, if instead of having to wait a year for the £20,000, and being deprived of the opportunity to invest it at 20 per cent, you could have some money now, what sum to be received now would you regard as exactly equivalent to getting £20,000 but having to wait a year for it?

We should obviously be happy to accept a lower amount if we could get it immediately than if we had to wait a year. This is because we could invest it at 20 per cent (in the alternative project). Logically, we should be prepared to accept the amount that, with a year's income, will grow to £20,000. If we call this amount PV (for present value) we can say:

$$PV + (PV \times 20\%) = £20,000$$

that is, the amount plus income from investing the amount for the year equals the £20,000.
If we rearrange this equation we find:

$$PV \times (1 + 0.2) = £20,000$$

Note that 0.2 is the same as 20 per cent, but expressed as a decimal.
Further rearranging gives:

$$PV = \frac{£20,000}{(1 + 0.2)}$$
$$= £16,667$$

Thus, rational investors who have the opportunity to invest at 20 per cent a year would not mind whether they have £16,667 now or £20,000 in a year's time. In this sense we can say that, given a 20 per cent investment opportunity, the present value of £20,000 to be received in one year's time is £16,667.

If we could derive the present value (PV) of each of the cash flows associated with Billingsgate's machine investment, we could easily make the direct comparison between the cost of making the investment (£100,000) and the various benefits that will derive from it in years 1 to 5. Fortunately we can do precisely this.

We can make a more general statement about the PV of a particular cash flow. It is:

PV of the cash flow of year n = Actual cash flow of year n divided by $(1 + r)^n$

where n is the year of the cash flow (that is, how many years into the future) and r is the opportunity investing rate expressed as a decimal (instead of as a percentage).

We have already seen how this works for the £20,000 inflow for year 1. For year 2 the calculation would be:

$$\text{PV of year 2 cash flow (that is, £40,000)} = \frac{£40,000}{(1 + 0.2)^2}$$

$$PV = \frac{£40,000}{(1.2)^2} = \frac{£40,000}{1.44} = £27,778$$

Thus the present value of the £40,000 to be received in two years' time is £27,778.

Activity 4.10

See if you can show that an investor would be indifferent to £27,778 receivable now, or £40,000 receivable in two years' time, assuming that there is a 20 per cent investment opportunity.

The reasoning goes like this:

	£
Amount available for immediate investment	27,778
Add Interest for Year 1 (20% × 27,778)	5,556
	33,334
Add Interest for Year 2 (20% × 33,334)	6,667
	40,001

(The extra £1 is only a rounding error.)

Thus, because the investor can turn £27,778 into £40,000 in two years, these amounts are equivalent. We can say that £27,778 is the present value of £40,000 receivable after two years (given a 20 per cent rate of return).

Now let us calculate the present values of all of the cash flows associated with the Billingsgate machine project and hence the *net present value (NPV)* of the project as a whole.

The relevant cash flows and calculations are as follows:

Time	Cash flow £000	Calculation of PV	PV £000
Immediately (time 0)	(100)	$(100)/(1 + 0.2)^0$	(100.00)
1 year's time	20	$20/(1 + 0.2)^1$	16.67
2 years' time	40	$40/(1 + 0.2)^2$	27.78
3 years' time	60	$60/(1 + 0.2)^3$	34.72
4 years' time	60	$60/(1 + 0.2)^4$	28.94
5 years' time	20	$20/(1 + 0.2)^5$	8.04
5 years' time	20	$20/(1 + 0.2)^5$	8.04
		NPV	24.19

Note that $(1 + 0.2)^0 = 1$

Once again, we must ask how we can decide whether the machine project is acceptable to the business. In fact, the decision rule is simple.

- For any project to be acceptable, the NPV must be positive.
- Where there are competing projects with positive NPVs, the one that gives the highest positive NPV should be accepted.

In this case, the NPV is positive (and there are no competing projects), so we should accept the project and buy the machine. The reasoning behind this decision rule is quite straightforward. Given the investment opportunities available to the business, investing in the machine will make the business £24,190 better off. The gross benefits from investing in this machine are worth a total of £124,190 today and since the business can 'buy' these benefits for just £100,000 today, the investment should be made. If, however, the gross benefits were below £100,000, they would be less than the cost of 'buying' them.

Activity 4.11

What is the *maximum* the Billingsgate Battery Company would be prepared to pay for the machine, given the potential benefits of owning it?

....

The business would be prepared to pay up to £124,190 since the wealth of the owners of the business would be increased up to this price – though the business would prefer to pay as little as possible.

Using discount tables

Deducing the present values of the various cash flows is a little laborious using the approach that we have just taken. To deduce each PV we took the relevant cash flow and multiplied it by $1/(1 + r)^n$. Fortunately, there is a quicker way. Tables exist that show values of this **discount factor** for a range of values of r and n. Such a table appears in Appendix A at the end of this book on p. 515. Take a look at it.

Look at the column for 20 per cent and the row for one year. We find that the factor is 0.833. Thus the PV of a cash flow of £1 receivable in one year is £0.833. So a cash flow of £20,000 receivable in one year's time is £16,660 (that is, $0.833 \times £20,000$), the same result as we found doing it in longhand.

Activity 4.12

What is the NPV of the Chaotic Industries project from Activity 4.2, assuming a 15 per cent opportunity cost of finance (discount rate)? You should use the discount table in Appendix A.

Remember that the inflows and outflow are expected to be:

Time		£000
Immediately	Cost of vans	(150)
1 year's time	Net saving before depreciation	30
2 years' time	Net saving before depreciation	30
3 years' time	Net saving before depreciation	30
4 years' time	Net saving before depreciation	30
5 years' time	Net saving before depreciation	30
6 years' time	Net saving before depreciation	30
6 years' time	Disposal proceeds from the machine	30

The calculation of the NPV of the project is as follows:

Time	Cash flows	Discount factor (15% – from the table)	Present value
	£000		£000
Immediately	(150)	1.000	(150.00)
1 year's time	30	0.870	26.10
2 years' time	30	0.756	22.68
3 years' time	30	0.658	19.74
4 years' time	30	0.572	17.16
5 years' time	30	0.497	14.91
6 years' time	30	0.432	12.96
6 years' time	30	0.432	12.96
		NPV	(23.49)

Activity 4.13

How would you interpret this result?

The fact that the project has a negative NPV means that the present values of the benefits from the investment are worth less than the cost of entering into it. Any cost up to £126,510 (the present value of the benefits) would be worth paying, but not £150,000.

The discount tables reveal how the value of £1 diminishes as its receipt goes further into the future. Assuming an opportunity cost of finance of 20 per cent a year, £1 to be received immediately, obviously, has a present value of £1. However, as the time before it is to be received increases, its present value diminishes significantly, as is shown in Figure 4.3.

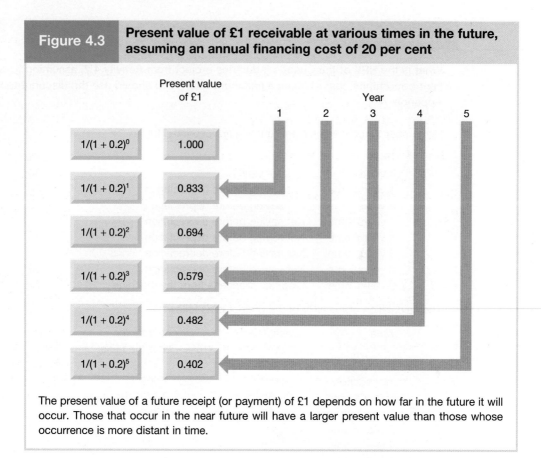

Figure 4.3	Present value of £1 receivable at various times in the future, assuming an annual financing cost of 20 per cent

The present value of a future receipt (or payment) of £1 depends on how far in the future it will occur. Those that occur in the near future will have a larger present value than those whose occurrence is more distant in time.

The discount rate and the cost of capital

We have seen that the appropriate discount rate to use in NPV assessments is the opportunity cost of finance. This is, in effect, the cost to the business of the finance that it will use to finance the investment, should it go ahead. This will normally be the cost of the mixture of funds (shareholders' funds and borrowings) used by the business. This is usually known as the **cost of capital**. We discuss this in more detail in Chapter 8.

Why NPV is superior to ARR and PP

From what we have seen, NPV seems to be a better method of appraising investment opportunities than either ARR or PP. This is because it fully takes account of each of the following:

- *The timing of the cash flows.* By discounting the various cash flows associated with each project according to when it is expected to arise, NPV takes account of the time value of money. Associated with this is the fact that by discounting, using the opportunity cost of finance (that is, the return that the next best alternative opportunity would generate), the net benefit after financing costs have been met is identified (as the NPV of the project).

- *The whole of the relevant cash flows.*   NPV includes all of the relevant cash flows irrespective of when they are expected to occur. It treats them differently according to their date of occurrence, but they are all taken into account in the NPV, and they all have an influence on the decision.
- *The objectives of the business.*   NPV is the only method of appraisal in which the output of the analysis has a direct bearing on the wealth of the shareholders of a business. (Positive NPVs enhance wealth; negative ones reduce it.) Since we assume that private sector businesses seek to maximise shareholders' wealth, NPV is superior to the methods previously discussed.

We saw earlier that a business should take on all projects with positive NPVs, when their cash flows are discounted at the opportunity cost of finance. Where a choice has to be made among projects, a business should normally select the one with the highest NPV.

Internal rate of return (IRR)

This is the last of the four major methods of investment appraisal that are found in practice. It is quite closely related to the NPV method in that, like NPV, it also involves discounting future cash flows. The **internal rate of return (IRR)** of a particular investment is the discount rate which, when applied to its future cash flows, will make them equal to the cash outlays. In essence, it represents the yield from an investment opportunity.

Activity 4.14

We should recall that, when we discounted the cash flows of the Billingsgate Battery Company machine investment opportunity at 20 per cent, we found that the NPV was a positive figure of £24,190 (see page 128). What does the NPV of the machine project tell us about the rate of return that the investment will yield for the business?

The fact that the NPV is positive when discounting at 20 per cent implies that the rate of return that the project generates is more than 20 per cent. The fact that the NPV is a pretty large figure implies that the actual rate of return is quite a lot above 20 per cent. We should expect increasing the size of the discount rate to reduce NPV, because a higher discount rate gives a lower discounted figure.

We have seen that the IRR can be defined as the discount rate that equates the discounted cash inflows with the cash outflows. To put it another way, the IRR is the discount rate that will have the effect of producing an NPV of precisely zero. It is somewhat laborious to deduce the IRR by hand, since it cannot usually be calculated directly. Iteration (trial and error) is the approach that must usually be adopted. Fortunately, computer spreadsheet packages can deduce the IRR with ease. The package will also use a trial and error approach, but at high speed.

For Billingsgate Battery Company, let us try a higher rate, say 30 per cent, and see what happens:

Time	Cash flow £000	Discount factor 30%	PV £000
Immediately (time 0)	(100)	1.000	(100.00)
1 year's time	20	0.769	15.38
2 years' time	40	0.592	23.68
3 years' time	60	0.455	27.30
4 years' time	60	0.350	21.00
5 years' time	20	0.269	5.38
5 years' time	20	0.269	5.38
		NPV	(1.88)

In increasing the discount rate from 20 per cent to 30 per cent, we have reduced the NPV from £24,190 (positive) to £1,880 (negative). Since the IRR is the discount rate that will give us an NPV of exactly zero, we can conclude that the IRR of Billingsgate Battery Company's machine project is very slightly below 30 per cent. Further trials could lead us to the exact rate, but there is probably not much point, given the likely inaccuracy of the cash flow estimates. It is probably good enough, for practical purposes, to say that the IRR is about 30 per cent.

The relationship between the NPV method discussed earlier and the IRR is shown graphically in Figure 4.4 using the information relating to the Billingsgate Battery Company.

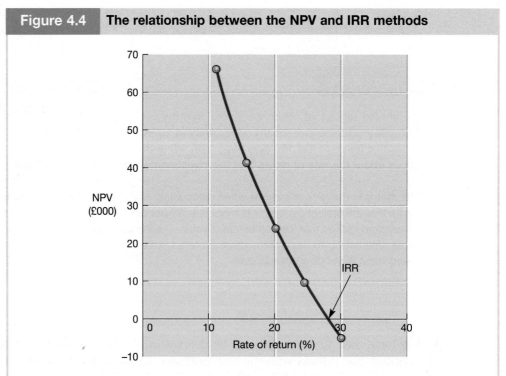

Figure 4.4 **The relationship between the NPV and IRR methods**

If the discount rate were zero, the NPV would be the sum of the net cash flows. In other words, no account would be taken of the time value of money. However, if we assume increasing discount rates, there is a corresponding decrease in the NPV of the project. When the NPV line crosses the horizontal axis there will be a zero NPV, and the point where it crosses is the IRR.

We can see that, where the discount rate is zero, the NPV will be the sum of the net cash flows. In other words, no account is taken of the time value of money. However, as the discount rate increases there is a corresponding decrease in the NPV of the project. When the NPV line crosses the horizontal axis there will be a zero NPV, and that represents the IRR.

Activity 4.15

What is the internal rate of return of the Chaotic Industries project from Activity 4.2. You should use the discount table at the end of this chapter. *Hint*: Remember that you already know the NPV of this project at 15 per cent.

Since we know (from Activity 4.12) that, at a 15 per cent discount rate, the NPV is a relatively large negative figure, our next trial is using a lower discount rate, say 10 per cent:

Time	Cash flows £000	Discount factor (10% – from the table)	Present value £000
Immediately	(150)	1.000	(150.00)
1 year's time	30	0.909	27.27
2 years' time	30	0.826	24.78
3 years' time	30	0.751	22.53
4 years' time	30	0.683	20.49
5 years' time	30	0.621	18.63
6 years' time	30	0.565	16.95
6 years' time	30	0.565	16.95
		NPV	(2.40)

This figure is close to zero NPV. However, the NPV is still negative and so the precise IRR will be a little below 10 per cent.

In answering Activity 4.15, we were fortunate in using a discount rate of 10 per cent for our second iteration as this happened to be very close to the IRR figure. But what if we had used 6 per cent? This discount factor will provide us with a large positive NPV as we shall see below.

Time	Cash flows £000	Discount factor (6% – from the table)	Present value £000
Immediately	(150)	1.000	(150.00)
1 year's time	30	0.943	28.29
2 years' time	30	0.890	26.70
3 years' time	30	0.840	25.20
4 years' time	30	0.792	23.76
5 years' time	30	0.747	22.41
6 years' time	30	0.705	21.15
6 years' time	30	0.705	21.15
		NPV	18.66

We can see that the IRR will fall somewhere between 15 per cent, which gives a negative NPV, and 6 per cent, which gives a positive NPV. We could undertake further iterations in order to derive the IRR. In practice, most businesses have computer software packages that will do this quickly. If, however, we have to calculate the IRR manually, further iterations can be time consuming.

We can get to the answer fairly quickly by first calculating the change in NPV arising from a 1 per cent change in the discount rate. This can be done by taking the differences between the two trials (that is, 15 per cent and 6 per cent) that we have already carried out:

Trial	Discount factor	Present value
		£000
1	15%	(23.49)
2	6%	18.66
Difference	9%	42.15

The change in NPV for every 1 per cent change in the discount rate will be:

$$\frac{42.15}{9} = 4.68\%$$

The reduction in the 15% discount rate required to achieve a zero NPV would therefore be:

$$\frac{23.49}{4.68} = 5.02\%$$

The IRR is therefore:

$$15.00 - 5.02 = \underline{9.98\%}$$

Note that this approach assumes a straight-line relationship between the discount rate and NPV. We can see from Figure 4.4, however, that this assumption is not strictly correct. Nevertheless, over a relatively short range, this simplifying assumption is not usually a problem and so we can still arrive at a reasonable approximation.

Managers using the IRR approach must have a minimum IRR requirement in mind. This is often referred to as the *hurdle rate* and, logically, this should be the opportunity cost of finance. The following decision rules should be applied:

● For any project to be acceptable, it must meet the minimum IRR requirement.
● Where there are competing projects, the one with the highest IRR should be selected.

IRR has certain attributes in common with NPV. All cash flows are taken into account, and their timing is handled logically. **Real World 4.5** lists the IRRs expected from the investment projects of three large businesses.

REAL WORLD 4.5

Rates of return

IRRs for investment projects can vary considerably. Here are a few examples of the expected returns from investment projects of large businesses.

● Associated British Ports, the UK's largest port operator, concentrates on projects that generate an IRR of at least 15 per cent;
● Brascan, a Canadian property and energy business, made a bid to acquire Canary Wharf, a property estate in London, and expected to generate an IRR of at least 20 per cent if the bid price was accepted.
● Hutchison Whampoa, a large conglomerate business, requires an IRR of at least 25 per cent from its telecom projects.

Sources: 'Brascan raises offer for Canary Wharf', FT.com, 13 February 2004; 'Spread of risks give ABP confident outlook', FT.com, 13 February 2003; Lex column: 'Hutchison Whampoa', 31 March 2004.

Problems with IRR

The main disadvantage of IRR is the fact that it does not correctly address the question of wealth generation. It could therefore lead to the wrong decision being made. This is because IRR would, for example, always consider an IRR of 25 per cent to be preferable to an IRR of 20 per cent, assuming an opportunity cost of finance of, say, 15 per cent. Although accepting the project with the higher percentage return will often generate more wealth, this may not always be the case. This is because IRR completely ignores the *scale of investment*. With a 15 per cent cost of finance, £15 million invested at 20 per cent [that is, 15m × (20 – 15)% = 0.75m] would make us richer than £5 million invested at 25 per cent [that is, 5m × (25 – 15)% = 0.50m]. IRR does not recognise this. This problem with percentages is another example illustrated by the Mexican road discussed in Real World 4.4. It should be acknowledged that it is not usual for projects to be competing where there is such a large difference in scale. Even though the problem may be rare and so, typically, IRR will give the same signal as NPV, a method (NPV) that is always reliable must be better to use than IRR.

A further problem with the IRR method is that it has difficulty handling projects with unconventional cash flows. In the examples studied so far, each project has a negative cash flow arising at the start of its life and then positive cash flows thereafter. However, in some cases, a project may have both positive and negative cash flows at future points in its life. Such a pattern of cash flows can result in there being more than one IRR, or even no IRR at all.

Example 4.2

Let us assume that a project had the following pattern of cash flows:

Time	Cash flows
	£000
Immediately	(4,000)
One year's time	9,400
Two years' time	(5,500)

These cash flows will give a zero NPV at both 10 per cent and 25 per cent. Thus, we will have two IRRs, which can be confusing for decision makers. Assume, for example, the minimum acceptable IRR is 15 per cent. Should the project be accepted or rejected?

Figure 4.5 shows the NPV of the above project for different discount rates. Once again, where the NPV line touches the horizontal axis, there will be a zero NPV and that will also represent the IRR.

| Figure 4.5 | The IRR method providing more than one solution |

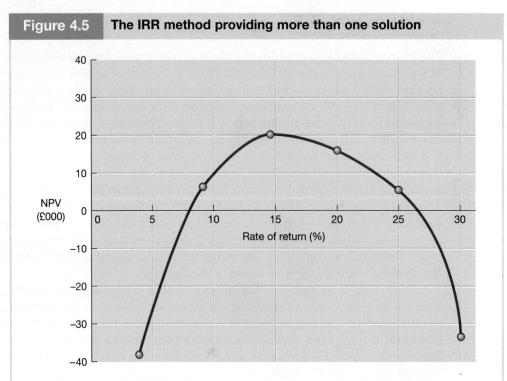

The point at which the NPV line touches the horizontal axis will be the IRR. The figure shows that the NPV of the project is zero at a 10 per cent discount rate and a 25 per cent discount rate. Hence there are two possible IRRs for this project.

Some practical points

When undertaking an investment appraisal, there are several practical points that we should bear in mind:

- *Past costs.* As with all decisions, we should only take account of **relevant costs** in our analysis. This means that only costs that vary with the decision should be considered. Thus, all past costs should be ignored as they cannot vary with the decision. In some cases, a business may incur costs (such as, development costs and market research costs.) *before* the evaluation of an opportunity to launch a new product. As they have already been incurred, these costs should be disregarded, even though the amounts may be substantial. Costs that have already been committed but not yet paid should also be disregarded. Where a business has entered into a binding contract to incur a particular cost, it becomes in effect a past cost even though payment may not be due until some point in the future.
- *Common future costs.* It is not only past costs that do not vary with the decision; some future costs may also be the same. Take, for example, a road haulage business that has decided that it will buy a new lorry and the decision lies between two different models. The load capacity, the fuel and maintenance costs are different for each lorry. The potential costs and revenues associated with these are all relevant items. The lorry will require a driver, so the business will need to employ one, but a

suitably qualified driver could drive either lorry equally well, for the same wage. The cost of employing the driver is thus irrelevant to the decision as to which lorry to buy. This is despite the fact that this cost is a future one. If, however, the decision did not concern a choice between two models of lorry but rather whether to operate an additional lorry or not, the cost of employing the additional driver would be relevant. This is because it would then be a cost that would vary with the decision made.

● *Opportunity costs.*   Opportunity costs arising from benefits forgone must be taken into account. Thus, for example, when considering a decision concerning whether or not to continue to use a machine already owned by the business, the realisable value of the machine might be an important **opportunity cost**.

These three points concerning costs are brought together in Activity 4.16 below.

Activity 4.16

A garage has an old car that it bought several months ago for £3,000. The car needs a replacement engine before it can be sold. It is possible to buy a reconditioned engine for £300. This would take seven hours to fit by a mechanic who is paid £8 an hour. At present the garage is short of work, but the owners are reluctant to lay off any mechanics or even to cut down their basic working week because skilled labour is difficult to find and an upturn in repair work is expected soon.

Without the engine, the car could be sold for an estimated £3,500. What is the minimum price at which the garage should sell the car, with a reconditioned engine fitted, to avoid making a loss? (Ignore any timing differences in receipts and payments.)

The minimum price is the amount required to cover the relevant costs of the job. At this price, the business will make neither a profit nor a loss. Any price below this amount, will result in a reduction in the wealth of the business. Thus, the minimum price is:

	£
Opportunity cost of the car	3,500
Cost of the reconditioned engine	300
Total	3,800

The original cost of the car is a past cost and is, therefore, irrelevant. However, we are told that, without the engine, the car could be sold for £3,500. This is the opportunity cost of the car, which represents real benefits forgone, and should be taken into account.

The cost of the new engine is relevant because, if the work is done, the garage will have to pay £300 for the engine, but will pay nothing if the job is not done. The £300 is a future cost that varies with the decision and should be taken into account.

The labour cost is irrelevant because the same cost will be incurred whether the mechanic undertakes the work or not. This is because the mechanic is being paid to do nothing if this job is not undertaken; thus the additional labour cost arising from this job is zero.

● *Taxation.*   Investors will be interested in the after-tax returns generated from the business and so taxation will usually be an important consideration when making an investment decision. The profits from the project will be taxed, the capital investment may attract tax relief, and so on. Tax is levied on these at significant rates. This means that, in real life, unless tax is formally taken into account, the wrong decision could easily be made. Some, if not all, of the taxation relating to the current year's profits will be paid in a later period (usually the following year). Thus, the timing of the tax outflow should also be taken into account when preparing the cash flows for the project.

- *Cash flows not profit flows.* We have seen that for the NPV, IRR and PP methods, it is cash flows rather than profit flows that are relevant to the evaluation of investment projects. In a problem requiring the application of any of these methods we may be given details of the profits for the investment period, and shall be required to adjust these in order to derive the cash flows. Remember, the net profit *before* non-cash items (such as depreciation) is an approximation to the cash flows for the period, and so we should work back to this figure.

  When the data are expressed in profit rather than cash flow terms, an adjustment in respect of working capital may also be necessary. Some adjustment should be made to take account of changes in working capital. For example, launching a new product may give rise to an increase in the net cash investment made in trade debtors (receivables), stock (inventories) and trade creditors (payables), requiring an immediate outlay of cash. This outlay for additional working capital should be shown in the NPV calculations as part of the initial cost. However, at the end of the life of the project, the additional working capital will be released. This disinvestment, resulting in an inflow of cash at the end the project should also be taken into account at the point at which it is received.

- *Year-end assumption.* In the examples above, we have assumed that cash flows arise at the end of the relevant year. This is a simplifying assumption that is used to make the calculations easier. (However, it is perfectly possible to deal more precisely with the cash flows.) The assumption is clearly unrealistic as money will have to be paid to employees on a weekly or monthly basis and customers will pay within a month or two of buying the product or service. Nevertheless, it is probably not a serious distortion. We should be clear, however, that there is nothing about any of the appraisal methods that demands that this assumption be made.

- *Interest payments.* When using discounted cash flow techniques, interest payments should not be taken into account in deriving the cash flows for the period. The discount factor already takes account of the costs of financing and so to take account of interest charges in deriving cash flows for the period would be double-counting.

- *Other factors.* Investment decision making must not be viewed as simply a mechanical exercise. The results derived from a particular investment appraisal method will be only one input to the decision-making process. There may be broader issues connected to the decision that have to be taken into account, but which may be difficult or impossible to quantify. For example, a regional bus company may be considering an investment in a new bus to serve a particular route that local residents would like to see operated. Although the NPV calculations may reveal that a loss will be made on the investment, it may be that by not investing in the new bus, and therefore not operating the route, the renewal of the company's licence to operate will be put at risk. In such a situation, the size of the expected loss from providing the route, as revealed by the calculations made, must be weighed against the prospect of losing the right to operate, before a final decision is made.

  The reliability of the forecasts and the validity of the assumptions used in the evaluation will also have a bearing on the final decision. We shall see in the following chapter that various techniques may be applied to the information concerning a proposed investment to take account of risk and to assess sensitivity to any inaccuracies in the figures used.

Activity 4.17

The directors of Manuff (Steel) Ltd are considering closing one of the business's factories. There has been a reduction in the demand for the products made at the factory in recent years, and the directors are not optimistic about the long-term prospects for these products. The factory is situated in the north of England, in an area where unemployment is high.

The factory is leased, and there are still four years of the lease remaining. The directors are uncertain as to whether the factory should be closed immediately or at the end of the period of the lease. Another business has offered to sublease the premises from Manuff at a rental of £40,000 a year for the remainder of the lease period.

The machinery and equipment at the factory cost £1,500,000, and have a balance sheet value of £400,000. In the event of immediate closure, the machinery and equipment could be sold for £220,000. The working capital at the factory is £420,000, and could be liquidated for that amount immediately, if required. Alternatively, the working capital can be liquidated in full at the end of the lease period. Immediate closure would result in redundancy payments to employees of £180,000.

If the factory continues in operation until the end of the lease period, the following operating profits (losses) are expected:

	Year 1 £000	Year 2 £000	Year 3 £000	Year 4 £000
Operating profit (loss)	160	(40)	30	20

The above figures include a charge of £90,000 a year for depreciation of machinery and equipment. The residual value of the machinery and equipment at the end of the lease period is estimated at £40,000.

Redundancy payments are expected to be £150,000 at the end of the lease period if the factory continues in operation. The business has an annual cost of capital of 12 per cent. Ignore taxation.

Required:
(a) Determine the relevant cash flows arising from a decision to continue operations until the end of the lease period rather than to close immediately.
(b) Calculate the net present value of continuing operations until the end of the lease period, rather than closing immediately.
(c) What other factors might the directors take into account before making a final decision on the timing of the factory closure?
(d) State, with reasons, whether or not the business should continue to operate the factory until the end of the lease period.

Your answer to this activity should be as follows:
(a) Relevant cash flows

	Year 0 £000	Year 1 £000	Year 2 £000	Year 3 £000	Year 4 £000
Operating cash flows (Note 1)		250	50	120	110
Sale of machinery (Note 2)	(220)				40
Redundancy costs (Note 3)	180				(150)
Sublease rentals (Note 4)		(40)	(40)	(40)	(40)
Working capital invested (Note 5)	(420)				420
	(460)	210	10	80	380

(b) Discount rate 12%	1.000	0.893	0.797	0.712	0.636
Present value	(460)	187.5	8.0	57.0	241.7
Net present value	34.2				

(c) Other factors that may influence the decision include:

Activity 4.17 continued

- *The overall strategy of the business.* The business may need to set the decision within a broader context. It may be necessary to manufacture the products made at the factory because they are an integral part of the business's product range. The business may wish to avoid redundancies in an area of high unemployment for as long as possible.
- *Flexibility.* A decision to close the factory is probably irreversible. If the factory continues, however, there may be a chance that the prospects for the factory will brighten in the future.
- *Creditworthiness of sub-lessee.* The business should investigate the creditworthiness of the sub-lessee. Failure to receive the expected sub-lease payments would make the closure option far less attractive.
- *Accuracy of forecasts.* The forecasts made by the business should be examined carefully. Inaccuracies in the forecasts or any underlying assumptions may change the expected outcomes.

(d) The NPV of the decision to continue operations rather than close immediately is positive. Hence, shareholders would be better off if the directors took this course of action. The factory should therefore continue in operation rather than close down. This decision is likely to be welcomed by employees and would allow the business to maintain its flexibility.

Notes
1. Each year's operating cash flows are calculated by adding back the depreciation charge for the year to the operating profit for the year. In the case of the operating loss, the depreciation charge is deducted.
2. In the event of closure, machinery could be sold immediately. Thus an opportunity cost of £220,000 is incurred if operations continue.
3. By continuing operations, there will be a saving in immediate redundancy costs of £180,000. However, redundancy costs of £150,000 will be paid in four years' time.
4. By continuing operations, the opportunity to sublease the factory will be foregone.
5. Immediate closure would mean that working capital could be liquidated. By continuing operations this opportunity is forgone. However, working capital can be liquidated in four years' time.

Investment appraisal in practice

As a footnote to our examination of investment appraisal techniques, it is interesting to consider their practical significance. Many surveys have been conducted in the UK into the methods of investment appraisal used by businesses. They have tended to show the following features:

- businesses using more than one method to assess each investment decision, increasingly so over time;
- an increased use of the discounting methods (NPV and IRR) over time, with these two becoming the most popular in recent years;
- continued popularity of ARR and PP, despite their theoretical shortcomings and the rise in popularity of the discounting methods;
- a tendency for larger businesses to use the discounting methods and to use more than one method in respect of each decision.

Real World 4.6 shows the results of the most recent survey conducted of UK businesses regarding their use of investment appraisal methods.

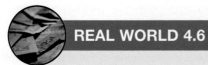

REAL WORLD 4.6

A survey of UK business practice

Method	Percentage of businesses using the method
Net present value	80
Internal rate of return	81
Payback period	70
Accounting rate of return	56
	287

Source: G. C. Arnold and P. Hatzopoulos, 'The theory-practice gap in capital budgeting: evidence from the United Kingdom'. *Journal of Business Finance and Accounting* (June/July 2000). Reproduced by kind permission of Blackwell Publishing Ltd.

A recent survey of US businesses also shows considerable support for the NPV and IRR methods. There is less support, however, for the payback method and accounting rate of return. **Real World 4.7** sets out some of the main findings.

REAL WORLD 4.7

A survey of US practice

A survey of the chief financial officers (CFOs) of 392 US businesses examined the popularity of various methods of investment appraisal. Figure 4.6 below shows the percentage of businesses surveyed that always or almost always used the four methods discussed in this chapter.

Figure 4.6 The use of investment appraisal methods among US businesses

The figure shows that the IRR and NPV methods are both widely used and are much more popular than the payback and accounting rate of return methods. Nevertheless, the payback method is still used always, or almost always, by a majority of US businesses.

Source: Based on information in R. Graham and C. Harvey, How do CFOs make capital budgeting and capital structure decisions? *Journal of Applied Corporate Finance* Vol 15 No 1 2002.

Activity 4.18

Earlier in the chapter we discussed the theoretical limitations of the payback method. How do you explain the fact that it still seems to be a popular method of investment appraisal among businesses?

A number of possible reasons may explain this finding:

● PP is easy to understand and use.
● It can avoid the problems of forecasting far into the future.
● It gives emphasis to the early cash flows when there is greater certainty concerning the accuracy of their predicted value.
● It emphasises the importance of liquidity. Where a business has liquidity problems, a short payback period for a project is likely to appear attractive.

PP can provide a convenient, though rough and ready, assessment of the profitability of a project, in the way that it is used in **Real World 4.8**.

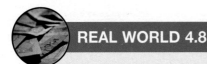

REAL WORLD 4.8

Space to earn

SES Global is the world's largest commercial satellite operator. This means that it rents satellite capacity to broadcasters, governments, telecommunications groups and Internet service providers. It is a risky venture that few are prepared to undertake. As a result, a handful of businesses dominate the market.

Launching a satellite requires a huge initial outlay of capital, but relatively small cash outflows following the launch. Revenues only start to flow once the satellite is in orbit. A satellite launch costs around €250m. The main elements of this cost are the satellite (€120m), the launch vehicle (€80m), insurance (€40m) and ground equipment €10m).

According to Romain Bausch, president and chief executive of SES Global, it takes three years to build and launch a satellite. However, the average lifetime of a satellite is fifteen years during which time it is generating revenues. The revenues generated are such that the payback period is around four to five years.

Source: 'Satellites need space to earn', Tim Burt, www.FT.com, 14 July 2003.

The popularity of PP may suggest a lack of sophistication among managers concerning investment appraisal. This criticism is most often made against managers of smaller businesses. In fact, both of the surveys discussed above, as well as other surveys, have found that smaller businesses are much less likely to use discounted cash flow methods (NPV and IRR) than larger ones.

The survey evidence suggests that many businesses use more than one method to appraise investments. The sum of percentage usage for each appraisal method in the UK survey, for example, is 287 per cent (see Real World 4.6). Real World 4.6 also suggests that most businesses use one of the two discounted cash flow methods. Generally, survey evidence has shown a strong increase in the rate of usage of both NPV and IRR, in the UK, over the years.

IRR may be as popular as NPV, despite its shortcomings, because it expresses outcomes in percentage terms rather than in absolute terms. This form of expression appears to be more acceptable to managers. This may be because managers are used to using percentage figures as targets (for example, return on capital employed).

Real World 4.9 shows extracts from the 2003 annual report of a well-known business: Rolls-Royce plc, the builder of engines for aircraft and other purposes.

REAL WORLD 4.9

The use of NPV at Rolls-Royce

In its 2003 annual report and accounts, Rolls-Royce plc stated that:

> The Group continues to subject all investments to rigorous examination of risks and future cash flows to ensure that they create shareholder value. All major investments require Board approval.
> The Group has a portfolio of projects at different stages of their life cycles. Discounted cash flow analysis of the remaining life of projects is performed on a regular basis.

Source: Rolls-Royce plc, *Annual Report and Accounts* 2003.

Rolls-Royce makes clear that it uses NPV (the report refers to creating shareholder value and to discounted cash flow, which strongly implies NPV). It is interesting to note that Rolls-Royce not only assesses new projects, but also reassesses existing ones. This must be a sensible commercial approach. Businesses should not continue with existing projects unless those projects have a positive NPV based on future cash flows. Just because a project seemed to have a positive NPV before it started does not mean that this will persist, in the light of changing circumstances. Activity 4.17 (p. 139) considered a decision to close down a project.

Self-assessment question 4.1

Beacon Chemicals plc is considering buying some equipment to produce a chemical named X14. The new equipment's capital cost is estimated at £100,000. If its purchase is approved now, the equipment can be bought and production can commence by the end of this year. £50,000 has already been spent on research and development work. Estimates of revenues and costs arising from the operation of the new equipment appear below:

	Year 1	Year 2	Year 3	Year 4	Year 5
Sales price (£ per litre)	100	120	120	100	80
Sales volume (litres)	800	1,000	1,200	1,000	800
Variable costs (£ per litre)	50	50	40	30	40
Fixed costs (£000)	30	30	30	30	30

If the equipment is bought, sales of some existing products will be lost, and this will result in a loss of contribution of £15,000 a year over its life.

The accountant has informed you that the fixed costs include depreciation of £20,000 a year on the new equipment. They also include an allocation of £10,000 for fixed overheads. A separate study has indicated that if the new equipment were bought, additional

Self-assessment question 4.1 continued

overheads, excluding depreciation, arising from producing the chemical would be £8,000 a year. Production would require additional working capital of £30,000.

For the purposes of your initial calculations ignore taxation.

Required:

(a) Deduce the relevant annual cash flows associated with buying the equipment.
(b) Deduce the payback period.
(c) Calculate the net present value using a discount rate of 8 per cent.

Hint: You should deal with the investment in working capital by treating it as a cash outflow at the start of the project and an inflow at the end.

The process of investment decision making

So far, we have been concerned with the methods of evaluating investment opportunities that have already been identified. This topic is given a great deal of emphasis in the literature relating to investment decisions. Though the evaluation of projects is undoubtedly important, we must bear in mind that it is only *part* of the process of investment decision making. There are other important aspects that managers must also consider.

It is possible to see the investment process as a sequence of six stages, each of which must be given proper consideration by managers. The six stages are set out in Figure 4.7 and described below.

Stage 1: Determine investment funds available

The amount of funds available for investment may be determined by the external market for funds or by internal management. In practice, it is often the latter that has the greater influence on the amount available. In either case, it may be that the funds will not be sufficient to finance the profitable investment opportunities available. When this occurs, some form of **capital rationing** has to be undertaken. This means that managers are faced with the task of deciding on the most profitable use of the investment funds available. To ensure that competing projects are prioritised correctly, some modification to the NPV decision rule is necessary. This point is discussed further in the next chapter.

Stage 2: Identify profitable project opportunities

A vitally important part of the investment process is the search for profitable investment opportunities. A business should be proactive and should adopt a systematic approach towards identifying investment opportunities. To maintain a competitive edge, the search for new investment opportunities should be considered a normal part of the planning process. The range of investment opportunities available to a business is likely to include the development of new products or services, improving existing products or services, entering new markets, and investing to increase capacity or

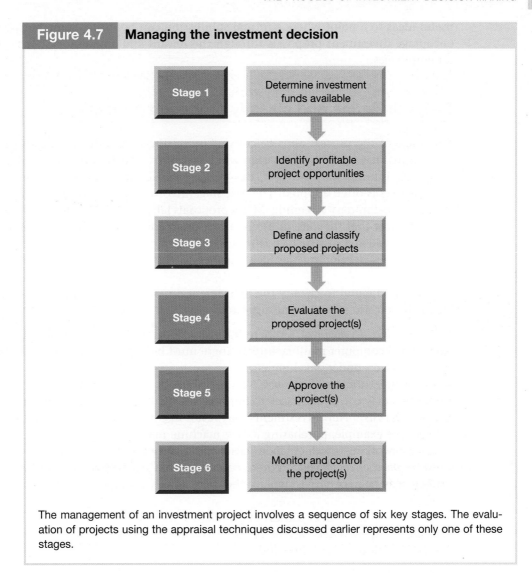

| Figure 4.7 | **Managing the investment decision** |

Stage 1 → Determine investment funds available

Stage 2 → Identify profitable project opportunities

Stage 3 → Define and classify proposed projects

Stage 4 → Evaluate the proposed project(s)

Stage 5 → Approve the project(s)

Stage 6 → Monitor and control the project(s)

The management of an investment project involves a sequence of six key stages. The evaluation of projects using the appraisal techniques discussed earlier represents only one of these stages.

efficiency. The search for new opportunities will often involve looking outside the business to identify changes in technology, customer demand, market conditions and so on. Information will need to be gathered, and this may take some time, particularly for unusual or non-routine investment opportunities.

It is important that the business's investments should fit in with its strategic plans. The business should seek out investment projects that use its strengths (such as management expertise in a particular activity) to exploit opportunities (for example, an expansion of the market). At the same time, investment projects selected should avoid exposing the business's weaknesses (such as a shortage of suitably skilled labour) to threats (for example, other businesses poaching skilled staff). The business is likely to be able to generate greater amounts of wealth by investing in particular types of project, rather than in others. It is also possible that the business will be able to generate greater benefits from a particular project than a business with different strengths and weaknesses.

The search for new opportunities is likely to be more successful where there is a culture that encourages employees at all levels to submit proposals. Various policies can be adopted to help develop such a culture. For example, some businesses encourage unrefined ideas to be submitted and will then invest resources to refine the potentially useful ideas to a point where a formal submission can be made. Some businesses will encourage investment proposals through the reward and appraisal systems operating for employees.

Stage 3: Refine and classify proposed project(s)

This stage of the process aims to convert promising ideas into full-blown proposals. This means that further information will be required, much of it of a detailed nature. Collecting information, however, can be time consuming and costly, and so a two-stage process is often adopted. The first stage involves collecting enough information to allow a preliminary screening. Many proposals fall at this first hurdle because it soon becomes clear that they are unprofitable or unacceptable for other reasons. Proposals that are considered worthy of further investigation continue to the second stage. This stage involves developing the ideas further so that more detailed screening can be carried out.

It is often helpful to classify the investment opportunities identified. The following broad classifications have been suggested:

● *New product development.* Where businesses operate in fast-changing markets (for example, computer manufacturers), there must be a regular stream of new, innovative products under development.
● *Improving existing product sales.* To maintain or enhance competitive position, a business may continually seek to improve the quality or design of existing products.
● *Reducing costs.* New investments may result in considerable savings over the longer term. For example, purchasing a new machine may reduce the costs incurred from scrap, reworking, product labour costs and quality inspection.
● *Replacement of equipment.* Where equipment has reached the end of its economic life it may be necessary to replace the items simply to maintain the existing level of output.
● *Welfare and safety.* A business may seek to achieve certain standards or be required to adhere to new regulations relating to such issues as employee safety, environmental pollution, recycling and so on.

Activity 4.19

What do you think are the benefits of classifying investment proposals in this way? Could it be helpful when gathering information and making decisions?

Classification can be useful in deciding on the level of information required for a particular proposal. For example, equipment replacement may be a routine occurrence and so a replacement proposal may only require evidence that the particular piece of equipment has reached the end of its economic life. New product development, on the other hand, may require market research evidence, a marketing plan and detailed costings to support the proposal.

Classification can also help in deciding on the acceptance criteria to be applied. For example, equipment replacement may be considered low risk and this may be reflected in a low required rate of return. New product development, on the other hand, may be considered to be high risk and this may be reflected in a high rate of return. (Risk and return in relation to investment proposals are considered in detail in the next chapter.)

Stage 4: Evaluate proposed project(s)

Once a project has passed the preliminary screening stage and has been fully developed, a detailed evaluation is usually carried out. For projects of any size, this may involve providing answers to a number of key questions, including:

- What is the nature and purpose of the project?
- Does the project align with the overall objectives of the business?
- How much finance is required? Does this fit with the funds available?
- What other resources (such as expertise, IT, factory space and so on) are required for successful completion of the project?
- How long will the project last and what are its key stages?
- What is the expected pattern of cash flows?
- What are the major problems associated with the project and how can they be overcome?
- What is the NPV/IRR of the project? How does this compare with other opportunities available?
- Have risk and inflation been taken into account in the appraisal process and, if so, what are the results?

It is important to appreciate that the ability and commitment of those responsible for proposing and managing the project will be vital to its success. Hence, when evaluating a new project, those proposing it may also be evaluated. In some cases, senior managers may decide not to support a project that appears profitable on paper if they lack confidence in the ability of key managers to see it through to completion.

Stage 5: Approve project(s)

Once the managers responsible for investment decision making are satisfied that the project should be undertaken, formal approval can be given. However, a decision on a project may be postponed if senior managers need more information from those proposing the project, or if revisions are required to the proposal. In some cases, the proposal may be rejected if it is considered unprofitable or likely to fail. Before rejecting a proposal, however, the implications of not pursuing the project for such areas as market share, staff morale and existing business operations must be carefully considered.

Approval may be authorised at different levels of the management hierarchy according to the type of investment and amount of finance required. For example, a plant manager may have authority to accept investment projects up to a maximum of, say, £100,000, and beyond this amount, authority from a capital expenditure committee, made up of senior managers and directors, may be required.

Stage 6: Monitor and control the project(s)

Making a decision to invest in, say, the plant needed to provide a new service does not automatically cause the investment to be made and provision of the service to go smoothly ahead. Managers will need to manage the project actively through to completion. This, in turn, will require further information gathering.

Management should receive progress reports at regular intervals concerning the project. These reports should provide information relating to the actual cash flows for each stage of the project, which can then be compared against the forecast figures provided when the proposal was submitted for approval. The reasons for significant variations should be ascertained, and corrective action taken where possible. Any changes in the expected completion date of the project or any expected variations in future cash flows from budget should be reported immediately; in extreme cases, managers may even abandon the project if circumstances appear to have changed dramatically for the worse. We saw in Real World 4.9 that Rolls-Royce undertakes this kind of reassessment of existing projects. No doubt most other well-managed businesses do this too.

In addition to financial measures, key non-financial measures, such as physical output, wastage rate, customer satisfactions scores and so on, may be used to monitor performance. Certain types of projects, such as civil engineering and construction projects, may have 'milestones' (that is, particular levels of completion) to be reached by certain dates. The progress towards each milestone should be monitored carefully and early warnings should be given of any problems that are likely to prevent their achievement. Project management techniques (for example, critical path analysis) should be employed wherever possible and their effectiveness reported to senior management.

An important part of the control process is a **post-completion audit** of the project. This is, in essence, a review of the project performance in order to see whether it lived up to expectations and whether any lessons can be learned from the way that the investment process was carried out. In addition to an evaluation of financial costs and benefits, non-financial measures of performance, such as the ability to meet deadlines and levels of quality achieved, should also be reported.

The fact that a post-completion audit is an integral part of the management of the project should also encourage those who submit projects to use realistic estimates. Where overoptimistic estimates are used in an attempt to secure project approval, the managers responsible will find themselves accountable at the post-completion audit stage.

Activity 4.20

Can you think of any drawbacks with the use of post-completion audits? Could they have an adverse effect on manager behaviour?

One problem that has been suggested is that a post-completion audit may inhibit managers from proposing and supporting projects that carry a high level of risk. If things go wrong, they could be blamed. This may result in only low-risk projects being submitted for consideration.

Another problem is that managers may feel threatened by the post-completion audit investigations and so will not cooperate fully with the audit team.

However, the behaviour of managers is likely to be influenced by the way in which the post-completion audit is conducted. If it is seen by managers as simply a device to apportion blame, then the problems mentioned in Activity 4.20 are more likely to occur. However, if it is used as a constructive tool where the main objective is to learn from experience, and the high-risk nature of particular projects is taken into account, the problems mentioned need not arise.

Post-completion audits can be difficult and time consuming to carry out, and so the likely benefits must be weighed against the costs involved. Senior management may feel, therefore, that only projects above a certain size should be subject to a post-completion audit.

Real World 4.10 outlines the main elements of the capital investment process for two large UK companies: Tesco plc and United Utilities plc. We can see that both businesses use post-completion audits when evaluating past investment projects. No doubt most well-managed businesses do the same.

REAL WORLD 4.10

The capital investment process

In its 2004 annual report, Tesco plc, the supermarket chain, said:

> The capital investment programme is subject to formalised review procedures requiring key criteria to be met. All major initiatives require business cases to be prepared, normally covering a minimum period of five years. Post investment appraisals are also carried out.

In its 2004 annual report, United Utilities plc, the electricity and water utility, said that it has:

> established procedures, set out in a group internal control manual, for planning, approving and monitoring major capital expenditure, major projects and the development of new business which includes short- and long-term budgets, risk evaluation, detailed appraisal and review procedures, defined authority levels and post-investment performance reviews.

Sources: The annual reports of the businesses concerned.

Investment decisions and human behaviour

The sequence of stages described above may give the impression that investment decision making is an entirely rational process. However, studies have shown that, in practice, this may not always be the case. It has been argued that an investment project will often gather support among managers as it is being developed and that the greater the level of support, the greater the potential for bias in the information used to evaluate the project. This may mean that future cash flows are overestimated or the risks associated with the project are underestimated. It has also been suggested that the project sponsors will often seek political support among senior managers so that final approval of the project is simply a formality (see reference 1 at the end of the chapter). These behavioural aspects are beyond the scope of this book. Nevertheless, it is important to recognise that investment decisions are made by individuals who may have their own interests to satisfy.

SUMMARY

The main points in this chapter may be summarised as follows:

Accounting rate of return (ARR) is the average accounting profit from the project expressed as a percentage of the average investment.

● Decision rule: projects with an ARR above a defined minimum are acceptable; the greater the ARR, the more attractive the project becomes.

● Conclusions on ARR:
  – it does not relate directly to shareholders' wealth – can lead to illogical conclusions
  – takes almost no account of the timing of cash flows
  – ignores some relevant information and may take account of some irrelevant
  – relatively simple to use
  – much inferior to NPV.

Payback period (PP) is the length of time that it takes for the cash outflow for the initial investment to be repaid out of resulting cash inflows.

● Decision rule: projects with a PP up to defined maximum period are acceptable, the shorter the PP, the more desirable.

● Conclusions on PP:
  – does not relate to shareholders' wealth; ignores inflows after the payback date
  – takes little account of the timing of cash flows
  – ignores much relevant information
  – does not always provide clear signals and can be impractical to use
  – much inferior to NPV, but it is easy to understand and can offer a liquidity insight, which might be the reason for its widespread use.

Net present value (NPV) is the sum of the discounted values of the net cash flows from the investment.

● Money has a time value.

● Decision rule: all positive NPV investments enhance shareholders' wealth; the greater the NPV, the greater the enhancement and the more desirable.

● PV of a cashflow = Cashflow × $1/(1 + r)^n$, assuming a constant discount rate.

● The act of discounting brings cash flows at different points in time to a common valuation basis (their present value), which enables them to be directly compared.

● Conclusions on NPV:
  – relates directly to shareholders' wealth objective
  – takes account of the timing of cash flows
  – takes all relevant information into account
  – provides clear signals and practical to use.

Internal rate of return (IRR) is the discount rate that, when applied to the cash flows of a project, causes it to have a zero NPV.

● Represents the average percentage return on the investment, taking account of the fact that cash may be flowing in and out of the project at various points in its life.

● Decision rule: projects that have an IRR greater than the cost of capital are acceptable; the greater the IRR, the more attractive the project.

- Cannot normally be calculated directly; a trial and error approach is often necessary.
- Conclusions on IRR:
  - does not relate directly to shareholders' wealth. Usually gives the same signals as NPV but can mislead where there are competing projects of different size
  - takes account of the timing of cash flows
  - takes all relevant information into account
  - problems of multiple IRRs when there are unconventional cash flows
  - inferior to NPV.

Use of appraisal methods in practice

- All four methods identified are widely used.
- The discounting methods (NPV and IRR) show a steady increase in usage over time.
- Many businesses use more than one method.
- Larger businesses seem to be more sophisticated in their choice and use of appraisal methods than smaller ones.

Management of the investment project has six stages

1 Determine investment funds available – dealing, if necessary with capital rationing problems.
2 Identify profitable project opportunities.
3 Refine and classify the project.
4 Evaluate the proposed project.
5 Approve the project.
6 Monitor and control the project – using a post-completion audit approach.

→ Key terms

Accounting rate of return (ARR) p. 115
Payback period (PP) p. 120
Net present value (NPV) p. 123
Risk p. 124
Risk premium p. 125
Inflation p. 125

Discount factor p. 128
Cost of capital p. 130
Internal rate of return (IRR) p. 131
Relevant costs p. 136
Opportunity cost p. 137
Capital rationing p. 144
Post-completion audit p. 148

For definitions of these terms see the Glossary, pp. 562–571.

Further reading

If you wish to explore the topics discussed in this chapter in more depth, try the following books:

Business Finance: Theory and Practice, *McLaney, E.*, 7th edn, Financial Times Prentice Hall, 2006, chapters 4–6.

Corporate Financial Management, *Arnold, G.*, 2nd edn, Financial Times Prentice Hall, 2002, chapters 2–4.

Corporate Finance and Investment, *Pike, R. and Neale, B.*, 4th edn, Prentice Hall International, 2002, chapters 5–7.

Investment Appraisal and Financial Decisions, *Lumby, S. and Jones, C.*, 7th edn, International Thomson Business Press, 2003, chapters 3, 5 and 6.

References

1 **Reckoning with Risk**, *Gigerenzer, G.*, Penguin Books, 2002.

2 'The theory–practice gap in capital budgeting: evidence from the United Kingdom', *Arnold, G. C. and Hatzopoulos, P. D.*, **Journal of Business Finance and Accounting**, June/July 2000, pp. 603–26.

3 'How do CFOs make capital budgeting and capital structure decisions?' *Graham, J. R. and Harvey, C. H.*, **Journal of Applied Corporate Finance**, vol. 15 (2002), no. 1.

4 **Accounting for Management Control**, *Emmanual, C., Otley, D. and Merchant, K.*, Chapman and Hall, 1990.

REVIEW QUESTIONS

Answers to these questions can be found in Appendix D at the back of the book.

4.1 Why is the net present value method of investment appraisal considered to be theoretically superior to other methods that are found in practice?

4.2 The payback method has been criticised for not taking the time value of money into account. Could this limitation be overcome? If so, would this method then be preferable to the NPV method?

4.3 Research indicates that the IRR method is a more popular method of investment appraisal than the NPV method. Why might this be?

4.4 Why are cash flows rather than profit flows used in the IRR, NPV and PP methods of investment appraisal?

EXERCISES

Exercises 4.4 to 4.7 are more advanced than 4.1 to 4.3. Those with coloured numbers have answers at the back of the book.

> If you wish to try more exercises, visit the students' side of the Companion Website.

4.1 The directors of Mylo Ltd are currently considering two mutually exclusive investment projects. Both projects are concerned with the purchase of new plant. The following data are available for each project:

	Project 1 £	Project 2 £
Cost (immediate outlay)	100,000	60,000
Expected annual net profit (loss):		
Year 1	29,000	18,000
2	(1,000)	(2,000)
3	2,000	4,000
Estimated residual value of the plant	7,000	6,000

The business has an estimated cost of capital of 10 per cent, and uses the straight-line method of depreciation for all non-current (fixed) assets when calculating net profit. Neither project would increase the working capital of the business. The business has sufficient funds to meet all capital expenditure requirements.

Required:
(a) Calculate for each project:
   (i) The net present value
   (ii) The approximate internal rate of return
   (iii) The payback period.

(b) State which, if any, of the two investment projects the directors of Mylo Ltd should accept, and why.

(c) State, in general terms, which method of investment appraisal you consider to be most appropriate for evaluating investment projects, and why.

4.2 Arkwright Mills plc is considering expanding its production of a new yarn, code name X15. The plant is expected to cost £1 million and have a life of five years and a nil residual value. It will be bought, paid for and ready for operation on 31 December Year 0. £500,000 has already been spent on development costs of the product, and this has been charged in the profit and loss account (income statement) in the year it was incurred.

The following results are projected for the new yarn are:

	Year 1	Year 2	Year 3	Year 4	Year 5
	£m	£m	£m	£m	£m
Sales	1.2	1.4	1.4	1.4	1.4
Costs, including depreciation	1.0	1.1	1.1	1.1	1.1
Profit before tax	0.2	0.3	0.3	0.3	0.3

Tax is charged at 50 per cent on annual profits (before tax and after depreciation) and paid one year in arrears. Depreciation of the plant has been calculated on a straight-line basis. Additional working capital of £0.6 million will be required at the beginning of the project and released at the end of Year 5. You should assume that all cash flows occur at the end of the year in which they arise.

Required:

(a) Prepare a statement showing the incremental cash flows of the project relevant to a decision concerning whether or not to proceed with the construction of the new plant.

(b) Compute the net present value of the project using a 10 per cent discount rate.

(c) Compute the payback period to the nearest year. Explain the meaning of this term.

4.3 The accountant of your business has recently been taken ill through overwork. In his absence his assistant has prepared some calculations of the profitability of a project, which are to be discussed soon at the board meeting of your business. His workings, which are set out below, include some errors of principle. You can assume that the statement below includes no arithmetical errors.

	Year 1 £000	Year 2 £000	Year 3 £000	Year 4 £000	Year 5 £000	Year 6 £000
Sales revenue		450	470	470	470	470
Less Costs						
Materials		126	132	132	132	132
Labour		90	94	94	94	94
Overheads		45	47	47	47	47
Depreciation		120	120	120	120	120
Working capital	180					
Interest on working capital		27	27	27	27	27
Write-off of development costs		30	30	30		
Total costs	180	438	450	450	420	420
Profit (loss)	(180)	12	20	20	50	50

$$\frac{\text{Total profit (loss)}}{\text{Cost of equipment}} = \frac{(£28,000)}{£600,000} = \text{Return on investment (4.7\%)}$$

You ascertain the following additional information:

1 The cost of equipment contains £100,000, being the book value of an old machine. If it were not used for this project it would be scrapped with a zero net realisable value. New equipment

costing £500,000 will be purchased on 31 December Year 0. You should assume that all other cash flows occur at the end of the year to which they relate.

2 The development costs of £90,000 have already been spent.

3 Overheads have been costed at 50 per cent of direct labour, which is the business's normal practice. An independent assessment has suggested that incremental overheads are likely to amount to £30,000 a year.

4 The business's cost of capital is 12 per cent.

Ignore taxation in your answer.

Required:

(a) Prepare a corrected statement of the incremental cash flows arising from the project. Where you have altered the assistant's figures you should attach a brief note explaining your alterations.

(b) Calculate:
(i)   The project's payback period
(ii) The project's net present value as at 31 December Year 0.

(c) Write a memo to the board advising on the acceptance or rejection of the project.

4.4 C. George (Controls) Ltd manufactures a thermostat that can be used in a range of kitchen appliances. The manufacturing process is, at present, semi-automated. The equipment used costs £540,000, and has a written-down (balance sheet) value of £300,000. Demand for the product has been fairly stable, and output has been maintained at 50,000 units a year in recent years.

The following data, based on the current level of output, have been prepared in respect of the product:

	Per unit	
	£	£
Selling price		12.40
Less		
Labour	3.30	
Materials	3.65	
Overheads: Variable	1.58	
Fixed	1.60	
		10.13
Profit		2.27

Although the existing equipment is expected to last for a further four years before it is sold for an estimated £40,000, the business has recently been considering purchasing new equipment that would completely automate much of the production process. The new equipment would cost £670,000 and would have an expected life of four years, at the end of which it would be sold for an estimated £70,000. If the new equipment is purchased, the old equipment could be sold for £150,000 immediately.

The assistant to the business's accountant has prepared a report to help assess the viability of the proposed change, which includes the following data:

	Per unit	
	£	£
Selling price		12.40
Less		
Labour	1.20	
Materials	3.20	
Overheads: Variable	1.40	
Fixed	3.30	
		9.10
Profit		3.30

Depreciation charges will increase by £85,000 a year as a result of purchasing the new machinery; however, other fixed costs are not expected to change.

In the report the assistant wrote:

'The figures shown above that relate to the proposed change are based on the current level of output and take account of a depreciation charge of £150,000 a year in respect of the new equipment. The effect of purchasing the new equipment will be to increase the net profit to sales ratio from 18.3% to 26.6%. In addition, the purchase of the new equipment will enable us to reduce our stock (inventories) level immediately by £130,000.

In view of these facts, I recommend purchase of the new equipment.'

The business has a cost of capital of 12 per cent. Ignore taxation.

Required:

(a) Prepare a statement of the incremental cash flows arising from the purchase of the new equipment.
(b) Calculate the net present value of the proposed purchase of new equipment.
(c) State, with reasons, whether the business should purchase the new equipment.
(d) Explain why cash flow forecasts are used rather than profit forecasts to assess the viability of proposed capital expenditure projects.

4.5   Newton Electronics Ltd has incurred expenditure of £5 million over the past three years researching and developing a miniature hearing aid. The hearing aid is now fully developed, and the directors are considering which of three mutually exclusive options should be taken to exploit the potential of the new product. The options are as follows:

● *Option 1*.   The business could manufacture the hearing aid itself. This would be a new departure, since the business has so far concentrated on research and development projects. However, the business has manufacturing space available that it currently rents to another business for £100,000 a year. The business would have to purchase plant and equipment costing £9 million and invest £3 million in working capital immediately for production to begin.

A market research report, for which the business paid £50,000, indicates that the new product has an expected life of five years. Sales of the product during this period are predicted as follows:

| | Predicted sales for the year ended 30 November | | | | |
	Year 1	Year 2	Year 3	Year 4	Year 5
Number of units (000s)	800	1,400	1,800	1,200	500

The selling price per unit will be £30 in the first year but will fall to £22 in the following three years. In the final year of the product's life, the selling price will fall to £20. Variable production costs are predicted to be £14 a unit, and fixed production costs (including depreciation) will be £2.4 million a year. Marketing costs will be £2 million a year.

The business intends to depreciate the plant and equipment using the straight-line method and based on an estimated residual value at the end of the five years of £1 million. The business has a cost of capital of 10 per cent a year.

● *Option 2*.   Newton Electronics Ltd could agree to another business manufacturing and marketing the product under licence. A multinational business, Faraday Electricals plc, has offered to undertake the manufacture and marketing of the product, and in return will make a royalty payment to Newton Electronics Ltd of £5 per unit. It has been estimated that the annual number of sales of the hearing aid will be 10 per cent higher if the multinational business, rather than if Newton Electronics Ltd, manufactures and markets the product.

● *Option 3*.   Newton Electronics Ltd could sell the patent rights to Faraday Electricals plc for £24 million, payable in two equal instalments. The first instalment would be payable immediately and the second at the end of two years. This option would give Faraday Electricals the exclusive right to manufacture and market the new product.

Ignore taxation. Assume it is now 30 November Year 0.

Required:
(a) Calculate the net present value of each of the options available to Newton Electronics Ltd.
(b) Identify and discuss any other factors that Newton Electronics Ltd should consider before arriving at a decision.
(c) State what you consider to be the most suitable option, and why.

4.6 Chesterfield Wanderers is a professional football club that has enjoyed considerable success in both national and European competitions in recent years. As a result, the club has accumulated £10 million to spend on its further development. The board of directors is currently considering two mutually exclusive options for spending the funds available.

The first option is to acquire another player. The team manager has expressed a keen interest in acquiring Basil ('Bazza') Ramsey, a central defender, who currently plays for a rival club. The rival club has agreed to release the player immediately for £10 million if required. A decision to acquire 'Bazza' Ramsey would mean that the existing central defender, Vinnie Smith, could be sold to another club. Chesterfield Wanderers has recently received an offer of £2.2 million for this player. This offer is still open but will only be accepted if 'Bazza' Ramsey joins Chesterfield Wanderers. If this does not happen, Vinnie Smith will be expected to stay on with the club until the end of his playing career in five years' time. During this period, Vinnie will receive an annual salary of £400,000 and a loyalty bonus of £200,000 at the end of his five-year period with the club.

Assuming 'Bazza' Ramsey is acquired, the team manager estimates that gate receipts will increase by £2.5 million in the first year and £1.3 million in each of the four following years. There will also be an increase in advertising and sponsorship revenues of £1.2 million for each of the next five years if the player is acquired. At the end of five years, the player can be sold to a club in a lower division and Chesterfield Wanderers will expect to receive £1 million as a transfer fee. During his period at the club, 'Bazza' will receive an annual salary of £800,000 and a loyalty bonus of £400,000 after five years.

The second option is for the club to improve its ground facilities. The west stand could be extended and executive boxes could be built for businesses wishing to offer corporate hospitality to clients. These improvements would also cost £10 million and would take one year to complete. During this period, the west stand would be closed, resulting in a reduction of gate receipts of £1.8 million. However, gate receipts for each of the following four years would be £4.4 million higher than current receipts. In five years' time, the club has plans to sell the existing grounds and to move to a new stadium nearby. Improving the ground facilities is not expected to affect the ground's value when it comes to be sold. Payment for the improvements will be made when the work has been completed at the end of the first year. Whichever option is chosen, the board of directors has decided to take on additional ground staff. The additional wages bill is expected to be £350,000 a year over the next five years.

The club has a cost of capital of 10 per cent. Ignore taxation.

Required:
(a) Calculate the incremental cash flows arising from each of the options available to the club.
(b) Calculate the net present value of each of the options.
(c) On the basis of the calculations made in (b) above, which of the two options would you choose and why?
(d) Discuss the validity of using the net present value method in making investment decisions for a professional football club.

4.7 Haverhill Engineers Ltd manufactures components for the car industry. It is considering automating its line for producing crankshaft bearings. The automated equipment will cost £700,000. It will replace equipment with a scrap value of £50,000 and a book written-down value of £180,000.

At present, the line has a capacity of 1.25 million units per year but typically it has only been run at 80 per cent of capacity because of the lack of demand for its output. The new line has a capacity of 1.4 million units per year. Its life is expected to be five years and its scrap value at that time £100,000.

The accountant has prepared the following cost estimates based on the expected output of 1,000,000 units per year:

	New line (per unit) pence	Old line (per unit) pence
Materials	40	36
Labour	22	10
Variable overheads	14	14
Fixed overheads	44	20
	120	80
Selling price	150	150
Profit per unit	30	70

Fixed overheads include depreciation on the old machine of £40,000 per year and £120,000 for the new machine. It is considered that, for the business overall, fixed overheads are unlikely to change.

The introduction of the new machine will enable stocks to be reduced by £160,000. The business uses 10 per cent as its cost of capital. You should ignore taxation.

Required:
(a) Prepare a statement of the incremental cash flows arising from the project.
(b) Calculate the project's net present value.
(c) Calculate the project's approximate internal rate of return.
(d) Explain the terms net present value and internal rate of return. State which method you consider to be preferable, giving reasons for your choice.

5

Making capital investment decisions: further issues

LEARNING OUTCOMES

When you have completed this chapter, you should be able to:

- Explain the modifications to the simple NPV decision rules that are required when there is capital rationing or when competing projects that have unequal lives are compared.

- Discuss the effect of inflation on investment appraisal and explain how inflation may be taken into account.

- Discuss the nature of risk and explain why it is important in the context of investment decisions.

- Describe the main approaches to the measurement of risk and discuss their limitations.

INTRODUCTION

This chapter deals with a number of important issues relating to the application of the investment appraisal methods considered in the previous chapter. The simple NPV decision rules that we considered in that chapter were: (1) that we should accept all projects with a positive NPV, as this would lead to the maximisation of shareholder wealth, and (2) that, where there are competing projects, the project with the higher (or highest) NPV should be selected. In practice, things are not always straightforward and there are certain circumstances that call for a modification to these simple decision rules. In this chapter, we consider three such circumstances.

Inflation has been a persistent problem for most industrialised economies. In this chapter we consider the problems that inflation creates for the evaluation of investment decisions. We also consider ways in which we can adjust for the effects of inflation when undertaking discounted cash flow analysis.

Financial decision making involves making estimates about the future. However, producing reliable estimates can be difficult. It can be particularly difficult where the environment is fast-changing or where new products are being developed. The issue of risk, which can be defined as the likelihood that what is estimated to occur will not actually occur, is, therefore, an important part of financial decision making. In this chapter we consider the problem of risk in the context of investment decision making. We shall see that methods proposed for dealing with risk vary greatly in their level of sophistication.

Investment decisions when funds are limited

We saw in the previous chapter that projects with a positive NPV should be undertaken if the business wishes to maximise shareholder wealth. However, what if there are insufficient funds available to undertake all the projects with a positive NPV? In practice, it may be that either the investors will not be prepared to provide the necessary funds or that senior management has decided to impose a limit on the amount of funds to be allocated to investment projects. Where, for any reason, finance is rationed, the basic NPV rules mentioned in the previous chapter require modification. To illustrate the modifications required, let us consider Example 5.1.

Example 5.1

Unicorn Engineering Ltd is considering three possible investment projects: X, Y and Z. The expected pattern of cash flows for each project is as follows:

	Project cash flows		
	X	Y	Z
	£m	£m	£m
Initial outlay	(8)	(9)	(11)
1 year's time	5	5	4
2 years' time	2	3	4
3 years' time	3	3	5
4 years' time	4	5	6.5

The business has a cost of finance of 12 per cent and the investment budget for the year that has just begun is restricted to £12 million. Each project is divisible (that is, it is possible to undertake part of a project if required).

Which investment project(s) should the business undertake?

Solution

If the cash flows for each project are discounted using the cost of finance as the appropriate discount rate, the NPVs are:

Project X			Project Y			Project Z		
Cash	Discount rate	PV	Cash	Discount rate	PV	Cash	Discount rate	PV
£m	12%	£m	£m	12%	£m	£m	12%	£m
(8)	1.00	(8.0)	(9)	1.00	(9.0)	(11)	1.00	(11.0)
5	0.89	4.5	5	0.89	4.5	4	0.89	3.6
2	0.80	1.6	3	0.80	2.4	4	0.80	3.2
3	0.71	2.1	3	0.71	2.1	5	0.71	3.6
4	0.64	2.6	5	0.64	3.2	6.5	0.64	4.2
		NPV 2.8			NPV 3.2			NPV 3.6

It is tempting to think that the best approach to dealing with the limited availability of finance would be to rank the projects according to their NPV. Hence, Project Z would be ranked first, Project Y would be ranked second and Project X would be ranked last. Given that £12 million is available, this would lead to the acceptance of Project Z (£11 million) and part of Project Y (£1 million). The total NPV from the £12 million invested would, therefore, be:

$$£3.6m + \frac{£3.2m}{9} = £4m$$

However, this solution would not represent the most efficient use of the limited finance available.

The best approach, when projects are divisible, is to maximise the *present value per £ of scarce finance*. By dividing the present values of the future cash inflows by the outlay for each project, a figure that represents the present value per £ of scarce finance is obtained. This figure provides a measure that is known as the **profitability index**.

Using the information in the example, the following figures would be obtained for the profitability index for each project. (*Note*: The top part of the fractions represent the future cash flows *before* deducting the investment outlays.)

	Project X	Project Y	Project Z
Profitability index:	$\frac{10.8}{8.0}$	$\frac{12.2}{9.0}$	$\frac{14.6}{11.0}$
	= 1.35	= 1.36	= 1.33

All the projects provide a profitability index of greater than 1. The profitability index will always be greater than 1 where the NPV from the project is positive.

Activity 5.1

What does the profitability index calculated in Example 5.1 suggest about the relative profitability of the projects? What would be the NPV of the £12 million invested, assuming the profitability index approach is used?

Activity 5.1 continued

The above calculations indicate that Project Y provides the highest present value per £ of scarce finance and so should be ranked first. Project X should be ranked second and Project Z should be ranked third. To maximise the use of the limited funds available (£12 million), the business should, therefore, undertake all of Project Y (£9 million) and part of Project X (£3 million).

The total NPV of the £12 million invested would be £3.2 million + (3/8 × £2.8 million) = £4.3 million. Note that this figure is higher than the total NPV obtained where projects were ranked according to their absolute NPVs.

There may be a need for projects to be financed over more than one year and limits may be placed on the availability of finance in each year. In such circumstances, there will be more than one constraint to consider. A mathematical technique known as **linear programming** can be used to maximise the NPV, given that not all projects with a positive NPV can be undertaken. This technique adopts the same approach (that is, it maximises the NPV per £ of scarce finance) as that illustrated above. Computer software is available to undertake the analysis required for this kind of multi-period, rationing problem. A detailed consideration of linear programming is beyond the scope of this book; however, if you are interested in this technique, take a look at the suggested further reading at the end of the chapter.

Non-divisible investment projects

The profitability index approach is only suitable where projects are divisible. Where this is not the case, the problem must be looked at in a different way. The investment project, or combination of whole projects, that will produce the highest NPV for the limited finance available should be selected.

Activity 5.2

Recommend a solution for Unicorn Engineering Ltd if the investment projects were not divisible (that is, it was not possible to undertake part of a project) and the finance available was:

(a) £12 million
(b) £18 million
(c) £20 million.

If the capital available was £12 million, only Project Z should be recommended as this would provide the highest NPV (£3.6 million) for the funds available for investment. If the capital available was £18 million, Projects X and Y should be recommended as this would provide the highest NPV (£6 million). If the capital available was £20 million, Projects Y and Z should be recommended as this would provide the highest NPV (£6.8 million).

Mutually exclusive projects

A business may be faced with a situation where investment projects are mutually exclusive. For example, a business may be able to invest in either one project or another, similar, project but not both. In this kind of situation, the possible combinations available within the finance limit should be compared to see which provides the highest NPV.

Activity 5.3

What investment solution should be recommended if all three projects were divisible but the business could select *either* Project X *or* Project Z (that is, they were mutually exclusive)? Assume the capital available is £12 million.

In this case, the combinations that are possible within the £12 million finance limit should be compared. There are really only two combinations:

1 Project Y plus part of Project X, or
2 Project Y plus part of Project Z.

The outcomes from each combination are as follows:

	Combination 1		Combination 2	
	Outlay	NPV	Outlay	NPV
	£m	£m	£m	£m
Project Y	9	3.2	9	3.2
Project X (3/8 of total)	3	1.1	–	–
Project Z (3/11 of total)	–	–	3	1.0
	12	4.3	12	4.2

The calculations reveal that the first combination is better as it has a slightly higher NPV.

Activity 5.4

Assume the budget limit was £18 million rather than £12 million. What would now be the recommended combination?

The calculations are as follows:

	Combination 1		Combination 2	
	Outlay	NPV	Outlay	NPV
	£m	£m	£m	£m
Project Y	9	3.2	9	3.2
Project X (whole)	8	2.8	–	–
Project Z (9/11)	–	–	9	2.9
	17	6.0	18	6.1

The calculations now reveal that the second combination is better as it would give a slightly higher NPV.

Comparing projects with unequal lives

In the previous section, we considered a situation where it may be necessary to modify the simple NPV decision rules in order to make optimal investment decisions. In this section, we consider another situation where some modification to these rules is required.

On occasions, a business may find itself in a position where it has to decide between two (or more) competing projects that are aimed at meeting a continuing need but which have different life spans. When this situation arises, accepting the project with the shorter life may offer the business the opportunity to reinvest sooner in another project with a positive NPV. This opportunity to reinvest sooner should be taken into account in any NPV analysis so that proper comparisons between competing projects can be made. This is not taken into account, however, in the simple form of NPV analysis.

To illustrate how direct comparisons between two (or more) competing projects with unequal lives can be made, under the circumstances described above, let us consider Example 5.2.

Example 5.2

Khan Engineering Ltd has the opportunity to invest in two competing machines. Details of each machine are as follows:

	Machine A £000	Machine B £000
Initial outlay	(100)	(140)
Cash flows		
1 year's time	50	60
2 years' time	70	80
3 years' time	–	32

The business has a cost of capital of 10 per cent.

State which of the two machines, if either, should be acquired.

Solution

One way to tackle this problem is to assume that the machines form part of a repeat chain of replacement and to compare the machines using the **shortest-common-period-of-time approach**. If we assume that investment in Machine A can be repeated every two years and that investment in Machine B can be repeated every three years, the *shortest common period of time* over which the machines can be compared is six years (that is, 2 × 3).

The first step in this process of comparison is to calculate the NPV for each project over their expected lives. Thus, the NPV for each project will be as follows:

	Cash flows £000	Discount rate 10%	Present value £000
Machine A			
Initial outlay	(100)	1.00	(100.0)
1 year's time	50	0.91	45.5
2 years' time	70	0.83	58.1
		NPV	3.6
Machine B			
Initial outlay	(140)	1.00	(140.0)
1 year's time	60	0.91	54.6
2 years' time	80	0.83	66.4
3 years' time	32	0.75	24.0
		NPV	5.0

The next step is to calculate the NPV arising for each machine, over a six-year period, using the reinvestment assumption discussed above. That is, investment in Machine A will be repeated three times and investment in Machine B will be repeated twice during the six-year period.

This means that, for Machine A, the NPV over the six-year period will be equal to the NPV above (that is, £3,600) plus equivalent amounts two years and four years later. The calculation (in £000) will be:

$$NPV = £3.6 + \frac{£3.6}{(1 + 0.1)^2} + \frac{£3.6}{(1 + 0.1)^4} = £9.1$$

These calculations can be shown in the form of a diagram as in Figure 5.1.

Figure 5.1   NPV for Machine A using a common period of time

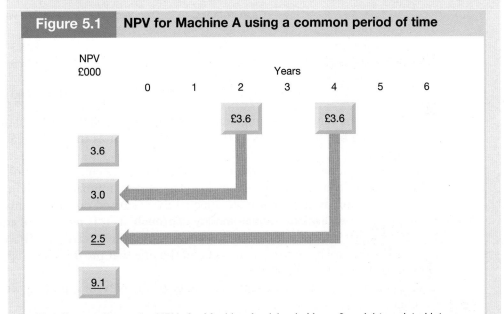

The diagram shows the NPVs for Machine A arising in Years 2 and 4 translated into present value terms.

Activity 5.5

What is the NPV for Machine B over the six-year period? Which machine is the better buy?

In the case of Machine B, the NPV over the six-year period will be equal to the NPV above plus the equivalent amount three years later. The calculation will be:

$$NPV = £5.0 + \frac{£5.0}{(1 + 0.1)^3} = £8.8$$

The calculations set out above suggest that Machine A is the better buy as it will have the higher NPV over the six-year period.

An alternative approach

We can imagine that when investment projects have a longer life span than those in the example above, the calculations required using this method can be time consuming. Fortunately, there is another method that can be used which avoids the need for laborious calculations. This approach uses the annuity concept to solve the problem. An **annuity** is simply an investment that pays a constant sum each year over a period of time. Thus, fixed payments made in respect of a loan or mortgage or a fixed amount of income received from an investment bond would be examples of annuities.

To illustrate the annuity principle, let us assume that we are given a choice of purchasing a new car by either paying £6,000 immediately or by paying three annual instalments of £2,410 commencing at the end of Year 1. Assuming interest rates of 10 per cent, the present value of the annuity payments would be:

	Cash outflows £	Discount rate 10%	Present value £
1 year's time	2,410	0.91	2,193
2 years' time	2,410	0.83	2,000
3 years' time	2,410	0.75	1,807
		NPV	6,000

As the present value of the immediate payment is £6,000, these calculations mean that we should be indifferent as to the form of payment as they are equal in present value terms.

In the example provided, a cash sum paid today is the equivalent of making three annuity payments over a three-year period. The second approach to solving the problem of competing projects that have unequal lives is based on the annuity principle. Put simply, the **equivalent-annual-annuity approach**, as it is referred to, converts the NPV of a project into an annual annuity stream over its expected life. This conversion is carried out for each competing project and the one that provides the highest annual annuity is the most profitable project.

To establish the equivalent annual annuity of the NPV of a project, we apply the formula:

$$\text{Annual annuity} = \frac{i}{1 - (1 + i)^{-n}}$$

where i is the interest rate and n is the number of years.

Thus, using the information from the car loan example above, the annual value of an annuity that lasts for three years, which has a present value of £6,000 and where the discount rate is 10 per cent, is:

$$\text{Annual annuity} = £6,000 \times \frac{0.1}{1 - (1 + 0.1)^{-3}}$$

$$= £6,000 \times 0.402 = £2,412$$

(*Note*: The small difference between this final figure and the one used in the example earlier is due to rounding.)

There are tables that make life easier by providing the annual equivalent factors for a range of possible discount rates. An example of such an annuity table is given in Appendix B at the end of this book.

Activity 5.6

Use the table provided in Appendix B to calculate the equivalent annual annuity for each machine referred to in Example 5.2 above. Which machine is the better buy?

The equivalent annual annuity for Machine A is:

$$£3.6 \times 0.5762 = £2.07$$

The equivalent annual annuity for Machine B is:

$$£5.0 \times 0.4021 = £2.01$$

Machine A is, therefore, the better buy as it provides the higher annuity value. This is consistent with the finding of the shortest-common-period-of-time approach described earlier.

Self-assessment question 5.1

Choi Ltd is considering the purchase of a new photocopier that could lead to considerable cost savings. There are two machines on the market that are suitable for the business. The two machines have the following outlays and expected cost savings:

	Lo-tek	Hi-tek
	£	£
Initial outlay	(10,000)	(15,000)
Cost savings		
1 year's time	4,000	5,000
2 years' time	5,000	6,000
3 years' time	5,000	6,000
4 years' time	–	5,000

The business has a cost of finance of 12 per cent and will have a continuing need for the chosen machine.

Required:
(a) Evaluate each machine using both the shortest-common-period-of-time approach and the equivalent-annual-annuity approach.
(b) Which machine would you recommend and why?

The NPV approach and the ability to delay

In recent years there has been some criticism of the NPV approach. One important criticism is that conventional theory does not recognise the fact that, in practice, it is often possible to delay making an investment decision. This ability to delay, so it is argued, can have a profound effect on the final investment decision.

Activity 5.7

What are the possible benefits of delaying an investment decision?

By delaying, it may be possible to acquire more information concerning the likely outcome of the investment proposal. If a business decides not to delay, the investment decision, once made, may be irreversible. This may lead to losses if conditions prove unfavourable.

It is argued, therefore, that if managers do not exercise their option to delay, there may be an opportunity cost in the form of the benefits lost from later information. This opportunity cost can be large, and so failure to take this into account may lead to grossly incorrect investment decisions. One way of dealing with this problem is to modify the NPV decision rule so that the present value of the future cash flows must exceed the initial outlay *plus* any expected benefits from delaying the decision in order to obtain additional information. These benefits, however, will often be difficult to quantify.

The problem of inflation

Inflation is a problem with which modern businesses have to cope. Although the rate of inflation may change over time, there has been a persistent tendency for the general price level to rise in most economies. It is important to recognise this phenomenon when evaluating investment projects, as inflation will have an effect on both the cash flows and the discount rate over the life of the project.

During a period of inflation, the physical monetary amount required to acquire resources will rise over time and the business may seek to pass on any increase to customers in the form of higher prices. Inflation will also have an effect on the cost of financing the business, as investors seek to protect their investment from a decline in purchasing power by demanding higher returns. As a result of these changes, the cash flows and discount rates relating to the investment project will be affected.

To deal with the problem of inflation in the appraisal of investment projects, two possible approaches can be used:

● *Either* include inflation in the calculations by adjusting annual cash flows by the expected rate of inflation, and by using a discount rate that is also adjusted for inflation. This will mean estimating the actual monetary cash flows expected from the project and using a market rate of interest that will take inflation into account.
● *Or* exclude inflation from the calculations by adjusting cash flows accordingly and by using a 'real' discount rate that does not include any element to account for inflation.

Both methods, properly applied, will give the same result.

If all cash flows are expected to increase in line with the general rate of inflation, it would be possible to use net cash flows as the basic for any adjustments. However, it is unlikely that the relationship between the various items that go to make up the net cash flows of the business will remain constant over time. In practice, inflation is likely to affect the various items differently. This means that separate adjustments for each of the monetary cash flows will be necessary.

Activity 5.8

Why is inflation likely to have a differing effect on the various items making up the net cash flow of a business?

Different costs may increase at different rates due to relative changes in demand. For example, labour costs may rise more quickly than materials costs if labour is in greater demand than the materials being used. Certain costs may be fixed over time (for example, lease payments) and may therefore be unaffected by inflation over the period of the project.

In a highly competitive environment, a business may be unable to pass on all of the increase in costs to customers and so will have to absorb some of the increase by reducing profits. Thus, cash inflows from sales may not fully reflect the rise in the costs of the various inputs.

To compute the real cash flows from a project, it will be necessary to calculate the monetary cash flows relating to each item and then deflate these amounts by the *general* rate of inflation. This adjustment will provide us with the *current general purchasing power* of the cash flows. This measure of general purchasing power is of more relevance to investors than if the cash flows were deflated by a specific rate of inflation relevant to each type of cash flow. Similarly, the real discount rate will be deduced by deflating the market rate of interest by the *general* rate of inflation.

Real World 5.1 sets out the findings of a survey of UK businesses which reveals how inflation is dealt with in practice.

REAL WORLD 5.1

Adjusting for inflation

The following table summarises the ways in which UK businesses adjust for inflation for investment appraisal purposes:

Approach used	Business size			
	Small %	Medium %	Large %	Total %
Specify cash flow in constant prices and apply a real rate of return	47	29	45	42
All cash flows expressed in inflated price terms and discounted at the market rate of return	18	42	55	39
Considered at risk analysis or sensitivity stage*	21	13	16	17
No adjustment	18	21	3	13
Other	0	0	3	1

* This approach is discussed later in the chapter.

> **Real World 5.1 continued**
>
> Two points worth noting from the summary table are:
>
> ● Large and medium-sized businesses are more likely to inflate cash flows and to use a market rate of return than to use real cash flows and a real discount rate. For small businesses, however, it is the other way around.
> ● Small and medium-sized businesses are more likely to make no adjustment for inflation than large businesses.
>
> *Source: Corporate Financial Management*, G. Arnold, 2nd edn, Financial Times Prentice Hall, 2002.

Risk and investment decisions

Risk arises where the future is unclear and where a range of possible future outcomes exists. As the future is uncertain, there is a chance (or risk) that estimates made concerning the future will not occur. Risk is particularly important in the context of investment decisions. This is because of:

● the relatively long timescales involved – there is more time for things to go wrong between the decision being made and the end of the project; and
● the size of the investment – if things do go wrong, the impact can be both significant and lasting.

Sometimes, a distinction is made in the literature between *risk* and *uncertainty*. However, this distinction is not particularly useful for our purposes and in this chapter the two words are used interchangeably.

In the sections that follow, we examine various methods that can be used to help managers deal with the problem of risk. This examination will focus on the more useful and systematic approaches to dealing with risk that have been proposed. In practice, crude methods of dealing with risk are sometimes used, such as shortening the required payback period and employing conservative cash flows. However, these methods rely on arbitrary assumptions and have little to commend them. They have, therefore, been excluded from our examination.

The first three methods of dealing with risk that we consider were discussed briefly in Chapter 2 during our examination of projected financial statements. We now consider them in more detail as they are also relevant to investment decisions.

Sensitivity analysis

A popular way of assessing the level of risk is to carry out **sensitivity analysis**. This method was briefly discussed when we considered projected financial statements in Chapter 2. We may recall that this method involves an examination of key input values in order to see how changes in each input might influence the likely outcomes. One form of sensitivity analysis involves posing a series of 'what if?' questions. For example:

● What if sales volume is 5 per cent higher than expected?
● What if sales volume is 10 per cent lower than expected?

By answering these 'what if?' questions, the managers will have a range of possible outcomes to consider, which can be useful for investment appraisal purposes as well as for profit planning.

There is, however, another form of sensitivity analysis that is particularly useful in the context of investment appraisal. Where the result from an appraisal, using the best estimates, is positive, the value for each key factor can be examined to see by how much it could be changed before the project became unprofitable for that reason alone.

Let us suppose that the NPV for an investment in a machine to provide a particular service is estimated to be a positive value of £50,000. To carry out sensitivity analysis on this investment proposal, each of the key input factors – cost of the machine, sales volume and price, operating costs, life of the machine, discount rate and so forth – is considered in turn. For each factor, the highest adverse value that it could have before the NPV figure becomes negative (that is, the value for the factor at which NPV is zero) will be calculated. The difference between the value for that factor at which the NPV is zero and the estimated value represents the 'margin of safety' for that particular factor. The process is set out in Figure 5.2.

| Figure 5.2 | **Factors affecting the sensitivity of NPV calculations for a new machine** |

Sensitivity analysis involves identifying the key factors that affect the project. In the figure, six factors have been identified for the particular project. (In practice, the key factors are likely to vary between projects.) Once identified, each factor will be examined in turn to find the highest adverse value it could have for the project to have a zero NPV.

When carrying out sensitivity analysis, a computer spreadsheet model of the project can be extremely valuable as the calculations can often be laborious. It then becomes a very simple matter to try various values for the key factors and to see the effect of changes in these factors on the NPV. Example 5.3 below, which illustrates sensitivity analysis, is, however, straightforward and can be undertaken without recourse to a spreadsheet.

Example 5.3

S. Saluja (Property Developers) Ltd intends to bid at an auction, to be held today, for a manor house that has fallen into disrepair. The auctioneer believes that the manor house will be sold for about £450,000. The business wishes to renovate the property and to divide it into luxury flats to be sold for £150,000 each. The renovation will be in two stages and will cover a two-year period. Stage 1 will cover the first year of the project. It will cost £500,000 and the six flats completed during this stage are expected to be sold for a total of £900,000 at the end of the first year. Stage 2 will cover the second year of the project. It will cost £300,000 and the three remaining flats are expected to be sold at the end of the second year for a total of £450,000.

The cost of renovation is subject to an agreed figure with local builders; however, there is some uncertainty over the remaining input values. The business estimates its cost of capital at 12 per cent a year.

Required:

(a) What is the NPV of the proposed project?
(b) Assuming none of the other inputs deviate from the best estimates provided:
   (i)   What auction price would have to be paid for the manor house to cause the project to have a zero NPV?
   (ii) What cost of capital would cause the project to have a zero NPV?
   (iii) What is the sale price of each of the flats that would cause the project to have a zero NPV? (Each flat will be sold for the same price: £150,000.)
(c) Is the level of risk associated with the project high or low?

Solution

(a) The NPV of the proposed project is as follows:

	Cash flows £	Discount factor 12%	Present value £
Year 1 (£900,000 – £500,000)	400,000	0.893	357,200
Year 2 (£450,000 – £300,000)	150,000	0.797	119,550
Less Initial outlay			(450,000)
		NPV	26,750

(b) (i) To obtain a zero NPV, the auction price for the manor house would have to be £26,750 higher than the current estimate (that is, the amount of the estimated NPV). This would make a total price of £476,750, which is about 6 per cent above the current estimated price.

    (ii) As there is a positive NPV, the cost of capital that would cause the project to have a zero NPV must be higher than 12 per cent. Let us try 20 per cent.

	Cash flows £	Discount factor 20%	Present value £
Year 1 (£900,000 – £500,000)	400,000	0.833	333,200
Year 2 (£450,000 – £300,000)	150,000	0.694	104,100
Less initial outlay			(450,000)
		NPV	(12,700)

As the NPV, using a 20 per cent discount rate, is negative, the 'break-even' cost of capital must lie somewhere between 12 per cent and 20 per cent. A reasonable approximation is obtained as follows:

	Discount rate %	NPV £
	12	26,750
	20	(12,700)
Difference	8	39,450

The change in NPV for every 1 per cent change in the discount rate will be:

$$\frac{39,450}{8} = 4,931$$

The reduction in the 20 per cent discount rate required to achieve a zero NPV would therefore be:

$$\frac{12,700}{4,931} = 2.6\%$$

The cost of capital (that is, the discount rate) would, therefore, have to be 17.4 per cent (20.0 – 2.6) for the project to have a zero NPV.

This calculation is, of course, the same as that used in the previous chapter when calculating the IRR of the project. In other words, 17.4 per cent is the IRR of the project.

(iii) To obtain a zero NPV, the sale price of each flat must be reduced so that the NPV is reduced by £26,750. In Year 1, six flats are sold, and in Year 2, three flats are sold. The discount factor for Year 1 is 0.893 and for Year 2 it is 0.797. We can derive the fall in value per flat (Y), to give a zero NPV, by using the equation:

$$(6Y \times 0.893) + (3Y \times 0.797) = £26,750$$
$$Y = £3,452$$

The sale price of each flat necessary to obtain a zero NPV is therefore:

$$£150,000 - £3,452 = £146,548$$

This represents a fall in the estimated price of 2.3 per cent.

(c) These calculations indicate that the auction price would have to be about 6 per cent above the estimated price before a zero NPV is obtained. The margin of safety is, therefore, not very high for this factor. The calculations also reveal that the price of the luxury flats would only have to fall by 2.3 per cent from the estimated price before the NPV is reduced to zero. Hence, the margin of safety for this factor is even smaller. However, the cost of capital is less sensitive to changes and there would have to be an increase from 12 per cent to 17.4 per cent before the project produced a zero NPV.

It seems from the calculations that the sale price of the flats is the most sensitive of the three inputs examined. A careful re-examination of the market value of the flats seems appropriate before a final decision is made.

Real World 5.2 shows that it is not only businesses that may carry out sensitivity analysis in order to assess risk. A supplier or lender may also use this tool to see whether the business is a credit risk.

REAL WORLD 5.2

No fear of flying   **FT**

Ryanair is a low-cost airline that has enjoyed considerable success over recent years. As part of its expansion programme, the business has ordered 153 Boeing 737-800 aircraft, with an option to purchase a further 125 aircraft, over a period up to 2009. It has been reported that these aircraft cost Ryanair around US$32 million each. This represents a huge order for the Boeing Corporation and, of course, a huge risk if the aircraft were built for Ryanair and the business was then unable to pay for them. Around the time of the sale agreement, therefore, Boeing decided to evaluate the future profitability of Ryanair.

Boeing prepared a computer model to test whether changes in key variables such as a fall in passenger demand, changes in currency exchange rates and a rise in aviation fuel prices would damage the profitability of the low cost airline. Ryanair passed the tests with flying colours: the worst scenario generated was that Ryanair would break even. According to Boeing's sales director for the UK and Ireland, the Ryanair model was probably the most robust that Boeing had encountered.

Sources: 'How low can you go?', *Financial Times Magazine*, 21 June 2003; 'Ryanair: feeding time at the zoo', 11 February 2003, Research Report, Goodbody Stockbrokers.

The following activity can also be attempted without recourse to a spreadsheet.

Activity 5.9

A business has the opportunity to invest £12 million immediately in new plant and equipment in order to produce a new product. The product will sell at £80 each and it is estimated that 200,000 units of the product can be sold in each of the next four years. Variable costs are £56 a unit and additional fixed costs (excluding depreciation) are £1.0 million in total. The residual value of the plant and machinery at the end of the life of the product is estimated to be £1.6 million.

The business has a cost of capital of 12 per cent.

Required:
(a) Calculate the NPV of the investment proposal.
(b) Carry out separate sensitivity analysis to indicate by how much the following factors would have to change in order to produce an NPV of zero.
   (i)   Initial outlay on plant and machinery.
   (ii) Residual value of the plant and machinery.
   (iii) Discount rate.

(a) Annual operating cash flows are as follows:

	£m	£m
Sales (200,000 × £80)		16.0
Less		
Variable costs (200,000 × £56)	11.2	
Fixed costs	1.0	12.2
		3.8

Estimated cash flows are as follows:

	Year 0 £m	Year 1 £m	Year 2 £m	Year 3 £m	Year 4 £m
Plant and equipment	(12.0)				1.6
Operating cash flows		3.8	3.8	3.8	3.8
	(12.0)	3.8	3.8	3.8	5.4

The NPV of the project is:

	Year 0 £m	Year 1 £m	Year 2 £m	Year 3 £m	Year 4 £m
Cash flows	(12.0)	3.8	3.8	3.8	5.4
Discount rate (12%)	1.0	0.89	0.80	0.71	0.64
Present value	(12.0)	3.38	3.04	2.70	3.46
	NPV 0.58				

(b) (i) The increase required in the initial outlay on plant and equipment to achieve an NPV of zero will be £0.58 million (as the plant and equipment are already expressed in present value terms). This represents a 4.8 per cent increase on the current estimated figure of £12 million.

(ii) Using a discount rate of 14 per cent, the NPV of the project is:

	Year 0 £m	Year 1 £m	Year 2 £m	Year 3 £m	Year 4 £m
Cash flows	(12.0)	3.8	3.8	3.8	5.4
Discount rate (14%)	1.0	0.88	0.77	0.68	0.59
Present value	(12.0)	3.34	2.92	2.58	3.18
	NPV 0.02				

This is very close to an NPV of zero and so 14 per cent is the approximate figure. This is 16.7 per cent higher than the cost of capital.

(iii) The fall in the residual value of the plant and equipment (R) that will lead to a zero NPV is:

(R × discount factor at the end of four years) − NPV of the project = 0

By rearranging this equation, we have:

$$(R \times \text{Discount factor at the end of four years}) = \text{NPV of the project}$$
$$R \times 0.64 = \text{£0.58 million}$$
$$R = \text{£0.58 million}/0.64$$
$$= \text{£0.90 million}$$

This represents a 43.8 per cent decrease in the current estimated residual value.

In your previous studies of accounting, you may have studied *break-even analysis*. Sensitivity analysis is, in essence, a form of break-even analysis. The point at which the NPV is zero is the point at which the project breaks even (that is, makes neither profit nor loss). The 'margin of safety' for a particular factor associated with the project can be interpreted in the same way as the margin of safety is interpreted in break-even analysis.

Sensitivity analysis should help managers to gain a feel for the investment project as they will be able to see the margin of safety for each factor. They should also be able to identify highly sensitive factors, which require careful study and which are also likely to require more detailed information. We should always bear in mind that the collection, reporting and evaluation of information can be costly and time consuming, and the more that managers can focus their efforts on the critical aspects of a decision the better. Sensitivity analysis can also be useful in directing the actions of managers. Where a project outcome has been identified as being highly sensitive to changes in a key factor, managers may decide to formulate plans to deal with possible variations from the estimated outcome.

Although sensitivity analysis is undoubtedly a useful tool for managers, it has two major drawbacks:

● It does not give managers clear decision rules concerning acceptance or rejection of the project. There is no single figure outcome that will indicate whether the project is worth undertaking. This means that managers must rely on their own judgement.
● It is a static form of analysis. Only one factor is considered at a time while the rest are held constant. In practice, however, it is likely that more than one factor value will differ from the best estimates provided.

Scenario analysis

 A slightly different approach, which overcomes the problem of dealing with a single variable at a time, is **scenario analysis**. This method was also briefly discussed in Chapter 2. We may recall that this approach changes a number of variables simultaneously so as to provide a particular 'state of the world', or scenario, for managers to consider. A popular form of scenario analysis is to provide three different 'states of the world', or scenarios, which set out:

● an optimistic view of likely future events
● a pessimistic view of likely future events
● a 'most likely' view of future events.

The approach is open to criticism because it does not indicate the likelihood of each scenario occurring nor does it identify the other possible scenarios that might occur. Nevertheless, the portrayal of optimistic and pessimistic scenarios may be useful in providing managers with some feel for the 'downside' risk and 'upside' potential associated with a project.

Simulations

 We saw in Chapter 2 that an approach using **simulations** is really a development of sensitivity analysis discussed earlier. The starting point for carrying out a simulation exercise is to model the investment project. This involves identifying the key factors affecting the project and their interrelationships. Thus, the cash flows will have to be modelled to reveal the key factors influencing both the cash receipts and the cash payments and their interrelationships. Let us illustrate this point using a simple example. The cash received from sales may be modelled by the following equation:

Sales revenue = Selling price per unit × (Market share × Market size)

The modelling process will also require equations showing the factors determining the cash expenses and the interrelationships between these factors. The relationship between the cash inflows and outflows must also be modelled. As investment projects usually extend over more than one year, there may also be a need to model the relationship between the cash flows occurring in different periods. Thus, a fairly large number of equations may be required to model even a fairly simple investment project proposal.

Once the key factors have been identified and their relationships have been modelled, the next step is to specify the possible values for each of the factors within the model. A computer is then used to select one of the possible values from each distribution on a random basis. It then generates projected cash flows using the selected values for each factor. This process represents a single trial. The process is then repeated using other values for each factor until many possible combinations of values for the key factors have been considered. The results of the repeated sampling allow us to obtain a probability distribution of the values of the cash flows for the project (see Figure 5.3).

The use of simulations is meant to help managers in two ways. First, the process of building a model helps managers to understand more fully the nature of the project and the issues that must be resolved. Second, it provides managers with a distribution of project outcomes that can be used to assess the riskiness of the project. However, these potential benefits must be weighed against the potential problems of producing simulations.

Simulation can be costly and time consuming. In practice, the task of producing a simulation model may be given to support staff, and managers may not be closely

Figure 5.3   The main steps in simulation

The figure sets out the sequence of steps involved in carrying out a simulation exercise.

involved with its construction. When this task is delegated, the first potential benefit referred to above may easily be lost. Furthermore, there are usually problems in modelling the relationship between factors and in establishing the distribution of outcomes for each factor. The more complex the project, the more complex these problems are likely to be.

Risk preferences of investors

So far, the methods discussed have sought to identify the level of risk associated with a project. However, this is not, of itself, enough. The attitude of investors towards risk should also be determined. Unless we know how investors are likely to react to the presence of risk in investment opportunities, we cannot really make an informed decision. It is important, therefore, to consider what the attitude of investors is likely to be towards risk.

In theory, investors may display three possible attitudes towards risk. They may be:

- **Risk-seeking investors.**   Some investors enjoy a gamble. Given two projects with the same expected return but with different levels of risk, the risk-seeking investor would choose the project with the higher level of risk.
- **Risk-neutral investors.**   Some investors are indifferent to risk. Thus, given two projects with the same expected return but with different levels of risk, the risk-neutral investor would have no preference. Both projects provide the same expected return and the fact that one project has a higher level of risk would not be an issue.
- **Risk-averse investors.**   Some investors are averse to risk. Given two projects with the same expected return but with different levels of risk, a risk-averse investor would choose the project that has a lower level of risk.

While some investors may be risk seekers and some investors may be indifferent to risk, the evidence suggests that the vast majority of investors are risk averse. It is important to appreciate that being risk averse does *not* mean that an investor will not be prepared to take on risky investments. It means, rather, that investors will require compensation in the form of higher returns from projects that have higher levels of risk. An explanation as to why this is the case can be found in *utility theory*.

Risk and utility theory

To describe utility theory, let us assume you can measure the satisfaction, or utility, you receive from money in the form of 'utils of satisfaction' and let us also assume that you are penniless. If a rich benefactor gives you £1,000, this may bring you a great deal of satisfaction as it would allow you to buy many things that you have yearned for. Let us say it provides you with 20 utils of satisfaction. If the benefactor gives you a further £1,000, this may also bring you a great deal of satisfaction, but not as much as the first £1,000 as your essential needs have now been met. Let us say, therefore, it provides you with 10 utils of satisfaction. If the benefactor then gives you a further £1,000, the additional satisfaction received from this additional sum may reduce to, say, 6 utils and so on. (The expression *diminishing marginal utility of wealth* is often used to describe the situation where the additional satisfaction received from wealth declines with each additional amount of wealth received.)

The relationship between the level of satisfaction received and the amount of wealth received can be expressed in the form of a **utility function**. For a risk-averse individual, the utility function, when shown graphically, would take the shape of a downward-sloping curve as shown in Figure 5.4. We can see clearly from this graph that each increment in wealth provides a diminishing level of satisfaction for the individual. We can also see that the increase in satisfaction from gaining additional wealth is not the same as the decrease in satisfaction from losing the same amount of wealth.

Figure 5.4	Utility function for a risk-averse individual

The figure shows the concave shape of the utility function for a risk-averse individual. We can see that each additional amount of wealth received provides a diminishing amount of satisfaction for the individual. The greater the aversion to risk, the more concave the utility function will become.

An individual with wealth of, say, £2,000 would receive satisfaction from this amount of 30 utils. If, however, the wealth of the individual fell by £1,000 for some reason, the loss of satisfaction would be greater than the satisfaction gained from receiving an additional £1,000. We can see the loss of satisfaction from a fall in wealth of £1,000 would be 10 utils, whereas the gain in satisfaction from receiving an additional £1,000 would only be 6 utils. As the satisfaction, or happiness, lost from a fall in wealth is greater than the satisfaction, or happiness, gained from acquiring an equivalent amount of wealth, the individual will be averse to risk and will only be prepared to undertake risk in exchange for the prospect of higher returns.

The particular shape of the utility curve will vary between individuals. Some individuals are likely to be more risk averse than others. The more risk averse an individual is, the more concave the shape of the curve will become. However, this general concave curve shape will apply to all risk-averse individuals.

For an individual who is indifferent to risk, the marginal satisfaction, or utility, of wealth will not diminish as described above. Instead, the marginal utility of wealth will remain constant. This means the individual's utility function will look quite different from that of a risk-averse individual.

Activity 5.10

Try to draw a graph that plots the utility of wealth against wealth for an individual who is indifferent to risk. Explain the shape of the graph line.

An individual who is indifferent to risk would have a utility function that can be plotted in the form of a straight line as shown in Figure 5.5.

This indicates that the satisfaction, or happiness, lost from a fall in wealth will be equal to the satisfaction, or happiness, gained from acquiring an equivalent amount of wealth.

Figure 5.5   Utility function for a risk-neutral individual

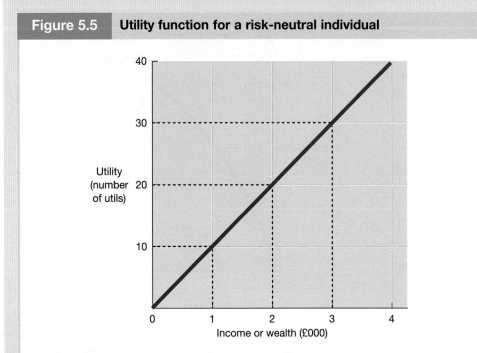

The figure shows the utility function for a risk-neutral individual. The straight line indicates that each additional util of wealth received will produce the same amount of satisfaction.

For a risk-seeking individual, the marginal satisfaction, or utility, of wealth will increase rather than decrease or remain constant. This means that the shape of a risk-seeking individual's utility function, when displayed in the form of a graph, will be quite different from the two described above.

Activity 5.11

Draw a graph plotting the utility of wealth against wealth for an individual who is risk seeking and explain the shape of the graph line.

The graph for a risk-seeking individual will be as shown in Figure 5.6. We can see from the graph that the curve is upward sloping. The satisfaction, or happiness, gained from an increase in wealth would be greater than the satisfaction, or happiness, lost from a decrease in wealth of an equivalent amount. This means the individual will be prepared to take on risks in order to obtain additional wealth.

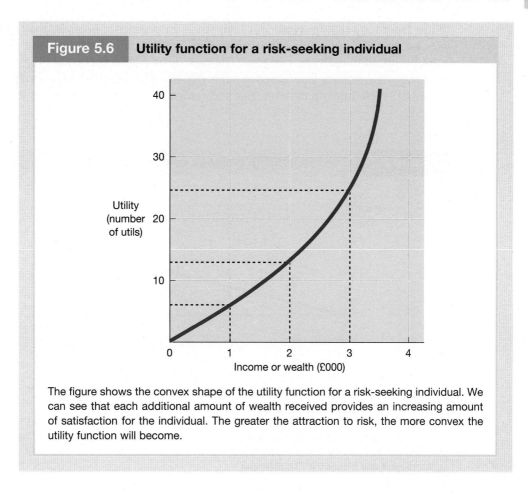

Figure 5.6   **Utility function for a risk-seeking individual**

The figure shows the convex shape of the utility function for a risk-seeking individual. We can see that each additional amount of wealth received provides an increasing amount of satisfaction for the individual. The greater the attraction to risk, the more convex the utility function will become.

Although utility theory helps us to understand why investors are risk averse, it would not be possible to identify the utility functions of individual investors and then combine these in some way so as to provide a guide for management decisions. The practical value of this theory is, therefore, limited. In the real world, managers may make decisions based on their own attitudes towards risk rather than those of investors, or make assumptions about the risk preferences of investors.

Risk-adjusted discount rate

We have seen from the section above that there is a relationship between risk and the rate of return required by investors. The reaction of a risk-averse individual will be to require a higher rate of return for risky projects. The higher the level of risk associated with a project, the higher the required rate of return. The **risk-adjusted discount rate** is based on this simple relationship between risk and return. Thus, when evaluating investment projects, managers will increase the NPV discount rate in the face of increased risk. In other words, a *risk premium* will be required for risky projects: the higher the level of risk, the higher the risk premium.

The risk premium is usually added to a 'risk-free' rate of return in order to derive the total return required. The risk-free rate is normally taken to be equivalent to the rate of return from long-term government loan stock. In practice, a business may divide projects up into risk categories (for example, low, medium and high risk) and then assign a risk premium to each risk category. The cash flows from a particular project will then be discounted using a rate based on the risk-free rate plus the appropriate risk premium. This relationship between risk and return is illustrated in Figure 5.7.

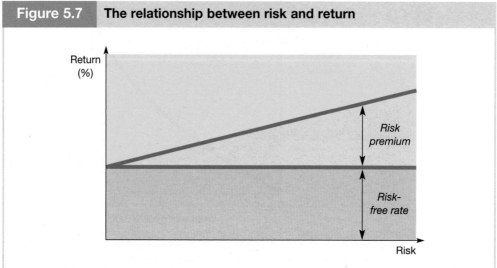

Figure 5.7   The relationship between risk and return

It is possible to take account of the riskiness of projects by changing the discount rate. A risk premium is added to the risk-free rate in order to derive the appropriate discount rate. A higher return will normally be expected from projects where the risks are higher. Thus, the more risky the project, the higher the risk premium.

The use of a risk-adjusted discount rate provides managers with a single-figure outcome that can be used when making a decision either to accept or to reject a project. Moreover, managers are likely to have an intuitive grasp of the relationship between risk and return and may well feel comfortable with this technique. However, there are practical difficulties with implementing this approach.

Activity 5.12

Can you think of what the practical problems with this approach might be?

Subjective judgement is required when assigning an investment project to a particular risk category and then in assigning a risk premium to each category. The choices made will reflect the personal views of the managers responsible and these may differ from the views of the shareholders they represent. The choices made can, nevertheless, make the difference between accepting or rejecting a particular project. (We shall see in Chapter 8, however, that there is a more sophisticated approach to deriving a risk premium that does not rely on subjective judgement.)

Expected values and risk assessment

A further method of assessing risk is through the use of *statistical probabilities*. It may be possible to identify a range of possible outcomes and to assign a probability of occurrence to each one of the outcomes in the range. Using this information, we can derive an **expected value**, which is a weighted average of the possible outcomes where the probabilities are used as weights. To illustrate this method in relation to an investment decision, let us consider Example 5.4.

Example 5.4

Patel Properties Ltd has the opportunity to acquire a lease on a block of flats that has only two years remaining before it expires. The cost of the lease would be £1,000,000. The occupancy rate of the block of flats is currently around 70 per cent and the flats are let almost exclusively to naval personnel. There is a large naval base located nearby and there is little other demand for the flats. The occupancy rate of the flats will change in the remaining two years of the lease depending on the outcome of a defence review. The navy is currently considering three options for the naval base. These are:

- *Option 1.* Increase the size of the base by closing down a naval base in another region and transferring the naval personnel to the base located near to the flats.
- *Option 2.* Close down the naval base near to the flats and leave only a skeleton staff there for maintenance purposes. The personnel would be moved to a base in another region.
- *Option 3.* Leave the naval base open but reduce staffing levels by 20 per cent.

The directors of Patel Properties Ltd have estimated the following net cash flows for each of the two years under each option and the probability of their occurrence:

	£	Probability
Option 1	800,000	0.6
Option 2	120,000	0.1
Option 3	400,000	0.3
		1.0

Note: The sum of the probabilities is 1.0 (that is, it is certain that one of the possible options will arise).

The business has a cost of capital of 10 per cent.
Should the business purchase the lease on the block of flats?

Solution

To answer the question, the **expected net present value (ENPV)** of the proposed investment can be calculated. To do this, the weighted average of the possible outcomes for each year must first be calculated. This involves multiplying each

Example 5.4 continued

cash flow by its probability of occurrence (as the probabilities are used as weights). The expected annual net cash flows will be:

	Cash flows £	Probability	Expected cash flows £
Option 1	800,000	0.6	480,000
Option 2	120,000	0.1	12,000
Option 3	400,000	0.3	120,000
Expected cash flows in each year			612,000

Having derived the expected annual cash flows in each year, they can be discounted using a rate of 10 per cent to reflect the cost of capital.

	Expected cash flows £	Discount rate 10%	Expected present value £
Year 1	612,000	0.909	556,308
Year 2	612,000	0.826	505,512
			1,061,820
Less Initial investment			1,000,000
Expected net present value (ENPV)			61,820

We can see that the ENPV is positive. Hence, the wealth of shareholders is expected to increase by purchasing the lease. (However, the size of the ENPV is small in relation to the initial investment and so the business may wish to check carefully the key assumptions used in the analysis before a final decision is made.)

The ENPV approach has the advantage of producing a single-figure outcome and of having a clear decision rule to apply (that is, if the ENPV is positive the business should invest, if it is negative it should not). However, this approach produces an average figure that may not be capable of actually occurring. This point was illustrated in the example above where the expected (net present) value does not correspond to any of the stated options.

Using an average figure can also obscure the underlying risk associated with the project. Simply deriving the ENPV, as in Example 5.4, can be misleading. Without some idea of the individual possible outcomes and their probability of occurring, the managers are in the dark. If either of Options 2 and 3 were to occur, the NPV of the investment would be negative (wealth destroying). It is 40 per cent probable that one of these options will occur, so this is a significant risk. Only if Option 1 were to occur (60 per cent probable), would investing in the flats represent a good decision. Of course, in advance of making the investment, which option will actually occur is not known.

None of the above should be taken to mean that the investment in the flats should not be made, simply that the managers are better placed to make a judgement where information on the possible outcomes is available. Thus, where the ENPV approach is being used, it is probably a good idea to reveal to managers the different possible outcomes and the probability attached to each outcome. By so doing, the managers will be able to gain an insight to the 'downside risk' attached to the project. This point is further illustrated by Activity 5.13.

Activity 5.13

Ukon Ltd is considering two competing projects. Details of each project are as follows:

● Project A has a 0.8 probability of producing a negative NPV of £500,000, a 0.1 probability of producing a positive NPV of £1.0 million, and a 0.1 probability of producing a positive NPV of £5.5 million.
● Project B has a 0.2 probability of producing a positive NPV of £125,000, a 0.3 probability of producing a positive NPV of £250,000, and a 0.5 probability of producing a positive NPV of £300,000.

What is the expected net present value (ENPV) of each project?

The ENPV of Project A is:

Probability	NPV	Expected value
	£	£
0.8	(500,000)	(400,000)
0.1	1,000,000	100,000
0.1	5,500,000	550,000
		ENPV 250,000

The ENPV of Project B is:

Probability	NPV	Expected value
	£	£
0.2	125,000	25,000
0.3	250,000	75,000
0.5	300,000	150,000
		ENPV 250,000

Although the ENPV of each project in Activity 5.13 is identical, this does not mean that the business will be indifferent about which project to undertake. Project A has a high probability of making a loss, whereas Project B is not expected to make a loss under either possible outcome. If we assume that investors are risk averse, they will prefer the business to take on Project B as this will provide the same level of expected return as Project A but has a lower level of risk.

It can be argued that the problem identified above may not be significant where the business is engaged in several similar projects, as it will be lost in the averaging process. However, in practice, investment projects may be unique events and this argument will not then apply. Also, where the project is large in relation to other projects undertaken the argument loses its force. There is also the problem that a factor that might cause one project to have an adverse outcome could also have adverse effects on other projects.

Event tree diagrams

When a range of possible outcomes can arise from a particular investment opportunity, it is sometimes helpful to identify each of the possible outcomes by preparing an **event tree diagram**. This diagram, as the name implies, is shaped like a tree where each branch represents a possible event, or outcome. Probabilities may be assigned to each of the events or outcomes identified and where individual outcomes can occur in different combinations, we can deduce the probability of each possible combination by multiplying together the probabilities associated with the individual outcomes.

Example 5.5 provides an illustration of how a simple event tree may be constructed for an investment project with possible outcomes that can be combined in different ways.

Example 5.5

Zeta Computing Services Ltd has recently produced some software for a client organisation. The software has a life of two years and will then become obsolete. The cost of developing the software was £60,000. The client organisation has agreed to pay a licence fee of £80,000 a year for the software if it is used in only one of its two divisions and £120,000 a year if it is used in both of its divisions. The client may use the software for either one or two years in either division but will definately use it in at least one division in each of the two years.

Zeta Computing Services Ltd believes there is a 0.6 chance that the licence fee received in any one year will be £80,000 and a 0.4 chance that it will be £120,000.

Produce an event tree diagram for the project.

Solution

The four possible outcomes attached to this project and their probability of occurrence (p) are as follows:

Outcome	Probability
1 Year 1 cash flow £80,000 ($p = 0.6$) and Year 2 cash flow £80,000 ($p = 0.6$). The probability of both years having cash flows of £80,000 will be (0.6×0.6)	= 0.36
2 Year 1 cash flow £120,000 ($p = 0.4$) and Year 2 cash flow £120,000 ($p = 0.4$). The probability of both years having cash flows of £120,000 will be (0.4×0.4)	= 0.16
3 Year 1 cash flow £120,000 ($p = 0.4$) and Year 2 cash flow £80,000 ($p = 0.6$). The probability of this sequence of cash flows occurring will be (0.4×0.6)	= 0.24
4 Year 1 cash flow £80,000 ($p = 0.6$) and Year 2 cash flow £120,000 ($p = 0.4$). The probability of this sequence of cash flows occurring will be (0.6×0.4)	= 0.24
	1.00

This information can be displayed in the form of an event tree diagram as shown in Figure 5.8.

Figure 5.8 — Event tree diagram showing different possible project outcomes

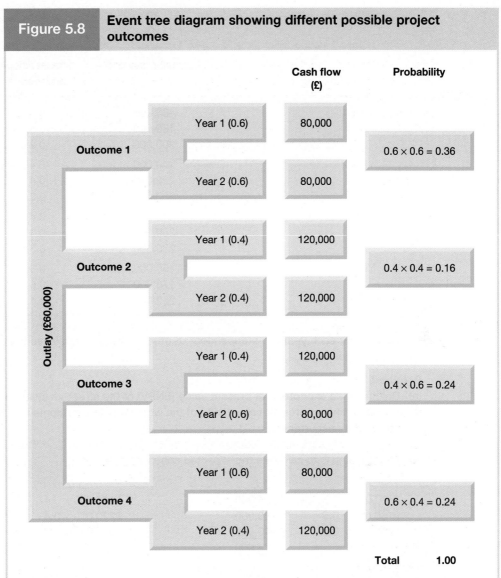

The event tree diagram sets out the different possible outcomes associated with a particular project and the probability of each outcome. We can see that each outcome is represented by a branch and that each branch has subsidiary branches. The sum of the probabilities attached to the outcomes must equal 1.00. In other words, it is certain that one of the possible outcomes will occur.

Activity 5.14

Kernow Cleaning Services Ltd provides street-cleaning services for local councils in the far south west of England. The work is currently labour intensive and few machines are employed. However, the business has recently been considering the purchase of a fleet of street-cleaning vehicles at a total cost of £540,000. The vehicles have a life of four years and are likely to result in a considerable saving of labour costs. Estimates of the likely labour savings and their probability of occurrence are set out below:

Activity 5.14 continued

	Estimated savings £	Probability of occurrence
Year 1	80,000	0.3
	160,000	0.5
	200,000	0.2
Year 2	140,000	0.4
	220,000	0.4
	250,000	0.2
Year 3	140,000	0.4
	200,000	0.3
	230,000	0.3
Year 4	100,000	0.3
	170,000	0.6
	200,000	0.1

Estimates for each year are independent of other years. The business has a cost of capital of 10 per cent.

Required:
(a) Calculate the expected net present value (ENPV) of the street-cleaning machines.
(b) Calculate the net present value (NPV) of the worst possible outcome and the probability of its occurrence.

(a) The first step is to calculate the expected annual cash flows:

Year 1	£	Year 2	£
£ 80,000 × 0.3	24,000	£140,000 x 0.4	56,000
£160,000 × 0.5	80,000	£220,000 x 0.4	88,000
£200,000 × 0.2	40,000	£250,000 x 0.2	50,000
	144,000		194,000

Year 3		Year 4	
£140,000 x 0.4	56,000	£100,000 x 0.3	30,000
£200,000 x 0.3	60,000	£170,000 x 0.6	102,000
£230,000 x 0.3	69,000	£200,000 x 0.1	20,000
	185,000		152,000

The expected net present value (ENPV) can now be calculated as follows:

Period	Expected cash flow £	Discount rate 10%	Expected PV £
0	(540,000)	1.000	(540,000)
1	144,000	0.909	130,896
2	194,000	0.826	160,244
3	185,000	0.751	138,935
4	152,000	0.683	103,816
		ENPV	(6,109)

(b) The worst possible outcome can be calculated by taking the lowest values of savings each year, as follows:

Period	Cash flow £	Discount rate 10%	PV £
0	(540,000)	1.000	(540,000)
1	80,000	0.909	72,720
2	140,000	0.826	115,640
3	140,000	0.751	105,140
4	100,000	0.683	68,300
			NPV (178,200)

The probability of occurrence can be obtained by multiplying together the probability of each of the worst outcomes above, that is, $0.3 \times 0.4 \times 0.4 \times 0.3 = 0.014$ (or 1.4 per cent).

Thus, the probability of occurrence is 1.4 per cent, which is very low.

Risk and the standard deviation

In the problems discussed so far, the number of possible outcomes relating to a particular project has been fairly small. Perhaps only two or three possible outcomes have been employed to illustrate particular principles. In reality, however, there may be a large number of outcomes that could occur. Indeed, a project may have thousands of possible outcomes, each with its own probability of occurrence. Although it would not be very realistic, let us suppose a particular project has a large number of possible outcomes and that we are able to identify each possible outcome and to assign a probability to it. This would mean that we could plot a probability distribution of the outcomes that could take the form of a continuous curve, such as the one shown in Figure 5.9.

Figure 5.9	**Probability distribution of outcomes for a single investment project**

[Figure: Curve plotting "Probability of outcome" on the vertical axis against "NPV of investment project (£000)" on the horizontal axis, with marks at 0, 10, 20, 30, 40.]

The figure shows the probability distribution of outcomes for a single investment project. We can see that the range of possible outcomes forms a continuous curve. The particular shape of the curve will vary according to the nature of the project.

The particular shape of the curve is likely to vary between investment projects. Variations in the shape of the curve can occur even where projects have identical expected values. To illustrate this point, the probability distribution for two separate projects that have the same expected value is shown in Figure 5.10. We can see, however, that Project A has a range of possible values that is much more tightly distributed around the expected value than Project B.

Figure 5.10	Probability distribution of two projects with the same expected value

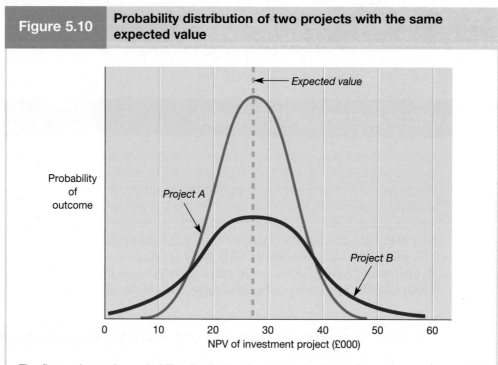

The figure shows the probability distribution for two projects that have the same expected value. We can see the distribution for each project around the expected value is quite different. Project A has a much tighter distribution than Project B. This means that Project A has less 'downside' risk but also has less 'upside' potential.

This difference in the shape of the two probability distributions can provide us with a useful indicator of risk. The graph shows that the tighter the distribution of possible future values, the greater the chance that the actual value will be close to the expected value. This means there is less 'downside' risk associated with the particular investment project (but also less 'upside' potential). We can say, therefore, *the tighter the probability distribution of outcomes, the lower the risk associated with the investment project.* The graph in Figure 5.10 shows that the possible outcomes for Project A are much less spread out than those of Project B. Hence, Project A will be considered a less risky venture than Project B.

The variability of possible future values associated with a project can be measured using a statistical measure called the **standard deviation**. This is a measure of spread that is based on deviations from the mean, or expected value. To demonstrate how the standard deviation is calculated, let us consider Example 5.6.

Example 5.6

Telematix plc is considering two mutually exclusive projects: Cable and Satellite. The possible NPVs for each project and their associated probabilities are as follows:

Cable			Satellite	
NPV	*Probability of occurrence*		*NPV*	*Probability of occurrence*
£m			*£m*	
10	0.1		15	0.6
20	0.5		20	0.2
25	0.4		40	0.2

To calculate the standard deviation, the ENPV for each project must be calculated. In the case of the Cable project, the ENPV is as follows:

(a)	*(b)*	*(c) = (a) × (b)*
NPV	*Probability of occurrence*	*ENPV*
£m	*£m*	*£m*
10	0.1	1.0
20	0.5	10.0
25	0.4	10.0
		21.0

The next step is to calculate the deviations around the ENPV by deducting the expected NPV from each possible outcome. For the Cable project, the following set of deviations will be obtained:

(a)	*(b)*	*(c) = (a) – (b)*
Possible NPV	*ENPV*	*Deviation*
£m		*£m*
10	21	–11
20	21	–1
25	21	4

The calculations reveal two of the deviations are negative and one is positive. To prevent the positive and negative deviations from cancelling each other out, we can eliminate the negative signs by squaring the deviations. The sum of the squared deviations is referred to as the *variance*. The variance for the Cable project will be:

Deviations	*Squared deviations*
–11	121
–1	1
4	16
	Variance 138

The problem with the variance is that it provides a unit of measurement that is the square of the NPV deviations. In this case, the variance is 138 $(£m)^2$ which is difficult to interpret. To make things easier, it is a good idea to take the square root of the variance. The final step in calculating the standard deviation is to do just that. The standard deviation is:

$$\text{Standard deviation} = \sqrt{\text{Variance}}$$

Example 5.6 continued

For the Cable project, the standard deviation is:

$$\text{Standard deviation} = \sqrt{£138m}$$
$$= £11.74m$$

It was mentioned earlier that the standard deviation is a measure of spread. Thus, we can say that the higher the standard deviation for a particular investment project, the greater the spread, or variability, of possible outcomes.

Activity 5.15

Calculate the standard deviation for the Satellite project. Which project has the higher level of risk?

To answer this activity, the steps outlined above must be followed. Thus:

Step 1. Calculate the ENPV:

(a)	(b)	(c) = (a) × (b)
NPV	Probability of occurrence	ENPV
£m		£m
15	0.6	9.0
20	0.2	4.0
40	0.2	8.0
		21.0

Step 2. Calculate the deviations around the ENPV:

(a)	(b)	(c) = (a) − (b)
Possible NPV	ENPV	Deviation
£m	£m	£m
15	21	−6
20	21	−1
40	21	19

Step 3. Calculate the variance (that is, sum the squared deviations):

Deviations	Squared deviations
−6	36
−1	1
19	361
	Variance 398

Step 4. Find the square root of the variance (that is, the standard deviation):*

$$\text{Standard deviation} = \sqrt{£398m}$$
$$= £19.95m$$

The Satellite project has the higher standard deviation and, therefore, the greater variability of possible outcomes. Hence, it has the higher level of risk.

* Computer software or calculators with statistical functions can be used to calculate the standard deviation and so this manual approach need not be used in practice. It is shown here for illustrative purposes.

The standard deviation and the normal distribution

If the distribution of possible outcomes has a symmetrical bell shape when plotted on a graph, it is referred to as a **normal distribution**. In Figure 5.11 we can see an example of a normal distribution. Note that this kind of distribution has a single peak and that there is an equal tapering off from the peak to each tail. In practice, distributions of data often display this pattern. Where a normal distribution occurs, it is possible to identify the extent to which possible outcomes will deviate from the mean or expected value. The following rules will apply:

● Approximately 68 per cent of possible outcomes will fall within one standard deviation from the mean or expected value.
● Approximately 95 per cent of possible outcomes will fall within two standard deviations from the mean or expected value.
● Approximately 100 per cent of possible outcomes will fall within three standard deviations from the mean or expected value.

Even when the possible outcomes do not form a precise symmetrical bell shape, or normal distribution, these rules can still be reasonably accurate. We shall see below how these rules may be useful in interpreting the level of risk associated with a project.

Figure 5.11	**The normal distribution and standard deviations**

The figure shows the probability of an outcome being one, two and three standard deviations from the mean or expected value. Note that approximately 100 per cent of possible outcomes will fall within three standard deviations of the mean (assuming a normal distribution). There is only a very small probability of an outcome being more than three standard deviations from the mean.

The expected value–standard deviation rules

Where the expected value of the returns of investment opportunities and their standard deviation are known, we have both a measure of return and a measure of risk that can be used for making decisions. If investors are risk averse, they will be seeking the highest level of return for a given level of risk (or the lowest level of risk for a given level of return). The following decision rules can, therefore, be applied where the possible outcomes for investment projects are normally distributed:

Where there are two competing projects, X and Y, Project X should be chosen when either:

● the expected return of Project X is equal to, or greater than, that of Project Y and the standard deviation of Project X is lower than that of Project Y, or
● the expected return of Project X is greater than that of Project Y and the standard deviation of Project X is equal to, or lower than, that of Project Y.

→   The **expected value-standard deviation rules** as they are known do not cover all possibilities. For example, the rules cannot help us discriminate between two projects where one has both a higher expected return and a higher standard deviation. Nevertheless, they provide some help for managers.

Activity 5.16

Refer back to Example 5.6 above. Which project should be chosen and why? (Assume the possible outcomes are normally distributed.)

We can see from our earlier calculations that the Cable and Satellite projects have an identical expected net present value. However, the Cable project has a much lower standard deviation, indicating less variability of possible outcomes. Applying the decision rules mentioned above, this means that the Cable project should be selected; or to put it another way, a risk-averse investor would prefer the Cable project as it provides the same expected return for a lower level of risk.

Measuring probabilities

As we might expect, assigning probabilities to possible outcomes can often be a problem. There may be many possible outcomes arising from a particular investment project and to identify each outcome and then assign a probability to it may prove to be an impossible task. Nevertheless, there are circumstances where it is feasible to use probabilities.

Probabilities may be derived using either an objective or a subjective approach.
→ **Objective probabilities** are based on information gathered from experience. For example, the transport manager of a business operating a fleet of motor vans may be able to provide information concerning the possible life of a newly purchased van based on the record of similar vans acquired in the past. From the information available, probabilities may be developed for different possible life spans. However, past experience

may not always be a reliable guide to the future, particularly during a period of rapid change. In the case of the motor vans, for example, changes in design and technology or changes in the purpose for which the vans are being used may undermine the validity of using past data. **Subjective probabilities** are based on opinion and will be used where past data are either inappropriate or unavailable. The opinions of independent experts may provide a useful basis for developing subjective probabilities, though even these may contain bias which will affect the reliability of the judgements made.

Despite these problems, we should not dismiss the use of probabilities. They help to make explicit some of the risks associated with a project and can help managers to appreciate the uncertainties that must be faced. Real World 5.3 provides an example of the use of probabilities to assess the risks associated with an investment project.

REAL WORLD 5.3

Assigning probabilities

The transport strategy for South Hampshire includes a light rail transit route linking Fareham, Gosport and Portsmouth. The proposed route is 14.3 km long and contains 16 stops. A thorough appraisal of the proposed investment has been undertaken which estimates an NPV of £272 million for the scheme. An integral part of the investment appraisal involved assigning probabilities to various risks identified with the scheme, including risks relating to design, construction and development, performance, operating costs, revenue streams and technology.

During the period of construction and development, a number of risks were identified. One such risk relates to cost overruns on the construction of a tunnel along part of the route. The total cost of the tunnel was estimated at £42.2 million but the following probabilities were assigned to various possible cost overruns.

Probability of occurrence %	Cost £000	Cost of risk £000	Expected cost £000
34	100	34	
46	1,000	460	
10	2,000	200	
5	4,000	200	
4	6,000	240	
1	10,000	100	1,234
100			

We can see from the table that it has been estimated that there is an 80 per cent chance that the cost overrun will be £1.0 million or less and a 90 per cent chance that it will be £2.0 million or less.

Source: South Hampshire Rapid Transit Fareham–Gosport–Portsmouth Investment Appraisal, www.hants.gov.uk

Portfolio effects and risk reduction

So far, our consideration of risk has looked at the problem from the viewpoint of an investment project being undertaken in isolation. However, in practice, a business will normally invest in a range, or *portfolio*, of investment projects rather than a single

project. This approach to investment provides a potentially useful way of reducing risk. The problem with investing all available funds in a single project is, of course, that an unfavourable outcome could have disastrous consequences for the business. By investing in a spread of projects, an adverse outcome from a single project is less likely to have severe repercussions. The saying, 'don't put all your eggs in one basket', neatly sums up the best advice concerning investment policy.

Investing in a range of different projects is referred to as **diversification**, and by holding a diversified portfolio of investment projects the total risk associated with the business can be reduced. Indeed, in theory, it is possible to combine two risky investment projects so as to create a portfolio of projects that is riskless. To illustrate this point let us consider Example 5.7.

Example 5.7

Frank N. Stein plc has the opportunity to invest in two investment projects in Transylvania. The possible outcomes from each project will depend on whether the ruling party of the country wins or loses the next election. (For the sake of simplicity, we shall assume the ruling party will either win or lose outright and there is no possibility of another outcome, such as a hung parliament.) The NPV from each project under each outcome is estimated as follows:

	Project 1 NPV £m	Project 2 NPV £m
Ruling party wins	(20)	30
Ruling party loses	40	(30)

What should the business do to manage the risks involved in each project?

Solution

By investing in *both* projects, the total NPV for the business under each outcome will be as follows:

	Project 1 NPV £m	Project 2 NPV £m	Total returns £m
Ruling party wins	(20)	30	<u>10</u>
Ruling party loses	40	(30)	<u>10</u>

We can see that, whatever the outcome of the election, the total NPV for the business will be the same (that is, £10 million). Although the possible returns from each project vary according to the results of the election, they are inversely related and so the total returns will be stabilised. As risk can be diversified away in this manner, the relationship between the returns from individual investment projects is an important issue for managers.

The coefficient of correlation

A business may eliminate the variability in total returns by investing in projects whose returns are inversely related, such as in the example above. Ideally, a business should invest in a spread of investment projects so that when certain projects generate low (or negative) returns, other projects are generating high returns, and vice versa. It is possible to measure the degree to which the returns from individual projects are related by using the **coefficient of correlation**. This coefficient is an abstract measure that ranges along a continuum between +1 and –1.

When the coefficient for two projects, X and Y, is positive, it means that increases in the returns from Project X will be accompanied by increases in returns from Project Y: the higher the positive measure, the stronger the relationship between the returns of the two projects. A coefficient of +1 indicates a perfect positive correlation and this means that the returns are moving together in perfect step. In Figure 5.12, we see a graph showing the returns for two investment projects that have a perfect positive correlation.

Figure 5.12	Two projects whose returns have a perfect positive correlation

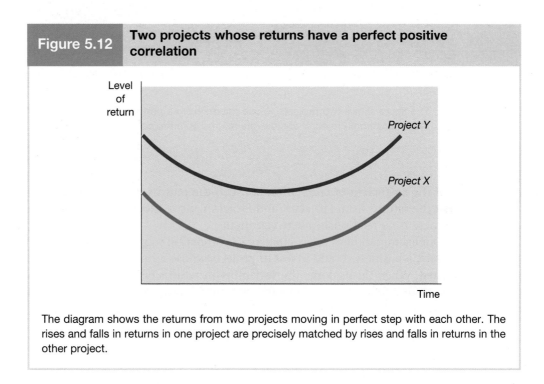

The diagram shows the returns from two projects moving in perfect step with each other. The rises and falls in returns in one project are precisely matched by rises and falls in returns in the other project.

If the coefficient of correlation is negative, increases in the returns from Project X will be accompanied by decreases in the returns from Project Y. A coefficient of –1 indicates a perfect negative correlation between two projects. In other words, the projects' returns will move together in perfect step, but in *opposite directions*.

Activity 5.17

Suppose the returns from Project Y had a perfect negative correlation with those of Project X. Draw a graph depicting the relationship between the two projects.

Activity 5.17 continued

The graph for two investment projects whose returns are perfectly negatively correlated is shown in Figure 5.13.

| Figure 5.13 | Two projects whose returns have a perfect negative correlation |

The figure shows two projects whose returns have a perfect inverse relationship. When the returns from Project Y are low, the returns from Project X are high, and vice versa.

If the coefficient of correlation between the returns of two projects is 0, this means that the returns from Project X and Project Y move independently of one another and so there is no relationship between them.

Our examination of the coefficient of correlation suggests that to eliminate risk completely, a business should invest in projects whose returns are perfectly negatively correlated. When this is done, the variability in returns between projects will cancel each other out and so risk is completely diversified away. So far, so good – unfortunately, however, it is rarely possible to follow such an investment policy. In the real world, projects whose returns are perfectly negatively correlated are extremely difficult to find. Nevertheless, risk can still be diversified away to some extent by investing in projects whose returns do not have a perfect positive correlation. Provided the correlation between projects is less than +1, some offsetting will occur. The further the coefficient of correlation moves away from +1 and towards –1 on the scale, the greater this offsetting effect will be.

Activity 5.18

Should the managers of a business seek project diversification as their primary objective?

The answer is no. Even if two projects could be found whose returns had a perfect negative correlation, this does not necessarily mean that they should be pursued. The expected returns from the projects must also be considered when making any investment decision.

One potential problem of diversification is that a range of different projects can create greater project management problems. Managers will have to deal with a variety of different projects with different technical and resource issues to resolve. The greater the number of projects, the greater the management problems are likely to be.

Real World 5.4 provides an example of diversification in practice.

REAL WORLD 5.4

Dealing with investment risk

3i Group plc is an investment business that focuses on ambitious, smaller businesses with high growth potential. When dealing with investment risk, diversification is a key issue as revealed in the following extract from its annual report and accounts for 2004:

> Investment levels are set, allocated and monitored by product area and geography. Within this framework 3i invests in all sectors of the economy except those where the opportunity to invest in . . . businesses meeting 3i's investment criteria is limited. Management periodically reviews the portfolio, which is well diversified by industry sector, to ensure that there is no undue exposure to any one sector.

Source: 3i Group plc Report and Accounts 2004.

Diversifiable and non-diversifiable risk

The benefits of risk diversification can be obtained by increasing the number of projects within the investment portfolio. As each investment project is added to the portfolio, the variability of total returns will diminish, providing that the projects are not perfectly correlated. However, there are limits to the benefits of diversification due to the nature of the risks faced. The total risk relating to a particular project can be divided into two types: **diversifiable risk** and **non-diversifiable risk**. As the names suggest, it is only the former type of risk that can be eliminated through diversification.

The two types of risk can be described as follows:

- *Diversifiable risk* is that part of the total risk that is specific to the project, such as changes in key personnel, legal regulations, the degree of competition and so on. By spreading available funds between investment projects, it is possible to offset adverse outcomes occurring in one project against beneficial outcomes in another. (Diversifiable risk is also referred to as avoidable risk, or unsystematic risk.)
- *Non-diversifiable risk* is that part of the total risk that is common to all projects and which, therefore, cannot be diversified away. This element of risk arises from general market conditions and will be affected by such factors as the rate of inflation, the general level of interest rates, exchange rate movements and the rate of growth within the economy. (Non-diversifiable risk is also referred to as unavoidable risk, or systematic risk.)

In Figure 5.14, the relationship between the level of portfolio risk and the size of the portfolio is shown. We can see that, as the number of projects increases, the diversifiable element of total risk is reduced. This does not mean, necessarily, that a business should invest in a large number of projects. Many of the benefits from diversification can often be reaped from investing in a relatively small number of projects. In Figure 5.14, we can see the additional benefits from each investment project diminish

Figure 5.14	Reducing risk through diversification

The figure shows that, as the size of the portfolio of projects is increased, the level of total risk is reduced. However, the rate of reduction in the level of total risk decreases quite sharply and soon reaches a point where investing in further projects to reduce risk is of little or no value.

quite sharply. This suggests that a business with a large portfolio of projects may gain very little from further diversification.

Non-diversifiable risk is based on general economic conditions and therefore all businesses will be affected. However, certain businesses are more sensitive to changes in economic conditions than others. For example, during a recession, some types of businesses will be badly affected, whereas others will be only slightly affected.

Activity 5.19

Provide two examples of businesses that are likely to be:

(a) badly affected by an economic recession
(b) only slightly affected by an economic recession.

The types of business that are likely to be badly hit by recession will include those selling expensive or luxury goods and services such as:

- hotels and restaurants
- travel companies
- house builders and construction
- airlines
- jewellers.

The types of business that are likely to be only slightly affected by recession will include those selling essential goods and services such as:

- gas and electricity suppliers
- water suppliers
- basic food retailers and producers
- undertakers.

The businesses that are likely to be badly affected by an economic recession will usually have a cyclical pattern of profits. Thus, during a period of economic growth, these businesses may make large profits, and during periods of recession they may make large losses. The businesses that are likely to be only slightly affected will tend to have a fairly stable pattern of profits over the economic cycle.

The distinction between diversifiable and non-diversifiable risk is an important issue that we shall return to when considering the cost of capital in the next chapter.

Risk assessment in practice

Surveys of UK businesses suggest that risk assessment methods have become more widely used over time. These surveys also suggest that sensitivity analysis and scenario analysis are the most popular methods of assessing risk. **Real World 5.5** sets out evidence from a survey by Arnold and Hatzopoloulus (see reference 1 at the end of the chapter).

REAL WORLD 5.5

Assessing risk

The following table summarises the extent to which various risk assessment methods are used by UK businesses.

| | Businesses | | | |
Technique	Small %	Medium %	Large %	Total %
Sensitivity/scenario analysis	82	83	89	85
Reduced payback period	15	42	11	20
Risk-adjusted discount rate	42	71	50	52
Probability analysis	27	21	42	31
Beta analysis*	3	0	5	3
Subjective assessment	44	33	55	46

* This approach is discussed in some detail in the next chapter.

The table shows that sensitivity/scenario analysis is the most popular way of dealing with risk and that there are often significant variations in the popularity of the other methods among businesses of different size. The fact that the percentage totals in each column are greater than 100 per cent indicates that some businesses are using more than one method.

Source: *Corporate Financial Management*, G. Arnold, 2nd edn, Financial Times Prentice Hall, 2002.

SUMMARY

The main points in this chapter may be summarised as follows:

Investment decisions when funds are limited

- When projects are divisible, managers should maximise the present value per £ of scarce finance.
- The profitability index provides a measure of the present value per £ of scarce finance.
- Where funding requirements extend beyond a single period, linear programming can be used to maximise NPV.

Comparing projects with unequal lives

- Can be dealt with by assuming the projects form part of a repeat chain of replacement and then make comparisons using the shortest-common-period-of-time approach.
- Alternatively, the equivalent-annual-annuity approach converts the NPV of a project into an annual annuity stream over its expected life.

The problem of inflation

- Either, include inflation by adjusting the annual cash flows and the discount rate to take account of price increases.
- Or, exclude inflation by adjusting the cash flow to real terms and by using a 'real' discount rate.

Risk

- Is important because of the long time scales and amounts involved in investment decisions.
- Various methods of dealing with risk are available.

Sensitivity analysis

- Provides an assessment, taking each input factor in turn, of how much each one can vary from estimate before a project is not viable:
  - provides useful insights to projects
  - does not give a clear decision rule, but provides an impression
  - it can be rather static.

Scenario analysis

- Changes a number of variables simultaneously to provide a particular 'state of the world'.
- Usually three different states – optimistic, pessimistic and most likely – are portrayed.
- Does not indicate the likelihood of each state occurring or the other possible states that may occur.

Simulations

- Involves identifying the key variables of the project and their key relationships.
- Possible values are attached to each factor and a computer is used to select one of the possible values on a random basis to produce a projected cash flow.

- The process is repeated many times to obtain a probability distribution of the values of the cash flows.
- It can be costly and time consuming.

Risk preferences of shareholders

- Given a choice between two projects with the same expected return but with different levels of risk:
  - risk-seeking investors will choose the project with the higher level of risk
  - risk-neutral investors will have no preference
  - risk-averse investors will choose the project with the lower level of risk.
- Most investors appear to be risk averse.

Risk-adjusted discount rate

- Risk-averse investors will require a risk premium for risky projects.
- Using a risk-adjusted discount rate, where a risk premium is added to the risk-free rate, is a logical response to risk.

Expected net present value (ENPV) approach

- Assigns probabilities to possible outcomes.
- The expected value is the weighted average of the possible outcomes where the probabilities are used as weights.
- The ENPV appoach:
  - provides a single value and a clear decision rule
  - the single ENPV figure can hide the real risk
  - useful for the ENPV figure to be supported by information on the range of possible outcomes
  - probabilities may be subjective (based on opinion) or objective (based on evidence).

The standard deviation

- Is a measure of spread based on deviations from the mean.
- Provides a measure of risk.

Portfolio effect

- By holding a diversified portfolio of investment projects, the total risk associated with the business can be reduced.
- Ideally, a business should hold a spread of projects, such that when certain projects generate low returns, others generate high returns.
- Only diversifiable risk can be eliminated through diversification.

→ **Key terms**

Profitability index p. 161	**Risk-adjusted discount rate** p. 181
Linear programming p. 162	**Expected value** p. 183
Shortest-common-period-of-time	**Expected net present value (ENPV)**
approach p. 164	p. 184
Annuity p. 166	**Event tree diagram** p. 186
Equivalent-annual-annuity	**Standard deviation** p. 190
approach p. 166	**Normal distribution** p. 193
Risk p. 170	**Expected value–standard deviation**
Sensitivity analysis p. 170	rules p. 194
Scenario analysis p. 176	**Objective probabilities** p. 194
Simulation p. 176	**Subjective probabilities** p. 195
Risk-seeking investors p. 178	**Diversification** p. 196
Risk-neutral investors p. 178	**Coefficient of correlation** p. 197
Risk-averse investors p. 178	**Diversifiable risk** p. 199
Utility function p. 179	**Non-diversifiable risk** p. 199

For definitions of these terms see the Glossary, pp. 562–571.

Further reading

If you wish to explore the topics discussed in this chapter in more depth, try the following books:

Business Finance: Theory and practice, *McLaney, E.*, 7th edn, Financial Times Prentice Hall, 2006, chapters 5 and 6.

Corporate Finance and Investment, *Pike, R. and Neale, B.*, 4th edn, Prentice Hall International, 2002, chapters 5 and 6.

Corporate Financial Management, *Arnold, G.*, 2nd edn, Financial Times Prentice Hall, 2002, chapters 3, 5 and 6.

Investment Appraisal and Financial Decisions, *Lumby, S. and Jones, C.*, 7th edn, International Thomson Business Press, 2003, chapters 7–9.

Reference

'The theory–practice gap in capital budgeting: evidence from the United Kingdom,' *Arnold, G. and Hatzopoulus, P.*, **Journal of Business Finance and Accounting**, June/July 2000, pp. 603–26, cited in **Corporate Financial Management**, *Arnold, G.*, 2nd edn, Financial Times Prentice Hall, 2002, p. 218.

REVIEW QUESTIONS

Answers to these questions can be found in Appendix D at the back of the book.

5.1 There is evidence to suggest that some businesses fail to take account of inflation in investment decisions. Does it really matter given that, in recent years, the level of inflation has been low? What would be the effect on NPV calculations (that is, would NPV be overstated or understated) of dealing with inflation incorrectly by (a) discounting nominal cash flows at real discount rates and (b) discounting real cash flows at nominal discount rates?

5.2 What is risk and why is it an important issue for investment decision making?

5.3 What practical problems arise when using the risk-adjusted discount rate to deal with the problem of risk?

5.4 Explain why the standard deviation may be useful in measuring risk.

EXERCISES

Exercises 5.5 to 5.7 are more advanced than 5.1 to 5.4. Those with coloured numbers have answers at the back of the book.

 If you wish to try more exercises, visit the students' side of the Companion Website.

5.1 Lee Caterers Ltd is about to make an investment in new kitchen equipment. It is considering whether to replace the existing kitchen equipment with cook/freeze or cook/chill technology. The following cash flows are expected from each form of technology:

	Cook/chill £000	Cook/freeze £000
Initial outlay	(200)	(390)
1 year's time	85	88
2 years' time	94	102
3 years' time	86	110
4 years' time	62	110
5 years' time	–	110
6 years' time	–	90
7 years' time	–	85
8 years' time	–	60

The business would expect to replace the new equipment purchased with similar equipment at the end of its life. The cost of finance for the business is 10 per cent.

Required:
Which type of equipment should the business invest in? Use both approaches considered in the chapter to support your conclusions.

5.2 D'Arcy (Builders) Ltd is considering three possible investment projects: A, B and C. The expected pattern of cash flows for each project is:

Project cash flows

	A	B	C
	£000	£000	£000
Initial outlay	(17)	(20)	(24)
1 year's time	11	12	9
2 years' time	5	7	9
3 years' time	7	7	11
4 years' time	6	6	13

The business has a cost of finance of 10 per cent and the capital expenditure budget for next year is £25 million.

Required:

Which investment project(s) should the business undertake assuming:

(a) each project is divisible; and

(b) each project is indivisible?

5.3 Simonson Engineers plc is considering the building of a new plant in Indonesia to produce products for the South-east Asian market. To date, £450,000 has been invested in market research and site surveys. The cost of building the plant will be £9 million and it will be in operation and paid for in one year's time. Estimates of the likely cash flows from the plant and their probability of occurrence are set out as follows:

	Estimated cash flows £m	Probability of occurrence
Year 2	2.0	0.2
	3.5	0.6
	4.0	0.2
Year 3	2.5	0.2
	3.0	0.4
	5.0	0.4
Year 4	3.0	0.2
	4.0	0.7
	5.0	0.1
Year 5	2.5	0.2
	3.0	0.5
	6.0	0.3

Estimates for each year are independent of each other. The cost of capital for the business is 10 per cent.

Required:

(a) Calculate the expected net present value of the proposed plant.

(b) Calculate the net present value of the worst possible outcome and the probability of its occurrence.

(c) Should the business invest in the new plant? Why?

5.4 Helena Chocolate Products Ltd is considering the introduction of a new chocolate bar into their range of chocolate products. The new chocolate bar will require the purchase of a new piece of equipment costing £30,000 which will have no other use and no residual value on completion of the project. Financial data relating to the new product are as follows:

	Per bar (£)
Selling price	0.60
Variable costs	0.22

Fixed costs of £20,000 a year will be apportioned to the new product. These costs represent a 'fair share' of the total fixed costs of the business. The costs are unlikely to change as a result of any decision to introduce new products into the existing range. Other developments currently being finalised will mean that the new product will have a life of only three years and the level of expected demand for the new product is uncertain. The marketing department has produced the following levels of demand and the probability of each for all three years of the product's life.

Year 1		Year 2		Year 3	
Sales (units)	Probability	Sales (units)	Probability	Sales (units)	Probability
100,000	0.2	140,000	0.3	180,000	0.5
120,000	0.4	150,000	0.3	160,000	0.3
125,000	0.3	160,000	0.2	120,000	0.1
130,000	0.1	200,000	0.2	100,000	0.1

A rival business has offered to buy the right to produce and sell the new chocolate bar for £100,000. The cost of finance is 10 per cent and interest charges on the money borrowed to finance the project are expected to be £3,000 per year.

Required:
(a) Compute the expected net present value of the product.
(b) Advise the directors on the appropriate course of action. Give reasons.

5.5 Devonia (Laboratories) Ltd has recently carried out successful clinical trials on a new type of skin cream which has been developed to reduce the effects of ageing. Research and development costs incurred by the business in relation to the new product amount to £160,000. In order to gauge the market potential of the new product, an independent firm of market research consultants was hired at a cost of £15,000. The market research report submitted by the consultants indicates that the skin cream is likely to have a product life of four years and could be sold to retail chemists and large department stores at a price of £20 per 100 ml container. For each of the four years of the new product's life, sales demand has been estimated as follows:

Number of 100 ml containers sold	Probability of occurrence
11,000	0.3
14,000	0.6
16,000	0.1

If the business decides to launch the new product it is possible for production to begin at once. The necessary equipment to produce the product is already owned by the business and originally cost £150,000. At the end of the new product's life it is estimated that the equipment could be sold for £35,000. If the business decides against launching the new product the equipment will be sold immediately for £85,000 as it will be of no further use to the business.

The new skin cream will require one hour's labour for each 100 ml container produced. The cost of labour for the new product is £8.00 an hour. Additional workers will have to be recruited to produce the new product. At the end of the product's life the workers are unlikely to be offered further work with the business and redundancy costs of £10,000 are expected. The cost of the ingredients for each 100 ml container is £6.00. Additional overheads arising from production of the product is expected to be £15,000 a year.

The new skin cream has attracted the interest of the business's competitors. If the business decides not to produce and sell the skin cream it can sell the patent rights to a major competitor immediately for £125,000.

Devonia (Laboratories) Ltd has a cost of capital of 12 per cent. Ignore taxation.

Required:
(a) Calculate the expected net present value (ENPV) of the new product.
(b) State, with reasons, whether or not Devonia (Laboratories) Ltd should launch the new product.
(c) Discuss the strengths and weaknesses of the expected net present value approach for making investment decisions.

5.6   Nimby plc is considering two mutually exclusive projects: Delphi and Oracle. The possible NPVs for each project and their associated probabilities are as follows:

Delphi		Oracle	
NPV	Probability of occurrence	NPV	Probability of occurrence
£m		£m	
20	0.2	30	0.5
40	0.6	40	0.3
60	0.2	65	0.2

Required:
(a) Calculate the expected net present value and the standard deviation associated with each project.
(b) Which project would you select and why? State any assumptions you have made in coming to your conclusions.
(c) Discuss the limitations of the standard deviation as a measure of project risk.

5.7   Plato Pharmaceuticals Ltd has invested £300,000 to date in developing a new type of insect repellent. The repellent is now ready for production and sale, and the marketing director estimates that the product will sell 150,000 bottles a year over the next five years. The selling price of the insect repellent will be £5 a bottle and variable costs are estimated to be £3 a bottle. Fixed costs (excluding depreciation) are expected to be £200,000 a year. This figure is made up of £160,000 additional fixed costs and £40,000 fixed costs relating to the existing business which will be apportioned to the new product.

In order to produce the repellent, machinery and equipment costing £520,000 will have to be purchased immediately. The estimated residual value of this machinery and equipment in five years' time is £100,000. The business calculates depreciation on a straight-line basis.

The business has a cost of capital of 12 per cent. Ignore taxation.

Required:
(a) Calculate the net present value of the product.
(b) Undertake sensitivity analysis to show by how much the following factors would have to change before the product ceased to be worthwhile:
(i)   The discount rate.
(ii)   The initial outlay on machinery and equipment.
(iii) The net operating cash flows.
(iv) The residual value of the machinery and equipment.

6

Financing a business 1: sources of finance

LEARNING OUTCOMES

When you have completed this chapter, you should be able to:

● Identify the main sources of external finance available to a business and explain the advantages and disadvantages of each source.

● Identify the main sources of internal finance available to a business and explain the advantages and disadvantages of each source.

● Discuss the factors to be taken into account when choosing an appropriate source of finance.

INTRODUCTION

This is the first of two chapters that examine the financing of businesses. In this chapter we identify the main sources of finance available to businesses and discuss the main features of each source. We also consider the factors to be taken into account when choosing among the various sources of finance that are available.

In the following chapter we go on to examine capital markets, including the role and efficiency of the London Stock Exchange and the ways in which share capital can be issued. We also consider the ways in which smaller businesses, which do not have access to the London Stock Exchange, may try to raise finance.

Sources of finance

When examining the various sources of finance available to a business, it is useful to distinguish between *external* and *internal* sources. By external sources of finance we mean those that require the agreement of someone beyond the directors and managers of the business. Thus, finance from an issue of new shares is an external source because it requires the agreement of potential shareholders. Internal sources of finance, on the other hand, do not require agreement from other parties and arise from management decisions. Thus, retained profits are a source of internal finance because the directors have the power to retain profits without the agreement of the shareholders (whose profits they are!).

In the sections that follow, we begin by examining external sources of finance and then go on to examine internal sources of finance. When considering the external sources of finance it is probably helpful to distinguish between *long-term* and *short-term* sources of finance. In practice, these terms are not tightly defined but, for the purposes of this chapter, long-term finance will be defined as a source of finance that is due for repayment after approximately one year, whereas short-term finance will be defined as a source of finance that is repayable within approximately one year.

Sources of external finance

Figure 6.1 summarises the main sources of long-term and short-term external finance available to a business.

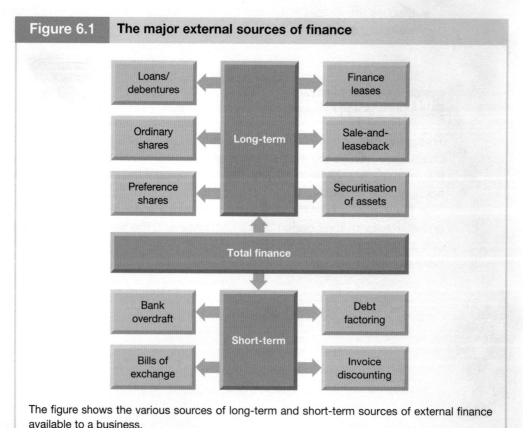

Figure 6.1 **The major external sources of finance**

The figure shows the various sources of long-term and short-term sources of external finance available to a business.

Long-term sources of external finance

As Figure 6.1 reveals, the major sources of long-term external finance are:

- ordinary shares
- preference shares
- loans and debentures
- finance leases
- sale-and lease-back arrangements
- securitisation of assets.

We now look at each of these sources in turn.

Ordinary shares

Ordinary shares form the backbone of the financial structure of a business. Ordinary share capital represents a business's risk capital. There is no fixed rate of dividend and ordinary shareholders will receive a dividend only if profits available for distribution still remain after other investors (preference shareholders and lenders) have received their returns in the form of dividend payments or interest. If the business is wound up, the ordinary shareholders will receive any proceeds from asset disposals only after lenders and creditors, and, in some cases, after preference shareholders, have received their entitlements. Because of the high risks associated with this form of investment, ordinary shareholders will normally require the business to provide a comparatively high rate of return.

Although ordinary shareholders have a limited loss liability, based on the amount they have invested or agreed to invest, the potential returns from their investment are unlimited. This is because, after preference shareholders and lenders have received their returns, all the remaining profits will accrue to the ordinary shareholders. Thus, their 'downside risk' is limited whereas their upside potential is not. Ordinary shareholders exercise control over the business through their voting rights. This gives them the power both to elect the directors and to remove them from office.

From the business's perspective, ordinary shares can be a valuable form of financing as, at times, it is useful to be able to avoid paying a dividend.

Activity 6.1

Under what circumstances might a business find it useful to avoid paying a dividend?

Two circumstances spring to mind. An expanding business may prefer to retain funds in order to fuel future growth. A business in difficulties may need the funds to meet its operating costs and so may find making a dividend a real burden. The drain on liquid resources may inhibit growth or recovery. Where the business is financed entirely by ordinary shares, this problem need not occur.

Although a business financed by ordinary shares can avoid making cash payments to shareholders when it is not prudent to do so, the market value of the shares may go down. The cost to the business of financing through ordinary shares may become higher if shareholders feel uncertain about future dividends. It is also worth pointing out that the business does not obtain any tax relief on dividends paid to shareholders, whereas interest on borrowings is tax deductible.

Preference shares

Preference shares offer investors a lower level of risk than ordinary shares. Provided there are sufficient profits available, preference shares will normally be given a fixed rate of dividend each year and preference dividends will be paid before ordinary dividends are paid. If a business is wound up, preference shareholders may be given priority over the claims of ordinary shareholders. (The business's particular documents of incorporation will state the precise rights of preference shareholders in this respect.)

Activity 6.2

Would you expect the returns to preference shares to be higher or lower than those to ordinary shares?

Because of the lower level of risk associated with this form of investment (preference shareholders have priority over ordinary shareholders regarding dividends, and perhaps capital repayment), investors will be offered a lower level of return than that normally expected by ordinary shareholders.

Preference shareholders are not usually given voting rights, although these may be granted where the preference dividend is in arrears.

There are various types of preference shares that may be issued. *Cumulative preference shares* give investors the right to receive arrears of dividends that have arisen as a result of there being insufficient profits in previous periods. The unpaid amounts will accumulate and will be paid when sufficient profits have been generated. *Non-cumulative preference shares* do not give investors this right. Thus, if a business is not in a position to pay the preference dividend due for a particular period, the preference shareholder loses the right to receive that dividend. *Participating preference shares* give investors the right to a further share in the profits available for dividend after they have been paid their fixed rate and after ordinary shareholders have been awarded a dividend. *Redeemable preference shares* allow the business to buy back the shares from shareholders at some agreed future date. Redeemable preference shares are seen as a lower-risk investment than non-redeemable shares and so tend to carry a lower dividend. A business can also issue redeemable ordinary shares, but these are rare in practice.

Activity 6.3

Would you expect the market price of ordinary shares or of preference shares to be the more volatile? Why?

The dividends of preference shares tend to be fairly stable over time, and there is usually an upper limit on the returns that can be received. As a result, the share price, which reflects the expected future returns from the share, will normally be less volatile than for ordinary shares.

Preference share capital is similar to loan capital in so far as both offer investors a fixed rate of return. However, preference share capital is a far less popular form of fixed-return capital than loan capital. An important reason for this is that dividends paid to preference shareholders are not allowable against the taxable profits of the business, whereas interest paid to lenders is allowable. From the perspective of the ordinary shareholders, it is preferable for prior claims to be allowable against taxation as this will leave a larger residual amount for them.

In the following chapter we shall look at the role of the Stock Exchange in raising share capital and the methods used by larger businesses to make share issues.

Loans and debentures

Most businesses rely on loans, as well as share capital, to finance operations. Lenders enter into a contract with the business in which the rate of interest, dates of interest payments, capital repayments and security for the loan are clearly stated. This means that if a business is successful, the lenders will not benefit from this success beyond the fact that their claim will become more secure. If, on the other hand, the business experiences financial difficulties, the lenders may receive less than the terms of their contract with the business.

The major risk facing those who invest in loan capital is that the business will default on interest payments and capital repayments. To protect themselves against this risk, lenders often seek some form of **security** from the business. This may take the form of assets pledged either by a **fixed charge** on particular assets held by the business, or a **floating charge**, which 'hovers' over the whole of the business's assets. A floating charge will cease to 'hover' and become fixed on particular assets in the event the business defaults on its obligations.

Activity 6.4

What do you think is the advantage for the business of having a floating charge rather than a fixed charge on its assets?

A floating charge on assets will allow the managers of the business greater flexibility in their day-to-day operations than a fixed charge. Assets can be traded without reference to the lenders.

Not all assets will be acceptable to investors as a form of security. Assets to be pledged must normally be non-perishable, be capable of being sold easily and be fairly high in value relative to their size. (Freehold land and premises normally meet these criteria and so are often favoured by lenders.) The availability of asset-based security means that lenders, in the event of default, have the right to seize the assets pledged and sell these in order to obtain the amount owing. Any amounts remaining from the proceeds of the sale, after the investors' claims have been satisfied, will be returned to the business. In some cases, security offered by the borrower may take the form of a personal guarantee by the owners of the business or, perhaps, some third party.

→   Lenders may seek further protection through the use of **loan covenants**. These are obligations, or restrictions, on the business that form part of the loan contract. Such covenants may impose:

- the right of lenders to receive particular financial reports concerning the business;
- an obligation to insure the assets that are offered as security;
- a restriction on the right to issue further loan capital without prior permission of the existing lenders;
- a restriction on the ability of the managers of the business to sell certain assets held;
- a restriction on the level of dividend payments or level of payments made to directors;
- minimum acceptable levels of liquidity or maximum acceptable levels of gearing.

Any breach of these restrictive covenants can have serious consequences for the business. The lender may demand immediate repayment of the loan in the event of a material breach. Real World 6.1 provides an example of one well-known business that warned investors of the risk that it would breach its loan covenants because it was in financial difficulty.

REAL WORLD 6.1

Bulmer warns of breach of covenants   FT

HP Bulmer, the cidermaker crippled by over-ambitious expansion plans, yesterday admitted for the first time that the new management might have to put up a 'for sale' sign.

The company, which leads the UK cider market with its Strongbow brand, also warned that deteriorating trading conditions might lead to a breach of its banking covenants in April.

But Miles Templeman, chief executive, said he was fully aware of the reality of the situation when he took up the post at the beginning of this month. His appointment followed the loss of the former chief executive and finance director as the company's problems unfolded.

'It may have got a little worse,' said Mr Templeman. 'But I still believe this is a good business and it is better for us to turn it round and build the value back in ourselves.'

In a statement on its working capital requirements, the company said that October and November had been difficult months for sales of its cider to pub-goers in the UK. At the same time the decision to quit the international businesses and to stop product innovation was proving more expensive than previously estimated.

In addition, margins in the take-home trade were still being squeezed, and the loss of a third-party contract for packing at the company's Belgian plant had cost £800,000. As a result, the company, which only in November announced that it had agreed new financing arrangements with its banks until November this year, was at risk of breaching its covenants.

Mr Templeman said the board would be examining all options, including initiating talks with potential buyers if necessary. It would also consider selling the Beer Seller, the company's wholesale business that specialises in supplies to independent pubs and restaurants, or a rights issue.

Regarded as an expert on brands, Mr Templeman wants to focus on the UK cider business, particularly Strongbow. Bulmer has about two-thirds of the UK market, and also owns Woodpecker and Scrumpy Jack.

Source: 'Bulmer warns of breach of covenants', *Financial Times*, 25 January 2003.

The use of security and loan covenants can significantly lower the risk to which lenders are exposed and may make the difference between a successful and an unsuccessful issue of loan capital. They can also lower the cost of loan capital to the business as the required rate of return for lenders will vary according to the perceived level of risk of a business defaulting on its obligations.

It is possible for a business to issue loan capital that is subordinated to (that is, ranked below) other loan capital already in issue. This means that holders of this form of loan capital will not receive interest payments or capital repayments until the claims of senior loan holders (that is, lenders ranked above the subordinated lenders) have been satisfied. Any restrictive covenants imposed by senior loan holders relating to the issue of further loan capital will often ignore the issue of **subordinated loans** as this should not pose a threat to their claims. Holders of subordinated loans will normally expect to be compensated for the higher risks involved by a higher level of interest payment than that given to senior loan holders.

Term loans

One common form of long-term loan is the **term loan**. This type of loan is offered by banks and other financial institutions, and is usually tailored to the needs of the client business. The amount of the loan, the time period, the repayment terms and the interest payable are all open to negotiation and agreement, which can be very useful. For example, where all of the funds to be borrowed are not required immediately, a business may agree with the lender that funds are drawn only as and when required. This means that interest will be paid only on amounts drawn and the business will not have to pay interest on amounts borrowed that are temporarily surplus to requirements. Term loans tend to be cheap to set up (from the borrower business's perspective) and can be quite flexible as to conditions.

Debentures

Another form of long-term loan finance is the **debenture**. This is simply a loan that is evidenced by a trust deed. The debenture loan is frequently divided into units (rather like share capital), and investors are invited to purchase the number of units they require. The debenture loan may be redeemable or irredeemable. Debentures of public limited companies are often traded on the Stock Exchange, and their listed value will fluctuate according to the fortunes of the business, movements in interest rates and so on.

Mortgages

A **mortgage** is a form of loan that is secured on an asset, typically freehold property. Financial institutions such as banks, insurance businesses and pension funds are often prepared to lend to businesses on this basis. The mortgage may be over a long period (20 years or more).

Eurobonds

Eurobonds are unsecured loan stocks issued by listed businesses (and other large organisations) in various countries, and the finance is raised on an international basis.

A distinguishing feature of eurobonds is that they are denominated in a currency other than the home currency of the business that issued them. Thus, for example, a UK business may issue a eurobond that is denominated in US dollars. (It is quite common for eurobonds to be issued in US dollars, although they may also be issued in other major currencies.) They are bearer bonds (that is, the owner of the bond is not registered and the holder of the bond certificate is regarded as the owner) and interest is normally paid (without deduction of tax) on an annual basis.

Eurobonds are part of an emerging international capital market and they are not subject to regulations imposed by authorities in particular countries. This may explain, in part, the fact that the cost of servicing eurobonds is usually lower than the cost of similar domestic **bonds**. Numerous financial institutions throughout the world have created a market for eurobonds, where holders of eurobonds are able to sell them to would-be holders. Eurobonds are usually issued by the issuing business and are made available to large banks and other financial institutions, which may either retain them as an investment or sell them to their clients.

The extent of borrowing, by UK businesses, in currencies other than sterling has expanded hugely in recent years. Businesses are often attracted to eurobonds because of the size of the international capital market. Access to a large number of international investors is likely to increase the chances of a successful issue. In addition, the lack of regulation in the eurobond market means that national restrictions regarding loan issues may be overcome.

Real World 6.2, which is an extract from an article in the *Financial Times*, provides an example of a eurobond issue by a well-known UK business.

REAL WORLD 6.2

Taking off with eurobonds FT

A growing number of companies are entering the eurobond market for the first time, encouraged by the opportunity to reach new investors with low financing costs . . . This week BAA, the operator of Heathrow and six other airports in the UK, raised €750m ($913m) from its first euro-denominated bond . . .

'This deal gave the company access to capital at a similar cost to what it could have done in sterling,' said Jean-Marc Mercier at HSBC's corporate syndicate desk, which managed the deal with BNP Paribas and Deutsche Bank.

'In addition, two-thirds of the investors in the deal were new to the company,' he added.

Diversifying the investor base is important for companies, as it increases their flexibility to raise capital when they need to.

Source: 'New appetite develops for eurobonds', *Financial Times*, 18 September 2004.

Activity 6.5

Both loan capital and preference shares provide fixed returns to investors. Would you expect the returns to loan capital to be higher or lower than those to preference shares?

Investors will normally view loans as being less risky than preference shares. Lenders have priority over any claims from preference shareholders, and will usually have security for their loans. As a result of the lower level of risk associated with this form of investment, investors are usually prepared to accept a lower rate of return.

The risk/return characteristics of loan, preference share and ordinary share finance are shown graphically in Figure 6.2.

| Figure 6.2 | The risk/return characteristics of long-term sources of finance |

The higher the level of risk associated with a particular form of long-term finance, the higher will be the expected returns from investors. Ordinary shares are the most risky and have the highest expected return and, as a general rule, loan capital is the least risky and has the lowest expected return.

Deep discount bonds

A business may issue redeemable loan capital that offers a rate of interest below the market rate. Such loans are issued at a discount to their redeemable value and are referred to as **deep discount bonds**. Thus, a business may issue loan capital at, say, £80 for every £100 of nominal value. In some cases, the loan capital may have a zero rate of interest. These are referred to as **zero coupon bonds**. Although lenders will receive little or no interest during the period of the loan, they will receive a gain when the loan is finally redeemed at the full £100. The redemption yield, as it is referred to, is often quite high and, when calculated on an annual basis, may compare favourably with returns from other forms of loan capital with the same level of risk.

Deep discount bonds may have particular appeal to businesses with short-term cash flow problems. They receive an immediate injection of cash and there are no significant cash outflows associated with the loan until the maturity date. From an investment perspective, the situation is reversed. Deep discount bonds are likely to appeal to investors who do not have short-term cash flow needs since a large part of the return is received on maturity of the loan. However, deep discount bonds can often be traded on the stock market if required, which will not affect the borrower but will enable the lender to obtain cash.

Convertible loans

A **convertible loan** (or debenture) gives an investor the right to convert a loan into ordinary shares at a given future date and at a specified price. The investor remains a lender to the business and will receive interest on the amount of the loan until such time as the conversion takes place. The investor is not obliged to convert the loan or debenture to ordinary shares. This will be done only if the market price of the shares at the conversion date exceeds the agreed conversion price.

An investor may find this form of investment a useful 'hedge' against risk (that is, it can reduce the level of risk). This may be particularly useful when investment in a new business is being considered. Initially, the investment is in the form of a loan and regular interest payments will be made. If the business is successful, the investor can then decide to convert the investment into ordinary shares.

A business may also find this form of financing useful. If the business is successful the loan becomes self-liquidating as investors will exercise their option to convert and there will be no redemption costs. The business may also be able to offer a lower rate of interest to investors because they expect future benefits to arise from the conversion. However, there will be some dilution of control and possibly a dilution of earnings for existing shareholders if holders of convertible loans exercise their option to convert. (Dilution of earnings available to shareholders will not automatically occur as a result of the conversion of loan capital to share capital. There will be a saving in interest charges that will have an offsetting effect.)

Real World 6.3 sets out details of one particular convertible loan issue.

REAL WORLD 6.3

The answer is blowin' in the wind

In June 2003, Scottish Power plc issued convertible bonds to help finance research into new methods of creating energy, including the development of wind farms. The business initially intended to raise $575m (£343m) from the issue, but the popularity of the bonds among investors allowed the business to raise $700m (£420m). The bonds were sold to specialist investors, mostly financial institutions. The investors can convert the bonds into 90 million ordinary shares in the future, which represent 5 per cent of Scottish Power's total share capital. Thus, there will not be a significant dilution of control for existing share-holders if the bonds are converted. The share price at which the bonds may be converted is 460 pence and, at the time of the issue, the market price of Scottish Power's shares was 372 pence.

Source: 'Generating cash from bonds', *Accountancy Age*, 17 July 2003, p. 7.

Measuring the riskiness of loan capital

A number of credit-rating agencies, including Moody's Investor Services and Standard and Poor Corporation (S&P), place loan capital issued by businesses into categories according to the level of default risk: the lower the risk of default, the higher the rating category assigned to the loan. The ratings used by the two leading agencies mentioned earlier are very similar and are set out below (see **Real World 6.4**). To arrive at an appropriate loan, or debt, rating, an agency will rely on the use of both published and unpublished information, interviews with key executives and visits to the business's premises. The rating classification assigned to the debt will be derived from an assessment of all the relevant information obtained.

REAL WORLD 6.4

The main debt-rating categories of two leading credit-rating agencies

Standard and Poor's	Moody's Investor Services	
AAA	Aaa	The lowest risk category. Lenders are well protected as the business has a strong capacity to pay the principal and interest.
AA	Aa	High quality debt. Slightly smaller capacity to pay than the earlier category.
A	A	Good capacity to pay the principal and interest but the business may be more susceptible to adverse effects of changing circumstances and economic conditions.
BBB	Baa	Medium quality debt. There is adequate capacity to pay the amounts due.
BB	Ba	Speculative aspects of the debt. Future capacity is not assured.
B	B	More speculative elements than the category above.
CCC	Caa	Poor quality debt. Interest or capital may be at risk.
CC	Ca	Poorer quality debt than the category above. The business is often in default.
C	C	Lowest quality debt. No interest is being paid and the prospects for the future are poor.

These are the main categories of debt rating used; there are also sub-categories.

Source: Adapted from Benninga, S. Z. and Sarig, O. H., *Corporate Finance: A valuation approach*, McGraw-Hill, 1997, p. 341. Copyright © 1997 The McGraw-Hill Companies, Inc.

Once debt has been assigned to a particular category, it will tend to remain in that category unless there is a significant change in circumstances.

Junk bonds (high yield bonds)

Loan capital falling within any of the first four categories identified in Real World 6.4 is generally considered to be of high quality (investment grade) and some financial institutions are restricted by their rules to investing only in these loan categories. Loan capital rated below these first four categories is often given the rather disparaging name of **junk bonds**. In many cases, loan capital with a junk bond rating started life with a high rating but, because the business had suffered misfortune, it had been downgraded. (Such a business is known as a 'fallen angel'.)

Activity 6.6

Does it really matter if the loan capital of a business is downgraded to 'junk' bond status?

A downgrade to 'junk' bond status is usually regarded as serious as it may well increase the cost of capital. Investors are likely to seek higher returns to compensate for the perceived increase in default risk.

Real World 6.5 describes the downgrading of the loan capital of one well-known UK business to junk bond status and the reaction of its management to this news.

REAL WORLD 6.5

Warning: low-flying airline   FT

Shares in British Airways dropped 6 per cent on Tuesday afternoon after Standard & Poor's downgraded the airline's long-term corporate credit rating to 'junk', triggering an angry response from the airline.

BA shares were down $8\frac{1}{2}$p to 143p in afternoon trade in London.

The credit rating agency downgraded the corporate rating to BB+ from BBB– and the carrier's long-term unsecured debt rating to BB– from BB+. The move follows a review to assess the group's creditworthiness in the wake of the war in Iraq and the outbreak of Sars.

Bob Ukiah, analyst at S&P, said: 'As a result of the more challenging industry environment, Standard & Poor's believes that British Airways' financial profile and credit measures are no longer, nor are likely to be, over the next several years, appropriate for an investment-grade rating.'

S&P said the rating reflected the group's high financial leverage (gearing), the need for additional pensions' contributions, competition in its core markets as well as its heavy exposure on the key North Atlantic route.

John Rishton, BA's chief financial officer, responded angrily to the downgrade, saying: 'I am astonished that Standard & Poor's has chosen to downgrade us at this time,' adding that since the last review 'we have exceeded all of our financial and restructuring targets under our Future Size and Shape programme and only last week Moody's confirmed its rating for the company and its debt.'

Tuesday's move comes in spite of recent efforts by BA to reduce costs in the face of a recent deterioration in its financial profile.

In May, BA said it had moved from a loss to a profit in the year to the end of March, climbing from a pre-tax loss of £200m the year before, its worst result in 20 years, to a pre-tax profit of £135m. Analysts attributed the airline's recovery to the fact BA started cost-cutting and restructuring measures earlier than some of its rivals. The restructuring, which started just before September 11, is on target to cut 13,000 jobs by September.

Mr Ukiah did, however, say on Tuesday that: 'British Airways should be able to improve its financial position, despite the challenges and uncertain outlook of the industry . . . This should allow it to achieve credit ratios appropriate for the revised ratings over the next year or two.'

Source: 'S&P cuts British Airways to "junk" status', www.FTcom, 1 July 2003.

In addition to increasing the cost of capital, a downgrade to junk bond status can adversely affect business relationships. Real World 6.6 describes the possible risks for a major IT business of a downgrade and the efforts made by its managers to avoid this fate.

REAL WORLD 6.6

EDS warns of dividend cut   **FT**

Electronic Data Systems yesterday warned it might cut its dividends as part of efforts to improve its financial position by about $1bn and avoid a downgrade to junk bond status.

The move comes as the world's second-largest IT outsourcing company is trying to execute a large turnround plan and position itself for growth. If it were to lose its investment grade rating it would hamper its efforts to win new business.

In documents filed with the SEC, the group said dividends could be cut by about two-thirds this year. It is also considering selling equity or equity-linked securities to raise capital.

Earlier this year, EDS had been placed under review for downgrade by leading credit ratings agencies.

Although EDS said a downgrade to junk status would not materially affect its current business relationships, it could raise its cost of capital.

A downgrade would also make it more challenging to win outsourcing contracts, which usually run between five and ten years. It has to prove to customers that it has capital resources for such long-term projects. EDS is competing against aggressive and well-capitalised competitors such as IBM and Hewlett-Packard.

Source: 'EDS warns of a dividend cut', *Financial Times*, 11 May 2004.

Not all junk bonds start life as investment-grade securities. Since the 1980s, loan capital with an initial low rating has been issued by some US businesses. This type of loan capital provides investors with high interest rates to compensate for the high level of default risk. Businesses that issue junk bonds are usually less financially stable than those offering investment-grade bonds and may offer lower levels of security and weaker loan covenants than those normally associated with standard loan agreements. As junk bonds provide relatively high levels of returns to investors, they are also referred to as *high yield bonds*.

Junk bonds, or high yield bonds, became very popular in the USA as they allowed some businesses to raise finance that was not available from other sources. Within a fairly short space of time, a market for this form of borrowing developed. Although junk bonds are used by many businesses to finance everyday needs such as investment in stocks, debtors and non-current assets, they came to the attention of the public through their use in financing hostile takeovers. In some cases, a small business would take on very high levels of gearing through the use of junk bonds in order to finance a takeover of a larger business. Once the takeover was achieved, non-core assets of the larger business would often be sold off in order to repay the junk bond holders.

The junk bond market in the USA has enjoyed a brief but turbulent history. There have been allegations of market manipulation, the collapse of a leading market maker and periods when default levels on junk bonds have been very high. Although such events have shaken investor confidence, the market has proved more resilient than many had expected and junk bonds are again enjoying a period of popularity. Nevertheless, there is always the risk that, in a difficult economic climate, investors will make a 'flight to quality' and the junk bond market will become illiquid.

In Europe, junk bonds have not enjoyed the same degree of popularity among investors: the European market is approximately one-tenth of the size of the US market. Perhaps this is because European investors tend to view ordinary shares as a high-risk/

high-return investment and view loan capital as a form of low-risk/low-return investment. Junk bonds are a hybrid form of investment lying somewhere between ordinary shares and conventional loan capital. It could be argued that this type of investment is not really necessary as investors could achieve the same result by holding a balanced portfolio of ordinary shares and conventional loan capital.

Activity 6.7

We have considered two major forms of long-term finance: preference shares and loan capital. Both forms of finance require the business to provide a particular rate of return to investors. What are the factors that may be taken into account by a business when deciding between these two sources of finance?

The main factors are as follows:

- Preference shares have a higher rate of return than loan capital. From the investors' point of view, preference shares are more risky. The amount invested cannot be secured and the return is paid after the returns paid to lenders.
- A business has a legal obligation to pay interest and make capital repayments on loans at the agreed dates. It will usually make every effort to meet its obligations, as failure to do so can have serious consequences, as mentioned earlier. Failure to pay a preference dividend, on the other hand, is less important. There is no legal obligation to pay if profits are not available for distribution. Although failure to pay a preference dividend may prove an embarrassment for the business, and may make it difficult to persuade investors to take up future preference share issues, the preference shareholders will have no redress against the business if there are insufficient profits to pay the dividend due.
- It was mentioned above that the UK taxation system permits interest on loans to be deducted from profits for taxation purposes whereas preference dividends cannot. As a result, the cost of servicing loan capital is usually much less than the cost of servicing preference shares.
- The issue of loan capital may result in the management of a business having to accept some restrictions on its freedom of action. We have seen that loan agreements often contain covenants that can be onerous. However, no such restrictions can be imposed by preference shareholders.

A further point that has not been dealt with so far is that preference shares issued form part of the permanent capital base of the business. If they are redeemed, the law requires that they be replaced, either by a new issue of shares or by a transfer from reserves, in order to ensure that the capital base of the business stays intact. However, loan capital is not viewed, in law, as part of the permanent capital base of the business and, therefore, there is no legal requirement to replace any loan capital that has been redeemed.

Public issues of ordinary shares, preference shares and loan stocks

Real World 6.7 provides an impression of the relative importance of the three principal types of securities: ordinary shares, preference shares and loan capital.

REAL WORLD 6.7

New issues by listed businesses

Figure 6.3 plots the issues of capital made by UK-listed businesses (excluding financial businesses such as banks) in recent years. The chart reveals that loan capital and ordinary shares are the major sources of long-term external finance. Preference shares are a much less important source of new finance.

| Figure 6.3 | Capital issues by UK Stock Exchange listed businesses (excluding financial businesses), 1993–2002 |

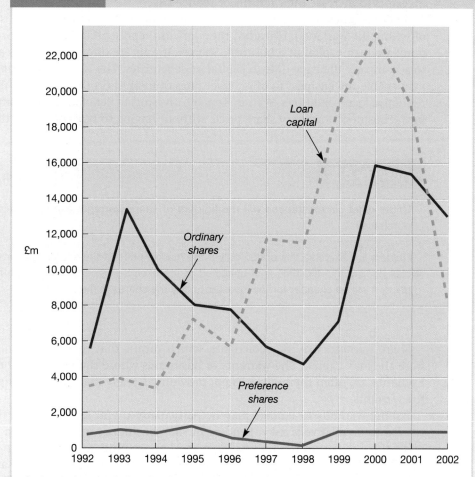

At times, the popularity of ordinary shares and that of loan capital seem to move counter to one another. When ordinary shares are popular, loan capital is unpopular, and vice versa. This tends to reflect the level of interest rates and business confidence. However, in recent years, ordinary share issues and loan capital issues have both moved in the same direction. Preference shares have dwindled to virtually nothing, in terms of new issues. The chart, of course, is not the whole story. Most finance from ordinary shareholders comes from profit retentions rather than share issues. In addition, bank loans are not included.

Source: *Financial Statistics*, Office for National Statistics, October 2004. Copyright © 2004 Crown copyright. Reproduced with the permission of the Controller of HMSO.

Warrants

→ Holders of **warrants** have the right, but not the obligation, to acquire ordinary shares in a business at a given price (the 'exercise' price). In the case of both convertible loan capital and warrants, the price at which shares may be acquired is usually higher than the market price of those ordinary shares at the time of issue. The warrant will usually state the number of shares that the holder may purchase and the time limit within which the option to buy shares can be exercised. Occasionally, perpetual warrants are issued that have no set time limits. Warrants do not confer voting rights or entitle the holders to make any claims on the assets of the business. They are neither shares nor

→ loan stocks and represent a form of **financial derivative**. A financial derivative is any form of financial instrument, based on share or loan capital, that can be used by investors to increase their returns or reduce risk.

To the business issuing the warrants, they represent a source of funds (the proceeds of selling the warrants). However, they can also represent an incentive for investors to purchase loan capital in a business. Share warrants are often provided as a 'sweetener' to accompany the issue of loan capital or debentures. The issue of warrants in this way may enable the business to offer lower rates of interest on the loan or to negotiate less restrictive loan conditions. Warrants enable investors to benefit from any future increases in the business's ordinary share price, without having to buy the shares themselves.

Activity 6.8

Under what circumstances will the holders of share warrants exercise their option to purchase?

···

Holders will exercise this option only if the market price of the shares exceeds the exercise price within the time limit specified. If the exercise price is higher than the market price, it will be cheaper for the investor to buy the shares in the market.

Share warrants may be detachable, which means that they can be sold separately from the loan capital. The warrants of businesses whose shares are listed on the Stock Exchange are often themselves listed, providing a ready market for buying and selling the warrants.

Issuing warrants to lenders may be particularly useful for businesses that are considered to be relatively risky. Lenders in such businesses may feel that a new project offers them opportunities for loss but no real opportunity to participate in any 'upside' potential from the risks undertaken. By issuing share warrants, lenders are given the opportunity to participate in future gains, which may make them more prepared to support risky projects.

Warrants have a gearing element, which means that changes in the value of the underlying shares can lead to a disproportionate change in value of the warrants. This makes them a speculative form of investment. To illustrate this gearing element, suppose that a share had a current market price of £2.50 and that an investor was able to exercise an immediate option to purchase a single share in the business at £2.00. The value of the warrant, in theory, would be £0.50 (that is, £2.50 − £2.00). Let us further suppose that the price of the share rose by 10 per cent to £2.75 before the warrant option was exercised. The value of the warrant would now rise to £0.75 (that is, £2.75 – £2.00), which represents a 50 per cent increase in value. This gearing effect can, of course, operate in the opposite direction as well.

It is probably worth mentioning the difference in status within a business between holders of convertible loan capital and holders of loans with share warrants attached if both groups decide to exercise their right to convert. Convertible loan holders become ordinary shareholders and are no longer lenders to the business. They will have used the value of the loans to 'buy' the shares. Warrant holders become ordinary shareholders by paying cash for the shares. If the warrant holders held loans as well, then their status as lenders is unaffected by exercising their right to buy the shares bestowed by the warrant. Thus they become both ordinary shareholders of and lenders to the business.

Both convertible loans and warrants are examples of financial derivatives.

Interest rates and interest rate risk

→ Interest rates on loan finance may be either floating or fixed. A **floating interest rate** means that the required rate of return from lenders will rise and fall with market rates of interest. (However, it is possible for a floating rate loan to be issued that sets a maximum rate of interest and/or a minimum rate of interest payable.) The market value of the lender's investment in the business is likely to remain fairly stable over time.

→ The converse will normally be true for loans and debentures with **fixed interest rates**. The interest payments will remain unchanged with rises and falls in market rates of interest but the value of the loan investment will fall when interest rates rise, and will rise when interest rates fall.

Activity 6.9

Why do you think the value of fixed-interest loan capital will rise and fall with rises and falls in interest rates?

This is because investors will be prepared to pay less for loan capital that pays a rate of interest below the market rate of interest and will be prepared to pay more for loan capital that pays a rate of interest above the market rate of interest.

Movements in interest rates can be a significant issue for businesses that have high levels of borrowing. A business with a floating rate of interest may find that interest rate rises will place real strains on cash flows and profitability. Conversely, a business that has a fixed rate of interest will find that, when interest rates are falling, it will not enjoy the benefits of lower interest charges. To reduce or eliminate these risks, a busi-

→ ness may enter into a **hedging arrangement**. This is an attempt to reduce or eliminate risk by taking some form of counteraction.

To hedge against the risk of interest rate movements, various devices may be

→ employed: One popular device is the **interest rate swap**. This is an arrangement between two businesses whereby each business assumes responsibility for the other's interest payments. Typically, it involves a business with a floating interest rate loan swapping interest payment obligations with a business with a fixed interest rate loan. A swap agreement can be undertaken through direct negotiations with another business, but it is usually easier to negotiate through a bank or other financial inter-mediary. Although there is an agreement to swap interest payments, the legal respons-ibility for these payments will still rest with the business that entered into the original loan agreement. Thus, the borrowing business may continue to make interest payments to the lender in line with the loan agreement. However, at the end of an agreed period, the two parties to the swap agreement will make a compensating cash adjustment between themselves.

A swap agreement can be a useful hedging device where there are different views concerning future movements in interest rates. For example, a business with a floating rate agreement may believe that interest rates are going to rise, whereas a business with a fixed rate agreement may believe that interest rates are going to fall. However, swap agreements may also be used to exploit imperfections in the capital markets. It is some-times the case that one business has an advantage over another when negotiating interest rates for a fixed loan agreement, but would prefer a floating loan agreement, whereas the other business is in the opposite position. When this occurs, both busi-nesses can benefit from a swap agreement.

Real World 6.8 sets out the policies of two large businesses towards dealing with interest rate risk.

REAL WORLD 6.8

Dealing with interest rate risk

Associated British Ports plc is the largest ports operator in the UK. Its policy towards inter-est rate risk is as follows:

> Risks arising from changes in interest rates are managed by maintaining an appropriate balance between fixed and floating rate debt. At the end of the year 70 per cent of the group's borrowings were fixed (2002: 68 per cent) the group uses derivative instruments, such as interest rate swaps, when appropriate to hedge against changes in interest rates and to adjust the balance between fixed and floating rate debt.

Source: Annual Report and Accounts 2003.

Bovis Homes plc is a major UK house builder. Its policy towards interest risk is as follows:

> By fixing £75.0 million of borrowings through interest rate swaps with varying maturities, the Group has made certain its interest costs on what is considered its core borrowing requirement. Borrowings in addition to those core borrowings are judged on a case by case basis at the time of drawing down the loans in terms of interest rate flexibility and loan maturity.

Source: Annual Report and Accounts 2003.

Finance leases

Instead of buying an asset, such as a piece of equipment, direct from a supplier, a busi-ness may arrange for another business (typically a financial institution such as a bank) to buy it and then lease it to the business. The business that purchases the asset and leases it out is known as a 'lessor' and the business that leases the asset is known as the 'lessee'.

→   A **finance lease**, as such an arrangement is known, is in essence a form of lending. This is because, had the lessee borrowed the funds and then used them to buy the asset itself, the effect would be much the same. The lessee would have use of the asset but would also have a financial obligation to the lender – just as with a leasing arrangement.

Although with finance leasing, legal ownership of the asset remains with the financial institution (the lessor), a finance lease agreement transfers to the user (the lessee) virtually all the rewards and risks that are associated with the item being leased. The finance lease agreement covers a significant part of the life of the item being leased and, often, cannot be cancelled. Real World 6.9 gives an example of the use of finance leasing by British Airways plc.

REAL WORLD 6.9

Finance leasing at British Airways

Many airline businesses use finance leasing as a means of acquiring new aeroplanes. The financial statements for British Airways plc for the year ended 31 March 2004 reveal that approximately 32 per cent (totalling £2,247 million) of the net book value of its fleet of aircraft had been acquired through this method.

Source: Annual Report and Accounts 2004.

→   A finance lease can be contrasted with an **operating lease** where the rewards and risks of ownership stay with the owner and where the lease is short term. An example of an operating lease is where a builder hires some earth-moving equipment for a week to carry out a particular job.

Over the years, some important benefits associated with finance leasing have disappeared. Changes in the tax laws no longer make it such a tax-efficient form of financing, and changes in accounting disclosure requirements no longer make it possible to conceal this form of 'borrowing' from investors. Nevertheless, the popularity of finance leases has continued. Other reasons must, therefore, exist for businesses to adopt this form of financing. These reasons are said to include the following:

- *Ease of borrowing.*   Leasing may be obtained more easily than other forms of long-term finance. Lenders normally require some form of security and a profitable track record before making advances to a business. However, a lessor may be prepared to lease assets to a new business without a track record and to use the leased assets as security for the amounts owing.
- *Cost.*   Leasing agreements may be offered at reasonable cost. As the asset leased is used as security, standard lease arrangements can be applied and detailed credit checking of lessees may be unnecessary. This can reduce administration costs for the lessor and, thereby, help in providing competitive lease rentals.
- *Flexibility.*   Leasing can help provide flexibility where there are rapid changes in technology. If an option to cancel can be incorporated into the lease, the business may be able to exercise this option and invest in new technology as it becomes available. This will help the business to avoid the risk of obsolescence.

● *Cash flows.* Leasing, rather than purchasing an asset outright, means that large cash outflows can be avoided. The leasing option allows cash outflows to be smoothed out over the asset's life. In some cases, it is possible to arrange for low lease payments to be made in the early years of the asset's life, when cash inflows may be low, and for these to increase over time as the asset generates positive cash flows.

Real World 6.10 provides some impression of the importance of finance leasing over recent years.

REAL WORLD 6.10

The importance of finance leasing in the UK

Figure 6.4 charts the growth in the value of finance leasing in the UK over the years 1999 to 2003.

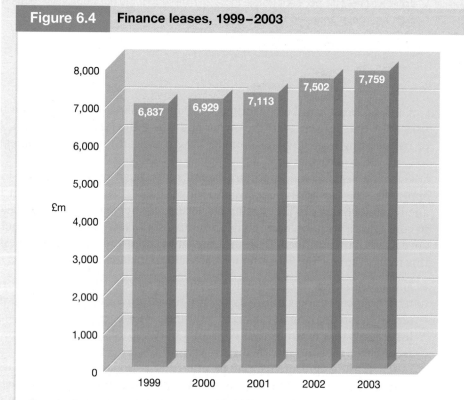

| Figure 6.4 | Finance leases, 1999–2003 |

Over the five-year period, there has been a steady increase in the amount of finance leasing. Overall, the increase was around 13 per cent.

Source: Chart constructed from data published by the Finance and Leasing Association (www.fla.org.uk). Copyright © 2003 Finance and Leasing Association.

Sale-and-leaseback arrangements

→ A **sale-and-leaseback** arrangement involves a business raising finance by selling an asset to a financial institution. The sale is accompanied by an agreement to lease the asset back to the business to allow it to continue to use the asset. The lease payment is a business expense that is allowable against profits for taxation purposes.

Freehold property is often the asset that is the subject of such an arrangement. When this is the case, there are usually rent reviews at regular intervals throughout the period of the lease, and the amounts payable in future years may be difficult to predict. At the end of the lease agreement, the business must either try to renew the lease or find alternative premises. Although the sale of the premises will result in an immediate injection of cash for the business, it will lose benefits from any future capital appreciation on the property. Where a capital gain arises on the sale of the premises to the financial institution, a liability for taxation may also arise.

A sale-and-leaseback agreement can be used to help a business focus on its core competences. Real World 6.11 reveals how sale-and-leaseback agreements can help hotel businesses to become hotel operators rather than a hotel operators and owners.

REAL WORLD 6.11

Rooms to manoeuvre
FT

Travelodge, the UK budget hotel operator owned by Permira, the venture capital firm, is to raise £400m via a sale and leaseback of 136 of its freehold properties.

The deal will see Travelodge dispose of its entire freehold estate, the first time a UK hotel operator has attempted such a move. The group has appointed CB Richard Ellis, the hotel and property consultancy, to manage the process. Thirty potential buyers have been targeted.

Sale and leasebacks were popular a few years ago with hotel operators ranging from Hilton to Le Meridien opting to sell their assets to release capital and then lease them back.

But, while several operators continue to be asset-heavy, the popularity of the financing mechanism appeared to have waned. The Travelodge deal will be the first significant sale and leaseback this year once completed.

Grant Hearn, the chain's chief executive, said in an interview with the *Financial Times* that the proceeds from the sale would be used to pay down debt. The group is still looking to buy new hotels but will take on any new properties on a leasehold basis. 'I suppose we are being opportunistic and taking advantage of buoyant property prices,' he said. 'CB Richard Ellis has told us there's £8bn chasing property at the moment. It doesn't make any sense for us to hang on to it.'

It is unclear which groups will invest in the scheme but there are several property funds and banks with an interest in acquiring freehold hotels that deliver regular yields.

Hilton Group raised more than £335m two years ago when it sold 10 of its UK hotels to a limited partnership vehicle that included Bank of Scotland.

Royal Bank of Scotland has also invested heavily in hotel purchases, buying 10 properties from Hilton in 2001 and leasing them back to the operator. In the same year the Scottish bank acquired 12 Le Meridien hotels for £1.25bn and leased them back to the upmarket hotel brand.

Travelodge has an aggressive development plan and aims to open a new hotel every 10 days during the next 12 months.

Source: 'Travelodge to raise £400m via sale and leaseback plan', *Financial Times*, 12 July 2004.

Securitisation

→ **Securitisation** involves bundling together illiquid financial or physical assets of the same type in order to provide backing for issuing interest-bearing securities, such as bonds. This financing method was first used by US banks, which bundled together residential mortgage loans in order to provide asset backing for the issue of bonds to investors. (Mortgage loans held by a bank are financial assets that offer future benefits to the bank in the form of interest receivable.) The bonds issued were considered to be low risk as they were also backed by a guarantee from the bank. It was therefore possible for a bank to offer lower rates of interest on the bonds issued than on the interest accruing to the mortgage loans, which provided the asset backing.

Securitisation has now spread beyond the banking industry and has become an important source of finance for businesses in a wide range of industries. Future benefits from a variety of illiquid assets are now used as backing for bond issues, including:

- credit card receipts
- water industry charges
- rental income from university accommodation
- ticket sales for football matches
- royalties from music copyright
- consumer instalment contracts
- beer sales to pub tenancies.

The effect of securitisation is to capitalise the claims to these future benefits. This capitalised amount is then sold to investors, through the financial markets, to raise finance for the business holding the claims.

Securitisation usually involves setting up a special-purpose vehicle (SPV) to acquire the bundle of illiquid assets from the business wishing to raise finance. This SPV will then arrange the issue of interest-bearing securities, such as a 10-year fixed rate bond, to investors. The interest to be paid on the securities to be issued will be met by the income generated from the securitised assets. When the securities mature, the amount to be repaid may come from receipts from the securitised assets, assuming maturity dates are co-terminus. In other cases, repayment may come from the issue of new securities or from income generated by the securitised assets in excess of that needed to pay interest charges.

Securitised assets tend to be of good quality with regular and predictable income streams. To reassure investors, however, the assets offered may be higher in value than the securities issued (known as *overcollateralisation*) or some form of credit insurance may be available from a third party, such as a bank.

In addition to being a useful source of finance, a securitisation issue may be used to help manage risk. Where, for example, a bank has lent large amounts to a particular industry sector, it can reduce its exposure to the sector by bundling together some of the outstanding loan contracts and making a securitisation issue.

Real World 6.12 provides an example of a pub and restaurant operator that has securitised the whole of its business.

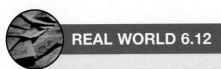

REAL WORLD 6.12

Cheers! **FT**

Mitchells & Butlers, the stock exchange-listed British group which owns All Bar One pubs and Harvester restaurants, priced the largest ever UK pub securitisation yesterday, selling £1.9bn in bonds.

UK investors were the largest buyers of the issue, which consisted of six tranches.

M&B is a managed business, which means its pubs are run by its employees and the main source of revenue is food and drink sales.

Most pub securitisations so far have been backed by revenue from leased or tenanted businesses, where the pubs are operated by independent retailers and the company's main source of cash is rental income and beer sales to the tenant.

Source: 'M&B prices largest UK pub securitisation', *Financial Times*, 7 November 2003.

Short-term sources of external finance

A short-term source of borrowing is one that is available for a short time period. We saw at the beginning of the chapter that, although there is no agreed definition of what 'short term' means, we shall define it as being approximately one year or less. Figure 6.1 revealed that the major sources of short-term external finance are:

● bank overdrafts
● bills of exchange
● debt factoring
● invoice discounting.

Each of these sources is discussed below.

Bank overdrafts

→ A **bank overdraft** enables a business to maintain a negative balance on its bank account. It represents a very flexible form of borrowing as the size of an overdraft can (subject to bank approval) be increased or decreased according to the financing requirements of the business. It is relatively inexpensive to arrange and interest rates are often very competitive. The rate of interest charged on an overdraft will vary, however, according to how creditworthy the customer is perceived to be by the bank. It is also fairly easy to arrange – sometimes an overdraft can be agreed by a telephone call to the bank. In view of these advantages, it is not surprising that this is an extremely popular form of short-term finance.

Banks prefer to grant overdrafts that are self-liquidating, that is, the funds applied will result in cash inflows that will extinguish the overdraft balance. The banks may ask for forecast cash flow statements from the business to see when the overdraft will be repaid and how much finance is required. The bank may also require some form of security on amounts advanced.

One potential drawback with this form of finance is that it is repayable on demand. This may pose problems for a business that is illiquid. However, many businesses operate for many years using an overdraft. This form of borrowing, though in theory regarded as short term, can often become a long-term source of finance.

Bills of exchange

→ A **bill of exchange** is similar, in some respects, to an IOU. It is a written agreement that is addressed by one person to another, requiring the person to whom it is addressed to pay a particular amount at some future date. Bills of exchange are used in trading transactions and are offered by a buyer to a supplier in exchange for goods. The supplier who accepts the bill of exchange may either keep the bill until the date the payment is due (this is usually between 60 and 180 days after the bill is first drawn up) or may present it to a bank for payment. The bank will usually be prepared to pay the supplier the face value of the bill, less a discount, and will then collect the full amount of the bill from the buyer at the specified payment date. The advantage of using a bill of exchange is that it allows the buyer to delay payment for the goods purchased but provides the supplier with an opportunity to receive immediate payment from a bank if required. Nowadays, bills of exchange are not widely used for trading transactions within the UK, but they are still used for overseas trading.

Debt factoring

→ **Debt factoring** is a service offered by a financial institution known as a factor. Many of the large factors are subsidiaries of commercial banks. Debt factoring involves the factor taking over the debt collection for a business. In addition to operating normal credit control procedures, a factor may offer to undertake credit investigations and advise on the creditworthiness of customers. It may also offer protection for approved credit sales. Two main forms of factoring agreement exist:

● *Recourse factoring*, where the factor assumes no responsibility for bad debts arising from credit sales.
● *Non-recourse factoring*, where, for an additional fee, the factor assumes responsibility for bad debts up to an agreed amount.

The factor is usually prepared to make an advance to the business of up to around 80 per cent of approved trade debtors (although it can sometimes be as high as 90 per cent). This advance is usually paid immediately after the goods have been supplied to the customer. The balance of the debt, less any deductions for fees and interest, will be paid after an agreed period or when the debt is collected. The charge made for the factoring service is based on total turnover and is often around 2–3 per cent of turnover. Any advances made to the business by the factor will attract a rate of interest similar to the rate charged on bank overdrafts.

Debt factoring is, in effect, outsourcing the trade debtors control to a specialist subcontractor. Many businesses find a factoring arrangement very convenient. It can result in savings in credit management and can create more certain cash flows. It can also release the time of key personnel for more profitable ends. This may be extremely important for smaller businesses that rely on the talent and skills of a few key individuals. In addition, the level of finance available will rise 'spontaneously' with the level of sales. The business can decide how much of the finance available is required and can use only that which it needs. However, there is a possibility that some will see a factoring arrangement as an indication that the business is experiencing financial difficulties. This may have an adverse effect on confidence in the business. For this reason, some businesses try to conceal the factoring arrangement by collecting outstanding debts on behalf of the factor.

Not all businesses will find factoring arrangements the answer to their financing problems. Factoring agreements may not be possible to arrange for very small businesses (those with a turnover of, say, less than £100,000) because of the high set-up costs. In addition, businesses engaged in certain sectors such as retailers or building contractors, where trade disputes are part of the business culture, may find that factoring arrangements are simply not available.

Figure 6.5 shows the factoring process diagrammatically.

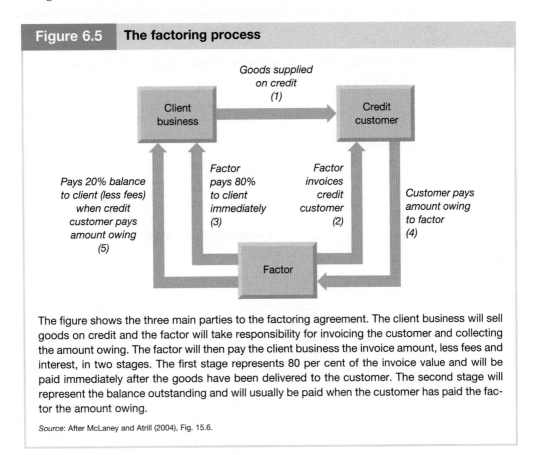

| Figure 6.5 | **The factoring process** |

The figure shows the three main parties to the factoring agreement. The client business will sell goods on credit and the factor will take responsibility for invoicing the customer and collecting the amount owing. The factor will then pay the client business the invoice amount, less fees and interest, in two stages. The first stage represents 80 per cent of the invoice value and will be paid immediately after the goods have been delivered to the customer. The second stage will represent the balance outstanding and will usually be paid when the customer has paid the factor the amount owing.

Source: After McLaney and Atrill (2004), Fig. 15.6.

When considering a factoring agreement, the costs and likely benefits arising must be identified and carefully weighed. Example 6.1 illustrates how this may be done.

| Example 6.1 |

Mayo Computers Ltd has an annual turnover of £20 million before taking into account bad debts of £0.1 million. All sales made by the business are on credit and, at present, credit terms are negotiable by the customer. On average, the settlement period for trade debtors is 60 days. The business is currently reviewing its credit policies to see whether more efficient and profitable methods could be used.

The business is considering whether it should factor its trade debts. The accounts department has recently approached a factoring business, which has agreed to provide an advance equivalent to 80 per cent of trade debtors (where the trade debtors figure is based on an average settlement period of 40 days) at an interest rate of 12 per cent. The factoring business will undertake collection of the trade debts and will charge a fee of 2 per cent of sales turnover for this service. The factoring service is also expected to eliminate bad debts and will lead to credit

Example 6.1 continued

administration savings of £90,000. The settlement period for trade debtors will be reduced to an average of 40 days, which is equivalent to that of its major competitors.

The business currently has an overdraft of £4.8 million at an interest rate of 14 per cent a year. The bank has written recently to the business stating that it would like to see a reduction in this overdraft.

In evaluating the factoring arrangement, it is useful to begin by considering the cost of the existing arrangements:

Existing arrangements

	£000
Bad debts written off each year	100
Interest cost of average debtors outstanding [(£20m × 60/365) × 14%]	460
Total cost	560

The cost of the factoring arrangement can now be compared with the above:

Factoring arrangement

	£000
Factoring fee (£20m × 2%)	400
Interest on factor loan (assuming 80% advance and reduction in average credit period) [(£16m × 40/365) × 12%]	210
Interest on overdraft (remaining 20% of debtors financed in this way) [(£4m × 40/365) × 14%]	61
	671
Less Savings in credit administration	90
Cost of factoring	581

The above calculations show that the net additional cost of factoring for the business would be £21,000 (£581,000 − £560,000).

Invoice discounting

Invoice discounting involves a business approaching a factor or other financial institution for a loan based on a proportion of the face value of credit sales outstanding. If the institution agrees, the amount advanced is usually 75–80 per cent of the value of the approved sales invoices outstanding. The business must agree to repay the advance within a relatively short period – perhaps 60 or 90 days. The responsibility for collecting the trade debts outstanding remains with the business and repayment of the advance is not dependent on the trade debts being collected. Invoice discounting will not result in such a close relationship developing between the business and the financial institution as occurs with factoring. It may be a one-off arrangement whereas debt factoring usually involves a longer-term arrangement between the client and the financial institution.

Nowadays, invoice discounting is a much more important source of funds to businesses than factoring (see Figure 6.6 in **Real World 6.13**). There are three main reasons for this.

- It is a confidential form of financing which the business's customers will know nothing about.

- The service charge for invoice discounting is only about 0.2–0.3 per cent of turnover compared to 2.0–3.0 per cent of turnover for factoring.
- Many businesses are unwilling to relinquish control of their customers' records. Customers are an important resource of the business and many businesses wish to retain control over all aspects of their relationship with their customers.

REAL WORLD 6.13

The popularity of invoice discounting and factoring

Figure 6.6 charts the relative importance of invoice discounting and factoring in terms of the value of client sales revenue.

| Figure 6.6 | Client sales revenue: invoice discounting and factoring, 1999–2003 |

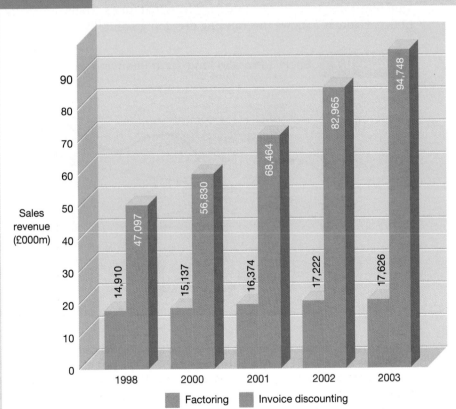

Over the five years, invoice discounting, as measured by client sales turnover, has risen much more sharply than for factoring. Client turnover for factoring has increased by around 18 per cent whereas invoice discounting has doubled. For 2003, client sales revenue for invoice discounting was more than five times greater than that for factoring.

Source: Chart constructed from data published by Factors and Discounters Association (www.factors.org.uk). Copyright © 2004 Factors and Discounters Association.

→ Factoring and invoice discounting are forms of **asset-based finance** as the assets of debtors are, in effect, used as security for the cash advances received by the business.

Long-term versus short-term borrowing

Having decided that some form of borrowing is required to finance the business, managers must then decide whether long-term borrowing or short-term borrowing is more appropriate. Some of the many issues that should be taken into account when making this decision are described below.

Matching

The business may attempt to match the type of borrowing with the nature of the assets held. Thus, long-term borrowing might finance assets that form part of the permanent operating base of the business, including non-current assets and a certain level of current assets. This leaves assets held for a short period, such as current assets held to meet seasonal increases in demand, to be financed by short-term borrowing, because short-term borrowing tends to be more flexible in that funds can be raised and repaid at short notice. Figure 6.7 shows this funding division graphically.

Figure 6.7 **Short-term and long-term financing requirements**

The broad consensus on financing seems to be that all of the permanent financial needs of the business should come from long-term sources. Only that part of current assets that fluctuates in the short term, probably on a seasonal basis, should be financed from short-term sources.

Source: After McLaney and Atrill (2004), Fig. 15.8.

A business may wish to match the asset life exactly with the period of the related loan; however, this may not be possible because of the difficulty of predicting the life of many assets.

Activity 6.10

Some businesses may take up a less cautious financing position than shown in Figure 6.7 and others may take up a more cautious one. How would the diagram differ under each of these options?

A less cautious position would mean relying on short-term finance to help fund part of the permanent capital base, so the arrow labelled 'short-term finance' would expand downwards. A more cautious position would mean relying on long-term finance to help finance the fluctuating assets of the business, so the arrow labelled 'long-term finance' would expand upwards.

Flexibility

Short-term borrowing may be a useful means of postponing a commitment to taking on a long-term loan. This may be seen as desirable if interest rates are high and it is forecast that they will fall in the future. Short-term borrowing does not usually incur penalties if there is early repayment of the amount outstanding whereas some form of financial penalty may have to be paid if long-term loans are repaid early.

Refunding risk

Short-term borrowing has to be renewed more frequently than long-term borrowing. This may create problems for the business if it is already in financial difficulties or if there is a shortage of funds available for lending.

Interest rates

Interest payable on long-term finance is often higher than for short-term finance, as lenders require a higher return where their funds are locked up for a long period. This fact may make short-term borrowing a more attractive source of finance for a business. However, there may be other costs associated with borrowing (arrangement fees, for example) that need to be taken into account. The more frequently that borrowings must be renewed, the higher these costs will be.

Internal sources of finance

In addition to external sources of finance there are certain internal sources of finance that a business may use to generate funds for particular activities. These sources usually have the advantage that they are flexible. They may also be obtained quickly – particularly working capital sources – and do not require the permission of other parties. The main sources of internal funds are described below and summarised in Figure 6.8.

| Figure 6.8 | **Major internal sources of finance** |

The major long-term source of internal finance is the profits that are retained rather than distributed to shareholders. The major short-term sources of internal finance involve reducing the level of debtors (receivables) and stocks (inventories) and increasing the level of creditors (payables).

Source: After McLaney and Atrill (2004), Fig. 15.1.

Long-term sources of internal finance

Retained profits

Retained profits are the major source of finance (internal or external) for most businesses. By retaining profits within the business rather than distributing them to shareholders in the form of dividends, the funds of the business are increased.

| Activity 6.11 |

Are retained profits a free source of finance for the business?

It is tempting to think that retained profits are a cost-free source of funds for a business. However, this is not the case. If profits are reinvested rather than distributed to shareholders, those shareholders cannot reinvest the profits made in other forms of investment. They will therefore expect a rate of return from the profits reinvested which is equivalent to what they would receive if the funds had been invested in another opportunity with the same level of risk.

The reinvestment of profit rather than the issue of new shares can be a useful way of raising finance from ordinary share investors. There are no issue costs associated with retaining profits and the amount raised is certain once the profit has been made. When issuing new shares, the issue costs may be substantial and there may be uncertainty over the success of the issue. Retaining profits will have no effect on the control of the business by existing shareholders. However, where new shares are issued to outside investors there will be some dilution of control suffered by existing shareholders.

The retention of profits is something that is determined by the directors of the business. They may find it easier simply to retain profits rather than to ask investors to subscribe to a new share issue. Retained profits are already held by the business and so it does not have to wait to receive the funds. Moreover, there is often less scrutiny when profits are being retained for reinvestment purposes than when new shares are being issued. Investors and their advisers will examine closely the reasons for any new share issue.

A problem with the use of profits as a source of finance, however, is that the timing and level of future profits cannot always be reliably determined. Some shareholders may prefer profits to be retained by the business rather than be distributed in the form of dividends. By ploughing back profits, it may be expected that the business will expand and share values will increase as a result. In the UK, not all capital gains are liable for taxation. (For the tax year 2004/05, an individual with capital gains of less than £8,200 would not be taxed on those gains.) A further advantage of capital gains over dividends is that the shareholder has a choice as to when the gain is realised. Research suggests that investors may be attracted to particular businesses according to the dividend/retention policies that they adopt. This point is considered in more detail in Chapter 8.

Retained profits and 'pecking order' theory

It has been argued that businesses have a 'pecking order' when taking on long-term finance. This pecking order can be summarised as follows:

- Retained profits will be used to finance the business if possible.
- Where retained profits are insufficient, or unavailable, loan capital will be used.
- Where loan capital is insufficient, or unavailable, share capital will be used.

The most plausible explanation for the above pecking order is that the managers of the business have access to information that investors do not. Let us suppose that the managers have reliable information indicating that the prospects for the business are better than that predicted by the market. This means that shares will be undervalued and, so, to raise finance by an issue of shares under such circumstances would involve selling them at an undervalued price. This would, in effect, result in a transfer of wealth from existing shareholders to those investors who take up the new share issue. Hence, the managers, who are employed to act in the best interests of existing shareholders, will prefer to rely on retained profit, followed by loan capital, instead.

Activity 6.12

Why should not the managers simply release any inside information to the market to allow the share price to rise and so make it possible to issue shares at a fair price?

There are at least two reasons why this may not be a good idea:

- It may be time consuming and costly to persuade the market that the prospects of the business are better than current estimates. Investors may find it hard to believe what the managers tell them.
- It may provide useful information to competitors about future developments.

Let us now suppose the managers of a business have access to bad news about the future. If the market knows that the business will rely on retained profit and loan capital when in possession of good news, it will assume that the issue of share capital can be taken as an indication that the business is in possession of bad news. Investors are, therefore, likely to feel the shares of the business are currently overvalued and will not be interested in subscribing to a new issue. (There is some evidence to show that the value of shares will fall when a share issue is announced.) Hence, this situation will again lead managers to favour retained profits followed by loan capital, with share capital as a last resort.

The pecking order theory may well help explain the heavy reliance of businesses on retained profits as a source of long-term finance, but it will not be the only influence on the financing decision. There are other factors to be taken into account when deciding on an appropriate source of finance, as we shall see in Chapter 8.

Short-term sources of internal finance

Figure 6.1 reveals that the major forms of short-term internal finance are:

- tighter credit control
- reducing stock levels
- delaying payments to creditors.

Each of these is discussed below.

Tighter credit control

By exerting tighter control over trade debtors (receivables) it may be possible for a business to reduce the proportion of assets held in this form and so release funds for other purposes. Having funds tied up in trade debts represents an opportunity cost in that those funds could be used for profit-generating activities. It is important, however, to weigh the benefits of tighter credit control against the likely costs in the form of lost customer goodwill and lost sales. To remain competitive, a business must take account of the needs of its customers and the credit policies adopted by rival businesses within the industry. We consider this further in Chapter 10.

Activity 6.13 below involves weighing the costs of tighter credit control against the likely future benefits.

Activity 6.13

H. Rusli Ltd provides a car valet service for car hire businesses when their cars are returned from hire. Details of the service costs are as follows:

	Per car	
	£	£
Car valet charge		20
Less Variable costs	14	
Fixed costs	4	18
Net profit		2

Sales revenue is £10 million a year and is all on credit. The average credit period taken by the car hire businesses is 45 days, although the terms of credit require payment within 30 days. Bad debts are currently £100,000 a year. Debtors are financed by a bank overdraft costing 15 per cent a year.

The credit control department of H. Rusli Ltd believes it can eliminate bad debts and can reduce the average credit period to 30 days if new credit control procedures are implemented. These will cost £50,000 a year and are likely to result in a reduction in sales of 5 per cent a year.

Should the business implement the new credit control procedures?

(*Hint*: To answer this activity it is useful to compare the current cost of trade credit with the costs under the proposed approach.)

The current cost of trade credit is:

	£
Bad debts	100,000
Overdraft [(£10m × 45/365) × 15%]	184,931
	284,931

The cost of trade credit under the new policy will be:

	£
Overdraft [(95% × £10m) × (30/365) × 15%]	117,123
Cost of control procedures	50,000
Net cost of lost sales [(£10m/£20 × 5%)(20 − 14*)]	150,000
	317,123

The above figures reveal that the business will be worse off if the new policies are adopted.

* The loss will be the contribution from valeting the car, that is, the difference between the valet charge and the variable costs. The fixed costs are ignored as they do not vary with the decision.

Reducing stock (inventory) levels

This is an internal source of funds that may prove attractive to a business. As with debtors, holding stocks imposes an opportunity cost on a business as the funds tied up cannot be used for other opportunities. By holding less stock, funds become available for those opportunities. However, a business must try to ensure there are sufficient stocks available to meet likely future sales demand. Failure to do so will result in lost customer goodwill and lost sales revenue.

The nature and condition of the stock held will determine whether it is possible to exploit this form of finance. A business may be overstocked as a result of poor buying decisions in the past. This may mean that a significant proportion of stocks held are slow moving or obsolete and cannot, therefore, be reduced easily. These issues are picked up again in Chapter 10.

Delaying payment to trade creditors (payables)

By providing a period of credit, suppliers are in effect offering a business an interest-free loan. If the business delays payment, the period of the 'loan' is extended and funds are retained within the business for other purposes. This may be a cheap form of finance for a business, although this is not always the case. If a business fails to pay within the agreed credit period, there may be significant costs: for example, the business may find it difficult to buy on credit when it has a reputation as a slow payer.

Self-assessment question 6.1

Helsim Ltd is a wholesaler and distributor of electrical components. The most recent financial statements of the business revealed the following:

Profit and loss account (income statement) for the year ended 31 May Year 10

	£m	£m
Sales revenue		14.2
Opening stock	3.2	
Purchases	8.4	
	11.6	
Closing stock	(3.8)	(7.8)
Gross profit		6.4
Administration expenses	(3.0)	
Selling and distribution expenses	(2.1)	
Finance charges	(0.8)	(5.9)
Net profit before taxation		0.5
Corporation tax		(0.2)
Net profit after taxation		0.3

Balance sheet as at 31 May Year 10

	£m	£m	£m
Non-current assets			
Land and buildings			3.8
Equipment			0.9
Motor vehicles			0.5
			5.2
Current assets			
Stock (inventory)		3.8	
Trade debtors (receivables)		3.6	
Cash at bank		0.1	
		7.5	
Less **Current liabilities**			
Trade creditors (payables)	1.8		
Bank overdraft	3.6	5.4	2.1
			7.3
Non-current liabilities			
Debentures (secured on freehold land)			3.5
			3.8
Equity			
£1 ordinary shares			2.0
Profit and loss account			1.8
			3.8

Notes

1 Land and buildings are shown at their current market value. Equipment and motor vehicles are shown at their written-down values.
2 No dividends have been paid to ordinary shareholders for the past three years.

In recent months, trade creditors have been pressing for payment. The managing director has, therefore, decided to reduce the level of trade creditors to an average of 40 days outstanding. In order to achieve this he has decided to approach the bank with a view to increasing the overdraft to finance the necessary payments. The business is currently paying 12 per cent interest on the overdraft.

Required:

(a) Comment on the liquidity position of the business.
(b) Calculate the amount of finance required in order to reduce trade creditors, as shown on the balance sheet, to an average of 40 days outstanding.
(c) State, with reasons, how you consider the bank would react to the proposal to grant an additional overdraft facility.
(d) Evaluate four sources of finance (internal or external, but excluding a bank overdraft) that may be used to finance the reduction in trade creditors and state, with reasons, which of these you consider the most appropriate.

SUMMARY

The main points in this chapter may be summarised as follows:

Sources of finance

● Long-term sources of finance are not due for repayment within approximately one year whereas short-term sources are due for repayment within approximately one year.

● External sources of finance require the agreement of anyone beyond the directors and managers of the business, whereas internal sources of finance do require the compliance of 'outsiders'.

● The higher the level of risk associated with investing in a particular form of finance, the higher the level of return that will be expected by investors.

External sources of finance

● The main external, long-term sources of finance are ordinary shares, preference shares, loans, leases and securitisation of assets.

● Ordinary shares are normally considered to be the most risky form of investment and, therefore, provide the highest expected returns to investors.

● Loan capital is normally the least risky and provides the lowest expected returns to investors.

● Preference shares normally provide returns somewhere between those offered by ordinary share capital and loan capital.

● Loan capital is relatively low risk because lenders are offered security for their loan; furthermore, covenants in the loan contract often impose obligations on managers, or restrictions on the actions of managers, that help protect the lenders.

- There are different types of loan capital including term loans, debentures, mortgages eurobonds and deep discount bonds.
- Convertible loan capital gives investors the right to convert their loan capital to ordinary (equity) share capital at a given future date and at a specified price. This will be done if the market price at the conversion date exceeds the specified price.
- A number of credit-rating agencies attempt to categorise loan capital issued by businesses according to the level of default risk.
- Junk bonds are those that do not fall within the investment grade categories established by the credit-rating agencies.
- Warrants give holders the right, but not the obligation, to buy ordinary shares at a given price and are often used as a sweetener to accompany a loan issue.
- Interest rates may be floating or fixed.
- Interest rate risk may be reduced, or eliminated, through the use of hedging arrangements such as interest rate swaps.
- A finance lease is, in essence, a form of lending that gives the lessee the use of an asset over most of its useful life in return for payment of a lease rental.
- A sale-and-leaseback arrangement involves the sale of an asset to a financial institution accompanied by an agreement to lease the asset back to the business.
- Securitisation involves bundling together homogeneous, illiquid assets to provide backing for the issue of bonds.
- The main sources of external *short-term* finance are bank overdrafts, debt factoring and invoice discounting.
- Bank overdrafts are flexible and cheap but are repayable on demand.
- Debt factoring and invoice discounting both use the trade debtors (receivables) of a business as a basis for borrowing, with the latter being more popular because of relative cost and flexibility.
- When considering the choice between long-term and short-term sources of borrowing, factors such as matching the type of borrowing with the nature of the assets held, the need for flexibility, refunding risk, and interest rates should be taken into account.

Internal sources of finance

- An internal source of long-term finance is retained profits. It is by far the most important source of new long-term finance (internal or external) for UK businesses.
- Retained profits are not a free source of finance as investors will require levels of return from retained profits similar to those from ordinary shares.
- The main short-term sources of internal finance are tighter credit control of debtors (receivables), reducing stock (inventory) levels and delaying payments to trade creditors (payables).

→ **Key terms**

Security p. 213	**Financial derivative** p. 224
Fixed charge p. 213	**Floating interest rate** p. 225
Floating charge p. 213	**Fixed interest rate** p. 225
Loan covenants p. 214	**Hedging arrangement** p. 225
Subordinated loans p. 215	**Interest rate swap** p. 225
Term loan p. 215	**Finance lease** p. 227
Debenture p. 215	**Operating lease** p. 227
Mortgage p. 215	**Sale and leaseback** p. 229
Eurobonds p. 215	**Securitisation** p. 230
Bonds p. 216	**Bank overdraft** p. 231
Deep discount bonds p. 217	**Bill of exchange** p. 232
Zero coupon bonds p. 217	**Debt factoring** p. 232
Convertible loan p. 217	**Invoice discounting** p. 234
Junk (high yield) bonds p. 219	**Asset-based finance** p. 236
Warrants p. 224	

For definitions of these terms see the Glossary, pp. 562–571.

Further reading

If you wish to explore the topics discussed in this chapter in more depth, try the following books:

Corporate Finance and Investment, *Pike, R. and Neale, B.*, 4th edn, Financial Times Prentice Hall, 2003, chapters 16–18.

Corporate Financial Management, *Arnold G.*, 2nd edn, Financial Times Prentice Hall, 2002, chapters 11 and 12.

Principles of Corporate Finance, *Brealey, R. and Myers, C.*, 7th edn, McGraw-Hill, 2002, chapters 23, 25 and 26.

REVIEW QUESTIONS

Answers to these questions can be found in Appendix D at the back of the book.

6.1 What are share warrants and what are the benefits to a business of issuing share warrants?

6.2 'Convertible loan capital is really a form of delayed equity.' Do you agree? Discuss.

6.3 What are the benefits of an interest swap agreement and how does it work?

6.4 Distinguish between invoice discounting and debt factoring.

EXERCISES

Exercises 6.4 to 6.7 are more advanced than 6.1 to 6.3. Those with coloured numbers have answers at the back of the book.

 If you wish to try more exercises, visit the students' side of the Companion Website.

6.1 Answer *all* parts below.

Required:
Provide reasons why a business may decide to:
(a) Lease rather than buy an asset which is to be held for long-term use
(b) Use retained profit to finance growth rather than issuing new shares
(c) Repay long-term loan capital earlier than the specified repayment date.

6.2 H. Brown (Portsmouth) Ltd produces a range of central heating systems for sale to builders' merchants. As a result of increasing demand for the business's products, the directors have decided to expand production. The cost of acquiring new plant and machinery and the increase in working capital requirements are planned to be financed by a mixture of long-term and short-term borrowing.

Required:
(a) Discuss the major factors that should be taken into account when deciding on the appropriate mix of long-term and short-term borrowing necessary to finance the expansion programme.
(b) Discuss the major factors that a lender should take into account when deciding whether to grant a long-term loan to the business.
(c) Identify three conditions that might be included in a long-term loan agreement, and state the purpose of each.

6.3 Securitisation is now used in a variety of different industries. In the music industry, for example, rock stars such as David Bowie, Michael Jackson and Iron Maiden have used this form of financing to their benefit.

Required:

(a) Explain the term 'securitisation'.

(b) Discuss the main features of this form of financing and the benefits of using securitisation.

6.4 Raphael Ltd is a small engineering business that has annual credit sales revenue of £2.4 million. In recent years, the business has experienced credit control problems. The average collection period for sales has risen to 50 days even though the stated policy of the business is for payment to be made within 30 days. In addition, 1.5 per cent of sales are written off as bad debts each year.

   The business has recently been in talks with a factor that is prepared to make an advance to the business equivalent to 80 per cent of debtors, based on the assumption that customers will, in future, adhere to a 30-day payment period. The interest rate for the advance will be 11 per cent a year. The trade debtors are currently financed through a bank overdraft, which has an interest rate of 12 per cent a year. The factor will take over the credit control procedures of the business and this will result in a saving to the business of £18,000 a year; however, the factor will make a charge of 2 per cent of sales revenue for this service. The use of the factoring service is expected to eliminate the bad debts incurred by the business.

Required:

Calculate the net cost of the factor agreement to the business and state whether or not the business should take advantage of the opportunity to factor its trade debts.

6.5 Cybele Technology Ltd is a software business that is owned and managed by two computer software specialists. Although sales have remained stable at £4 million per year in recent years, the level of debtors has increased significantly. A recent financial report submitted to the owners indicates an average settlement period for debtors of 60 days compared with an industry average of 40 days. The level of bad debts has also increased in recent years and the business now writes off approximately £20,000 of bad debts each year.

   The recent problems experienced in controlling credit have led to a liquidity crisis for the business. At present, the business finances its debtors by a bank overdraft bearing an interest rate of 14 per cent a year. However, the overdraft limit has been exceeded on several occasions in recent months and the bank is now demanding a significant decrease in the size of the overdraft. To comply with this demand, the owners of the business have approached a factor who has offered to make an advance equivalent to 85 per cent of trade debtors, based on the assumption that the level of debtors will be in line with the industry average. The factor will charge a rate of interest of 12 per cent a year for this advance. The factor will take over the sales ledger of the business and, for this service, will charge a fee based on 2 per cent of sales. The business believes that the services offered by the factor should eliminate bad debts and should lead to administrative cost savings of £26,000 per year.

Required:

(a) Calculate the effect on the net profit of Cybele Technology Ltd of employing a debt factor. Discuss your findings.

(b) Discuss the potential advantages and disadvantages for a business that employs the services of a debt factor.

6.6 Telford Engineers plc, a medium-sized Midlands manufacturer of automobile components, has decided to modernise its factory by introducing a number of robots. These will cost £20 million and will reduce operating costs by £6 million a year for their estimated useful life of 10 years starting next year (Year 10). To finance this scheme, the business can raise £20 million either:

1 by the issue of 20 million ordinary shares at 100p, or

2 by loan capital at 14 per cent interest a year, capital repayments of £3 million a year commencing at the end of Year 11.

Extracts from Telford Engineers' financial statements appear below:

Summary of balance sheet at 31 December

	Year 6	Year 7	Year 8	Year 9
	£m	£m	£m	£m
Non-current assets	48	51	65	64
Current assets	55	67	57	55
Current liabilities				
Trade creditors (payables)	(20)	(27)	(25)	(18)
Bank overdraft	(5)	–	(6)	(8)
	78	91	91	93
Equity	48	61	61	63
Non-current liabilities	30	30	30	30
	78	91	91	93
Number of issued 25p shares	80 million	80 million	80 million	80 million
Share price	150p	200p	100p	145p

Summary of profit and loss accounts (income statements) for years ended 31 December

	Year 6	Year 7	Year 8	Year 9
	£m	£m	£m	£m
Sales revenue	152	170	110	145
Profit before interest and taxation	28	40	7	15
Interest payable	(4)	(3)	(4)	(5)
Profit before taxation	24	37	3	10
Taxation	(12)	(16)	(0)	(4)
Profit after taxation	12	21	3	6
Dividends	(6)	(8)	(3)	(4)
Retained profit	6	13	0	2

For your answer you should assume that the corporate tax rate for Year 10 is 30 per cent, that sales revenue and operating profit will be unchanged except for the £6 million cost saving arising from the introduction of the robots, and that Telford Engineers will pay the same dividend per share in Year 10 as in Year 9.

Required:
(a) Prepare, for each financing arrangement, Telford Engineers' projected profit and loss account for the year ending 31 December Year 10 and a statement of its share capital, reserves and loans on that date.
(b) Calculate Telford's projected earnings per share for Year 10 for both schemes.
(c) Which scheme would you advise the business to adopt? You should give your reasons and state what additional information you would require.

6.7   Gainsborough Fashions Ltd operates a small chain of fashion shops in North Wales. In recent months the business has been under pressure from its trade creditors to reduce the average credit period taken from three months to one month. As a result, the directors of the business have approached the bank to ask for an increase in the existing overdraft for one year to be able to comply with the creditors' demands. The most recent accounts of the business are as follows:

Balance sheet as at 31 May 2005

	£	£	£
Non-current assets			
Fixtures and fittings at cost		90,000	
Less Accumulated depreciation		23,000	67,000
Motor vehicles at cost		34,000	
Less Accumulated depreciation		27,000	7,000
			74,000
Current assets			
Stock (inventory) at cost		198,000	
Trade debtors (receivables)		3,000	
		201,000	
Current liabilities			
Trade creditors (payables)	162,000		
Accrued expenses	10,000		
Bank overdraft	17,000		
Taxation	5,000	194,000	7,000
			81,000
Non-current liabilities			
Debentures payable in just over one year's time			40,000
			41,000
Equity			
£1 ordinary shares			20,000
General reserve			4,000
Retained profit			17,000
			41,000

**Abbreviated profit and loss account (income statement)
for the year ended 31 May 2005**

	£
Sales	740,000
Net profit before interest and taxation	38,000
Interest charges	5,000
Net profit before taxation	33,000
Taxation	10,000
Net profit after taxation	23,000
Dividend paid	10,000
Retained profit for the year	13,000

Notes

1 The debentures are secured by personal guarantees from the directors.
2 The current overdraft bears an interest rate of 12 per cent a year.

Required:

(a) Identify and discuss the major factors that a bank would take into account before deciding whether or not to grant an increase in the overdraft of a business.

(b) State whether, in your opinion, the bank should grant the required increase in the overdraft for Gainsborough Fashions Ltd. You should provide reasoned arguments and supporting calculations where necessary.

7

Financing a business 2: raising long-term finance

LEARNING OUTCOMES

When you have completed this chapter, you should be able to:

- Discuss the role and nature of the Stock Exchange.

- Discuss the nature and implications of stock market efficiency.

- Outline the ways in which share capital may be issued.

- Identify the problems that smaller businesses experience in raising funds.

- Describe the ways in which smaller businesses can gain access to long-term finance.

INTRODUCTION

In this chapter we continue our examination of the financing issue by examining the ways in which businesses may raise long-term finance. We begin by looking at the role of the London Stock Exchange (which we shall refer to as simply the Stock Exchange) in raising finance for large businesses, and then go on to consider whether shares listed on the Stock Exchange are efficiently priced. We shall see that the efficiency with which the Stock Exchange prices shares has important implications for the financing of a business. To complete our discussion of the Stock Exchange, we discuss the different ways in which share capital may be issued.

Smaller businesses do not have access to the Stock Exchange and so must look elsewhere to raise long-term finance. In this chapter, we discuss some of the main providers of long-term finance for smaller businesses.

The Stock Exchange

→ In the sections that follow, we examine the role that the **Stock Exchange** plays in raising long-term finance for businesses and discuss some of the key features of this important financial market. We then go on to examine the extent to which shares, or other financial claims such as loans and debentures, are efficiently priced by the Stock Exchange.

The role of the Stock Exchange

The Stock Exchange acts as an important *primary* and *secondary* capital market for businesses. As a primary market its main function is to enable businesses to raise new capital. Thus, businesses may use the Stock Exchange to raise funds by issuing shares to new shareholders or to existing shareholders. The Stock Exchange also enables businesses to raise funds through the issue of loan capital and debentures. In order to issue shares or loan capital through the Stock Exchange, a business must be 'listed' with it. This means that it must meet fairly stringent Stock Exchange requirements concerning size, profit history, information disclosure, and so on.

As a secondary market, the function of the Stock Exchange is to enable investors to transfer their securities (that is, shares and loan capital) with ease. It provides a 'second-hand' market where shares and loan capital already in issue may be bought and sold. This role can bring real benefits to a business as investors are likely to be more prepared to invest if they know their investment can be easily turned into cash whenever required. As a result, businesses whose shares are traded on the Stock Exchange are likely to find it easier to raise long-term finance and to do so at lower cost.

Though investors are not obliged to use the Stock Exchange as the means of transferring shares in a listed business, it is usually the most convenient way of buying or selling shares.

Ownership of UK listed shares

Shares in Stock Exchange listed businesses are held principally by large financial institutions such as insurance companies, pension funds, unit trusts and investment trusts. These institutions have strengthened their grip on the Stock Exchange over time, while the proportion of listed shares held directly by individuals has declined steadily. In 1963, for example, 54 per cent of listed shares were held by individuals, whereas in 2003 this had fallen to 15 per cent (see reference 1 at the end of the chapter).

Real World 7.1 provides an analysis of the ownership of shares in UK listed businesses at the end of 2003.

REAL WORLD 7.1

Ownership of UK listed shares

At the end of 2003, the proportion of shares of UK listed businesses held by various groups were as shown in Figure 7.1 below.

Figure 7.1   Ownership of UK listed shares, end-2003

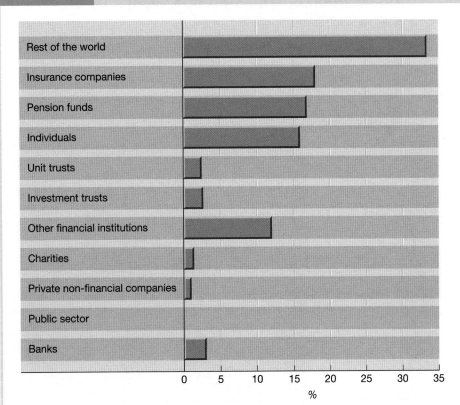

Ownership of UK listed shares is now dominated by large financial institutions. These figures do not fully portray the shareholdings of individuals, however, as they will also hold shares in unit trusts.

Source: Financial Statistics, Office for National Statistics, October 2004. Copyright © 2004 Crown copyright. Reproduced with the permission of the Controller of HMSO.

We saw in Chapter 1 that the growing influence of financial institutions has contributed to the rise in shareholder activism in recent years.

The size of listed businesses

Businesses listed on the Stock Exchange vary considerably in size, with market capital-isations ranging from below £2 million to more than £2,000 million. **Real World 7.2** below sets out the distribution of businesses across this wide range.

REAL WORLD 7.2

Distribution of UK listed businesses by equity market value

The distribution of UK listed businesses by equity market value is as shown in Figure 7.2 below.

| Figure 7.2 | Distribution of UK listed businesses by equity market value |

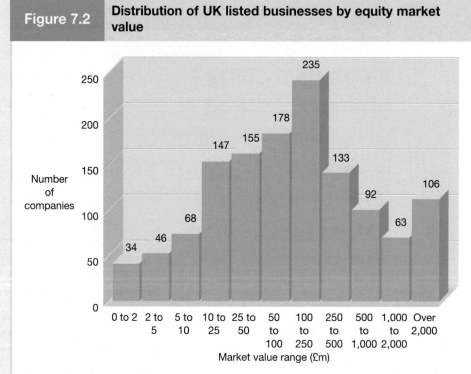

The graph shows that 295 businesses have a market capitalisation of less than £25 mil-lion and more than 450 businesses have a market capitalisation of less than £50 million. However, 106 businesses have a market capitalisation of more than £2,000 million.

Source: Adapted from www.londonstockexchange.com, Primary Market Fact Sheet, November 2004.

Share price indices

There are various indices available to help monitor trends in overall share price move-ments of Stock Exchange listed businesses. **FTSE (Footsie) indices**, as they are called, derive their name from the organisations behind them: the Financial Times (FT) and Stock Exchange (SE). The most common indices are:

- *FTSE 100.*   This is probably the most well known share price index. It is based on share price movements of the 100 largest businesses, by **market capitalisation**, listed on the Stock Exchange. (Market capitalisation is the total market value of the shares of the business.) Businesses within this index are often referred to as 'large cap' businesses.
- *FTSE Mid 250.*   An index based on share price movements of the next 250 largest businesses, by market capitalisation, listed on the Stock Exchange.
- *FTSE A 350.*   This index combines businesses in the FTSE 100 and FTSE Mid 250 indices.
- *FTSE Actuaries All Share Index.*   An index based on share price movements of more than 800 shares, which account for more than 90 per cent of the market capitalisation of all listed businesses.

Each index is constructed using a base date and a base value (the FTSE 100 index, for example, was constructed in 1984 with a base of 1,000) and is updated throughout each trading day. Each index is also reviewed on a quarterly basis, and businesses within a particular index may be replaced as a result of changes in their relative size.

Advantages and disadvantages of a Stock Exchange listing

In addition to the advantages already mentioned, it is claimed that a Stock Exchange listing can also help a business by:

- raising its profile, which may be useful in dealings with customers and suppliers;
- ensuring that its shares are valued in an efficient manner (a point to which we return later);
- broadening its investor base;
- acquiring other businesses by using its own shares as payment rather than cash;
- attracting and retaining employees by offering incentives based on share ownership schemes.

Before a decision is made to float (that is, list), however, these advantages must be weighed against the possible disadvantages of a listing.

Raising finance through the Stock Exchange can be a costly business. Share issues that arise from the initial listing of the business are known as an *initial public offering (IPO)*. To make such an offering, a business will rely on the help of various specialists such as lawyers, accountants and bankers. However, their services are not cheap. **Real World 7.3** provides an example.

REAL WORLD 7.3

Floating under heavy fees   **FT**

Benfield has earmarked almost 10 per cent of the proceeds from its initial public offering on fees and commissions for a host of bankers, lawyers and accountants.

The reinsurance broker is seeking to raise £100m through a global institutional offering as part of a plan to float on the London Stock Exchange later this month.

However, it has emerged that £9.2m of that sum will be swallowed up by the dozen companies involved in the flotation . . .

Source: 'Benfield earmarks almost 10 per cent for fees in £100m flotation', *Financial Times*, Business section, 9 June 2003, p. 26.

In addition to these out-of-pocket expenses, a huge amount of management time is usually required to undertake an IPO through the Stock Exchange, which can result in missed business opportunities.

Another important disadvantage is the regulatory burden placed on listed businesses. Once a business is listed, there are continuing requirements that must be met, covering issues such as:

- disclosure of financial information
- informing shareholders of significant developments
- the rights of shareholders and lenders
- the obligations of directors.

These requirements can be onerous and can also involve substantial costs for the business.

Another potential disadvantage is that the activities of listed businesses are closely monitored by financial analysts, financial journalists and other businesses. Such scrutiny may be unwelcome, particularly if the business is dealing with sensitive issues or is experiencing operational problems.

If investors become disenchanted with the business, and the price of its shares falls, this may make it vulnerable to a takeover bid from another business. This risk has led some businesses to withdraw from the Stock Exchange. Sir Richard Branson, the principal shareholder of Virgin, floated this business on the Stock Exchange in 1986. However, eighteen months later he decided to de-list the business. The value of the shares in Virgin fell substantially during a crash in stock market prices in 1987 and Sir Richard believed that this made the business vulnerable to a takeover. He wanted to retain control of the business and decided, therefore, to de-list the business (after buying back shares he had sold at the time of the listing).

A potential disadvantage for smaller listed businesses is that they may be overlooked by investors and so may not reap the key benefit of a listing. **Real World 7.4** explains why larger businesses tend to dominate the minds of investors.

REAL WORLD 7.4

Big is beautiful

The 100 largest businesses account for more than three-quarters of the value of the market and it is these large companies that provide the main focus of interest for investors. Large institutional investors, in particular, are normally only interested in large businesses because of the size of the investments that they make in each business. It has been suggested that businesses valued at less than £100 million are unlikely to be of interest. This makes it hard for smaller businesses to raise new capital, unless, perhaps, they can convince investors that they are fast growing. Thus, for some small businesses the advantages of listing are outweighed by the disadvantages.

Source: Based on information in 'Climbing aboard the flight from flotation', Philip Coggan, *Financial Times*, 6 September 2003.

A final disadvantage claimed is that Stock Exchange investors suffer from a short-term investment perspective. It is argued that the investment myopia of investors puts pressure on listed businesses to produce good results in the short term, even though this may have adverse long-term effects. This claim is worthy of further investigation and so will be considered in a later section.

Raising finance through the Stock Exchange

The Stock Exchange can be a useful vehicle for a successful entrepreneur wishing to realise the value of the business that has been built up. By floating the shares on the Stock Exchange, and thereby making the shares available to the public, the entrepreneur will usually benefit from a gain in the value of the shares held and will be able to realise that gain easily, if required, by selling some shares. **Real World 7.5** provides an example of a business floating on the Stock Exchange and making its owners a lot of money.

REAL WORLD 7.5

Privatised stationer 'to float'

Ray Peck is an entrepreneur who runs a business that was the government's former stationery division. Newspaper reports revealed that he wished to float the business on the Stock Exchange and that stock market investors were likely to value the business at around £80m to £100m. Mr Peck, his senior managers and a financial institution bought the whole business for about £10m two years before the intention to float the business was reported. At the time, Ray Peck owned 20 per cent of the shares of the business, which means that his stake in the business would be valued somewhere between £16 million and £20 million, assuming that predictions concerning the value of the business were accurate.

Source: Sunday Times, Business section, 30 June 2002, p. 3.

Shares sold through an initial listing on the Stock Exchange may be new shares or shares already in issue, which the existing owners wish to sell.

It seems that we should be cautious when invited to subscribe to the sale of shares arising from an initial listing. **Real World 7.6** tells us why investing in new business flotations, may be bad for our wealth.

REAL WORLD 7.6

New issues but old problems   **FT**

Back in 1940 Benjamin Graham and David Dodd, the fathers of security analysis wrote: 'the odds are so strongly against the man who buys into these new flotations that he might as well throw three-quarters of the money out the window and keep the rest in the bank.'

Now confirmation of the poor record of recent new issues comes from an Ernst and Young survey. The accountancy group looked at the records of 200 companies that floated on the UK market between 1998 and 2002. It found that only 39 per cent of the sample had increased profits since flotation (although 82 per cent had seen their sales grow).

This should not come as too much of a surprise. Companies are most likely to float on the market when their recent trading record is impressive. But periods of rapid growth can be very dangerous for a company – costs and management ambitions can get out of hand.

Real World 7.6 continued

Furthermore, no business can grow rapidly forever, and there is a risk that the flotation occurs just at the moment when the decline is beginning.

And, as Ernst and Young points out, the very act of flotation incurs significant costs and can divert management focus from the business. The money raised can also burn a hole in the management's pockets, leading to a flurry of spending that would disgrace a football manager.

All this is slightly discouraging, given that the primary role of the stock market is to allow growing businesses to raise capital. But perhaps a certain amount of investor greed (and gullibility) is necessary if industry is to gain access to finance. New issue investors have been fooled before; they will be fooled again.

Source: Financial Times, 8 August 2003, p. 22.

The Stock Exchange and the problem of short termism

It seems to be the conventional wisdom that listed businesses are under pressure to perform well over the short term by Stock Exchange investors. Furthermore, as a result of this pressure, businesses are inhibited from undertaking projects that will only yield benefits in the longer term. Instead, they will opt for investments that perform well over the short term, even though the long-term prospects may be poor. Although this view of Stock Exchange investors seems to be widely held, it is not well supported by the evidence. Indeed, there is some compelling evidence to the contrary.

Evidence of share price behaviour can be cited that suggests that investors take a long-term view when making investment decisions. Two such examples are:

- *Share price reaction to investment plans.* If a short-term view is taken by investors, any announcement by a business that it plans to undertake long-term investment or research would be treated as bad news. It should lead investors to sell their shares and this, in turn, would result in a fall in the company's share price. Conversely, any announcement by a business that long-term investment plans are to be scrapped would be treated as good news and should result in a rise in share price. In fact, the opposite share price reaction to that stated will usually occur.
- *Dividend payments.* Investors demanding short-term returns would be expected to value businesses with a high dividend yield more highly than businesses with a low dividend yield. This kind of behaviour would allow an astute investor to buy shares in low-yielding businesses at a lower price than their 'true' value and so, over time, make higher returns. However, the evidence suggests that businesses with low dividend yields are more highly regarded by investors than businesses with high dividend yields (see reference 2 at the end of the chapter).

If Stock Exchange investors are not to blame for the short-term perspective of managers, then who is to blame? Some believe that it is the managers themselves. It has been argued, for example, that managers have incorrect views about what Stock Exchange investors are really looking for. (There is certainly survey evidence to support the view that managers *believe* that investors have a short-term investment perspective.) It has also been suggested that managers adopt a short-term view because their rewards are linked to short-term results or because frequent job changes encourage the quest for short-term results. Finally, it has been suggested that the particular appraisal methods adopted by managers to evaluate investment opportunities encourage a short-term view (see reference 2 at the end of the chapter).

Activity 7.1

Can you think of an investment appraisal method, dealt with in Chapter 4, which may encourage a short-term view?

The payback method places emphasis on how quickly an investment repays its initial outlay. This method is widely used and may encourage a short-term approach by managers. (An alternative explanation, however, is that the payback method is selected by managers because they adopt a short-term perspective.)

Some believe, however, that managers are not the real culprits and that it is high inflation and economic instability during the post-war years that have given managers a short-term perspective. Thus, to encourage long-term thinking we need a sustained period of stable monetary conditions.

The efficiency of the Stock Exchange

It was mentioned above that the Stock Exchange helps share prices to be efficiently priced. The term 'efficiency' in this context does not relate to the way in which the Stock Exchange is administered but rather to the way in which information is processed. An **efficient stock market** is one in which information is processed quickly and accurately and so share prices faithfully reflect all relevant information available. In other words, prices are determined in a rational manner and represent the best estimate of the 'true worth' of the shares.

The term 'efficiency' does not imply that investors have perfect knowledge concerning a business and its future prospects and that this knowledge is reflected in the share price. Information may come to light concerning the business that investors did not previously know about and which may indicate that the current share price is higher or lower than its 'true worth'. However, in an efficient market, the new information will be quickly absorbed by investors and this will lead to an appropriate share price adjustment.

We can see that the term 'efficiency' in relation to the Stock Exchange is not the same as the economists' concept of perfect markets, which you may have come across in your previous studies. The definition of an efficient capital market does not rest on a set of restrictive assumptions regarding the operation of the market (for example, that relevant information is freely available, that all investors have access to all relevant information, and so on). In reality, such assumptions will not hold. The term 'efficient market' is a narrower concept that has been developed by studying the behaviour of stock markets in the real world. It simply describes the situation where relevant information is *quickly* and *accurately* reflected in share prices. The speed at which new information is absorbed in share prices will mean that not even nimble-footed investors will have time to make superior gains by buying or selling shares when new information becomes available.

To understand why the Stock Exchange may be efficient, it is important to bear in mind that securities listed on the Stock Exchange are scrutinised by many individuals, including skilled analysts, who are constantly seeking to make gains from identifying securities that are inefficiently priced. They are alert to new information and will react quickly when new opportunities arise. If, for example, a share can be identified as being below its 'true worth' investors would immediately exploit this information by buying shares in that business. When this is done on a large scale, the effect will be to drive up the price of the share, thereby eliminating any inefficiency within the market. Thus, as a result of the efforts to make gains from inefficiently priced securities, investors will, paradoxically, promote the efficiency of the market.

Three levels of efficiency have been identified concerning the operation of stock markets. These are as follows.

The weak form of efficiency

The weak form reflects the situation where movements in share prices follow a random path. Current share price movements are independent of past share price movements and any information contained in past share prices will already be reflected in current share prices. The random nature of share price movements means that any attempt to study past prices in order to detect a pattern of price movements will fail. It is not, therefore, possible to make gains from simply studying past price movements. Thus, investors and analysts who draw up charts of share price changes (which is known as technical analysis) in order to predict future price movements will be wasting their time.

The semi-strong form of efficiency

The semi-strong form takes the notion of efficiency a little further and describes the situation where all publicly available information, including past share prices, is reflected in the current share price. Other publicly available forms of information will include published accounts, business announcements, newspaper reports, economic forecasts, and so on. These forms of information, which will become available at random intervals, are quickly absorbed by the market and so investors who study relevant reports and announcements (known as fundamental analysis), in an attempt to make above-average returns on a consistent basis, will be disappointed. The information will already be incorporated into share prices.

The strong form of efficiency

The strong form is the ultimate form of efficiency and describes the situation where share prices fully reflect all available information, whether or not it is publicly available. This means that the share price will be a good approximation to the 'true' value of the share. As all relevant information is absorbed in share prices, even those who have 'inside' information concerning a business, such as unpublished reports or confidential management decisions, will not be able to make superior returns, on a consistent basis, from using this information.

The various forms of efficiency described above can be viewed as a progression where each higher form of efficiency incorporates the previous form(s). Thus, if a stock market is efficient in the semi-strong form it will also be efficient in the weak form. Similarly, if a stock market is efficient in the strong form, it will also be efficient in the semi-strong and weak forms (see Figure 7.3).

Figure 7.3   The three levels of market efficiency

The weak form of efficiency

↓

The semi-strong form of efficiency

↓

The strong form of efficiency

The figure shows the three forms of efficiency that have been identified for stock markets. These forms of efficiency represent a progression where each form incorporates the previous level(s).

Activity 7.2

Can you explain why the relationship between the various forms of market efficiency explained above should be the case?

If a stock market is efficient in the semi-strong form it will reflect all publicly available information. This will include past share prices. Thus, the semi-strong form will incorporate the weak form. If the stock market is efficient in the strong form, it will reflect all available information; which includes publicly available information. Thus, it will incorporate the semi-strong and weak forms.

It is worth noting that, within each of the three forms discussed above, there are varying degrees of efficiency. In other words, efficiency within each form should be viewed as a continuum ranging from total efficiency to total inefficiency. Thus, Keane (see reference 3 at the end of the chapter) argues that a stock market may be totally efficient in the weak form, near-totally efficient in the semi-strong form and totally inefficient in the strong form.

Activity 7.3

Dornier plc is a large civil engineering business that is listed on the Stock Exchange. On 1 May it received a confidential letter stating that it had won a large building contract from an overseas government. The new contract is expected to increase the profits of the business by a substantial amount over the next five years. The news of the contract was announced publicly on 4 May.

How would the shares of the business react to the formal announcement on 4 May assuming (a) a semi-strong and (b) a strong form of market efficiency?

Under the semi-strong form, the formal announcement would lead to an increase in the value of the shares. Under the strong form of efficiency, however, there would be no share reaction as the information would already be impounded in the share price.

Evidence on stock market efficiency

You may wonder what evidence exists to support each of the above forms of efficiency. For the weak form there is a very large body of evidence that spans many countries and many time periods. Much of this evidence has resulted from researchers checking whether security price movements follow a random pattern: that is, checking to find out whether successive price changes were independent of each other. The results point overwhelmingly to the existence of a random pattern of share prices. There has also been some research involving the examination of trading rules that are used by some investors. These rules are based on the identification of trend-like patterns to determine the point at which to buy or sell shares in order to achieve superior returns. Given the earlier findings on the random nature of share price movements, it is not surprising that the evidence suggests that the trading rules developed are useless.

Activity 7.4

If share prices follow a random pattern, does this not mean that the market is acting in an irrational (and inefficient) manner?

No. New information concerning a business is likely to arise at random intervals and so share price adjustments to the new information will arise at those random intervals. The randomness of share price movements is, therefore, to be expected if markets are efficient.

Despite the evidence concerning the random nature of price movements, some analysts (known as technical analysts) believe that price movements in financial markets do exhibit repetitive patterns of behaviour. **Real World 7.7** illustrates some of the techniques used by these analysts to help predict future price movements.

 REAL WORLD 7.7

Reading the signs

The charts in Figure 7.4 are taken from the *Independent* and show the techniques used by technical analysts being applied to different markets: the Dow Jones Index (a share price index of 30 industrial companies listed on the New York Stock Exchange), the share price of Vodafone plc (a major mobile phone operator) and to currency markets.

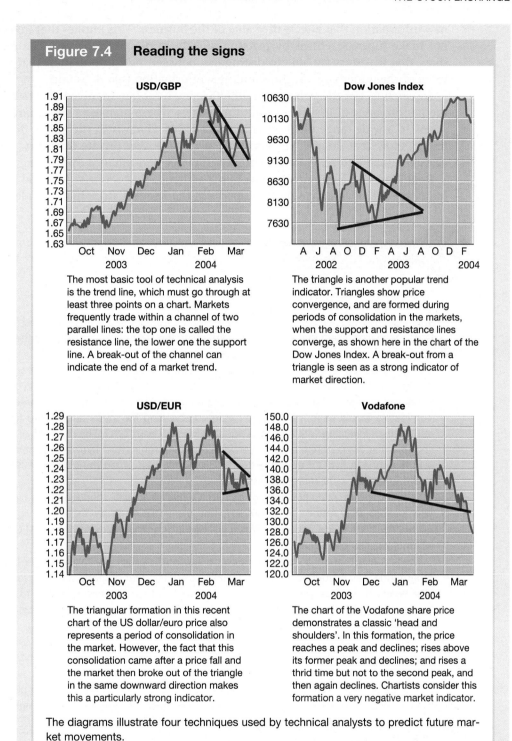

Figure 7.4 Reading the signs

USD/GBP

The most basic tool of technical analysis is the trend line, which must go through at least three points on a chart. Markets frequently trade within a channel of two parallel lines: the top one is called the resistance line, the lower one the support line. A break-out of the channel can indicate the end of a market trend.

Dow Jones Index

The triangle is another popular trend indicator. Triangles show price convergence, and are formed during periods of consolidation in the markets, when the support and resistance lines converge, as shown here in the chart of the Dow Jones Index. A break-out from a triangle is seen as a strong indicator of market direction.

USD/EUR

The triangular formation in this recent chart of the US dollar/euro price also represents a period of consolidation in the market. However, the fact that this consolidation came after a price fall and the market then broke out of the triangle in the same downward direction makes this a particularly strong indicator.

Vodafone

The chart of the Vodafone share price demonstrates a classic 'head and shoulders'. In this formation, the price reaches a peak and declines; rises above its former peak and declines; and rises a thrid time but not to the second peak, and then again declines. Chartists consider this formation a very negative market indicator.

The diagrams illustrate four techniques used by technical analysts to predict future market movements.

Source: 'Reading the signs', The Independent, 27 March 2004.

Research to test the semi-strong form of efficiency has usually involved monitoring the reaction of the share price to new information, such as profit announcements. This is done to see whether the market reacts to new information in an appropriate manner. The results usually show that share prices readjust quickly and accurately to any new information that affects the value of the business. This implies that investors cannot make superior returns by reacting quickly to new information. The results also show that investors are able to distinguish between new information that affects the value of the underlying business and new information that does not.

Research to test the strong form of efficiency has often involved an examination of the performance of investment fund managers. These managers are assumed to have access to a wide range of information, not all of which is in the public domain. The results show that despite this apparent advantage over private investors, fund managers are unable to generate consistently superior performance over time.

Real World 7.8 summarises some of the evidence that actively managed investment funds are unable to consistently outperform the relevant stock market index.

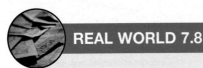

REAL WORLD 7.8

Trying to beat the index   **FT**

Well-documented research . . . shows that returns from most actively managed funds – at least those that invest in the big, liquid markets in the UK or US – do not beat their benchmark index.

Legal & General summarises much of the data. It shows that over five years the FTSE All-Share index outperformed 55 per cent of actively managed funds investing in UK shares – before fees. After high initial fees, just a quarter of funds managed to beat the index.

Investors would have made more money by backing the index and aiming for market returns than investing with most individual managers, says L&G. The chances of picking a UK fund that will continue to turn in an index-beating return over five years is considerably less than one in five. Of the 72 active funds that outperformed the index in 1998 just 31 active funds were still doing so in 2003.

The longer term statistics are just as bad. Of the 44 actively managed trusts with a 20-year performance history, eight outperfomed the FTSE All-Share index, highlighting just how difficult it is to identify which trusts will be long-term winners, said the WM Company, which assesses performance.

Those funds that do outperform often do so because they are taking higher risks than other funds, say academics, and are unlikely to sustain that outperformance over successive years. If there is any evidence of persistent outperformance it is due to luck and momentum rather than judgement – that is, a fund holds a stock that produces a high return in one year and carries on to the next.

Once you adjust returns for risk that the managers have taken, the only evidence of consistency is on the downside – that is, poor managers systematically underperform benchmarks.

'Losers generally repeat, while winners do not necessarily repeat,' was the bleak summation reached by professors David Blake of Birkbeck College and Allan Timmerman of the University of California in a study for the Financial Services Authority.

Source: 'It does not always pay to follow the stars', *Financial Times*, 15 May 2004.

The implications of stock market efficiency for managers

Having identified the various forms of market efficiency and the evidence in support of each form, we need to be clear what the implications are for the managers of a business. It seems that there are six important lessons that they should learn.

Lesson 1: Timing doesn't matter

Where the managers of a business are considering a new issue of shares, they may feel that the timing of the issue is important. If the stock market is inefficient, there is always a risk that the price of a share will fall below its 'true worth' and making a new issue at such a point could be very costly for the business. This would mean the timing of new issues is a critical management decision. However, if the market is efficient then, by definition, the price quoted for shares will faithfully reflect the available information. This implies that the timing of issues will not be critical as there is no optimal point in time for making a new issue. Even if the market is very depressed and share prices are very low, it cannot be assumed that things will improve. The share prices prevailing at the low point will still reflect the market's estimate of the future returns from the shares.

Activity 7.5

Why might a financial manager who accepts that the market is efficient in the semi-strong form nevertheless be justified in delaying the issue of new shares until what he or she believes will be a more appropriate time?

The justification for delaying a new issue under the circumstance described would be that the manager believes the market has got it wrong. This situation could arise if the market has inadequate information with which to price securities correctly. The manager may have access to inside information which, when made available to the market, will lead to an upward adjustment in share prices.

Lesson 2: Don't search for undervalued businesses

If the stock market accurately absorbs information concerning businesses, the prices quoted for shares and other securities will represent the best estimates available of their 'true worth'. This means that investors should not spend time trying to find undervalued shares in order to make gains. Unless they have access to information which the market does not have, they will not be able to 'beat the market' on a consistent basis. To look for undervalued shares will only result in time being spent and transaction costs being incurred to no avail. Similarly, managers should not try to identify undervalued shares in other businesses with the intention of identifying possible takeover targets. While there may be a number of valid and compelling reasons for taking over another business, the argument that shares of the target business are undervalued by the stock market is not one of them.

Lesson 3: Take note of market reaction

The investment plans and decisions of managers will be quickly and accurately reflected in the share price. Where these plans and decisions result in a fall in share price, managers may find it useful to review them. In effect, the market provides managers with a 'second opinion', which is both objective and informed. This opinion should not go unheeded.

Lesson 4: You can't fool the market

Some managers appear to believe that form is as important as substance when communicating new information to investors. This may induce them to 'window dress' the financial statements in order to provide a better picture of financial health than is warranted by the facts. However, the evidence suggests that the market is able to see through any cosmetic attempts to improve the financial picture. The market quickly and accurately assesses the economic substance of the business and will price the shares accordingly. Thus, accounting policy changes (such as switching from one depreciation method to another in order to boost profits in the current year) will be a waste of time.

We saw earlier that businesses may issue mixed forms of securities. Convertible loan capital, for example, has a loan element and an ordinary share element. It is not possible, however, to fool an efficient stock market by the issue of such securities and, thereby, obtain a 'cheap' form of finance. The hybrid nature of convertible loan capital would be recognised and priced accordingly.

Activity 7.6

Convertible loan capital will usually be issued with rates of interest that are lower than conventional loan capital. Is this evidence that the market has been misled and is, therefore, inefficient?

If the market is prepared to accept a lower rate of interest for convertible loan capital than for more conventional forms of loan capital, this need not imply the market has been misled and that it is, therefore, inefficient. Indeed, it may well mean that the market is efficient and has taken account of all relevant information. Investors may be prepared to accept a lower rate of interest in return for the likely future benefits arising from the conversion rights.

Lesson 5: The market decides the level of risk, not the business

Investors will correctly assess the level of risk associated with an investment and will impose an appropriate rate of return. Moreover, this rate of return will apply to whichever business undertakes that investment. Managers will not be able to influence the required rate of return by adopting particular financing strategies. This means, for example, that the issue of certain types of security, or combinations of securities, will not reduce the rate of return required by the market.

Lesson 6: Champion the interests of shareholders

It was mentioned in Chapter 1 that the primary objective of a business is the maximisation of shareholder wealth. If managers take decisions and actions that are consistent with this objective, it will be reflected in the share price. This is likely to benefit the managers of the business as well as the shareholders.

Are the stock markets really efficient?

The view that capital markets, at least in the major industrialised countries, are efficient is now part of the conventional wisdom of finance. However, there is a growing body of evidence that casts doubt on the efficiency of capital markets and which has reopened the debate on this topic. Below we consider some of the evidence.

Stock exchange regularities

Researchers have unearthed regular share price patterns in some of the major stock markets. This suggests an element of inefficiency as it would be possible to exploit these patterns in order to achieve superior returns over time. Some of the more important 'regularities' that have been identified are as follows:

● *Business size.* There is now a substantial body of evidence indicating that, other things being equal, small businesses yield higher returns than large businesses. The evidence concerning this phenomenon also shows that the superior returns from small businesses will change over time. The size effect, as it is called, is more pronounced at the turn of the year, for example, than at any other point.

● *Price/earnings (P/E) ratio.* We saw in Chapter 3 that the P/E ratio is a measure of market confidence in a particular share: the higher the P/E ratio, the greater the expected future returns from that share. However, research has shown that a portfolio of shares held in businesses with a low P/E ratio will outperform a portfolio of shares held in businesses with a high P/E ratio. This suggests that investors can make superior returns from investing in businesses with low P/E ratios.

● *Investment timing.* There are various studies indicating that superior returns may be gained by timing investment decisions appropriately. For example, it has been found that higher returns can be achieved by buying shares at the beginning of April, in the UK, and then selling them at the end of this month, than similar share trading in any other month. Some studies have shown that on Mondays there is an above-average fall in share prices. This may be because investors review their portfolio of shares at the weekend and then decide to sell unwanted shares when the market opens on Monday morning, thereby depressing prices. This suggests, of course, that it is better to buy rather than sell shares on a Monday. Other studies have revealed that the particular time of the day in which shares are traded can lead to superior returns.

Activity 7.7

Can you suggest why April may provide better returns than other months of the year?

One reason may be that a new tax year begins in this month. Investors may sell loss-making shares in March to offset any capital gains tax on shares sold at a profit during the tax year. As a result of these sales, share prices will become depressed. At the start of the new tax year, however, investors will start to buy shares again and so share prices will rise.

The key question is whether these regularities seriously undermine the idea of market efficiency. Many believe that they are of only minor importance and that, on the whole, the markets are efficient for most of the time. The view taken is that, in the real world, there are always likely to be inefficiencies. It can also be argued that if investors discover share price patterns, they will try to exploit these patterns in order to make higher profits. By so doing, they will eliminate the patterns and so make the markets even more efficient. However, others believe that these regularities reveal that previous research that supported the notion of market efficiency is seriously flawed and that we must seek alternative explanations for the way in which stock markets behave.

Bubbles, bull markets and behavioural finance

In recent years, a new discipline called **behavioural finance** has emerged, which offers an alternative explanation of the way in which markets behave. This new discipline rejects the notion that investors behave in a rational manner, and there is a plethora of research evidence in psychology to support this view. Many studies have shown that individuals make systematic errors when processing information. It seems that individuals are prone to various biases and, when making investment decisions, these biases can result in the mispricing of shares. Where this occurs, there are profitable opportunities that can be exploited. A detailed study of these behavioural biases is beyond the scope of this book. However, it is worth providing one example to illustrate the challenge they pose to the notion of efficient markets.

One well-documented bias is the overconfidence that individuals have in their own information processing skills and judgement. In the context of investment decisions, overconfidence may lead to a number of errors including:

- an underreaction to new share price information, which arises from a tendency to place more emphasis on new information confirming an original share valuation than new information challenging this valuation;
- a reluctance to sell shares that have incurred losses because it involves admitting to past mistakes;
- incorrectly assessing the riskiness of future returns;
- a tendency to buy and sell shares more frequently than is prudent.

Such errors may help to explain share price 'bubbles' and overextended 'bull' markets, where investor demand keeps share prices buoyant despite evidence suggesting that share prices are too high.

Share price bubbles, which inflate and then burst, appear in stock markets from time to time. When they inflate there is a period of high prices and high trading volumes, which is sustained by the enthusiasm of investors rather than by the fundamentals affecting the shares. During a bubble, investors appear to place too much faith in their optimistic views of future share price movements, and, for a while at least, ignore warning signals concerning future growth prospects. However, as the warning signals become stronger, the disparity between investors' views and reality eventually becomes too great and a correction occurs, bringing investors' views more into line with fundamental values. This realignment of investors' views leads to a large correction in share prices – in other words, the bubble bursts.

For similar reasons, overconfidence can result in overextended bull markets, where share prices become detached from fundamental values.

How should managers act?

At present, the debate concerning the efficiency of markets continues and further research is required before a clear picture emerges. Although this situation may be fine for researchers, we are left with the problem of how managers should respond to an increasingly mixed set of messages concerning the behaviour of the stock markets. Probably the best advice is for managers to assume that, as a general rule, the markets are efficient. The weight of evidence still supports this view, and failure to act in this way could be very costly indeed. Where it is clear, however, that some market inefficiency exists, managers should be prepared to take advantage of the opportunities that it provides.

Share issues

A business may issue shares in a number of different ways. These may involve direct appeals by the business to investors or may involve the use of financial intermediaries. The most common methods of share issue are as follows:

- rights issues
- bonus issues
- offers for sale

- public issues
- placings.

Each of these is considered in turn below.

Rights issues

➡ **Rights issues** are made when businesses that have been established for some time seek to raise finance by issuing additional shares for cash. Company law gives existing shareholders the right of first refusal on these new shares, which are offered to them in proportion to their existing shareholding. Only where the existing shareholders waive their right would the share be offered to the investing public generally.

Rights issues, which are now the most common form of share issue, are a relatively cheap and straightforward way of issuing shares: issue expenses are quite low and issue procedures are simpler than for other forms of share issue. The fact that those offered new shares already have an investment in the business, which presumably suits their risk/return requirements, is likely to increase the chances of a successful issue.

Activity 7.8

What is the advantage to shareholders of having the right of first refusal on new shares issued for cash?

The main advantage is that control of the business by existing shareholders will not be diluted, provided they take up the offer of new shares.

A rights offer usually allows existing shareholders to acquire shares in the business at a price below the current market price. This means that entitlement to participate in a rights offer has a cash value. Existing shareholders who do not wish to take up the rights offer can sell their rights to other investors. Calculating the cash value of the rights entitlement is quite straightforward. An example can be used to illustrate how this is done.

Example 7.1

Shaw Holdings plc has 20 million ordinary shares of 50p in issue. These shares are currently valued on the Stock Exchange at £1.60 per share. The directors of Shaw Holdings plc believe the business requires additional long-term capital and have decided to make a one-for-four issue (that is, one new share for every four shares held) at £1.30 per share. What is the value of the rights per new share?

Solution

The first step in the valuation process is to calculate the price of a share following the rights issue. This is known as the *ex-rights price* and is simply a weighted average of the price of shares before the issue of rights and the price of the rights shares. In the above example we have a one-for-four rights issue. The theoretical ex-rights price is, therefore, calculated as follows:

Example 7.1 continued

	£
Price of four shares before the rights issue (4 × £1.60):	6.40
Price of taking up one rights share:	1.30
	7.70
	7.70
Theoretical ex-rights price:	5
	£1.54

As the price of each share, in theory, should be £1.54 following the rights issue and the price of a rights share is £1.30, the value of the rights offer will be the difference between the two:

£1.54 – £1.30 = £0.24 per new share

Market forces will usually ensure the actual price of rights and the theoretical price will be fairly close.

Activity 7.9

An investor with 2,000 shares in Shaw Holdings plc (see Example 7.1) has contacted you for investment advice. She is undecided whether to take up the rights issue, sell the rights or allow the rights offer to lapse.
Calculate the effect on the net wealth of the investor of each of the options being considered.

If the investor takes up the rights issue, she will be in the following position:

	£
Value of holding after rights issue [(2,000 + 500) × £1.54]	3,850
Less Cost of buying the rights shares (500 × £1.30)	650
	3,200

If the investor sells the rights, she will be in the following position:

	£
Value of holding after rights issue (2,000 × £1.54)	3,080
Sale of rights (500 × £0.24)	120
	3,200

If the investor lets the rights offer lapse, she will be in the following position:

	£
Value of holding after rights issue (2,000 × £1.54)	3,080

As we can see, the first two options should leave her in the same position concerning net wealth as she was before the rights issue. Before the rights issue she had 2,000 shares worth £1.60 each, or £3,200. However, she will be worse off if she allows the rights offer to lapse than under the other two options. In practice, the business may sell the rights offer on behalf of the investor and pass on the proceeds in order to ensure that she is not worse off as a result of the issue.

When considering a rights issue, the directors of a business must first consider the amount of funds that it needs to raise. This will depend on the future plans and commitments of the business. The directors must then decide on the issue price of the rights shares. Generally speaking, this decision is not of critical importance. In the example above, the business made a one-for-four issue with the price of the rights shares set at £1.30. However, it could have raised the same amount by making a one-for-two issue and setting the rights price at £0.65, or a one-for-one issue and setting the price at £0.325 and so on. The issue price that is finally decided upon will not affect the value of the underlying assets of the business or the proportion of the underlying assets and earnings of the business to which the shareholder is entitled. The directors must, however, ensure that the issue price is not *above* the current market price of the shares in order for the issue to be successful.

Activity 7.10

Why will a rights issue fail if the issue price of the shares is above the current market price of the shares?

If the issue price is above the current market price, it would be cheaper for the investor to purchase shares in the business in the open market (assuming transaction costs are not significant) than to acquire the shares by taking up the rights offer.

In practice, a rights issue will usually be priced at a significant discount to the market price of shares at the date of the rights announcement. Time will elapse between the announcement date of the rights issue and the date at which the rights shares must be subscribed, and during this period there is always a risk that the market price of the shares will fall and the rights issue price will be higher than the market price at the subscription date. If this occurs, the rights issue will fail for the reasons mentioned in Activity 7.10. The higher the discount offered, therefore, the lower the risk of such failure.

Despite the attractions of rights issues, it can be argued that the rights given to existing shareholders will prevent greater competition for new shares in the business. This may, in turn, increase the costs of raising finance for the business because other forms of share issue may be able to raise the required finance more cheaply.

Rights issues are frequently made to raise cash for expansion, but **Real World 7.9** gives an example of where a rights issue was made for exactly the opposite reason.

REAL WORLD 7.9

Laura Ashley to close 35 European stores   **FT**

Laura Ashley has taken the unusual step of launching a rights issue, not to fund expansion but to assist it in the closure of 35 of its loss-making European stores, including all its remaining shops in Germany.

The UK clothing and home furnishing retailer, which earlier this month warned that full-year results would be below market expectations, is hoping to raise £9m ($14.6m) through the issue priced at about 8p a share.

It will go some way to pay for the estimated £7.7m cost of closing the stores, which have dragged down results at the group that is known for its floral offerings, both in clothing and furniture.

In its Christmas trading statement Laura Ashley blamed the fall in profits, that knocked almost 20 per cent off its already battered shares, on the heavy discounting in its European stores.

KC Ng, chief executive, said the rights issue and closures would place the company on a 'firmer footing' for further development.

Laura Ashley said that it remained committed to its remaining 18 European stores, despite the closure of 35 stores. The group is looking for franchise partners to keep the profitable stores going . . .

Source: 'Laura Ashley to close 35 European stores', Lisa Urquhart, *Financial Times*, 23 January 2003, www.FT.com

Bonus issues

→ A **bonus issue** should not be confused with a rights issue of shares. A bonus, or scrip, issue also involves the issue of new shares to existing shareholders in proportion to their existing shareholdings. However, shareholders do not have to pay for the new shares issued. The bonus issue is achieved by transferring a sum from the reserves to the paid-up share capital of the business and then issuing shares, equivalent in value to the amount transferred, to existing shareholders. As the reserves are already owned by the shareholders, they do not have to pay for the shares issued. In effect, a bonus issue will simply convert reserves into paid-up capital. To understand this conversion process, and its effect on the financial position of the business, let us consider Example 7.2.

Example 7.2

Wickham plc has the following abbreviated balance sheet as at 31 March:

	£m
Net assets	20
Financed by	
Share capital (£1 ordinary shares)	10
Reserves	10
	20

The directors decide to convert £5 million of the reserves to paid-up capital. As a result, it was decided that a one-for-two bonus issue should be made. Following the bonus issue, the balance sheet of Wickham plc will be as follows:

	£m
Net assets	20
Financed by	
Share capital (£1 ordinary shares)	15
Reserves	5
	20

We can see in Example 7.2 that the share capital of the business has increased and there has been a corresponding decrease in the reserves of the business. The net assets of the business remain unchanged by the bonus issue. Although each shareholder will own more shares following the bonus issue, the proportion held of the total number of shares in issue will remain unchanged and so the stake in the business and the net assets of the business will remain unchanged. Thus, bonus issues do not, of themselves, result in an increase in shareholder wealth. They will simply switch part of the owners claim from reserves to share capital.

Activity 7.11

Assume that the market price per share in Wickham plc (see Example 7.2) before the bonus issue was £2.10. What will be the market price per share following the share issue?

The business has made a one-for-two issue. A holder of two shares would therefore be in the following position before the bonus issue:

2 shares held at £2.10 market price = £4.20

As the wealth of the shareholder has not increased as a result of the issue, the total value of the shareholding will remain the same. This means that, as the shareholder holds one more share following the issue, the market value per share will now be:

$$\frac{£4.20}{3} = \underline{£1.40}$$

You may wonder from the calculations above why bonus issues are made by businesses, particularly as the effect of a bonus issue may be to reduce the reserves available for dividend payments. A number of reasons have been put forward to explain this type of share issue, which includes the following:

● *Share price.* The share price of a business may be very high and, as a result, its share may become more difficult to trade on the Stock Exchange. It seems that shares that trade within a certain price range generate more interest and activity within the market. By increasing the number of shares in issue, the market price of each share will be reduced, which may make the shares more marketable.
● *Lender confidence.* The effect of making a transfer from distributable reserves to paid-up share capital will be to increase the permanent capital base of the business. This move may increase confidence among lenders. In effect, a bonus issue will lower the risk of the business reducing its ordinary shareholders' investment through dividend distributions, thereby leaving lenders in an exposed position.
● *Market signals.* The directors may use a bonus issue as an opportunity to signal to investors their confidence in the future prospects of the business. The issue may be accompanied by the announcement of good news concerning the business (for example, securing a large contract or achieving an increase in profits). Under these circumstances, the share price of the business may rise in the expectation that earnings/dividends per share will be maintained. Shareholders would, therefore, be better off following the issue. However, it is the *information content* of the bonus issue, rather than the issue itself, that will create this increase in wealth.

Real World 7.10 provides an example of a bonus issue by a well-known business.

REAL WORLD 7.10

Bonus on the cards

In October 2003, Clinton Cards plc announced a one-for-two bonus issue. The company said that the objective of this was to increase the liquidity/marketability of the shares by reducing the market price per share. This is the first of the three reasons mentioned above for making bonus issues. The company's share price had increased steeply on the back of strong past, and expected future, profit growth.

Clinton Cards plc is the UK's largest specialist greetings card retailer.

Source: Based on information in FT Money, Markets week world, 'Clinton Cards', *Financial Times*, 4 October 2003, www.FT.com

Offer for sale

An **offer for sale** involves a business, trading as a public limited company, selling a new issue of shares to a financial institution known as an issuing house. However, shares that are already in issue may also be sold to an issuing house. In the latter case, existing shareholders agree to sell their shares to the issuing house. The issuing house will, in turn, sell the shares purchased from either the business or its shareholders to the public. The issuing house will publish a prospectus that sets out details of the business and the type of shares to be sold, and investors will be invited to apply for shares.

The advantage of this type of issue, from the business's viewpoint, is that the sale proceeds of the shares are certain. The issuing house will take on the risk of selling the shares to investors. This type of issue is often used when a business seeks a listing on the Stock Exchange and wishes to raise a large amount of funds.

Public issue

A **public issue** involves a business making a direct invitation to the public to purchase shares in the business. Typically, this is done through a newspaper advertisement, and the invitation to the public will be accompanied by the publication of a prospectus. The shares may, once again, be either a new issue or shares already in issue. An issuing house may be asked by the business to help administer the issue of the shares to the public and to offer advice concerning an appropriate selling price. However, the business rather than the issuing house will take on the risk of selling the shares. An offer for sale and a public issue will both result in a widening of share ownership in the business.

Setting a share price

When making an issue of shares, the business or the issuing house will usually set a price for the shares. However, establishing a share price may not be an easy task, particularly where the market is volatile or where the business has unique characteristics. If the share price is set too high, the issue will be undersubscribed and the business (or issuing house) will not receive the amount expected. If the share price is set too low, the issue will be oversubscribed and the business (or issuing house) will receive less than could have been achieved.

One way of dealing with the pricing problem is to make a **tender issue** of shares. This involves the investors determining the price at which the shares are issued. Although the business (or issuing house) may publish a reserve price to help guide investors, it will be up to the individual investor to determine the number of shares to be purchased and the price he or she wishes to pay. Once the offers from investors have been received, a price at which all the shares can be sold will be established (known as the striking price). Investors that have made offers at, or above, the striking price will be issued shares at the striking price and offers received below the striking price will be rejected. Note that *all* of the shares will be issued at the same price, irrespective of the prices actually offered by individual investors.

Example 7.3 illustrates the way in which a striking price is achieved.

Example 7.3

Celibes plc made a tender offer of shares and the following offers were received by investors:

Share price £	No. of shares tendered at this partuclar price 000s	Cumulative no. of shares tendered 000s
£2.80	300	300
£2.40	590	890
£1.90	780	1,670
£1.20	830	2,500

The directors of Celibes plc wish to issue 2,000,000 shares, at a minimum price of £1.20.

The striking price would have to be £1.20 as, above this price, there would be insufficient interest to issue 2,000,000 shares. At the price of £1.20, the total number of shares tendered exceeds the number of shares available and so a partial allottment would be made. Normally, each investor would receive 4 shares for every 5 shares tendered (that is 2,000/2,500).

Activity 7.12

Assume that, rather than issue a fixed number of shares, the directors of Celibes plc (see Example 7.3) wish to maximise the amount raised from the share issue. What would be the appropriate striking price?

The price at which the amount raised from the issue can be maximised is calculated as follows:

Share price £	Cumulative no. of shares 000s	Share sale proceeds £000
£2.80	300	840
£2.40	890	2,136
£1.90	1,670	3,173
£1.20	2,500	3,000

The table shows that the striking price should be £1.90 to maximise the share sale proceeds.

Although tender issues are used occasionally, they are not popular with investors and are, therefore, not in widespread use.

Placing

A **placing** does not involve an invitation to the public to subscribe to shares. Instead, the shares are 'placed' with selected investors, such as large financial institutions. This can be a quick and relatively cheap method of raising funds because savings can be made in advertising and legal costs. However, it can result in the ownership of the business being concentrated in a few hands and may prevent small investors from participating in the new issue of shares. Usually, businesses seeking relatively small amounts of cash will employ this form of issue.

Real World 7.11 describes how Tesco plc, the supermarket chain, has used a placing to raise finance.

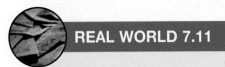

REAL WORLD 7.11

Tesco well placed

FT

Tesco on Tuesday revealed better than expected trading over the Christmas period and announced it was planning to raise £810m ($1.5bn) through a placing of shares.

Tesco said the placing, which will see it put 315m new ordinary shares into the market, equivalent to 4.4 per cent of its issued share capital, would give it the flexibility and firepower to take advantage of further opportunities to grow.

The placing also includes an over allotment option of 45m new ordinary shares.

As part of its expansion plans, Tesco will be using the money to accelerate its non-food offering, introducing more Tesco Extra formats allowing it to expand further into clothing and health and beauty.

As well as concentrating on the larger end of the market, the group said it would be increasing its presence in the convenience market, with the expansion of the Tesco Express brand.

Tesco said it would be well placed to buy some of the Safeway stores up for sale following Morrison's acquisition of the chain.

Terry Leahy, chief executive, said: 'Now is the right time to strengthen our finances further so we can take full advantage of the opportunities available.'

Source: 'Tesco raises £810m in placing as sales rise', *Financial Times*, 13 January 2004.

Providing long-term finance for the smaller business

Although the Stock Exchange provides an important source of long-term finance for large businesses, it is not really suitable for smaller businesses. The aggregate market value of shares that are to be listed on the Stock Exchange must be at least £700,000 and, in practice, the amounts are much higher because of the listing costs identified earlier. Thus, smaller businesses must look elsewhere for help in raising long-term finance. However, various reports and studies over the past seventy years have highlighted the problems that they encounter in doing so. These problems, which can be a major obstacle to growth, include:

- a lack of financial management skills (leading to difficulties in developing credible business plans that will satisfy lenders);
- a lack of knowledge concerning the availability of sources of long-term finance;
- providing sufficient security for loan capital;
- meeting rigorous assessment criteria (for example, a good financial track record over five years);
- an excessively bureaucratic screening process for loan applications (see reference 4 at the end of the chapter).

In addition to the problems identified, it is worth pointing out that the cost of finance is often higher for smaller businesses than for larger businesses because of the higher risks involved.

Not all of the financing constraints are externally imposed; some arise from the attitude of owners. It seems that many owners of small businesses are unwilling to consider raising new finance through the issue of ordinary shares to outsiders as it involves a dilution of control. It has also been claimed that some owners do not take out loans because they do not believe in borrowing (see reference 5 at the end of the chapter).

Although obtaining long-term finance is not always easy for smaller businesses (and one consequence may be excessive reliance on short-term sources of finance, such as bank overdrafts), things have improved over recent years. Some of the more important sources of long-term finance that are now available are considered below.

Venture capital

Venture capital is long-term capital provided to small and medium-sized businesses wishing to grow but which do not have ready access to stock markets. The supply of venture capital (or *private equity* capital as it is sometimes called) has increased rapidly in the UK over recent years since both government and corporate financiers have shown greater commitment to entrepreneurial activity. The main types of investments that are likely to be of interest to venture capitalists and the process by which investments are undertaken are considered below.

Types of investment

Venture capitalists are interested in investing in small and medium-sized businesses. The businesses must have good growth potential and the owners and managers must have the ambition and determination to realise this potential. Businesses financed by venture capitalists have higher levels of risk than would be acceptable to other providers of finance, but will also have the potential for higher returns. Venture capitalists will usually invest for a period of five years or more, with the amount varying according to need.

Venture capitalists provide share capital and loan finance for different types of business situations, including the following:

- *Start-up capital.*   This is available to businesses that are still at the concept stage of development through to those businesses that are ready to commence trading. The finance provided is usually to help design, develop or market new products and services.
- *Other early stage capital.*   This is available to businesses that have undertaken their development work and are ready to begin operations.
- *Expansion (development) capital.*   This aims to provide funding for growing businesses for additional working capital, new equipment, and so on. It may also include rescue finance, which is used to turn around a business after a period of poor performance.
- *Refinancing bank borrowings.*   This is aimed at reducing the level of gearing.
- *Secondary purchases.*   This refers to finance used to purchase shares in order to buy out part of the ownership of a business or to buy out another venture capitalist.
- *Buy-out capital.*   This is capital available to acquire an existing business. A management buy-out (MBO) is where the funds are used to help the existing management team to acquire the business, and an institutional buy-out (IBO) is where the venture capitalist acquires the business and installs a management team of its choice.

● *Buy-in capital.* This is capital available to acquire an existing business by an external management team. This kind of acquisition is known as a management buy-in (MBI). Buy-outs/buy-ins often occur when a large business wishes to divest itself of one of its operating units or when a family business wishes to sell out because of succession problems.

In practice, venture capitalists make much higher levels of investment in growth businesses and management acquisitions than in business start-ups. Although business start-ups may be important to the health of the economy, they are very high risk: investing in existing businesses is a much safer bet. Furthermore, start-up businesses often require relatively small amounts of finance and so the high cost of investigating and monitoring the investment can make this type of investment unprofitable.

Real World 7.12 provides an impression of venture capital investment in UK businesses.

REAL WORLD 7.12

Nothing ventured, nothing gained

Figures 7.5 and 7.6 show the investments made by venture capitalists during 2003 according to financing stage.

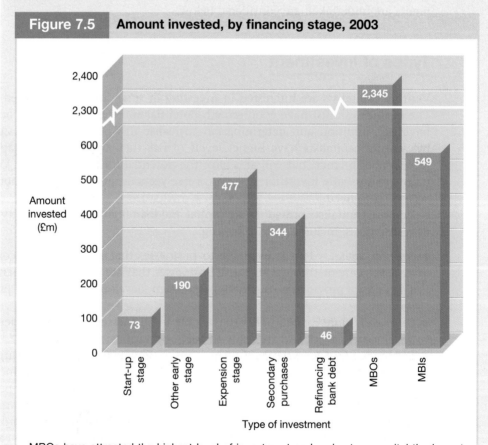

Figure 7.5 Amount invested, by financing stage, 2003

MBOs have attracted the highest level of investment and early-stage capital the lowest level of investment.

Source: Charts compiled from information in BVCA (2004) *BVCA Report on Investment Activity 2003*, British Venture Capital Association.

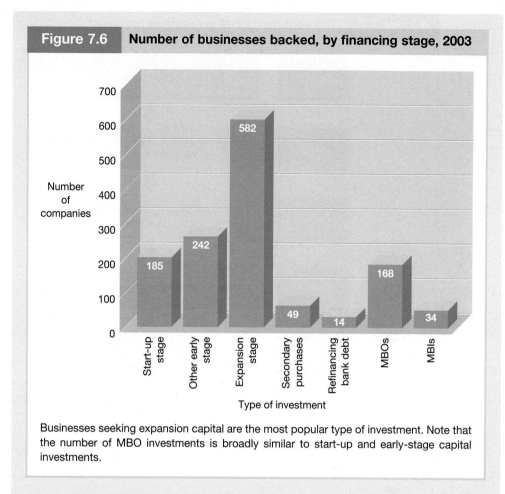

Figure 7.6   Number of businesses backed, by financing stage, 2003

Businesses seeking expansion capital are the most popular type of investment. Note that the number of MBO investments is broadly similar to start-up and early-stage capital investments.

When comparing the two figures above, we can see that the number of start-up businesses backed is slightly more than the number of MBOs. However, MBOs receive, on average, much higher levels of funding than start-ups: the average funding for MBOs is £17.7 million compared with £0.4 million for start-ups.

Source: Charts compiled from information in BVCA (2004) *BVCA Report on Investment Activity 2003*, British Venture Capital Association.

The venture capital process

Venture capital investment involves a five-step process that is similar to the investment process undertaken within a business. The five steps are set out in Figure 7.7, and below we consider each of these five steps.

Step 1: Obtaining the funds

Venture capitalists obtain their funds from various sources including large financial institutions (for example, pension funds), wealthy individuals and direct appeals to the public. Having obtained the funds, there is often a two- or three-year time lag between obtaining the required amount of funds and investing in appropriate investment opportunities. This is partly because new investment opportunities may take some time to identify and partly because, once found, these opportunities require careful investigation.

Figure 7.7   The venture capital investment process

The figure shows the five steps that a venture capitalist will go through when making an investment in a business.

Source: Van der Wayer (see reference 6 at the end of the chapter).

Step 2: Evaluating investment opportunities and making a selection

Once opportunities have been identified, the business plans prepared by the management team will be reviewed and an assessment will be made of the investment potential, including the potential for growth. When making an assessment, the following areas will be considered:

● the market for the products
● the business processes and the ways in which they can be managed
● the ambition and quality of the management team
● the opportunities for improving performance
● the types of risks involved and the ways in which they can be managed
● the track record and future prospects of the business.

The venture capitalists will also be interested to see whether the likely financial returns are commensurate with the risks that have to be taken. The internal rate of return (IRR) method is often used in helping to make this assessment, and an IRR in excess of 20 per cent is normally required (see reference 7 at the end of the chapter).

Step 3: Structuring the terms of the investment

When structuring the financing agreement, venture capitalists will try to ensure that their own exposure to risk is properly managed. This will involve establishing control mechanisms within the financing agreements to protect their investment. One important control mechanism is the requirement to receive information on the progress of the business at regular intervals. The venture capitalists will often stage the injection of funds over time rather than providing all the required funds at the beginning of the venture. They will use the information provided by the business, as well as information collected from other sources, as a basis for agreeing each staged payment. In this way, the progress of the business is reviewed on a regular basis and, where serious problems arise, the venture capitalists will retain the option of abandoning the project in order to contain any loss.

In some cases, the venture capitalist may manage the risk by sharing the financing requirements of the business with other venture capitalists. Establishing a financing syndicate will reduce the potential risks for the venture capitalist but it will also reduce the potential returns. The use of financing syndicates can also lead to the possibility of disputes between its members, particularly when things do not go according to plan.

The finance provided may be in the form of ordinary shares, loan stock or preference shares, and often a combination of these is employed. Convertible loans can offer the venture capitalists a useful hedge against risk. If things do not go according to plan and the venture becomes unprofitable, the venture capitalists will have the loan agreement as a protection for the investment. If, however, the venture is profitable, the venture capitalist can exercise the option to convert the loan stock to ordinary shares and thereby participate in the success of the business. Preference shares are similar to loans in so far as they confer priority over ordinary shares in respect of annual returns and asset distributions and, like loan capital, they can provide the option to convert to ordinary shares at some future date. Preference shares have the added advantage, however, of not taking up the debt capacity of the business that may be useful to the future financing needs of the business.

Venture capitalists will usually expect the owner/managers to demonstrate their commitment by investing in the business. Although the amounts they invest may be small in relation to the total investment, they should be large in relation to their personal wealth.

Step 4: Implementing the deal and monitoring progress

Venture capitalists usually have a close working relationship with client businesses throughout the period of the investment. It is quite common for the venture capitalists to have a representative on the board of directors in order to keep an eye on the investment. During the investment period it is usual for the venture capitalists to offer expert advice on technical and marketing matters. In this respect they provide a form of consultancy service to their clients. The venture capitalists will be keen to see whether the business plans prepared at the time of the initial investment are achieved. Those businesses that meet their key targets are likely to find the presence of the venture capitalists less intrusive than those businesses that do not. Monitoring by the venture capitalists is likely to be much closer at the early stages of the investment until certain problems, such as the quality of management and cost overruns, become less of a risk (see reference 8 at the end of the chapter).

Step 5: Achieving returns and exiting from the investment

A major part of the total returns from the investment is usually achieved through the final sale of the investment. The particular method of divestment is, therefore, of great concern to the venture capitalist. The most common forms of divestment are through:

● a trade sale (that is, where the investment is sold to another business)
● flotation of the business on the Stock Exchange, or the sale or quoted equity
● sale of the investment to the management team (buy-back)
● sale of the investment to another venture capitalist or financial institution.

In some cases, there will be an 'involuntary exit' when the business fails. The venture capitalist will then have to write off the investment.

Real World 7.13 shows the amounts divested by various methods during 2002 by venture capitalists.

REAL WORLD 7.13

Looking for an exit route

| Figure 7.8 | Amounts divested by venture capitalists during 2002 |

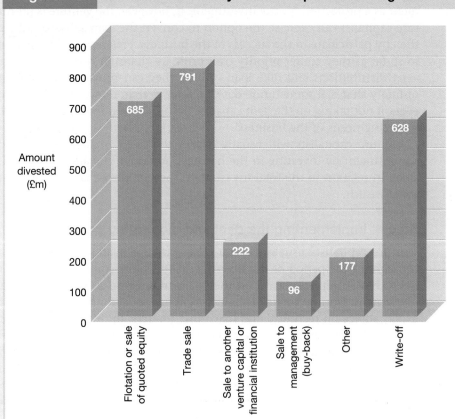

Trade sales generated the largest proceeds, followed by flotations and sale of quoted equities. These two categories account for more than half of the total divestments during the year.

Source: Complied from information in *BVCA Report on Investment Activity 2002*, British Venture Capital Association, www.bvca.co.uk

Venture capital and borrowing

A venture capitalist may require a business to borrow a significant proportion of its financing needs from a bank or other financial institution, thereby reducing the amount that it needs to invest in the business. In some cases, the cash flows generated by the business during the period in which the venture capitalist invests may then be used to reduce, or eliminate the outstanding loan.

Example 7.4 provides a simple illustration of this process.

Example 7.4

Ippo Ltd is a venture capitalist that has recently purchased Andante Ltd for £80 million. The business requires an immediate injection of £60 million to meet its needs and Ippo Ltd has insisted that this be raised by a 10 per cent bank loan. Ippo Ltd intends to float Andante Ltd in four years' time to exit from the investment and then expects to receive £160 million on the sale of its shares. During the next four years, the cash flows generated by Andante Ltd (after interest has been paid) will be used to eliminate the outstanding loan.

The net cash flows (before interest) of the business over the four years leading up to the flotation, are predicted to be as follows:

Year	1	2	3	4
	£m	£m	£m	£m
	20.0	20.0	20.1	15.0

Ippo Ltd has a cost of capital of 18 per cent and uses the internal rate of return (IRR) method to evaluate investment projects.

The following calculations reveal that the loan can be entirely repaid over the next four years.

	Yr 1	Yr 2	Yr 3	Yr 4
	£m	£m	£m	£m
Net cash flows	20.0	20.0	20.1	15.0
Loan interest (10%)	(6.0)	(4.6)	(3.1)	(1.4)
Cash available to repay loan	14.0	15.4	17.0	13.6
Loan at start of year	60.0	46.0	30.6	13.6
Cash available to repay loan	14.0	15.4	17.0	13.6
Loan at end of year	46.0	30.6	13.6	–

There are no cash flows remaining after the loan is repaid and so Ippo Ltd will receive nothing until the end of the fourth year, when the shares are sold.

The IRR of the investment will be the discount rate which, when applied to the net cash inflows, will provide an NPV of zero. Thus,

$$(£160m \times \text{Discount factor}) - £80m = 0$$
$$\text{Discount factor} = 0.50$$

A discount rate of approximately 19 per cent will give a discount factor of 0.5 in four years' time.

Thus, the IRR of the investment is approximately 19 per cent. This is higher than the costs of capital of Ippo Ltd and so the investment will increase the wealth of its shareholders.

Taking on a large loan imposes a tight financial discipline on the managers of a business as there must be always be enough cash to make interest payments and capital repayments. This should encourage them to be aggressive in chasing sales and to bear down on costs. Taking on a loan may also boost the returns to the venture capitalist.

Activity 7.13

Assume that:

(i) Ippo Ltd (see Example 7.4) provides additional ordinary share capital at the beginning of the investment period of £60 million, thereby eliminating the need for Andante Ltd to take on a bank loan;

(ii) any cash flows generated by Andante Ltd would be received by Ippo Ltd in the form of annual dividends.

What would be the IRR of the total investment in Andante Ltd for Ippo Ltd?

The IRR can be calculated using the trial and error method as follows. At discount rates of 10 per cent and 16 per cent, the NPV of the investment proposal is:

		Trial 1		Trial 2	
Year	Cash flows	Discount rate	Present value	Discount rate	Present value
	£m	10%	£m	16%	£m
0	(140.0)	1.00	(140.0)	1.00	(140.0)
1	20.0	0.91	18.2	0.86	17.2
2	20.0	0.83	16.6	0.74	14.8
3	20.1	0.75	15.1	0.64	12.9
4	175.0	0.68	119.0	0.55	96.3
			NPV 28.9		NPV 1.2

The calculations reveal that, at a discount rate of 16 per cent, the NPV is close to zero. Thus, the IRR of the investment is approximately 16 per cent, which is lower than the cost of capital. This means that the investment will reduce the wealth of the shareholders of Ippo Ltd.

The calculations in Example 7.4 and Activity 7.13 show that, by Andante Ltd taking on a bank loan, the returns to the venture capitalist are increased. This 'gearing effect', as it is called, is discussed in more detail in the next chapter.

Real World 7.14 discusses some of the benefits and problems of using venture (private equity) finance.

REAL WORLD 7.14

Venture capitalists – saints or sinners?   **FT**

Job creation, sales growth and export growth were far greater in private equity-backed businesses than in their publicly listed counterparts, a study released on Monday says.

The British Venture Capital Association's economic impact survey estimates that companies backed by the industry generate annual sales of £187bn ($343bn) and employ 2.7m people, or 18 per cent of private sector workforce.

Employment in private equity businesses rose an average 20 per cent a year in the five years to 2004, more than five times the increase in FTSE 100 companies.

Their sales rose 23 per cent a year over the five-year period, more than twice that of FTSE 100 companies, while exports grew 20 per cent a year compared with a national growth rate of 3.3 per cent.

In the last two decades, private equity has supplied £48bn worth of capital to 21,000 UK companies, of which nearly 12,000 are still trading, according to the BVCA.

John Mackie, BVCA chief executive, said: 'It demonstrates the continued importance of the private equity industry to the economy.'

Mark Pacitti, private equity partner at Deloitte, said private companies differed from public companies because there was better alignment of shareholder, management and business objectives.

'A public company with thousands of shareholders ends up being a very regulated business whereas private equity has only two big shareholders, a financial sponsor and a management team. That makes them much easier businesses to grow without the burden of heavy regulation.'

Critics argue, however, that private equity is an expensive source of capital. The large amounts of debt required to fund private equity deals significantly increase the risks to the company, sometimes to unacceptable levels.

Le Meridien, the hotels group, Welcome Break, the motorway service station operator, and Boxclever, the UK television rental business, struggled with debt burdens under private equity ownership.

Source: 'Survey highlights UK private equity growth', *Financial Times*, 31 October 2004.

Self-assessment question 7.1

Ceres plc is a large conglomerate which, following a recent strategic review, has decided to sell its agricultural foodstuffs division. The managers of this operating division believe that it could be run as a separate business and are considering a management buyout. The division has made an operating profit of £10 million for the year to 31 May Year 6 and the board of Ceres plc has indicated that it would be prepared to sell the division to the managers for a price based on a multiple of 12 times the operating profit for the most recent year.

The managers of the operating division have £5 million of the finance necessary to acquire the division and have approached Vesta Ltd, a venture capital business, to see whether it would be prepared to assist in financing the proposed management buy-out. The divisional managers have produced the following forecast of operating profits for the next four years:

Year to 31 May	Year 7 £m	Year 8 £m	Year 9 £m	Year 10 £m
Operating profit	10.0	11.0	10.5	13.5

To achieve the profit forecasts shown above, the division will have to invest a further £1 million in working capital during the year to 31 May Year 8. The division has freehold premises costing £40 million and plant and machinery costing £20 million. In calculating net operating profit for the division, these assets are depreciated, using the straight line method, at the rate of $2\frac{1}{2}$ per cent on cost and 15 per cent on cost, respectively.

Self-assessment question 7.1 continued

Vesta Ltd has been asked to invest £45 million in return for 90 per cent of the ordinary shares in a new company specifically created to run the operating division. The divisional managers would receive the remaining 10 per cent of the ordinary shares in return for their £5 million investment. The managers believe that a bank would be prepared to provide a 10 per cent loan for any additional finance necessary to acquire the division. (The freehold premises of the division are currently valued at £80 million and so there would be adequate security for a loan up to this amount.) All net cash flows generated by the new company during each financial year will be applied to reducing the balance of the loan and no dividends will be paid to shareholders until the loan is repaid. (There are no other cash flows apart from those mentioned above.) The loan agreement will be for a period of eight years. However, if the company is sold during this period, the loan must be repaid in full by the shareholders.

Vesta Ltd intends to realise its investment after four years when the fixed assets and working capital (excluding the bank loan) of the company are expected to be sold to a rival business at a price based on a multiple of 12 times the most recent annual operating profit. Out of these proceeds, the bank loan will have to be repaid by existing shareholders before they receive their returns. Vesta Ltd has a cost of capital of 25 per cent and employs the internal rate of return method to evaluate investment proposals.

Ignore taxation.

Workings should be in £millions and should be made to one decimal place.

Required:

(a) Calculate:
  (i) The amount of the loan outstanding at 31 May Year 10 immediately prior to the sale of the company
  (ii) The approximate internal rate of return for Vesta Ltd of the investment proposal described above

(b) State, with reasons, whether or not Vesta Ltd should invest in this proposal.

REAL WORLD 7.15

Learning Venturespeak

If you have to deal with venture capitalists it is important for you to be able to speak their language. 3i plc, a leading venture capitalist, has produced an interesting and amusing guide to this new language. Some of the vocabulary is reproduced or adapted from this guide below:

MBO　Management buy-out. A team of managers employed by a business purchases the business, usually with the help of an institutional investor.
MBI　Management buy-in. An incoming management team buys a business, again it is usually with the help of an institutional investor.
BIMBO　A combination of MBI and MBO.
COLOMBO　Colossally over-priced MBO.
DINGO　Don't invest, no growth opportunity.
Dog　A bad investment.

Flagpole syndrome   The start of a slippery slope for a hitherto successful business when the chairman decides the business is important enough to have a flagpole in the car park.

RAMBO   Rescue after MBO.

Spreadsheet jockey   Someone who loves analysing performance for the sake of it, but his or her spreadsheets don't really add much to the sum of human knowledge.

Source: Venturespeak 2000, 3i plc.

Business angels

→ **Business angels** are often wealthy individuals who have been successful in business. They are usually willing to invest somewhere between £10,000 and £250,000 in a start-up business or a business that is at an early stage of development through a share-holding. In some cases, larger amounts may be raised by a single angel or by a syndicate of angels. Business angels fill an important gap in the market as the nature and size of investments that they find appealing will often be unappealing to venture capitalists. The investment is usually made for a period of three to five years and the exit routes are basically the same as those used by venture capitalists. In addition to providing finance, a business angel can usually offer a wealth of business experience to budding tycoons.

Although business angels are looking for financial returns they may also be looking for interest and involvement. This may lead them to accept lower returns than would normally be expected for the risks involved. A further advantage of using business angels is that they can often make investment decisions quickly, particularly where they have expertise in the relevant business sector. However, the amounts of finance available are generally lower than venture capitalists can provide (see reference 9 at the end of the chapter).

Business angels offer an informal source of share finance and it is not always easy for owners of small businesses to locate a suitable angel. However, a number of business angel networks have now developed to help owners of small businesses find their 'perfect partner'. These networks provide a variety of services including information for angels concerning investment opportunities and advice to businesses on developing business plans. Regular meetings may be organised where entrepreneurs can present their business plans to potential angels. Many business angel networks belong to the National Business Angels Network (NBAN), which is a not-for-profit trade association.

Government assistance

One of the most effective ways in which the government assists small businesses is through the Small Firms Loan Guarantee Scheme. This scheme aims to help small businesses that have viable business plans but which lack the security to obtain a loan. The scheme guarantees loans made over a 2–10-year period to small businesses from participating banks for sums of £5,000 to £100,000 (increased to £250,000 for businesses that have been trading for at least two years). The government will guarantee 75 per cent of the amount borrowed in return for a premium of 2 per cent on the amount of the loan. Only businesses with sales of no more than £3 million per year (£5 million per year for manufacturing businesses) are eligible for the scheme.

The government also provides financial help through grants (for example, research and development) and by providing investors in small businesses with tax incentives (for example, through Venture Capital Trusts). In addition, it helps small businesses by providing information (for example, through Business Links) concerning the sources of finance available and by providing practical advice. It was mentioned earlier that lack of knowledge concerning funding sources can be a real problem for small businesses.

Finally, EU grants may be available to certain businesses, such as those located in deprived areas or those operating in an innovative sector.

Alternative Investment Market (AIM)

Several European stock markets have been established recently that specialise in the shares of smaller businesses. These include the **Alternative Investment Market (AIM)**, which is the largest and most successful. AIM is a second-tier market of the London Stock Exchange that was established in 1995. It offers businesses many of the benefits of a listing without the burdensome regulatory environment that accompanies a listing on the main market. The main regulatory differences between the two markets' tiers can be summarised as follows:

Main market	AIM
● Minimum 25 per cent shares in public hands	● No minimum shares to be in public hands
● Normally, 3-year trading record required	● No trading record requirement
● Prior shareholder approval required for substantial acquisitions and disposals	● No prior shareholder approval for transactions
● Pre-vetting of admission documents by the UK Listing Authority	● Admission documents not pre-vetted by the Stock Exchange or UK Listing Authority
● Minimum market capitalisation	● No minimum market capitalisation

Source: Adapted from information on www.londonstockexchange.com

AIM can provide venture capitalists with a useful means of liquidating an investment and can provide growing businesses with a stepping stone to the main market. **Real World 7.16** shows the distribution of businesses, by market capitalisation, in this market.

REAL WORLD 7.16

Distribution of AIM listed businesses by equity market value

Figure 7.9   Distribution of AIM businesses by equity market value

The graph shows that 681 businesses have a market capitalisation of less than £25 million and more than 816 businesses have a market capitalisation of less than £50 million. However, five businesses have a market capitalisation of more than £500 million.

Source: After www.londonstockexchange.com, AIM market statistics, November 2004.

AIM has attracted investors as well as businesses. Research shows that shares of smaller businesses are more actively traded on AIM than similar-size businesses on the main market (see reference 10 at the end of the chapter). **Real World 7.17** reveals the international ambitions of this second-tier market.

REAL WORLD 7.17

AIM markets its appeal around the world   **FT**

Last week's flotation of China Wonder, the first Chinese company to be listed on the Alternative Investment Market, is a sign of the market's international ambitions. The lightly regulated market for smaller companies has attracted 87 international companies out of 930 listings since its inception.

Real World 7.17 continued

'There are very few places for smaller companies to get access to public equity, and you certainly don't have those markets in Europe,' said Martin Graham, who is head of Aim as well as director of the London Stock Exchange's market services.

Aim next week becomes an exchange-regulated market to preserve its minimalist approach to regulation and avoid being subject to European Union directives. Companies listing on Aim are not governed by the UK Listing Authority rules, for example.

The market has been expanding so fast in the past two years, that its popularity could even eclipse that of the LSE's main market in coming years.

But Mr Graham plays down any rivalry. 'Both the main market and Aim will grow as a whole. You could have a situation in three to six years where they have the same numbers [of companies listed], especially as we internationalise Aim.'

There are currently 1,486 UK companies and 359 international companies, including investment trusts, listed on the main market. The market capitalisation of Aim is £24bn compared with trillions for the main market.

'The philosophy here is that we have a range of markets to suit different companies with different needs,' Mr Graham said. 'In the main market there is far greater access to capital and greater prestige.'

But a trickle of listed companies has flowed from the main market to Aim in recent months, partly to escape bureaucracy. About 190 companies have moved to Aim while 95 have moved up.

Fund managers' growing interest in smaller companies has put the spotlight on Aim in the past couple of years. A fifth of the £13bn raised on the market has come this year with 211 companies joining up to the end of August.

With a dearth of flotations on established stock markets across Europe this year, Aim has been the host to 60 per cent of Europe's initial public offerings by number.

Canada, Australia and Ireland are the countries of origin for most overseas listings on Aim but there is interest in the rest of the EU where start-up markets such as Germany's Neuer Markt have closed in the wake of the dotcom boom.

There are 20 companies from Canada and 19 from Australia listed on Aim but so far only two from Germany and two from Italy.

'It is not just important to bring the companies but also the local investors and brokers, without that, the companies will just drift back to their home markets,' said Mathew Wootton, deputy head of Aim.

Mr Graham and Mr Wootton are looking to attract more companies from China and India to the market. 'We have traditionally undersold ourselves we've got to encourage investors to be more international.'

Source: 'Aim markets its appeal around the world', FT.com, 4 October 2004.

Amazon.com: a case history

The internet retailer Amazon.com has grown considerably during its short life. Below we can see how that growth was financed in the early years. To begin with, the business relied heavily on the founder and his family for finance. However, as the business grew, other ways of raising finance, as described in the chapter, have become more important. **Real World 7.18** charts the progress of the business in its early years.

REAL WORLD 7.18

Financing Amazon.com – the early years

Financing of Amazon.com (1994–99)

Dates	Share price	Source of funds
1994: July to November	$0.0010	**Founder:** Jeff Bezos starts Amazon.com with $10,000; borrows $44,000
1995: February to July	$0.1717	**Family:** founder's father and mother invest $245,000
1995: August to December	$0.1287–0.3333	**Business angels:** 2 angels invest $54,408
1995/96: December to May	$0.3333	**Business angels:** 20 angels invest $937,000
1996: May	$0.3333	**Family:** founder's siblings invest $20,000
1996: June	$2.3417	**Venture capitalists:** 2 venture capital funds invest $8m
1997: May	$18.00	**IPO*:** 3m shares issued raising $49.1m
1997/98: December to May	$52.11	**Bond issue:** $326m bond issue

* Initial public offering of shares.

Source: Reproduced from Van Osnabrugge, M. and Robinson, R. J., *Angel Investing: Matching Start-up Funds with Start-up Companies – A Guide for Entrepreneurs and Individual Investors*. Copyright © 2000 Jossey-Bass Inc. Reprinted with permission of John Wiley & Sons, Inc.

SUMMARY

The main points in the chapter may be summarised as follows:

The Stock Exchange

- The Stock Exchange is an important primary and secondary market in capital for large businesses.
- Obtaining a Stock Exchange listing can help a business to raise finance and help to raise its profile but obtaining a listing can be costly and the regulatory and other burdens can be onerous.
- Stock Exchange investors are often accused of adopting a short-term perspective although there is no real evidence to support this.
- The Stock Exchange is efficient if information is processed by investors quickly and accurately so that prices faithfully reflect all relevant information.
- Three forms of efficiency have been suggested: the weak form, the semi-strong form and the strong-form.
- If the Stock Exchange is efficient, managers of a listed business should recognize six important lessons:
  - timing doesn't matter
  - don't search for undervalued businesses

    – take note of market reaction
    – you can't fool the market
    – the market decides the level of risk
    – champion the interests of shareholders.

● Stock Exchange 'regularities' and research into investor behaviour has cast doubt on the efficiency of stock markets.

Share issues

● Share issues that involve the payment of cash by investors can take the form of a rights issue, public issue, offer for sale or a private placing.

● A rights issue is made to existing shareholders. Most share issues are of this type as the law requires that shares that are to be issued for cash must first be offered to existing shareholders.

● A public issue involves a direct issue to the public and an offer for sale involves an indirect issue to the public.

● A private placing is an issue of shares to selected investors.

● A bonus (scrip) issue involves issuing shares to existing shareholders but the shareholders do not have to pay for them. The issue is achieved by transferring a sum from reserves to the share capital of the business.

● A tender issue allows the investors to determine the price at which the shares are issued.

Smaller businesses

● Smaller businesses do not have access to the Stock Exchange main market and so must look elsewhere for funds.

● Venture capital (private equity) is long-term capital for small or medium-sized businesses that are not listed on the Stock Exchange. These businesses often have higher levels of risk but provide the venture capitalist with the prospect of higher levels of return.

● Venture capitalists are interested in businesses with good growth prospects and offer finance for start-ups, business expansions and buy-outs.

● The investment period is five years or more and the venture capitalists may exit by a trade sale, flotation, buy-back or sale to another financial institution.

● Business angels are wealthy individuals who are willing to invest in businesses at an early stage of development.

● A number of business angel networks exist to help businesses find a suitable angel.

● The government assists small businesses through guaranteeing loans and by providing grants and tax incentives.

● The Alternative Investment Market (AIM) specialises in the shares of smaller businesses.

● AIM is a second-tier market of the Stock Exchange, which offers businesses the benefits of listing without the burdensome regulatory environment.

→ Key terms

Stock Exchange p. 252	**Public issue** p. 274
FTSE (Footsie) indices p. 254	**Tender issue** p. 274
Market capitalisation p. 255	**Placing** p. 275
Efficient stock market p. 259	**Venture capital** p. 277
Behavioural finance p. 267	**Business angels** p. 287
Rights issue p. 269	**Alternative Investment Market (AIM)**
Bonus issue p. 272	p. 288
Offer for sale p. 274	

For definitions of these terms see the Glossary, pp. 562–571.

Further reading

If you wish to explore the topics discussed in this chapter in more depth, try the following books:

Corporate Finance and Investment, *Pike, R. and Neale, B.*, 4th edn, Financial Times Prentice Hall, 2003, chapter 2.

Corporate Financial Management, *Arnold, G.*, 2nd edn, Financial Times Prentice Hall, 2002, chapters 9 and 10.

Principles of Corporate Finance, *Brealey, R. and Myers, C.*, 7th edn, McGraw-Hill, 2002, chapter 13.

The Inefficient Stock Market, *Haugen, R.*, 2nd edn, Prentice Hall, 2002.

References

1 **Financial Statistics**, Office for National Statistics, October 2004.

2 **Myths Surrounding Short-termism**, *Marsh P.*, Mastering Finance, Financial Times Pitman Publishing, 1998, pp. 168–74.

3 **Stock Market Efficiency: Theory, evidence, implications**, *Keane, S.*, Philip Allan, 1983.

4 **SME Finance and Regulation**, *Institute of Chartered Accountants in England and Wales*, 2000.

5 **Report of the Committee of Inquiry on Small Firms** (Bolton Committee), 1971, Cmnd 4811, HMSO.

6 'The venture capital vacuum', *Van der Wayer, M.*, **Management Today**, July 1995, pp. 60–4.

7 **A Guide to Private Equity**, British Venture Capital Association, 2004, www.bvca.co.uk

8 'Venture capital as an alternative means to allocate capital: an agency-theoretic view', *Norton, E.*, **Entrepreneurship**, Winter 1995, pp. 19–30.

9 **Business Angel Finance 2003/2004**, British Venture Capital Association, 2004, www.bvca.co.uk

10 'Aim makes its mark on the investment map', **Financial Times**, 9 February 2004.

REVIEW QUESTIONS

Answers to these questions can be found in Appendix D at the back of the book.

7.1 UK venture capitalists have been criticised for the low level of funding invested in business start-ups by comparison with the levels invested by their US counterparts. Can you think of possible reasons why such a difference may exist?

7.2 Why might a public business that has a stock exchange listing revert to being an unlisted business?

7.3 Distinguish between an offer for sale and a public issue of shares.

7.4 What kind of attributes do you think the owners and managers of a business should possess to attract venture capital finance?

EXERCISES

Exercises 7.5 to 7.7 are more advanced than 7.1 to 7.4. Those with coloured numbers have answers at the back of the book.

  If you wish to try more exercises, visit the students' side of the Companion Website.

7.1 'Venture capital is an important source of risk capital for smaller businesses.'

Required:
(a) Explain the term 'venture capital' and discuss the main types of business venture that are likely to prove attractive to a venture capital business.
(b) Identify the main issues that the board of directors of a business should take into account when deciding whether to use venture capital finance.
(c) Identify and discuss the factors that a venture capitalist will take into account when assessing an investment proposal.

7.2 (a) Explain what is meant by the term 'efficient market hypothesis' and discuss the three main forms of market efficiency.
(b) Explain the implications of an efficient market for the managers of a business that is listed on the London Stock Exchange.

7.3 'Smaller businesses experience greater problems in raising finance than larger businesses.'

Required:
(a) Discuss the problems that smaller businesses may confront when trying to obtain long-term finance.
(b) Describe how smaller businesses may gain access to long-term finance.

7.4 Pizza Shack plc operates a chain of pizza restaurants in the south of England. The business started operations five years ago and has enjoyed uninterrupted and rapid growth. The directors of the business, however, believe that future growth can only be achieved if the company seeks a listing on the London Stock Exchange. If the directors go ahead with a listing, the financial advisers to the business have suggested that an issue of ordinary shares by tender at a minimum price of £2.20 would be an appropriate method of floating the business. The advisers have suggested that 3 million ordinary shares should be issued in the first instance although the directors of the business are keen to raise the maximum amount of funds possible.

Initial research carried out by the financial advisers suggests that the following demand for shares at different market prices is likely:

Share price	Number of shares tendered at each share price
£	000s
3.60	850
3.20	1,190
2.80	1,380
2.40	1,490
2.00	1,540
1.60	1,560
	8,010

Required:

(a) Discuss the advantages and disadvantages of making a tender issue of shares.

(b) Calculate the expected proceeds from the tender issue, assuming the business:
   (i) Issues 3 million shares
   (ii) Wishes to raise the maximum amount of funds possible.

7.5 The board of directors of Wicklow plc is considering an expansion of production capacity following an increase in sales over the past two years. The most recent accounts for the business are set out below.

Balance sheet as at 30 November Year 5

	£m	£m
Non-current assets		
Freehold premises at cost	28.0	
Less Accumulated depreciation	6.0	22.0
Machinery and equipment at cost	32.0	
Less Accumulated depreciation	21.0	11.0
Fixtures and fittings at cost	10.0	
Less accumulated depreciation	2.0	8.0
		41.0
Current assets		
Stock (inventory) at cost	14.0	
Debtors (receivables)	22.0	
Cash at bank	2.0	
	38.0	
Current liabilities		
Trade creditors (payables)	20.0	18.0
		59.0
Non-current liabilities		
12% loan – Donegal Bank		20.0
		39.0
Equity		
£0.50 ordinary shares		20.0
Retained profit		19.0
		39.0

Profit and loss account (income statement) for the year ended 30 November Year 5

	£m
Sales revenue	95.0
Profit before interest and taxation	8.0
Interest charges	2.4
Profit before taxation	5.6
Corporation tax (30%)	1.7
Profit after taxation	3.9
Dividend proposed and paid	1.2
Retained profit for the year	2.7

The business plans to invest a further £15 million in machinery and equipment and is considering two possible financing options. The first option is to make a one-for-four rights issue. The current market price per share is £2.00 and the rights shares would be issued at a discount of 25 per cent on this market price. The second option is to take a further loan that will have an initial annual rate of interest of 10 per cent. This is a variable rate and, while interest rates have been stable for a number of years, there has been recent speculation that interest rates will begin to rise in the near future.

The outcome of the expansion is not certain. The management team involved in developing and implementing the expansion plans has provided three possible outcomes concerning profit before interest and tax for the following year:

	Change in profits before interest and tax from previous year
Optimistic	+30%
Most likely	+10%
Pessimistic	−20%

The dividend per share for the forthcoming year is expected to remain the same as for the year ended 30 November Year 5.

Wicklow plc has a lower level of gearing than most of its competitors. This has been in accordance with the wishes of the Wicklow family, which has a large shareholding in the company. The share price of the company has shown rapid growth in recent years and the P/E ratio for the business is 20.4 times, which is much higher than the industry average of 14.3 times.

Costs of raising finance should be ignored.

Required:

(a) Prepare calculations that show the effect of each of the possible outcomes of the expansion programme on:
  (i) Earnings per share
  (ii) The gearing ratio (based on year-end figures), and
  (iii) The interest cover ratio of Wicklow plc, under both of the financing options.

(b) Assess each of the financing options available to Wicklow plc from the point of view of an existing shareholder and compare the possible future outcomes with the existing situation.

7.6 Devonian plc has the following long-term capital structure as at 30 November Year 4:

	£m
Ordinary shares 25p fully paid	50.0
General reserve	22.5
Retained profit	25.5
	98.0

The company has no long-term loans.

In the year to 30 November Year 4, the operating profit (net profit before interest and taxation) was £40 million and it is expected that this will increase by 25 per cent during the forthcoming year. The business is listed on the London Stock Exchange and the share price as at 30 November Year 4 was £2.10.

The business wishes to raise £72 million in order to re-equip one of its factories and is considering two possible financing options. The first option is to make a one-for-five rights issue at a discount price of £1.80 per share. The second option is to take out a long-term loan at an interest rate of 10 per cent a year. If the first option is taken, it is expected that the price/earnings (P/E) ratio will remain the same for the forthcoming year. If the second option is taken, it is estimated that the P/E ratio will fall by 10 per cent by the end of the forthcoming year.

Assume a corporation tax rate of 30 per cent.

Required:
(a) Assuming a rights issue of shares is made, calculate:
  (i) The theoretical ex-rights price of an ordinary share in Devonian plc
  (ii) The value of the rights for each original ordinary share.
(b) Calculate the price of an ordinary share in Devonian plc in one year's time assuming:
  (i) A rights issue is made
  (ii) A loan issue is made.
  Comment on your findings.
(c) Explain why rights issues are usually made at a discount.
(d) From the business's viewpoint, how critical is the pricing of a rights issue likely to be?

7.7 Carpets Direct plc wishes to increase the number of its retail outlets in the south of England. The board of directors has decided to finance this expansion programme by raising the funds from existing shareholders through a one-for-four rights issue. The most recent profit and loss account of the business is as follows:

Profit and loss account (income statement) for the year ended 30 April

	£m
Sales revenue	164.5
Profit before interest and taxation	12.6
Interest	6.2
Profit before taxation	6.4
Corporation tax	1.9
Profit after taxation	4.5
Ordinary dividends proposed and paid	2.0
Retained profit for the year	2.5

The share capital of the company consists of 120 million ordinary shares with a par value of £0.50 per share. The shares of the business are currently being traded on the Stock Exchange at a price/earnings ratio of 22 times and the board of directors has decided to issue the new shares at a discount of 20 per cent on the current market value.

Required:
(a) Calculate the theoretical ex-rights price of an ordinary share in Carpets Direct plc.
(b) Calculate the price at which the rights in Carpets Direct plc are likely to be traded.
(c) Identify and evaluate, at the time of the rights issue, each of the options arising from the rights issue to an investor who holds 4,000 ordinary shares before the rights announcement.

8

The cost of capital and the capital structure decision

LEARNING OUTCOMES

When you have completed this chapter, you should be able to:

- Calculate the cost of capital for a business and explain its relevance to investment decision making.

- Calculate the degree of financial gearing for a business and explain its significance.

- Evaluate different capital structure options available to a business.

- Identify and discuss the main points in the debate concerning the optimal capital structure for a business.

INTRODUCTION

When appraising investment opportunities, the cost of capital has an important role to play. In this chapter, we shall see how the cost of capital may be computed. Following this examination, we turn our attention to the factors that should be taken into account when making capital structure decisions and, in particular, the impact of gearing on the risks and returns to ordinary shareholders. We touched on this area in Chapter 3 and will now consider it in more detail. We end the chapter by examining the debate concerning whether an optimal capital structure exists for a business.

Cost of capital

We saw in Chapter 4 that the cost of capital is used as the appropriate discount rate in NPV calculations and as the appropriate 'hurdle rate' when assessing IRR calculations. As investment projects are normally financed from long-term capital, the discount rate, or hurdle rate, that should be applied to new investment projects should reflect the expected returns required by the providers of these various forms of capital. From the viewpoint of the business, these expected returns by investors will represent the **cost of capital** that it employs. This cost is an *opportunity cost* as it represents the return that investors would expect to earn from investments with a similar level of risk.

As the cost of capital is an essential element of investment appraisal, its calculation must be undertaken with care. Failure to do so could lead to adverse consequences for the business.

Activity 8.1

What adverse consequences could result from failing to calculate correctly the cost of capital for a business?

Where a business, which uses the NPV approach to investment appraisal, calculates its cost of capital incorrectly, it will apply the wrong discount rate to investment projects. If the cost of capital figure is understated, this may result in the acceptance of projects that will reduce shareholder wealth. This can arise when the understated cost of capital produces a positive NPV, whereas the correct cost of capital produces a negative NPV. Applying the NPV decision rule of accepting projects that have a positive NPV would, in this case, result in acceptance of unprofitable projects. If, on the other hand, the cost of capital figure is overstated, this may result in the rejection of profitable projects. This can arise when the overstated cost of capital produces a negative NPV whereas the correct cost of capital produces a positive NPV.

Similar problems can occur where a business adopts the IRR method and uses the cost of capital as the hurdle rate.

In Chapter 6, we saw that the main forms of *external* long-term capital for businesses include:

- ordinary shares
- preference shares
- loan capital.

In addition, an important form of *internal* long-term capital is:

- retained profit.

In the sections that follow, we shall see how the cost of each element of long-term capital may be deduced. We shall also see that there is a strong link between the cost of a particular element of capital and its value: both are determined by the level of return. As a result, our discussions concerning the cost of capital will also embrace the issue of value. For reasons that should soon become clear, we consider first how each element of capital is valued and then go on to deduce its cost to the business.

Ordinary shares

There are two major approaches to determining the cost of ordinary shares to a business: the dividend-based approach and the risk/return-based approach. Each approach is discussed below.

Dividend-based approach

Investors hold assets (including ordinary shares) in the expectation of receiving future benefits. In broad terms, the value of an asset can be defined in terms of the stream of future benefits that arise from holding that asset. When considering ordinary shares, we can say that the value of an ordinary share can be defined in terms of the future dividends that investors receive by holding the share. To be more precise, the value of an ordinary share will be the present value of the expected future dividends from the particular share.

In mathematical terms, the value of an ordinary share (P_0) can be expressed as follows:

$$P_0 = \frac{D_1}{(1+K_0)^1} + \frac{D_2}{(1+K_0)^2} + \frac{D_3}{(1+K_0)^3} + \cdots + \frac{D_n}{(1+K_0)^n}$$

where: P_0 = the current market value of the share
D = the expected future dividend in years 1 to n
n = the number of years over which the business expects to issue dividends
K_0 = the cost of ordinary shares to the business (that is, the required return for investors).

Activity 8.2

The valuation approach above takes into account the expected dividend stream over the whole life of the business. Is this really relevant for an investor who holds a share for a particular period of time (say five years) and then sells the share?

The valuation approach should still be relevant. Put simply, an investor will receive only dividends from the business in which shares are held, and so the market value of the share at the time of sale should reflect the present value of the (remaining) future dividends. Thus, when determining an appropriate selling price, the expected dividend stream beyond the point at which the share is held should be highly relevant to the investor.

The valuation model above can be used to determine the *cost* of ordinary shares to the business (K_0). Assuming the value of an ordinary share and the expected future dividends is known, the cost of an ordinary share will be the discount rate that, when applied to the stream of expected future dividends, will produce a present value that is equal to the current market value of the share. Thus, the required rate of return for ordinary share investors (that is, the cost of ordinary shares to the business) is similar to the internal rate of return (IRR) used to evaluate investment projects.

To deduce the required rate of return for investors, we can use the same trial and error approach as that used to deduce the internal rate of return for investment projects. In practice, however, this trial and error approach is rarely used, as simplifying assumptions are normally employed concerning the pattern of dividends, which make the calculations easier. The need for simplifying assumptions arises because of the problems associated with predicting the future dividend stream from an ordinary share.

Often, one of two simplifying assumptions concerning the pattern of future dividends will be employed. The first assumption is that dividends will remain constant over time. Where dividends are expected to remain constant for an infinite period, the fairly complicated equation to deduce the current market value of a share stated above can be reduced to:

$$P_0 = \frac{D_0}{K_0}$$

This equation (which is the equation for capitalising a perpetual annuity) can be rearranged to provide an equation for deducing the *cost* of ordinary shares to the business. Hence:

$$K_0 = \frac{D_0}{P_0}$$

Activity 8.3

Kowloon Investments plc has ordinary shares in issue that have a current market value of £2.20. The annual dividend to be paid by the business in future years is expected to be 40p. What is the cost of the ordinary shares to the business?

The cost of the ordinary shares will be:

$$K_0 = \frac{D_0}{P_0}$$

$$= \frac{0.40}{2.20}$$

$$= 0.182 \text{ or } 18.2\%$$

The second simplifying assumption that may be employed is that dividends will grow at a constant rate over time. Where dividends are expected to have a constant growth rate, the equation to deduce the current market value of a share shown above can be reduced to:

$$P_0 = \frac{D_1}{K_0 - g}$$

where g is the expected annual growth rate. (The model assumes K_0 is greater than g.)

This equation can also be rearranged to provide an equation for deducing the *cost* of ordinary share capital. Hence:

$$K_0 = \frac{D_1}{P_0} + g$$

Determining the future growth rate in dividends (g) is often a problem in practice. One approach is to use the average past rate of growth in dividends (adjusted, perhaps, for any new information concerning future prospects). There are, however, several other approaches and a business must select whichever is likely to give the most accurate results.

Activity 8.4

Avalon plc has ordinary shares in issue that have a current market price of £1.50. The dividend expected for next year is 20p per share and future dividends are expected to grow at a constant rate of 3 per cent a year.
  What is the cost of the ordinary shares to the business?

The cost is calculated as follows:

$$K_0 = \frac{D_1}{P_0} + g = \frac{0.20}{1.50} + 0.03 = 0.163 \text{ or } 16.3\%$$

It should now be clear why we began by looking at how a share is valued before going on to deduce its cost. We have now seen how the value of an ordinary share to an investor and the cost of capital for the business are linked and how valuation models can help in deriving the required returns from investors. This relationship between value and the cost of capital also applies to preference shares and loan capital, as we shall see in a later section.

Risk/return approach

An alternative approach to deducing the returns required by ordinary shareholders is to use the **capital asset pricing model (CAPM)**. This approach builds on the ideas that we discussed in Chapter 5.

We may recall that, when discussing the attitude of investors towards risk and the risk adjusted discount rate, the following points were made:

● Investors who are risk averse will seek additional returns to compensate for the risks associated with a particular investment. These additional returns are referred to as the *risk premium*.
● The higher the level of risk, the higher the risk premium that will be demanded.
● The risk premium is an amount required by investors that is over and above the returns from investing in risk-free investments.
● The total returns required from a particular investment will, therefore, be made up of a risk-free rate plus any risk premium.

The relationship between risk and return is depicted in Figure 8.1.

Although the above ideas were made in respect of investment projects undertaken by a business, they are equally valid when considering investments in ordinary shares. CAPM (pronounced 'cap-M') is based on the above ideas and so the required rate of return to ordinary share investors (and, therefore, the cost of ordinary shares to the business) is viewed as being made up of a risk-free rate of return *plus* a risk premium. This means that, to calculate the required return, we have to derive the risk-free rate of return and the risk premium associated with a particular share.

Figure 8.1	The relationship between risk and return

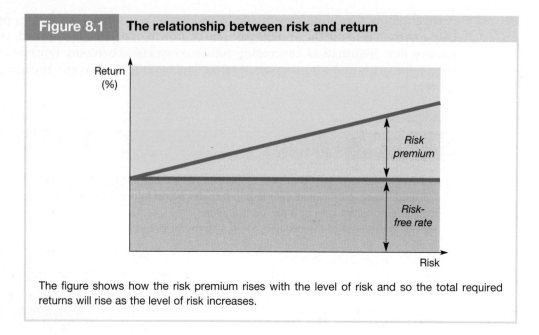

The figure shows how the risk premium rises with the level of risk and so the total required returns will rise as the level of risk increases.

Deriving the risk-free rate of return is not normally a major problem as the returns from government securities can be used as an approximation. They provide the most secure return available as the government guarantees payment. A more difficult problem, however, is deriving the risk premium for a particular share. CAPM does this by adopting a three-stage process, which is as follows:

1 Measure the risk premium for the ordinary share market as a whole. This figure will be the difference between the returns from the ordinary share market and the returns from an investment in risk-free investments.
2 Measure the returns from a particular share in relation to the returns from the ordinary share market as a whole.
3 Apply this relative measure of returns to the ordinary share market risk premium (calculated in stage 1) to derive the risk premium for the particular share.

The second and third stages of the process require further explanation.

We may recall from Chapter 6 that total risk is made up of two elements: *diversifiable* and *non-diversifiable* risk. Diversifiable risk is that part of the risk that is specific to the investment project and which can be eliminated by spreading available funds among investment projects. Non-diversifiable risk is that part of total risk that is common to all projects and which, therefore, cannot be diversified away. This element of risk arises from general market conditions.

This distinction between the two types of risk is also relevant to investors. The total risk associated with holding shares is also made up of diversifiable and non-diversifiable risk. By holding a portfolio of shares, an investor can eliminate diversifiable risk, which is specific to the share, leaving only non-diversifiable risk, which is common to all shares.

We know that risk-averse investors will only be prepared to take on increased risk if there is the prospect of increased returns. However, as diversifiable risk can be eliminated through holding a diversified portfolio, there is no reason why investors should receive additional returns for taking on this form of risk. It is, therefore, only the non-diversifiable risk element of total risk for which investors should expect additional returns.

The non-diversifiable risk element for a particular share can be measured using **beta**. This is a measure of the non-diversifiable risk of the share in relation to the market as a whole, or, to put it another way, it is the degree to which a share fluctuates with movements in the market as a whole. A risky share is one that experiences greater fluctuations than those of the market as a whole and, therefore, has a high beta value. It follows that the expected returns for such a share should be greater than the average returns of the market.

Using the above ideas, the required rate of return for investors for a particular share can be calculated as follows:

$$K_0 = K_{RF} + b(K_m - K_{RF})$$

where: K_0 = the required return for investors for a particular share
K_{RF} = the risk-free rate on government securities
b = beta of the particular share
K_m = the expected returns to the market for the next period
$(K_m - K_{RF})$ = the expected market average risk premium for the next period.

This equation reflects the idea that the required return for a particular share is made up of two elements: the risk-free return plus a risk premium. We can see the risk premium is equal to the expected risk premium for the market as a whole multiplied by the beta of the particular share. This adjustment to the market risk is undertaken to derive the relative risk associated with the particular share. (As stated earlier, beta measures the non-diversifiable risk of a particular share in relation to the market as a whole.)

The expected market average risk premium can be derived by reference to past periods, on the assumption that past periods provide a good predictor of future periods. A market average for a relatively long period is usually calculated, as share returns can fluctuate wildly over the short term. The CAPM equation shows that the risk premium can be deduced by subtracting the returns from government securities (the risk-free rate) from the average returns to the market. **Real World 8.1** shows the returns from gilts (government securities), the average market returns and the equity market risk premium for a variety of time periods.

 REAL WORLD 8.1

Ordinary share risk premiums

The following table shows the returns from the equity market, the returns from gilts and the equity risk premium over different time periods, each ending in 2003.

	(a) Equity market returns %	(b) Gilt returns %	(a) – (b) Equity market risk premium %
1900–2003	5.0	1.1	3.9
1920–2003	6.8	2.8	4.0
1940–2003	6.7	1.1	5.6
1960–2003	5.5	2.5	3.0
1980–2003	8.8	6.9	1.9

Source: Barclays Capital, www.barcap.com

A share with a return that moves in perfect step with the market will have a beta measure of 1.0. A share that is only half as volatile as the market will have a beta of 0.5 and a share that is twice as volatile as the market will have a beta of 2.0. The evidence suggests that many shares have a beta that is fairly close to the market measure of 1.0. Betas are normally measured using regression analysis on past data, again, on the assumption that past periods provide a good predictor of future periods. The monthly returns from a particular share (that is, dividends plus any increase in share value) for a period are regressed against the returns from the market as a whole (as represented by some Stock Exchange index such as the FTSE 100).

To illustrate this approach, let us assume that the monthly returns from a particular share and the returns to the market are plotted on a graph, as shown in Figure 8.2. A line of best fit can then be drawn, using regression analysis. Note the slope of this line. We can see that, for this particular share, the returns do not change as much as the returns for the market as a whole. In other words, the beta is less than 1.

| Figure 8.2 | **Relationship between the returns from an individual share and returns from the market** |

The figure shows the relationship between the returns from an individual share and the movements for the market. A linear relationship is assumed and linear regression analysis is used to establish a line of best fit.

Measures of beta for the shares of UK listed businesses are available from various information agencies such as the London Business School Risk Measurement Service and Bloomberg. Calculating beta, therefore, is not usually necessary. **Real World 8.2** provides examples of betas of some well-known UK listed businesses.

REAL WORLD 8.2

Betas in practice

Betas for some well-known UK listed businesses are set out in Figure 8.3 below.

Figure 8.3   Betas for a sample of well-known UK listed businesses

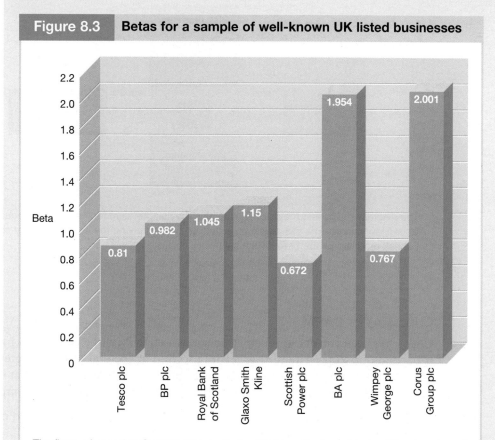

The figure shows that Scottish Power plc (a utility) has the lowest beta of the sample and Corus Group plc (a steel producer) has the highest beta.

Source: Graph compiled from information taken from www.bloomberg.com, 2 January 2005.

Activity 8.5

Lansbury plc has recently obtained a measure of its beta from a business information agency. The beta obtained is 1.2. The expected returns to the market for the next period is 10 per cent and the risk-free rate on government securities is 3 per cent. What is the cost of ordinary shares to the business?

Using the CAPM formula we have:

$$K_0 = K_{RF} + b(K_m - K_{RF}) = 3\% + 1.2(10\% - 3\%) = 11.4\%$$

Figure 8.4 below illustrates the main elements in calculating the cost of ordinary shares using CAPM.

Figure 8.4 **Calculating the cost of ordinary shares using CAPM**

The diagram shows that the risk-free rate plus the risk premium for the share will equal the cost of ordinary shares. The risk premium is derived by multiplying the equity (ordinary share) market risk premium by the beta for the share.

Criticisms of CAPM

CAPM has been subject to much criticism, which will not be considered in detail as it is beyond our scope. The further reading section at the end of this chapter, however, provides some useful references. It is, nevertheless, worth mentioning that some of the key assumptions of CAPM have been challenged. These include the assumptions that:

● investors hold a well-diversified portfolio of shares (and therefore need not be compensated for diversifiable risk);
● the return on a share will be influenced *only* by general market changes;
● there is a linear relationship between beta and expected returns.

All theoretical models contain simplifying assumptions and these criticisms could be overlooked if CAPM provided a good explanation of the relationship between risk and return. Unfortunately, various studies have shown that it fails to do this. Until a more complete model of the risk/return relationship is developed, however, CAPM remains the best way to estimate ordinary share returns.

CAPM and business practice

Having ploughed through the above sections on CAPM, it may be reassuring to know that it is actually used in practice. **Real World 8.3** briefly sets out the findings of two surveys, which shed some light on how UK listed businesses compute their cost of ordinary share capital.

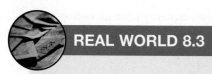

REAL WORLD 8.3

A beta way to do it

Two surveys have revealed that CAPM is the most popular way of computing the cost of ordinary share capital among UK listed businesses:

- A postal survey of 193 UK listed business revealed that CAPM is used by 47.2 per cent of respondents. The dividend-based approach came a poor second with only 27.5 per cent of respondents using it (see reference 1 at the end of the chapter).
- An interview-based survey of 18 UK listed businesses revealed that CAPM is used by 13 (78 per cent) of respondents (see reference 2 at the end of the chapter).

Differences in usage of CAPM between these two surveys may be due to the fact that the first survey included businesses of all sizes whereas the second survey looked only at very large businesses. Larger businesses may adopt a more sophisticated approach to calculating the cost of ordinary shares than smaller businesses.

Retained profit

Retained profit is an important source of finance from ordinary shareholders and, as we saw in Chapter 6, it cannot be regarded as 'cost free'. If profits are reinvested by the business, the shareholders will expect to receive returns on these funds that are equivalent to the returns expected from investments in opportunities with similar levels of risk. The ordinary shareholders' interest in the business is made up of ordinary share capital plus any retained profits, and the expected returns from each will, in theory, be the same. Hence, when we calculate the cost of ordinary share capital we are also calculating the cost of any retained profits. (In practice, however, we may require a slightly higher return from any new shares issued to compensate for the issue costs.)

Loan capital

We begin this section concerning loan capital as we began the sections relating to ordinary shares. That is, we shall consider the value of this element first and then go on to consider its cost. It cannot be emphasised enough that these two aspects are interrelated. Indeed, they may be seen as two sides of the same coin.

Loan capital may be irredeemable (that is, the business is not expected to repay the principal sum and so interest will be paid indefinitely). Where the rate of interest on the loan is fixed, the equation used to derive the value of irredeemable loan capital is similar to the equation used to derive the value of ordinary shares where the dividends remain constant over time. The equation for the value of irredeemable loan capital is:

$$P_d = \frac{I}{K_d}$$

where: P_d = the current market value of the loan capital

K_d = the cost of loan capital to the business

I = the annual rate of interest on the loan capital.

This equation can be rearranged to provide an equation for deducing the *cost* of loan capital. Hence:

$$K_d = \frac{I}{P_d}$$

Interest payments on loan capital are an allowable expense for taxation purposes and so the net cash flows incurred in servicing the loan capital will be the rate of interest payable *less* the tax charge, which can be offset. For investment appraisal purposes we take the post-tax net cash flows resulting from a project, and so, when calculating the appropriate discount rate, we should be consistent and use the post-tax rates for the cost of capital. The post-tax cost of loan capital will be:

$$K_d = \frac{I(1-t)}{P_d}$$

where t is the rate of corporation tax payable.

Activity 8.6

Tan and Co plc has irredeemable loan capital outstanding on which it pays an annual rate of interest of 10 per cent. The current market value of the loan capital is £88 per £100 nominal value and the corporation tax rate is 20 per cent. What is the cost of the loan capital to the business?

Using the above formula, the cost of loan capital is:

$$K_d = \frac{I(1-t)}{P_d}$$

$$= \frac{10(1-0.20)}{88}$$

$$= 9.1\%$$

Note that the rate of interest payable on the nominal value of the loan capital does not represent the relevant cost for investment appraisal purposes. Rather, we are concerned with the *opportunity cost* of the loan capital. This represents the return that can be earned by investing in an opportunity that has the same level of risk. The *current market rate of interest* of the loan capital, as calculated above, will provide us with a measure of the relevant opportunity cost.

Where the loan capital is redeemable, deriving the cost of capital figure is a little more complex. However, the principles and calculations required to derive the relevant figure have already been covered in Chapter 4. An investor who purchases redeemable loan capital will pay an initial outlay and then expect to receive annual interest payments plus a repayment of capital at the end of the loan period. The required rate of return for the investor will be the discount rate which, when applied to the future cash flows, will produce a present value that is equal to the current market value of the investment. Thus, the rate of return can be computed in the same way as the IRR is computed for other forms of investment opportunity. Let us consider Example 8.1.

Example 8.1

Lim Associates plc issues £20 million loan capital on which it pays an annual rate of interest of 10 per cent on the nominal value. The issue price of the loan capital is £88 per £100 nominal value and the rate of corporation tax is 20 per cent. The loan capital is due to be redeemed in four years' time at its nominal value.

What are the annual cash flows for this issue?

Solution

The cash flows for this issue of loan capital will be as follows:

		Cash flows £m
Year 0	Current market value [£20m × (88/100)]	17.6
Years 1–3	Interest payable (£20m × 10%)	(2.0)
Year 4	Redemption value (−£20m) + Interest (−£2m)	(22.0)

To derive the cost of loan capital to the business, the trial and error approach that is used in calculating the IRR can be used.

Activity 8.7

Calculate the cost of loan capital for Lim Associates plc. (*Hint*: Start with a discount rate of 10 per cent.)

Using a discount rate of 10 per cent, the NPV is calculated as follows:

	Cash flows £m	Discount rate 10%	PV of cash flows £m
Year 0	17.6	1.00	17.6
Year 1	(2.0)	0.91	(1.8)
Year 2	(2.0)	0.83	(1.7)
Year 3	(2.0)	0.75	(1.5)
Year 4	(22.0)	0.68	(15.0)
		NPV	(2.4)

This discount rate is too low as the discounted future cash outflows exceed the issue price of the loan capital – that is the NPV is negative. Let us try 15 per cent.

	Cash flows £m	Discount rate 15%	PV of cash flows £m
Year 0	17.6	1.00	17.6
Year 1	(2.0)	0.87	(1.7)
Year 2	(2.0)	0.76	(1.5)
Year 3	(2.0)	0.66	(1.3)
Year 4	(22.0)	0.57	(12.5)
		NPV	0.6

This discount rate is a little too high as the discounted cash outflows are less than the issue price of the loan capital. Thus, the appropriate rate lies somewhere between 10 and 15 per cent.

→

Activity 8.7 continued

We can see that the NPV changed by £3.0 million (that is, £2.4 million + £0.6 million) for a 5 per cent (that is, 10 – 15) change in the discount rate, which is equivalent to £0.6m for every 1 per cent change. Thus, a discount rate of 14 per cent would achieve an NPV of zero as a 15 per cent discount rate produced an NPV of £0.6 million. This represents the pre-tax cost of loan capital. The rate of corporation tax is 20 per cent and so the post-tax cost of loan capital is 14 per cent × (1 – 0.2) = 11.2 per cent.

Preference shares

Let us again begin by a consideration of the value of this element of capital before moving on to calculate its cost. Preference shares may be either redeemable or irredeemable. They are similar to loan capital in so far as the holders receive an agreed rate of return each year (which is expressed in terms of the nominal value of the shares). However, preference shares differ from loan capital in that the annual dividends paid to preference shareholders do not represent a tax-deductible expense. Thus, the full cost of the annual dividend payments must be borne by the business. Where the rate of dividend on the preference shares is fixed (that is, there is no right to participate in additional profits), the equation used to derive the value of irredeemable preference shares is again similar to the equation used to derive the value of ordinary shares where the dividends remain constant over time. The equation for irredeemable preference shares is:

$$P_p = \frac{D_p}{K_p}$$

where: P_p = the current market price of the preference shares
K_p = the cost of preference shares to the business
D_p = the annual dividend payments.

This equation can be rearranged to provide an equation for deducing the *cost* of irredeemable preference shares. Hence:

$$K_p = \frac{D_p}{P_p}$$

Activity 8.8

Iordanova plc has 12 per cent preference shares in issue with a nominal (par) value of £1. The shares have a current market price of £0.90 (excluding dividends).
  What is the cost of the preference shares?

The cost of the preference shares is:

$$K_p = \frac{D_p}{P_p} = \frac{12}{90} = 13.3\%$$

In the case of redeemable preference shares, the cost of capital can be deduced using the IRR approach, which was used earlier to determine the cost of redeemable loan capital.

Activity 8.9

L. C. Conday plc has £50 million 10 per cent £1 preference shares in issue. The current market price is £0.92 and the shares are due to be redeemed in three years' time at their nominal value. What is the cost of the preference shares? (*Hint*: Start with a discount rate of 11 per cent.)

The annual cash flows are as follows:

		Cash flows £m
Year 0	Current market value (£50m × 0.92)	46.0
Years 1–2	Dividends (£50m × 10%)	5.0
Year 3	Redemption value (£50m) + Dividend (£5m)	55.0

Using a discount rate of 11 per cent, the NPV is as follows:

	Cash flows £m	Discount rate 11%	PV of cash flows £m
Year 0	46.0	1.00	46.0
Year 1	(5.0)	0.90	(4.5)
Year 2	(5.0)	0.81	(4.0)
Year 3	(55.0)	0.73	(40.1)
		NPV	(2.6)

This discount rate is too low as the discounted future cash outflows exceed the issue price of the preference share capital. Let us try 13 per cent:

	Cash flows £m	Discount rate 13%	PV of cash flows £m
Year 0	46.0	1.00	46.0
Year 1	(5.0)	0.89	(4.4)
Year 2	(5.0)	0.78	(3.9)
Year 3	(55.0)	0.69	(38.0)
		NPV	(0.3)

The discounted cash outflows are almost equal to the issue price of the preference share capital. Thus, the cost of preference shares is approximately 13 per cent.

Weighted average cost of capital (WACC)

When making financing decisions, it is argued that managers of a business have a target capital structure in mind. Although the relative proportions of equity and loans may vary over the short term, these proportions, it is claimed, remain fairly stable when viewed over the medium to longer term. The existence of a fairly stable capital structure is consistent with the view that managers believe that a particular financing mix will minimise the cost of capital of the business, or, to put it another way, a particular financing mix provides an optimal capital structure for the business. (Whether or not there is such a thing as an optimal capital structure is discussed later in the chapter.) However, a target capital structure is unlikely to be set in stone. It may change from time to time in response to changes in the tax rates, interest rates, and so on, which affect the cost of particular elements of the capital structure.

The existence of a stable capital structure (presumably reflecting the target capital structure) has important implications for the evaluation of investment projects. It has already been argued that the required rates of return from investors (that is, the costs of capital to the business) should provide the basis for determining an appropriate discount rate for investment projects. If we accept that a business will maintain a fairly stable capital structure over the period of the project, then the average cost of capital can provide an appropriate discount rate. The average cost of capital can be calculated by taking the cost of the individual elements and then weighting each element in proportion to the target capital structure (by market value) of the business. Example 8.2 illustrates how the **weighted average cost of capital (WACC)** is calculated.

Example 8.2

Danton plc has 10 million ordinary shares in issue with a current market value of £2.00 per share. The expected dividend for next year is 16p per share and this is expected to grow each year at a constant rate of 4 per cent. The business also has:

- 10.0 million 9 per cent £1 irredeemable preference shares in issue with a market price of £0.90 per share, and
- £20 million of irredeemable loan capital in issue with a nominal rate of interest of 6 per cent and which is quoted at £80 per £100 nominal value.

Assume a rate of corporation tax of 20 per cent and that the current capital structure reflects the target capital structure of the business.

What is the weighted average cost of capital of the business?

Solution

The first step is to calculate the cost of the individual elements of capital. The cost of ordinary shares in Danton plc is calculated as follows:

$$K_0 = \frac{D_1}{P_0} + g \quad \text{(see note)}$$

$$= \frac{16}{200} + 0.04$$

$$= 12\%$$

Note: The dividend valuation model has been used to calculate the cost of ordinary shares; however, the CAPM model could have been used instead if the relevant information had been available.

The cost of the preference share capital is as follows:

$$K_p = \frac{D_p}{P_p}$$

$$= \frac{9}{90}$$

$$= 10\%$$

The cost of loan capital is:

$$K_d = \frac{I(1-t)}{P_d} = \frac{6(1-0.2)}{80} = 6.0\%$$

Having derived the cost of the individual elements, the weighted average cost of these elements can now be calculated. The WACC will be:

	(a) Market value £m	(b) Proportion of total market value	(c) Cost %	(d) = (b × c) Contribution to WACC
Ordinary shares (10m × £2) (see note)	20	0.44	12	5.3
Preference shares (10m × £0.90)	9	0.20	10	2.0
Loan capital (£20m × 0.8)	16	0.36	6	2.2
	45	1.00		
WACC				**10.5%**

Note: The market value of the capital rather than the nominal value has been used in the calculations. This is because we are concerned with the opportunity cost of capital invested, as explained earlier.

Figure 8.5 sets out the approach used to calculate the WACC of a business.

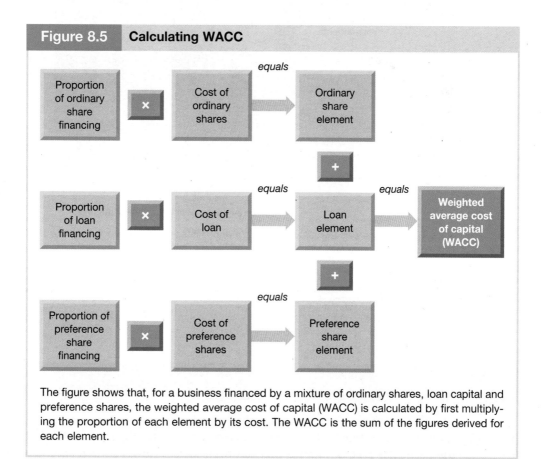

| Figure 8.5 | Calculating WACC |

The figure shows that, for a business financed by a mixture of ordinary shares, loan capital and preference shares, the weighted average cost of capital (WACC) is calculated by first multiplying the proportion of each element by its cost. The WACC is the sum of the figures derived for each element.

Whether businesses maintain a target capital structure in practice has been the subject of some debate. **Real World 8.4** provides some evidence from the US concerning this issue.

REAL WORLD 8.4

Targets in practice

A survey of 392 US businesses reveals mixed support for the idea of a target capital structure. Figure 8.6 below sets out the evidence.

| Figure 8.6 | **Use of target capital structures by US businesses** |

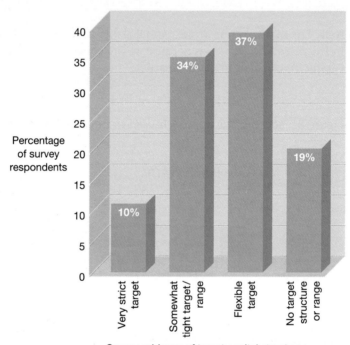

The figure reveals that only 10 per cent of businesses surveyed adhered to a strict target capital structure and 19 per cent of businesses had no target capital structure at all.

Source: How do CFOs make capital budgeting and capital structure decisions? J. Graham and C. Harvey. Paper prepared for *Journal of Applied Corporate Finance*, Vol. 15, No. 1 2002.

Specific or average cost of capital?

An investment project may be financed by raising funds from a particular source. As a result, it is tempting to argue that the cost of capital for the project should be based on the particular type of finance that has been raised. However, this argument would be incorrect. When new funds are required for a particular project, it is not normally feasible to raise the funds in exactly the same proportions as in the existing capital structure. To minimise the cost of raising funds, it will usually make sense for a business to raise funds from one source and, later, to raise funds from another, even though this may lead to deviations in the required capital structure over the short term. The fact that a particular source of new funds is used for a project will be determined by the requirements for the long-term capital structure of the business rather than the requirements of the project.

Using the specific cost of funds raised for the project could lead to illogical decisions being made. Assume a business is considering an investment in two new machines that are identical in every respect and that each machine has an estimated IRR of 12 per cent. Let us further assume that the first machine will be financed using loan capital with a post-tax cost of 10 per cent. However, as debt capacity of the business will then be used up, the second machine must be financed by ordinary share capital at a cost of 14 per cent. If the specific cost of capital is used to evaluate investment decisions, the business would be in the peculiar position of accepting the investment in the first machine, because the IRR exceeds the cost of capital, and rejecting the second (identical) machine because the IRR is lower than the cost of capital! By using the WACC, we avoid this kind of problem. Each machine will be evaluated according to the average cost of capital, which should then result in consistent decisions being made.

Limitations of the WACC approach

The WACC approach has been criticised for not taking proper account of risk in investment decisions. In practice, different investment opportunities are likely to have different levels of risk and so it can be argued that the cost of capital for each project should be adjusted accordingly. We may recall from Chapter 5 that investors who are normally risk averse require higher returns to compensate for higher levels of risk. This means that the WACC is really only suitable where an investment project is expected to have the same level of risk as existing investments, or the proposed project is fairly small and is, therefore, not expected to have a significant effect on the overall risk level of the business.

It was mentioned earlier that the WACC approach assumes that the capital structure of the business remains stable over the period of the investment project. However, if this is not the case, the validity of the WACC approach is undermined. Changes in capital structure can result in changes in the proportions of the individual capital elements and, perhaps, changes in the costs of these elements.

Cost of capital in practice

Real World 8.5 below provides some evidence on the frequency with which the cost of capital is reviewed in practice and the use of WACC as the appropriate discount rate in capital investment decisions.

REAL WORLD 8.5

Counting the cost

The survey of 193 UK listed businesses mentioned in Real World 8.3 above revealed the frequency with which businesses reassess their cost of capital. As the financial environment continually changes, we should expect businesses to reassess their cost of capital fairly frequently. The frequency with which the businesses surveyed reassess their cost of capital is shown in Figure 8.7. These findings indicate that an annual reassessment is preferred by more than half of respondents.

A further finding concerns the extent to which the weighted average cost of capital was used in evaluating investment decisions. Figure 8.8 shows the discount rates that were used for investment projects. We saw above that WACC is normally the appropriate discount rate to use when evaluating investment projects. The reasons for using the cost of ordinary shares only or a long-term borrowing rate require further investigation. The use of the ordinary share cost of capital would be appropriate only where the business was entirely financed by ordinary shares and the riskiness of the project was in line with that of the business as a whole. The use of a long-term borrowing rate is even more difficult to understand as it fails to take into account the required rate of return to investors.

Figure 8.7	**Frequency with which businesses reassess their cost of capital**

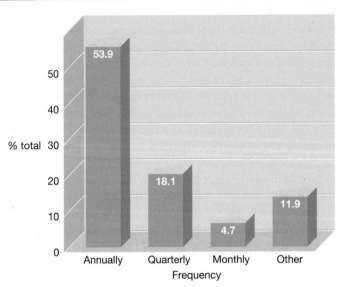

The figure shows that nearly all of the businesses surveyed reassess their cost of capital on at least an annual basis. Those falling into the 'other' category reassess every six months (2.6 per cent) when long-term interest rates change (3.1 per cent) and on a project-by-project basis (6.2 per cent).

Source: Adapted from E. McLaney, J. Pointon, M. Thomas and J. Tucker, Practioners' perspectives on the UK cost of capital, *European Journal of Finance*, 10, pp. 123–138, April 2004.

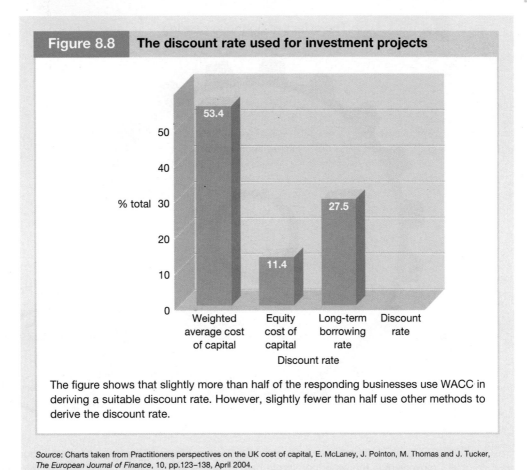

Figure 8.8   The discount rate used for investment projects

The figure shows that slightly more than half of the responding businesses use WACC in deriving a suitable discount rate. However, slightly fewer than half use other methods to derive the discount rate.

Source: Charts taken from Practitioners perspectives on the UK cost of capital, E. McLaney, J. Pointon, M. Thomas and J. Tucker, *The European Journal of Finance*, 10, pp.123–138, April 2004.

Financial gearing

We have already seen that the presence of capital with a fixed rate of return, such as loan capital and preference share capital, in the long-term capital structure of a business is referred to as 'gearing' (or to be more precise 'financial gearing'). The term 'gearing' is used to convey the point that fixed-return capital can accentuate the changes in profit before interest and taxation (PBIT) and on the returns to ordinary shareholders. The effect is similar to the effect of two intermeshing cog wheels of unequal size (see Figure 8.9). The movement in the larger cog wheel (profit before interest and taxation) causes a more than proportionate movement in the smaller cog wheel (returns to ordinary shareholders).

The effect of financial gearing on the returns to ordinary shareholders is demonstrated in the Example 8.3.

Figure 8.9	The effect of financial gearing

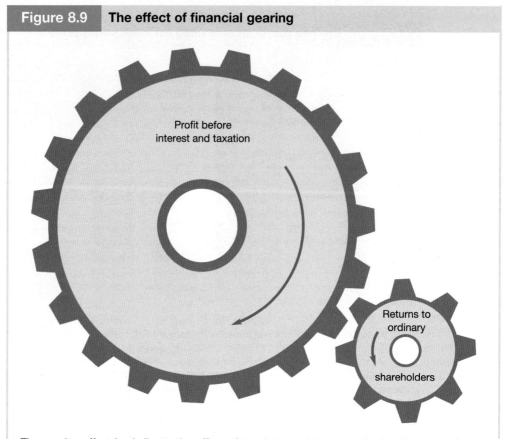

The gearing effect is similar to the effect of two intermeshing cog wheels of unequal size. A movement in the larger cog (profit before interest and taxation) brings about a disproportionately large movement in the smaller cog (returns to ordinary shareholders).

Example 8.3

Alpha plc and Gamma plc are similar businesses and have generated identical profits before interest and taxation (PBIT) for Year 1 of £80 million. The long-term capital structure of each business is as follows:

	Alpha plc £m	Gamma plc £m
£1 ordinary shares	200	340
12% preference shares	100	50
10% loan stock	100	10
	400	400

Although both businesses have the same total long-term capital, we can see that the level of financial gearing differs significantly between the two businesses.

A widely used measure of gearing, which we came across in Chapter 3, is as follows:

$$\text{Financial gearing ratio} = \frac{\text{Loan capital} + \text{Preference shares (if any)}}{\text{Total long-term capital}} \times 100\%$$

For Alpha plc and Gamma plc, the ratios are 50 per cent [(200/400) × 100%] and 15 per cent [(60/400) × 100%], respectively. These ratios indicate that Alpha has a high level of financial gearing, that is, a high proportion of fixed return capital (loan capital plus preference shares) in relation to its total long-term capital, and Gamma has a relatively low level of financial gearing.

Let us now consider the effect of financial gearing on the returns to ordinary shareholders. The earnings per share (EPS) for the ordinary share investors of each business for Year 1 can be calculated as follows:

	Alpha plc £m	Gamma plc £m
PBIT	80.0	80.0
Less Loan interest	10.0	1.0
Profit before taxation	70.0	79.0
Less Corporation tax (say, 30%)	21.0	23.7
Profit after taxation	49.0	55.3
Less Preference dividend paid	12.0	6.0
Profit available to ordinary shareholders	37.0	49.3

The EPS for ordinary share investors of Alpha plc are 18.5p (that is, £37m/200m) and for Gamma plc they are 14.5p (that is, £49.3m/340m).

In this example, we can see that ordinary share investors in Alpha plc earn higher returns in Year 1 than ordinary share investors in Gamma plc. This arises from the use of a higher level of fixed-return capital (loan capital and preference share capital) in the capital structure. The advantage of financial gearing is that when additional profits generated from the use of fixed-return capital exceed the additional fixed payments (interest and preference dividends) incurred, the surplus will accrue to the ordinary shareholders. The more gearing in the capital structure, the higher the potential benefits and so, in this case, the ordinary share investors of Alpha plc achieve a higher return.

However, the financial gearing effect can operate in both directions. To illustrate this point, let us assume that the profit before interest and taxation for the following year is £40 million for each business. The earnings per share for ordinary share investors for Year 2 would be as follows:

	Alpha plc £m	Gamma plc £m
PBIT	40.0	40.0
Less Loan interest	10.0	1.0
Profit before taxation	30.0	39.0
Less Corporation tax (say, 30%)	9.0	11.7
Profit after taxation	21.0	27.3
Less Preference dividend	12.0	6.0
Profit available to ordinary shareholders	9.0	21.3
EPS	4.5p	6.3p

In this case, we can see that the returns to ordinary shareholders of Alpha plc are lower than those of Gamma plc. The cost of servicing the loan capital and preference share capital will remain the same as in Year 1 and so the fall in profit before interest and taxation will be borne entirely by the ordinary shareholders. We can also see from the example that the decrease in earnings per share is much greater for ordinary shareholders in the higher-geared business than in the lower-geared business. This illustrates the point made earlier that the effect of financial gearing is to accentuate changes in returns to ordinary share investors arising from changes in profit before interest and taxation.

Real World 8.6 shows how Tesco plc, the UK and, increasingly, international supermarket chain has been able to use increasing loan financing to boost ROSF in the early 2000s.

REAL WORLD 8.6

Tesco gears up for shareholders' returns

The following information relates to Tesco plc for its accounting years to the end of February 1999 to 2003:

	1999	2000	2001	2002	2003
ROCE (%)	17.2	16.1	16.6	16.1	15.3
Interest cover (times)	10.7	10.5	9.4	8.7	8.4
ROSF (%)	21.3	20.9	22.7	23.2	23.3

Over the five years, there was a decline in ROCE, but a steady increase in gearing (as measured by a decline in the interest cover ratio) had the effect of broadly increasing ROSF. The business must have been able to borrow at a lower rate of interest rate than its rate of ROCE. This boosted the returns to shareholders.

There is absolutely no suggestion here that Tesco's increased gearing was unwise. This is an extremely well managed and successful business.

Source: Tesco plc Annual Report and Financial Statements 2003.

Degree of financial gearing

The effect of financial gearing, as we have just seen, is that any increase in the profit before interest and taxation for a financially geared business will result in a disproportionate increase in earnings per share, and any decrease in profit before interest and taxation will result in a disproportionate decrease in earnings per share. The higher the level of financial gearing, the more sensitive earnings per share become to changes in profit before interest and taxation for any given level. The **degree of financial gearing** provides a measure of the financial gearing effect and can be calculated as follows:

$$\text{Degree of financial gearing} = \frac{\text{\% change in EPS}}{\text{\% change in PBIT}}$$

For Alpha plc, the degree of financial gearing, based on the changes between Year 1 and Year 2, will be:

$$\text{Degree of financial gearing} = \frac{-75.7\%}{-50\%}$$

$$= 1.5$$

Activity 8.10

What is the degree of financial gearing for Gamma plc?

For Gamma plc, the degree of financial gearing will be:

$$\text{Degree of financial gearing} = \frac{\% \text{ change in EPS}}{\% \text{ change in PBIT}}$$

$$= \frac{-56.6\%}{-50\%}$$

$$= 1.1$$

In both cases, the figure derived is greater than 1, which indicates the presence of financial gearing. The higher the figure derived, the greater the sensitivity of earnings per share to changes in profit before interest and taxation. This measure of financial gearing indicates that, in the case of Alpha plc, a 1.0 per cent change in profit before interest and taxation from the base level of £80 million will result in a 1.5 per cent change in earnings per share, whereas for Gamma plc, a 1.0 per cent change in profit before interest and taxation from the base level of £80 million will only result in a 1.1 per cent change in earnings per share.

Another way of arriving at the degree of financial gearing for a particular level of profit before interest and taxation is as follows:

$$\textbf{Degree of financial gearing} = \frac{\textbf{PBIT}}{\textbf{PBIT} - I - [P \times 100/(100 - t)]}$$

where: I = interest charges
P = preference dividend
t = tax rate.

(Note that the preference dividend is 'grossed up' to a pre-tax amount by multiplying the dividend by $100/(100 - t)$. This is done to ensure consistency with the other variables in the equation.)

The above equation has the advantage that a single measure of PBIT is all that is required to derive the degree of financial gearing. For Alpha plc, the measure will be calculated as follows for Year 1:

$$\text{Degree of financial gearing} = \frac{80}{80 - 10 - [12 \times 100/(100 - 30)]}$$

$$= \frac{80}{52.9}$$

$$= 1.5$$

This equation will yield the same results as the earlier equation shown above.

Activity 8.11

Calculate the degree of financial gearing for Gamma plc for Year 1 using the above equation.

The calculation is:

$$\text{Degree of financial gearing} = \frac{\text{PBIT}}{\text{PBIT} - I - [P \times 100/(100 - t)]}$$

$$= \frac{80}{80 - 1 - [6 \times 100/(100 - 30)]}$$

$$= \frac{80}{70.4}$$

$$= 1.1$$

It is important to appreciate that the impact of financial gearing for a business will become less pronounced as the level of profit before interest and taxation increases in relation to fixed capital payments (interest and preference dividends). Where profit before interest and taxation barely covers the fixed capital payments, even small changes in the former figure can have a significant impact on earnings per share. This high degree of sensitivity will be reflected in the degree of financial gearing measure. However, as profit before interest and taxation increases in relation to fixed capital charges, earnings per share will become less sensitive to changes. As a result, the degree of financial gearing measure will be lower.

Activity 8.12

What is the degree of financial gearing for Alpha plc and Gamma plc for Year 2?

For Alpha plc, the degree of financial gearing in Year 2 (when profit before interest and taxation is much lower) will be:

$$\text{Degree of financial gearing} = \frac{\text{PBIT}}{\text{PBIT} - I - [P \times 100/(100 - t)]}$$

$$= \frac{40}{40 - 10 - [12 \times 100/(100 - 30)]} = 3.1$$

For Gamma plc, the degree of financial gearing in Year 2 will be:

$$\text{Degree of financial gearing} = \frac{\text{PBIT}}{\text{PBIT} - I - [P \times 100/(100 - t)]}$$

$$= \frac{40}{40 - 1 - [6 \times 100/(100 - 30)]} = 1.3$$

We can see that EPS for both businesses is now more sensitive to changes in the level of PBIT than in the previous year when profits were higher. However, returns to ordinary shareholders in Alpha plc, which has a higher level of financial gearing, have become much more sensitive to change than returns to ordinary shareholders in Gamma plc.

Gearing and the evaluation of capital structure decisions

When evaluating capital structure decisions, the likely impact of gearing on the expected risks and returns for ordinary shareholders must be taken into account. The use of projected financial statements and gearing ratios, which were examined in earlier chapters, can help assess the likely effect of different capital structure options on the risks and returns for ordinary shareholders. Example 8.4 illustrates the way in which capital structure options may be evaluated.

Example 8.4

Semplice Ltd manufactures catering equipment for restaurants and hotels. The balance sheet of the business as at 31 May Year 4 is as follows:

Balance sheet as at 31 May Year 4

	£m	£m	£m
Non-current assets			
Freehold property at cost		48.7	
Less Accumulated depreciation		8.5	40.2
Machinery and equipment at cost		24.6	
Less Accumulated depreciation		7.2	17.4
			57.6
Current assets			
Stock (inventory) at cost	22.5		
Trade debtors (receivables)	27.6		
Cash at bank	1.3	51.4	
Less **Current liabilities**			
Trade creditors (payables)	25.2		
Taxation	2.6	27.8	23.6
			81.2
Less **Non-current liabilities**			
12% loan			20.0
			61.2
Equity			
£0.25 ordinary shares			15.0
Retained profit			46.2
			61.2

An abridged profit and loss account for the year ended 31 May Year 4 is as follows:

Abridged profit and loss account (income statement) for the year ended 31 May Year 4

	£m
Sales revenue	137.4
Profit before interest and taxation	23.2
Interest payable	2.4
Profit before taxation	20.8
Corporation tax	5.2
Profit after taxation	15.6
Dividend paid	6.0
Retained profit for the year	9.6

→

Example 8.4 continued

The board of directors of Semplice Ltd has decided to invest £20 million in new machinery and equipment to meet an expected increase in sales for the business's products. The expansion in production facilities is expected to result in an increase of £6 million in annual profit before interest and taxation.

To finance the proposed investment, the board of directors is considering either:

1 a rights issue of 8 million ordinary shares at a premium of £2.25 per share, or
2 the issue of £20 million 10 per cent debentures at par.

The directors wish to increase the dividend per share by 10 per cent in the forthcoming year irrespective of the financing method chosen.

Assume a rate of corporation tax of 25 per cent.

Share issue costs can be ignored.

Which financing option should be chosen?

Solution

A useful starting point in tackling this problem is to prepare a forecast profit and loss account for the year ended 31 May Year 5 under each financing option.

Projected profit and loss account for the year ended 31 May Year 5

	Shares £m	Debentures £m
Profit before interest and taxation	29.2	29.2
Interest payable	2.4	4.4
Profit before taxation	26.8	24.8
Corporation tax (25%)	6.7	6.2
Profit after taxation	20.1	18.6
Dividend	7.5	6.6
Retained profit for the year	12.6	12.0

Having prepared the forecast profit and loss accounts, the impact of each financing option on the overall capital structure of the business should be considered. The projected capital structure under each option will be:

	Shares £m	Debentures £m
Equity		
Share capital £0.25 ordinary shares	17.0	15.0
Share premium	18.0	
Retained profit	58.8	58.2
	93.8	73.2
Loan capital	20.0	40.0

Notes

1 The share premium account represents the amount received from the issue of shares that is above the nominal value of the shares. The amount is calculated as follows: 8 million × £2.25 = £18 million.
2 The number of shares in issue (25p shares) for the share issue option is 68 million (£17m/£0.25) and for the debenture option is 60 million (£15m/£0.25).

To help us further, gearing ratios and profitability ratios may be calculated under each option.

Activity 8.13

Using the forecast figures that have been calculated, compute the return on ordinary shareholders' funds ratio, earnings per share, interest cover ratio and gearing ratio, assuming:

(a) The business issues shares
(b) The business issues debentures.

These ratios are as follows:

	Shares	Debentures

Return on ordinary shareholders' funds (ROSF)

$$\text{ROSF} = \frac{\text{Earnings available to ordinary shareholders}}{\text{Ordinary shares plus reserves}}$$

	Shares	Debentures
Share issue $= \dfrac{\pounds12.6m}{\pounds93.8m} \times 100\%$	13.4%	
Debenture issue $= \dfrac{\pounds12.0m}{\pounds73.2m} \times 100\%$		16.4%

Earnings per share (EPS)

$$\text{EPS} = \frac{\text{Earnings available to ordinary shareholders}}{\text{No. of ordinary shares}}$$

	Shares	Debentures
Share issue $= \dfrac{\pounds20.1m}{68m}$	29.6p	
Debenture issue $= \dfrac{\pounds18.6m}{60m}$		31.0p

Interest cover ratio

$$\frac{\text{Profit before interest and taxation}}{\text{Interest payable}}$$

	Shares	Debentures
Share issue $= \dfrac{\pounds29.2m}{\pounds2.4m}$	12.2 times	
Debentures $= \dfrac{\pounds29.2m}{\pounds4.4m}$		6.6 times

Gearing ratio
Gearing ratio

$$= \frac{\text{Loan capital}}{\text{(Ordinary shares + Reserves + Loan capital)}} \times 100\%$$

Share issue

$$= \frac{\pounds20.0m}{(93.8 + 20)} \times 100\%$$ 17.6%

Debenture issue

$$= \frac{(\pounds20.0m + \pounds20.0m)}{(73.2 + 40)} \times 100\%$$ 35.3%

The calculations we have undertaken in Activity 8.13 should help us assess the implications of each financing option.

Activity 8.14

Briefly evaluate each of the proposed financing options from the perspective of an existing shareholder.

The debenture option provides the investor with better returns. We can see that EPS is slightly higher and the ROSF is 3 per cent higher than under the share option. However, the debenture option also produces a higher level of gearing and, therefore, a higher level of risk. Although the gearing ratio for the debenture option does not seem excessive, it does represent a significant increase to the existing level of 24.6 per cent (that is, £20m/£81.2m) and is twice as high as the share option. The interest cover for the debenture option is almost half that for the share option. Nevertheless, the profit before interest and taxation comfortably exceeds the interest charges.

The investor must decide whether the fairly small increase in returns warrants the increase in gearing that must be undertaken to achieve those returns.

Gearing and signalling

Managers must be aware that when a decision to change the existing level of gearing is announced, investors may interpret this as a signal concerning future prospects. Thus, an increase in the level of gearing may be interpreted by investors as indicating management confidence in future profitability and, as a result, share prices may rise. Managers must therefore be sensitive to the possible signals that are being transmitted to the market by their actions and, where necessary, provide further explanation.

Constructing a PBIT–EPS indifference chart

When making a financing decision, managers may wish to know the returns to ordinary shareholders at different levels of profit before interest and taxation under the different financing options available. It is often useful to present this information to managers in the form of a chart. To provide an illustration of such a chart, we can use the information contained in our answer to Example 8.4 above. The chart, which is referred to as a **PBIT–EPS indifference chart**, is set out in Figure 8.10. We can see that the vertical axis of the chart plots the earnings per share and the horizontal axis plots the profit before interest and taxation.

To show the returns to shareholders at different levels of profit, we need two co-ordinates for each financing scheme. The first of these will be the profit before interest and taxation necessary to cover the fixed capital charges. For the debenture issue, the relevant amount is £4.4 million and for the ordinary share issue, the amount is £2.4 million (see profit and loss accounts above). This is because, at these amounts, there will be nothing available to the ordinary shareholders and so earnings per share will be zero. These points will be plotted on the vertical axis.

Figure 8.10	PBIT–EPS indifference chart for two financing options

The chart reveals the returns to shareholders, as measured by earnings per share, for different levels of profit before interest and taxation of two financing options. The point at which the two lines intersect represents the level of profit before interest and tax at which both financing options provide the same rate of return to shareholders. This is referred to as the indifference point.

The second coordinate for each financing scheme will be the earnings per share at the expected profit before interest and taxation. (However, an arbitrarily determined level of profit before interest and taxation could also be used.) For the debenture issue the earnings per share at the expected profit before interest and taxation is 31.0p, and for the ordinary share issue it is 29.6p (see earlier calculations). By joining the two co-ordinates relevant to each financing scheme, we have a straight line that reveals the earnings per share at different levels of profit before interest and taxation.

We can see from the chart that at lower levels of profit before interest and taxation, the ordinary share issue provides better returns to shareholders. However, the debenture issue line has a steeper slope and returns to ordinary shareholders rise more quickly. We can see that beyond a profit before interest and taxation of £19.4 million, ordinary shareholders begin to reap the benefits of gearing and their returns become higher under this alternative. The profit before interest and taxation of £19.4 million is referred to as the **indifference point** (that is, the point at which the two financing schemes provide the same level of return to ordinary shareholders).

The distance between the indifference point and the expected level of profit before interest and taxation provides us with a 'margin of safety'. The chart reveals that there is a reasonable margin of safety for the debenture alternative: there would have to be a fall in profit before interest and taxation of about 34 per cent before the ordinary share alternative became more attractive. Thus, provided the managers were confident that the expected levels of profit could be maintained, the debenture alternative would be more attractive.

A business may consider issuing preference shares to finance a particular project. As preference dividends are paid out of profits *after taxation* this means that, when calculating the first coordinate for the chart, the profits *before* interest and taxation must be sufficient to cover both the dividends and the relevant corporation tax payments.

In other words, we must 'gross up' the preference dividend by the relevant corporation tax rate to derive the profits before interest and taxation figure.

The indifference point between any two financing options can also be derived by using a simple mathematical approach. Example 8.5 illustrates the process.

Example 8.5

The information for Semplice plc in Example 8.4 above can be used to illustrate how the indifference point is calculated.

Let x be the PBIT at which the two financing options provide the same EPS.

	Shares £m	Debentures £m
Profit before interest and taxation	x	x
Interest payable	2.4	4.4
Profit before taxation	$(x - 2.4)$	$(x - 4.4)$
Corporation tax (25%)	$0.25(x - 2.4)$	$0.25(x - 4.4)$
Profit after taxation	$0.75(x - 2.4)$	$0.75(x - 4.4)$
EPS	$\dfrac{0.75(x - £2.4m)}{68m}$	$\dfrac{0.75(x - £4.4m)}{60m}$

Thus, the EPS of the two financing options will be equal when:

$$\frac{0.75(x - £2.4m)}{68m} = \frac{0.75(x - £4.4m)}{60m}$$

We can solve this equation as follows:

$$\frac{(0.75x - £1.8m)}{68m} = \frac{(0.75x - £3.3m)}{60m}$$

$$45x - £108m = 51x - £224.4m$$

$$6x = £116.4m$$

$$x = \underline{£19.4m}$$

Self-assessment question 8.1

Russell Ltd installs and services heating and ventilation systems for commercial premises. The most recent balance sheet and profit and loss account of the business are set out below:

Balance sheet as at 31 May Year 4

	£000	£000	£000
Non-current assets			
Machinery and equipment at cost		883.6	
Less Accumulated depreciation		328.4	555.2
Motor vehicles at cost		268.8	
Less Accumulated depreciation		82.2	186.6
			741.8

Current assets	£000	£000	£000
Stock (inventory) at cost	293.2		
Trade debtors (receivables)	510.3		
Cash at bank	18.4		
		821.9	
Current liabilities			
Trade creditors (payables)	417.3		
Corporation tax	64.0	481.3	340.6
			1,082.4
Non-current liabilities			
12% debentures (repayable Year 10/11)			250.0
			832.4
Equity			
£1 ordinary shares			400.0
General reserve			50.2
Retained profit			380.2
			832.4

Profit and loss account (income statement) for the year ended 31 May Year 4

	£000
Sales revenue	5,207.8
Net profit before interest and taxation	542.0
Interest payable	30.0
Net profit before taxation	512.0
Corporation tax (25%)	128.0
Net profit after taxation	384.0
Dividend paid	153.6
Retained profit for the year	230.4

The business wishes to invest in more machinery and equipment in order to cope with an upsurge in demand for its services. An additional profit before interest and taxation of £120,000 per year is expected if an investment of £600,000 is made in plant and machinery.

The directors of the business are considering an offer from a venture capital business to finance the expansion programme. The finance will be made available immediately through either:

(i) an issue of £1 ordinary shares at a premium on par of £3 per share, or
(ii) an issue of £600,000 10% debentures at par.

The directors of the business wish to maintain the same dividend payout ratio in future years as in past years, whichever method of finance is chosen.

Required:
(a) For each of the financing schemes:
  (i) Prepare a projected profit and loss account for the year ended 31 May Year 5
  (ii) Calculate the projected earnings per share for the year ended 31 May Year 5
  (iii) Calculate the projected level of gearing as at 31 May Year 5.
(b) Briefly assess both of the financing schemes under consideration from the viewpoint of the existing shareholders.
(c) Calculate the level of profit before interest and taxation at which the earnings per share under each of the financing options will be the same.

What determines the level of gearing?

In practice, the level of gearing adopted by a business is likely to be influenced by the attitude of owners, managers and lenders. The factors that each of these groups is likely to bear in mind when making gearing decisions are considered below.

The attitude of the owners

The attitude of owners is likely to be influenced by the following factors:

- *Control.* Owners may be reluctant to issue new ordinary share capital where it results in a dilution of control. This may lead them to view loan capital as a better financing option.
- *Flexibility.* Too high a level of gearing may eliminate the potential for future borrowing. As a result, financial flexibility may be lost. Loan capital can often be raised much more quickly than share capital, which can be important when a business operates in a fast-changing environment.
- *Risk.* Risk-averse investors will only be prepared to take on more risk if there is the opportunity for higher rates of return. Thus, the additional risks of higher gearing must be outweighed by the prospect of higher returns.
- *Returns.* The potential benefits for owners of gearing have been discussed earlier. Where owners are receiving relatively poor returns, they may be reluctant to provide additional share capital and may try to lift their returns through higher gearing.

Real World 8.7 describes the reluctance of investors to inject further share capital into water utilities, leading these businesses to take on higher levels of borrowing to raise the finance required.

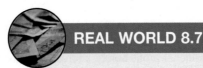

REAL WORLD 8.7

Turning off the equity tap   **FT**

The ability of privatised water companies to pay for future large investment schemes required by the government and the European Union is threatened by the reluctance of shareholders and lenders to pump more money into the sector, a survey warns today.

Companies have spent £50bn, since privatisation in 1989, to improve water quality and protect the environment. Spending is expected to remain high over the next 10 years because of new EU directives affecting issues such as sewage treatment.

Investors, representing more than half of UK managed funds, have said they would be reluctant to support share issues to pay for further capital investment unless returns improved.

Water companies say average price cuts in household bills of 12 per cent, imposed by the regulator in 1999, have impaired their ability to tap shareholders for fresh funds. They are pressing the regulator to raise returns by increasing bills when the next five-year price controls are triggered in April 2005.

Lenders have also cautioned that there are limits to the extent to which companies may be able to raise borrowing. The sector's net debt has risen from £4bn in 1995 to £15.6bn last year.

The survey was conducted for Water UK, the industry trade association, by Angela Whelan, former utilities analyst at Credit Lyonnais, in conjunction with Ofwat, the regulator.

It says: 'Overall, equity investors are not very enthusiastic about supporting a rights issue, especially to fund the capital programme. The majority indicated that returns would have to be above the current cost of capital.'

Pressure on finances has prompted water companies to raise more debt. Glas Cymru, which acquired Welsh Water, is 100 per cent debt financed while Anglian Water, owned by AWG, is almost 90 per cent financed by borrowings. Gearing across the sector has risen from 21 per cent in 1995 to 56 per cent last year.

More than 80 per cent of debt investors told the survey that lending risks would increase 'if more companies were to restructure their capital base and significantly increase gearing above 80 per cent'.

Pamela Taylor, Water UK chief executive, said: 'It looks certain that major capital investment will have to continue. The survey shows that it would be unwise to take for granted availability of funding at the required level and price.'

Source: 'Water companies' plans threatened by investor reluctance', *Financial Times*, 7 April 2003.

The attitude of management

Although managers are employed to operate a business in the owners' best interests, they may not always do this. Managers may object to high levels of gearing if they feel that it places their income and job security at risk. They make a big investment of 'human capital' in the business and become dependent on its continuing financial health. Managers cannot diversify this 'human capital' risk in the way that investors can diversify their financial capital risk. Managers may also object to the tight financial discipline that loan capital imposes on them. They may feel under constant pressure to ensure that sufficient cash is available to cover interest payments and capital repayments.

These objections may lead them to avoid making investments that require funding through loan capital.

The attitude of lenders

When deciding whether to provide loan finance, lenders will be concerned with the ability of the business to repay the amount borrowed and to pay interest at the due dates. There are various factors that will have a bearing on these issues.

Activity 8.15

What factors are likely to influence the ability of a business to repay the amount borrowed and to pay interest at due dates?

The following factors are likely to be important:

● *Profitability.*   Where a business has a stable level of profits, lenders may feel that there is less risk to their investment than where profits are volatile. Profit stability will depend on such factors as the nature of the products sold, the competitive structure of the industry and so on.
● *Cash-generating ability.*   Where a business is able to generate strong, predictable cash flows, lenders may feel there is less risk to their investment.

Activity 8.15 continued

- *Security for the loan*.   The nature and quality of assets held by a business will deter-mine whether there is adequate security for a loan. Generally speaking, lenders prefer assets that have a ready market value, which can be easily transferred and which will not deteriorate quickly (for example, freehold land).
- *Fixed costs*.   A business that operates with a high level of fixed costs has a high level of risk as fixed costs have to be paid irrespective of the level of sales and profits. Lenders may feel that a business with high fixed costs will only add to these by bor-rowing and this may increase the overall level of risk to unacceptable levels.

This is not an exhaustive list: you may have thought of other factors.

Levels of gearing can vary significantly between industries. Generally speaking, levels of gearing will be higher in industries where profits are stable (which lenders are likely to prefer). Thus, higher levels of gearing are likely to occur in utilities such as electricity, gas and water businesses, which are less affected by economic recession, changes in consumer tastes and so forth, than most businesses.

The capital structure debate

It may come as a surprise to discover that there is some debate in the finance literature over whether the capital structure decision really is important. There is some contro-versy over whether the 'mix' of long-term funds employed can have an effect on the overall cost of capital of a business. If a particular mix of funds can produce a lower cost of capital, then the way in which the business is financed is important as it can affect its value. (In broad terms, the value of a business can be defined as the net pre-sent value of its future cash flows. By lowering the cost of capital, which is used as the discount rate, the value of the business will be increased.)

The traditional view

The issue as to whether it really matters how the business is financed has been the subject of intense debate between two schools of thought: the traditional school and the modernist school. According to the traditional view, the capital structure decision is very important. The traditionalists point out that the cost of loan capital is cheaper than the cost of ordinary (equity) share capital (see Chapter 6). This difference in the relative cost of finance suggests that by increasing the level of borrowing (or gearing), the overall cost of capital of the business can be reduced. However, there are drawbacks to taking on additional borrowing. As the level of borrowing increases, ordinary share-holders will require higher levels of return on their investments to compensate for the higher levels of financial risk that they will have to bear. Existing lenders will also require higher levels of return.

The traditionalists argue, however, that at fairly low levels of borrowing, the benefits of raising finance through the use of loan capital will outweigh any costs that arise. This is because ordinary shareholders and lenders will not view low levels of borrow-ing as having a significant effect on the level of risk that they have to bear and so will not require a higher level of return in compensation. As the level of borrowing increases, however, things will start to change. Ordinary shareholders and existing lenders will become increasingly concerned with the higher interest charges that must be met and the risks this will pose to their own claims on the income and assets of the business. As a result, they will seek compensation for this higher level of risk in the form of higher expected returns.

The situation just described is set out in Figure 8.11. We can see that, where there are small increases in borrowing, ordinary shareholders and existing lenders do not require greatly increased returns. However, at significantly higher levels of borrowing, the risks involved take on greater importance for investors and this is reflected in the sharp rise in the returns required from each group. Note that the overall cost of capital (which is a weighted average of the cost of ordinary shares and loan capital) declines when small increases in the level of borrowing occur. However, at significantly increased levels of borrowing, the increase in required returns from equity shareholders and lenders will result in a sharp rise in the overall cost of capital.

An important implication of the above analysis is that managers of the business should try to establish that mix of loan/equity finance that will minimise the overall cost of capital. At this point, the business will be said to achieve an **optimal capital structure**. By minimising the overall cost of capital in this way, the value of the business (that is, the net present value of future cash flows) will be maximised. This relationship between the level of borrowing, the cost of capital and business value is illustrated in Figure 8.12.

We can see that the graph of the value of the business displays an inverse pattern to the graph of the overall cost of capital. (This is because a lower cost of capital will result

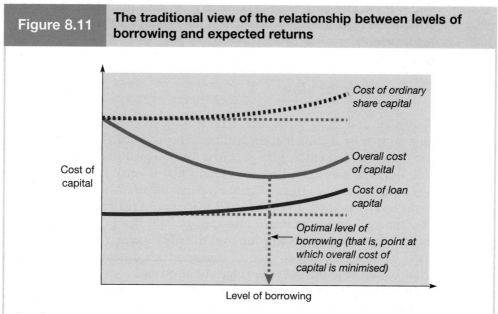

| Figure 8.11 | The traditional view of the relationship between levels of borrowing and expected returns |

The figure assumes that at low levels of borrowing, ordinary (equity) shareholders will not require a higher level of return to compensate for the higher risk incurred. As loan finance is cheaper than ordinary share finance, this will lead to a fall in the overall cost of capital. However, this situation will change as the level of borrowing increases. At some point, the increased returns required by ordinary shareholders will begin to outweigh the benefits of cheap loan capital and so the overall cost of capital will start to rise. The implication is, therefore, that there is an optimum level of gearing for a business.

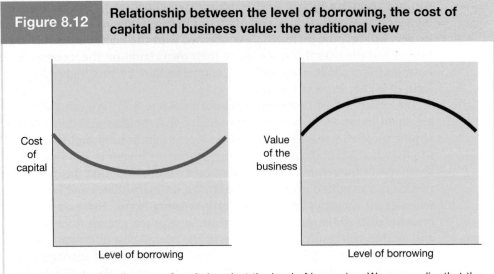

Figure 8.12 **Relationship between the level of borrowing, the cost of capital and business value: the traditional view**

The first graph plots the cost of capital against the level of borrowing. We saw earlier that the traditionalist view suggests that, in the first instance, the cost of capital will fall as the level of borrowing increases. However, at higher levels of borrowing, the overall cost of capital will begin to increase. The second graph plots the level of borrowing against the value of the business. This is the inverse of the first graph. As the cost of capital decreases so the value increases, and vice versa.

in a higher net present value for the future cash flows of the business.) This relationship suggests that the financing decision is critically important. Failure to identify and achieve the right financing 'mix' could have serious adverse consequences for shareholder wealth.

The modernist view

Modigliani and Miller (MM), who represent the modernist school, challenged the traditional view by arguing that the required returns to shareholders and to lenders would not follow the pattern as set out above. They argued that shareholders in a business with financial gearing will expect a return that is equal to the returns expected from investing in a similar ungeared business plus a premium, which rises in *direct proportion* to the level of gearing. Thus, the increase in returns required for ordinary shareholders as compensation for increased financial risk will rise in constant proportion to the increase in the level of borrowing over the *whole range of borrowing*. This pattern contrasts with the traditional view, of course, which displays an uneven change in the required rate of return over the range of borrowing.

The MM analysis also assumes that the returns required from borrowers would remain constant as the level of borrowing increases. This latter point may appear strange at first sight. However, if lenders have good security for the loans made to the business, they are unlikely to feel at risk from additional borrowing and will not, therefore, seek additional returns. This is provided, of course, that the business does not exceed its borrowing capacity.

The MM position is set out in Figure 8.13. As you can see, the overall cost of capital remains constant at varying levels of borrowing. This is because the benefits obtained from raising finance through borrowing, which is cheaper than share capital, is exactly offset by the increase in required returns from ordinary shareholders.

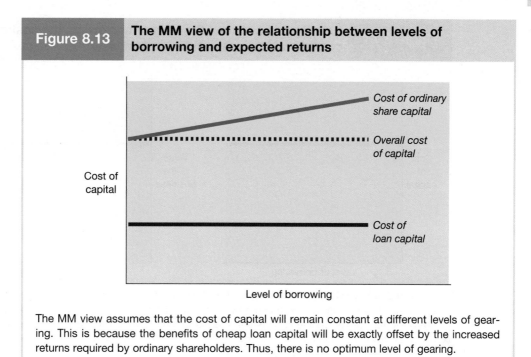

Figure 8.13   **The MM view of the relationship between levels of borrowing and expected returns**

The MM view assumes that the cost of capital will remain constant at different levels of gearing. This is because the benefits of cheap loan capital will be exactly offset by the increased returns required by ordinary shareholders. Thus, there is no optimum level of gearing.

An important implication of the MM view is that the financing decision is not really important. Figure 8.13 shows that there is no optimal capital structure for a business, as suggested by the traditionalists, because the overall cost of capital remains constant. This means that one particular capital structure is no better or worse than any other and so managers should not spend time on evaluating different forms of financing 'mixes' for the business. Instead, they should concentrate their efforts on evaluating and managing the investments of the business.

Activity 8.16

In Figure 8.12 we saw the traditional view of the relationships between the cost of capital and the level of borrowing and the value of the business and the level of borrowing. How would the MM view of these two relationships be shown in graphical form?

The relationship between (i) the level of borrowing and the cost of capital and (ii) the level of borrowing and the value of the business, as viewed by MM, is set out in Figure 8.14.

Although the views of Modigliani and Miller were first published in the late 1950s, they are often described as modernists because they base their position on economic theory (unlike the traditional school). They argue that the value of a business is determined by the future income from its investments, and the risk associated with those investments, and not by the way in which this income is divided among the different providers of finance. In other words, it is not possible to increase the value of a business (that is, lower the overall cost of capital) simply by borrowing, as the traditionalists suggest. MM point out that borrowing is not something that only businesses are able to undertake. Borrowing can also be undertaken by individual investors. As business borrowing can be replicated by individual investors, there is no reason why it

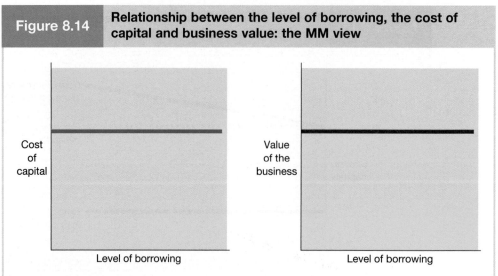

Figure 8.14 Relationship between the level of borrowing, the cost of capital and business value: the MM view

The first graph shows that, according to MM, the cost of capital will remain constant at different levels of borrowing. The second graph shows the implication of this for the value of the business. As the cost of capital is constant, the net present value of future cash flows from the business will not be affected by the level of borrowing. Hence, the value of the business will remain constant.

should create additional value for the investor. **(Un)Real World 8.8** explains the theory from a lighter perspective.

(UN)REAL WORLD 8.8

If you want to understand the arguments of MM . . . start with a pizza

We have just seen that it is the income-generating power and risks associated with the underlying investments of the business, rather than the different ways in which a business may be financed, that determine the value of a business. This point was once explained by Miller (of Modigliani and Miller fame) as follows:

> Think of the firm as a gigantic pizza, divided into quarters. If now, you cut each quarter in half into eighths, the M&M proposition says that you will have more pieces, but not more pizza.

In other words, different financing methods will have an effect on how the business investments and income stream will be divided up but will not affect the value of these.

However, Miller's view of pizzas, like his view of capital structure, may be controversial. When Yogi Berra, a US baseball player, was asked whether he would like his pizza cut into six or eight pieces he is reputed to have said, 'Better make it six, I don't think I can eat eight' (see Hawawini, G. and Viallet, C., 2nd edn, South Western, Thomson Learning, 2002, p. 353).

A simple example may help to illustrate the MM position that business borrowing should not create additional value for a business.

Example 8.6

Two businesses, Delta plc and Omega plc, are identical except for the fact that Delta plc is financed entirely by ordinary shares and Omega plc is 50 per cent financed by loans. The profits before interest for each business for the year is £2 million. The ordinary shareholders of Delta plc require a return of 12 per cent and the ordinary shareholders of Omega plc require a return of 14 per cent. Omega plc pays 10 per cent interest per year on the £10 million loans outstanding. (Taxation is to be ignored for reasons that we shall discuss later.)

	Delta plc £m	Omega plc £m
Profits before interest	2.0	2.0
Interest payable	–	1.0
Available to ordinary shareholders	2.0	1.0

The market value of the total ordinary shares of each business will be equivalent to the profits capitalised at the required rate of return. Thus, the market value of each business is as follows:

	Delta plc £m	Omega plc £m
Market value of ordinary (equity) shares:		
(£2m/0.12)	16.7	
(£1m/0.14)		7.1
Market value of loan capital		10.0
Market value of each business	16.7	17.1

MM argue that differences in the way in which each business is financed cannot result in a higher value for Omega plc as shown above. This is because an investor who owns, say, 10 per cent of the shares in Omega plc would be able to obtain the same level of income from investing in Delta plc, for the same level of risk as the investment in Omega plc and for a lower net investment. The investor, by borrowing an amount equivalent to 10 per cent of the loans of Omega plc (that is, an amount proportional to the ownership interest in Omega plc), and selling the shares held in Omega plc in order to finance the purchase of a 10 per cent equity stake in Delta plc, would be in the following position:

	£000
Return from 10% equity investment in Delta plc	200
Less Interest on borrowing (£1,000 × 10%)	100
Net return	100
Purchase of shares (10% × £16.7m)	1,670
Less Amount borrowed	1,000
Net investment in Delta plc	670

The investor with a 10 per cent stake in the ordinary share capital of Omega plc is, currently, in the following position:

	£000
Return from 10% investment in Omega plc	100
Net investment in Omega plc: existing shareholding (10% × £7.1m)	710

As we can see, the investor would be better off by taking on personal borrowing in order to acquire a 10 per cent share of the ordinary share capital of the

Example 8.6 continued

ungeared business, Delta plc, than by continuing to invest in the geared business, Omega plc. The effect of a number of investors switching investments in this way would be to reduce the value of the shares in Omega plc (thereby increasing the returns to ordinary shareholders in Omega plc), and to increase the value of shares in Delta plc (thereby reducing the returns to equity in Delta plc). This switching from Omega plc to Delta plc (which is referred to as **arbitrage transactions**) would continue until the returns from each investment were the same, and so no further gains could be made from such transactions. At this point, the value of each business would be identical.

The MM analysis, while extremely rigorous and logical, is based on a number of restrictive assumptions. These include the following.

Perfect capital markets

The assumption of perfect capital markets means that there are no share transaction costs and investors and businesses can borrow unlimited amounts at the same rates of interest. Although these assumptions may be unrealistic, they may not have a significant effect on the arguments made. Where the prospect of 'arbitrage' gains (that is, selling shares in an overvalued business and buying shares in an undervalued business) are substantial, share transaction costs are unlikely to be an important issue as the potential benefits will outweigh the costs. It is only at the margin that share transaction costs will take on significance.

Similarly, the assumption that investors can borrow unlimited amounts at the same rate of interest may only take on significance at the margin. We have seen that the UK stock market is dominated by large investment institutions such as pension funds, unit trusts and insurance businesses that hold a very large proportion of all shares issued by listed businesses. These institutions may well be able to borrow very large amounts at similar rates to those offered to a business.

No bankruptcy costs

Assuming that there are no bankruptcy costs means that, if a business were liquidated, no legal and administrative fees would be incurred and the business assets could be sold at a price that would enable shareholders to receive cash equal to the market value of their shareholding prior to the liquidation. This assumption will not hold true in the real world where bankruptcy costs can be very high.

However, it is only at high levels of gearing that bankruptcy costs are likely to be a real issue. We saw in Chapter 6 that borrowing leads to a commitment to pay interest and to repay capital: the higher the level of borrowing, the higher the level of commitment and the higher the risk that this commitment will not be met. In the case of a low-geared, or moderately geared, business it may be possible to take on additional borrowing, if necessary, to meet commitments whereas a highly geared business may have no further debt capacity.

Risk

It is assumed that businesses exist that have identical operating risks but which have different levels of borrowing. Although this is unlikely to be true, it does not affect the validity of MM's arguments.

No taxation

A world without corporate or personal income taxes is clearly an unrealistic assumption. The real issue, however, is whether this undermines the validity of MM's arguments. We shall, therefore, consider next the effect of introducing taxes on the MM position.

MM and the introduction of taxation

MM were subject to considerable criticism for not dealing with the problem of taxation in their analysis. This led them to revise their position so as to include taxation. They acknowledged in their revised analysis that the tax relief from interest payments on loans provides a real benefit to ordinary shareholders. The more the level of borrowing increases, the more tax relief the business receives and so the smaller the tax liability of the business will become.

We should recall that the original MM position was that the benefits of cheap loan capital will be exactly offset by increases in the required rate of return by ordinary share investors. Tax relief on loan interest should, therefore, represent an additional benefit to shareholders. As the amount of tax relief increases with the amount of borrowing, the overall cost of capital (after tax) will be lowered as the level of borrowing increases. The implication of this revised position is that there is an optimum level of gearing and it is at 100 per cent gearing. In Figure 8.15, we can see the MM position after taxation has been introduced.

Thus, the MM position moves closer to the traditional position in so far as it recognises that there is a relationship between the value of the business and the way in which it is financed. It also recognises that there is an optimum level of gearing.

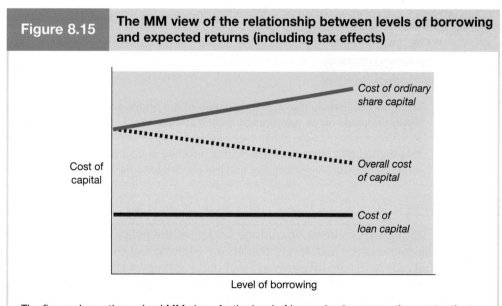

| **Figure 8.15** | **The MM view of the relationship between levels of borrowing and expected returns (including tax effects)** |

The figure shows the revised MM view. As the level of borrowing increases, the greater the tax benefits to ordinary (equity) shareholders. These tax benefits will increase with the level of borrowing and so the overall cost of capital (after tax) will be lowered as the level of borrowing increases. This means that there is an optimum level of gearing and it is at the 100 per cent level of gearing.

The relationship between (a) the level of borrowing and the cost of capital and (b) the level of borrowing and business value, after taking into account the tax effects, is set out in Figure 8.16.

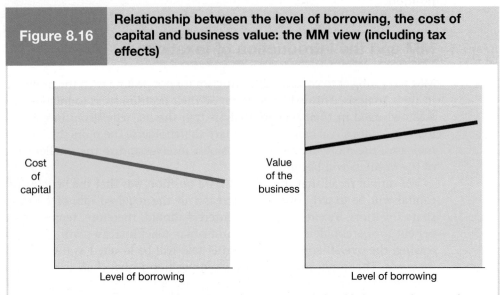

Figure 8.16	Relationship between the level of borrowing, the cost of capital and business value: the MM view (including tax effects)

The first graph displays the MM (including tax) view of the relationship between the cost of capital and the level of borrowing. We can see that as the level of borrowing increases, the overall cost of capital decreases. The second graph shows the relationship between the value of the business and the level of borrowing. A decrease in the overall cost of capital results in a rise in the value of the business and so, as the level of borrowing increases, the value of the business increases.

Activity 8.17

What do you think is the main implication of the above analysis for managers who are trying to decide on an appropriate capital structure?

This revised MM analysis implies that a business should borrow to capacity as this will lower the post-tax cost of capital and thereby increase the value of the business.

In practice, however, few businesses follow the policy just described. When borrowing reaches very high levels, lenders are likely to feel that their security is threatened and ordinary share investors will feel that bankruptcy risks have increased. Thus, both groups are likely to seek higher returns, which will, in turn, increase the overall cost of capital. (A business would have to attract *risk-seeking* investors in order to prevent a rise in its cost of capital.)

The debate concerning capital structure still rumbles on. Although the arguments of the traditional school have been undermined by the inexorable logic of MM, it does seem that, in the real world, businesses tend to settle for moderate rather than high levels of gearing as recommended by the MM (including tax) arguments. We have just seen that the risk of bankruptcy and the effect of this on the attitudes of shareholders and lenders may prevent a business from taking on very high levels of gearing. Nevertheless, it could be argued that, from an ordinary share investor's viewpoint, the business should continue to borrow until the risks of incurring bankruptcy costs outweigh the benefits from higher gearing.

Real World 8.9 describes how investment trust businesses, which invest in other businesses, change their level of gearing according to the perceived level of risk.

REAL WORLD 8.9

Gearing levels fall amid fears over risks

Investment trust managers, who control £62bn of assets, have almost halved their levels of borrowing, or gearing, over the past two years because of fears about the strength of the stock market recovery and regulatory concerns.

The average level of gearing of the conventional investment trust has fallen from 20 per cent at the end of March 2003 to 11 per cent at the end of March this year (2005), according to the Association of Investment Trust Companies. Some specialist sectors, including UK high income, have maintained higher levels of gearing.

'Managers are taking a cautious view of markets and boards are becoming wary of taking any risk at all in terms of gearing,' says Iain Scouller, analyst at UBS.

JP Morgan Fleming's European Fledgling investment trust cut its gearing from 18 to 2 per cent at the beginning of this month. 'The managers felt there had been a period of strong performance and it was time to slightly reduce its risk profile,' says David Barron, head of investment trusts. 'We felt it was time to lock in some of those gains.'

Some managers are maintaining their gearing levels but switching from expensive long-term borrowing into short-term arrangements. 'Long-term arrangements worked well in the 1990s but managers were hit hard in the bear [sellers] market,' said Charles Cade, analyst at Close Wins, a market maker. 'Now they want flexible gearing that changes with market conditions.'

Investment trusts make a selling point of their ability to gear up in the good times. They contrast themselves with unit trusts which are only permitted to borrow up to 10 per cent of their net asset value.

There is no official upper limit on investment trust borrowing but trusts are limited by what investors would think was prudent and by the willingness of banks to lend. One manager said gearing of more than 25 per cent could make a trust hard to market.

Investment trusts gear up when they believe they can make a higher return on their investment than the interest they are paying on their borrowing. Additional borrowing also means they can take advantage of opportunities without having to sell existing investments.

The downside of gearing is that if markets fall and the performance of the assets in the portfolio is poor, then the losses will be magnified by high borrowings.

'Gearing levels fall amid fears over risks', www.ft.com, 30 April 2005.

SUMMARY

The main points in this chapter may be summarised as follows:

Cost of capital

- An opportunity cost, which reflects the returns that investors would expect to earn from investments with the same level of risk.

- Two major approaches to determining the cost of ordinary (equity) shares, the dividend-based approach and the risk/return (CAPM) approach.

- The dividend-based approach reflects the fact that a share can be valued according to the future dividends received.

- Dividend valuation models often assume constant dividends over time ($K_0 = D_0/P_0$) or that dividends will grow at a constant rate [$K_0 = (D_1/P_0) + g$].

- The risk/return approach is based on the idea that the cost of an ordinary share is made up of a risk-free rate of return plus a risk premium.

- The risk premium is calculated by measuring the risk premium for the market as a whole, then measuring the returns from a particular share in relation to the market and applying this measure to the market risk premium [$K_0 = K_{RF} + b(K_m - K_{RF})$].

- The cost of irredeemable loan capital can be derived in a similar way to that of ordinary shares where the dividend stays constant ($K_d = I(1 - t)/P_d$).

- The cost of redeemable loan capital can be computed using an IRR approach.

- The cost of preference share capital can be derived in a similar way to that of ordinary shares where the dividend stays constant ($K_p = D_p/P_p$).

- The weighted average cost of capital (WACC) is derived by taking the cost of each element of capital and weighting each element in proportion to the target capital structure.

Financial gearing

- The effect of financial gearing is that changes in profit before interest and taxation (PBIT) result in disproportionate changes in the returns to ordinary shareholders.

- The degree of financial gearing measures the sensitivity of changes in returns to ordinary shareholders to changes in PBIT.

- A PBIT–EPS indifference chart can be constructed to reveal the returns to shareholders at different levels of PBIT for different financing options.

- In practice, gearing levels will be determined by the attitude of owners, managers and lenders.

The capital structure debate

- Two schools of thought.

- The traditional view is that the capital structure decision is important whereas the modernist view is that it is not.

Traditional viewpoint

- Traditionalists argue that, at lower levels of gearing, shareholders and lenders are unconcerned about risk; however, at higher levels they become concerned and demand higher returns.

- This leads to an increase in WACC.

- WACC decreases at lower levels of gearing (because investors do not demand increased returns) but then increases.
- This means that there is an optimum level of gearing.

Modernist viewpoint

- Modernists (MM) argue that shareholders are always concerned about the level of gearing.
- Cheaper loan finance is offset by increasing cost of ordinary shares and so the cost of capital remains constant.
- This means that there is no optimum level of gearing.
- If tax is introduced, the modernist view is changed.
- There are benefits arising from tax relief on loan capital which should be exploited by taking on loan capital up to the point where these benefits are offset by the potential costs of bankruptcy.

→ Key terms

Cost of capital   p. 300
Capital asset pricing model (CAPM)
   p. 303
Beta   p. 304
Weighted average cost of capital
   (WACC)   p. 314

Degree of financial gearing   p. 322
PBIT–EPS indifference chart
   p. 328
Indifference point   p. 329
Optimal capital structure   p. 335
Arbitrage transactions   p. 340

For definitions of these terms see the Glossary, pp. 562–571.

Further reading

If you wish to explore the topics discussed in this chapter in more depth, try the following books:

Business Finance: Theory and Practice McLaney E 7th Edn Financial Times Prentice Hall 2006 Chapters 10 and 11.

Corporate Finance and Investment, *Pike, R. and Neale, B.*, 4th edn, Financial Times Prentice Hall, 2003, Chapters 20 and 21.

Corporate Financial Management, *Arnold G.*, Financial Times Prentice Hall, 2002, Chapter 18.

Financial Management, *Brigham, E. and Ehrhardt, M.*, 10th edn, Harcourt, 2002, Chapters 16 and 17.

References

1 'Practitioners' perspectives on the UK cost of capital', *McLaney, E., Pointon, J., Thomas, M. and Tucker J.*, **European Journal of Finance**, April 2004, pp. 123–38.

2 **The Cost of Capital in the UK**, *Gregory, A. and Rutterford, J.* (with Zaman, M.), Chartered Institute of Management Accountants Research Monograph, 1999.

3 'How do CFOs make capital budgeting and capital structure decisions?', *Graham, J. and Harvey, C.*, **Journal of Applied Corporate Finance**, vol. 15 (2002), no. 1.

4 Quoted in **Finance for Executives**, *Hawawini, G. and Viallet, C.*, 2nd edn, South Western/ Thomson Learning, 2002, p. 353.

REVIEW QUESTIONS

Answers to these questions can be found in Appendix D at the back of the book.

8.1 How might a business find out whether a particular planned level of gearing would be acceptable to investors?

8.2 What factors might a prospective lender take into account when deciding whether to make a long-term loan to a particular business?

8.3 Should the specific cost of raising finance for a particular project be used as the appropriate discount rate for investment appraisal purposes?

8.4 What are the main implications for the financial manager who accepts the arguments of:

(a) the traditional approach
(b) the MM (excluding tax effects) approach
(c) the MM (including tax effects) approach

concerning capital structure?

EXERCISES

Exercises 8.5 to 8.7 are more advanced than 8.1 to 8.4. Those with coloured numbers have answers at the back of the book.

 If you wish to try more exercises, visit the students' side of the Companion Website.

8.1 Riphean plc and Silurian plc are two businesses operating in different industries from one another. They are both financed by a mixture of ordinary share and loan capital and both are seeking to derive the cost of capital for investment decision making purposes. The following information is available concerning the two businesses for the year to 30 November Year 8:

	Riphean plc	Silurian plc
Net profit after taxation	£3.0m	£4.0m
Gross dividends	£1.5m	£2.0m
Market value per ordinary share	£4.00	£1.60
Number of ordinary shares	5m	10m
Gross interest yield on loan capital	8%	12%
Market value of loan capital	£10m	£16m

The annual growth rate in dividends is 5 per cent for Riphean plc and 8 per cent for Silurian plc.

Assume a 30 per cent rate of corporation tax.

Required:

(a) Explain what is meant by the term 'cost of capital' and state why it is important for a business to calculate its cost of capital correctly.

(b) Calculate the weighted average cost of capital of Riphean plc and Silurian plc using the information provided.

(c) Discuss two possible reasons why the cost of ordinary share capital differs between the two businesses.

(d) Discuss two limitations of using the weighted average cost of capital when making investment decisions.

8.2 Celtor plc is a property development business operating in the London area. The business has the following capital structure as at 30 November Year 9:

	£000
£1 ordinary shares	10,000
Retained profit	20,000
9% debentures	12,000
	42,000

The ordinary shares have a current market value of £3.90 and the current level of dividend is 20p per share. The dividend has been growing at a compound rate of 4 per cent a year in recent years. The debentures of the business are irredeemable and have a current market value of £80 per £100 nominal. Interest due on the debentures at the year end has recently been paid.

The business has obtained planning permission to build a new office block in a redevelopment area. The business wishes to raise the whole of the finance necessary for the project by the issue of more irredeemable 9 per cent debentures at £80 per £100 nominal. This is in line with a target capital structure set by the business where the amount of debt capital will increase to 70 per cent of ordinary share capital within the next two years. The rate of corporation tax is 25 per cent.

Required:

(a) Explain what is meant by the term 'cost of capital'. Why is it important for a business to calculate its cost of capital correctly?

(b) Calculate the weighted average cost of capital of Celtor plc that should be used for future investment decisions.

8.3 Grenache plc operates a chain of sports shops throughout the UK. In recent years competition has been fierce and profits and sales have declined. The most recent accounts of the business are as follows:

Balance sheet as at 30 April Year 7

	£m	£m	£m
Non-current assets			
Freehold premises at cost		56.5	
Less Accumulated depreciation		10.2	46.3
Fixtures, fittings and equipment at cost		23.6	
Less Accumulated depreciation		7.5	16.1
			62.4
Current assets			
Stock (inventory) at cost		52.4	
Trade debtors (receivables)		2.3	
Cash		1.2	
		55.9	
Current liabilities			
Trade creditors (payables)	48.1		
Corporation tax	1.6	49.7	6.2
			68.6

	£m	£m	£m
Non-current liabilities			
10% debenture			25.0
			43.6
Equity			
£1 ordinary shares			25.0
Retained profit			18.6
			43.6

Profit and loss account (income statement) for the year ended 30 April Year 7

	£m
Sales revenue	148.8
Profit before interest and taxation	15.7
Interest payable	2.5
Profit before taxation	13.2
Corporation tax (25%)	3.3
Profit after taxation	9.9
Dividends paid	5.2
Retained profit for the year	4.7

A new managing director was appointed during Year 7 to improve the performance of the business. She plans a 'sand and surf' image for the business in order to appeal to the younger market. This will require a large investment in new stocks and a complete redesign and refurbishment of the shops. The cost of implementing the plan is estimated to be £30 million.

The business is considering two possible financing options. The first option is to issue further 10 per cent debentures at par. The second option is to make a rights issue based on a 20 per cent discount on the current market value of the shares. The market capitalisation of the business is currently £187.5 million.

The future performance following the relaunch of the business is not certain. Three scenarios have been prepared concerning the possible effects on annual profits before interest and taxation:

Scenario	Change in profits before interest and taxation compared to most recent year
	%
Optimistic	+40
Most likely	+15
Pessimistic	−25

The dividend per share will increase by 10 per cent during the forthcoming year if there is an increase in profit but will decrease by 20 per cent if there is a reduction in profit.

The business has a current gearing ratio that is broadly in line with its competitors.

Required:

(a) Prepare, in so far as the information allows, a forecast profit and loss account for the forthcoming year for each scenario assuming:
  (i) A loan issue is made
  (ii) A rights issue is made.
  Workings should be in £m and to one decimal place.

(b) Calculate the earnings per share and gearing ratio for the forthcoming year for each scenario assuming:
  (i) A loan issue is made
  (ii) A rights issue of shares is made.

(c) Assess the future plans and financing options being considered from the perspective of a current shareholder and state what additional information, if any, you may require to make a more considered assessment.

8.4 Trexon plc is a major oil and gas exploration business that has most of its operations in the Middle East and South East Asia. Recently, the business acquired rights to explore for oil and gas in the Gulf of Mexico. Trexon plc proposes to finance the new operations from the issue of ordinary shares. At present, the business is financed by a combination of ordinary share capital and loan capital. The ordinary shares have a nominal value of £0.50 and a current market value of £2.60. The current level of dividend is £0.16 per share and this has been growing at a compound rate of 6 per cent a year in recent years. The loan capital is irredeemable and has a current market value of £94 per £100 nominal. Interest on the loan capital is at the rate of 12 per cent and interest due at the year end has recently been paid. At present, the business expects 60 per cent of its finance to come from ordinary share capital and the rest from loan capital. In the future, however, the business will aim to finance 70 per cent of its operations from ordinary share capital.

When the proposal to finance the new operations via the rights issue of shares was announced at the annual general meeting of the business, objections were raised by two shareholders present, as follows:

● *Shareholder A argued*: 'I fail to understand why the business has decided to issue shares to finance the new operation. Surely it would be better to reinvest profit, as this is, in effect, a free source of finance.'
● *Shareholder B argued*: 'I also fail to understand why the business has decided to issue shares to finance the new operation. However, I do not agree with the suggestion made by Shareholder A. I do not believe that shareholder funds should be used at all to finance the new operation. Instead, the business should issue more loan capital, as it is cheap relative to ordinary share capital and would, therefore, reduce the overall cost of capital of the business.'

Corporation tax is at the rate of 35 per cent.

Required:
(a) Calculate the weighted average cost of capital of Trexon plc that should be used in future investment decisions.
(b) Comment on the remarks made by:
    (i)   Shareholder A, and
    (ii) Shareholder B.

8.5 Ashcroft plc, a family-controlled business, is considering raising additional funds to modernise its factory. The scheme is expected to cost £2.34 million and will increase annual profits before interest and tax from 1 January Year 4 by £0.6 million. A summarised balance sheet and profit and loss account are shown below. Currently the share price is 200p.

Two schemes have been suggested. First, 1.3 million shares could be issued at 180p (net of issue costs). Second, a consortium of six City institutions has offered to buy debentures from the business totalling £2.34 million. Interest would be at the rate of 13 per cent per annum and capital repayments of equal annual instalments of £234,000 starting on 1 January Year 5 would be required.

Balance sheet as at 31 December Year 3

	£m	£m
Non-current assets (net)		1.4
Current assets		
Stock (inventory)	2.4	
Debtors (receivables)	2.2	
	4.6	
Current liabilities		
Creditors (payables)	3.2	
Corporation tax	0.3	
	3.5	
Net current assets		1.1
Total assets *less* current liabilities		2.5
Equity		
Called-up share capital, 25p ordinary shares		1.0
Profit and loss account		1.5
		2.5

Profit and loss account (income statement) for the year ended 31 December Year 3

	£m
Sales revenue	11.2
Profit on ordinary activities before tax	1.2
Taxation on profit on ordinary activities	0.6
Profit on ordinary activities after tax	0.6
Dividends paid	0.3
Retained profit for the financial year	0.3

Assume corporation tax is charged at the rate of 50 per cent.

Required:

(a) Compute the earnings per share for Year 4 under the debenture and the ordinary share alternatives.

(b) Compute the level of profits before debenture interest and tax at which the earnings per share under the two schemes will be equal.

(c) Discuss the considerations the directors should take into account before deciding upon debenture finance or ordinary share finance.

8.6   Hatleigh plc is a medium-sized engineering business based in South Wales. The accounts for the year ended 30 April 2005 are as follows:

Balance sheet as at 30 April 2005

	£000	£000	£000
Non-current assets			
Freehold premises at valuation			3,885
Plant and machinery at cost less depreciation			2,520
Motor vehicles at cost less depreciation			1,470
			7,875
Current assets			
Stock (inventory): Raw materials		824	
Work in progress		2,120	
Finished goods		5,436	
Trade debtors (receivables)		8,578	
		16,958	

Less Current liabilities	£000	£000	£000
Trade creditors (payables)	3,322		
Bank overdraft	4,776		
Corporation tax	201	8,299	
			8,659
			16,534
Less Non-current liabilities			
10% debentures 2010–11 (secured on freehold premises)			3,500
			13,034
Equity			
Share capital (25p shares)			8,000
Retained profit			5,034
			13,034

Profit and loss account (income statement) for the year ended 30 April 2005

	£000
Sales revenue	34,246
Cost of sales	24,540
Gross profit	9,706
Expenses	7,564
Operating profit	2,142
Interest	994
Profit before taxation	1,148
Corporation tax (35%)	402
Net profit after taxation	746
Dividends paid	600
Retained profit for the year	146

The business made a one-for-four rights issue of ordinary shares during the year. Sales for the forthcoming year are forecast to be the same as for the year to 30 April 2005. The gross profit margin is likely to stay the same as in previous years but expenses (excluding interest payments) are likely to fall by 10 per cent as a result of economies.

The bank has been concerned that the business has persistently exceeded the agreed overdraft limits and, as a result, the business has now been asked to reduce its overdraft to £3 million over the next three months. The business has agreed to do this and has calculated that interest on the bank overdraft for the forthcoming year will be £440,000 (after taking account of the required reduction in the overdraft). In order to achieve the reduction in overdraft, the chairman of Hatleigh plc is considering either the issue of more ordinary shares for cash to existing shareholders at a discount of 20 per cent, or the issue of more 10% debentures redeemable 2010–11 at the end of July 2005. It is believed that the share price will be £1.50 and the 10% debentures will be quoted at £82 per £100 nominal value at the end of July 2005. The bank overdraft is expected to remain at the amount shown in the balance sheet until that date. Any issue costs relating to new shares or debentures should be ignored.

Required:
(a) Calculate:
 (i) the total number of shares, and
 (ii) the total par value of debentures
 which will have to be issued in order to raise the funds necessary to reduce the overdraft to the level required by the bank.
(b) Calculate the expected earnings per share for the year to 30 April 2006 assuming:
 (i) the issue of shares, and
 (ii) the issue of debentures
 are carried out to reduce the overdraft to the level required by the bank.

(c) Critically evaluate the proposal of the chairman to raise the necessary funds by the issue of:
  (i) shares, and
  (ii) debentures.

8.7 Jubilee plc operates four wholesale food outlets in Scotland. After several years of sales and profits growth the business has recently experienced some financial problems. The accounts for the year ended 31 May Year 6 are shown below:

Balance sheet as at 31 May Year 6

	£000	£000	£000
Non-current assets			
Freehold land and buildings at valuation			4,600
Fixtures and fittings at cost		150	
Less Accumulated depreciation		60	90
Motor vans at cost		160	
Less Accumulated depreciation		45	115
			4,805
Current assets			
Stock (inventory) at cost		5,208	
Trade debtors (receivables)		5,240	
Cash		6	
		10,454	
Less **Current liabilities**			
Trade creditors (payables)	4,100		
Corporation tax	53		
Bank overdraft	3,200	7,353	3,101
			7,906
Less **Non-current liabilities**			
11% debentures Years 10–11 (secured			
on freehold land and buildings)			3,800
			4,106
Equity			
£1 ordinary shares			1,400
Retained profit			2,706
			4,106

Profit and loss account (income statement) for the year ended 31 May Year 6

	£000
Sales revenue	45,000
Cost of sales	36,000
Gross profit	9,000
Expenses	7,600
Operating profit	1,400
Interest payable	1,050
Profit before taxation	350
Corporation tax (30%)	105
Net profit after taxation	245
Dividends paid	140
Retained profit	105

Stock levels remained constant throughout the year. All sales and purchases are on credit.
In recent months the business has failed to pay trade creditors within the agreed credit periods. In order to restore its credit standing, the business wishes to reduce its trade creditors

to an average of 30 days' credit (all purchases are on credit). In addition, the business wishes to refurbish its outlets and to acquire a computerised accounting system at a total cost of £700,000. To finance these requirements, the business is considering making a rights issue of shares at a discount of 25 per cent on the market value. At present, shares are trading on the Stock Exchange at £1.60. Alternatively, the business may make an issue of 10% debentures at a price of £96 per £100 nominal value to be secured on the freehold property.

In the forthcoming year, sales are expected to increase by 10 per cent and the gross profit margin is likely to remain the same as for the year ended 31 May Year 6. Expenses are likely to rise by 5 per cent during the forthcoming year. Interest charges on the overdraft are expected to be lower, due largely to falling interest rates, at £260,000. Dividends per share are planned to be the same as the year to 31 May Year 6.

The raising of the necessary finance is expected to take place at the beginning of the year to 31 May Year 7. Issue costs relating to new shares and debentures can be ignored.

Required:
(a) Treating separately each method of raising finance, calculate:
    (i)   the total number of shares, and
    (ii) the total par (nominal) value of debentures
    which have to be issued in order to raise the finance required.
(b) Calculate the forecast earnings per share for the year to 31 May Year 7 assuming:
    (i)   a rights issue of shares is made, and
    (ii) an issue of debentures is made
    to raise the necessary finance.
(c) Calculate the gearing ratio as at 31 May Year 7 assuming:
    (i)   a rights issue of shares is made, and
    (ii) an issue of debentures is made.
(d) Discuss the major factors to be considered by Jubilee plc when deciding between a rights issue of shares and an issue of debentures to raise the necessary finance.

Workings should be to the nearest £000.

9

Developing a dividend policy

LEARNING OUTCOMES

When you have completed this chapter, you should be able to:

- Describe the nature of dividends and the way in which they are paid.

- Explain why dividends should have no effect on shareholder wealth in a world of perfect and efficient markets.

- Discuss the factors that influence dividend policy in practice.

- Discuss the alternatives to cash dividends that may be used.

INTRODUCTION

The issue of dividend policy has aroused much controversy over the years. At the centre of this controversy is whether the pattern of dividends adopted by a business has any effect on shareholders' wealth. In this chapter, we examine the arguments that have been raised. Although the importance of dividend policy to shareholders remains a moot point, there is evidence to suggest that managers *perceive* the dividend decision to be important. We consider the attitudes of managers towards dividends and examine the factors that are likely to influence dividend policy in practice. We also consider the alternatives to a cash dividend that might be used.

The payment of dividends

It is probably a good idea to begin our examination of dividends and dividend policy by describing briefly what dividends are and how they are paid. **Dividends** represent a return by a business to its shareholders. This return is normally paid in cash, although it would be possible for it to be paid with assets other than cash. In your previous studies, you may have discovered that there are legal limits on the amount that can be distributed in the form of dividend payments to shareholders.

Activity 9.1

Why does the law impose limits on the amount of cash that can be distributed as dividends?

If there were no legal limits, it would be possible for shareholders to withdraw their investment from the business and so leave the lenders and creditors in an exposed financial position. The law tries to protect lenders and creditors by preventing excessive withdrawals of shareholder capital. One way in which this can be done is through placing restrictions on dividend payments.

The law states that dividends can only be paid to shareholders of private limited companies out of *realised* profits. In essence, the maximum amount available for distribution will be the accumulated trading profits (less any losses) *plus* any profits on the disposal of fixed assets. Any surpluses arising from the revaluation of fixed assets will represent an unrealised profit that cannot be distributed. However, shareholders of public companies can be paid out of the net accumulated profits whether the profits are realised or unrealised.

Activity 9.2

Bio-tech Ltd started trading in Year 1 and made a trading profit of £200,000 in this year. In Year 2, the business made a trading loss of £150,000 but made a profit on the sale of freehold buildings of £30,000. Other fixed assets were revalued during the year leading to an increase in the revaluation reserve of £60,000. Assuming that no dividend was paid in Year 1, what is the maximum dividend that could be paid by Bio-tech Ltd in Year 2?

Bio-tech Ltd is a private limited company, hence the maximum dividend is calculated as follows:

	£
Trading profit Year 1	200,000
Profit on sale of fixed asset Year 6	30,000
	230,000
Less Trading loss Year 2	150,000
Maximum amount available for distribution	80,000

It should be noted that businesses rarely distribute the maximum amount available for distribution. Indeed, the dividend paid is normally much lower than the trading profits for the year in which the dividend is declared. In other words, the trading profits usually 'cover' the dividend payment by a comfortable margin.

Dividends can also take the form of bonus shares. Instead of receiving cash, the shareholders may receive additional shares in the business. We consider this particular form of dividend (often referred to as a scrip dividend) later in the chapter.

Dividends are often paid twice yearly by large listed businesses. The first dividend is paid after the interim (half yearly) results have been announced. It represents a sort of 'payment on account'. The second and final dividend is paid after the year end. The final dividend will be paid after the annual financial reports have been published, and after the shareholders have agreed, at the annual general meeting, to the dividend payment proposed by the directors.

As shares are bought and sold continuously by investors, it is important to establish which investors have the right to receive the dividends declared. To do this, a **record date** is set by the business. Investors whose names appear in the share register on the record date will receive the dividends payable. When the share prices quoted on the Stock Exchange include accrued dividends payable, they are said to be quoted **cum dividend**. However, on a specified day before the record date, the quoted share prices will exclude the accrued dividend and so will become **ex dividend**. Assuming no other factors affect the share price, the ex-dividend price should be lower than the cum dividend price by the amount of the dividend payable. This is because a new shareholder would not qualify for the dividend and so the share price can be expected to fall by the amount of the dividend.

Most listed businesses produce a financial calendar for investors. The calendar, which is included in the published financial reports and websites, sets out the key dates for investors for the forthcoming year. **Real World 9.1** provides an example of such a calendar for a well-known business.

REAL WORLD 9.1

Financial calendar

The financial calendar for 2004 for Scottish and Newcastle Group plc, a leading brewer, was set out in its 2003 Report and Accounts as follows:

2004

Late March	Report and Accounts mailed
31 March	Shares traded ex-dividend
2 April	Record date for final dividend
29 April	Annual general meeting
4 May	Payment of final dividend on ordinary shares
30 June	Half year end
Early August	Half year results to be announced
Early October	Payment of interim dividend on ordinary shares
31 December	Financial year end

Source: Scottish and Newcastle Group plc Report and Accounts 2003.

Dividend policies in practice

It was mentioned above that businesses rarely distribute all of the profits available to shareholders in the form of dividend. Usually the dividends paid are lower than the profits available for this purpose. The extent to which the profits generated during a particular period, and available for distribution, cover the dividend payment can be expressed in the **dividend cover ratio**. This ratio is calculated as follows:

$$\text{Dividend cover} = \frac{\text{Earnings for the year available for dividends}}{\text{Dividends announced for the year}}$$

The dividend cover ratio has already been discussed in Chapter 3. We may recall that the higher the ratio, the lower the risk that dividends to shareholders will be affected by adverse trading conditions. The inverse of this ratio is known as the *dividend payout ratio*, which was also discussed in Chapter 3. The lower this ratio, the lower the risk that dividends will be affected by adverse trading conditions.

Many businesses express their dividend policy in terms of either a target dividend cover ratio or a target dividend payout ratio. **Real World 9.2** sets out the targets established by particular businesses.

REAL WORLD 9.2

Setting target ratios

Scottish Power plc, an international energy business, expresses its dividend policy in terms of dividend cover and states that it seeks to maintain:

a target dividend cover based on full year earnings, within a range of 1.5 to 2.0 times and ideally towards the middle of that range.

Source: Scottish Power plc Annual Report and Accounts 2003/4.

mmO2, a mobile phone operator, has announced its dividend policy as follows:

Going forward, the Board is committed to implement a policy of regular, sustainable dividends, growing by reference to the Group's underlying earnings per share . . . with a medium-term target payout ratio of 50%.

Source: www.mmO2.com, November 2004.

Real World 9.3 reveals the average dividend coverage ratios for listed businesses over a range of industries. The factors that determine the particular level of dividend cover adopted are considered later in the chapter.

REAL WORLD 9.3

Dividend coverage ratios

Figure 9.1 shows the average dividend coverage ratios chosen by listed businesses in a range of industries.

Figure 9.1	Average dividend cover ratios for businesses in a range of industries

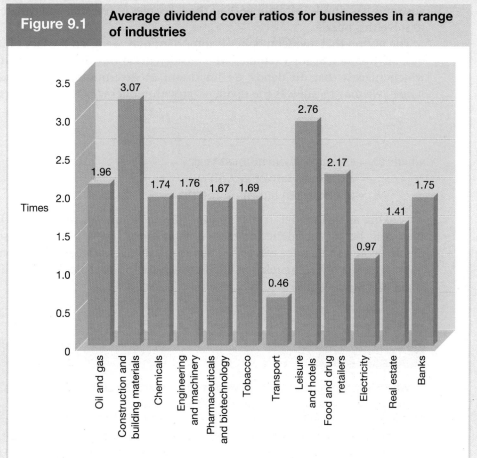

From this diagram, we can see that the average dividend cover ratio for most of the various industries selected falls roughly within the range of 1.0 to 2.5 times.

Source: Compiled from data in *Financial Times*, 2–3 October 2004.

For various reasons, dividend cover ratios tend to vary between countries. Where there is access to capital markets, for example, profit retention becomes less important for businesses and so dividend distributions can be higher. Other factors such as the different treatment of dividends for taxation purposes and differences in the extent to which corporate governance procedures and shareholder activism exert pressure on managers to distribute dividends, can also be important.

Dividend policy and shareholder wealth

Much of the interest surrounding dividend policy has been concerned with the relationship between dividend policy and shareholder wealth. Put simply, the key question to be answered is: can the pattern of dividends adopted by a business influence shareholder wealth? (Note that it is the *pattern* of dividends rather than dividends themselves which is the issue. Shareholders must receive cash at some point in order for their shares to have any value.) While the question may be stated simply, the answer is less simple. After more than three decades of research and debate we have yet to solve this puzzle.

The notion that dividend policy is important may seem, on the face of it, to be obvious. In Chapter 8, for example, we considered various dividend valuation models, which suggest that dividends are important in determining share price. One such model, we may recall, was the dividend growth model which is as follows:

$$P_0 = \frac{D_1}{K_0 - g}$$

where: D_1 = expected dividend next year
g = a constant rate of growth
K_0 = the expected return on the share.

Looking at this model, it may appear that by simply increasing the dividend (D_1) there will be an automatic increase in share price (P_0). If the relationship between dividends and share price was as just described, then, clearly, dividend policy would be important. However, the relationship between these two variables is not likely to be as straightforward as this.

Activity 9.3

Why might an increase in the dividend (D_1) not lead to an increase in share price (P_0)? (*Hint*: Think of the other variables in the equation.)

An increase in dividend payments will only result in an increase in share price if there is no consequential effect on the dividend growth rate. It is likely, however, that an increase in dividend will result in a fall in this growth rate, as there will be less cash to invest in the business. Thus, the beneficial effect on share price arising from an increase in next year's dividend may be cancelled out by a decrease in future years' dividends.

The traditional view of dividends

The dividend policy issue, like the capital structure issue discussed in the previous chapter, has two main schools of thought. The early finance literature accepted the view that dividend policy was important for shareholders. It was argued that a shareholder would prefer to receive £1 today rather than to have £1 reinvested in the business, even though this might yield future dividends. The reasoning for this was that future dividends (or capital gains) are less certain and so will be valued less highly. The saying 'a bird in the hand is worth two in the bush' is often used to describe this argument. Thus, if a business decides to replace an immediate and certain cash dividend with uncertain future dividends, shareholders will discount the future dividends at a higher rate in order to take account of this greater uncertainty. Referring back to the dividend growth model, the traditional view suggests that K_0 will rise if there is an increase in D_1, as dividends received later will not be valued so highly.

If this line of reasoning is correct, the effect of applying a higher discount rate to future dividends will mean that the share value of businesses that adopt a high retention policy will be adversely affected. The implication for corporate managers is, therefore, quite clear. They should adopt as generous a dividend distribution policy as possible, given the investment and financing policies of the business, as this will represent the optimal dividend policy for the business. In view of the fact that the level of payout will affect shareholder wealth, the dividend payment decision will be an important policy decision for managers.

The modernist (MM) view of dividends

Modigliani and Miller (MM) have challenged this view of dividend policy. They argue that, given perfect and efficient markets, the pattern of dividend payments adopted by a business will have no effect on shareholder wealth. Where such markets exist, the wealth of shareholders will be affected solely by the investment projects that the business undertakes. To maximise shareholder wealth, therefore, the business should take on all investment projects that have a positive NPV. The way in which the returns from these investment projects are divided between dividends and retention is unimportant. Thus, a decision to pay a lower dividend will simply be compensated for by an increase in share price.

MM point out that it is possible for an individual investor to 'adjust' the dividend policy of a business to conform to his or her particular requirements. If a business does not pay a dividend, the shareholder can create 'home-made' dividends by selling a portion of the shares held. If, on the other hand, a business provides a dividend that the shareholder does not wish to receive, the amount can be reinvested in additional shares in the business. In view of this fact, there is no reason for an investor to value the shares of one business more highly than another simply because it adopts a particular dividend policy.

The implications of the MM position for corporate managers are quite different from the implications of the traditional position described earlier. The MM view suggests that there is no such thing as an optimal dividend policy, and that one policy is as good as another (that is, the dividend decision is irrelevant to shareholder wealth). Thus managers should not spend time considering the most appropriate policy to adopt, but should, instead, devote their energies to finding and managing profitable investment opportunities.

The MM position explained

MM believe that dividends simply represent a movement of funds from inside the business to outside the business. This change in the location of funds should not have any effect on shareholder wealth. The MM position is set out in Example 9.1.

Example 9.1

Merton Ltd has the following balance sheet as at 31 December Year 5:

Balance sheet as at 31 December Year 5

	£000
Assets at market value (exc. cash)	100
Cash	30
	130
Less Loan capital	40
Net assets	90
Ordinary (equity) capital (30,000 shares) plus reserves	90

Suppose that the business decides to distribute all the cash available (that is, £30,000) to shareholders by making a 100p dividend per share. This will result in a fall in the value of net assets to £60,000 (that is, £90,000 – £30,000) and a fall in the value of its shares from £3 (that is, £90,000/30,000) to £2 (that is, £60,000/30,000). The balance sheet following the dividend payment will therefore be as follows:

Balance sheet following the dividend payment

	£000
Assets at market value (exc. cash)	100
Cash	–
	100
Less Loan capital	40
Net assets	60
Ordinary (equity) capital (30,000 shares) plus reserves	60

Before the dividend distribution, an investor holding 10 per cent of the shares in Merton Ltd will have 3,000 shares worth £9,000 (that is, 3,000 × £3). Following the distribution, the investor will have 3,000 shares worth £6,000 (that is, 3,000 × £2.00) plus a cash dividend of £3,000 (that is, 3,000 × £1.00) = £9,000. In other words, the total wealth of the investor remains the same.

If the investor did not want to receive the dividends, the cash received could be used to purchase more shares in the business. Although the number of shares held by the investor will change as a result of this decision, his or her *total wealth* will remain the same. If, on the other hand, Merton Ltd did not issue a dividend, and the investor wished to receive one, he or she could create the desired dividend by simply selling a portion of the shares held. Once again, this will change the number of shares held by the investor, but will not change the total amount of wealth held.

What about the effect of a dividend payment on the amounts available for investment? We may feel that a high dividend payment will mean that less can be retained by the business, and this may, in turn, mean that the business will be unable to invest in projects that have a positive NPV. If this occurs, then shareholder wealth will be adversely affected. However, if we assume perfect and efficient capital markets exist, the business will be able to raise the finance required for investment purposes and will not have to rely on profit retention. In other words, dividend policy and investment policy can be regarded as quite separate issues.

The wealth of existing shareholders should not be affected by raising finance from new issues rather than retention. Activity 9.4 reinforces this point.

Activity 9.4

Suppose that Merton Ltd (see Example 9.1) replaces the £30,000 paid out as dividends by an issue of shares to new shareholders. Show the balance sheet after the new issue and calculate the value of shares held by existing shareholders after the issue.

The balance sheet following the new issue will be almost the same as before the dividend payment was made. However, the number of shares in issue will increase. If we assume the new shares can be issued at a fair value (that is, current market value), the number of shares in issue will increase by 15,000 shares (£30,000/£2.00 = 15,000).

Balance sheet following the issue of new shares

	£000
Assets at market value (exc. cash)	100
Cash	30
	130
Less Loan capital	40
Net assets	90
Ordinary (equity) capital (45,000 shares) plus reserves	90

The existing shareholders will own 30,000 of the 45,000 shares in issue and will therefore own net assets worth £60,000 (30,000/45,000 × £90,000). In other words, their wealth will not be affected by the financing decision.

What about the traditional argument in support of dividend policy (that is, should investors prefer 'a bird in the hand')? The answer to this question is: probably not. The problem with the argument described earlier is that it is based on a misconception of the nature of risk. The risks borne by a shareholder will be determined by the level of business borrowing and the nature of the business operations. These risks do not necessarily increase over time and are not affected by the dividend policy of the business. Dividends will only reduce risk if the amount received by the shareholder is then placed in a less risky form of investment (with a lower level of return). This could equally be achieved, however, through the sale of the shares in the business.

Activity 9.5

There is one situation where even MM would accept that 'a bird in the hand is worth two in the bush' (that is, that immediate dividends are preferable). Can you think what it is? (*Hint*: Think of the way in which shareholder wealth is increased.)

Shareholder wealth is increased by the business accepting projects that have a positive NPV. If the business starts to accept projects with a negative NPV, this would decrease shareholder wealth. In such circumstances, a rational shareholder would prefer to receive a dividend rather than to allow the business to reinvest the profits of the business.

The MM assumptions

The logic of the MM arguments has proved to be unassailable and it is now widely accepted that, in a world of perfect and efficient capital markets, dividend policy should have no effect on shareholder wealth. The burning issue, however, is whether or not the MM analysis can be applied to the real world of imperfect markets. There are three key assumptions on which the MM analysis rests, and which have aroused much debate. These assumptions are, in essence, that we live in a 'frictionless' world where there are:

● no share issue costs
● no share transaction costs, and
● no taxation.

The first assumption means that money paid out in dividends can be replaced by the business through a new share issue without incurring additional costs. Thus, a business need not be deterred from paying a dividend simply because it needs cash to invest in a profitable project, as the amount can be costlessly replaced. In the real world, however, share issue costs can be significant.

The second assumption means that investors can make 'home-made' dividends or reinvest in the business at no extra cost. In other words, there are no barriers to investors pursuing their own dividend and investment strategies. Once again, in the real world, costs will be incurred when shares are purchased or sold by investors. The creation of 'home-made' dividends as a substitute for business dividend policy may pose other practical problems for the shareholder, such as the indivisibility of shares, resulting in shareholders being unable to sell the exact amount of shares required, and the difficulty of selling shares in unlisted companies. These problems, it is argued, can lead to investors becoming reliant on the dividend policy of the business as a means of receiving cash income. It can also lead them to have a preference for one business rather than another, because of the dividend policies adopted.

The third assumption concerning taxation is unrealistic and, in practice, tax may be an important issue for investors. It is often argued that, in the UK, the taxation rules can have a significant influence on investor preferences. It may be more tax efficient for an investor to receive benefits in the form of capital gains rather than dividends because, below a certain threshold (£8,200 or less for 2004/05), capital gains arising during a particular financial year are not taxable, whereas all dividends are taxable. In addition, it is possible for an investor to influence the timing of capital gains by choosing when to sell shares, whereas the timing of dividends is normally outside the investor's control.

Activity 9.6

In a world where taxation is an important issue for investors, how will the particular dividend policy adopted by a business affect its share price?

If, as a result of the tax system, investors prefer capital gains rather than dividends, a business with a high dividend payout ratio would be valued less than a similar business with a low payout ratio.

Although differences between the tax treatment of dividend income and capital gains still exist, changes in taxation policy have narrowed these differences in recent years. One important policy change has been the creation of tax shelters (for example, Individual Savings Accounts, or ISAs), which allow investors to receive dividend income and capital gains free of taxation. Another important change has been the calculation of capital gains tax liability at the investors' marginal rate of taxation, which brings the treatment of capital gains more into line with the treatment of income from dividends. These changes have reduced the impact of taxation on dividend policy.

The three assumptions discussed undoubtedly weaken the MM analysis when applied to the real world. However, this does not necessarily mean that their analysis is destroyed. Indeed, the research evidence tends to support their position. One direct way to assess the validity of MM's arguments, in the real world, is to see whether there is a positive relationship between the dividends paid by businesses and their share price. If such a relationship exists then MM's arguments would lose their force. The majority of studies, however, have failed to find any significant correlation between dividends and share prices.

The importance of dividends

Whether or not we accept the MM analysis, there is little doubt that, in practice, the pattern of dividends is seen by investors and corporate managers to be important. It seems that there are three possible reasons to explain this phenomenon. These are:

● the clientele effect
● the information signalling effect
● the need to reduce agency costs.

Each of these reasons is considered below.

The clientele effect

It was mentioned earlier that transaction costs may result in investors becoming reliant on the dividend policies of businesses. It was also argued that the tax position of investors can exert an influence on whether dividends or capital gains are preferred. These factors may, in practice, mean that dividend policy will exert an important influence on investor behaviour. Investors may seek out businesses whose dividend policies match closely their particular needs. Thus businesses with particular dividend policies will attract particular types of investors. This phenomenon is referred to as the
clientele effect.

The existence of a clientele effect has important implications for managers. First, dividend policy should be clearly set out and consistently applied. Investors attracted to a particular business because of its dividend policy will not welcome unexpected changes. Secondly, managers need not concern themselves with trying to accommodate all the different needs of shareholders. The particular distribution policy adopted by the business will tend to attract a certain type of investor depending on his or her cash needs and taxation position.

Investors should be wary, however, of making share investment decisions based primarily on dividend policy. Minimising costs may not be an easy process for investors. Those, for example, requiring a regular cash income, and who seek out businesses with high dividend payout ratios, may find that any savings in transaction costs are cancelled out by incurring other forms of cost.

Activity 9.7

What kind of costs may be borne by investors who invest in high-dividend payout businesses, do you think?

Being committed to a high-dividend payout may prevent a business from investing in profitable projects that would have increased shareholder wealth. Hence, there could be a loss of future benefits for the investor. If, however, a business decides to raise finance to replace the amount distributed in dividends, the cost of raising the required finance will be borne by existing shareholders.

Investors must, therefore, look beyond the dividend policy of a business in order to make a sensible investment decision.

The evidence concerning the clientele effect is fairly mixed. Although there are studies, based on both US and the UK data, that support the existence of a clientele effect, other studies have cast doubt on these findings. More research, perhaps using different approaches to examining the issue, is required for a clearer picture to emerge.

Information signalling

In an imperfect world, managers of a business will have greater access to information regarding the profits and performance of the business than investors. This **information asymmetry**, as it is called, between managers and investors allows dividends to be used by managers as a means of passing on to investors information concerning the business. Thus, new information relating to future prospects may be signalled through changes in dividend policy. If, for example, managers are confident about the business's prospects, there may be **information signalling** to this effect through an increase in dividends.

Activity 9.8

Why would managers wish to use dividends as a means of conveying information about the business's prospects? Why not simply issue a statement to shareholders? Try to jot down at least two reasons why managers may prefer a less direct approach.

At least three reasons have been put forward to explain why dividend signalling may be preferred. First, it may be that the managers do not want to disclose the precise nature of the events that improve the business's prospects. Suppose, for example, that a business has signed a large government defence contract, which will be formally announced by the government at some time in the future. In the intervening period, however, the price of the shares in the business may be depressed and the managers may be concerned that the business is vulnerable to a takeover. The managers might, under the circumstances, wish to boost the share price without specifying the nature of the good news.

Second, issuing a statement about, say, improved future prospects may not be convincing, particularly if earlier statements by managers have proved incorrect. Statements are 'cheap' whereas an increase in dividends would be more substantial evidence of the managers' confidence in the future. Third, managers may feel that an explicit statement concerning future prospects will attract criticism from shareholders if things do not work out as expected. They may, therefore, prefer more coded messages to avoid being held to account at a later date.

Sending a positive signal to the market by increasing dividends is an expensive way to send a message. It may also seem wasteful (particularly where investors do not wish to receive higher dividends for tax reasons). However, it may be the only feasible way of ensuring that investors take seriously the good news that managers wish to convey.

Various studies have been carried out to establish the 'information content' of dividends. Some of these studies have looked at the share price reaction to *unexpected* changes in dividends. If signalling exists, an unexpected dividend announcement should result in a significant share price reaction. The results from these studies provide convincing evidence that signalling does exist, that is, a dividend increase (positive signal) results in an increase in share price, and a dividend decrease (negative signal) results in a decrease in share price. One interesting feature of the evidence is that the market reaction to dividend reductions is much greater than the market reaction to dividend increases. It appears that investors regard dividend reductions much more seriously.

Managers must avoid sending mixed signals to investors. **Real World 9.4** reveals how confusion over the future dividend policy of one leading business led to an adverse investor reaction.

REAL WORLD 9.4

In the hot seat

Jonathan Bloomer, the chief executive of Prudential, was under pressure last night after he signalled that the insurer's dividend was likely to be cut despite recent assurances that the twice-yearly payment was not under threat.

He faces a crucial round of discussions with large investors after the company lost almost a fifth of its stock market value amid confusion about the extent of dividend cuts. The company also reduced its payouts to policyholders for the third time in six months.

Despite the Pru reporting a 2% rise in operating profit to £1.1bn, its shares fell 69.25p to 323.75p and affected other insurers who are due to report results in coming days. Aviva fell 5% while L&G lost 11% of its stock market value.

Major investors had believed the Pru had indicated it was unlikely to cut its dividend. Yesterday they punished the insurer for its apparent change of heart and for not giving more details about future policy. One shareholder said: 'The manner in which this is being done lacks clarity.'

The company's decision comes months after Michael McLintock, who runs the Pru's M&G fund management arm, urged blue chip businesses to maintain their payouts to shareholders.

Source: 'Irate City puts Pru chief under pressure: investors seek explanation for confused signals about dividend policy', *Guardian*, 26 February 2003.

Reducing agency costs

In recent years, *agency theory* has become increasingly influential in the financial management literature. Agency theory views a business as a coalition of different interest groups (managers, shareholders, lenders, and so on) in which each group is seeking to maximise its own welfare. According to this theory, one group connected with the business may engage in behaviour that results in costs being borne by another group.

However, the latter group may try to restrain the action of the former group, through contractual or other arrangements, so as to minimise these costs. Two examples of where a conflict of interest arises between groups, and the impact on dividend policy, are considered below.

The first example concerns a conflict of interest between shareholders and managers. If the managers (who are agents of the shareholders) decide to invest in lavish offices, expensive cars and other 'perks', they will be pursuing their own interests at a cost to the shareholders. (This potential conflict was briefly discussed in Chapter 1.) Shareholders may avoid incurring these agency costs, however, by reducing the cash available for managers to spend. They may insist that surplus cash be distributed to them in the form of a dividend. Managers may decide to support this policy to demonstrate their commitment to the shareholders' interests. Agency costs can prevent managers from receiving full recognition for their achievements, and helping to reduce these costs could be to their benefit.

The second example concerns a conflict between shareholders and lenders. Shareholders may seek to reduce their stake in the business by withdrawing cash in the form of dividends. This may be done to reduce their exposure to the risks associated with the business. However, this is likely to be to the detriment of lenders, who will become more exposed to these risks. The lenders may, therefore, try to prevent this kind of behaviour by restricting the level of dividends to be paid to shareholders.

Activity 9.9

How can lenders go about restricting shareholders' rights to dividends? (*Hint*: Think back to Chapter 6.)

Lenders can insist that loan covenants, which restrict the level of dividend payable, be included in the loan agreement.

Agency costs will be more of an issue where there is a clear separation between the shareholders and the managers of the business.

Figure 9.2 sets out the main reasons why dividends seem to be important in the real world.

Figure 9.2   Reasons for the importance of dividends

The figure shows the main reasons for the importance of dividends as discussed in the text.

Factors determining the level of dividends

We have now seen that there are three possible reasons why investors and managers regard dividends as being important. In addition, there are various practical issues that have a bearing on the *level* of dividends paid by a business. These include the following.

Investment opportunities

Businesses that have good investment opportunities may try to retain profits rather than distribute them. As we saw in Chapter 6, retained profits come first in the 'pecking order' when raising long-term finance, and is easily the most important source of long-term finance for businesses.

Investment opportunities may vary over the life cycle of a business and so its retention/dividend policies may also vary. In the early phase, when businesses are growing quickly, a policy of either low dividends or no dividends may be chosen in order to retain profits for reinvestment, but at a more mature stage of the business cycle, when investment opportunities are restricted, a policy of higher dividends may be chosen.

Real World 9.5 provides an example of how one business varied its dividend policy over time.

REAL WORLD 9.5

The joys of middle age   FT

With depressing regularity, we are told that it is essential to plan early for our later years. Surely this applies to companies as well as individuals? And perhaps even to one that is, rightly, lauded as one of Asia's great corporate growth stories at the moment: Samsung Electronics.

This year will be Samsung's best yet. Net profits at the high-tech conglomerate are expected to more than double to $10bn – more than Dell and Nokia put together, as South Korean analysts have gleefully pointed out. But 2004 could also turn out to be a high-water mark for Samsung.

The growth rate for semiconductors, which contributes half of operating profits, is likely to halve to single digits in the coming year – as most chip-makers, including Samsung and most recently Philips, have warned. Margins on mobile phones and prices of liquid crystal displays, the other two money spinners, are also under pressure. All in all, Samsung is unlikely to be firing on all cylinders again for quite a while and consensus estimates expect a 12 per cent drop in earnings in 2005.

Beyond the various industry cycles it is exposed to, Samsung faces the trickier problem of increasing size. With revenues above $50bn, it is now so large that it will take a spectacular new best-seller to have much impact on its top and bottom lines. It seems likely, therefore, that when profit growth resumes in 2006, as analysts expect, it will be more sedentary. LG Securities forecasts compound three-year earnings growth of less than 10 per cent for 2005, compared with 35 per cent over the past three years.

Encouragingly, Samsung has recently started to acknowledge its approaching maturity – at least implicitly. In July, the group doubled its interim dividend and earlier this month it announced a $1.75bn share buy-back, its fourth in two years. Taken together, this amounts to a payout ratio of nearly 50 per cent for the first half of 2004. Assuming a similarly sized final dividend, Samsung will hand back about 30 per cent of its annual profits to shareholders.

Source: 'Samsung and the joys of middle age: sharing out the cash', www.Ft.com, 27 September 2004.

Financing opportunities

In some cases, raising external finance for new investment may be a problem and so profit retention may be the only option available. It can be argued that, where such a problem exists, and investors are indifferent about dividends, it would make sense for managers to regard dividends as simply a residual, that is, the managers should make dividend distributions only where the expected return from investment opportunities is below the required return for investors. The implication of this policy is that dividends could fluctuate each year according to the investment opportunities available: the greater the investment needs of the business, the less that is available for distribution, and vice versa. This line of argument is consistent with the **residual theory of dividends**. Where, however, a business is able to finance easily and cheaply from external sources, there is less need to rely on retained profits, which can then be distributed in the form of dividends.

Legal requirements

Company law restricts the amount that a business can distribute in the form of dividends. We saw earlier that the law states that, for private limited companies, dividends can only be paid to shareholders out of *realised* profits. In essence, the maximum amount available for distribution will be the accumulated trading profits (less any losses) *plus* any profits on the disposal of assets.

Loan covenants

There may be covenants included in a loan contract that restrict the level of dividends available for distribution to shareholders during the loan period. These covenants, as we saw in Chapter 6, are designed to protect the lenders' investment in the business.

Profit stability

Businesses that have a stable pattern of profits over time are in a better position to make higher dividend payouts than businesses that have a volatile pattern of profits.

Activity 9.10

Why should this be the case?

Businesses that have a stable pattern of profits are able to plan with greater certainty and are less likely to feel a need to retain profits for unexpected events.

Control

A high profit retention/low dividend policy can help avoid the need to issue new shares, and so existing shareholders' control will not be diluted. (Even though existing shareholders have pre-emptive rights, they may not always be in a position to purchase new shares issued by the business.)

Threat of takeover

A further aspect of control concerns the relationship between dividend payments and the threat of takeover. It has been suggested, for example, that a high retention/low distribution policy can increase the vulnerability of a business to takeover.

Activity 9.11

Why might it be suggested that a low payout policy increases the threat of takeover? Is this a very convincing point?

If a predator is seeking to acquire the business, it may be able to convince shareholders that the dividends paid are too low and that the existing management is not maximising their wealth. Thus, a low dividend policy may make the task of acquisition much easier. Such arguments, however, are only likely to appeal to unsophisticated shareholders. More sophisticated shareholders will recognise that dividends represent only part of the total return from the shares held. (However, if profits are retained rather than distributed, they must be employed in a profitable manner. Failure to do this will make the threat of takeover greater.)

Dividend policy may, however, help avert the threat of takeover. Issuing a large dividend may signal to the market the managers' confidence in the prospects of the business. This should, in turn, increase the value of the shares and so make a takeover more costly for the predator business. However, the market may not necessarily interpret a large dividend in this way. Investors may regard a large dividend as a desperate attempt by the directors to gain their support and so will discount the dividend received.

Market expectations

Investors may have developed certain expectations concerning the level of dividend to be paid. These expectations may be formed as a result of earlier statements made by the managers of the business. If these expectations are not met, there may be a loss of investor confidence in the business.

Inside information

The managers of a business may have inside information concerning the prospects of a business which cannot be published but which indicates that the shares are currently undervalued by investors. In such a situation, it may be sensible to rely on internal shareholder funds (that is, retained profit) rather than issuing more shares. Although this may lead to lower dividends, it could enhance the wealth of the existing shareholders.

Figure 9.3 sets out the main influences on the level of dividends declared by a business.

The dividend policy of other businesses

The dividend policy adopted by a business may be considered in relation to other, comparable businesses. Indeed, it has been suggested that investors make comparisons between businesses and that a significant deviation in dividend policy from the sector norm will attract criticism. The implication seems to be that managers should shape the dividend policy of their business according to what comparable businesses are doing. This however, may be neither practical nor desirable.

To begin with, there is the problem of identifying comparable businesses. In practice, there may be real differences between businesses concerning risk characteristics,

| Figure 9.3 | **Factors influencing the level of dividends** |

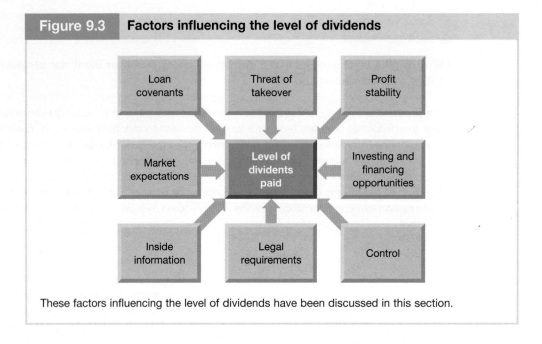

These factors influencing the level of dividends have been discussed in this section.

rate of growth and accounting policies adopted. There may also be real differences between businesses concerning the influences mentioned above such as investment opportunities, loan covenants, and so on. Even if comparable businesses could be found, the use of such businesses as a benchmark assumes that they adopt dividend polices that are optimal, which may not be the case.

These problems suggest that dividend policy is best determined according to the particular requirements of the business. If the policy adopted differs from the norm, the managers should be able to provide reasons to investors.

Dividend policy and management attitudes: some evidence

An interesting aspect of dividend policy concerns the attitudes and behaviour of managers. One of the earliest pieces of research on this topic was undertaken in the USA by Lintner (see reference 1 at the end of the chapter) who carried out interviews with managers in 28 businesses. Although this research is now quite old, it is still considered to be one of the most accurate descriptions of how managers set dividend policy in practice.

Lintner found that managers considered the dividend decision to be an important one and were committed to long-term target dividend payout ratios. He also found that managers were concerned more with variations in dividends than the absolute amount of dividends paid. Managers held the view that investors preferred a smooth increase in dividends payments over time and were reluctant to increase the level of dividends in response to a short-term increase in profits. They wished to avoid a situation where dividends would have to be cut in the future, and so dividends were increased only when it was felt that the higher level of dividends could be sustained through a permanent increase in earnings. As a result, there was a time lag between dividend growth and earnings growth.

Activity 9.12

Are these attitudes of managers described above consistent with another view of dividends discussed earlier?

The attitude of managers described by Lintner is consistent with more recent work concerning the use of dividends as a means of information signalling. The managers interviewed seem to be aware of the fact that a dividend cut would send negative signals to investors.

In a later study, Fama and Babiak (see reference 2 at the end of the chapter) found that businesses distributed about half of their profits in the form of dividends. However, significant increases in earnings would only be followed by a *partial adjustment* to dividends in the first year. On average, the increase in dividends in the first year was only about one-third of the increase that would have been consistent with maintaining the target payout ratio. The smooth and gradual adjustment of dividends to changes in profits revealed by this study is consistent with the earlier study by Lintner and confirms that managers wish to ensure a sustainable level of dividends.

Where a business experiences adverse trading conditions, DeAngelo and others (see reference 3 at the end of the chapter) found that managers are often reluctant to reduce dividend payments immediately. Instead, they will try to maintain the existing level of dividends until it is clear that the former profit levels cannot be achieved. At this point, the managers will usually make a single large reduction, rather than a series of small reductions to a new level of dividends.

An important study by Baker and others (see reference 4 at the end of the chapter) asked US managers to express their views concerning dividend policy. Some of the key findings regarding managers' attitudes are shown in **Real World 9.6**.

 ## REAL WORLD 9.6

Managers' attitudes towards dividends   **FT**

Baker and others surveyed 188 managers of US, dividend-paying, listed businesses. The researchers wished to establish the views of managers concerning dividend policies adopted, why dividends are important and whether dividends affected the value of the business. Figure 9.4 sets out some of the key statements that managers were asked to consider and their responses.

Source: 'Revisiting managerial perspectives on dividend policy', H. Baker, G. Powell and E. Theodore Veit, *Journal of Economics and Finance*, Fall, 2002, pp. 267–83.

Real World 9.6 continued

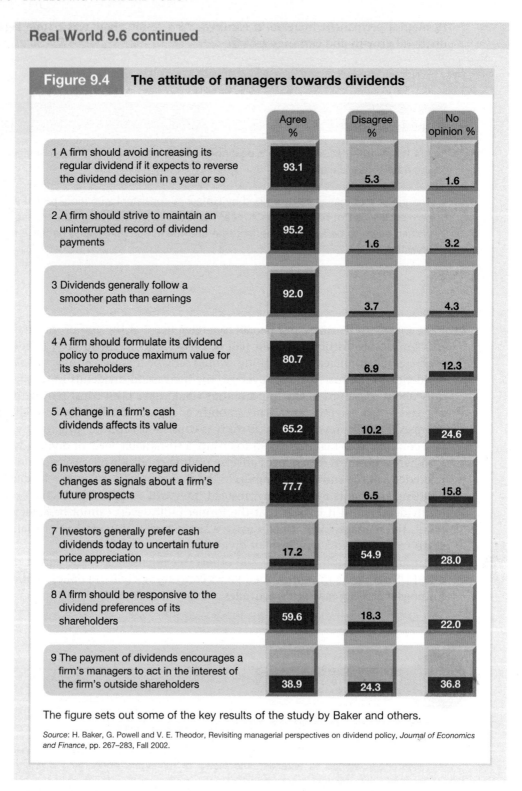

| Figure 9.4 | The attitude of managers towards dividends |

	Agree %	Disagree %	No opinion %
1 A firm should avoid increasing its regular dividend if it expects to reverse the dividend decision in a year or so	93.1	5.3	1.6
2 A firm should strive to maintain an uninterrupted record of dividend payments	95.2	1.6	3.2
3 Dividends generally follow a smoother path than earnings	92.0	3.7	4.3
4 A firm should formulate its dividend policy to produce maximum value for its shareholders	80.7	6.9	12.3
5 A change in a firm's cash dividends affects its value	65.2	10.2	24.6
6 Investors generally regard dividend changes as signals about a firm's future prospects	77.7	6.5	15.8
7 Investors generally prefer cash dividends today to uncertain future price appreciation	17.2	54.9	28.0
8 A firm should be responsive to the dividend preferences of its shareholders	59.6	18.3	22.0
9 The payment of dividends encourages a firm's managers to act in the interest of the firm's outside shareholders	38.9	24.3	36.8

The figure sets out some of the key results of the study by Baker and others.

Source: H. Baker, G. Powell and V. E. Theodor, Revisiting managerial perspectives on dividend policy, *Journal of Economics and Finance*, pp. 267–283, Fall 2002.

The study reveals that the majority of managers acknowledge the importance of a smooth, uninterrupted pattern of dividends. This is in line with the earlier findings of Lintner. The study also reveals that the majority of managers acknowledge the signalling effect and clientele effect but not the role of dividends in reducing agency costs. These views, therefore, do not chime precisely with the theories concerning why dividends are important. Finally, the study reveals that the majority of managers do not support the bird-in-the-hand argument, and they therefore reject the traditional view.

Dividend smoothing in practice

The attitude of managers towards dividend smoothing, as described by the Lintner study and by other studies, seems to be reflected in practice. For many businesses, the pattern of dividends is much smoother than the pattern of underlying earnings. **Real World 9.7** provides an example.

REAL WORLD 9.7

A real smoothie

BPB plc is a major supplier of materials for building construction. Over the five-year period to 31 March 2004 the basic earnings per share (EPS) and dividend per share (DPS) for the business were as set out in Figure 9.5 below.

| Figure 9.5 | **Earnings and dividends per share for BPB plc over time** |

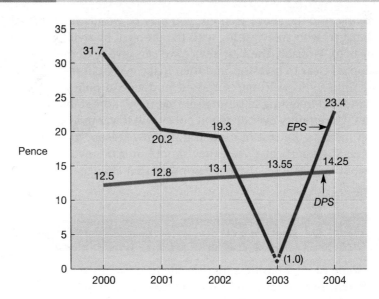

The figure shows that, although earnings per share have been fairly erratic, dividends per share have followed a smooth upward path over the five-year period.

Source: Chart compiled from information in BPB plc Annual Report 2004.

Self-assessment question 9.1

Sandarajan plc is a business that has recently obtained a listing on the Stock Exchange. The business operates a chain of supermarkets in Northern Ireland and was the subject of a management buy-out five years ago. In the period since the buy-out, the business has grown rapidly. The managers and a venture capital organisation owned 80 per cent of the shares prior to the Stock Exchange listing. However, this has now been reduced to 20 per cent. The record of the business over the past five years is as follows:

Year	Net profit after tax £000	Dividend £000	No. of shares issued 000s
1	420	220	1,000
2	530	140	1,000
3	650	260	1,500
4	740	110	1,500
5 (most recent)	880	460	1,500

Required:
(a) Comment on the dividend policy of the business prior to the Stock Exchange listing.
(b) What advice would you give to the managers of the business concerning future dividend policy?

What should managers do?

Having read the above sections, you may be wondering what advice we should give to managers who are wrestling with the problem of dividend policy and who are looking for help. Probably the best advice we can give is to make the dividend policy that is adopted clear to investors and then make every effort to keep to that policy. Investors are unlikely to welcome 'surprises' in dividend policy and may react by selling their shares and investing in businesses that have more stable and predictable dividend policies. Uncertainty over dividend policy will lower the value of the business's shares and will increase the cost of capital. If, for any reason, managers have to reduce the dividends for a particular year, they should prepare investors for the change in dividend payout and state clearly the reasons for that change.

Alternatives to cash dividends

In some cases, a business may decide to make distributions to shareholders in a form different from a cash dividend. The two most important of these are scrip dividends and share repurchases. Below we consider each of these options.

Scrip dividends

A business may make a **scrip dividend** (or bonus share dividend) rather than making a cash distribution to shareholders. Thus, if a business announced a 20 per cent scrip dividend this would mean that each shareholder would receive a 20 per cent increase in the number of shares held. We saw in Chapter 6, however, that scrip issues (or bonus issues) do not result in an increase in shareholder wealth. Making a scrip issue is, in essence, a bookkeeping transaction that will not, of itself, create value. Nevertheless, the market may respond positively to a scrip dividend if it is seen as a sign of the directors' confidence concerning the future. The scrip issue may suggest that the directors will maintain the same dividend per share in the future, despite the increase in the number of shares in issue. Various research studies have shown a positive response to scrip dividend announcements by the market. However, if a business does not maintain or increase its dividend per share in subsequent periods, the positive effect on share prices will be lost.

In some cases, shareholders may be given the choice between a scrip dividend and a cash dividend. Those shareholders who choose the scrip dividend will increase their proportion of the total shares issued relative to that held by the shareholders who take the cash option. For tax purposes, shareholders who receive a scrip dividend will be treated, broadly speaking, as having received the cash dividend option from the business.

Share repurchase

In recent years, share repurchases have become a popular way of making distributions to shareholders. They are usually undertaken for one or more of the following reasons:

- to return cash to shareholders that is surplus to requirements;
- to buy out unwelcome shareholders;
- to adjust the capital structure to a more suitable level of gearing;
- to support the share price when it has temporarily fallen.

A repurchase can be achieved by acquiring shares through the stock market, through agreements with particular shareholders or through a tender offer to all shareholders. In the case of a tender offer, the business will offer to purchase a particular number of shares for a specified price during the offer period. Shares that are repurchased by the business are cancelled. A share repurchase is a voluntary agreement between the business and its shareholders, which means that shareholders wishing to keep their shares can do so.

Businesses with surplus cash may prefer to repurchase shares rather than to pay higher dividends. It has the advantage that it is a one-off event which does not oblige the business to make similar distributions in the future. Although the same effect may be achieved by a 'special' dividend to shareholders, a repurchase focuses on those shareholders wishing to receive cash. There is also the advantage that payments to shareholders can be spread over a longer period.

Real World 9.8 provides a rare example of a business that decided to make a share repurchase *and* a special dividend.

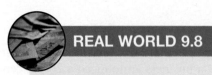

REAL WORLD 9.8

Cash bonanza

Microsoft said yesterday it would dig into its cash mountain to pay a $32bn (£19bn) special dividend to its shareholders in the biggest corporate pay-out of its kind.

Together with plans to buy back $30bn of its shares over the next four years and double its regular dividend payment, the plan answers critics who have attacked the software giant for being too conservative with its finances in the past.

However, even after the payment Microsoft will be left with some $25bn of cash. 'We will have a high-class problem to deal with,' said John Connors, chief financial officer.

Microsoft's shares rose about 5 per cent in after-hours trading yesterday after the cash plan was unveiled. However, the news disappointed some investors and analysts who had wanted the software giant to take a far more radical approach.

The company will still keep more than $25bn in reserve, and executives said it planned to maintain a 'conservative' stance on its finances. Bill Gates, its chairman and founding father, will make an estimated $3bn from the pay-out.

Commenting on the delay in the dividend and buyback plans, Charles Di Bona, an analyst at Bernstein Research, said: 'I would have preferred to see more of that upfront rather than over four years.' He also questioned Microsoft's decision to leave its dividend yield below the level of the broader stock market. Microsoft's shares will yield 1.1 per cent, compared with 2 per cent for the S&P 500.

Microsoft had resisted calls to pay out cash in the past, arguing that antitrust cases against it left too much uncertainty.

In particular, it was concerned that strident regulatory intervention could jeopardise its business model, undermining its ability to keep churning out cash.

The recent resolutions of a series of legal challenges laid the ground for yesterday's decision. In particular, the last remaining challenge to the company's settlement with the US justice department was thrown out by a court last month, while the two biggest private antitrust suits, from Time Warner and Sun Microsystems, have been settled.

Microsoft has hesitated in the past about handing over its excess cash to shareholders, preferring to keep the money back for investments.

However, several investments have drawn criticism, including $10bn of losses from cable and telecommunications companies at the height of the 1990s.

The special dividend of $3 a share, equivalent to $32bn, will be paid out on December 2, subject to the approval of shareholders. It also doubled its annual dividend to 32 cents a share.

Microsoft has amassed a cash mountain of $56bn, and is set to add to its free cash reserves at the rate of about $12bn a year, according to Rick Sherlund, an analyst at Goldman Sachs.

Source: 'Microsoft $32bn special dividend smashes corporate pay-out records', *Financial Times*, 21 July 2004.

When a business undertakes a repurchase, the shareholders can benefit from the adjustment to the capital structure. The gearing effect, which arises from changes in the relative proportions of equity and loan capital, can boost returns to shareholders, which can in turn boost the share price. However, a rise in share price will not automatically occur: the additional benefits of higher gearing must outweigh the additional risks.

Managers must take care to ensure equity between shareholders during a share repurchase. In some cases, the market may undervalue the shares of a business, perhaps because it does not have access to information known to the managers of the business. If this situation exists, the shareholders who hold on to their shares will benefit at the expense of those who sell. In other cases, the market for shares in the business may be slow and the effect of repurchasing a large number of shares may be to create an artificially high price. This will benefit those who sell at the expense of those who continue to hold shares.

SUMMARY

The main points in this chapter may be summarised as follows:

Dividends

- Represent a return by a business to its shareholders.
- There are legal limits on dividend distributions to protect creditors and lenders.
- They are usually paid twice a year by large businesses.
- Cum dividend share prices include the accrued dividend; ex dividend prices exclude the dividend.
- Businesses often have a target dividend cover ratio or target dividend payout ratio.

Dividend policy and shareholder wealth

- Two major schools of thought concerning the effect of dividends on shareholder wealth.
- The traditional school argues that investors prefer dividends now because the amounts are more certain.
- The implications for managers are that they should adopt as generous a dividend policy as possible.
- The modernists (MM) argue that, given perfect and efficient markets, the pattern of dividends has no effect on shareholder wealth.
- The implication for managers is that one policy is as good as another and so they should not spend time considering which policy should be adopted.
- The MM position assumes no share issue costs, no share transaction costs and no taxation; these assumptions weaken (but do not necessarily destroy) their arguments.

Dividends in practice

- Dividends appear to be important to investors.
- The clientele effect, signalling effect and the need to reduce agency costs may explain this.
- The level of dividends distributed is dependent on various factors, including: investment and financing opportunities, legal and loan requirements, profit stability, control issues (including takeover threats), market expectations and inside information.

Management attitudes

- Managers perceive dividends as being important for investors.
- They prefer a smooth increase in dividends and are reluctant to cut dividends.

Alternatives to cash dividends

● Scrip dividends are a bookkeeping transaction, but the market may see them as a sign of managers' confidence in the future, and respond positively.

● Share repurchases involves repurchasing and then cancelling shares.

→ **Key terms**

Dividend   p. 356
Record date   p. 357
Cum dividend   p. 357
Ex dividend   p. 357
Dividend cover ratio   p. 358

Clientele effect   p. 365
Information asymmetry   p. 366
Information signalling   p. 366
Residual theory of dividends   p. 370
Scrip dividend   p. 377

For definitions of these terms see the Glossary, pp. 562–571.

Further reading

If you wish to explore the topics discussed in this chapter in more depth, try the following books:

Business Finance: Theory and practice, *McLaney, E.*, 7th edn, Financial Times Prentice Hall, 2006, chapter 12.

Corporate Finance and Investment, *Pike, R. and Neale, B.*, 4th edn, Financial Times Prentice Hall, 2003, chapter 19.

Corporate Financial Management, *Arnold, G.*, Financial Times Prentice Hall, 2002, chapter 19.

Financial Management, *Brigham, E. and Ehrhardt, M.*, 10th edn, Harcourt, 2002, chapters 17 and 18.

References

1 'Distribution of incomes of corporations among dividends, retained earnings and taxes', *Lintner, J.*, **American Economic Review**, no. 46, May 1956, pp. 97–113.

2 'Dividend policy: an empirical analysis', *Fama, E. F. and Babiak, H.*, **Journal of the American Statistical Association**, December 1968.

3 'Dividends and losses', *DeAngelo, H., DeAngelo, L. and Skinner, D.*, **Journal of Finance**, December 1992, pp. 281–9.

4 'Revisiting managerial perspectives on dividend policy', *Baker, H., Powell, G. and Theodore Veit, E.*, **Journal of Economics and Finance**, Fall 2002, pp. 267–83.

REVIEW QUESTIONS

Answers to these questions can be found in Appendix D at the back of the book.

9.1 Can you think of three reasons why a business should wish to repurchase some of its shares?

9.2 'The business's dividend decision is really a by-product of its capital investment decision.' Discuss.

9.3 Is it really important for a business to try to meet the needs of different types of investors when formulating its dividend policy?

9.4 Describe how agency theory may help to explain the dividend policy of businesses.

EXERCISES

Exercises 9.3 to 9.6 are more advanced than 9.1 and 9.2. Those with coloured numbers have answers at the back of the book.

 If you wish to try more exercises, visit the students' side of the Companion Website.

9.1 The dividend policy of businesses has been the subject of much debate in the financial management literature.

Required:
Discuss the view that dividends can increase the wealth of shareholders.

9.2 Identify and discuss the factors that may influence the dividend policies of businesses.

9.3 The following listed businesses each have different policies concerning distributions to shareholders:

● *North plc* pays all profits available for distribution to shareholders in the form of a cash dividend each year.
● *South plc* has yet to pay any cash dividends to shareholders and has no plans to make dividend payments in the foreseeable future.
● *West plc* repurchases shares from shareholders as an alternative to a dividend payment.
● *East plc* offers shareholders the choice of either a small but stable cash dividend or a scrip dividend each year.

Required:
Discuss the advantages and disadvantages of each of the above policies.

9.4 Fellingham plc has 20 million ordinary £1 shares in issue. No shares have been issued during the past four years. The business's earnings and dividends record taken from the historic accounts showed:

	Year 1	Year 2	Year 3	Year 4 (most recent)
Earnings per share	11.00p	12.40p	10.90p	17.20p
Dividend per share	10.00p	10.90p	11.88p	12.95p

At the annual general meeting for Year 1, the chairman had indicated that it was the intention to consistently increase annual dividends by 9 per cent, anticipating that, on average, this would maintain the spending power of shareholders and provide a modest growth in real income.

In the event, subsequent average annual inflation rates, measured by the general index of prices, have been:

Year 2	11%
Year 3	10%
Year 4	8%

The ordinary shares are currently selling for £3.44, excluding the year 4 dividend.

Required:
Comment on the declared dividend policy of the business and its possible effects on both Fellingham plc and its shareholders, illustrating your answer with the information provided.

9.5   Mondrian plc is a new business that aims to maximise the wealth of its shareholders. The board of directors is currently trying to decide upon the most appropriate dividend policy to adopt for the business's shareholders. However, there is strong disagreement among three of the directors concerning the benefits of declaring cash dividends:

- *Director A* argues that cash dividends would be welcome by investors and that as high a dividend payout ratio as possible would reflect positively on the market value of the business's shares.
- *Director B* argues that whether a cash dividend is paid or not is irrelevant in the context of shareholder wealth maximisation.
- *Director C* takes an opposite view to Director A and argues that dividend payments should be avoided as they would lead to a decrease in shareholder wealth.

Required:
(a) Discuss the arguments for and against the position taken by each of the three directors.
(b) Assuming the board of directors decides to pay a dividend to shareholders, what factors should be taken into account when determining the level of dividend payment?

9.6   Traminer plc provides software solutions for the airline industry. At present, shares in the business are held by the senior managers and by a venture capital business. However, Traminer plc intends to seek a Stock Exchange listing and to make 75 per cent of the ordinary shares available to the investing public. The board of directors recently met to decide upon a dividend policy for the business once it has become listed. However, the meeting ended without agreement. The chairman argued that the existing dividend policy need not be changed whereas the managing director argued that it should be changed. The operations director expressed the view that, as the pattern of dividends had no effect on the shareholders' wealth, the debate was irrelevant.

Information relating to the business over the past five years is set out below:

Year ended 30 April	Ordinary shares in issue 000	Net profits after taxation £000	Ordinary dividends £000
2001	500	840	420
2002	500	1,190	580
2003	800	1,420	340
2004	1,000	1,940	450
2005	1,000	2,560	970

Required:

(a) Explain the rationale for the view expressed by the operations director.

(b) Evaluate the rationale explained in (a) above and include in your evaluation two reasons why, in practice, managers consider the pattern of dividends to be important to shareholders.

(c) Evaluate the dividend policy pursued by Traminer plc over the past five years and comment on the points expressed by the chairman and the managing director.

10

Managing working capital

INTRODUCTION

In this chapter we consider the factors that must be taken into account when managing the working capital of a business. Each element of working capital is identified, and the major issues surrounding them are discussed. Working capital represents a significant investment for many businesses and so its proper management and control can be vital. We saw in Chapter 4 that it may be an important aspect of new investment proposals. Some useful tools in the management of working capital are forecasts, which we explored in Chapter 2, and financial ratios, which were considered in Chapter 3.

The nature and purpose of working capital

→ **Working capital** is usually defined as current assets less current liabilities. The major elements of current assets are:

- stocks (inventories)
- trade debtors (receivables)
- cash (in hand and at bank).

The major elements of current liabilities are

- trade creditors (payables)
- bank overdrafts.

The size and composition of working capital can vary between industries. For some types of business, the investment in working capital can be substantial. For example, a manufacturing business will typically invest heavily in raw materials, work in progress and finished goods, and will often sell its goods on credit, thereby generating trade debtors. A retailer, on the other hand, will hold only one form of stock (finished goods), and will usually sell goods for cash. Many service businesses hold no stocks. Most businesses buy goods and/or services on credit, giving rise to trade creditors. Few, if any, businesses operate without a cash balance, though in some cases it is a negative one (bank overdraft).

Working capital represents a net investment in short-term assets. These assets are continually flowing into and out of the business, and are essential for day-to-day operations. The various elements of working capital are interrelated, and can be seen as part of a short-term cycle. For a manufacturing business, the working capital cycle can be depicted as shown in Figure 10.1.

Figure 10.1	**The working capital cycle**

Cash is used to pay trade creditors for raw materials, or raw materials are bought for immediate cash settlement; cash is spent on labour and other aspects that turn raw materials into work in progress and, finally, into finished goods. The finished goods are sold to customers either for cash or on credit. In the case of credit customers, there will be a delay before the cash is received from the sales. Receipt of cash completes the cycle.

For a retailer the situation would be as in Figure 10.1, except that there would be no work in progress and the raw materials and the finished stock would be the same. For a purely service business, the working capital cycle would also be similar to that depicted in Figure 10.1, except that there would be no stock of raw materials and finished goods. There may well be work in progress, however, since many services, for example a case handled by a firm of solicitors, will take some time to complete and costs will build up before the client is billed for them.

Managing working capital

The management of working capital is an essential part of the business's short-term planning process. It is necessary for management to decide how much of each element should be held. As we shall see later in this chapter, there are costs associated with holding either too much or too little of each element. Management must be aware of these costs, which include opportunity costs, in order to manage effectively. Hence, the potential benefits must be weighed against the likely costs in an attempt to achieve the optimum investment.

The working capital needs of a particular business are likely to change over time as a result of changes in the business environment. This means that working capital decisions are constantly being made. Managers must try to identify changes in an attempt to ensure that the level of investment in working capital is appropriate.

Activity 10.1

What kinds of changes in the commercial environment might lead to a decision to change the level of investment in working capital? Try to identify four possible changes that could affect the working capital needs of a business.

These may include the following:

- changes in interest rates
- changes in market demand
- changes in the seasons
- changes in the state of the economy.

You may have thought of others.

In addition to changes in the external environment, changes arising within the business could alter the required level of investment in working capital. Examples of such internal changes include using different production methods (resulting, perhaps, in a need to hold less stock) and changes in the level of risk that managers are prepared to take.

The scale of working capital

We might imagine that, compared with the scale of investment in non-current assets by the typical business, the amounts involved with working capital are pretty trivial. This would be a false assessment of reality – the scale of the working capital elements for most businesses is vast.

Real World 10.1 gives some impression of the working capital investments for five UK businesses that are either very well known by name or whose products are everyday commodities for most of us. These businesses were randomly selected, except that that each one is high profile and from a different industry. For each business, the major balance sheet items are expressed as a percentage of the total investment by the providers of long-term finance.

REAL WORLD 10.1

A summary of the balance sheets of five UK businesses

	GUS plc	Go-Ahead Group plc	Astra-Zeneca plc	Tesco plc	United Utilities plc
Balance sheet date	31.3.04	28.6.03	31.12.03	28.2.04	31.3.04
	%	%	%	%	%
Non-current assets	81	126	67	119	98
Current assets					
Stock	18	2	19	9	–
Trade debtors	18	23	20	–	3
Other debtors	18	29	17	6	3
Cash and near cash	14	16	25	9	13
	68	70	81	24	19
Current liabilities					
Trade creditors	10	25	19	19	1
Tax and dividends	9	15	16	7	4
Other short-term liabilities	19	55	12	12	11
Overdrafts and short-term loans	11	1	1	5	1
	49	96	48	43	17
Working capital	19	(26)	33	(19)	2
Total long-term investment	100	100	100	100	100

The non-current assets, current assets and current liabilities are expressed as a percentage of the total net investment (equity plus non-current liabilities) of the business concerned. The businesses were randomly selected, except that they were deliberately taken from different industries. GUS is a major retail and business services group, which owns Argos and other businesses. Go-Ahead is a major passenger transport provider, principally through buses and trains. It runs much of the central London bus service and owns South Central and Thames Trains. Astra-Zeneca is a major pharmaceutical business. Tesco is one of the major UK supermarkets. United Utilities is a major distributor of electricity and water, particularly in the north west of England.

Source: The table was constructed from information appearing in the annual reports of the five businesses concerned.

The totals for current assets are pretty large when compared with the total long-term investment. This is particularly true of GUS, Go-ahead and Astra-Zeneca. The amounts vary considerably from one type of business to the next. When we look at the nature of working capital held we can see that Astra-Zeneca, GUS and Tesco, which produce and/or sell goods, are the only ones that hold significant amounts of stock. The other two businesses are service providers and so stocks are not a significant item. We can see from the table that Tesco does not sell on credit and very few of United Utilities sales are on credit as these businesses have little or nothing invested in trade debtors. It is interesting to note that Tesco's trade creditors are much higher than its stock. Since most of these creditors will be suppliers of stock, it means that the business is able, on average, to have the cash from a particular sale in the bank before it needs to pay for the goods concerned.

These types of variation in the amounts and types of working capital elements are typical of other businesses. In the sections that follow, we consider each element of working capital separately and how it might be properly managed.

Managing stocks (inventories)

A business may hold stocks for various reasons, the most common of which is to meet the immediate day-to-day requirements of customers and production. However, a business may hold more than is necessary for this purpose if it is believed that future supplies may be interrupted or scarce. Similarly, if the business believes that the cost of stocks will rise in the future, it may decide to stockpile.

For some types of business the stock held may represent a substantial proportion of the total assets held. For example, a car dealership that rents its premises may have nearly all of its total assets in the form of stock. In the case of manufacturing businesses, stock levels tend to be higher than in many other types of business as it is necessary to hold three kinds of stock: raw materials, work in progress and finished goods. Each form of stock represents a particular stage in the production cycle. For some types of business, the level of stock held may vary substantially over the year owing to the seasonal nature of the industry. An example of such a business is a greetings card manufacturer. For other businesses, stock levels may remain fairly stable throughout the year.

Where a business holds stock simply to meet the day-to-day requirements of its customers and for production, it will normally seek to minimise the amount of stock held. This is because there are significant costs associated with holding stocks. These include storage and handling costs, financing costs, the risks of pilferage and obsolescence, and the opportunities forgone by tying up funds in this form of asset. However, a business must also recognise that if the level of stocks held is too low, there will also be associated costs.

Activity 10.2

What costs might a business incur as a result of holding too low a level of stocks? Try to jot down at least three types of cost.

You may have thought of the following costs:

- Loss of sales, from being unable to provide the goods required immediately.
- Loss of goodwill from customers, for being unable to satisfy customer demand.
- High transport costs incurred to ensure that stocks are replenished quickly.
- Lost production due to shortage of raw materials.
- Inefficient production scheduling due to shortages of raw materials.
- Purchasing stocks at a higher price than might otherwise have been possible in order to replenish stocks quickly.

One problem faced by management is that many of the costs of holding stock mentioned above will not be separately identified by conventional accounting systems. Cost classification methods used in practice are likely to include some of these costs within a broad cost category, or as part of an overall total for the business. For example, storage costs may be included under the broad heading of 'security and maintenance', financing costs may be included as part of the total finance charges incurred by the business, and so on. Furthermore, other costs, such as lost sales or the opportunity cost of tying up funds, will not be directly recorded by the accounting system. This lack of information concerning the costs of holding particular levels of stock makes the management of stock more difficult.

Before we go on to deal with the various approaches that can be taken to managing stock, **Real World 10.2** provides an example of how badly things can go wrong if stock is not adequately controlled.

REAL WORLD 10.2

Pallets lost at Brambles

Brambles Industries plc (BI) is an Anglo-Australian industrial services business, formed in 2001 when the industrial services subsidiary of GKN plc, the UK engineering business, was merged with the Australian business Brambles Ltd.

BI uses pallets on which it delivers its products to customers. These are returnable by customers so BI holds a stock, or pool, of pallets. Each pallet costs the business about £10. Unfortunately, BI lost 14 million pallets during the year ended in June 2002 as a result of poor stock control, and this led to a significant decline in the business's profits and share price.

At BI's annual general meeting in Sydney, Australia, one of the shareholders was quoted as saying: 'Running a pallet pool is not rocket science. I can teach one of my employees about pallets in 20 minutes.'

Source: Based on an article in the *Financial Times*, 27 November 2002.

To try to ensure that the stocks are properly managed, a number of procedures and techniques may be used. These are reviewed below.

Forecasting future demand

One of the best means of a business trying to ensure that there will be stock (inventory) available to meet future production requirements and sales is to make appropriate plans. These forecasts should deal with each product that the business makes and/or sells. It is important that every attempt is made to ensure the accuracy of forecasts, as they will determine future ordering and production levels. The forecasts may be derived in various ways. We saw in Chapter 2 that they may be developed using statistical techniques such as time series analysis, or they may be based on the judgement of the sales and marketing staff.

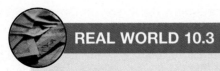

REAL WORLD 10.3

Dreaming of a bright Christmas

Wal-Mart is the world's largest retailer and has extremely sophisticated stock planning and control systems. Nevertheless, things can still go wrong. During 2002, there was a rise in sales revenue of 12 per cent and a rise in stock levels of 10 per cent. The large rise in stock in relation to the rise in sales revenue was unplanned and was largely due to sales revenue over the Christmas period falling below expectations. This represents poor stock management by Wal-Mart standards. The business, however, expects to get back on track and to ensure that stocks grow by less than half the rate of sales revenue in the future.

Source: Based on an article in the *Financial Times*, Lex column, 19 February 2003.

Financial ratios

One ratio that can be used to help monitor stock levels is the average stock turnover period, which we examined in Chapter 3. As we should recall, this ratio is calculated as follows:

$$\text{Average stock turnover period} = \frac{\text{Average stock held}}{\text{Cost of sales}} \times 365$$

This will provide a picture of the average period for which stocks are held, and can be useful as a basis for comparison. It is possible to calculate the average stock turnover period for individual product lines as well as for stocks as a whole.

Recording and reordering systems

The management of stocks in a business of any size requires a sound system of recording stock movements. There must be proper procedures for recording stock purchases and sales. Periodic stock checks may be required to ensure that the amount of physical stocks held is consistent with what is indicated by the stock records.

There should also be clear procedures for the reordering of stocks. Authorisation for both the purchase and the issue of stocks should be confined to a few senior staff. This should avoid problems of duplication and lack of coordination. To determine the point at which stock should be reordered, information will be required concerning the **lead time** (that is, the time between the placing of an order and the receipt of the goods) and the likely level of demand.

Activity 10.3

An electrical retailer keeps a particular type of light switch in stock. The annual demand for the light switch is 10,400 units, and the lead time for orders is four weeks. Demand for the stock is steady throughout the year. At what level of stock should the business reorder, assuming that it is confident of the information given above?

Activity 10.3 continued

The average weekly demand for the stock item is 10,400/52 = 200 units. During the time between ordering the stock and receiving it, the stock sold will be 4 × 200 units = 800 units. So the business should reorder no later than when the stock level reaches 800 units, in order to avoid a 'stockout'.

In most businesses, there will be some uncertainty surrounding the above factors and so a buffer or safety stock level may be maintained in case problems occur. The amount of buffer stock to be held is really a matter of judgement. This judgement will depend on:

● the degree of uncertainty concerning the above factors
● the likely costs of running out of stock
● the cost of holding the buffer stock.

The effect of holding buffer stock will be to raise the reorder point for goods.

Activity 10.4

Assume the same facts as in Activity 10.3 above. However, we are also told that the business maintains a buffer stock of 300 units. At what level of stock should the business reorder?

Reorder point = Expected level of demand during the lead time + Level of buffer stock
         = 800 + 300 = 1,100 units

Carrying buffer stock will increase the cost of holding stocks; however, this must be weighed against the cost of running out of stock, in terms of lost sales, production problems, and so on.

Real World 10.4 provides an example of how small businesses can use technology in stock reordering to help compete against their larger rivals.

REAL WORLD 10.4

Taking on the big boys

The use of technology in stock recording and reordering may be of vital importance to the survival of small businesses that are being threatened by larger rivals. One such example is that of small independent bookshops. Technology can come to their rescue in two ways. First, electronic point-of-sale (EPOS) systems can record books as they are sold and can constantly update stocks held. Thus, books that need to be reordered can be quickly and easily identified. Second, the reordering process can be improved by using web-based technology, which allows books to be ordered in real time. Many large book wholesalers provide free web-based software to their customers for this purpose and try to deliver books ordered during the next working day. This means that a small bookseller, with limited shelf space, may keep one copy only of a particular book but maintain a range of books that competes with that of a large bookseller.

Source: Based on information in 'Small stores keep up with the big boys', www.FT.com, 5 February 2003.

Levels of control

Senior managers must make a commitment to the management of stocks. However, the cost of controlling stocks must be weighed against the potential benefits. It may be possible to have different levels of control according to the nature of the stocks held. The **ABC system of stock control** is based on the idea of selective levels of control.

A business may find that it is possible to divide its stock into three broad categories: A, B and C. Each category will be based on the value of stock held, as is illustrated in Example 10.1.

Example 10.1

Alascan Products plc makes door handles and door fittings. It makes them in brass, in steel and in plastic. The business finds that brass fittings account for 10 per cent of the physical volume of the finished stock that it holds, but these represent 65 per cent of its total value. This is treated as Category A stock. There are sophisticated recording procedures, tight control is exerted over stock movements and there is a high level of security at the stock's location. This is economic because the stock represents a relatively small proportion of the total volume.

The business finds that steel fittings account for 30 per cent of the total volume of finished stock and represent 25 per cent of its total value. This is treated as Category B stock, with a lower level of recording and management control being applied.

The remaining 60 per cent of the volume of stock is plastic fittings, which represent the least valuable items that account for only 10 per cent of the total value of finished stock held. This is treated as Category C stock, so the level of recording and management control would be lower still. Applying to this stock the level of control that is applied to Category A or even Category B stock, would be uneconomic.

Categorising stock in this way seeks to direct management effort to the most important areas, and tries to ensure that the costs of controlling stock are proportional to the stock's importance.

Figure 10.2 shows the logic of the ABC approach to stock (inventory) control.

Stock (inventory) management models

It is possible to use decision models to help manage stock. The **economic order quantity (EOQ)** model is concerned with answering the question: how much stock should be ordered? In its simplest form, the EOQ model assumes that demand is constant, so that stocks will be depleted evenly over time, and replenished just at the point that the stock runs out. These assumptions would lead to a 'saw tooth' pattern to represent stock movements within a business, as shown in Figure 10.3.

The EOQ model recognises that the key costs associated with stock management are the costs of holding it and the cost of ordering it. The model can be used to calculate the optimum size of a purchase order by taking account of both of these cost elements. The cost of holding stock can be substantial, and so management may try to minimise the average amount of stock held. However, by reducing the level of stock held, and therefore the holding costs, there will be a need to increase the number of orders during the period, and so ordering costs will rise.

Figure 10.2	ABC method of analysing and controlling stock

Category A contains stock that, though relatively few in quantity, accounts for a large proportion of the total value. Category B stock consists of those items that are less valuable but more numerous. Category C comprises those stock items that are very numerous but relatively low in value. Different stock control rules would be applied to each category. For example, only Category A stock would attract the more expensive and sophisticated controls.

Source: After McLaney and Atrill (2004), Fig. 16.3.

Figure 10.3	Patterns of stock movements over time

Here we assume that there is a constant rate of usage of the stock item, and that stock is reduced to zero just as new stock arrives. At time 0 there is a full level of stock. This is steadily used as time passes; just as it falls to zero it is replaced. This pattern is then repeated.

Source: After McLaney and Atrill (2004), Fig. 16.3.

Figure 10.4 shows how, as the level of stock and the size of stock orders increase, the annual costs of placing orders will decrease because fewer orders will be placed. However, the cost of holding stock will increase, as there will be higher average stock levels. The total costs curve, which is based on the sum of holding costs and ordering costs, will fall until the point E is reached, which represents the minimum total cost.

Figure 10.4 **Stockholding and stock order costs**

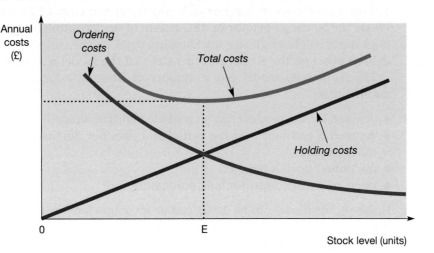

Small stock levels imply frequent reordering and high annual ordering costs. Small stock levels also imply relatively low stockholding costs. High stock levels imply exactly the opposite. There is, in theory, an optimum order size that will lead to the sum of ordering and stockholding costs (total costs) being at a minimum.

Source: After McLaney and Atrill (2004), Fig. 16.3.

Thereafter, total costs begin to rise. The EOQ model seeks to identify point E at which total costs are minimised. This will represent half of the optimum amount that should be ordered on each occasion. Assuming, as we are doing, that stock is used evenly over time and that stock falls to zero before being replaced, the average stock level equals half of the order size.

The EOQ model, which can be used to derive the most economic order quantity, is:

$$EOQ = \sqrt{\frac{2DC}{H}}$$

where: D = the annual demand for the item of stock (expressed in units of the stock)
C = the cost of placing an order
H = the cost of holding one unit of stock for one year.

Activity 10.5

HLA Ltd sells 2,000 bags of cement each year. It has been estimated that the cost of holding one bag of cement for a year is £4. The cost of placing an order for stock is estimated at £250.
Calculate the EOQ for bags of cement.

....

Your answer to this activity should be as follows:

$$EOQ = \sqrt{\frac{2 \times 2,000 \times 250}{4}} = 500 \text{ units}$$

This will mean that the business will have to order bags of cement four times each year so that sales demand can be met.

Note that the cost of the stock concerned, that is the price paid to the supplier, does not directly impact on the EOQ model. The EOQ model is only concerned with the administrative costs of placing each order and the costs of looking after the stock. Where the business operates an ABC system of stock control, however, more expensive stock items will have greater stockholding costs. So the cost of the stock may have an indirect effect on the economic order size that the model recommends.

The basic EOQ model has a number of limiting assumptions. In particular, it assumes that:

● demand for the product can be predicted with accuracy
● demand is constant over the period and does not fluctuate through seasonality or other reasons
● no 'buffer' stock is required
● there are no discounts for bulk purchasing.

However, the model can be developed to accommodate the problems of each of these limiting assumptions. Many businesses use this model (or a development of it) to help in the management of stocks.

Materials requirement planning systems

A **materials requirement planning (MRP) system** takes planned sales demand as its starting point. It then uses a computer package to help schedule the timing of deliveries of bought-in parts and materials to coincide with production requirements. It is a coordinated approach that links materials and parts deliveries to the scheduled time of their input to the production process. By ordering only those items that are necessary to ensure the flow of production, stock levels are likely to be reduced. MRP is really a 'top-down' approach to stock management, which recognises that stock ordering decisions cannot be viewed as being independent from production decisions. In recent years, this approach has been extended to provide a fully integrated approach to production planning. The approach also takes account of other manufacturing resources such as labour and machine capacity.

Just-in-time stock (inventory) management

In recent years, many businesses have tried to eliminate the need to hold stocks by adopting **just-in-time (JIT) stock management**. This approach was originally used in the US defence industry during the Second World War, but in more recent times its scope has broadened. It was first used on a wide scale by Japanese manufacturing businesses. The essence of JIT is, as the name suggests, to have supplies delivered to a business just in time for them to be used in the production process or in a sale. By adopting this approach the stockholding costs rest with suppliers rather than with the business itself. On the other hand, a failure by a particular supplier to deliver on time could cause enormous problems and costs to the business. Thus JIT can save cost, but it tends to increase risk.

For JIT to be successful, it is important that the business informs suppliers of its stock requirements in advance, and that suppliers, in their turn, deliver materials of the right quality at the agreed times. Failure to do so could lead to a dislocation of production or supply to customers and could be very costly. Thus a close relationship is required between the business and its suppliers.

Although a business that applies JIT will not have to hold stocks, there may be other costs associated with this approach. As the suppliers will be required to hold stocks for the business, they may try to recoup this additional cost through increased prices. The close relationship necessary between the business and its suppliers may also prevent the business from taking advantage of cheaper sources of supply if they become available.

Many people view JIT as more than simply a stock control system. The philosophy underpinning this approach is concerned with eliminating waste and striving for excellence. There is an expectation that suppliers will always deliver stock on time and that there will be no defects in the items supplied. There is also an expectation that, for manufacturers, the production process will operate at maximum efficiency. This means there will be no production breakdowns and the queuing and storage times of products manufactured will be eliminated, as only that time spent directly on processing the products is seen as adding value. While these expectations may be impossible to achieve, they do help to create a culture that is dedicated to the pursuit of excellence and quality.

Real Worlds 10.5 and 10.6 show how two well-known businesses operating in the UK (one a retailer, the other a manufacturer) use JIT to advantage.

REAL WORLD 10.5

JIT at Boots

The Boots Company plc, the UK's largest healthcare retailer, has recently improved the stock management at its stores. The business is working towards a JIT system where a stock delivery from its one central warehouse in Nottingham will be made every day to each retail branch, with nearly all of the stock lines being placed directly on to the sales shelves, not into a branch stock room. The business says that this will bring significant savings of stores staff time and lead to significantly lower levels of stock being held, without any lessening of the service offered to customers. The new system is expected to lead to major economic benefits for the business.

Source: Based on information in The Boots Company plc Annual Report and Accounts 2003.

REAL WORLD 10.6

JIT at Nissan

Nissan Motors UK Limited, the UK manufacturing arm of the world-famous Japanese car business, has a plant in Sunderland in the north east of England. Here it operates a well-developed JIT system. Sommer supplies carpets and soft interior trim from a factory close to the Nissan plant. It makes deliveries to Nissan once every 20 minutes on average, so as to arrive exactly as they are needed in production. This is fairly typical of all of the 200 suppliers of components and materials to the Nissan plant.

Source: Based on information in Partnership Sourcing Best Practice case study, www.pslcbi.com/studies/docnissan.htm

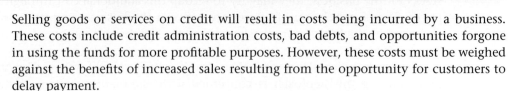

Managing debtors (receivables)

Selling goods or services on credit will result in costs being incurred by a business. These costs include credit administration costs, bad debts, and opportunities forgone in using the funds for more profitable purposes. However, these costs must be weighed against the benefits of increased sales resulting from the opportunity for customers to delay payment.

Selling on credit is widespread, and appears to be the norm outside the retail trade. When a business offers to sell its goods or services on credit, it must have clear policies concerning:

● which customers should receive credit
● how much credit should be offered
● what length of credit it is prepared to offer
● whether discounts will be offered for prompt payment
● what collection policies should be adopted
● how the risk of non-payment can be reduced.

We consider each of these issues below.

Which customers should receive credit?

A business offering credit runs the risk of not receiving payment for goods or services supplied. Thus, care must be taken over the type of customer to whom credit facilities are offered. When considering a proposal from a customer for the supply of goods or services on credit, the business must take a number of factors into account. The following **five Cs of credit** provide a business with a useful checklist.

● *Capital.* The customer must appear to be financially sound before any credit is extended. Where the customer is a business, its financial statements should be examined. Particular regard should be given to the customer's likely future profitability and liquidity. In addition, any major financial commitments (for example, capital expenditure, contracts with suppliers) must be taken into account.
● *Capacity.* The customer must appear to have the capacity to pay amounts owing. Where possible, the payment record of the customer to date should be examined. If the customer is a business, the type of business operated and the physical resources of the business will be relevant. The value of goods that the customer wishes to buy on credit must be related to the customer's total financial resources.
● *Collateral.* On occasions, it may be necessary to ask for some kind of security for goods supplied on credit. When this occurs, the business must be convinced that the customer is able to offer a satisfactory form of security.
● *Conditions.* The state of the industry in which the customer operates, and the general economic conditions of the particular region or country, may have an important influence on the ability of a customer to pay the amounts outstanding on the due date.
● *Character.* It is important for a business to make some assessment of the customer's character. The willingness to pay will depend on the honesty and integrity of the individual with whom the business is dealing. Where the customer is a limited company, this will mean assessing the characters of its directors. The business must feel satisfied that the customer will make every effort to pay any amounts owing.

It is clear from the above that a business will need to gather information concerning the ability and willingness of the customer to pay the amounts owing at the due dates.

Activity 10.6

Assume that you are the credit manager of a business and that a limited company approaches you with a view to buying goods on credit. What sources of information might you decide to use to help assess the financial health of the potential customer?

There are various possibilities. You may have thought of some of the following:

- *Trade references.* Some businesses ask potential customers to supply them with references from other suppliers who have made sales on credit to them. This may be extremely useful, provided that the references supplied are truly representative of the opinions of a customer's suppliers. There is a danger that a potential customer will attempt to be selective when giving details of other suppliers, in order to gain a more favourable impression than is deserved.
- *Bank references.* It is possible to ask the potential customer for a bank reference. Although banks are usually prepared to supply references, the contents of such references are not always very informative. If customers are in financial difficulties, the bank may be unwilling to add to their problems by supplying poor references. It is worth remembering that the bank's loyalty is likely to be to the customer rather than the enquirer. In addition, the bank will usually charge a fee for providing a reference.
- *Published financial statements.* A limited company is obliged by law to file a copy of its annual financial statements with the Registrar of Companies. These financial statements are available for public inspection and provide a useful source of information. Apart from the information contained in the financial statements, company law requires public limited companies to state in the directors' report the average time taken to pay suppliers. Nowadays, the annual reports of many companies are available on the website or on computer-based information systems (for example, FAME).
- *The customer.* Interviews with the directors of the customer business and visits to its premises may be carried out to gain some impression of the way that the customer conducts its business. Where a significant amount of credit is required, the business may ask the customer for access to internal budgets and other unpublished financial information to help assess the level of risk involved.
- *Credit agencies.* Specialist agencies exist to provide information that can be used to assess the creditworthiness of a potential customer. The information that a credit agency supplies may be gleaned from various sources, including the financial statements of the customer and news items relating to the customer from both published and unpublished sources. The credit agencies may also provide a credit rating for the business.
- *Register of County Court Judgments.* Any money judgments given against the business or an individual in a county court will be maintained on the register for six years. This register is available for inspection by any member of the public for a small fee.
- *Other suppliers.* Similar business will often be prepared to exchange information concerning slow payers or defaulting customers through an industry credit circle. This can be a reliable and relatively cheap way of obtaining information.

How much credit should be offered?

Once a customer is considered creditworthy, credit limits for the customer should be established and procedures should be laid down to ensure that these limits are adhered to. Unfortunately, there are no theories or models to help a business decide on the appropriate credit limit to adopt; it is really a matter of judgement. Some businesses adopt simple 'rule of thumb' methods based on either the amount of sales made to the customer (say, twice the monthly sales figure for that customer) or a maximum the business is prepared to be owed (say, a maximum of 20 per cent of the working capital).

Length of credit period

A business must determine what credit terms it is prepared to offer its customers. The length of credit offered to customers can vary significantly between businesses, and may be influenced by such factors as:

- the typical credit terms operating within the industry
- the degree of competition within the industry
- the bargaining power of particular customers
- the risk of non-payment
- the capacity of the business to offer credit
- the marketing strategy of the business.

The last point identified may require some explanation. The marketing strategy of a business may have an important influence on the length of credit allowed. For example, if a business wishes to increase its market share it may decide to be more generous in its credit policy in an attempt to stimulate sales. Potential customers may be attracted by the offer of a longer credit period. However, any such change in policy must take account of the likely costs and benefits arising.

To illustrate this point, consider Example 10.2.

Example 10.2

Torrance Ltd produces a new type of golf putter. The business sells the putter to wholesalers and retailers and has an annual turnover of £600,000. The following data relate to each putter produced.

	£	£
Selling price		40
Variable costs	20	
Fixed cost apportionment	6	26
Net profit		14

The business's cost of capital is estimated at 10 per cent a year.

Torrance Ltd wishes to expand the sales volume of the new putter. It believes that offering a longer credit period can achieve this. The business's average collection period is currently 30 days. It is considering three options in an attempt to increase sales revenue. These are as follows:

	Option		
	1	2	3
Increase in average collection period (days)	10	20	30
Increase in sales revenue (£)	30,000	45,000	50,000

To enable the business to decide on the best option to adopt, it must weigh the benefits of the options against their respective costs. The benefits arising will be represented by the increase in profit from the sale of additional putters. From the cost data supplied we can see that the contribution (that is, selling price (£40) less variable costs (£20)) is £20 a putter, that is, 50 per cent of the selling price. So, whatever increase there may be in sales revenue, the additional contributions will be half of that figure. The fixed costs can be ignored in our calculations, as they will remain the same whichever option is chosen.

The increase in contribution under each option will therefore be:

	Option		
	1	2	3
50% of the increase in sales revenue (£)	15,000	22,500	25,000

The increase in debtors under each option will be as follows:

	Option		
	1	2	3
	£	£	£
Projected level of debtors			
40 × £630,000/365 (Note 1)	69,041		
50 × £645,000/365		88,356	
60 × £650,000/365			106,849
Less Current level of debtors			
30 × £600,000/365	49,315	49,315	49,315
Increase in debtors	19,726	39,041	57,534

The increase in debtors that results from each option will mean an additional finance cost to the business.

The net increase in the business's profit arising from the projected change is:

	Option		
	1	2	3
	£	£	£
Increase in contribution (see above)	15,000	22,500	25,000
Less Increase in finance cost (Note 2)	1,973	3,904	5,753
Net increase in profits	13,027	18,596	19,247

The calculations show that Option 3 will be the most profitable one.

Notes

1 If the annual sales revenue total £630,000 and 40 days' credit are allowed (both of which will apply under Option 1), the average amount that will be owed to the business by its customers, at any point during the year, will be the daily sales revenue (that is, £630,000/365) multiplied by the number of days that the customers take to pay (that is, 40).

Exactly the same logic applies to Options 2 and 3 and to the current level of debtors.

2 The increase in the finance cost for Option 1 will be the increase in debtors (£19,726 × 10%). The equivalent figures for the other options are derived in a similar way.

Example 10.2 illustrates the way in which a business should assess changes in credit terms. However, if there is a risk that, by extending the length of credit, there will be an increase in bad debts, this should also be taken into account in the calculations, as should any additional collection costs that will be incurred.

Real World 10.7 provides some insight to the typical length of credit taken by UK businesses.

REAL WORLD 10.7

Length of credit taken by UK businesses

In their annual reports, UK limited companies are legally obliged to disclose the average length of trade credit that they take from their suppliers. For a random sample of 21 UK Stock Exchange listed businesses, the following applied:

Shortest period taken by any business	8 days
Longest period taken by any business	60 days
Mean (simple average) period for all of the businesses	38 days
Median (middle ranking) period of all of the businesses	38 days

Source: Based on information in the 2003 and 2004 annual reports of a random sample of UK Stock Exchange listed businesses.

An alternative approach to evaluating the credit decision

It is possible to view the credit decision as a capital investment decision. The granting of credit involves an outlay of resources in the form of cash (which has been temporarily forgone) in the expectation that future cash flows will be increased (through higher sales) as a result. A business will usually have choices concerning the level of investment to be made in credit sales and the period over which credit is granted. These choices will result in different returns and different levels of risk. There is no reason in principle why the NPV investment appraisal method, which we considered in Chapter 4, should not be used to evaluate these choices. We have seen that the NPV method takes into account both the time value of money and the level of risk involved.

Cash discounts

A business may decide to offer a **cash discount** in an attempt to encourage prompt payment from its credit customers. The size of any discount will be an important influence on whether a customer decides to pay promptly.

From the business's viewpoint, the cost of offering discounts must be weighed against the likely benefits in the form of a reduction both in the cost of financing debtors and in the amount of bad debts.

In practice, there is always the danger that a customer may be slow to pay and yet may still take the discount offered. Where the customer is important to the business it may be difficult to insist on full payment. An alternative to allowing the customer to take discounts by reducing payment, is to agree in advance to provide discounts for prompt payment through quarterly credit notes. As credit notes will only be given for those debts paid on time, the customer will often make an effort to qualify for the discount.

Self-assessment question 10.1

Williams Wholesalers Ltd at present requires payment from its customers by the end of the month after the month of delivery. On average, customers take 70 days to pay. Sales revenue amounts to £4 million a year and bad debts to £20,000 a year.

It is planned to offer customers a cash discount of 2 per cent for payment within 30 days. Williams estimates that 50 per cent of customers will accept this facility but that the remaining customers, who tend to be slow payers, will not pay until 80 days after the sale. At present the business has an overdraft facility at an interest rate of 13 per cent a year. If the plan goes ahead, bad debts will be reduced to £10,000 a year and there will be savings in credit administration expenses of £6,000 a year.

Required:

Should Williams Wholesalers Ltd offer the new credit terms to customers? You should support your answer with any calculations and explanations that you consider necessary.

Debt factoring and invoice discounting

We saw in Chapter 6 that trade debts can, in effect, be turned into cash by either factoring them or having sales invoices discounted. These both seem to be fairly popular approaches to managing trade debtors.

Collection policies

A business offering credit must ensure that amounts owing are collected as quickly as possible. Various steps can be taken to achieve this, as outlined below.

Develop customer relationships

For major customers it is often useful to cultivate a relationship with the key staff responsible for paying sales invoices. By so doing, the chances of prompt payment may be increased. For less important customers, the business should at least identify key staff who can be contacted in the event of a payment problem.

Publicise credit terms

The credit terms of the business should be made clear in all relevant correspondence, such as order acknowledgements, invoices and statements. In early negotiations with the prospective customer, credit terms should be discussed openly and an agreement reached.

Issue invoices promptly

An efficient collection policy requires an efficient accounting system. Invoices (bills) must be sent out promptly to customers, as must regular monthly statements. Reminders must also be dispatched promptly to customers who are late in paying. If a customer fails to respond to a reminder, the accounting system should alert managers so that a stop can be placed on further deliveries.

Monitor outstanding debts

Management can monitor the effectiveness of collection policies in a number of ways. One method is to calculate the **average settlement period for debtors** ratio, which we dealt with in Chapter 3. This ratio, we should recall, is calculated as follows:

$$\text{Average settlement period for debtors} = \frac{\text{Trade debtors}}{\text{Credit sales revenue}} \times 365$$

Although this ratio can be useful, it is important to remember that it produces an *average* figure for the number of days for which debts are outstanding. This average may be badly distorted by a few large customers who are very slow or very fast payers.

Produce an ageing schedule of debtors

A more detailed and informative approach to monitoring debtors may be to produce an **ageing schedule of debtors**. Debts are divided into categories according to the length of time the debt has been outstanding. An ageing schedule can be produced, on a regular basis, to help managers see the pattern of outstanding debts. An example of an ageing schedule is set out in Example 10.3.

Example 10.3

Ageing schedule of debtors at 31 December

Customer	Days outstanding				Total
	1–30	31–60	61–90	90+	
	£	£	£	£	£
A Ltd	20,000	10,000	–	–	30,000
B Ltd	–	24,000	–	–	24,000
C Ltd	12,000	13,000	14,000	18,000	57,000
Total	32,000	47,000	14,000	18,000	111,000

This shows a business's trade debtor figure at 31 December, which totals £111,000. Each customer's balance is analysed according to how long the debt has been outstanding.

Thus we can see from the schedule that A Ltd has £20,000 outstanding for 30 days or less (that is, arising from sales during December), and £10,000 outstanding for between 31 and 60 days (arising from November sales). This information can be very useful for credit control purposes.

Many accounting software packages now include this ageing schedule as one of the routine reports available to managers. Such packages often have the facility to put customers 'on stop' when they reach their credit limits. Putting a customer 'on stop' means that no further credit sales will be made to that customer until debts arising from past sales have been settled.

Identify the pattern of receipts

A slightly different approach to exercising control over debtors is to identify the pattern of receipts from credit sales on a monthly basis. This involves monitoring the percentage of trade debtors that pays (and the percentage of debts that remain unpaid) in the month of sale and the percentage that pays in subsequent months. To do this, credit sales for each month must be examined separately. To illustrate how a pattern of credit sales receipts is produced, consider a business that made credit sales of £250,000 in

June and received 30 per cent of the amount owing in the same month, 40 per cent in July, 20 per cent in August and 10 per cent in September. The pattern of credit sales receipts and amounts owing is shown in Example 10.4.

Example 10.4

Pattern of credit sales receipts

	Receipts from June credit sales £	Received %	Amount outstanding from June sales at month end £	Outstanding %
June	75,000	30	175,000	70
July	100,000	40	75,000	30
August	50,000	20	25,000	10
September	25,000	10	–	–

Example 10.4 shows how sales made in June were received over time. This information can be used as a basis for control. The actual pattern of receipts can be compared with the expected (budgeted) pattern of receipts in order to see if there was any significant deviation (see Figure 10.5). If this comparison shows that debtors are paying more slowly than expected, management may decide to take corrective action.

Figure 10.5 Comparison of actual and budgeted receipts over time for Example 10.4

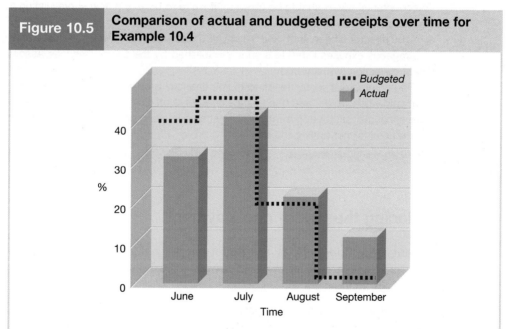

The graph shows the actual pattern of cash receipts from credit sales made in June. It can be seen that 30 per cent of the sales income for June is received in that month; the remainder is received in the three following months. The (assumed) budgeted pattern of cash receipts for June sales is also depicted. By comparing the actual and budgeted pattern of receipts, it is possible to see whether credit sales are being properly controlled and to decide whether corrective action is required.

Answer queries quickly

It is important for relevant staff to deal with customer queries quickly and efficiently. Payment is unlikely to be made by customers until their queries have been dealt with.

Deal with slow payers

It is almost inevitable that a business making significant sales on credit will sometimes be faced with customers who do not pay. When this occurs, there should be agreed procedures for dealing with the situation. However, the cost of any action to be taken against delinquent debtors must be weighed against the likely returns. For example, there is little point in taking legal action against a customer, incurring large legal expenses, if there is evidence that the customer does not have the necessary resources to pay. Where possible, an estimate of the cost of bad debts should be taken into account when setting prices for products or services.

As a footnote to our consideration of managing debtors, **Real World 10.8** outlines some of the excuses that long-suffering credit managers must listen to when chasing payment for outstanding debt.

REAL WORLD 10.8

It's in the post

Accountants' noses should be growing, if we're to believe a new survey listing the bizarre excuses given by businesses that fail to pay their debts.

'The director's been shot' and 'I'll pay you when God tells me to' are just two of the most outrageous excuses listed in a survey published by the Credit Services Association, the debt collection industry body.

The commercial sector tends to blame financial problems, and excuses such as 'you'll get paid when we do' and 'the finance director is off sick' are common. However, those in the consumer sector apparently feel no shame in citing personal relationship problems as the reason for not paying the bill.

Source: Accountancy, April 2000, p. 18.

Reducing the risk of non-payment

Efficient collection policies are important in reducing the risk of non-payment. However, there are other ways in which a business can reduce this type of risk. Possibilities include:

- Requiring customers to pay part of their sales value in advance of the goods being sent.
- Agreeing to offset amounts owed for the purchase of goods against amounts due for goods supplied to the same business.
- Requiring a third-party guarantee from a financially sound business such as a bank or parent company.
- Making it a condition of sale that the legal title of the goods is not passed to the customer until the goods are paid for.

- Taking out insurance to cover the costs of any legal expenses incurred in recovering the debt. (Some customers may refuse to pay if they feel the business does not have the resources to pursue the debt through the courts.)
- Taking out insurance against risk of non-payment. Trade credit insurance can cover the whole of the credit sales of the business up to an agreed limit or can cover a number of specified customers.

The practical circumstances will determine which of the above methods is appropriate to use. For example, it would not be feasible to try to retain the legal title of raw materials or components which are intended to become part of a finished product. Remember also that, in a highly competitive environment, customers may be unwilling to accept stringent conditions. The risk of non-payment must always be weighed against the risk of lost sales.

Managing cash

Why hold cash?

Most businesses hold a certain amount of cash. The amount of cash held tends to vary considerably between businesses.

Activity 10.7

Why do you think a business may decide to hold at least some of its assets in the form of cash? (*Hint*: There are broadly three reasons.)

The three reasons are as follows:

1 To meet day-to-day commitments, a business requires a certain amount of cash. Payments for wages, overhead expenses, goods purchased and so on must be made at the due dates. Cash has been described as the lifeblood of a business. Unless it circulates through the business and is available for the payment of maturing obligations, the survival of the business will be at risk. Profitability is not enough: a business must have sufficient cash to pay its debts when they fall due.
2 If future cash flows are uncertain for any reason, it would be prudent to hold a balance of cash. For example, a major customer that owes a large sum to the business may be in financial difficulties. Given this situation, the business can retain its capacity to meet its obligations by holding a cash balance. Similarly, if there is some uncertainty concerning future outlays, a cash balance will be required.
3 A business may decide to hold cash to put itself in a position to exploit profitable opportunities as and when they arise. For example, by holding cash, a business may be able to acquire a competitor business that suddenly becomes available at an attractive price.

How much cash should be held?

Although cash can be held for each of the reasons identified in Activity 10.7, this may not always be necessary. If a business is able to borrow quickly, the amount of cash it needs to hold can be reduced. Similarly, if the business holds assets that can easily be converted to cash (for example, marketable securities such as shares in Stock Exchange listed businesses or government bonds), the amount of cash held can be reduced.

The decision as to how much cash a particular business should hold is a difficult one. Different businesses will have different views on the subject.

Activity 10.8

What do you think are the major factors that influence how much cash a business will hold? See if you can think of five possible factors.

You may have thought of the following:

- *The nature of the business.* Some businesses such as utilities (for example, water, electricity and gas suppliers) may have cash flows that are both predictable and reasonably certain. This will enable them to hold lower cash balances. For some businesses, cash balances may vary greatly according to the time of year. A seasonal business may accumulate cash during the high season to enable it to meet commitments during the low season.
- *The opportunity cost of holding cash.* Where there are profitable opportunities it may not be wise to hold a large cash balance.
- *The level of inflation.* Holding cash during a period of rising prices will lead to a loss of purchasing power. The higher the level of inflation, the greater will be this loss.
- *The availability of near-liquid assets.* If a business has marketable securities or stocks that may easily be liquidated, the amount of cash held may be reduced.
- *The availability of borrowing.* If a business can borrow easily (and quickly), there is less need to hold cash.
- *The cost of borrowing.* When interest rates are high, the option of borrowing becomes less attractive.
- *Economic conditions.* When the economy is in recession, businesses may prefer to hold cash so that they can be well placed to invest when the economy improves. In addition, during a recession, businesses may experience difficulties in collecting debts. They may therefore hold higher cash balances than usual in order to meet commitments.
- *Relationships with suppliers.* Too little cash may hinder the ability of the business to pay suppliers promptly. This can lead to a loss of goodwill. It may also lead to discounts being forgone.

Controlling the cash balance

Several models have been developed to help control the cash balance of the business. One such model proposes the use of upper and lower control limits for cash balances and the use of a target cash balance. The model assumes that the business will invest in marketable investments that can easily be liquidated. These investments will be purchased or sold, as necessary, in order to keep the cash balance within the control limits.

The model proposes two upper and two lower control limits (see Figure 10.6). If the business exceeds an *outer* limit, the managers must decide whether or not the cash balance is likely to return to a point within the *inner* control limits set, over the next few days. If this seems likely, then no action is required. If, on the other hand, it does not seem likely, management must change the cash position of the business by either lending or borrowing (or possibly by buying or selling marketable securities).

In Figure 10.6 we can see that the lower outer control limit has been breached for four days. If a four-day period is unacceptable, managers must sell marketable securities to replenish the cash balance.

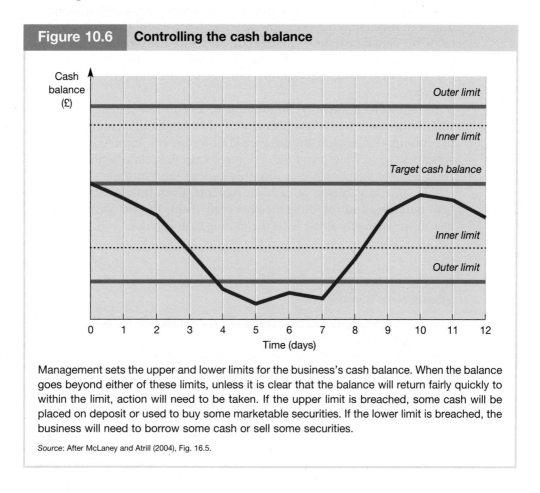

Figure 10.6	Controlling the cash balance

Management sets the upper and lower limits for the business's cash balance. When the balance goes beyond either of these limits, unless it is clear that the balance will return fairly quickly to within the limit, action will need to be taken. If the upper limit is breached, some cash will be placed on deposit or used to buy some marketable securities. If the lower limit is breached, the business will need to borrow some cash or sell some securities.

Source: After McLaney and Atrill (2004), Fig. 16.5.

The model relies heavily on management judgement to determine where the control limits are set and the period within which breaches of the control limits are acceptable. Experience may be useful in helping managers decide on these issues. There are other models, however, that do not rely on management judgement. Instead, these use quantitative techniques to determine an optimal cash policy. One model proposed, for example, is the cash equivalent of the stock economic order quantity model, discussed earlier in the chapter.

Projected cash flow statements and the management of cash

To manage cash effectively, it is useful for a business to prepare a projected cash flow statement. This is a very important tool for both planning and control purposes.

Projected cash flow statements were considered in Chapter 2, and so we shall not consider them again in detail here. However, it is worth repeating the point that these statements enable managers to see the expected impact of planned events on the cash balance. The projected cash flow statements will identify periods when cash surpluses and cash deficits are expected.

When a cash surplus is expected to arise, managers must decide on the best use of the surplus funds. When a cash deficit is expected, managers must make adequate provision by borrowing, liquidating assets or rescheduling cash payments or receipts to deal with this. Projected cash flow statements are useful in helping to control the cash held. The actual cash flows can be compared with the projected, or forecast, cash flows for the period. If there is a significant divergence between the forecast cash flows and the actual cash flows, explanations must be sought and corrective action taken where necessary.

To refresh your memory, an example of a cash flow statement is given in Example 10.5. Remember there is no set format for this statement. Managers can determine how the information should be presented. However, the format set out in the example appears to be in widespread use. Projected cash flow statements covering a short term are usually broken down into monthly periods (and in some cases weekly periods) to enable close monitoring of cash movements. Cash inflows are usually shown above cash outflows, and the difference between them (the net cash flow) for a month is identified separately along with the closing cash balance.

Example 10.5

Projected cash flow statement for the six months to 30 November

	June £	July £	August £	September £	October £	November £
Cash inflows						
Credit sales	–	–	4,000	5,500	7,000	8,500
Cash sales	4,000	5,500	7,000	8,500	11,000	11,000
	4,000	5,500	11,000	14,000	18,000	19,500
Cash outflows						
Motor vehicles	6,000					
Equipment	10,000					7,200
Freehold premises	40,000					
Purchases	–	29,000	9,250	11,500	13,750	17,500
Wages/salaries	900	900	900	900	900	900
Commission	–	320	440	560	680	680
Overheads	500	500	500	500	650	650
	57,400	30,720	11,090	13,460	15,980	26,930
Net cash flow	(53,400)	(25,220)	(90)	540	2,020	(7,430)
Opening balance	60,000	6,600	(18,620)	(18,710)	(18,170)	(16,150)
Closing balance	6,600	(18,620)	(18,710)	(18,170)	(16,150)	(23,580)

Although cash budgets are prepared primarily for internal management purposes, prospective lenders sometimes require them when a loan to a business is being considered.

Operating cash cycle

When managing cash, it is important to be aware of the **operating cash cycle** (OCC) of the business. For a retailer, for example, this may be defined as the time period between the outlay of cash necessary for the purchase of stocks and the ultimate receipt of cash from the sale of the goods. In the case of a business, for example a wholesaler, that purchases goods on credit for subsequent resale on credit, the OCC is as shown in Figure 10.7.

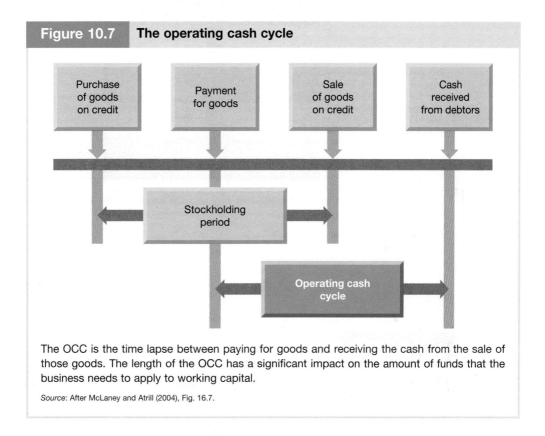

Figure 10.7	The operating cash cycle

The OCC is the time lapse between paying for goods and receiving the cash from the sale of those goods. The length of the OCC has a significant impact on the amount of funds that the business needs to apply to working capital.

Source: After McLaney and Atrill (2004), Fig. 16.7.

Figure 10.7 shows that payment for goods acquired on credit occurs some time after the goods have been purchased, and therefore no immediate cash outflow arises from the purchase. Similarly, cash receipts from debtors will occur some time after the sale is made, and so there will be no immediate cash inflow as a result of the sale. The OCC is the period between making the payment made to the creditor for goods supplied and receiving the cash from the debtor. Although Figure 10.7 depicts the position for a retailing or wholesaling business, the precise definition of the OCC can easily be adapted for both service and manufacturing businesses.

The OCC is important because it has a significant influence on the financing requirements of the business: the longer the cycle, the greater the financing requirements of the business and the greater the financial risks. For this reason, a business is likely to want to reduce the OCC to the minimum possible period.

For the type of business mentioned above, which buys and sells on credit, the OCC can be calculated from the financial statements by the use of certain ratios. It is calculated as shown in Figure 10.8.

Figure 10.8   Calculating the operating cash cycle

The figure shows that for businesses that buy and sell on credit, three ratios are required to calculate the OCC.

Source: After McLaney and Atrill (2004), Fig. 16.7.

Activity 10.9

The financial statements of Freezeqwik Ltd, a distributor of frozen foods, are set out below for the year ended 31 December last year.

Profit and loss account (income statement) for the year ended 31 December last year

	£000	£000
Sales revenue		820
Less Cost of sales		
Opening stock	142	
Purchases	568	
	710	
Less Closing stock	166	544
Gross profit		276
Administration expenses	(120)	
Selling and distribution expenses	(95)	
Financial expenses	(32)	(247)
Net profit		29
Corporation tax		(7)
Net profit after tax		22

Balance sheet as at 31 December last year

Non-current assets	£000	£000	£000
Property, plant and equipment			
Freehold premises at valuation			180
Fixtures and fittings at written-down value			82
Motor vans at written-down value			102
			364
Current assets			
Stock (inventory)		166	
Trade debtors (receivables)		264	
Cash		24	
		454	
Less **Current liabilities**			
Trade creditors (payables)	159		
Corporation tax	7	166	288
			652
Equity			
Ordinary share capital			300
Preference share capital			200
Retained profit			152
			652

All purchases and sales are on credit. There has been no change in the level of debtors or creditors over the period.

Calculate the length of the OCC for the business and go on to suggest how the business may seek to reduce this period.

The OCC may be calculated as follows:

	No. of days

Average stockholding period:

$$\frac{\text{(Opening stock + Closing stock)/2}}{\text{Cost of sales}} \times 365 = \frac{(142 + 166)/2}{544} \times 365 \qquad 103$$

Average settlement period for debtors:

$$\frac{\text{Trade debtors}}{\text{Credit sales}} \times 365 = \frac{264}{820} \times 365 \qquad \underline{118}$$

$$221$$

Less Average settlement period for creditors:

$$\frac{\text{Trade creditors}}{\text{Credit purchases}} \times 365 = \frac{159}{568} \times 365 \qquad \underline{102}$$

OCC $\qquad \underline{119}$

The business can reduce the length of the OCC in a number of ways. The average stockholding period seems quite long. At present, average stocks held represent more than three months' sales revenue. Lowering the level of stocks held will reduce this. Similarly, the average settlement period for debtors seems long, at nearly four months' sales revenue. Imposing tighter credit control, offering discounts, charging interest on overdue accounts and so on, may reduce this. However, any policy decisions concerning stocks and debtors must take account of current trading conditions.

Extending the period of credit taken to pay suppliers could also reduce the OCC. However, for reasons that will be explained later, this option must be given careful consideration.

Cash transmission

A business will normally wish to benefit from receipts from customers at the earliest opportunity. The benefit is immediate where payment is made in cash. However, when payment is made by cheque, there is normally a delay of three to four working days before the cheque can be cleared through the banking system. The business must therefore wait for this period before it can benefit from the amount paid in. In the case of a business that receives large amounts in the form of cheques, the opportunity cost of this delay can be significant.

To avoid this delay, a business could require payments to be made in cash. This is not usually very practical, mainly because of the risk of theft and the expense of conveying cash securely. Another option is to ask for payment to be made by standing order or by direct debit from the customer's bank account. This should ensure that the amount owing is always transferred from the bank account of the customer to the bank account of the business on the day that has been agreed.

It is also possible for funds to be transferred directly to a business's bank account. As a result of developments in computer technology, customers can pay for items by using debit cards, which results in the appropriate account being instantly debited and the seller's bank account being instantly credited with the required amount. This method of payment is widely used by large retail businesses, and may well extend to other types of business.

Bank overdrafts

Bank overdrafts are simply bank current accounts that contain a negative amount of cash. They are a type of bank loan. We looked at these in Chapter 6 in the context of short-term bank lending. They can be a useful tool in managing the business's cash flow requirements. Bank overdrafts are a flexible form of borrowing and are cheap relative to other sources of finance. For this reason, the majority of UK businesses use bank overdrafts to finance their operations. Although, in theory, bank overdrafts are a short-term source of finance, in practice, they can extend over a long period of time, as many businesses continually renew their overdraft facility with the bank. Although renewal may not usually be a problem, there is always a danger that the bank will demand repayment at short notice, as it has the right to do. If the business is highly dependent on borrowing, and alternative sources of borrowing are difficult to find, this could raise severe problems.

When deciding whether or not to have a bank overdraft, the business should first consider the purpose of the borrowing. Overdrafts are most suitable for overcoming short-term funding problems (for example, increases in stockholding requirements owing to seasonal fluctuations), and should be self liquidating, as explained in Chapter 6. For longer-term funding problems or for borrowings that are not self liquidating, other sources of finance may be more suitable.

It is important to agree the correct facility with the bank, as borrowings in excess of the overdraft limit may incur high charges. To determine the amount of the overdraft facilities the business should produce projected cash flow statements. There should also be regular reporting of cash flows to ensure that the overdraft limit is not exceeded.

Managing trade creditors (payables)

Trade credit arises from the fact that most businesses buy their goods and service requirements on credit. In effect, suppliers are lending the business money, interest free, on a short-term basis. Trade creditors are the other side of the coin from trade debtors. One business's trade creditor is another one's trade debtor, in respect of a particular transaction. Trade creditors are an important source of finance for most businesses. It has been described as a 'spontaneous' source, as it tends to increase in line with the increase in the level of activity achieved by a business. Trade credit is widely regarded as a 'free' source of finance and, therefore, a good thing for a business to use. There may, however, be real costs associated with taking trade credit.

First, customers who take credit may not be as well treated as those who pay immediately. For example, when goods are in short supply, credit customers may receive lower priority when allocating the stock available. In addition, credit customers may be less favoured in terms of delivery dates or the provision of technical support services. Sometimes, the goods or services provided may be more costly if credit is required. Nevertheless, in most industries, trade credit is the norm. As a result, the above costs will not apply except, perhaps, to customers that abuse the credit facilities. A business purchasing supplies on credit may also have to incur additional administration and accounting costs in dealing with the scrutiny and payment of invoices, maintaining and updating creditors' accounts and so on.

REAL WORLD 10.9

Can't pay, won't pay

In some cases, delaying payment to creditors can be a sign of financial distress. One such example occurred in 2001 when Kmart, a large US retailer, suffered a cash crisis. The crisis was largely as a result of one manager ordering $850m worth of stocks, which was later described in an internal report as 'excessive'. To conserve cash, the business implemented Project Slow It Down. This involved systematically delaying or reducing payments to trade creditors. The project also involved denying creditors access to records of the amounts owed by Kmart and giving false reasons as to why they had not been paid on time.

Source: Based on information in 'Kmart's fall is tale of poor governance', *Financial Times*, 29 January 2003.

Where a supplier offers a discount for prompt payment, the business should give careful consideration to the possibility of paying within the discount period. Example 10.6 illustrates the cost of foregoing possible discounts.

Example 10.6

Hassan Ltd takes 70 days to pay for goods from its supplier. To encourage prompt payment, the supplier has offered the business a 2 per cent discount if payment for goods is made within 30 days.

Hassan Ltd is not sure whether it is worth taking the discount offered.

Example 10.6 continued

If the discount is taken, payment could be made on the last day of the discount period (that is, the thirtieth day). However, if the discount is not taken, payment will be made after 70 days. This means that by not taking the discount the business will receive an extra 40 days' (that is, 70 – 30) credit. The cost of this extra credit to the business will be the 2 per cent discount foregone. If we annualise the cost of this discount foregone, we have:

$$\frac{365}{40} \times 2\% = 18.3\%*$$

We can see that the annual cost of foregoing the discount is very high, and it may be profitable for the business to pay the supplier within the discount period, even if it means that it will have to borrow to enable it to do so.

* This is an approximate annual rate. For the more mathematically minded, the precise rate is:

$$\{[(1 + 2/98)^{9.125}] - 1\} \times 100\% = 20.2\%$$

The above points are not meant to imply that taking credit is a burden to a business. There are of course real benefits that can accrue. Provided that trade credit is not abused, it can represent a form of interest-free loan. It can be a much more convenient method of paying for goods and services than paying by cash, and during a period of inflation there will be an economic gain by paying later rather than sooner for goods and services purchased. For most businesses, these benefits will exceed the costs involved.

Controlling trade creditors (payables)

To help monitor the level of trade credit taken, management can calculate the **average settlement period for creditors**. As we saw in Chapter 3, this ratio is:

$$\text{Average settlement period} = \frac{\text{Trade creditors}}{\text{Credit purchases}} \times 365$$

Once again, this provides an average figure, which could be misleading. A more informative approach would be to produce an ageing schedule for creditors. This would look much the same as the ageing schedule for debtors described earlier.

Since, as was pointed out earlier in this section, one business's trade creditor is another's trade debtor, the information contained in Real World 10.7 provides some indication of typical lengths of trade credit taken by UK businesses.

Working capital problems of the small business

We saw earlier (Real World 10.1, p. 388) that the amounts invested by businesses in working capital are often high in proportion to the total assets employed. It is, therefore, important that these amounts are properly managed. Although this point applies to businesses of all sizes, it may be of particular importance to small businesses. It is often claimed that many small businesses suffer from a lack of capital and, where this is the case, tight control over working capital investment becomes critical. There is evidence, however, that small businesses are not very good at managing their working capital, and this has been cited as a major cause of their high failure rate compared with that of large businesses. In this section, we consider the working capital management problems associated with small businesses.

Credit management

Small businesses often lack the resources to manage their trade debtors (receivables) effectively. It is not unusual for a small business to operate without a separate credit control department. This tends to mean that both the expertise and the information required to make sound judgements concerning terms of sale and so on, may not be available. A small business may also lack proper debt collection procedures, such as prompt invoicing and sending out regular statements. This will increase the risks of late payment and defaulting debtors.

These risks probably tend to increase where there is an excessive concern for growth. In an attempt to increase sales, small businesses may be too willing to extend credit to customers that are poor credit risks. While this kind of problem can occur in businesses of all sizes, small businesses seem particularly susceptible.

Another problem faced by small businesses is their lack of market power. They will often find themselves in a weak position when negotiating credit terms with larger businesses. Moreover, when a large customer exceeds the terms of credit, the small supplier may feel inhibited from pressing the customer for payment in case future sales are lost.

It seems that small businesses have a much greater proportion of overdue debts than large businesses. **Real World 10.10** refers to evidence of this.

REAL WORLD 10.10

Small businesses wait longer

A survey undertaken by the Credit Management Research Centre (CMRC) during April and June 2003, indicates that small businesses (that is, those with annual sales turnover of less than £5 million) are likely to have to wait an average of 60 days for their trade debtors to pay. This contrast with the average of 32 to 33 days for the large businesses mentioned earlier (see Real World 10.7).

Source: Based on 'Small firms still have to wait for their money', Doug Morrison, *Sunday Telegraph*, 14 September 2003. Morrison's article discussed the CMRC research.

The reason for the delay suffered by small businesses probably relates to one of the factors mention above, namely the bargaining power of customers. The customers of small businesses may well be larger ones, which can use a threat, perhaps an implied one, of withdrawing custom, to force small businesses to accept later trade debtor settlement.

In the UK, the government has intervened to help deal with this problem and the law now permits small businesses to charge interest on overdue accounts. In addition, large companies are now required to disclose in their published financial statements the payment policy adopted towards suppliers, in the hope that this will improve the behaviour of those that delay payments. However, it is unlikely that legislation alone will make a significant improvement. Although small businesses may be able to charge interest on overdue accounts, they will often avoid doing so because they fear that large customers will view this as a provocative act. What is really needed to help small businesses is a change in the payment culture.

We saw in Chapter 6 that one way of dealing with the credit management problem is to factor the outstanding debts. Under this kind of arrangement, the factor will take over the sales ledger of the business and will take responsibility for the prompt collection of debts. However, some businesses are too small to take advantage of this facility. The set-up costs of a factoring arrangement often make businesses with a small turnover (up to, say, £100,000 a year) an uneconomic proposition for the factor.

Managing stock (inventory)

A lack of financial management skills within a small business often creates problems in managing stock in an efficient and effective way. The owners of small businesses are not always aware that there are costs involved in holding too much stock and that there are also costs involved in holding too little. These costs, which were discussed earlier, may be very high in certain industries such as manufacturing and wholesaling, where stock accounts for a significant proportion of the total assets held.

It was mentioned earlier in the chapter that the starting point for an effective stock management system is good planning and budgeting systems. In particular, there should be reliable sales forecasts, or budgets, available for stock ordering purposes. However, it seems that not all small businesses prepare these forecasts or budgets. A survey by Chittenden and others (see reference 1 at the end of the chapter) of small and medium-sized businesses indicated that only 78 per cent of those replying prepared a sales budget. Stock management can also benefit from good reporting systems and the application of quantitative techniques (for example, the economic order quantity model) to try to optimise stock levels. However, the same survey found that more than one-third of small businesses relied on manual methods of stock control, and the majority did not use stock optimisation techniques.

Managing cash

The management of cash raises similar issues to those relating to the management of stocks. There are costs involved both in holding too much and too little cash. Thus, there is a need for careful planning and monitoring of cash flows over time. The survey by Chittenden and others found, however, that only 63 per cent of those replying prepared a cash forecast. It was also found that cash balances are generally proportionately higher for smaller businesses than for larger ones. More than half of those in the survey held surplus cash balances on a regular basis. Although this may reflect a more conservative approach to liquidity among the owners of smaller businesses, it may suggest a failure to recognise the opportunity costs of cash balances.

Managing credit suppliers

In practice, small businesses often try to cope with the late payment of credit customers by delaying payments to their credit suppliers. We saw earlier in the chapter, however, that this can be an expensive option. Where discounts are foregone, the annual cost of this financing option compares unfavourably with most other forms of short-term financing. Nevertheless, the vast majority of small and medium-sized businesses are unaware of the very high cost of delaying payment, according to the Chittenden survey.

SUMMARY

The main points in this chapter may be summarised as follows:

Working capital

- Working capital (WC) is the difference between current assets and current liabilities.
- That is, WC = Stock + Debtors + Cash – Creditors – Bank overdrafts.
- An investment in WC cannot be avoided in practice – typically large amounts are involved.

Stock in trade (inventories)

- There are costs of holding stock, which include:
  - lost interest
  - storage cost
  - insurance cost
  - obsolescence.
- There are also costs of not holding sufficient stock, which include:
  - loss of sales and customer goodwill
  - production dislocation
  - loss of flexibility – cannot take advantage of opportunities
  - reorder costs – low stock implies more frequent ordering.
- Practical points on stock management include:
  - identify optimum order size – models can help with this
  - set stock reorder levels
  - use forecasts
  - keep reliable stock records
  - use accounting ratios (for example, stock turnover period ratio)
  - establish systems for security of stock and authorisation
  - consider just-in-time (JIT) stock management.

Trade debtors (receivables)

- When assessing which customers should receive credit, the five Cs of credit can be used:
  - capital
  - capacity
  - collateral
  - condition
  - character.
- The costs of allowing credit include:
  - lost interest
  - lost purchasing power
  - costs of assessing customer creditworthiness
  - administration cost
  - bad debts
  - cash discounts (for prompt payment).
- The costs of denying credit include:
  - loss of customer goodwill.

- Practical points on debtor management:
  - establish a policy
  - assess and monitor customer creditworthiness
  - establish effective administration of debtors
  - establish a policy on bad debts
  - consider cash discounts
  - use financial ratios (for example, average settlement period for debtors ratio)
  - use ageing summaries.

Cash

- The costs of holding cash include:
  - lost interest
  - lost purchasing power.
- The costs of holding insufficient cash include:
  - loss of supplier goodwill if unable to meet commitments on time
  - loss of opportunities
  - inability to claim cash discounts
  - costs of borrowing (should an obligation need to be met at short notice).
- Practical points on cash management:
  - establish a policy
  - plan cash flows
  - make judicious use of bank overdraft finance – it can be cheap and flexible
  - use short-term cash surpluses profitably
  - bank frequently
  - operating cash cycle (for a retailer) = length of time from buying stock to receiving cash from debtors less creditors' payment period (in days)
  - transmit cash promptly
- An objective of WC management is to limit the length of the operating cash cycle, subject to any risks that this may cause.

Trade creditors (payables)

- The costs of taking credit include:
  - higher price than purchases for immediate cash settlement
  - administrative costs
  - restrictions imposed by seller.
- The costs of not taking credit include:
  - lost interest-free borrowing
  - lost purchasing power
  - inconvenience – paying at the time of purchase can be inconvenient.
- Practical points on creditor management:
  - establish a policy
  - exploit free credit as far as possible
  - use accounting ratios (for example, average settlement period ratio).

Working capital and the small business

- Small businesses often lack the skills and resources to manage working capital effectively.
- Small businesses often suffer from large businessses delaying payments for goods supplied.
- Changes in the law designed to help small businesses have had limited success.

> → **Key terms**

Working capital   p. 386
Lead time   p. 391
ABC system of stock control   p. 393
Economic order quantity (EOQ)
   p. 393
Materials requirement planning (MRP)
   system   p. 396
Just-in-time (JIT) stock management
   p. 396

Five Cs of credit   p. 398
Cash discount   p. 402
Average settlement period for
   debtors   p. 403
Ageing schedule of debtors   p. 404
Operating cash cycle (OCC)   p. 411
Average settlement period for
   creditors   p. 416

For definitions of these terms see the Glossary, pp. 562–571.

Further reading

If you wish to explore the topics discussed in this chapter in more depth, try the following books:

Business Finance: Theory and practice, *McLaney, E.*, 7th edn, Financial Times Prentice Hall, 2006, chapter 13.

Corporate Finance and Investment, *Pike, R. and Neale, B.*, 4th edn, Prentice Hall International, 2003, chapters 14 and 15.

Corporate Financial Management, *Arnold, G.*, 2nd edn, Financial Times Prentice Hall, 2002, chapter 13.

Financial Management and Decision Making, *Samuels, J., Wilkes, F. and Brayshaw, R.*, International Thomson Business Press, 1999, chapter 18.

Reference

1 **Financial Management and Working Capital Practices in UK SMEs**, *Chittenden, F., Poutziouris, P. and Michaelis, N.*, Manchester Business School, 1998.

REVIEW QUESTIONS

Answers to these questions can be found in Appendix D at the back of the book.

10.1 Tariq is the credit manager of Heltex plc. He is concerned that the pattern of monthly sales receipts shows that credit collection is poor compared with budget. Heltex's sales director believes that Tariq is to blame for this situation, but Tariq insists that he is not. Why might Tariq not be to blame for the deterioration in the credit collection period?

10.2 How might each of the following affect the level of stocks held by a business?

(a) An increase in the number of production bottlenecks experienced by the business.
(b) A rise in the level of interest rates.
(c) A decision to offer customers a narrower range of products in the future.
(d) A switch of suppliers from an overseas business to a local business.
(e) A deterioration in the quality and reliability of bought-in components.

10.3 What are the reasons for holding stocks? Are these reasons different from the reasons for holding cash?

10.4 Identify the costs of holding:

(a) Too little cash
(b) Too much cash.

EXERCISES

Exercises 10.4 to 10.7 are more advanced than 10.1 to 10.3. Those with coloured numbers have answers at the back of the book.

 If you wish to try more exercises, visit the students' side of the Companion Website.

10.1 Hercules Wholesalers Ltd has been particularly concerned with its liquidity position in recent months. The most recent profit and loss account and balance sheet of the business are as follows:

Profit and loss account (income statement) for the year ended 31 December last year

	£000	£000
Sales revenue		452
Less Cost of sales		
Opening stock	125	
Add purchases	341	
	466	
Less Closing stock	143	323
Gross profit		129
Expenses		132
Net loss for the period		(3)

Balance sheet as at 31 December last year

	£000	£000	£000
Non-current assets			
Property, plant and equipment			
Freehold premises at valuation			280
Fixtures and fittings at cost less depreciation			25
Motor vehicles at cost less depreciation			52
			357
Current assets			
Stock (inventory)		143	
Debtors (receivables)		163	
		306	
Less **Current liabilities**			
Trade creditors (payables)	145		
Bank overdraft	140	285	21
			378
Less **Non-current liabilities**			
Loans			120
			258
Equity			
Ordinary share capital			100
Retained profit			158
			258

The debtors and creditors were maintained at a constant level throughout the year.

Required:
(a) Explain why Hercules Wholesalers Ltd is concerned about its liquidity position.
(b) Calculate the operating cash cycle for Hercules Wholesalers Ltd based on the information above. (Assume a 360-day year.)
(c) State what steps may be taken to improve the operating cash cycle of the business.

10.2 International Electric plc at present offers its customers 30 days' credit. Half the customers, by value, pay on time. The other half take an average of 70 days to pay. The business is considering offering a cash discount of 2 per cent to its customers for payment within 30 days.

The credit controller anticipates that half of the customers who now take an average of 70 days to pay (that is, one-quarter of all customers) will pay in 30 days. The other half (the final quarter) will still take an average of 70 days to pay. The scheme will also reduce bad debts by £300,000 a year.

Annual sales revenue of £365 million is made evenly throughout the year. At present the business has a large overdraft (£60 million) with its bank at 12 per cent a year.

Required:
(a) Calculate the approximate equivalent annual percentage cost of a discount of 2 per cent, which reduces the time taken by debtors to pay from 70 days to 30 days. (*Hint*: This part can be answered without reference to the narrative above.)
(b) Calculate debtors outstanding under both the old and new schemes.
(c) How much will the scheme cost the business in discounts?
(d) Should the business go ahead with the scheme? State what other factors, if any, should be taken into account.
(e) Outline the controls and procedures that a business should adopt to manage the level of its debtors.

10.3 The managing director of Sparkrite Ltd, a trading business, has just received summary sets of statements for last year and this year:

Sparkrite Ltd
Profit and loss accounts for years ended 30 September last year and this year

	Last year		This year	
	£000	£000	£000	£000
Sales revenue		1,800		1,920
Less Cost of sales				
Opening stock	160		200	
Purchases	1,120		1,175	
	1,280		1,375	
Less Closing stock	200		250	
		1,080		1,125
Gross profit		720		795
Less Expenses		680		750
Net profit		40		45

Balance sheets as at 30 September last year and this year

	Last year		This year	
	£000	£000	£000	£000
Non-current assets		950		930
Current assets				
Stock (inventory)	200		250	
Debtors (receivables)	375		480	
Bank	4		2	
	579		732	
Less Current liabilities	195		225	
		384		507
		1,334		1,437
Equity				
Fully paid £1 ordinary shares		825		883
Reserves		509		554
		1,334		1,437

The finance director has expressed concern at the increase in stock and debtors levels.

Required:
(a) Show, by using the data given, how you would calculate ratios that could be used to measure stock and debtor levels during last year and this year.
(b) Discuss the ways in which the management of Sparkrite Ltd could exercise control over:
(i) Stock levels
(ii) Debtor levels.

10.4 Your superior, the general manager of Plastics Manufacturers Limited, has recently been talking to the chief buyer of Plastic Toys Limited, which manufactures a wide range of toys for young children. At present, Plastic Toys is considering changing its supplier of plastic granules and has offered to buy its entire requirement of 2,000 kg a month from you at the going market rate, provided that you will grant it three months' credit on its purchases. The following information is available:

1 Plastic granules sell for £10 a kg, variable costs are £7 a kg, and fixed costs £2 a kg.
2 Your own business is financially strong, and has sales revenue of £15 million a year. For the foreseeable future it will have surplus capacity, and it is actively looking for new outlets.
3 Extracts from Plastic Toys' financial statements:

	Year 1 £000	Year 2 £000	Year 3 £000
Sales revenue	800	980	640
Profit before interest and tax	100	110	(150)
Capital employed	600	650	575

	Year 1 £000	Year 2 £000	Year 3 £000
Current assets			
Stocks	200	220	320
Debtors	140	160	160
	340	380	480
Current liabilities			
Creditors	180	190	220
Overdraft	100	150	310
	280	340	530
Net current assets	60	40	(50)

Required:

(a) Write some short notes suggesting sources of information that you would use to assess the creditworthiness of potential customers who are unknown to you. You should critically evaluate each source of information.

(b) Describe the accounting controls that you would use to monitor the level of your business's trade debtors.

(c) Advise your general manager on the acceptability of the proposal. You should give your reasons and do any calculations you consider necessary. (*Hint*: To answer this question you must weigh the costs of administration and cash discounts against the savings in bad debts and interest charges.)

10.5 Mayo Computers Ltd has an annual turnover of £20 million before taking into account bad debts of £0.1 million. All sales made by the business are on credit, and, at present, credit terms are negotiable by the customer. On average, the settlement period for trade debtors is 60 days. Trade debtors are financed by an overdraft bearing a 14 per cent rate of interest per year. The business is currently reviewing its credit policies to see whether more efficient and profitable methods could be employed. Only one proposal has so far been put forward concerning the management of trade credit.

The credit control department has proposed that customers should be given a $2\frac{1}{2}$ per cent discount if they pay within 30 days. For those who do not pay within this period, a maximum of 50 days' credit should be given. The credit department believes that 60 per cent of customers will take advantage of the discount by paying at the end of the discount period, and the remainder will pay at the end of 50 days. The credit department believes that bad debts can be effectively eliminated by adopting the above policies and by employing stricter credit investigation procedures, which will cost an additional £20,000 a year. The credit department is confident that these new policies will not result in any reduction in sales revenue.

Required:

Calculate the net annual cost (savings) to the business of abandoning its existing credit policies and adopting the proposals of the credit control department. (*Hint*: To answer this question you must weigh the costs of administration and cash discounts against the savings in bad debts and interest charges.)

10.6 Boswell Enterprises Ltd is reviewing its trade credit policy. The business, which sells all of its goods on credit, has estimated that sales revenue for the forthcoming year will be £3 million under the existing policy. Thirty per cent of trade debtors are expected to pay one month after being invoiced and 70 per cent are expected to pay two months after being invoiced. These estimates are in line with previous years' figures.

At present, no cash discounts are offered to customers. However, to encourage prompt payment, the business is considering giving a $2\frac{1}{2}$ per cent cash discount to debtors who pay in one month or less. Given this incentive, the business expects 60 per cent of trade debtors to pay one month after being invoiced and 40 per cent of debtors to pay two months after being invoiced. The business believes that the introduction of a cash discount policy will prove attractive to some customers and will lead to a 5 per cent increase in total sales revenue.

Irrespective of the trade credit policy adopted, the gross profit margin of the business will be 20 per cent for the forthcoming year and three months' stock will be held. Fixed monthly expenses of £15,000 and variable expenses (excluding discounts), equivalent to 10 per cent of sales revenue, will be incurred and will be paid one month in arrears. Trade creditors will be paid in arrears and will be equal to two months' cost of sales. The business will hold a fixed cash balance of £140,000 throughout the year, whichever trade credit policy is adopted. No dividends will be proposed or paid during the year.

Ignore taxation.

Required:
(a) Calculate the investment in working capital at the end of the forthcoming year under:
   (i) The existing policy
   (ii) The proposed policy.
   (*Hint*: The investment in working capital will be made up of stock, debtors and cash, *less* trade creditors and any unpaid expenses at the year end.)
(b) Calculate the expected net profit for the forthcoming year under:
   (i) The existing policy
   (ii) The proposed policy.
(c) Advise the business as to whether it should implement the proposed policy.

10.7 Delphi plc has recently decided to enter the expanding market for minidisc players. The business will manufacture the players and sell them to small TV and hi-fi specialists, medium-sized music stores and large retail chain stores. The new product will be launched next February and predicted sales revenue for the product from each customer group for February and the expected rate of growth for subsequent months are as follows:

Customer type	February sales revenue £000	Monthly compound sales revenue growth %	Credit sales months
TV and hi-fi specialists	20	4	1
Music stores	30	6	2
Retail chain stores	40	8	3

The business is concerned about the financing implications of launching the new product, as it is already experiencing liquidity problems. In addition, it is concerned that the credit control department will find it difficult to cope. This is a new market for the business and there are likely to be many new customers who will have to be investigated for creditworthiness.

Workings should be in £000 and calculations made to one decimal place only.

Required:
(a) Prepare an ageing schedule of the monthly debtors balance relating to the new product for each of the first four months of the new product's life, and comment on the results. The schedule should analyse the debts outstanding according to customer type. It should also indicate, for each customer type, the relevant percentage outstanding in relation to the total amount outstanding for each month.
(b) Identify and discuss the factors that should be taken into account when evaluating the creditworthiness of the new business customers.

11

Measuring and managing for shareholder value

LEARNING OUTCOMES

When you have completed this chapter, you should be able to:

- Describe the shareholder value approach and explain its implications for the management of a business.

- Discuss the reasons why new ways of measuring shareholder value are necessary.

- Explain SVA and EVA® and describe their role in measuring and delivering shareholder value.

- Explain MVA and TSR and evaluate their usefulness for investors.

INTRODUCTION

For some years, shareholder value has been a 'hot' issue among managers. Many leading businesses now claim that the quest for shareholder value is the driving force behind their strategic and operational decisions. In this chapter we begin by asking what is meant by the term 'shareholder value', and in the sections that follow, we look at some of the main approaches to measuring shareholder value.

The quest for shareholder value

Let us start by considering what the term **shareholder value** means. In simple terms, it is about putting the needs of shareholders at the heart of management decisions. It is argued that shareholders invest in a business with a view to maximising their financial returns in relation to the risks that they are prepared to take. As managers are appointed by the shareholders to act on their behalf, management decisions and actions should reflect a concern for maximising shareholder returns. Although the business may have other 'stakeholder' groups, such as employees, customers and suppliers, it is the shareholders that should be seen as the most important group.

This, of course, is not a new idea. Take a look at most books on finance or economics, including this one, and you will see that maximising shareholder returns is assumed to be the key objective of a business. However, not everyone accepts this idea. Some believe that a balance must be struck between the competing claims of the various stakeholders. A debate about whether shareholders should be regarded as the most important group is beyond the scope of this chapter. What we can say, however, is that changes in the economic environment over recent years have often forced managers to focus their attention on the needs of shareholders.

In the past, shareholders have been accused of being too passive and of accepting too readily the profits and dividends that managers have delivered. However, this has changed. Nowadays, shareholders are much more assertive and, as owners of the business, are in a position to insist that their needs are given priority. Since the 1980s we have witnessed the deregulation and globalisation of business as well as enormous changes in technology. The effect has been to create a much more competitive world. This has meant not only competition for products and services but also competition for funds. Businesses must now compete more strongly for shareholder funds and so must offer competitive rates of return.

Thus, self-interest may be the most powerful reason for managers to commit themselves to maximising shareholder returns. If they do not do this, there is a real risk that shareholders will either replace them with managers who will, or shareholders will allow the business to be taken over by another business, with managers who are dedicated to maximising shareholder returns.

Creating shareholder value

Creating shareholder value involves a four-stage process. The first stage is to set objectives for the business that recognise the central importance of maximising shareholder returns. This will set a clear direction for the business. The second stage is to establish an appropriate means of measuring the returns, or value, that have been generated for shareholders. For reasons that we shall discuss later, the traditional methods of measuring returns to shareholders are inadequate for this purpose. The third stage is to manage the business in order to ensure that shareholder returns are maximised. This means setting demanding targets and then achieving them through the best possible use of resources, the use of incentive systems and the embedding of a shareholder value culture throughout the business. The final stage is to measure the shareholder returns over a period of time to see whether the objectives have actually been achieved. These stages are set out in Figure 11.1.

| Figure 11.1 | **Creating shareholder value** |

The figure sets out the four-stage process required to create shareholder value.

The need for new forms of measurement

Given a commitment to maximise shareholder returns, an appropriate measure must be selected that will help assess the returns to shareholders over time. It has been argued that the conventional methods for measuring shareholder returns are seriously flawed and so should not be used for this purpose.

Activity 11.1

What are the conventional methods of measuring shareholder returns?

Managers normally use accounting profit or some ratio that is based on accounting profit, such as return on shareholders' funds or earnings per share.

One problem of using accounting profit, or a ratio based on profit, is that profit is measured over a relatively short period of time (usually one year). However, when we talk about maximising shareholder returns, we are concerned with maximising returns over the long term. It has been suggested that using profit as the key measure will run the risk that managers will take decisions that improve performance in the short term but which may have an adverse effect on long-term performance. For example, profits may be increased in the short term by cutting back on staff training and research expenditure. This type of expenditure, however, may be vital to long-term survival.

A second problem that arises with conventional methods of measuring shareholder returns is that risk is ignored. We saw in Chapter 5 that there is a linear relationship between the level of returns achieved and the level of risk that must be taken to achieve those returns. The higher the level of returns required, the higher the level of risk that must be taken to achieve the returns. A management strategy that produces an increase in profits can reduce shareholder value if the increase in profits achieved is not commensurate with the increase in the level of risk. Thus, profit alone is not enough.

A third problem with the use of profit, or a ratio based on profit, is that it does not take account of all of the costs of the capital invested by the business. The conventional approach to measuring profit will deduct the cost of loan capital (that is, interest charges) in arriving at net profit but there is no similar deduction for the cost of shareholder funds. (Remember that dividends are deducted *after* arriving at the net profit figure and represent only part of the total return to shareholders.) Critics of the conventional approach point out that a business will not make a profit, in an economic sense, unless it covers the cost of all capital invested, including shareholder funds. Unless this is done, the business will operate at a loss and so shareholder value will be reduced.

A final problem is that the accounting profit reported by a business can vary according to the particular policies that have been adopted. Some businesses adopt a very conservative approach, which would be reflected in particular accounting policies such as the immediate writing off of intangible assets (for example, research and development and goodwill), the use of the reducing balance method of depreciation (which favours high depreciation charges in the early years), and so on. Businesses that do not adopt conservative accounting policies would report profits more quickly. The writing off of intangible assets over a long period (or perhaps, not writing off intangible assets at all), the use of the straight-line method of depreciation, and so forth, will mean that profits are reported more quickly.

In addition, there are some businesses that may adopt particular accounting policies or structure transactions in a particular way in order to portray a picture of financial health that is in line with what those who prepared the financial statements would like to see rather than what is a true and fair view of financial performance and position. This practice, which we discussed in Chapter 3, is referred to as 'creative accounting' and has been a major problem for accounting rule makers.

Net present value (NPV) analysis

To summarise the points made above, we can say that in order to measure changes in shareholder value, what we really need is a measure that will consider the long term, take account of risk and the cost of shareholders' funds, and will not be affected by accounting policy choices. Fortunately, we have a measure that can, in theory, do just this.

Net present value analysis was discussed in Chapter 4. We saw that if we want to know the net present value (NPV) of an asset (whether this is a physical asset such as a machine or a financial asset such as a share), we must discount the future cash flows generated by the asset over its life. Thus:

$$NPV = C_1 \frac{1}{(1 + r)^1} + C_2 \frac{1}{(1 + r)^2} + C_3 \frac{1}{(1 + r)^3} + \ldots$$

where: C = cash flows at time t (1, 2, 3, . . .)
r = the required rate of return.

Shareholders have a required rate of return and managers must strive to generate long-term cash flows for shares (in the form of dividends or proceeds that investors receive from the sale of the shares) that meet this rate of return. A negative present value will indicate that the cash flows generated do not meet the minimum required rate of return. If a business is to create value for its shareholders, it must generate cash flows that exceed the required returns of shareholders. In other words, the cash flows generated must produce a positive present value.

The NPV method fulfils the criteria that we mentioned earlier for the following reasons:

● It considers the long term. The returns from an investment, such as shares, are considered over the whole of the investment's life.
● It takes account of the cost of capital and risk. Future cash flows are discounted using the required rates of returns from investors (that is, both long-term lenders and shareholders). Moreover, this required rate of return will reflect the level of risk associated with the investment. The higher the level of risk, the higher the required level of return.
● It is not sensitive to the choice of accounting policies. Cash rather than profit is used in the calculations and is a more objective measure of return.

Extending NPV analysis: shareholder value analysis

We know from our earlier study of NPV that, when evaluating an investment project, shareholder wealth will be maximised when the net present value of cash flows generated by the project are maximised. In essence, the business is simply a portfolio of investment projects and so the same principles should apply when considering the business as a whole. **Shareholder value analysis (SVA)** is founded on this basic idea.

The SVA approach involves evaluating strategic decisions according to their ability to maximise value, or wealth, for shareholders. To undertake this evaluation, conventional measures are discarded and replaced by discounted cash flows. We have seen that the net present value of a project represents the value of that particular project. Given that the business can be viewed as a portfolio of projects, the value of the business as a whole can, therefore, be viewed as the net present value of the cash flows that it generates. SVA seeks to measure the discounted cash flows of the business as a whole and then seeks to identify that part which is available to the shareholders.

Activity 11.2

If the net present value of future cash flows generated by the business represents the value of the business as a whole, how can we derive that part of the value of the business that is available to shareholders?

A business will normally be financed by a combination of loan capital and ordinary shareholders' funds. Thus, holders of loan capital will also have a claim on the total value of the business. That part of the total business value that is available to ordinary shareholders can therefore be derived by deducting from the total value of the business (total NPV), the market value of any loans outstanding. Hence:

Shareholder value = Total business value − Market value of outstanding loans

Measuring free cash flows

→ The cash flows used to measure total business value are the **free cash flows**. These are the cash flows generated by the business that are available to ordinary shareholders and long-term lenders. In other words, they are equivalent to the net cash flows from operations after deducting tax paid and cash for additional investment. These free cash flows can be deduced from information contained within the profit and loss account and balance sheet of a business.

It is probably worth going through a simple example to illustrate how the free cash flows can be calculated in practice.

Example 11.1

Sagittarius plc generated sales of £220 million during the year and has an operating profit margin of 25 per cent of sales. Depreciation charges for the year were £8.0 million and the cash tax rate for the year was 20 per cent of operating profit. During the year, £11.3 million was invested in additional working capital and £15.2 million was invested in additional non-current (fixed) assets. A further £8.0 million was invested in the replacement of existing non-current assets.

The free cash flows are calculated as follows:

	£m	£m
Sales		220.0
Operating profit (25% × £220m)		55.0
Add Depreciation charge		8.0
Operating cash flows		63.0
Less Cash tax (20% × £55m)		11.0
Operating cash flows after tax		52.0
Less Additional working capital	11.3	
Additional non-current assets	15.2	
Replacement non-current assets	8.0	34.5
Free cash flows		17.5

We can see from Example 11.1 that, to derive the operating cash flows, the depreciation charge is added back to the operating profit figure. We can also see that the cost of replacement of existing non-current (fixed) assets is deducted from the operating cash flows in order to deduce the free cash flows. When we are trying to predict future free cash flows, one way of arriving at an approximate figure for the cost of replacing existing assets is to assume that the depreciation charge for the year is equivalent to the replacement charge for non-current assets. This would mean that the two adjustments mentioned cancel each other out and the calculation in Example 11.1 could be shortened to:

	£m	£m
Sales		220.0
Operating profit (25% × £220m)		55.0
Less Cash tax (20% × £55m)		11.0
		44.0
Less: Additional working capital	11.3	
Additional non-current assets	15.2	26.5
Free cash flows		17.5

This shortened approach enables us to identify the key variables in determining free cash flows as being:

- sales
- operating profit margin
- cash tax rate
- additional investment in working capital
- additional investment in non-current assets.

Figure 11.2 sets out the process in the form of a flow chart.

The five variables identified are **value drivers** of the business that reflect key business decisions. These decisions convert into free cash flows and finally into shareholder value.

The free cash flows should be measured over the life of the business. However, this is usually a difficult task. To overcome the problem, it is helpful to divide the future cash flows into two elements:

- cash flows over the planning horizon and which may be forecast with a reasonable level of reliability; and
- cash flows occurring beyond the planning horizon, which will be represented by a terminal value.

It is a good idea to try to make the planning horizon as long as possible. This is because the discounting process ensures that values beyond the planning horizon are given little weight. As can be imagined, cash flows in the distant future can be extremely difficult to forecast with accuracy and so the less weight given to them, the better.

Figure 11.2   **Measuring free cash flows**

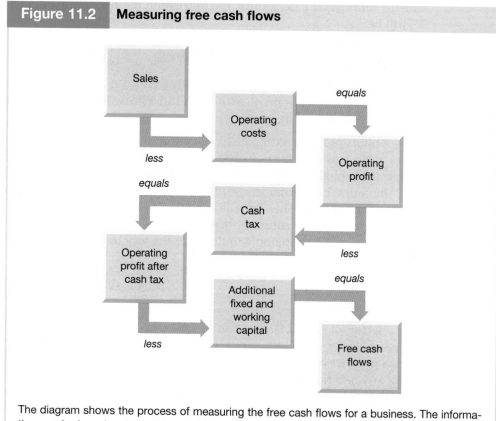

The diagram shows the process of measuring the free cash flows for a business. The information required can be gleaned from the profit and loss account and balance sheet of a business.

Activity 11.3

Libra plc has an estimated terminal value (representing cash flows beyond the planning horizon) of £100 million. What is the present value of this figure assuming a discount rate of 12 per cent and a planning horizon of:

(a) 5 years
(b) 10 years
(c) 15 years?

(You may find it helpful to refer to the discount tables in Appendix A at the end of the text.)

The answers are:

(a) £100m × 0.567 = £56.7m
(b) £100m × 0.322 = £32.2m
(c) £100m × 0.183 = £18.3m

We can see that there is a dramatic difference in the present value of the terminal calculation between the three time horizons, given a 12 per cent discount rate.

To calculate the terminal value of a business, it is usually necessary to make simplifying assumptions. It is beyond the scope of this book to discuss this topic in detail. However, one common assumption is that returns beyond the planning horizon will remain constant (perhaps at the level achieved in the last year of the planning period). Using the formula for a perpetuity, the calculation for determining the terminal value (TV) will be:

$$TV = C_1/r$$

where: C_1 = the free cash flows in the following year
r = the required rate of return from investors (that is, the weighted average cost of capital).

This formula provides a capitalised value for future cash flows. Thus, if an investor receives a constant cash flow of £100 per year and has a required rate of return of 10 per cent, the capitalised value of these cash flows will be £100/0.1 = £1,000. In other words, the future cash flows are worth £1,000, when invested at the required rate of return, to the investor. This formula is similar to the dividend formula, where dividends are assumed to be constant, that we covered in Chapter 8.

Let us go through an example to illustrate the way in which shareholder value can be calculated.

Example 11.2

The directors of United Pharmaceuticals plc are considering the purchase of all the shares in Bortex plc, which produces vitamins and health foods. Bortex plc has a strong presence in the UK and it is expected that the directors of the business will reject any bids that value the shares of the business at less than £11.00 per share.

Bortex plc generated sales for the most recent year end of £3,000 million. Extracts from the balance sheet of the business at the end of the most recent year are as follows:

	£m
Equity	
Share capital £1 ordinary shares	400.0
Reserves	380.0
	780.0
Non-current liabilities	
Loan capital	120.0

Forecasts that have been prepared by the business planning department of Bortex plc are as follows:

- Sales will grow at 10 per cent a year for the next five years.
- The operating profit margin is currently 15 per cent and is likely to be maintained at this rate in the future.
- The cash tax rate is 25 per cent.
- Replacement non-current asset investment (RNCAI) will be in line with the annual depreciation charge each year.
- Additional non-current asset investment (ANCI) over the next five years will be 10 per cent of sales growth.
- Additional working capital investment (AWCI) over the next five years will be 5 per cent of sales growth.

After five years, the sales of the business will stabilise at their Year 5 level.

The business has a cost of capital of 10 per cent and the loan capital figure in the balance sheet reflects its current market value.

The free cash flow calculation will be as follows:

	Year 1 £m	Year 2 £m	Year 3 £m	Year 4 £m	Year 5 £m	After Year 5 £m
Sales	3,300.0	3,630.0	3,993.0	4,392.3	4,831.5	4,831.5
Operating profit (15%)	495.0	544.5	599.0	658.8	724.7	724.7
Less Cash tax (25%)	(123.8)	(136.1)	(149.8)	(164.7)	(181.2)	(181.2)
Operating profit after cash tax	371.2	408.4	449.2	494.1	543.5	543.5
Less						
ANCAI (Note 1)	(30.0)	(33.0)	(36.3)	(39.9)	(43.9)	–
AWCI (Note 2)	(15.0)	(16.5)	(18.2)	(20.0)	(22.0)	–
Free cash flows	326.2	358.9	394.7	434.2	477.6	543.5

Notes

1 The additional non-current asset investment is 10 per cent of sales growth. In the first year, sales growth is £300m (that is, £3,300m – £3,000m). Thus, the investment will be 10% × £300m = £30m. Similar calculations are carried out for the following years.
2 The additional working capital investment is 5 per cent of sales growth. In the first year the investment will be 5% × £300m = £15m. Similar calculations are carried out in following years.

Having derived the free cash flows (FCF), the total business value can be calculated as follows:

Year	FCF £m	Discount rate 10.0%	Present value £m
1	326.2	0.91	296.8
2	358.9	0.83	297.9
3	394.7	0.75	296.0
4	434.2	0.68	295.3
5	477.6	0.62	296.1
Terminal value 543.5/0.10	5,435.0	0.62	3,369.7
Total business value			4,851.8

Activity 11.4

What is the shareholder value figure for the business in Example 11.2? Would the sale of the shares at £11 per share really add value for the shareholders of Bortex plc?

Shareholder value will be the total business value less the market value of the loan capital. Hence, shareholder value is:

	£m
£4,851.8m – £120m	= 4,731.8
The proceeds from the sale of the shares to	
United Pharmaceuticals would yield 400m × £11	= 4,400.0

Thus, from the point of view of the shareholders of Bortex plc, the sale of the business at the share price mentioned, would not increase shareholder value.

Figure 11.3 sets out the key steps in calculating SVA.

Figure 11.3 **Deriving shareholder value**

The figure shows how shareholder value is derived. The five value drivers mentioned earlier – sales, operating profit, cash tax, additional non-current assets and additional working capital – will determine the free cash flows. These cash flows will be discounted using the required rate of return from investors to determine the total value of the business. If we deduct the market value of any loan capital from this figure, we are left with a measure of shareholder value.

Managing the business with shareholder value analysis

We saw earlier that the adoption of SVA indicates a commitment to managing the business in a way that maximises shareholder returns. Those who support this approach argue that SVA can be a powerful tool for strategic planning. For example, SVA can be extremely useful when considering major shifts of direction such as:

● acquiring new businesses
● selling existing businesses
● developing new products or markets
● reorganising or restructuring the business.

This is because SVA takes account of all the elements that determine shareholder value.

To illustrate this point let us suppose that a business develops a new product that is quite different from those within its existing range of products and appeals to a quite different market. Profit forecasts may indicate that the product is likely to be profitable, and so a decision to launch the product may be made. However, this decision may increase the level of risk for the business and, if so, investors will demand higher levels of return. In addition, there may have to be a significant investment in additional non-current assets and working capital in order to undertake the venture. When these factors are taken into account, using the type of analysis shown above, it may be found that the present value of the venture is negative. In other words, shareholder value will be destroyed.

SVA is also useful in focusing attention on the value drivers that create shareholder wealth. For example, we saw earlier that the key variables in determining free cash flows were:

● sales
● operating profit margin
● cash tax rate
● additional investment in working capital
● additional investment in non-current assets.

In order to improve free cash flows and, in turn, shareholder value, management targets can be set for improving performance in relation to each value driver and responsibility assigned for achieving these targets.

Activity 11.5

What do you think are the practical problems of adopting an SVA approach?

Two practical problems spring to mind:

● Forecasting future cash flows lies at the heart of this approach. In practice, forecasting can be difficult and simplifying assumptions will usually have to be made.
● SVA requires more comprehensive information (for example, information concerning the value drivers) than the traditional measures discussed earlier.

You may have thought of other problems.

Implications of SVA

It is worth emphasising that supporters of SVA believe that this measure should replace the traditional accounting measures of value creation such as profit, earnings per share and return on ordinary shareholders' funds. To see whether shareholder value has increased or decreased, we must compare shareholder value at the beginning and the end of a period.

We can see that SVA is a radical departure from the conventional approach to managing a business. It will require different performance indicators, different financial reporting systems, and different management incentive methods. It may also require a change of culture within the business to accommodate the shareholder value philosophy as not all employees may be focused on the need to maximise shareholder wealth.

Economic value added (EVA®)

→ **Economic value added (EVA®)** has been developed and trademarked by a US management consultancy firm, Stern Stewart. However, EVA® is based on the idea of economic profit, which has been around for many years. The measure reflects the point made earlier that for a business to be profitable in an economic sense, it must generate returns that exceed the required returns from investors. It is not enough simply to make an accounting profit because this measure does not take full account of the returns required from investors.

EVA® indicates whether the returns generated exceed the required returns from investors. The formula is as follows:

$$EVA® = NOPAT - (R \times C)$$

where: NOPAT = net operating profit after tax

R = required returns from investors (that is, the weighted average cost of capital)

C = capital invested (that is, the net assets of the business).

Only when EVA® is positive can we say that the business is increasing shareholder wealth. To maximise shareholder wealth, managers must increase EVA® by as much as possible.

Activity 11.6

What can managers do in order to increase EVA®? (*Hint:* Use the formula shown above as your starting point.)

The formula suggests that in order to increase EVA®, managers may try the following tactics:

● Increase NOPAT. This may be done by either reducing expenses or by increasing sales.

- Use capital invested more efficiently. This means selling off assets that are not generating returns that exceed their cost and investing in assets that do.
- Reduce the required rates of return for investors. This may be achieved by changing the capital structure in favour of loan capital (which is cheaper to service than share capital). This strategy, however, can create problems, as discussed in Chapter 8.

EVA® relies on conventional financial statements to measure the wealth created for shareholders. However, the NOPAT and capital figures shown on these statements are used only as a starting point. They have to be adjusted because of the problems and limitations of conventional measures. According to Stern Stewart, the major problem is that profit and capital are understated because of the conservative bias in accounting measurement. Profit is understated as a result of arbitrary write-offs such as goodwill written off or research and development expenditure written off and also as a result of excessive provisions being created (such as a provision for doubtful debts). Capital is also understated because assets are reported at their original cost (less amounts written off), which can produce figures considerably below current market values. In addition, certain assets such as internally generated goodwill and brand names are omitted from the financial statements because no external transactions have occurred.

Stern Stewart has identified more than 100 adjustments that could be made to the conventional financial statements to eliminate the conservative bias. However, the firm believes that, in practice, only a handful of adjustments are probably needed to the accounting figures of any particular business. Unless an adjustment is going to have a significant effect on the calculation of EVA®, it is really not worth making. The adjustments made should reflect the nature of the particular business. Each business is unique and so must customise the calculation of EVA® to its particular circumstances. (This aspect of EVA® can be seen as either indicating flexibility or as being open to manipulation depending on whether you support this measure.)

The most common adjustments that have to be made are as follows:

- *Research and development (R&D) costs and marketing costs.* These costs should be written off over the period that they benefit. In practice, however, they are often written off in the period in which they are incurred. This means that any amounts written off immediately should be added back to the assets on the balance sheet, thereby increasing invested capital, and then written off over time.
- *Goodwill.* In theory, goodwill should receive the same treatment as R&D and marketing costs. However, Stern Stewart suggests leaving goodwill on the balance sheet. One argument in favour of this treatment is that goodwill is really a 'catch-all' that includes intangible items such as brand names and reputation that have potentially infinite lives. Thus, any amounts written off should be added back to assets.
- *Restructuring costs.* This item can be viewed as an investment in the future rather than an expense to be written off. Supporters of EVA® argue that by restructuring, the business is better placed to meet future challenges and so any amounts incurred should be added back to assets.
- *Marketable investments.* Investment in shares and loan capital are not included as part of the capital invested in the business. This is because the income from marketable investments is not included in the calculation of operating profit. (Income from this source will be added in the profit and loss account *after* operating profit has been calculated.)

Let us now consider a simple example to show how EVA® may be calculated.

Example 11.3

Scorpio plc was established two years ago and has produced the following balance sheet and profit and loss account at the end of the second year of trading.

Balance sheet as at the end of the second year

	£m	£m	£m
Non-current assets			
Goodwill		24.0	
Plant and equipment		56.0	
Motor vehicles		12.4	
Marketable investments		6.6	99.0
Current assets			
Stock (inventory)		34.5	
Debtors (receivables)		29.3	
Cash		2.1	
		65.9	
Current liabilities			
Trade creditors (payables)	30.3		
Taxation	0.9	31.2	34.7
			133.7
Non-current liabilities			
Loan capital			50.0
			83.7
Equity			
Share capital			60.0
Reserves			23.7
			83.7

Profit and loss account (income statement) for the second year

	£m	£m
Sales revenue		148.6
Cost of sales		76.2
Gross profit		72.4
Wages	24.5	
Depreciation of plant and equipment	8.8	
Goodwill written off	4.0	
Marketing costs	22.5	
Provision for doubtful debts	4.5	64.3
Operating profit		8.1
Income from investments		0.4
		8.5
Interest payable		0.5
Ordinary profit before taxation		8.0
Restructuring costs		2.0
Profit before taxation		6.0
Corporation tax		1.8
Profit after taxation		4.2

Discussions with the finance director reveal the following:

1 Goodwill was purchased during the first year of trading when another business was acquired. The goodwill cost £32.0 million and this amount is being written off over an eight-year period (starting in the first year of the business).

2 Marketing costs relate to the launch of a new product. The benefits of the marketing campaign are expected to last for three years (including this most recent year).

3 The provision for doubtful debts was created this year and the amount of the provision is very high. A more realistic figure for the provision would be £2.0 million.

4 Restructuring costs were incurred as a result of a collapse in a particular product market. By restructuring the business, benefits are expected to flow for an infinite period.

5 The business has a 10 per cent required rate of return for investors.

The first step in calculating EVA® is to adjust the net operating profit after tax to take account of the various points revealed from the discussion with the finance director. The revised figure is calculated as follows:

NOPAT adjustment

	£m	£m
Operating profit		8.1
Less Corporation tax		1.8
		6.3

EVA® adjustments (to be added back to profit)

Goodwill	4.0	
Marketing costs (2/3 × 22.5)	15.0	
Excess provision	2.5	21.5
Adjusted NOPAT		27.8

The next step is to adjust the net assets (as represented by equity and loan capital) to take account of the points revealed.

Adjusted net assets (or capital invested)

	£m	£m
Net assets per balance sheet		133.7
Add Goodwill adjustment (Note 1)	8.0	
Marketing costs (Note 2)	15.0	
Provision for doubtful debts	2.5	
Restructuring costs (Note 3)	2.0	27.5
		161.2
Less Marketable investments (Note 4)		6.6
Adjusted net assets		154.6

Notes

1 The goodwill adjustment takes account of the fact that there was a £4.0 million write-off in both Years 1 and 2.

2 The marketing costs represent two years' benefits added back (2/3 × £22.5m).

3 The restructuring costs are added back to the net assets as they provide benefits over an infinite period. (Note they were not added back to the operating profit as these costs were deducted *after* arriving at operating profit in the profit and loss account.)

4 The marketable investments do not form part of the operating assets of the business and the income from these investments is not part of the operating income.

Activity 11.7

What is the EVA® for the second year of the business in Example 11.3?

EVA® can be calculated as follows:

$$EVA® = NOPAT - (R \times C) = £27.8m - (10\% \times £154.6m)$$
$$= \underline{£12.3m} \text{ (to one decimal place)}$$

We can see that EVA® is positive and so the business increased shareholder wealth during the year.

The main advantage of this measure is the discipline to which managers are subjected as a result of the charge for capital that has been invested. Before any increase in shareholder wealth can be recognised, an appropriate deduction is made for the use of business resources. Thus, EVA® encourages managers to use these resources efficiently. Where managers are focused simply on increasing profits, there is a danger that the resources used to achieve any increase in profits will not be taken into proper account. **Real World 11.1** provides an example of one business that is using EVA® to help managers refocus.

REAL WORLD 11.1

VW changes gear   **FT**

Volkswagen, Europe's biggest carmaker, is shaking up executive pay in an attempt to make managers more cautious about investment and increase loyalty to the group rather than the seven individual brands.

VW will base up to 40 per cent of this year's bonus on returns above the cost of capital, a big step in an industry renowned for destroying capital – and a move that is likely to lead to a lower payout.

The switch to economic value added measures to determine pay is part of an attempt by Bernd Pischetsrieder, chief executive, and Hans Dieter Pötsch, incoming finance director, to make managers think harder before making investments.

The company has abandoned return on sales targets in favour of measuring return on invested capital. It is also clamping down on investment and research spending, widely seen as out of control.

'People will understand that this is probably the main driver to end up with a higher bonus,' Mr Pötsch told the Financial Times. 'We think it will be a good motivator.'

In addition to EVA, the bonus structure adds group performance measures to the individual and brand measures used in an attempt to make the brands work with each other, rather than competing.

The system is being introduced this year, although the poor performance of the company – which saw operating profits fall severely in the first six months of this year – means the first bonus will be small.

All managers have been on a course on EVA, a measure created by Stern Stewart, the management consultants. The idea of EVA is to gauge return on investment above the cost of raising the capital to fund it.

VW made a return on invested capital of 7.4 per cent last year, below its 7.7 per cent cost of capital – equivalent to destroying €134m ($147m) of value.

Source: 'VW to alter management focus', www.FT.com, 31 August 2003.

EVA® and SVA compared

Although at first glance it may appear that EVA® and SVA are worlds apart, this is not the case. In fact the opposite is true. EVA® and SVA are closely related and, in theory at least, should produce the same figure for shareholder value. The way in which shareholder value is calculated using SVA has already been described. The EVA® approach to calculating shareholder value adds the capital invested to the present value of future EVA® flows and then deducts the market value of any loan capital. Figure 11.4 illustrates the two approaches to determining shareholder value.

Figure 11.4   Two approaches to determining shareholder value

The figure shows how EVA® and SVA can both provide a measure of shareholder value. Total business value can be derived either by discounting the free cash flows over time or by discounting the EVA® flows over time and adding the capital invested. Whichever approach is used, the market value of loan capital must then be deducted to derive shareholder value.

Let us go through a simple example to illustrate this point.

Example 11.4

Leo Ltd has just been formed and has been financed by a £20 million issue of share capital and a £10 million issue of loan capital. The proceeds of the issue have been invested in non-current (fixed) assets with a life of three years and during this period these assets will depreciate by £10 million per year. The operating profit after tax is expected to be £15 million each year. There will be no replacement of non-current assets during the three-year period and no investment in working capital. At the end of the three years, the business will be wound up and the non-current assets will have no residual value.

The required rate of return by investors is 10 per cent.

Example 11.4 continued

The SVA approach to determining shareholder value will be as follows:

Year	FCF	Discount rate	Present value
	£m	10%	£m
1	25.0*	0.91	22.8
2	25.0	0.83	20.7
3	25.0	0.75	18.7
		Total business value	62.2
		Less Loan capital	10.0
		Shareholder value	52.2

* The free cash flows will be the operating profit after tax *plus* the depreciation charge (that is, £15m + £10m). In this case, there are no replacement non-current assets against which the depreciation charge can be netted off. It must therefore be added back.

The EVA® approach to determining shareholder value will be as follows:

Year	Opening capital invested (C)	Capital charge (10% × C)	Operating profit after tax	EVA®	Discount rate 10%	Present value of EVA®
	£m	£m	£m	£m		£m
1	30.0*	3.0	15.0	12.0	0.91	10.9
2	20.0	2.0	15.0	13.0	0.83	10.8
3	10.0	1.0	15.0	14.0	0.75	10.5
						32.2
				Opening capital		30.0
						62.2
				Less Loan capital		10.0
				Shareholder value		52.2

* The capital invested decreases each year by the depreciation charge (that is, £10 million).

EVA® or SVA?

Although both EVA® and SVA are consistent with the objective of maximising shareholder wealth and, in theory, should produce the same decisions and results, the supporters of EVA® claim that this measure has a number of practical advantages over SVA. One such advantage is that EVA® sits more comfortably with the conventional financial reporting systems and financial reports. There is no need to develop entirely new systems to implement EVA® as it can be calculated by making a few adjustments to the conventional profit and loss accounts and balance sheets.

It is also claimed that EVA® is more useful as a basis for rewarding managers. Both EVA® and SVA support the idea that management rewards be linked to increases in shareholder value. This should ensure that the interests of managers are closely aligned to the interests of shareholders. Under the SVA approach, management rewards will be determined on the basis of the contribution made to the generation of long-term cash flows. However, there are practical problems in using SVA for this purpose.

Activity 11.8

What are the practical problems that may arise when using SVA calculations to reward managers? (*Hint*: Think about how SVA is calculated.)

The SVA approach measures changes in shareholder value by reference to predicted changes in future cash flows and it is unwise to pay managers on the basis of predicted rather than actual achievements. If the predictions are optimistic, the effect will be that the business rewards optimism rather than real achievement. There is also a risk that unscrupulous managers will manipulate predicted future cash flows in order to increase their rewards.

Under EVA®, managers can receive bonuses based on actual achievement during a particular period. If management rewards are linked to a single period, however, there is a danger that managers will place undue attention to increasing EVA® during this period rather than over the long term. The objective should be to maximise EVA® over the longer term. Where a business has a stable level of sales, operating assets and borrowing, a current-period focus is likely to be less of a problem than where these elements are unstable over time. A stable pattern of operations minimises the risk that improvements in EVA® during the current period are achieved at the expense of future periods. Nevertheless, any reward system for managers must encourage a long-term perspective and so rewards should be based on the ability of managers to improve EVA® over a number of years rather than a single year.

Real World 11.2 describes the way in which one business uses EVA® to reward its managers.

REAL WORLD 11.2

Rewarding managers

Hanson PLC, a major supplier of heavy building materials, adopts a bonus system for its directors based on EVA®. EVA® generated is accumulated in a 'bonus bank' and the directors are paid a portion of the EVA® bonus bank during a particular year; the remainder is carried forward for payment in future years. The following is an extract from the 2004 Annual Report and Form 20-F of the business:

Annual bonus scheme
The annual bonus scheme for the Executive Directors and other senior executives is aligned with changes in shareholder value through the economic value added methodology. The main principle of economic value added is to recognise that over time a company should generate returns in excess of its operating costs and the cost of capital – the return that lenders and shareholders expect of the Company each year.

The annual bonus scheme is calibrated by reference to target levels of bonus. Each year the participant receives one-third of an accumulated bonus bank, which is updated for the year's performance compared to target. The bonus bank has two main functions; firstly it ensures that individuals do not make short-term decisions such as deferring essential expenditure from one year to the next and receive a bonus for doing so; and secondly, the bonus bank can act as a retention tool.

Source: Hanson PLC Annual Report and Form 20-F 2004.

It is worth noting that Stern Stewart believes that bonuses, calculated as a percentage of EVA®, should form a very large part of the total remuneration package for managers. Thus, the higher the EVA® figure, the higher the rewards to managers – with no upper limits. The philosophy is that EVA® should make managers wealthy provided it makes shareholders extremely wealthy. A bonus system should encompass as many managers as possible in order to encourage a widespread commitment to implementing EVA®.

EVA® in practice

Real World 11.3 contains some advice on how to implement EVA®.

REAL WORLD 11.3

The thoughts of Robert Goizueto

Robert Goizueto was the chief executive of Coca-Cola Co. for many years and was an ardent supporter of EVA®. He offered two pieces of advice for those wishing to implement this technique:

● *Keep it simple.*   By this he meant that EVA® should be the only method of value measurement used by managers. To do otherwise would lessen the impact of EVA® and would also make the management of the business unnecessarily complicated.
● *Make it accountable.*   By this he meant that managers should be rewarded for increasing EVA®. In this way, the managers' own interests become indistinguishable from those of the owners of the business.

Source: see *EVA: The real key to creating wealth*, A. Ehrbar, John Wiley, 1998.

Real World 11.4 gives some indication of the extent of the usage of value-based management (of which SVA and EVA® are examples) in the USA.

REAL WORLD 11.4

The extent of the use of value-based management in practice

A survey of US businesses, conducted in 2003, revealed that 52 per cent use value-based management, with a further 40 per cent considering using this approach in the future.

Source: 2003 Survey of Management, Ernst and Young, 2003.

Market value added (MVA)

Stern Stewart developed EVA® to provide a means of motivating managers and other employees to achieving shareholder value. It is really designed for internal management purposes. However, a further measure has been developed by the same management consultants to complement EVA® and to provide shareholders with a way of tracking changes in shareholder value over time. **Market value added (MVA)** attempts to measure the gains or losses in shareholder value by measuring the difference between the market value of the business and the total investment that has been made in it over the years. The market value of the business is usually taken to be the market value of shares and loan capital. The total investment is the long-term capital invested, which is made up of loan capital plus share capital plus retained earnings. Figure 11.5 illustrates the derivation of market value added.

Figure 11.5	Market value added (MVA)

This figure shows how market value added represents the difference between the total market value (loan capital plus share capital) and the total amount invested in the business.

It is worth going through a simple example to show how market value can be calculated.

Example 11.5

Cosmo plc began trading ten years ago. It has 2 million £1 ordinary shares in issue that have a current market value of £5 per share. These shares were issued at their nominal value when the business was founded. The business also has £6 million 10 per cent loan capital. The book value of the loan capital is the same as its current market value. In addition the business has retained earnings of £3 million.

The market value added can be calculated as follows:

	£m	£m
Market value of investments		
Ordinary shares (2m × £5)		10
Loan capital		6
		16
Total amount invested		
Ordinary shares (2m × £1)	2	
Retained earnings	3	
Loan capital	6	11
Market value added		5

We can see that market valued added is, in essence, a very simple idea. The cash value of the investment is compared with the cash invested. If the cash value of the investment is more than the cash invested, there has been an increase in shareholder value. If the cash value of the investment is less than the cash invested, there has been a decrease in shareholder value. There are, however, complications in measuring the figure for cash invested, which arises because of the conservative bias in accounting measurement. Thus, the adjustments to the balance sheet that are necessary for the proper calculation of EVA® are also required when measuring MVA.

The measurement of the cash value of capital invested is straightforward. The market value of each share is simply multiplied by the number of shares in issue in order to derive the total market value of the shares. If shares are not listed on the stock exchange it is not really possible to measure MVA, unless perhaps a bid for the business has been received from a possible buyer.

In Example 11.5, it was assumed that the market value and book value of loan capital are the same. This is a common assumption used in practice, and where this assumption is made, the calculation of MVA reduces to the difference between the market value of shares and the sum of the nominal value of those shares and retained earnings. Thus, in the example, MVA is simply the difference between £10m and £5m (£2m + £3m) = £5m.

In the example, we calculated MVA over the whole life of the business. The problem with doing this, in the case of an established business, is that it would not be clear when the value was actually created. The pattern of value creation over time may be useful in the assessment of past and likely future performance. It is perfectly feasible, however, to measure the change in MVA over any period by comparing the opening and closing positions for that period.

The link between MVA and EVA®

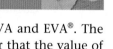

Stern Stewart argues that there is a strong relationship between MVA and EVA®. The theoretical underpinning of this relationship is clear. We saw earlier that the value of a business is equal to the present value of future expected EVA® plus the capital invested. Thus:

$$\text{Business value} = \text{Capital invested} + \text{PV of future EVA}®$$

This equation could be rearranged so that:

$$\text{PV of future EVA}® = \text{Business value} - \text{Capital invested} \tag{11.1}$$

We have also seen that market value added is the difference between the value of the business and the capital invested. Thus:

$$\text{MVA} = \text{Business value} - \text{Capital invested} \tag{11.2}$$

By comparing equations (11.1) and (11.2) we can see that:

$$\textbf{PV of future EVA}® = \textbf{MVA}$$

Stern Stewart states that the relationship described holds in practice as well as in theory. The firm has produced evidence to show that the correlation between MVA and EVA® is much stronger than the correlation between MVA and other measures of performance such as earnings per share, return on shareholders' funds, or cash flows.

Given that MVA reflects the expected future EVA® of a business, it follows that an investor using this measure will be able to see whether a business generates returns above the cost of capital invested. If a business only manages to provide returns in line with the cost of capital, the EVA® will be zero and so there will be no MVA. Thus, MVA can be used to impose a capital discipline on managers in the same way that EVA® does.

Limitations of MVA

MVA has a number of limitations as a tool for investors. To begin with, it has a fairly narrow scope. As mentioned earlier, MVA relies on market share prices and so it can only really be calculated for those businesses that are listed on a stock exchange. Similarly, MVA can only be used to assess the business as a whole as there are no separate market share prices available for strategic business units.

The interpretation of MVA can also be a problem. It is a measure of the absolute change occurring over time and so its significance is difficult to assess when deciding among competing investment opportunities involving businesses of different sizes or trading over different periods. Consider the following financial information relating to three separate businesses:

Business	Total market value (a) £m	Total capital invested (b) £m	Market value added (a) − (b) £m	No. of years trading
Alpha	250	120	130	18
Beta	480	350	130	16
Gamma	800	670	130	15

The table shows that each business has an identical MVA; but does this mean that each business has performed equally well? We can see that they operate with different amounts of capital invested and have operated over different periods.

The problems identified are not insurmountable but they reveal the difficulties of relying on an absolute measure when making investment decisions.

Activity 11.9

How could the problems of interpretation mentioned above be overcome?

The problem of the different time periods is probably best dealt with by comparing the businesses over the same time period. The problem of scale is probably best dealt with by comparing the MVA for each business with the capital invested in the business. (MVA/Capital provides a relative measure of wealth creation for investors.)

Real World 11.5 shows the MVA and EVA® measures for some well-known US businesses.

REAL WORLD 11.5

Has value been added?

Stern Stewart publishes an annual list of large US businesses, ranked according to their MVA. Information relating to some well-known businesses included on the list for 2002 is set out below.

Company	MVA	EVA®	Return on capital* %
Microsoft Corp.	212,340	2,201	22.0
Intl Business Machine Corp.	90,422	(8,032)	3.7
Exxon Mobil Corp.	85,108	(2,175)	6.6
Coca-Cola Co.	82,413	2,496	17.3
Intel Corp.	77,395	(3,736)	6.2
Dell Computer Corp.	69,425	360	17.4

* Calculated by dividing NOPAT by average capital employed

It is interesting to note that, in three cases the EVA® measure revealed a significant loss in shareholder value during 2002. However, the return on capital for each of these businesses was positive. This apparent anomaly can be explained by the fact that EVA® takes account of the required returns from shareholders, which incorporate risk.

Source: Adapted from 2002 EVA/MVA Annual Ranking Database, www.eva.com. Copyright © Stern Stewart & Co.

The most successful businesses at generating MVA are also the largest. Because MVA is an absolute measure of performance, large businesses have a greater potential to generate MVA. However, they also have a greater potential to destroy MVA.

Self-assessment question 11.1

Cupid plc produced the following balance sheet at the end of the third year of trading:

Balance sheet as at the end of the third year

	£m	£m	£m
Non-current assets			
Freehold land		60.0	
Computing equipment		90.0	
Motor vehicles		22.0	172.0
Current assets			
Stock (inventory)		39.0	
Debtors (receivables)		53.0	
Cash		12.0	
		104.0	

	£m	£m	£m
Current liabilities			
Trade creditors (payables)		45.0	59.0
			231.0
Non-current liabilities			
Loan capital			90.0
			141.0
Equity			
£1 ordinary shares			60.0
Reserves			81.0
			141.0

An analysis of the underlying records reveals the following:

1 Goodwill was purchased during the first year of trading when an existing business was acquired. The goodwill cost £50 million and this amount was immediately written off.

2 R&D costs relating to the development of a new product in the current year had been written off at a cost of £10 million. However, this is a prudent approach and the benefits are expected to last for ten years.

3 Freehold property has a current value of £200 million.

4 The current market value of an ordinary share is £8.50.

5 The book value of the loan capital reflects its current market value.

Required:
Calculate the MVA for the business over its period of trading.

Total shareholder return

→ **Total shareholder return (TSR)** has been used for many years by investors as a means of assessing value created and is often used as a basis for management reward systems. The total return from a share is made up of two elements: the increase (or decrease) in share value over a period plus (minus) any dividends paid during the period. To illustrate how total shareholder return is calculated, let us assume that a business commenced trading by issuing shares of £0.50 each at their nominal value (P_0) and by the end of the first year of trading the shares had increased in value to £0.55 (P_1). Furthermore, the business paid a dividend of £0.06 (D_1) per share during the period. We can calculate the total shareholder return as follows:

$$\text{Total shareholder return} = \frac{D_1 + (P_1 - P_0)}{P_0} \times 100\%$$

$$= \frac{0.06 + (0.55 - 0.50)}{0.50} \times 100\%$$

$$= 22\%$$

The figure calculated has little information value when taken alone. It can only really be used to assess performance when compared with some benchmark.

Activity 11.10

What benchmark would be most suitable?

Perhaps the best benchmark to use would be the returns made by similar businesses operating in the same industry over the same period of time.

The reason that a benchmark using the returns of similar businesses is usually suitable is because it will compare the returns generated by the business with those generated from other investment opportunities that have the same level of risk. We have seen in earlier chapters that the level of return from an investment should always be related to the level of risk that has to be taken.

TSR in practice

Real World 11.6 provides an example of a business that sets a target TSR in relation to other, broadly similar, businesses.

REAL WORLD 11.6

Setting a target TSR

Unilever plc is a leading consumer goods business selling well-known brands of washing powder, toothpaste, creams, oils and so on. The business calculates TSR over a three-year rolling period and states:

> The target for the business is to be in the top third of a reference group of 21 international consumer goods companies on a three-year rolling basis.

During 2002 it was positioned twelfth within its peer group but rose to sixth during 2003, thereby achieving its target.

Source: www.unilever.com

Many large businesses now publish total shareholder returns in their annual reports. **Real World 11.7** provides an example.

REAL WORLD 11.7

Tesco's TSR

Tesco plc, a major food retailer, publishes its TSR for a five-year period, along with movements in the FTSE 100 index for the same period. The TSR for the business, which is displayed graphically, is reproduced in Figure 11.6.

Source: Tesco plc Annual Report and Financial Statements 2004.

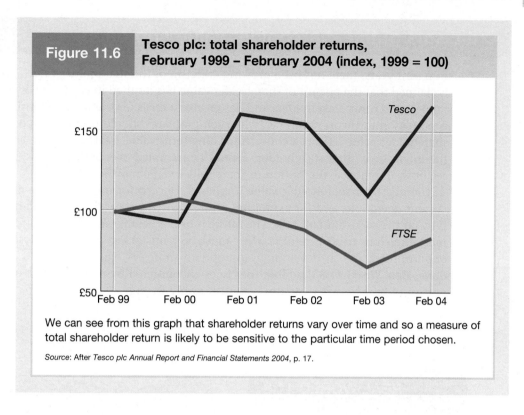

Figure 11.6   **Tesco plc: total shareholder returns, February 1999 – February 2004 (index, 1999 = 100)**

We can see from this graph that shareholder returns vary over time and so a measure of total shareholder return is likely to be sensitive to the particular time period chosen.

Source: After Tesco plc Annual Report and Financial Statements 2004, p. 17.

TSR and managers' rewards

Where TSR is to be used as a basis for management reward, the issue of risk is very important. Higher returns can be achieved by taking on higher risk projects. Managers should not be given rewards for increasing returns through this means.

Figure 11.7 sets out the main value measures that we have discussed in this chapter.

Figure 11.7   **The main value measures**

The figure above shows the main value measures discussed in this chapter. SVA and EVA® are primarily for internal management use, and TSR and MVA are primarily for use by investors.

Criticisms of the shareholder value approach

In recent years, there has been growing criticism of the shareholder value approach. It is claimed that the pursuit of shareholder value has resulted in conflicts between shareholders and other stakeholders and has created a crisis for the world of business. There is no reason in theory, however, why such problems should occur. We have seen that shareholder value reflects a concern for long-term value creation, and to achieve this, the interests of other stakeholders cannot be trampled over. Nevertheless, it is easy to see how, in practice, the notion of shareholder value may be corrupted.

The quest for shareholder value implies a concern for improving the efficiency of current operations and for exploiting future growth opportunities. The latter of these is by far the more difficult task. The future is unpredictable and risks abound. Managers must therefore tread carefully. They must be painstaking in their analysis of future opportunities and in developing appropriate strategies. However, this is not always done. **Real World 11.8** describes the issues encountered by mobile phone operators in pursuit of growth and why things went horribly wrong.

REAL WORLD 11.8

Future imperfect

Telecoms companies adopted a vision of future customers using mobile phones as the medium of choice for internet use, picture and video exchange, game and music downloads and other applications, enabled by G3 technology. There was little in the way of detailed research or planning to support this vision.

Which customers would use these services? What would they pay? How quickly would present generation technology fade? Without strongly worked-out growth strategies, they accepted, in line with investor pressure, the fashionable belief of massive uptake of G3 services. A poorly detailed vision gave them little support to evaluate an expensive investment in G3. It led them to grossly overvalue G3 licences and ultimately to destroy large portions of shareholder value.

Source: 'Companies must achieve the right balance for a successful strategy', *Financial News*, 22 February 2004.

Given the problems of exploiting future growth opportunities, managers may prefer to focus on improving efficiency. This is usually achieved by bearing down on costs through working assets harder, shedding staff and putting pressure on suppliers to lower prices. If, however, these cost reduction measures are taken too far, the result will be an emaciated business which is unable to take advantage of future growth opportunities and which has its major stakeholder groups locked in conflict.

To be successful, the shareholder value approach must strike the right balance between a concern for efficiency and a concern for future growth; a concern for efficiency alone is not enough. In order to achieve this balance, the way in which managers are assessed and rewarded must reflect the importance of both.

Measuring the value of future growth

If managers are to be assessed and rewarded, at least in part, on the basis of developing future growth potential, a suitable measure of this potential is required. According to Stern Stewart, the EVA® approach can provide such a measure.

We saw earlier that the value of a business can be described as:

$$\text{Business value} = \text{Capital invested} + \text{PV of future EVA}^\circledR$$

If a business has no growth potential and EVA® remains constant, we can use the formula for a perpetuity, so that the present value of future EVA® is:

$$\text{PV of future EVA}^\circledR = \frac{\text{EVA}^\circledR}{r}$$

where: r = required returns from investors (that is, the weighted average cost of capital). Thus, the value of a business with no growth potential is:

$$\text{Business value} = \text{Capital invested} + \frac{\text{EVA}^\circledR}{r}$$

Where the business has growth potential (as measured by growth in EVA®), business value (as measured by the market value of share and loan capital), will be greater than this. The value placed on future growth potential by investors is, therefore:

$$\frac{\text{Value of future}}{\text{growth potential}} = \frac{\text{Business}}{\text{value}} - \left(\text{Capital invested} + \frac{\text{EVA}^\circledR}{r} \right)$$

Stern Stewart refers to the above value as **future growth value (FGV®)**, and by using this measure periodically we can see whether managers are creating or destroying future value.

The percentage contribution to the value of the business arising from investor expectations concerning future growth in EVA® is:

$$\text{Percentage contribution to business value} = \left(\frac{\text{FGV}^\circledR}{\text{Business value}} \right) \times 100\%$$

This measure can be used to see whether managers are striking the right balance between efficiency and future growth.

Activity 11.11

Centaur plc has 5 million shares in issue with a market value of £8.40 per share. The company has £14.2 million capital invested and for the most recent year, EVA® was £1.8 million. The required return from investors is 10 per cent a year.

What is the percentage contribution to the market value of the business arising from future growth?

Activity 11.11 continued

$$\text{Assuming no growth, PV of future EVA}^® = \frac{\text{EVA}^®}{r}$$

$$= \frac{£1.8m}{0.10}$$

$$= £18.0m$$

$$\text{Value of future growth potential (FGV}^®) = \text{Business value} - \left(\text{Capital invested} + \frac{\text{EVA}^®}{r}\right)$$

$$= (5m \times £8.40) - (£14.2m + £18.0m)$$

$$= £9.8m$$

$$\text{Percentage contribution to business value} = \left(\frac{\text{FGV}^®}{\text{Business value}}\right) \times 100\%$$

$$= \frac{£9.8m}{5m \times £8.40} \times 100\%$$

$$= 23.3\%$$

Implementing the shareholder value approach

We have seen above that shareholder value may not always be implemented properly within a business. **Real World 11.9** sets out four different levels of implementation of shareholder value that may be found in practice, using an analogy of mobility to describe each level.

REAL WORLD 11.9

Walking the talk

The extent to which businesses implement a fully developed shareholder value approach can be described in terms of four distinct levels.

Level 1. Sitting

At the lowest level, shareholder value is embraced as a slogan and only as a slogan. Shareholder value appears in the company's mission statement, its investor communications or its managerial lexicon. Existing cost-cutting programmes may be relabelled as shareholder value initiatives. Nothing concrete is done to promote actual value gain.

Level 2. Hopping

Shareholder value is adopted with an exclusive emphasis on efficiency. The programme is formally communicated within the firm, organisational structures such as shareholder value committees and champions are created, shareholder value metrics such as EVA are introduced and used to measure the performance of divisions, departments and projects. The rewards of at least the senior management are tied in some way to the achievement of shareholder value targets.

Level 3. Shuffling

The two legs of shareholder value are recognised in principle by the statement of a growth vision or mission alongside the focus on efficiency. However, the use of the growth strategy is limited to communicating to investors that the firm is adopting fashionable strategies – we will focus on our core business and grow it organically and through overseas acquisitions. It is not 'lived' inside the company – if a value-creating opportunity is spotted that is at odds with the stated strategy, it will nevertheless be pursued.

Managers are judged by today's value created and not by how they prepare the stage for tomorrow's growth. The growth vision is not deep rooted and [is] likely to be abandoned under external pressure, such as investor desire to see a move into internet-related business.

Level 4. Marching

Both legs of shareholder value are adopted and implemented. A clear growth strategy is developed and used as the template for future investments. The growth strategy is communicated and sold to investors. The strategy is stuck to even under pressure. Metrics and rewards are instituted around both the attainment of efficiency improvements and the attainment of growth strategy goals. The growth strategy is owned and lived throughout the organisation.

Source: 'Companies must achieve the right balance for a successful strategy', *Financial News*, 22 February 2004.

SUMMARY

The main points in this chapter may be summarised as follows:

Shareholder value

- Means putting shareholders' interests at the heart of management decisions.
- To create shareholder value, the objectives of the business must reflect a concern for shareholder value, there must be appropriate methods of measurement, the business must be managed to create shareholder value and there must be periodic assessment of whether shareholder value has been achieved.

Measuring shareholder value – internal (management) measures

- Conventional forms of accounting measurement are inadequate – they focus on the short term, ignore risk, fail to take proper account of the cost of capital invested and are influenced by accounting methods employed.
- Two main approaches used to measure shareholder value: shareholder value analysis (SVA) and economic value added (EVA®).
- SVA is based on the concept of net present value analysis.
- It identifies key value drivers for generating shareholder value.
- EVA® provides a means of measuring whether the returns generated by the business exceed the required returns from investors.

- $EVA^® = NOPAT - (R \times C)$
- EVA® relies on conventional financial statements, which are adjusted because of their limitations.
- In theory, EVA® and SVA should produce the same decisions and results.

Measuring shareholder value – external (investor) measures

- Two main approaches: market value added (MVA) and total shareholder return (TSR).
- MVA measures the difference between the market value of the business and the investment made in the business.
- MVA = Present value of EVA®.
- MVA is really only suitable for listed businesses.
- Interpreting MVA can be a problem.
- TSR measures the total return to shareholder over a period.
- TSR is made up of the increase (decrease) in share value and the dividends paid.
- TSR can be sensitive to the time period chosen.

Criticisms of the shareholder value approach

- Two elements to shareholder value: efficiency of current operations and future growth.
- Undue emphasis on efficiency can undermine the prospects for future growth.

Measuring the value of future growth

- One approach is to use the EVA® methodology.
- Value of future growth potential = Market value of the business – (Capital invested + EVA®/r).
- To check whether managers strike the right balance between efficiency and future growth, the future growth potential can be compared with the market value of the business.

→ **Key terms**

Shareholder value   p. 428
Shareholder value analysis (SVA)
   p. 431
Free cash flows   p. 432
Value drivers   p. 433

Economic value added (EVA®)
   p. 438
Market value added (MVA)   p. 447
Total shareholder return (TSR)   p. 451
Future growth value (FGV®)   p. 455

For definitions of these terms see the Glossary, pp. 562–571.

Further reading

If you wish to explore the topic of shareholder value in more depth, try the following books:

Executive Corporate Finance: The business of enhancing shareholder value, *Asaf, S.*, Financial Times Prentice Hall, 2004.

Measuring Value for Shareholders, *Institute of Chartered Accountants in England and Wales Faculty of Finance and Management*, Good Practice Guideline No. 33, March 2001.

The Dynamics of Shareholder Value, *Mills, R.*, Mars Business Associates, 1998.

The EVA Challenge: Implementing valued added changes in an organization, *Stern, J. and Shielly, J.*, John Wiley, 2003.

References

1 **EVA: The real key to creating wealth**, *Ehrbar, A.*, John Wiley, 1998.
2 **2003 Survey of Management Accounting**, *Ernst and Young*, Ernst and Young, 2003.

REVIEW QUESTIONS

Answers to these questions can be found in Appendix D at the back of the book.

11.1 The shareholder value approach to managing businesses takes a different approach from the stakeholder approach to managing businesses. In the latter case, the different stakeholders of the business (employees, customers, suppliers and, so on) are considered of equal importance and so the interests of shareholders will not dominate. Is it possible for these two approaches to managing businesses to coexist in harmony within a particular economy?

11.2 Why is MVA not really suitable as a tool for internal management purposes?

11.3 Should managers take changes in the total market value of the shares (that is, share price × number of shares issued) over time as an indicator of shareholder value created (or lost)?

11.4 It has been argued that many businesses are overcapitalised. If this is true, what may be the reasons for businesses having too much capital and how can EVA® help avoid this problem?

EXERCISES

Questions 11.4 and 11.5 are more advanced than 11.1 to 11.3. Those with coloured numbers have answers at the back of the book.

 If you wish to try more exercises, visit the students' side of the Companion Website.

11.1 Aquarius plc has estimated the following free cash flows for its five-year planning period:

Year	Free cash flows
	£m
1	35.0
2	38.0
3	45.0
4	49.0
5	53.0

Required:
How might it be possible to check the accuracy of these figures? What internal and external sources of information might be used to see whether the figures are realistic?

11.2 Aries plc was recently formed and issued 80 million £0.50 shares at par and loan capital of £24m. The business used the proceeds from the capital issues to purchase the remaining lease on some commercial properties that are rented out to small businesses. The lease will expire in four years' time and during that period the annual operating profits are expected to be £12 million each year. At the end of the three years, the business will be wound up and the lease will have no residual value.

The required rate of return by investors is 12 per cent.

Required:

Calculate the expected shareholder value generated by the business over the four years, using:

(a) The SVA approach
(b) The EVA® approach.

11.3 Virgo plc is considering introducing a system of EVA® and wants its managers to focus on the longer term rather than simply focus on the year-to-year EVA® results. The business is seeking your advice as to how a management bonus system could be arranged so as to ensure the longer term is taken into account. The business is also unclear as to how much of the managers' pay should be paid in the form of a bonus and when such bonuses should be paid. Finally, the business is unclear as to where the balance between individual performance and corporate performance should be struck within any bonus system.

The finance director has recently produced figures that show that if Virgo plc had used EVA® over the past three years, the results would have been as follows:

	£m
2003	25
2004	(20)
2005	10

Required:

Set out your recommendations for a suitable bonus system for the divisional managers of the business.

11.4 Leo plc is considering entering a new market. A new product has been developed at a cost of £5 million and is now ready for production. The market is growing and estimates from the finance department concerning future sales of the new product are as follows:

Year	Sales
	£m
1	30.0
2	36.0
3	40.0
4	48.0
5	60.0

After Year 5, sales are expected to stabilise at the Year 5 level.
You are informed that:

● The operating profit margin from sales in the new market is likely to be a constant 20 per cent of sales revenue.
● The cash tax rate is 25 per cent of operating profit.
● Replacement non-current asset investment (RNC) will be in line with the annual depreciation charge each year.
● Additional non-current asset investment (ANC) over the next five years will be 15 per cent of sales growth.
● Additional working capital investment (AWCI) over the next five years will be 10 per cent of sales growth.

The business has a cost of capital of 12 per cent. The new market is considered to be no more risky than the markets in which the business already has a presence.

Required:

Using an SVA approach, indicate the effect of entering the new market on shareholder value. (Workings should be to one decimal place.)

11.5   Pisces plc produced the following balance sheet and profit and loss account at the end of the
third year of trading:

Balance sheet as at the end of the third year

	£m	£m	£m
Non-current assets			
Goodwill		40.0	
Machinery and equipment		80.0	
Motor vans		18.6	
Marketable investments		9.0	147.6
Current assets			
Stock (inventory)		45.8	
Debtors (receivables)		64.6	
Cash		1.0	
		111.4	
Current liabilities			
Trade creditors (payables)		62.5	48.9
			196.5
Non-current liabilities			
Loan capital			80.0
			116.5
Equity			
Share capital			80.0
Reserves			36.5
			116.5

Profit and loss account (income statement) for the third year

	£m	£m
Sales revenue		231.5
Cost of sales		143.2
Gross profit		88.3
Wages	33.5	
Depreciation of machinery and equipment	14.8	
Goodwill written off	10.0	
R&D costs	40.0	
Provision for doubtful debts	10.5	108.8
Operating loss		(20.5)
Income from investments		0.6
		(19.9)
Interest payable		(0.8)
Ordinary loss before taxation		(20.7)
Restructuring costs		(6.0)
Profit before taxation		(26.7)
Corporation tax		–
Loss after tax		(26.7)

An analysis of the underlying records reveals the following:

1 Goodwill was purchased during the first year of trading when an existing business was
   acquired. The goodwill cost £70 million and this amount is being written off over a seven-year
   period (starting in the first year of the business).
2 R&D costs relate to the development of a new product in the previous year. These costs are
   written off over a two-year period (starting last year). However, this is a prudent approach and
   the benefits are expected to last for 16 years.

3 The provision for doubtful debts was created this year and the amount of the provision is very high. A more realistic figure for the provision would be £4 million.
4 Restructuring costs were incurred at the beginning of the year and are expected to provide benefits for an infinite period.
5 The business has an 8 per cent required rate of return for investors.

Required:
Calculate the EVA® for the business for the third year of trading.

12

Mergers, takeovers and the valuation of shares

LEARNING OUTCOMES

When you have completed this chapter, you should be able to:

- Identify and discuss the main reasons for mergers and takeovers.

- Discuss the advantages and disadvantages of each of the main forms of purchase consideration used in a takeover.

- Identify the likely winners and losers from takeover activity.

- Outline the tactics that may be used to defend against a hostile bid.

- Identify and discuss the main methods of valuing the shares of a business.

INTRODUCTION

In this chapter, we consider various aspects of mergers and takeovers. We begin by examining the reasons for mergers and takeovers and then go on to consider the ways in which they can be financed. We also identify the likely winners and losers in a takeover and the defences available to a business seeking to fend off a hostile bid. In the final part of this chapter, we consider how the shares of a business can be valued. This is relevant to a range of financial decisions, including mergers and takeovers.

Mergers and takeovers

When two (or possibly more) businesses combine, it can take the form of either a **merger** or a **takeover**. The term 'merger' is normally used to describe a situation where the two businesses are of roughly equal size and there is agreement among the managers and owners of each business on the desirability of combining them. A merger is usually effected by creating an entirely new business from the assets of the two existing businesses, with both shareholder groups receiving a substantial ownership stake in the new business.

The term 'takeover' is normally used to describe a situation where a larger business acquires control of a smaller business, which is then absorbed by the larger business. When a takeover occurs, the shareholders of the target business may cease to have any financial interest in the business and the resources of the business may come under entirely new ownership. (The particular form of consideration used to acquire the shares in the target business will determine whether the shareholders continue to have a financial interest in the business.) Although the vast majority of takeovers are not contested, there are occasions when the management of the target business will fight to retain its separate identity.

In practice, however, many business combinations do not fit into these neat categories and it may be difficult to decide whether a merger or a takeover has occurred. The distinction between the two forms of combination is really only important in the context of financial reporting, as different forms of accounting exist for each type of combination. It is beyond the scope of this book to describe the merger and acquisition methods of accounting, and readers who wish to pursue this topic should consult a book on financial accounting. However, it is worth noting that the merger method of accounting can often provide a much better picture of financial health than the acquisition method of accounting for the combined business. In the past, there has been some misuse of merger accounting methods, and so business combinations must now meet strict criteria before they can adopt the merger accounting method. In this chapter, no real distinction will be made between the terms 'merger' and 'takeover' and we shall use the terms interchangeably.

Mergers and takeovers can be classified according to the relationship between the businesses being merged.

- A **horizontal merger** occurs when two businesses in the same industry, and at the same point in the production/distribution process, decide to combine.
- A **vertical merger** occurs when two businesses in the same industry, but at different points in the same production/distribution process, decide to combine.
- A **conglomerate merger** occurs when two businesses in unrelated industries decide to combine.

Activity 12.1

Can you think of an example of each type of merger for a tyre retailer?

An example of a horizontal merger would be where a tyre retailer merges with another tyre retailer to form a larger retail business. An example of a vertical merger would be where a tyre retailer merges with a manufacturer of tyres. This would mean that the combined business operates at different points in the production/distribution chain. An example of a conglomerate merger would be where a tyre retailer merges with an ice cream manufacturer.

Merger and takeover activity

Although mergers and takeovers are a normal part of the business landscape, there are surges in merger and takeover activity from time to time. **Real World 12.1** shows that there have been quite dramatic surges in the early 1970s and in the late 1980s, with each surge having its own particular combination of economic, political and technological factors that create the required environment. Important economic factors are, usually, rising share prices and low interest rates, which make financing mergers and takeovers much easier.

REAL WORLD 12.1

The urge to merge

Figure 12.1 below shows the pattern of takeover activity in the UK in recent years.

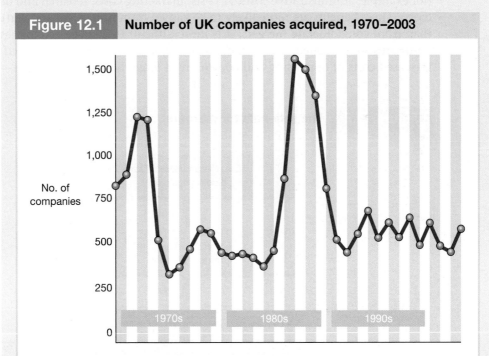

| Figure 12.1 | Number of UK companies acquired, 1970–2003 |

The chart shows that takeover activity surged in the early 1970s and late 1980s and, between these surges, the number of businesses acquired each year stayed broadly within the range 300–600.

Source: Based on http://www.statistics.gov.uk Office for National Statistics.

The rationale for mergers

In economic terms, a merger will be worthwhile only if combining the two businesses will lead to gains that would not arise if the two businesses had stayed apart. We saw in the previous chapter that the value of a business can be defined in terms of the *present value of its future cash flows*. Thus, if a merger is to make economic sense, the present value of the combined business should be equal to the present value of future cash flows of the bidding and target businesses *plus* a gain from the merger. Figure 12.2 illustrates this point.

There are various ways in which an economic gain may be achieved through a merger or takeover, the more important of these are described below.

Benefits of scale

A merger or takeover will result in a larger business being created that may enable certain benefits of scale to be achieved. For example, a larger business may be able to negotiate lower prices with suppliers in exchange for larger orders. A merger or takeover may also provide the potential for savings, as some operating costs may be duplicated (for example, administrative costs, IT costs, marketing costs, research and development costs). These benefits are more likely to be gained from horizontal and vertical mergers than from conglomerate mergers; it is more difficult to achieve economies where the businesses are unrelated. The benefits outlined, however, must be weighed against the increased costs of organising and controlling a larger business.

| Figure 12.2 | **The rationale for mergers** |

The figure shows that, to make economic sense, the present value of the merged business should be equal to the present value of the bidding and target businesses, when taken separately, plus an economic gain from the merger.

Real World 12.2 describes the anticipated cost savings arising from a merger between a Spanish bank, Santander Central Hispano, and a UK bank, Abbey National plc.

REAL WORLD 12.2

Banking on savings   **FT**

Alfredo Saenz, chief executive of Santander Central Hispano, recently suggested the bank could extract €500m (£330m) a year in costs if it took over Abbey National.

The acquisition would make SCH the eighth largest bank in the world and the UK's second biggest provider of mortgages and savings. It would also diversify SCH's revenue stream from Latin America and bring the bulk of its revenues from retail banking.

But as well as the commercial logic of the deal, SCH could also seek to stress potential cost savings from Abbey to make the deal more palatable to SCH investors. On Friday, some shareholders asked why the bank wanted a presence in the mature UK banking market.

The cost savings being talked about would represent about one-sixth of Abbey's £1.8bn cost base in its key personal financial services arm.

SCH has little presence in the UK and unlike a UK bidder, it could not merge overlapping call centres or close bank branches to cut costs.

However, it will rely on making savings particularly in Abbey's computer systems. Much of the costs would be saved by replacing the out-of-date technology platform. 'This is a technology story and cost synergies will be subtle,' one person close to the situation said.

Abbey is already mid-way through a programme of targeting cost savings in excess of £200m by 2005 and reinvesting in the branch network. It has also outsourced work to India and closed 10 operational sites to remove duplication.

However, it has not yet started to tackle the issue of its old legacy IT systems.

By contrast, SCH has a sophisticated platform, one of the best in Europe, which it bought when it acquired Banesto.

Integrating IT systems has been a crucial part of other bid battles for banks.

Royal Bank of Scotland won its £22bn takeover battle for NatWest in 2000 and integrating IT systems played a crucial role in its success. RBS migrated NatWest's 446 IT systems over 18 months to the RBS IT system that was a quarter of its size. The two systems held 18m accounts worth £158bn, with huge daily transaction volumes.

In 2002, RBS said the cumulative benefits realised by the end of the NatWest integration programme would be £5.5bn, about £1.4bn more than its original plan.

Source: 'Technology key to Abbey takeover', *Financial Times*, 26 July 2004.

Activity 12.2

Is it necessary for a business to merge with, or take over, another business in order to reap the benefits of scale? Can these benefits be obtained by other means?

A business may be able to obtain lower prices from suppliers, reduced research and development costs, and so forth, by joining a consortium of businesses or by entering into joint ventures with other businesses. This form of cooperation can result in benefits of scale and yet avoid the costs of a merger. (However, there will be costs in negotiating a detailed joint venture agreement.)

Eliminating competition

A business may combine with, or take over another business in order to eliminate competition and to increase the market share of its goods. This, in turn, can lead to increased profits.

Activity 12.3

What type of merger will achieve this objective? What are the potential problems of this kind of merger from the consumer's point of view?

A horizontal merger will normally be required to increase market share. The potential problems of such mergers are that consumers will have less choice following the merger and that the market power of the merged business will lead to an increase in consumer prices. For these reasons, governments often try to ensure that the interests of the consumer are protected when mergers resulting in a significant market share are proposed. (This point is considered in more detail later in the chapter.)

Underutilised resources

The full potential of a business may not be achieved because of a weak management team. In such a situation, there is an opportunity to install a stronger management team that could do better. This argument is linked to what is sometimes referred to as the 'market for corporate control'. The term is used to describe the idea that mergers and takeovers are motivated by teams of managers that compete for the right to control business resources. The market for corporate control ensures that weak management teams will not survive and that, sooner or later, they will be succeeded by stronger management teams. The threat of takeover, however, may motivate managers to improve their performance. This suggests that mergers and takeovers are good for the economy as they help to ensure that resources are fully utilised and that shareholder wealth maximisation remains the top priority.

Complementary resources

Two businesses may have complementary resources which, when combined, will allow higher profits to be made than if the businesses remain separate. By combining the two businesses, the relative strengths of each business will be brought together and this may lead to additional profits being generated. It may be possible, of course, for each business to overcome its particular deficiency and continue as a separate entity. Even so, it may still make sense to combine.

Activity 12.4

Why might there still be an argument in favour of a merger, even though a business could overcome any deficiency on its own?

Combining the resources of two businesses may lead to a quicker exploitation of the strengths of each business than if the businesses remained separate.

Real World 12.3 sets out the overtures made by the chief executive of Comcast, a major cable networks business, to Michael Eisner, chief executive of the Walt Disney Company, for a merger of the two businesses. These overtures, which were made in an open letter, pointed to the complementary resources of each business.

REAL WORLD 12.3

Dear Mickey   **FT**

Dear Michael,

I am writing following our conversation earlier this week in which I proposed that we enter into discussions to merge Disney and Comcast to create a premier entertainment and communications company. It is unfortunate that you are not willing to do so. Given this, the only way for us to proceed is to make a public proposal directly to you and your Board.

We have a wonderful opportunity to create a company that combines distribution and content in a way that is far stronger and more valuable than either Disney or Comcast can be standing alone. . . .

Under our proposal, your shareholders would own approximately 42% of the combined company. The combined company would be uniquely positioned to take advantage of an extraordinary collection of assets. Together, we would unite the country's premier cable provider with Disney's leading filmed entertainment, media networks and theme park properties.

In addition to serving over 21 million cable subscribers, Comcast is also the country's largest high speed internet service provider with over 5 million subscribers. As you have expressed on several occasions, one of Disney's top priorities involves the aggressive pursuit of technological innovation that enhances how Disney's content is created and delivered.

We believe this combination helps accelerate the realisation of that goal – whether through existing distribution channels and technologies such as video-on-demand and broadband video streaming or through emerging technologies still in development – to the benefit of all our shareholders, customers and employees.

We believe that improvements in operating performance, business creation opportunities and other combination benefits will generate enormous value for the shareholders of both companies.

Together, as an integrated distribution and content company, we will be best positioned to meet our respective competitive challenges. We have a stable and respected management team with a great track record for creating shareholder value. . . .

Very truly yours

Brian L. Roberts

Source: 'Dear Mickey: open letter to Disney', www.FT.com, 11 February 2004.

Footnote: Alas, Mickey did not write back and so the merger proposal was withdrawn.

Surplus funds

A business may operate within an industry that offers few investment opportunities. In such a situation, the management may find that it has surplus cash which is not earning a reasonable return. The solution to this problem may be to invest in a new industry where there is no shortage of profitable investment opportunities. By acquiring an existing business within the new industry, the necessary specialist managerial and technical know-how will be quickly acquired.

Activity 12.5

Could management deal with the problem of surplus funds in some other way? Why might this other way not be acceptable to shareholders and managers?

The surplus funds could be distributed to shareholders through a special dividend or a share repurchase arrangement. However, shareholders may not like this idea because there may be a tax liability arising from the distribution. Managers may also not like this idea as it will result in reduced resources for them to manage. (It is also worth mentioning that lenders may not like the idea of funds being returned to shareholders, as it may increase their (the lenders') exposure to risk.)

The motives for mergers and takeovers considered above are consistent with the objective of enhancing the wealth of shareholders. However, other motives, which are more difficult to justify, may provide the driving force for business combinations. The following are examples.

Diversification

A business may invest in another business, operating in a different industry, in order to reduce risk. We may recall that in Chapter 5 the benefits of diversification in dealing with the problem of risk were discussed. At first sight, such a policy may seem appealing. However, we must ask ourselves whether diversification by *management* will provide any benefits to shareholders that the *shareholders themselves* cannot provide more cheaply. It is often easier and cheaper for a shareholder to deal with the problem of risk by holding a diversified portfolio of shares than for the business to acquire another. It is quite likely that the latter approach will be expensive, as a premium may have to be paid to acquire the shares and external investment advisers and consultants may have to be hired at substantial cost.

Activity 12.6

Who do you think might benefit from diversification?

Diversification may well benefit the managers of the bidding business. Managers cannot diversify their investment of time and effort in the business easily. By managing a more diversified business, the risks of unemployment and lost income for managers are reduced.

There may be circumstances, however, where shareholders are in a similar position to managers. For example, owner-managers may find it difficult to diversify their time and wealth because they are committed to the business. In these particular circumstances, there is a stronger case for diversifying the business.

Real World 12.4 describes the problems that some banks experienced as a result of diversification and their attempts to extricate themselves from these problems.

REAL WORLD 12.4

Wealth warning! Businesses diversifying   FT

At the dawn of this decade there seemed no limits to the ambitions of the global banking industry. In the US the Gramm–Leach–Bliley Act dismantled Depression-era barriers between banks and other businesses, clearing the way for the creation of more 'financial services supermarkets' that would tempt customers with a one-stop outlet for everything from managed funds to travel insurance. In Europe, the advent of the eurozone seemed set to herald sweeping cross-border consolidation.

That has not happened. While bankers worldwide have been pursuing deals, their ambitions have grown humble. They are building scale in businesses they like and abandoning those that prove disappointing; but they are avoiding attempts at diversification. . . .

Underlying banks' new-found risk aversion is an acknowledgement that the diversification strategies fashionable during the 1990s seem to have produced minimal benefits for investors. Attempts at cross-selling – marketing as many products as possible to a customer – have proved disappointing in many cases.

According to Morgan Stanley: 'Investor doubts on bank managements' core competences have risen in recent years . . . the value to shareholders of banks increasing the diversity of the business model – fanning out in both geographic and activity terms – has given way to wholly legitimate concerns on both the risks and value added of diversity as an end in itself.'

In Europe, diversification has produced many casualties, particularly where banks' ventures into insurance are concerned. Indeed, the market risk acquired by banks has recently proved a bigger problem than the credit risk that is their stock in trade. Since Lloyds TSB of the UK bought Scottish Widows, the life assurer, in 2000, losses on its investment funds have been just as heavy as the group's hits on bad loans in both 2001 and 2002. Lloyds TSB, now under new leadership, has since tried to sell Scottish Widows but found no takers at the price it wanted.

Equally, Switzerland's Credit Suisse came to rue the day in 1997 when it took over the Winterthur insurance company. When combined with the disastrous consequences for earnings of having bought Donaldson Lufkin & Jenrette, the investment bank, at the top of the market, Credit Suisse found that its acquisitions had created a serious capital risk. Officially, the bank remains wedded to its investment bank, despite dissent on the board. But it has been much quicker to sell off large parts of its insurance operation, sometimes for excellent prices.

Nor has the argument for diversification been bolstered by the results when insurers have bought banks. Allianz has seen its reputation as one of Germany's finest companies shattered by its takeover of Dresdner Bank. Declining revenues and bad loans at the bank forced the insurer into a humiliatingly discounted equity-raising this year. Ironically, the move away from diversification probably began with Citigroup, the company most closely associated with the financial supermarket idea.

One big reason for the 1998 merger between Travelers and Citicorp that created Citigroup was to make cross-selling easier. This has happened in businesses ranging from branch banking to corporate finance. But Citigroup has run into curious results in other areas. When it offered vehicle and home insurance to banking customers, it attracted the wrong kind of people: bad drivers, for example.

'It just didn't play well together,' Sandy Weill, Citigroup's chairman, said at the time.

Source: 'The myth of the mega-bank: after the failures of diversification, wary lenders scale back their global ambitions', *Financial Times*, 6 January 2004.

Management interests and goals

A merger or takeover may be undertaken to fulfil the personal goals or interests of managers. They may acquire another business simply to reduce the risks that they face or to increase the amount of resources that they control. **Real World 12.5** also points out that managers may enjoy the excitement of mergers and takeovers.

REAL WORLD 12.5

Mergers can be fun

Mergers and acquisitions can be very exciting and managers often enjoy 'the thrill of the chase'. Warren Buffet, one of the world's most successful investors and chief executive officer of Berkshire Hathaway, has stated:

> Leaders, business or otherwise, seldom are deficient in animal spirits and often relish increased activity and challenge. At Berkshire, the corporate pulse never beats faster than when an acquisition is in prospect.

Source: Warren Buffett's letter to Berkshire Hathaway Inc. shareholders, 1981, www.berkshirehathaway.com

The personal goals and interests of managers may also explain why some proposed takeovers are fiercely contested by them.

Management interests and the agency problem

Although shareholders have the final say concerning whether a business should be acquired, they will rely heavily on information supplied to them by the managers. If the managers are determined to pursue their own goals, shareholders may not receive all the information required to make the correct decision. This is linked to the agency problem that was first discussed in Chapter 1. As we may recall, there is a risk that managers, who are employed to act on behalf of shareholders, will operate in a way that is designed to maximise their own benefits.

A merger, however, can sometimes be the solution to the agency problem. Where managers are not acting in the interests of the shareholders and are busy pursuing their own interests and goals, the effect is likely to be a decline in business performance and share price. The market for corporate control, mentioned earlier, should ensure that the business is taken over by another whose managers are committed to serving the interests of shareholders.

Forms of purchase consideration

When a business takes over another business, payment for the shares acquired may be made in different ways.

Activity 12.7

What different methods of payment may be used?

The main methods of payment are:

- cash
- shares in the bidding business
- loan capital in the bidding business.

Some combination of the methods listed in Activity 12.7 may, of course, also be used. Below we consider the advantages and disadvantages of each form of payment from the point of view of both the bidding business's shareholders and the target business's shareholders.

Cash

Payment by cash means the amount of the purchase consideration will be both certain and clearly understood by the target business's shareholders. This may improve the chances of a successful bid. It will also mean that shareholder control of the bidding business will not be diluted as no additional shares will be issued.

Raising the necessary cash, however, can create problems for the bidding business, particularly when the target business is large. It may only be possible to raise the amount required by a loan or share issue or by selling off assets, which the bidding business's shareholders may not like. On occasions, it may be possible to spread the cash payments over a period. However, deferred payments are likely to weaken the attraction of the bid to the target business's shareholders.

The receipt of cash will allow the target business's shareholders to adjust their share portfolios without incurring transaction costs on disposal. However, transaction costs will be incurred when new shares or loan capital are acquired to replace the shares sold. Moreover, the receipt of cash may result in a liability to capital gains tax (which arises on gains from the disposal of certain assets, including shares).

Shares

The issue of shares in the bidding business as purchase consideration will avoid any strain on its cash position. However, some dilution of existing shareholder control will occur and there may also be a risk of dilution in earnings per share. (Dilution will occur if the additional earnings from the merger divided by the number of new shares issued is lower than the existing earnings per share.) The directors must ensure that the authorised share capital of the business is sufficient to make a new issue and, more importantly, that the market value of the business's shares does not fall during the course of the takeover. A substantial fall in share price will reduce the value of the bid and could undermine the chances of acceptance. The cost of this form of financing must also be taken into account. We saw in Chapter 8 that the cost of servicing share capital is relatively expensive.

The target business's shareholders may find a share-for-share exchange attractive. As they currently hold shares, they may wish to continue with this form of investment rather than receive cash or other forms of security. A share-for-share exchange does not result in a liability for capital gains tax. (For capital gains tax purposes, no disposal is deemed to have occurred when this type of transaction takes place.) The target shareholders will also have a continuing ownership link with the original business, although it will now be part of a larger business. However, the precise value of the offer may be difficult to calculate owing to movements in the share prices of the two businesses.

Loan capital

Like the issue of shares, the issue of loan capital is simply an exchange of paper and so it avoids any strain on the cash resources of the bidding business. It has, however, certain advantages over shares in that the issue of loan capital involves no dilution of shareholder control and the service costs will be lower. A disadvantage of a loan-capital-for-share exchange is that it will increase the gearing of the bidding business and, therefore, the level of financial risk. The directors of the bidding business must ensure that the issue of loan capital is within its borrowing limits.

Loan capital may be acceptable to shareholders in the target business if they have doubts over the future performance of the combined business. Loan capital provides investors with both a fixed level of return and security for their investment. When a takeover bid is being made, convertible loan capital may be offered as purchase consideration.

Activity 12.8

What is the attraction of this form of loan capital from the point of view of the target business's shareholders?

The issue of convertible loan capital would give target business shareholders a useful hedge against uncertainty. This type of loan capital will provide relative security in the early years with an option to convert to ordinary shares at a later date. Investors will, of course, only exercise this option if things go well for the combined business.

There may be various factors influencing the form of consideration used by bidding businesses. Market conditions may be a critical factor. Research evidence suggests that ordinary shares are more likely to be used following a period of strong stock market performance. Recent high returns are seen as making shares more attractive to investors. Accounting policies are also cited as an important influence on the choice of bid consideration. There is some evidence to suggest that ordinary shares may be used to ensure that the combined business is treated as a merger rather than a takeover. (It was mentioned earlier that merger accounting methods often provide a better financial picture than other methods of accounting for business combinations.)

Activity 12.9

If accounting policies can influence the choice of bid consideration, what does this suggest to you about the efficiency of the stock market?

If the stock market is efficient, we would expect the particular method of accounting for a business combination to make no difference to investors' perceptions. Investors will not be fooled by accounting techniques that are designed to enhance the appearance of financial position.

Businesses with good growth opportunities are more likely to use ordinary shares when financing acquisitions. It seems that growth businesses prefer to use ordinary shares as this form of finance is less constraining than the issue of loan capital or the payment of cash. Businesses with poor growth opportunities, however, may not be able to offer ordinary shares in payment.

Real World 12.6 reveals the ways in which mergers have been financed in recent years.

REAL WORLD 12.6

How mergers are financed

The popularity of each form of bid consideration varies over time. Figure 12.3 shows that, in recent years, cash has usually been the most popular.

| Figure 12.3 | Bid consideration in mergers and acquisitions, 1994–2003 |

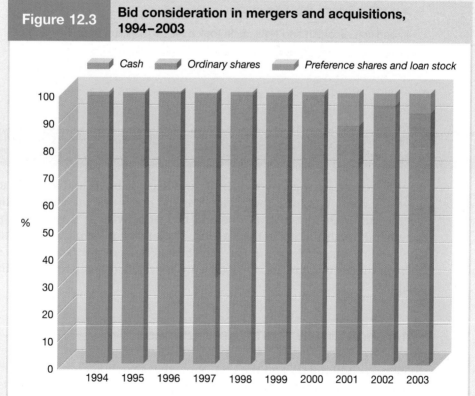

The figure shows that cash is the most popular form of bid consideration over the period followed by ordinary shares. Preference shares and loan capital are fairly insignificant forms of bid consideration.

Source: Based on http://www.statistics.gov.uk Office for National Statistics.

It is interesting to note that research in the UK and the USA suggests that businesses using ordinary shares as a means of acquisition achieve significantly poorer returns following the acquisition than those using cash (see reference 1 at the end of the chapter). The reasons for this are not entirely clear. Perhaps the relatively poor performance of share-for-share deals indicates that the bidding businesses' shares were too highly valued to begin with.

When purchasing another business, the debts of that business may be taken over. This can, of course, be regarded as part payment for the assets acquired. **Real World 12.7** shows how the acquisition of HP Bulmer Holdings, the cider maker, was financed by Scottish and Newcastle plc.

REAL WORLD 12.7

Paying for Bulmer

In 2003, the Boards of Scottish and Newcastle plc and HP Bulmer Holdings agreed terms for the acquisition of Bulmer. The total consideration amounted to £200 million, which was made up of:

- £64 million in cash and loans
- £136 million by the issue of 38m ordinary shares.

In addition, Scottish and Newcastle took over £107 million of Bulmer's debt.

Source: Scottish and Newcastle plc Annual Report 2003.

Who benefits?

In this section, we shall try to identify the likely winners and losers in a merger. We begin by considering the shareholders as the pursuit of shareholder value is usually claimed to be the driving force behind merger activity. It is worth asking, however, whether the reality matches the rhetoric. The answer, it seems, will depend on whether the bidding shareholders or the target shareholders are being discussed. Overall, mergers do create value, but it is unevenly allocated. (See reference 2 at the end of the chapter).

Shareholders in the target business

Studies, both in the UK and the USA, show that shareholders in the target business are usually the main beneficiaries. They are likely to receive substantial benefits from a takeover through a premium on the share price. Rose has summed up the position as follows:

> The bidder usually has to pay a premium over the pre-bid price of up to 100 per cent of the latter, with a mean of about 25 per cent in the UK and some 15 per cent in the US. In some cases the premium may appear to be small but this may merely reflect the fact that the 'pre-bid' price had already incorporated the possibility of a forthcoming bid. Bid premia tend to be higher in the case of contested bids, depending very much on whether another bidder is thought to be in the wings. (See reference 3 at the end of the chapter).

Activity 12.10

Why might a bidding business be prepared to pay a premium above the market value for the shares of a business?

Various reasons have been put forward to explain this phenomenon. They include the following:

● The managers of the bidding business have access to information that is not available to the market and which is not, therefore, reflected in the share price.
● The managers of the bidding business may simply misjudge the value of the target business.
● The managers may feel that there will be significant gains arising from combining the two businesses that are worth paying for. In theory, the maximum price a buyer will be prepared to pay will be equivalent to the present value of the business plus any gains from the merger.
● 'Management hubris.' Where there is more than one bidder or where the takeover is being resisted, the managers of a bidding business may fail to act rationally and may raise the bid price above an economically justifiable level. This may be done in order to salvage management pride as they may feel humiliated by defeat.

Share prices in the target business will usually reflect the bid premium for as long as the bid is in progress. Where a takeover bid is unsuccessful and the bid withdrawn, the share price of the target business will usually return to its pre-offer level. However, shares may fall below their pre-bid prices if investors believe that the managers have failed to exploit a profitable opportunity. The same fate may be experienced by shares in the bidding business.

Real World 12.8 below sets out details of merger and takeover bids.

REAL WORLD 12.8

Bids and bidders   **FT**

The following is an extract from a table concerning takeover bids and mergers that was published in the *Financial Times*.

Current takeover bids and mergers

Company bid for	Value of bid per share‡	Market price‡	Pre-bid price	Value of bid‡ £m	Bidder
ADL	40*	68	23	0.91	Nabarro Wells
Big Food Group	95*	$94\frac{1}{4}$	$92\frac{1}{2}$	326.47	Giant BidCo
Burtonwood	550*	550	$512\frac{1}{2}$	110.28	Wolves&Dudley
Countryside Props	275*	276	271	218.18	Copthorne
ebookers	320*	$316\frac{1}{2}$	312	203.09	Cendant
Kidde	165*	165	159	1.39bn	United Tech
Linx Printing	550*	$545\frac{1}{2}$	470	84.46	Danaher
NHP	260*	$256\frac{1}{2}$	257	539.56	TBG Careco
QXL Ricardo	800*	868	850	13.6	B.Florissant
RMC	855*	$847\frac{1}{2}$	599	2.28bn	Cemex
Royal Doulton	12*	$11\frac{3}{4}$	$10\frac{1}{4}$	39.88	Waterfd Wedgwd
TBI†	$92\frac{1}{2}$*	93	$88\frac{1}{2}$	517.00	Airport Concns
UA Group	1470†	1435	1200	51.90	Elphinstone

Prices in pence unless otherwise indicated. * All-cash offer. † Unconditional. ‡ Based on closing prices 14 January 2005.

Source: Financial Times, Money section, 15–16 January 2005, p. M18.

Activity 12.11

Calculate the bid premium for each of the target businesses and comment on the findings.

The size of the bid premia can be calculated as follows:

Company bid for	Value of bid per share	Pre-bid price	Bid premium percentage
	(a)	(b)	$\dfrac{(a) - (b)}{(b)} \times 100$
ADL	40*	23	73.9
Big Food Group	95*	$92\frac{1}{2}$	2.7
Burtonwood	550*	$512\frac{1}{2}$	7.3
Countryside Props	275*	271	1.5
ebookers	320*	312	2.6
Kidde	165*	159	3.8
Linx Printing	550*	470	17.0
NHP	260*	257	1.2
QXL Ricardo	800*	850	(5.9)
RMC	855*	599	42.7
Royal Doulton	12*	$10\frac{1}{4}$	17.1
TBI[†]	$92\frac{1}{2}$*	$88\frac{1}{2}$	4.5
UA Group	1470[†]	1435	2.4

We can see that the bid premia covers a wide range from 1.5 per cent to 73.9 per cent. Note that in one case, the bid offer is lower than the pre-bid price. One possible reason for this is that the market anticipated a bid before any formal announcement was made. The current market value exceeds the bid price, which may suggest that the market expects a higher offer to be made at a future date.

In most cases, the current market value of the shares has increased since the bid and has moved closer to the bid price. In some cases, it is higher than the bid price. Once again, this may be in anticipation of a higher offer being made.

All the bids included in this extract were in the form of cash and the overwhelming majority of bids in the complete table were in the form of cash.

Shareholders in the bidding business

Shareholders of the bidding business usually have little to celebrate. Although early studies offered some evidence that a merger provided them with either a small increase or no increase in the value of their investment, more recent studies suggest that, over the long run, takeovers produce a significant decrease in shareholder value (see reference 4 at the end of the chapter). Some studies also suggest that conglomerate takeovers provide the worst performance as indicated by both lower profitability and higher subsequent sell-offs of the acquired business (see reference 5 at the end of the chapter).

Activity 12.12

Why might shares in the bidding business lose value as a result of a takeover of a target business? Try to think of two reasons why this may be so.

Various reasons have been suggested. These include:

- *Overpayment.* The bidding business may pay too much to acquire the target business. We saw earlier that large premiums are often paid to acquire another business and this may result in a transfer of wealth from the bidding business shareholders to the target business shareholders.
- *Integration problems.* Following a successful bid, it may be difficult to integrate the target business's operations. There may be problems relating to organisational structure, key personnel, management style, management rivalries, and so on, which work against successful integration. These problems are most likely to arise in horizontal mergers where an attempt is made to fuse the systems and operations of the two separate businesses into a seamless whole. There are likely to be fewer problems where a conglomerate merger is undertaken and where there is no real attempt to adopt common systems or operations.
- *Management neglect.* There is a risk that, following the takeover, managers may relax and expect the combined business to operate smoothly. If the takeover has been bitterly contested, the temptation for management to ease back after the struggle may be very strong.
- *Hidden problems.* Problems relating to the target business may be unearthed following the takeover. This is most likely to arise where a thorough investigation was not carried out prior to the takeover.

Managers

Any discussion concerning winners and losers in a merger should include the senior managers of the bidding business and the target business. They are important stakeholders in their respective businesses and play an important role in takeover negotiations. This does not always mean, however, that they will benefit from a merger.

Activity 12.13

Following a successful bid, what is the likelihood of the senior managers in (a) the bidding business, and (b) the target business, benefiting from the merger?

(a) The managers of the bidding business are usually beneficiaries as they will manage an enlarged business, which will, in turn, result in greater status, income and security.

(b) The position of senior managers in the acquired business is less certain. In some cases, they may be retained and may even become directors of the enlarged business. In other cases, however, the managers may lose their jobs. A study by Franks and Mayer found that nearly 80 per cent of executive directors in a target business either resign or lose their job within two years of a successful takeover (see reference 6 at the end of the chapter).

Where managers in the target business lose their job, compensation may be payable. **Real World 12.9** outlines the compensation due to the directors of Safeway plc, a supermarket chain, in the event of a takeover. The business was subject to a number of takeover bids during 2003 and was eventually taken over by another supermarket chain, Wm Morrison plc.

REAL WORLD 12.9

Easing the pain   FT

Safeway's executive directors will be paid a total of more than £5.5m in compensation in the event that the supermarket group is taken over.

According to the group's annual report, published yesterday, David Webster, executive chairman, was paid £810,000 last year. He is entitled to one-and-a-half times his salary in the event of a takeover.

Carlos Criado-Perez, chief executive, was paid £802,000. He will be paid his basic annual salary of £654,000 – plus a change-of-control payment that could be more than £1m.

Long-serving executives Simon Laffin, finance director, and Lawrence Christensen, operations director, are each entitled to two years' notice – and would double their basic salaries of £343,000 and £301,000 respectively.

Richard Williams and Jack Sinclair – information technology director and trading and marketing director – are each on one-year's notice periods and would be paid their basic annual salaries of £301,000 and £291,000 respectively.

Source: 'Safeway directors' £5.5m compensation', *Financial Times*, 10 June 2003.

Advisers

Mergers and takeovers can be very rewarding for investment advisers and lawyers employed by each business during the bid period. It seems that, whatever the outcome of the bid, they are winners. **Real World 12.10** describes a particularly rewarding merger for advisers.

REAL WORLD 12.10

Nice work (if you can get it)

Britain's biggest merger of the year – the £13 billion marriage of lumbering energy giants Lattice and National Grid – generated City fees of more than £100 million it was disclosed today.

The fee bill, one of the highest totals ever seen for a single transaction, was spread around an A-list of City advisers and came in a year of depressed merger and acquisition activity.

The chief beneficiaries were investment bank NM Rothschild, the main financial advisers to electricity pylons group National Grid and JP Morgan Chase and Cazenove, joint financial advisers to Lattice, which operated the Transco national gas pipeline. . . .

Of the total bill of £105 million, the bulk, £67 million, was spent by Lattice and the remaining £38 million by National Grid. The total figure is far higher than the £76 million forecast in the merger documentation.

Source: 'UK's biggest merger generates £100 million in advisers' fees', *Evening Standard*, 26 November 2002.

Why do mergers occur?

The substantial body of evidence that now exists, covering different time periods and across several different countries, indicating the dubious value of takeovers for bidding business shareholders, raises the question as to why businesses persist in acquiring other businesses. The answer is still unclear. Perhaps it is because takeovers satisfy the interests of managers, or perhaps it reflects Samuel Johnson's view of remarriage – the triumph of hope over experience.

Real World 12.11 sets out the thoughts of Warren Buffet on why mergers occur.

REAL WORLD 12.11

A modern fairy tale

Many managements apparently were overexposed in impressionable childhood years to the story in which the imprisoned handsome prince is released from a toad's body by a kiss from a beautiful princess. Consequently, they are certain their managerial kiss will do wonders for the profitability of Company T[arget] . . . Investors can always buy toads at the going price for toads. If investors instead bankroll princesses who wish to pay double for the right to kiss the toad, those kisses had better pack some real dynamite. We've observed many kisses but very few miracles. Nevertheless, many managerial princesses remain serenely confident about the future potency of their kisses – even after their corporate backyards are knee-deep in unresponsive toads. . . .

We have tried occasionally to buy toads at bargain prices with results that have been chronicled in past reports. Clearly our kisses fell flat. We have done well with a couple of princes – but they were princes when purchased. At least our kisses didn't turn them into toads. And, finally, we have occasionally been quite successful in purchasing fractional interests in easily identifiable princes at toadlike prices.

Source: Warren Buffett's letter to Berkshire Hathaway Inc. shareholders, 1981, www.berkshirehathaway.com

Ingredients for successful mergers

Although many mergers and takeovers do not add value for shareholders, not all are unsuccessful. Why do some succeed? What are the magic ingredients of success? PA Consulting Group, a leading firm of management consultants, has tried to address these questions. Based on work with clients and research into mergers and acquisitions, the Group argues that consistent success in acquiring businesses can only be achieved if the following three factors are present:

● *Commitment.* This involves maintaining a clear focus on creating long-term value and committing the required resources to the merger process. It also involves reviewing performance in managing a merger in order to learn lessons for next time.
● *Competence.* To assess properly the risks and opportunities of a merger, a business must be able to assess its own strengths and weaknesses. It must be able to assess whether the areas of competence that it possesses will create value from the merger.

Business platforms (such as IT and manufacturing processes) that support core competences should be designed in such a way that they can be easily and quickly expanded to accommodate newly acquired businesses.

● *Control.* There must be strategic analysis of acquisitions to help determine when, where and what to buy. There must also be a careful assessment of risks, including financial and operating risks. Systematic and rigorous planning must be applied throughout the whole transaction – starting with the bid and continuing throughout the subsequent integration process. (See reference 7 at the end of the chapter.)

These key elements are set out in Figure 12.4.

Figure 12.4	Key factors required to ensure long-term merger and acquisition (M&A) capability

The diagram shows the main factors necessary to ensure consistent success in mergers and takeovers.

Source: Creating Long-term Value through Mergers and Acquisitions, PA Consulting Group, PA Knowledge Ltd, 2003.

Rejecting a takeover bid

A takeover bid may, of course, be rejected. This need not imply that the bid is unwelcome and that shareholders are committed to maintaining the business as an independent entity. It may simply be a tactic to increase the bid premium and, thereby, increase shareholder wealth. If, however, it is not a negotiating tactic but a genuine attempt to remain independent, there is no certainty that rejection will be the end of the story. The spurned business may decide to press ahead with a hostile bid. Some of the defensive tactics that can be used against such a bid are considered below.

Defensive tactics

Various tactics may be used to fend off a hostile bid. Some of these must be put in place before receiving a hostile bid whereas others can be deployed when the bid has been made. Defensive tactics include the following:

- *Conversion to private company status.* By converting to private limited company status, the shares of the business become more difficult to acquire. This conversion must, however, be undertaken before a bid has been received.
- *Employee share option schemes.* By encouraging employees to acquire shares in the business, the proportion of shareholders that are likely to resist a bid is increased. This is a further example of a defence that must be in place before a bid is received.
- *Circularising shareholders.* When an offer has been received, the managers (directors) of the target business will normally notify the shareholders in a circular letter. In this letter the case for rejection may be set out. It might be argued, for example, that it is not in the long-term interests of the shareholders to accept the offer, or that the price offered is too low. In support of such arguments, the managers may disclose hitherto confidential information such as profit forecasts, future dividend payments, asset valuations, details of new contracts, and so on. This may have the effect of boosting the share price thereby making the takeover more expensive.
- *Making the business unattractive.* The managers may take steps to make the business unattractive to a bidder. In the colourful language of mergers, this may involve taking a **poison pill** through the sale of prized assets of the business (the **crown jewels**). Other tactics include agreements to pay large sums to directors for loss of office resulting from a takeover (**golden parachutes**) and the purchase of certain assets that the bidding business does not want. In the past, some regional electricity businesses in the UK tried to fend off unwelcome takeover bids by making large dividend distributions to shareholders. These distributions resulted in both a reduction in cash balances and an increase in the gearing of the businesses.
- **Pac-man defence.** This involves the target business launching a counterbid for the bidding business. However, this tactic is difficult to carry out where the target business is much smaller than the predator business. (The name given to this particular tactic derives from a well-known computer game.)
- **White knight.** A target business may avoid a takeover by an unwelcome bidder by seeking out another business (a 'white knight') with which to combine. This tactic will normally be used only as a last resort, however, as it will result in the loss of independence. There is also a risk that the white knight will be less gallant after the merger than was hoped.
- **White squire.** This is a variation of the white knight tactic. In this case, another business that is regarded as supportive will purchase a block of shares in the target business that is big enough to prevent any real prospect of a takeover but will not provide a controlling interest. The white squire will usually be given some incentive to 'ride to the rescue' of the target business. This might take the form of a seat on the board or a discount on the price of the shares purchased.

Real World 12.12 shows that modern tactics used to resist takeover attempts are pretty tame when compared with those used in the USA during the nineteenth century.

REAL WORLD 12.12

Defensive tactics – Western style

The following is a brief description of a 'Wild West' style takeover battle that involved an attempt to take control of the Eirie Railroad in 1868:

> The takeover attempt pitted Cornelius Vanderbilt against Daniel Drew, Jim Fisk and Jay Gould. As one of the major takeover defences, the defenders of the Eirie Railroad issued themselves large quantities of stock (that is, shares), even though they lacked the authorisation to do so. At that time, bribery of judges and elected officials was common, and so legal remedies for violating corporate laws were particularly weak. The battle for control of the railroad took a violent turn when the target corporation hired guards, equipped with firearms and cannons, to guard their headquarters. The takeover attempt ended when Vanderbilt abandoned his assault on the Eirie Railroad and turned his attention to weaker targets.

Source: Mergers and Acquisitions, P. Gaughan, HarperCollins, 1991, p. 13.

Overcoming resistance to a bid

Managers of the bidding business may try to overcome resistance to the bid by circularising shareholders of the target business with information that counters any claims made against the commercial logic of the bid or the offer price. They may also increase the offer price for the shares in the target business. In some cases, the original offer price may be pitched at a fairly low level as a negotiating ploy. The offer price will then be increased at a later date, thereby allowing the target business's managers and shareholders to feel that they have won some sort of victory.

Protecting the interests of shareholders and the public

To protect the interests of shareholders of both the bidding business and the target business, there is the City Code on Takeovers and Mergers. This Code seeks to ensure that shareholders are supplied with all the information necessary to make a proper decision and that the information supplied gives a fair and accurate representation of the facts. Any forecasts supplied by the bidding business or the target business must be carefully prepared and the key assumptions underpinning the forecast figures must be stated. The Code expects all shareholders to be treated equally when a merger or takeover is being negotiated.

Protecting the interests of the public also becomes a consideration when larger businesses combine. Where a business with UK turnover in excess of £70 million is being taken over, or where the combined business has a 25 per cent share of a particular market, the proposed merger can be referred to the **Competition Commission**. This is an independent public body that considers the effect of mergers and takeovers on the level of competition operating within particular markets. If the Commission believes a merger would result in a substantial lessening of competition in a particular market, it has the power to take action. This includes preventing the merger from taking place. When a merger is referred to the Commission (usually by the Office of Fair Trading), detailed enquiries are carried out, which may take some time. A large business that is the target of a hostile bid may, therefore, seek a referral in the hope that the delays and trouble caused by a Commission enquiry will make it less attractive to the bidding business.

In addition to national rules, the European Union has competition rules to eliminate restrictive practices that may affect trade between EU member states. These rules can restrict mergers that could distort competition or could lead to an abuse of a dominant market position. Recent reforms now mean that EU member states will normally enforce EU competition rules.

Restructuring a business: divestments and demergers

A business may wish to decrease, rather than increase, its scale of their operations. Restructuring a business in this way can be achieved through either a divestment or a demerger. Each of these is discussed below.

Divestment

A divestment or *sell-off* of business operations may be undertaken for various reasons including:

● *Financial problems.*   A business that is short of cash or too highly geared may sell off certain operations to improve its financial position.
● *Defensive tactics.*   A business that is vulnerable to a takeover may take pre-emptive action by selling its 'crown jewels'.
● *Strategic focus.*   A business may wish to focus exclusively on core operations that are in line with its strategic objectives. As a result, non-core operations will be sold off.
● *Poor performance.*   Where the performance of a particular business operation is disappointing, it may be sold off to enable more profitable use of resources.

Divestment and the agency problem

When a sell-off is undertaken, the managers of the particular business operations may bid to become the new owners. This, however, may give rise to an agency problem for the shareholders.

Activity 12.14

What kind of agency problem may arise for shareholders?

The managers have a duty to act in the interests of the shareholders. However, when a management buy-out is in prospect, the managers have a conflict of interest. On the one hand, they have a duty to ensure that the sale of the business will maximise the wealth of the owners and, on the other, they will be keen to acquire the business for as low a price as possible. There is a risk, therefore, that unscrupulous managers will suppress important information or will fail to exploit profitable opportunities in the period leading up to a buy-out in order to obtain the business operations at a cheap price. Shareholders must be aware of this risk and must seek independent advice concerning the value and potential of the business operations for which the managers are bidding.

If the bid by managers is successful, the purchase arrangement is referred to as a *management buy-out*. We saw in Chapter 7 that management buy-outs are often financed by venture capitalists, who usually acquire a shareholding in the business.

Demerger

Rather than selling off business operations to a third party, they may be transferred to a new business. This kind of restructuring is referred to as a **demerger** or **spin-off**. In this case, ownership of the business operations remains unchanged as the current owners will be given shares in the newly created business. The allocation of shares to the owners is usually made in proportion to their shareholdings in the existing business. A demerger can be undertaken for various reasons, including:

● *Market appeal.* Where part of the business operations is unattractive to investors (for example, very high risk), sentiment towards the business as a whole may be adversely affected. By spinning off the unattractive operations, the business may increase its market appeal.

● *Defensive tactics.* A business may have certain operations that are prized by another business. By spinning off particular operations, the business may successfully avoid the risk of takeover. (As mentioned above, a divestment can also be used for this purpose.)

● *Unlocking potential.* Where a business is a conglomerate, it is usually extremely difficult to manage effectively a diverse range of businesses. A decision to spin off part of its operations should make the business easier to manage and more focused. It will also give the managers of the operations that have been spun off greater autonomy, which may in turn lead to improved performance.

● *Investors' needs.* Investors in a conglomerate are unlikely to find the various operations in which the business is engaged equally attractive. By creating separate businesses for different kinds of business operations, investors should benefit as they will be able to adjust their portfolios to reflect more accurately the required level of investment for each business operation.

Real World 12.13 provides an example of a business considering both a divestment and a spin-off of some of its operations.

REAL WORLD 12.13

Spinning toys

FT

Toys R Us, the largest speciality toy retailer in the US, yesterday said it was exploring the possible sale of its core toy business and a spin-off of its Babies R Us division, in a move that could reshape the industry.

The global toy business comprises its Toys R Us stores in the US and overseas as well as toysrus.com, its online unit. The fast-growing Babies R Us unit sells toys, clothing and accessories for newborns and toddlers.

Toys R Us has struggled with falling sales amid fierce competition from large discounters such as Wal-Mart and Target, as well as electronics retailers such as Best Buy, which sells video games. . . .

John Eyler, chairman and chief executive, said the global toy and Babies R Us businesses operated 'in distinct markets' and were 'at fundamentally different phases' in their growth cycle.

> 'By ultimately operating them as separate entities, we will provide a better opportunity for Babies R Us to continue its healthy growth,' Mr Eyler said. 'Whatever form the separation takes, these steps should facilitate the execution of a restructured – and substantially leaner and more focused – global toy business that we believe can generate significant cash.'
>
> Mark Rowen, senior analyst at Prudential Equity Group, said the announcement was 'extremely positive' for investors, as one of the critical pieces to unlocking shareholder value in the company was 'separating its crown jewel – Babies R Us'.
>
> *Source*: 'Toys Я Us mulls spin-off of baby unit', *Financial Times*, 12 August 2004.

As a footnote to the topics of divestment and demerger, it is worth pointing out that both forms of restructuring result in a smaller business. Thus some of the benefits of size, such as the benefits of scale, will be lost.

The valuation of shares

An important aspect of any merger or takeover negotiation is the value to be placed on the shares of the businesses to be merged or acquired. In this section, we explore the various methods that can be used to derive an appropriate share value for a business. Share valuation methods are not, of course, used only in the context of merger or takeover negotiations. They will also be required in other circumstances such as business flotations and liquidations. Nevertheless, mergers and takeovers are an important area for the application of share valuation methods.

In theory, the value of a share can be defined either in terms of the current value of the assets held or the future cash flows generated from those assets. In a world of perfect information and perfect certainty, share valuation would pose few problems. However, in the real world, measurement and forecasting problems conspire to make the valuation process difficult. Various valuation methods have been developed to deal with these problems, but they often produce quite different results.

The main methods employed to value a share can be divided into three broad categories:

● methods based on the value of the business's assets
● methods that use stock market information
● methods that are based on future cash flows.

Let us now examine some of the more important methods falling within each of these categories using the following example.

Example 12.1

CDC Ltd owns a chain of tyre and exhaust fitting garages in the west of England. The business has been approached by ATD plc, which owns a large chain of petrol stations, with a view to a takeover of CDC Ltd. ATD plc is prepared to make an offer in cash or a share-for-share exchange. The most recent financial statements of CDC Ltd are summarised below.

Example 12.1 continued

Profit and loss account (income statement) for the year ended 30 November 2005

	£m
Sales revenue	18.7
Profit before interest and tax	6.4
Interest	1.6
Profit before taxation	4.8
Corporation tax	1.2
Net profit after taxation	3.6
Dividend paid	1.0
Retained profit	2.6

Balance sheet as at 30 November 2005

Non-current assets	£m	£m	£m
Freehold land and premises at cost		4.6	
Less Accumulated depreciation		0.6	
			4.0
Plant and machinery at cost		9.5	
Less Accumulated depreciation		3.6	
			5.9
			9.9
Current assets			
Stock (inventory)		2.8	
Debtors (receivables)		0.4	
Bank		2.6	
		5.8	
Less **Current liabilities**			
Trade creditors (payables)	5.9		
Corporation tax	0.6	6.5	(0.7)
Total assets less current liabilities			9.2
Less **Non-current liabilities**			
Loans			3.6
			5.6
Equity			
£1 ordinary shares			2.0
Profit and loss account			3.6
			5.6

The accountant for CDC Ltd has estimated the future free cash flow of the business to be as follows:

2006	2007	2008	2009	2010
£4.4m	£4.6m	£4.9m	£5.0m	£5.4m

Note: After 2010, the free cash flows remain constant at £5.4 million for the following 12 years.

The business has a cost of capital of 10 per cent.

CDC Ltd has recently had a professional valuer establish the current resale value of its assets. The current resale value of each asset was as follows:

	£m
Freehold land and premises	18.2
Plant and machinery	4.2
Stock	3.4

The current resale values of the remaining assets are considered to be in line with their book values.

A company that is listed on the Stock Exchange and which is in the same business as CDC Ltd has a gross dividend yield of 5 per cent and a price/earnings ratio of 11 times.

The financial director believes that replacement costs are £1 million higher than the resale values for both freehold land and premises, and plant and machinery, and £0.5 million higher than the resale value of the stock. The replacement costs of the remaining assets are considered to be in line with their balance sheet values. In addition, the financial director believes the goodwill of the business has a replacement value of £10 million. The balance sheet values of the liabilities of the company also reflect their current market values.

Asset-based methods

Asset-based methods attempt to value a share by reference to the value of the assets held by the business. Shareholders own the business and, therefore, own the underlying net assets (total assets less liabilities) of the business. This means that a single share can be valued by dividing the value of the net assets of the business by the number of shares in issue.

Balance sheet method

The simplest method is to use the balance sheet values of the assets held. The **balance sheet**, or **net book value**, approach will determine the value of an ordinary share (P_0) as follows:

$$P_0 = \frac{\text{Total assets at balance sheet values} - \text{Total liabilities}}{\text{Number of ordinary shares issued}}$$

Where the business has preference shares in issue, these must also be deducted (at their book value) from the total assets in order to obtain the net book value of an ordinary share.

Activity 12.15

Calculate the net book value of an ordinary share in CDC Ltd.

The net book value of an ordinary share will be:

$$P_0 = \frac{(9.9 + 5.8) - (6.5 + 3.6)}{2.0} = £2.80$$

The balance sheet method has the advantage that the valuation process is straightforward and the data are easy to obtain. However, the balance sheet value, or net book value, of a share is likely to represent a conservative value. This is because certain intangible assets, such as internally generated goodwill and brand names, may not be recorded on the balance sheet and will, therefore, be ignored for the purposes of valuation. In addition, those assets that are shown on the balance sheet are usually recorded at their historic cost (less any depreciation to date, where relevant), and these figures may be below their current market values. During a period of inflation, the current market values of certain assets held, such as freehold land and buildings, will normally exceed the historic cost figures recorded on the balance sheet.

Often, a share value based on balance sheet values is calculated to obtain a minimum value for a share. A bidder, for example, may compare the bid price with the net book value to measure the 'downside' risk associated with acquiring a business. Where the bid price is close to the balance sheet value, the level of investment risk is likely to be small. It is fairly rare for the shares of a business to have a current market value that is below the net book value.

Current market value methods

Another approach to share valuation is to use the current market value, rather than balance sheet value, of assets held. In economic theory, the value of any asset (including a share in a business) should reflect the present value of the future benefits that it generates. The current market value of an asset should reflect the market's view of the present value of these future benefits as investors will be prepared to pay up to the present value of the future benefits to acquire the asset. Current market values can be expressed in terms of either **net realisable values** or **replacement costs**. In practice, both valuation approaches are used.

Liquidation method   The **liquidation method** values the assets held according to the net realisable values (that is, selling price less any costs of selling) that could be obtained in an orderly liquidation of the business. This method adopts the same basic equation as before, but uses net realisable values instead of balance sheet values for assets and liabilities. Thus, the liquidation value for an ordinary share is calculated as follows:

$$P_0 = \frac{\text{Total assets at net realisable values} - \text{Total liabilities at current market values}}{\text{Number of ordinary shares issued}}$$

Activity 12.16

Calculate the value of an ordinary share in CDC Ltd using the liquidation method.

The liquidation value for an ordinary share will be:

$$P_0 = \frac{[(18.2 + 4.2 + 3.4 + 0.4 + 2.6) - (6.5 + 3.6)^*]}{2.0}$$

$$= £9.35$$

* We are told in Example 12.1 that the balance sheet value of liabilities reflect their current market values.

Although an improvement on the balance sheet method, the liquidation method is also likely to reflect a conservative value. This is because it fails to take account of the value of the business as a going concern. Usually, the going concern value of a business will be higher than the sum of the individual values of the assets when sold piecemeal, because of the benefits of combining the assets. Net realisable values represent a lower limit for the current market value of assets held. The value of an asset *in use* is likely to be greater than the net realisable value of that asset. If this were not the case, a business would, presumably, sell the asset rather than keep it.

Using net realisable values can pose a number of practical problems. Where, for example, the asset is unique, such as a custom-built piece of equipment, it may be particularly hard to obtain a reliable value. Realisable values can vary according to the circumstances of the sale. The amount obtained in a hurried sale may be considerably below that which could be obtained in an orderly, managed sale.

Replacement cost method   Replacement cost can also be used as an indicator of the market value of the assets held by a business. Replacement will represent the cost of replacing a particular asset with an identical asset. The value of an ordinary share, based on replacement cost, will be calculated as follows:

$$P_0 = \frac{\text{Total assets at replacement cost} - \text{Total liabilities at current market values}}{\text{Number of ordinary shares issued}}$$

The replacement cost approach will take account of assets that can be sold on an individual basis as well as of goodwill, which will exist only where the business is a going concern. When this is done, the amount derived will represent an upper limit for the market value of assets held.

Activity 12.17

Calculate the value of an ordinary share in CDC Ltd using the replacement cost method.

The replacement cost approach will yield the following value for an ordinary share:

$$P_0 = \frac{[(19.2 + 5.2 + 3.9 + 0.4 + 2.6 + 10.0) - (3.6 + 6.5)]}{2.0}$$

$$= £15.6$$

Adopting the replacement cost method can lead to practical difficulties. Factors such as technological change may make it difficult to calculate an accurate replacement cost as the asset may no longer be in production.

Stock market methods

Where a business is listed on the Stock Exchange, the quoted share price provides an indication of value. We saw in Chapter 6 that there is evidence to suggest that share prices react quickly and in an unbiased manner to new information that becomes publicly available, and so, in that sense, the stock market can be described as efficient. As information is fully absorbed in share prices it can be argued that, until new information becomes available, shares are correctly valued. The efficiency of the stock market is largely due to the efforts of investors who closely monitor listed businesses in an attempt to identify undervalued shares. The activities of these investors ensure that undervalued shares do not stay undervalued for very long as they will buy the shares and so drive up the price.

It is possible to use stock market information and ratios to help value the shares of an unlisted business. The first step in this process is to find a listed business within the same industry that has similar risk and growth characteristics. Stock market ratios relating to the listed business can then be applied to the unlisted business in order to derive a share value. Two ratios that can be used in this way are the price/earnings (P/E) ratio and the dividend yield ratio.

Price/earnings (P/E) ratio method

The P/E ratio relates the current share price to the current earnings of the business. We may recall from Chapter 3 that the ratio is calculated as follows:

$$\text{P/E ratio} = \frac{\text{Market value per share}}{\text{Earnings per share}}$$

The P/E ratio reflects the market's view of the likely future growth in earnings. The higher the P/E ratio, the more highly regarded are the future growth prospects.

The equation above can be rearranged so that:

Market value per share (P_0) = P/E ratio × Earnings per share

Thus, we can see that the market value is a multiple of the benefits (earnings) that the share will provide.

The P/E ratio of a listed business can be applied to the earnings of a similar unlisted business to derive a share value. Using the rearranged equation above, the value of an ordinary share of an unlisted business is calculated as follows:

P_0 = P/E ratio of similar listed business × Earnings per share (of unlisted business)

Activity 12.18

Calculate the value of an ordinary share in CDC Ltd, using the P/E ratio method.

The value of an ordinary share using the P/E ratio method will be:

$$P_0 = 11 \times \frac{\text{£3.6 (earnings available to shareholders)}}{\text{2.0 (number of ordinary shares)}}$$

$$= \text{£19.80}$$

Although the calculations are fairly simple, this valuation approach should not be viewed as a mechanical exercise. Care must be taken to ensure that differences between the two businesses do not invalidate the valuation process. As can be imagined, a potential problem with this method is finding a listed business with similar risk and growth characteristics. Other differences, such as differences in accounting policies and accounting year ends between the two businesses, can lead to problems when applying the P/E ratio to the earnings of the unlisted business. An unlisted business may adopt different policies on such matters as directors' remuneration, which will require adjustment before applying the P/E ratio.

It should be borne in mind that shares in unlisted businesses are less marketable than those of similar listed businesses. To take account of this difference, a discount is usually applied to the share value derived by using the above equation. A discount of

30 per cent is not uncommon, although determining an appropriate discount figure is difficult.

Dividend yield ratio method

→ The **dividend yield ratio** offers another approach to valuing the shares of an unlisted business. This ratio relates the cash return from dividends to the current market value per share and we saw in Chapter 3 that it is calculated as follows:

$$\text{Dividend yield} = \frac{\text{Gross dividend per share}}{\text{Market value per share}} \times 100$$

The dividend yield can be calculated for shares listed on the Stock Exchange as both the market value per share and gross dividend per share will normally be known. However, for unlisted businesses, the market value per share is not normally known and, therefore, this ratio cannot normally be applied.

The above equation can be expressed in terms of the market value per share by re-arranging as follows:

$$\text{Market value per share } (P_0) = \frac{\text{Gross dividend per share}}{\text{Dividend yield}} \times 100$$

This rearranged equation can be used to value the shares of an unlisted business. For this purpose, the gross dividend per share of the unlisted business, whose shares are to be valued, and the dividend yield of a similar listed business is used in the equation.

Activity 12.19

Calculate the value of an ordinary share in CDC Ltd using the dividend yield method. (Assume a lower rate of income tax of 10 per cent.)

The value of an ordinary share using the dividend yield method will be:

$$P_0 = \frac{0.5 \times 100/90^*}{5} \times 100$$

$$= £11.11$$

* We may recall from Chapter 3 that the dividend as shown in the accounts must be 'grossed up' in order to obtain the gross dividend required for the equation.

This approach to share valuation has a number of weaknesses. Once again, we are faced with the problem of finding a similar listed business as a basis for the valuation. We must also recognise that dividend policies may vary considerably between businesses in the same industry, and may also vary between listed and unlisted businesses. Unlisted businesses, for example, are likely to be under less pressure to distribute profits in the form of dividends than listed businesses.

Dividends represent only part of the earnings stream of a business, and to value shares on this basis may be misleading. The valuation obtained will be largely a function of the dividend policy adopted (which is at the discretion of management) rather than the earnings generated. Where a business does not make dividend distributions, this method cannot be applied.

Cash flow methods

We have already seen that the value of an asset is equivalent to the present value of the future cash flows that it generates. The most direct, and theoretically appealing, approach is therefore, to value a share on this basis. The dividend valuation method and free cash flow method adopt this approach and both are discussed below.

Dividend valuation method

The cash returns from holding a share take the form of dividends received. It is possible, therefore, to view the value of a share in terms of the stream of future dividends that are received. We have already seen in Chapter 7, the value of a share will be the *discounted value of the future dividends received* and can be shown as:

$$P_0 = \frac{D_1}{(1 + K_0)} + \frac{D_2}{(1 + K_0)^2} + \ldots + \frac{D_n}{(1 + K_0)^n}$$

where: $D_{1,2\ldots,n}$ = the dividend received in periods 1, 2 . . . , n
K_0 = the required rate of return on the share.

Although this model is theoretically appealing, there are practical problems in forecasting future dividend payments and in calculating the required rate of return on the share. The first problem arises because dividends tend to fluctuate over time. If, however, dividends can be assumed to remain constant over time, we have already seen that the discounted dividend model can be reduced to:

$$P_0 = \frac{D_1}{K_0}$$

where D_1 = the dividend received at the end of period 1.

Activity 12.20

Assume that CDC Ltd has a constant dividend payout and the cost of ordinary share capital is estimated at 12 per cent. Calculate the value of an ordinary share in the business using the discounted dividend approach.

The value of an ordinary share using the discounted dividend approach will be:

$$P_0 = \frac{0.5 \text{ (that is, 1.0m/2.0m)}}{0.12}$$

$$= £4.17$$

The assumption of constant dividends, however, may not be very realistic, as many businesses attempt to increase their dividends to shareholders over time.

We saw in Chapter 7 that, where businesses increase their dividends at a constant rate of growth, the discounted dividend model can be revised to:

$$P_0 = \frac{D_1}{(K_0 - g)}$$

where g = the constant growth rate in dividends (the model assumes K_0 is greater than g).

In practice, an attempt may be made to forecast dividend payments for a manageable period (say, five years). After this period, accurate forecasting may become too difficult, and so a constant growth rate may be assumed for dividends received beyond the forecast horizon. Thus, the future dividend stream is divided into two separate elements: the first element based on dividend estimates over a particular forecast horizon, and the second representing dividends beyond the forecast horizon (and involving the use of a simplifying assumption). Although avoiding one problem, this approach creates another of deciding on an appropriate growth rate to use.

Figure 12.5 illustrates the process just described.

Figure 12.5   The dividend valuation method

The figure shows how the future dividend stream is divided into two elements in order to provide a value for a share. In the previous chapter a similar approach was used when making SVA calculations beyond the planning horizon.

The use of dividends as a basis for valuation can create difficulties because of their discretionary nature. Different businesses will adopt different dividend payout policies and this can affect the calculation of share values. In some cases, no dividends may be declared by a business for a considerable period. There are, for example, high-growth businesses that prefer to plough back profits into the business rather than make dividend payments.

Free cash flow method

Another approach to share valuation is to value the free cash flows that are generated by a business over time. Free cash flows were considered in Chapter 11. They represent the cash flows available to lenders and shareholders after any new investments in assets. In other words, they are equivalent to the net cash flows from operations after deducting tax paid and cash for investment.

The valuation process is the same as the process that we looked at in the preceding chapter. To value shares using free cash flows, we have to discount the future free cash flows over time, using the cost of capital. The present value of the free cash flows, after deducting amounts owing to long-term lenders at current market values, will represent that portion of the free cash flows that accrue to the ordinary shareholders. If this amount is divided by the number of ordinary shares in issue, we have a figure for the value of an ordinary share. Hence, the value of an ordinary share will be:

$$P_0 = \frac{\text{Present value of future free cash flows} - \text{Long-term loans at current market values}}{\text{Number of ordinary shares issued}}$$

Activity 12.21

Calculate the value of an ordinary share in CDC Ltd, using the free cash flow method.

The value of an ordinary share will be:

	Cash flow £m	Discount rate 10%	Present value £m
2006	4.4	0.91	4.00
2007	4.6	0.83	3.82
2008	4.9	0.75	3.68
2009	5.0	0.68	3.40
Next 13 years	5.4	4.90*	26.46
			41.36

$$P_0 = \frac{\text{PV} - \text{Long-term loans at current market value}^\dagger}{\text{Number of ordinary shares}}$$

$$= \frac{41.36 - 3.6^\ddagger}{2.0}$$

$$= £18.88$$

* This is the total of the individual discount rates for the 13-year period. This short-cut can be adopted where cash flows are constant. For the sake of simplicity, it is assumed that there are no cashflows after the 13-year period.

† This method, unlike the balance sheet methods discussed earlier, does not deduct short-term liabilities in arriving at a value per share. This is because they are dealt with in the calculation of free cash flows.

‡ We are told in the example that the balance sheet values of liabilities reflect their current market values.

We have seen in Chapter 11 that a major problem with this method is that of accurate forecasting. However, this can be tackled in the same way as described above. Free cash flows may be forecast over a manageable time horizon (say, five years) and then a terminal value substituted for free cash flows arising beyond that period. Determining the terminal value is, of course, a problem – and an important one – as it may be a significant proportion of the total cash flows.

In the previous chapter we used an example to illustrate the valuation of a business where it was assumed that returns remained constant after the planning period and used the following formula for a perpetuity in order to determine the terminal value (TV):

$$\text{TV} = \frac{C_1}{r}$$

where: C_1 = the free cash flows in the following year
r = the required rate of return from investors.

However, another approach would be to assume a constant growth rate over time, just as we did with dividends earlier. The terminal value of the business as a whole (TV_B) would then be:

$$\text{TV}_B = \frac{C_1}{(r - g)}$$

where: C = free cash flows in the following year
r = the cost of capital
g = the constant rate of growth in free cash flows.

Although free cash flows may appear to be clearly defined, in practice there may be problems. The discretionary policies of management concerning new investments will have a significant influence on the free cash flow figure calculated. Free cash flows are likely to fluctuate considerably between periods. Unlike earnings, management has no incentive to smooth out cash flows over time. However, for valuation purposes, it may be useful to smooth out cash flow fluctuations between periods in order to establish trends over time.

Other methods of share valuation

We have now discussed the main methods of valuing shares, however, other methods can be found in practice. One such method is to use the ratio between a key financial measure, such as sales, and share value using information from a similar business. Example 12.2 illustrates how this method works in practice.

Example 12.2

Aztec Ltd has sales of £12 million and has 500,000 shares in issue. A similar business, Inca plc, has sales of £30 million and a market capitalisation (that is, total value of ordinary shares in issue) of £10 million.

What is the value of an ordinary share in Aztec Ltd?

Solution

Inca plc has £3 of sales for every £1 of market capitalisation. Using this ratio of 3:1, the total value of the ordinary shares in Aztec Ltd will be £4 million (that is, £12m/3).

Dividing £4 million (the total value of shares) by 500,000 (the number of shares in issue) will provide a value of £8 for each share.

Although the calculations required are straightforward, it is assumed that the relationship between sales and market capitalisation will hold from one business to another. This, however, may be a 'heroic' assumption. The fact that a business sells the same kind of products or services does not mean that it will have the same profitability, asset structure, risk and growth prospects. Ultimately, it is these factors that determine value.

The relationship between market capitalisation and other key financial measures, such as net profit or the net book value of assets, may also be used as a basis for valuation. The approach used in each case is basically the same – and so are the problems.

A further method of valuing shares is the EVA® method that we discussed in Chapter 11. We may recall that the value of a business could be derived as follows:

Business value = Capital invested + PV of future EVA®

To derive the total value of the ordinary shares, the value of any loan capital must be deducted. By dividing total value of shares by the number of shares in issue, we can derive a value for an ordinary share. (We saw in Chapter 11 that this method should arrive at the same business value as the free cash flow approach discussed earlier.)

Valuing a newly established business: an example

Although valuing well-established businesses poses problems, those problems can appear trivial when struggling with the difficulties of valuing newly established businesses. These businesses will have no track record and may be making little or no profit. **Real World 12.14** reveals how analysts might go about valuing a biotech business that is making losses but which has promising new drugs in the pipeline.

REAL WORLD 12.14

Putting a price on a promise   **FT**

So how do you put a realistic valuation on companies that offer little more than promise. Is it just made up?

No. While it may appear more art than a science, there is a generally accepted approach to how analysts value loss-making biotech companies. It is far from perfect and carries the ever-present risk of drugs failing, but it does allow for a form of comparison between companies.

Where do they start?

In a similar way to how analysts might work out a discounted cash flow for an entire company, in which they try to put a value on what predicted future income would be worth today. In a sense, the analysts treat each promising experimental drug within a portfolio as a mini-company. They then carry out a discounted cash flow of each drug to establish a net present value. They then add together the net present value of each drug, along with any cash in the bank, and come up with a present value for the company.

Do they include every drug in a company's development pipeline?

No. Generally, they only include drugs that are already being tested on humans. This is a contentious issue for smaller companies with drugs at the research stage, which are usually assigned no value. They would need to know the potential future sales of a drug to work out a net present value.

How do they do that?

The key thing is to determine what expected peak sales would be if – and it is a big if – a drug successfully makes it all the way through human trials. The year of peak sales is usually taken to be five years from the launch.

Will this depend on the number of potential patients?

Absolutely. The analyst will look at information provided by the company and the wealth of source material available on the internet to determine the size of the patient group that could be treated by a certain drug – that is, how many people actually suffer from a certain disease or condition.

And do they look at the worldwide potential?

They concentrate on North America, western Europe and Japan, the places where people will pay lots of money for drugs.

What if there is competition from existing drugs to treat a condition?

If there is a competitive market with limited advantage offered by the new drug in terms of reducing side-effects or increasing effectiveness, the assumption will be that it will win 10 per cent market share. If there is no other treatment that addresses the same needs as the new drug, a penetration rate of about 50 per cent is assumed.

We have worked out the potential size of the patient population and market share, how do they come up with a price?

This is obviously tricky for a drug that addresses an unmet need, which would involve a certain amount of guesswork. But for those that will compete, you look at the price of the existing drugs. For example, a cancer treatment could cost $15,000 (£8,900). So, if we multiply the potential number of patients by the price, this gives us estimated peak yearly sales.

Does the biotech company receive all of this?

Not likely. Most biotech businesses do not have a sales and marketing division capable of selling large numbers of drugs, and relatively little capital. They often need to license promising drugs to bigger pharmaceutical companies, which help pay for development and would be responsible for sales. Because of this, they will only usually expect a royalty on future sales.

How much of a percentage should they expect on a royalty deal?

This depends on how canny management is when negotiating, but the most important aspect is how far along in development a drug is when a licensing deal is signed. The later it is, the better the royalty level the small biotech can expect.

For Phase I drugs, the earliest stage of human trials, the royalty is usually in the single digits. For Phase II it would be double digits. But this is very changeable, depending on how promising a drug is and the analyst would expect some guidance from a company.

Are there any other costs that need to be taken into account?

Yes. The cost of overheads needs to be factored in. This would usually reduce by another 30 per cent the return expected by the biotech from each drug.

What about tax?

Most biotechs are lossmaking, but if you wanted to be conservative you could take off another 30 per cent. So, we have a figure that represents the potential return on a drug. But that assumes it makes it through human trials and is approved by regulators.

We know that rarely happens.

Very true. For this reason, the analyst applies a probability factor for each drug to account for risk, depending on what stage they are at in development.

If it is in Phase I, the chance of success is 10 per cent, Phase II 30 per cent and Phase III 50–70 per cent. This can vary according to the quality of the data and the inherent riskiness of some drugs, but consistency is important to allow for the comparison of one company's drug pipeline with another's. Add all these factors together and we have an expected peak return for a drug that takes account of risk.

How do we translate that into what it is worth now – its net present value?

The assumption is that a patent on a drug will usually last about 10 years. So, for the first five years the expected return increases until it hits the peak. The peak sales figure is then carried forward for another five years. The analyst discounts the expected returns for each of these 10 years to determine what each amount is worth now, and adds those numbers together to give the net present value.

Real World 12.14 continued

What is discounting?

A discounted cash flow puts a figure on what someone should be willing to pay today to receive the anticipated cash flow in future years. Biotech drugs are assigned a relatively high discount rate of 13 per cent because people would expect a return commensurate with the risk. This means that if someone were to invest £100 in their drugs now, they should expect a return of 13 per cent for each year the drug was available on the market. A safer bet, such as Tesco, has a discount rate of between 7 and 8 per cent, which reflects the much higher likelihood that you will actually see a return on your investment.

Source: 'Trying to put a price on a promise', *Financial Times*, 9 March 2004.

Self-assessment question 12.1

Permian Holdings plc is a large conglomerate company that is listed on the London Stock Exchange. The board of directors of Permian Holdings plc has decided to restructure the business and, as part of the restructuring plan, it has been agreed to spin-off one of its largest subsidiaries, Miocene plc, as a separate business. Miocene plc will not seek an immediate Stock Exchange listing.

The most recent financial statements of Miocene plc are set out below.

Balance sheet as at 30 November 2005

	£m	£m	£m
Non-current assets			
Freehold buildings at cost		48.4	
Less Accumulated depreciation		15.2	33.2
Plant and equipment at cost		36.7	
Less Accumulated depreciation		12.4	24.3
Fixtures and fittings at cost		18.9	
Less Accumulated depreciation		8.5	10.4
			67.9
Current assets			
Stock (inventory)	34.8		
Trade debtors (receivables)	29.6	64.4	
Less **Current liabilities**			
Trade creditors (payables)	35.9		
Taxation	3.9		
Bank overdraft	11.4	51.2	13.2
			81.1
Less **Non-current liabilities**			
10% loan			21.0
			60.1
Equity			
Ordinary £0.25 shares			10.0
Share premium account			5.0
Profit and loss account			45.1
			60.1

**Profit and loss account (income statement) for the year
ended 30 November 2005**

	£m	£m
Sales revenue		153.6
Less Cost of sales		102.4
Gross profit		51.2
Less Selling and distribution expenses	12.3	
Administrative expenses	10.2	
Finance expenses	3.6	26.1
Net profit before taxation		25.1
Corporation tax		7.9
Net profit after taxation		17.2
Dividend paid		8.2
Retained profit for the year		9.0

The following additional information has been gathered concerning Miocene plc:

1   A firm of independent valuers has recently established the current realisable value of
the business's assets as:

	£m
Freehold land and buildings	65.4
Plant and equipment	18.8
Fixtures and fittings	4.6
Stocks	38.9

The balance sheet value of trade debtors reflects their current realisable values.

2   A similar business to Miocene plc is listed on the London Stock Exchange and has a
price/earnings (P/E) ratio of 11.

3   The profit after taxation for Miocene plc for the forthcoming year is expected to be the
same as for the year to 30 November 2005. The dividend payout ratio is expected to be
40 per cent and dividends are expected to grow at 4 per cent per annum for the foreseeable future.

4   The business has an estimated cost of ordinary shares of 10 per cent.

Required:
(a)   Calculate the value of a share in Miocene plc using the following valuation methods:
   (i)   Balance sheet (net book value) basis
   (ii)   Liquidation basis
   (iii)   P/E basis
   (iv)   Dividend growth basis.
(b)   Explain what is meant by the term 'spin-off' in the context of restructuring and suggest reasons why Permian plc might undertake this form of restructuring.

Choosing a valuation model

When deciding on the appropriate valuation model to employ, the purpose for which
the shares are being valued should be considered. Different valuation models may be
appropriate for different circumstances. For example, an 'asset stripper' (that is, someone who wishes to acquire a business with a view to selling off its individual assets)

would probably be most interested in the liquidation basis of valuation. A financial adviser to a new business being floated on the stock market, on the other hand, may rely more heavily on the P/E ratio method or the free cash flow method. We saw earlier that the former approach takes account of share values of similar businesses already listed on the Stock Exchange.

In cases such as mergers and takeovers, share valuations derived from the models can be used as a basis for negotiation. In such circumstances, they can be used to help set boundaries within which a final share value will be determined. The final figure will, however, be influenced by various factors including the negotiating skills and the relative bargaining position of the parties.

SUMMARY

The main points in this chapter may be summarised as follows:

Mergers and takeovers

- A merger is when two businesses of equal size combine; a takeover is when a larger business absorbs a smaller business.
- Mergers can be achieved through horizontal or vertical integration or by combining with unrelated businesses.
- There are surges in merger activity from time to time, usually as a result of a combination of political, economic and technological factors.
- To make economic sense, the merged business should generate greater cash flows than if the two businesses remained apart.

Rationale for mergers

- There are various reasons for a merger, which include:
  - benefits of scale
  - eliminating competition
  - exploiting underutilised resources
  - combining complementary resources
  - using surplus funds
  - diversification
  - pursuing managers' interests.
- The last two of these may not be consistent with the objective of maximising shareholder wealth.

Forms of purchase consideration

- Payment for the shares in an acquired business may take the form of:
  - cash
  - shares
  - loan capital.

Who benefits?

- Shareholders in the target business see an increase in the value of their investment.
- Shareholders in the bidding business often see a decrease in the value of their investment.

- Managers of the bidding business may gain through an increase in status, income and security.
- Managers of the target business often leave within a few years of the takeover.
- Financial advisers and lawyers usually benefit from a merger.

Resisting a takeover bid

- Various tactics may be employed to resist a bid, including:
  - conversion to private company status
  - employee share option schemes
  - circularising shareholders
  - making the business unattractive
  - pac-man defence
  - white knight defence
  - white squire defence.
- Managers of the bidding business may try to overcome resistance by circularising shareholders to explain the logic of the case or by increasing the bid price.

Protecting shareholders and the public

- The City Code on Mergers and Takeovers aims to ensure that shareholders are given every opportunity to evaluate a merger on its merits.
- To protect the public interest, the Competition Commission has the power to investigate mergers where a substantial lessening of competition may occur, and to take appropriate action.
- In the case of cross-border mergers, the EU has rules to protect competition.

Restructuring the business

- A divestment involves selling off part of the business operations.
- A demerger, or spin-off, involves transferring business operations to a new business that is owned by the current shareholders.

Valuing shares in a business

- Shares may be valued on the following bases:
  - methods based on the value of the assets (balance sheet method, liquidation method, replacement cost method)
  - methods based on stock market ratios (P/E ratio method and dividend yield method)
  - methods based on future cash flows (dividend valuation method and free cash flow method).
- The choice of valuation methods will depend on the reasons for the valuation.

→ **Key terms**

Merger p. 466	**White squire** p. 485
Takeover p. 466	**Competition Commission** p. 486
Horizontal merger p. 466	**Divestment** p. 487
Vertical merger p. 466	**Demerger (spin-off)** p. 488
Conglomerate merger p. 466	**Balance sheet (net book value)**
Poison pill p. 485	**basis** p. 491
Crown jewels p. 485	**Net realisable value** p. 492
Golden parachutes p. 485	**Replacement cost** p. 492
Pac-man defence p. 485	**Liquidation method** p. 492
White knight p. 485	**Dividend yield ratio** p. 495

For definitions of these terms see the Glossary, pp. 562–571.

Further reading

If you wish to explore the topics discussed in this chapter in more depth, try the following books:

Corporate Financial Management, *Arnold, G.*, 2nd edn, Financial Times Prentice Hall, 2002, chapters 17 and 20.

Corporate Finance and Investment, *Pike, R. and Neale, B.*, 3rd edn, Financial Times Prentice Hall, 2003, chapters 4 and 22.

Determining Value, *Barker, R.*, Financial Times Prentice Hall, 2001.

Takeovers, Restructuring and Corporate Governance, *Weston, F., Siu, J. and Johnson, B.*, 3rd edn, Prentice Hall, 2001.

References

1 'The long-run performance of UK acquirers: motives underlying the method of payment and their influence on subsequent performance', *Gregory, A.*, University of Exeter Discussion Paper, 1998.

2 **Takeovers, Restructuring and Corporate Governance**, *Weston, F., Siu, J. and Johnson, B.*, 3rd edn, Prentice Hall, 2001, chapter 8.

3 *The market for corporate control*, *Rose, H.*, Financial Times Mastering Management Series, supplement issue no. 2, February 1996.

4 'An examination of the long run performance of UK acquiring firms', *Gregory, A.*, **Working Papers in Accounting and Finance**, The University of Wales, Aberystwyth, 1997.

5 'Gains and losses from mergers: the evidence', *Ravenscroft, D.*, **Managerial Finance**, vol. 17, (1991), no. 1.

6 'Corporate ownership and corporate control: a study of France, Germany and the UK', *Franks, J. and Mayer, C.*, **Economic Policy**, no. 10 (1994).

7 **Creating Long-term Value through Mergers and Acquisitions**, *PA Consulting Group*, PA Knowledge Ltd, 2003.

8 **Mergers and Acquisitions**, *Gaughan, P.*, HarperCollins, 1991, p. 13.

REVIEW QUESTIONS

Answers to these questions can be found in Appendix D at the back of the book.

12.1 Distinguish between a merger and a takeover. What is the significance of this distinction?

12.2 Identify and discuss four reasons why a business may undertake divestment of part of its operations.

12.3 Identify four reasons why a business seeking to maximise the wealth of its shareholders may wish to take over another business.

12.4 Identify four tactics the directors of a target business might employ to resist an unwelcome bid.

EXERCISES

Exercises 12.4 to 12.7 are more advanced than 12.1 to 12.3. Those with coloured numbers have answers at the back of the book.

> If you wish to try more exercises, visit the students' side of the Companion Website.

12.1 When a business wishes to acquire another, it may make a bid in the form of cash, a share-for-share exchange, or loan capital-for-share exchange.

Required:

Discuss the advantages and disadvantages of each form of consideration from the viewpoint of:

(a) The bidding business's shareholders
(b) The target business's shareholders.

12.2 Dawn Raider plc has just offered 1 of its shares for 2 shares in Sleepy Giant plc, a business in the same industry as itself. Extracts from the financial statements of each business for the year ended 31 May Year 8, appear below:

	Dawn Raider £m	Sleepy Giant £m
Profits and loss accounts		
Sales revenue	150	360
Profits after tax	18	16
Dividends proposed and paid	4	14
Balance sheet data		
Non-current assets	150	304
Net current assets (Note 1)	48	182
	198	486
Less Loans	80	40
	118	446
Share capital (Note 2)	50	100
Reserves	68	346
	118	446

Notes

	Dawn Raider	Sleepy Giant
1 Includes cash/(overdrafts):	(£60m)	£90m
2 Shares:	25p	50p

Stock market data for each business is as follows:

	31 May Year 6	31 May Year 7	31 May Year 8
Dawn Raider plc			
Share price (pence)	120.0	144.0	198.0
Earnings per share (pence)	5.3	6.9	9.0
Dividends per share (pence)	2.0	2.0	2.0
Sleepy Giant plc			
Share price (pence)	45.0	43.0	72.0
Earnings per share (pence)	8.4	7.4	8.0
Dividends per share (pence)	8.0	7.0	7.0

If the takeover succeeds, Dawn Raider plans to combine Sleepy Giant's marketing and distribution channels with its own, with a post-tax saving of £1 million a year. In addition it expects to be able to increase Sleepy Giant's profits after tax by at least £5 million a year by better management. Dawn Raider's own profits after tax are expected to be £23 million (excluding the £1 million saving already mentioned), in the year ended 31 May Year 9.

One of the shareholders of Sleepy Giant has written to its chairman arguing that the bid should not be accepted. The following is an extract from his letter: 'The bid considerably undervalues Sleepy Giant since it is below Sleepy Giant's net assets per share. Furthermore, if Dawn Raider continues its existing policy of paying only 2p a share as a dividend, Sleepy Giant's shareholders will be considerably worse off.'

Required:

(a) Calculate:
   (i)   The total value of the bid and the bid premium.
   (ii) Sleepy Giant's net assets per share at 31 May Year 8.
   (iii) The dividends the holder of 100 shares in Sleepy Giant would receive in the year before and the year after the takeover.
   (iv) The earnings per share for Dawn Raider in the year after the takeover.
   (v)   The share price of Dawn Raider after the takeover assuming that it maintains its existing price/earnings ratio.

(b) Comment on:
   (i)   The points that the shareholder in Sleepy Giant raises in his letter.
   (ii) The amount of the bid consideration.

12.3 An investment business is considering taking a minority stake in two businesses, Monaghan plc and Cavan plc. Both are in the same line of business and both are listed on the London Stock Exchange.

Monaghan plc has had a stable dividend policy over the years. In the financial reports for the current year, the chairman stated that a dividend of 30p a share would be paid in one year's time and financial analysts employed by the investment business expect dividends to grow at an annual compound rate of 10 per cent for the indefinite future.

Cavan plc has had an erratic dividend pattern over the years and future dividends have been difficult to predict. However, to defend itself successfully against an unwelcome takeover, the business recently announced that dividends for the next three years were expected to be as follows:

Year	Dividend per share (pence)
1	20
2	32
3	36

Financial analysts working for the investment business believe that, after Year 3, Cavan plc would enjoy a smooth pattern of growth, and dividends would be expected to grow at a compound rate of 8 per cent for the indefinite future.

The investment business believes that a return of 14 per cent is required to compensate for the risks associated with the type of business in which the two businesses are engaged. Ignore taxation.

Required:
(a) State the arguments for and against valuing a share on the basis of its future dividends.
(b) Calculate the value of a share in:
   (i) Monaghan plc, and
   (ii) Cavan plc
   based on the expected future dividends of each business.

12.4 The directors of Simat plc have adopted a policy of expansion based on the acquisition of other businesses. The special projects division of Simat has been given the task of identifying suitable businesses for takeover.

Stidwell Ltd has been identified as being a suitable business and negotiations between the board of directors of each business have begun. Information relating to Stidwell Ltd is set out below:

Balance sheet as at 31 May Year 9

	£	£
Non-current assets		
Freehold land at cost		180,000
Plant and machinery at cost	120,000	
Less Accumulated depreciation	30,000	90,000
Motor vehicles at cost	35,000	
Less Accumulated depreciation	16,000	19,000
		289,000
Current assets		
Stock (inventory)	84,000	
Debtors (receivables)	49,000	
Cash	24,000	
	157,000	
Less Current liabilities		
Creditors (payables) and accruals	42,000	115,000
		404,000
Less Non-current liabilities		
10% debentures		140,000
		264,000
Equity		
Ordinary shares 50p each		150,000
Retained profit		114,000
		264,000

The net profit after tax of Stidwell Ltd for the year ended 31 May Year 9 was £48,500 and the dividend paid for the year £18,000. Profits and dividends of the business have shown little change over the past five years.

The realisable values of the assets of Stidwell Ltd, at the balance sheet date, were estimated to be as follows:

	£
Freehold land	285,000
Plant and machinery	72,000
Motor vehicles	15,000

For the remaining assets, the balance sheet values were considered to reflect current realisable values.

The special projects division of Simat plc has also identified another business, Asgard plc, which is listed on the Stock Exchange and which is broadly similar to Stidwell Ltd. The following details were taken from a recent copy of a financial newspaper:

Years 8–9 High	Low	Stock	Price	± or	Dividend (net)	Cover (times)	Yield (gross %)	P/E (times)
560p	480p	Asgard plc	500p	+4p	10.33p	4.4	2.76	11

Assume a lower rate of income tax of 10 per cent.

Required:

(a) Calculate the value of an ordinary share of Stidwell Ltd using each of the following valuation methods:
  (i)   Net assets (liquidation) basis
  (ii) Dividend yield
  (iii) Price/earnings ratio.
(b) Critically evaluate each of the valuation methods identified in (a) above.

12.5 Alpha plc, a dynamic, fast-growing business in microelectronics, has just made a bid of 17 of its own shares for every 20 shares of Beta plc, which manufactures a range of electric motors. Balance sheets and profit and loss accounts for the two businesses are as follows:

Profit and loss accounts (income statements) for the year ended 31 March Year 9

	Alpha plc £000	Beta plc £000
Sales revenue	3,000	2,000
Operating profit	300	140
Interest	100	10
Profit on ordinary activities before tax	200	130
Taxation on profit on ordinary activities	100	65
Profit on ordinary activities after tax	100	65
Dividends proposed and paid	20	30
Retained profit for the financial year	80	35

Other information:

	Alpha plc	Beta plc
Number of issued shares (million)	1.0	0.5
Earnings per share	10p	13p
Price/earnings ratio	20	10
Market price per share	200p	130p
Capitalisation (that is, market price per share × number of shares)	£2m	£0.65m
Dividend per share	2p	6p

Historical share prices (in pence) at 31 March each year have been:

	Year 4	Year 5	Year 6	Year 7	Year 8
Alpha plc	60	90	150	160	200
Beta plc	90	80	120	140	130

Balance sheets at 31 March Year 9

	Alpha plc £000	Beta plc £000
Non-current assets	1,200	900
Current assets	900	700
Current liabilities	(300)	(600)
Net current assets	600	100
Total assets *less* current liabilities	1,800	1,000
Less Long-term loans	(800)	(120)
	1,000	880
Share capital: 25p ordinary shares	250	125
Profit and loss account	750	755
	1,000	880

The merger of the two businesses will result in post-tax savings of £15,000 per year to be made in the distribution system of Alpha.

One of the shareholders of Beta has queried the bid and has raised the following points. First, he understands that Alpha normally pays only small dividends and that his dividend per share will decrease. Secondly, he is concerned that the bid undervalues Beta since the current value of the bid is less than the figure for shareholders' funds in Beta's balance sheet.

Required:
(a) Calculate the bid consideration.
(b) Calculate the earnings per share for the combined group.
(c) Calculate the theoretical post-acquisition price of Alpha shares assuming that the price/earnings ratio stays the same.
(d) Comment on the shareholder's two points.
(*Hint*: In order to answer this question you need to calculate the number of shares to be issued by Alpha and the total profit after tax following the merger. The market value of the shares following the merger can be found by rearranging the P/E ratio equation and inserting the relevant figures.)

12.6   Larkin Conglomerates plc owns a subsidiary, Hughes Ltd, which sells office equipment. Recently, Larkin Conglomerates plc has been reconsidering its future strategy and has decided that Hughes Ltd should be sold off. The proposed divestment of Hughes Ltd has attracted considerable interest from other businesses wishing to acquire this type of business. The most recent financial statements of Hughes Ltd are as follows:

Balance sheet as at 31 May Year 5

	£000	£000	£000
Non-current assets			
Freehold premises at cost		240	
Less Accumulated depreciation		40	200
Motor vans at cost		32	
Less Accumulated depreciation		21	11
Fixtures and fittings at cost		10	
Less Accumulated depreciation		2	8
			219

	£000	£000	£000
Current assets			
Stock (inventory)	34		
Debtors (receivables)	22		
Cash at bank	20	76	
Current liabilities			
Trade creditors (payables)	52		
Taxation and accrued expenses	14	66	10
			229
Non-current liabilities			
12% loan: Cirencester bank			100
			129
Equity			
£1 ordinary shares			60
General reserve			14
Retained profit			55
			129

Profit and loss account (income statement) for the year ended 31 May Year 5

	£000
Sales revenue	352.0
Profit before interest and taxation	34.8
Interest charges	12.0
Profit before taxation	22.8
Corporation tax	6.4
Profit after taxation	16.4
Dividend proposed and paid	4.0
	12.4
Transfer to general reserve	3.0
Retained profit for the year	9.4

The subsidiary has shown a stable level of sales and profits over the past three years. An independent valuer has estimated the current realisable values of the assets of the business as follows:

	£000
Freehold premises	235
Motor vans	8
Fixtures and fittings	5
Stock	36

For the remaining assets, the balance sheet values were considered to reflect their current realisable values.

Another business in the same industry, which is listed on the Stock Exchange, has a gross dividend yield of 5 per cent and a price/earnings ratio of 12. Assume a rate of income tax of 25 per cent.

Required:
(a) Calculate the value of an ordinary share in Hughes Ltd using the following methods:
   (i)   Net assets (liquidation) basis
   (ii) Dividend yield
   (iii) Price/earnings ratio.
(b) Briefly state what other information, besides the information provided above, would be useful to prospective buyers in deciding on a suitable value to place on the shares of Hughes Ltd.

12.7 The senior management of Galbraith Ltd is negotiating a management buy-out of the business from the existing shareholders. The most recent financial statements of Galbraith Ltd are as follows:

Balance sheet as at 30 November Year 6

	£	£	£
Non-current assets			
Freehold land and buildings at cost		320,000	
Less Accumulated depreciation		28,000	292,000
Plant and machinery at cost		209,000	
Less Accumulated depreciation		64,000	145,000
Motor vehicles at cost		76,000	
Less Accumulated depreciation		34,000	42,000
			479,000
Current assets			
Stock (inventory)		128,000	
Trade debtors (receivables)		146,000	
		274,000	
Less Current liabilities			
Trade creditors (payables)	147,000		
Taxation	19,000		
Bank overdraft	53,000	219,000	55,000
			534,000
Less Non-current liabilities			
13% debentures (secured)			180,000
			354,000
Equity			
Ordinary £0.50 shares			100,000
General reserve			85,000
Retained profit			169,000
			354,000

Profit and loss account (income statement) for the year ended 30 November Year 6

	£	£
Sales revenue		1,430,000
Less Cost of sales		870,000
Gross profit		560,000
Less Selling and distribution expenses	253,000	
Administration expenses	167,000	
Finance expenses	35,000	455,000
Net profit before taxation		105,000
Corporation tax		38,000
Net profit after taxation		67,000
Dividends proposed and paid		5,000
Retained profit		62,000

The following additional information is available:

1 A professional surveyor has recently established the current realisable value of the business's assets as being:

	£
Freehold land and buildings	365,000
Plant and machinery	84,000
Motor vehicles	32,000
Stocks	145,000

The current realisable value of trade debtors was considered to be the same as their balance sheet book values.

2 The free cash flows of the business over the next ten years are estimated as follows:

	£
Year 7	97,000
Year 8	105,000
Years 9–16	150,000

3 The cost of capital for the business is 10 per cent.
4 A similar business which is listed on the Stock Exchange has a price/earnings ratio of eight and a gross dividend yield of 2.2 per cent.

Assume a 20 per cent rate of income tax.

Required:
(a) Calculate the value of a share in Galbraith Ltd using the following valuation methods:
   (i)   Liquidation basis
   (ii) Price/earnings basis
   (iii) Dividend yield basis
   (iv) Free cash flow basis (assuming a ten-year life for the business).
(b) Briefly evaluate each of the share valuation methods set out in (a) above.
(c) Which share valuation method, if any, do you consider to be most valid as a basis for negotiation and why?
(d) What potential problems will a management buy-out proposal pose for the shareholders of Galbraith Ltd?

Appendix A

Present value table

Present value of 1, that is, $(1 + r)^{-n}$
where: r = discount rate
n = number of periods until payment.

Discount rate (r)

Period (n)	1%	2%	3%	4%	5%	6%	7%	8%	9%	10%	Period (n)
1	0.990	0.980	0.971	0.962	0.952	0.943	0.935	0.926	0.917	0.909	1
2	0.980	0.961	0.943	0.925	0.907	0.890	0.873	0.857	0.842	0.826	2
3	0.971	0.942	0.915	0.889	0.864	0.840	0.816	0.794	0.772	0.751	3
4	0.961	0.924	0.888	0.855	0.823	0.792	0.763	0.735	0.708	0.683	4
5	0.951	0.906	0.863	0.822	0.784	0.747	0.713	0.681	0.650	0.621	5
6	0.942	0.888	0.837	0.790	0.746	0.705	0.666	0.630	0.596	0.564	6
7	0.933	0.871	0.813	0.760	0.711	0.665	0.623	0.583	0.547	0.513	7
8	0.923	0.853	0.789	0.731	0.677	0.627	0.582	0.540	0.502	0.467	8
9	0.914	0.837	0.766	0.703	0.645	0.592	0.544	0.500	0.460	0.424	9
10	0.905	0.820	0.744	0.676	0.614	0.558	0.508	0.463	0.422	0.386	10
11	0.896	0.804	0.722	0.650	0.585	0.527	0.475	0.429	0.388	0.350	11
12	0.887	0.788	0.701	0.625	0.557	0.497	0.444	0.397	0.356	0.319	12
13	0.879	0.773	0.681	0.601	0.530	0.469	0.415	0.368	0.326	0.290	13
14	0.870	0.758	0.661	0.577	0.505	0.442	0.388	0.340	0.299	0.263	14
15	0.861	0.743	0.642	0.555	0.481	0.417	0.362	0.315	0.275	0.239	15

	11%	12%	13%	14%	15%	16%	17%	18%	19%	20%	
1	0.901	0.893	0.885	0.877	0.870	0.862	0.855	0.847	0.840	0.833	1
2	0.812	0.797	0.783	0.769	0.756	0.743	0.731	0.718	0.706	0.694	2
3	0.731	0.712	0.693	0.675	0.658	0.641	0.624	0.609	0.593	0.579	3
4	0.659	0.636	0.613	0.592	0.572	0.552	0.534	0.516	0.499	0.482	4
5	0.593	0.567	0.543	0.519	0.497	0.476	0.456	0.437	0.419	0.402	5
6	0.535	0.507	0.480	0.456	0.432	0.410	0.390	0.370	0.352	0.335	6
7	0.482	0.452	0.425	0.400	0.376	0.354	0.333	0.314	0.296	0.279	7
8	0.434	0.404	0.376	0.351	0.327	0.305	0.285	0.266	0.249	0.233	8
9	0.391	0.361	0.333	0.308	0.284	0.263	0.243	0.225	0.209	0.194	9
10	0.352	0.322	0.295	0.270	0.247	0.227	0.208	0.191	0.176	0.162	10
11	0.317	0.287	0.261	0.237	0.215	0.195	0.178	0.162	0.148	0.135	11
12	0.286	0.257	0.231	0.208	0.187	0.168	0.152	0.137	0.124	0.112	12
13	0.258	0.229	0.204	0.182	0.163	0.145	0.130	0.116	0.104	0.093	13
14	0.232	0.205	0.181	0.160	0.141	0.125	0.111	0.099	0.088	0.078	14
15	0.209	0.183	0.160	0.140	0.123	0.108	0.095	0.084	0.074	0.065	15

Appendix B
Annual equivalent factor table

Annual equivalent factor $A_{N,i}^{-1}$

	i	0.04	0.06	0.08	0.10	0.12	0.14	0.16	0.18	0.20
N	1	1.0400	1.0600	1.0800	1.1000	1.1200	1.1400	1.1600	1.1800	1.2000
	2	0.5302	0.5454	0.5608	0.5762	0.5917	0.6073	0.6230	0.6387	0.6545
	3	0.3603	0.3741	0.3880	0.4021	0.4163	0.4307	0.4453	0.4599	0.4747
	4	0.2755	0.2886	0.3019	0.3155	0.3292	0.3432	0.3574	0.3717	0.3863
	5	0.2246	0.2374	0.2505	0.2638	0.2774	0.2913	0.3054	0.3198	0.3344
	6	0.1908	0.2034	0.2163	0.2296	0.2432	0.2572	0.2714	0.2859	0.3007
	7	0.1666	0.1791	0.1921	0.2054	0.2191	0.2332	0.2476	0.2624	0.2774
	8	0.1485	0.1610	0.1740	0.1874	0.2013	0.2156	0.2302	0.2452	0.2606
	9	0.1345	0.1470	0.1601	0.1736	0.1877	0.2022	0.2171	0.2324	0.2481
	10	0.1233	0.1359	0.1490	0.1627	0.1770	0.1917	0.2069	0.2225	0.2385
	11	0.1141	0.1268	0.1401	0.1540	0.1684	0.1834	0.1989	0.2148	0.2311
	12	0.1066	0.1193	0.1327	0.1468	0.1614	0.1767	0.1924	0.2086	0.2253
	13	0.1001	0.1130	0.1265	0.1408	0.1557	0.1712	0.1872	0.2037	0.2206
	14	0.0947	0.1076	0.1213	0.1357	0.1509	0.1666	0.1829	0.1997	0.2169
	15	0.0899	0.1030	0.1168	0.1315	0.1468	0.1628	0.1794	0.1964	0.2139

Appendix C
Solutions to self-assessment questions

Chapter 2

2.1 Quardis Ltd

(a) The projected profit and loss account (income statement) for the year ended 31 May 2006 is:

	£000	£000
Sales revenue		280
Less Cost of sales		
Opening stock	24	
Purchases	186	
	210	
Closing stock	30	180
Gross profit		100
Wages	34	
Other overhead expenses	21	
Interest payable	12	
Depreciation – Freehold premises	9	
– Fixtures	6	82
Net profit before tax		18
Corporation tax (35%)		6
Net profit after tax		12
Dividend paid and proposed		10
Retained profit for the year		2

(b) Projected balance sheet as at 31 May 2006:

	£000	£000	£000
Non-current assets			
Freehold premises at cost		460	
Less Accumulated depreciation		39	421
Fixtures and fittings at cost		60	
Less Accumulated depreciation		16	44
			465
Current assets			
Stock-in-trade		30	
Trade debtors (60% × £280 × 3/12)		42	
		72	
Current liabilities			
Trade creditors (£186 × 2/12)	31		
Accrued expenses (3 + 4)	7		
Bank overdraft (balancing figure)	55		
Corporation tax (50% × 6)	3	96	(24)
			441

	£000	£000	£000
Non-current liabilities			
Loan – Highland Bank			95
			346
Equity			
£1 ordinary shares			200
Retained profit			146
			346

(c) The projected statements reveal a poor profitability and liquidity position for the business. The liquidity position at 31 May 2006 reveals a serious deterioration when compared with the previous year.

As a result of preparing these projected statements the management of Quardis Ltd may wish to make certain changes to their original plans. For example, the repayment of part of the loan may be deferred or the dividend may be reduced in order to improve liquidity. Similarly, the pricing policy of the business and the level of expenses proposed may be reviewed in order to improve profitability.

Chapter 3

3.1   Ali plc and Bhaskar plc

In order to answer this question you may have used the following ratios:

	Ali plc	Bhaskar plc
Current ratio	$=\dfrac{£853.0}{£422.4}$	$=\dfrac{£816.5}{£293.1}$
	$= 2.0$	$= 2.8$
Acid test ratio	$=\dfrac{£(853.0-592.0)}{£422.4}$	$=\dfrac{£(816.5-403.0)}{£293.1}$
	$= 0.6$	$= 1.4$
Gearing ratio	$=\dfrac{£190}{£(687.6+190)}\times 100$	$=\dfrac{£250}{£(874.6+250)}\times 100$
	$= 21.6\%$	$= 22.2\%$
Interest cover ratio	$=\dfrac{£151.3}{£19.4}$	$=\dfrac{£166.9}{£27.5}$
	$= 7.8$ times	$= 6.1$ times
Dividend payout ratio	$=\dfrac{£135.0}{£99.9}\times 100$	$=\dfrac{£95.0}{£104.6}\times 100$
	$= 135\%$	$= 91\%$
Price/earnings ratio	$=\dfrac{£6.50}{31.2\text{p}}$	$=\dfrac{£8.20}{41.8\text{p}}$
	$= 20.8$ times	$= 19.6$ times

Ali plc has a much lower current ratio and acid test ratio than that of Bhaskar plc. The reasons for this may be partly due to the fact that Ali plc has a lower average settlement period for debtors. The acid test ratio of Ali plc is substantially below 1.0: this may suggest a liquidity problem.

The gearing ratio of each business is quite similar. Neither business has excessive borrowing. The interest cover ratio for each business is also similar. The respective ratios indicate that both businesses have good profit coverage for their interest charges.

The dividend payout ratio for each business seems very high indeed. In the case of Ali plc the dividends announced for the year are considerably higher than the earnings generated during the year that are available for dividend. As a result part of the dividend was paid out of retained profits from previous years. This is an unusual occurrence. Although it is quite legitimate to do this, such action may nevertheless suggest a lack of prudence on the part of the directors.

The P/E ratio for both businesses is high, which indicates market confidence in their future prospects.

Chapter 4

4.1 Beacon Chemicals Ltd

(a) The relevant cash flows are:

				Year		
	0	1	2	3	4	5
	£000	£000	£000	£000	£000	£000
Sales revenue	–	80	120	144	100	64
Loss of contribution		(15)	(15)	(15)	(15)	(15)
Variable costs		(40)	(50)	(48)	(30)	(32)
Fixed costs		(8)	(8)	(8)	(8)	(8)
Operating cash flows		17	47	73	47	9
Working capital	(30)					30
Capital cost	(100)					
Net relevant cash flows	(130)	17	47	73	47	39

Notes
1 Only the fixed costs that are incremental to the project (only existing because of the project) are relevant. Depreciation is irrelevant because it is not a cash flow.
2 The research and development cost is irrelevant since it has been spent irrespective of the decision on X14 production.

(b) The payback period is deduced as follows:

	Year 0	Year 1	Year 2	Year 3
	£000	£000	£000	£000
Cumulative cash flows	(130)	(113)	(66)	7

Thus the equipment will have repaid the initial investment by the end of the third year of operations.

(c) The calculation for the net present value is:

	Year 0	Year 1	Year 2	Year 3	Year 4	Year 5
	£000	£000	£000	£000	£000	£000
Discount factor	1.00	0.926	0.857	0.794	0.735	0.681
Present value	(130)	15.74	40.28	57.96	34.55	26.56
Net present value	45.09 (that is, the sum of the present values for years 0 to 5)					

Chapter 5

5.1 Choi Ltd

(a) In evaluating the two machines, the first step is to calculate the NPV of each project over their respective time periods:

Lo-tek	Cash flows £	Discount rate 12%	Present value £
Initial outlay	(10,000)	1.00	(10,000)
1 year's time	4,000	0.89	3,560
2 years' time	5,000	0.80	4,000
3 years' time	5,000	0.71	3,550
		NPV	1,110

Hi-tek	Cash flows £	Discount rate 12%	Present value £
Initial outlay	(15,000)	1.00	(15,000)
1 year's time	5,000	0.89	4,450
2 years' time	6,000	0.80	4,800
3 years' time	6,000	0.71	4,260
4 years' time	5,000	0.64	3,200
		NPV	1,710

The shortest common period of time over which the machines can be compared is 12 years (that is, 3 × 4). This means that Lo-tek will be repeated four times and Hi-tek will be repeated three times during the 12-year period.

The NPV for Lo-tek will be:

$$\text{Total NPV} = £1,110 + \frac{£1,110}{(1 + 0.12)^6} + \frac{£1,110}{(1 + 0.12)^9} + \frac{£1,110}{(1 + 0.12)^{12}}$$

$$= £2,358.8$$

The NPV for Hi-tek will be:

$$\text{Total NPV} = £1,710 + \frac{£1,710}{(1 + 0.12)^8} + \frac{£1,710}{(1 + 0.12)^{12}}$$

$$= £2,840.3$$

The equivalent-annual-annuity approach will provide the following results for Lo-tek:

$$£1,110 \times 0.4163 = £462.09$$

and the following results for Hi-tek:

$$£1,710 \times 0.3292 = £562.93$$

(b) Hi-tek is the better buy because calculations show that it has the higher NPV over the shortest common period of time and provides the higher equivalent-annual-annuity value.

Chapter 6

6.1 Helsim Ltd

(a) The liquidity position may be assessed by using the liquidity ratios discussed in Chapter 3.

$$\text{Current ratio} = \frac{\text{Current assets}}{\text{Current liabilities}}$$

$$= \frac{£7.5\text{m}}{£5.4\text{m}}$$

$$= 1.4$$

$$\text{Acid test ratio} = \frac{\text{Current assets (less stock)}}{\text{Current liabilities}}$$

$$= \frac{£3.7\text{m}}{£5.4\text{m}}$$

$$= 0.7$$

The ratios calculated above reveal a fairly weak liquidity position. The current ratio seems quite low and the acid test ratio seems very low. This latter ratio suggests that the business does not have sufficient liquid assets to meet its maturing obligations. It would, however, be useful to have details of the liquidity ratios of similar businesses in the same industry in order to make a more informed judgement. The bank overdraft represents 67 per cent of the short-term liabilities and 40 per cent of the total liabilities of the business. The continuing support of the bank is therefore important to the ability of the business to meet its commitments.

(b) The finance required to reduce trade creditors to an average of 40 days outstanding is calculated as follows:

	£m
Trade creditors at balance sheet date	1.80
Trade creditors outstanding based on	
40 days' credit (40/365 × £8.4m) (that is, credit purchases)	0.92
Finance required	0.88 (say £0.9m)

(c) The bank may not wish to provide further finance to the business. The increase in overdraft will reduce the level of trade creditors but will increase the exposure of the bank. The additional finance invested by the bank will not generate further funds and will therefore not be self-liquidating. The question does not make it clear whether the business has sufficient security to offer the bank for the increase in overdraft facility. The profits of the business will be reduced and the interest cover ratio, based on the profits generated to the year ended 31 May, would reduce to 1.5 times if the additional overdraft were granted (based on interest charged at 12 per cent a year). This is very low and implies that a relatively small decline in profits would mean that interest charges would not be covered.

(d) A number of possible sources of finance might be considered. Four possible sources are as follows:

● *Issue of ordinary shares.* This option may be unattractive to investors. The return on shareholders' funds is fairly low at 7.9 per cent and there is no evidence that the profitability of the business will improve. If profits remain at their current level the effect of issuing more shares will be to further reduce the returns to ordinary shareholders.

● *Issue of loans.* This option may also prove unattractive to investors. The effect of issuing further loans will be similar to that of increasing the overdraft. The profits of the business will be reduced and the interest cover ratio will decrease to a low level. The gearing ratio of the business is already quite high at 48 per cent and it is not clear what security would be available for the loan.

● *Chase debtors.* It may be possible to improve cash flows by reducing the level of credit outstanding from debtors. At present the average settlement period is 93 days, which seems quite high. A reduction in the average settlement period by approximately one-quarter would generate the funds required. However, it is not clear what effect this would have on sales.

- *Reduce stock.* This appears to be the most attractive of the four options discussed. At present the average stock turnover period is 178 days, which seems to be very high. A reduction in this stock turnover period by less than one-quarter would generate the funds required. However, if the business holds a large amount of slow-moving and obsolete stock it may be difficult to reduce stock levels easily.

Chapter 7

7.1 Ceres plc

(a) (i) *Preliminary calculations*

Annual depreciation is £4m [that is, freehold property (£40m $\times$ $2\frac{1}{2}$%) and plant (£20m $\times$ 15%)].

Cost of acquiring the business is £120m (that is, £10m $\times$ 12).

Loan finance required is £70m (that is, £120m − £50m).

Loan outstanding at 31 May Year 10

Year to 31 May	Yr 7	Yr 8	Yr 9	Yr 10
	£m	£m	£m	£m
Operating profit	10.0	11.0	10.5	13.5
Add Annual depr'n	4.0	4.0	4.0	4.0
	14.0	15.0	14.5	17.5
Less Working capital	–	(1.0)	–	–
Loan interest	(7.0)	(6.3)	(5.5)	(4.6)
Cash to repay loan	7.0	7.7	9.0	12.9
Loan at start of year	70.0	63.0	55.3	46.3
Cash to repay loan	7.0	7.7	9.0	12.9
Loan at end of year	63.0	55.3	46.3	33.4

(ii) **Internal rate of return (IRR)**

The net amount to be received in Year 10 by the venture capitalist is calculated as follows:

	£m
Sale proceeds (12 $\times$ £13.5m)	162.0
Less Loan repayment	33.4
Proceeds to shareholders	128.6
Less	
Amount to shareholder/managers (10%)	12.9
For venture capitalist	115.7

Trial 1 – Discount rate 24%
NPV is:

$$(£115.7m \times 0.42) - £45m = £3.6m$$

As it is positive, the IRR is higher.

Trial 2 – Discount rate 28%
NPV is:

$$(£115.7m \times 0.37) - £45m = (£2.2m)$$

As it is negative, the IRR is lower.

A 4% change in the discount rate leads to a £5.8m (£3.6m + £2.2m) change in the NPV. Thus, a 1% change in the discount rate results in a £1.45m change in NPV. The IRR is:

$$24\% + \left(\frac{£3.6m}{£1.45m}\right)\% = \underline{\underline{26.5\%}}$$

(b) The IRR exceeds the cost of capital – but only just. It is likely to be sensitive to forecast inaccuracies. The forecast inputs should be re-examined, particularly the forecast profit in the year of sale. It is much higher than in previous years and forms the basis for calculating the sale price.

Chapter 8

8.1   Russell Ltd

(a) (i)

**Projected profit and loss accounts (income statements)
for the year ended 31 May Year 5**

	Shares	Debentures
	£000	£000
Net profit before interest and tax	662.0	662.0
Interest	30.0	90.0
Net profit before tax	632.0	572.0
Corporation tax (25%)	158.0	143.0
Net profit after tax	474.0	429.0
Dividend	189.6	171.6
Retained profit	284.4	257.4

(ii) **Earnings per share (EPS)**

	Shares	Debentures
$EPS = \dfrac{\text{Profit available to ordinary shareholders}}{\text{No. of ordinary shares}}$	$\dfrac{474}{(400 + 150)}$	$\dfrac{429}{400}$
	£0.86	£1.07

(iii) **Gearing ratio**

	Shares	Debentures
$\dfrac{\text{Loan capital}}{\text{Share capital + Reserves + Loan capital}} \times 100\%$	$\dfrac{250}{(832.4 + 284.4 + 600.0 + 250)} \times 100\%$	$\dfrac{850}{(832.4 + 257.4 + 850)} \times 100\%$
	12.7%	43.8%

(b) The debenture option provides a significantly higher EPS figure than the share option. The EPS for the most recent year is £0.96 (384/400) and this lies between the two options being considered. On the basis of the EPS figures, it seems that the debenture option is the more attractive. Pursuing the share option will lower EPS compared with the current year, and will result in a single shareholder obtaining 25 per cent of the voting share capital. As a result, this option is unlikely to be attractive. However, the gearing ratio under the debenture option is significantly higher than the share option. This ratio is also much higher than the current gearing ratio of the business of 23.1 per cent (250/1,082.4). The investor must balance the significant increase in financial risk with the additional returns that are generated.

(c) The level of profit before interest and taxation at which EPS under each option is the same will be:

Ordinary shares *Ordinary shares plus debentures*

$$\frac{(x - 30.0)(1 - 0.25)}{(400.0 + 150.0)} = \frac{(x - 90.0)(1 - 0.25)}{400.0}$$

$$400(0.75x - 22.5) = 550(0.75x - 67.5)$$
$$300x - 9,000 = 412.5x - 37,125$$
$$112.5x = 28,125$$
$$x = \underline{250\ (000)}$$

The above figure could also have been calculated using a PBIT-EPS indifference chart as shown in the chapter.

Chapter 9

9.1 Sandarajan plc

(a) The dividend per share and dividend payout ratio over the five-year period under review is as follows:

Year	Dividend per share	Dividend payout %
1	22.0p	52.4
2	14.0p	26.4
3	17.3p	40.0
4	7.3p	14.9
5	30.7p	52.3

The figures above show an erratic pattern of dividends over the five years. Such a pattern is unlikely to be welcomed by investors. In an imperfect world, dividends may be important to investors because of taxation policy and information signalling.

(b) Managers should, therefore, decide on a payout policy and then make every effort to stick with this policy. This will ensure that dividends are predictable and contain no 'surprises' for investors. Any reduction in the dividend is likely to be seen as a sign of financial weakness and the share price is likely to fall. If a reduction in dividends cannot be avoided, the managers should make clear the change in policy and the reasons for the change.

Chaper 10

10.1 Williams Wholesalers Ltd

	£	£
Existing level of debtors (£4m × 70/365)		767,123
New level of debtors: (£2m × 80/365)	438,356	
(£2m × 30/365)	164,384	602,740
Reduction in debtors		164,383
Costs and benefits of policy		
Cost of discount (£2m × 2%)		40,000
Less Savings		
Interest payable (£164,383 × 13%)	21,370	
Administration costs	6,000	
Bad debts (20,000 − 10,000)	10,000	37,370
Net cost of policy		2,630

Chapter 11

11.1 Cupid plc

Adjusted net assets (capital invested)

	£m	£m
Total assets less current liabilities as per the balance sheet		231.0
Add Freehold land (£200m – £60m)	140.0	
Goodwill	50.0	
R&D (9/10 × £10m)	9.0	199.0
Adjusted total assets less current liabilities		430.0*

* This figure represents the adjusted figure for share and loan capital.

Market value added calculation

	£m
Market value of shares (60m × £8.50)	510.0
Less Capital invested (see above)	430.0
MVA	80.0

Chapter 12

12.1 Miocene plc

(a) (i) **Balance sheet basis**

$$\text{Price of an ordinary share } (P_0) = \frac{\text{Net assets at balance sheet values}}{\text{Number of ordinary shares}}$$

$$= \frac{£60.1m}{40m}$$

$$= £1.50$$

(ii) **Liquidation basis**

$$P_0 = \frac{\text{Net assets* at current realisable values}}{\text{Number of ordinary shares}}$$

$$= \frac{£85.1m}{40m}$$

$$= £2.13$$

* The net assets figure is derived as follows:

	£m	£m
Freehold land and buildings		65.4
Plant and equipment		18.8
Fixtures and fittings		4.6
Stocks		38.9
Trade debtors		29.6
		157.3
Less **Creditors**		
Current	51.2	
Non-current	21.0	72.2
		85.1

(iii) **Price/earnings basis**

$$P_0 = \frac{\text{Price/earnings ratio} \times \text{Net profit after tax}}{\text{Number of ordinary shares}}$$

$$= \frac{11 \times £17.2m}{40m}$$

$$= \frac{£189.2m}{40m}$$

$$= £4.73$$

(iv) **Dividend growth basis**

$$P_0 = \frac{D_1}{K_0 - g}$$

$$= \frac{[(£17.2m \times 40\%)/40m]}{(0.10 - 0.04)}$$

$$= £2.87$$

(b) This topic is covered in the chapter. Refer as necessary.

Appendix D
Solutions to review questions

Chapter 1

1.1 The key tasks of the finance function are:

- financial planning and forecasting
- investment appraisal
- financing decisions
- capital market operations
- financial control.

1.2 Wealth maximisation is considered to be superior to profit maximisation for the following reasons:

- The term 'profit' is ambiguous. Different measures of profit can lead to different decisions being made, as we saw in the chapter.
- Profit maximisation in the short term may be at the expense of profit maximisation in the long term.
- Profit maximisation ignores the issue of risk. This may lead to decisions that result in investments in risky projects in order to gain higher returns. However, this may not meet with shareholders' needs.

Wealth maximisation takes both risk and long-run returns into account.

1.3 Survival may be viewed as a necessary objective for the existence of a business. However, shareholders will expect to receive returns from their investment and will not normally be interested in businesses that embrace this as their primary objective. Nevertheless, there may be points in the economic cycle when survival becomes the dominant objective. It can be argued, of course, that, in a highly competitive economy, a business will have to pursue a wealth maximisation objective in order to survive. Under such circumstances, wealth maximisation and survival may be seen as different sides of the same coin.

1.4 There are various problems that are associated with such an incentive plan. These include:

- It is a 'one-way bet'. There are no penalties if the managers fail to deliver.
- It fails to take risk into account. One way of increasing profits is to increase the investment risks.
- The profits generated may not be entirely due to the actions of managers. Other factors (for example, general economic conditions) may have an important influence.

Chapter 2

2.1   When a business is growing fast, it is vitally important that the managers maintain a balance between increases in the level of sales and the finance available to sustain this increase. The business must not pursue sales growth to the point where it becomes financially overstretched and then collapses. Projected financial statements will show the impact of future changes in sales on the profitability, liquidity and financing requirements of the business. If the business shows signs of being unable to sustain the level of sales growth in the future, corrective action can be taken.

2.2   It is correct to state that the future is uncertain. It is also probably correct to state that projected financial statements will prove to be inaccurate. Most businesses, however, find that, despite the inaccuracies that are inherent in the forecasting process, it is better to produce such statements than not to do so. The question that must be asked is: how can a business function if no projections are made available to managers? The problem of uncertainty should not prevent some form of financial planning occurring. It is far better for the business to deal with this problem through such techniques as sensitivity analysis and scenario analysis.

2.3   An existing business is likely to find the preparation of projected financial statements easier than a new business for several reasons. These include:

● The existence of past data concerning sales, overheads and so on for a number of years which can be used as a basis for extrapolation.
● Close links with customers, suppliers and so on which will help to identify likely future changes within the industry and future price changes.
● A team of managers who are experienced in producing forecasts over a number of years and who have an understanding of the competition within the industry.

A new business may find it difficult to predict its likely market share or the rate of growth that it will achieve. This will be the case particularly where it is offering a new product or service.

2.4   The sales forecast is of critical importance because it will determine the overall level of operations of the business. Thus, the future levels of investment, financing and overheads will be influenced by the level of sales. The cash received from sales will be an important factor in deriving the projected cash flows, and the sales revenue will be an important factor in deriving the projected profits. The projected cash flows and profits will, in turn, be important factors in preparing the projected balance sheet. For these reasons, care must be taken in deriving a sales forecast for the business.

Chapter 3

3.1   The fact that a business operates on a low profit margin indicates that a small percentage of profit is being produced for each £1 of sales revenue generated. However, this does not mean necessarily that the return on capital employed will be low as a result. If the business is able to generate a large amount of sales revenue during a period, the total profit may be very high even though the net profit per £1 of sales revenue is low. If the net profit generated is high, this can lead, in turn, to a high return on capital employed, since it is the total net profit that is used as the numerator (top part of the fraction) in this ratio. Many businesses (including supermarkets) pursue a strategy of 'low margin, high turnover'.

3.2   The balance sheet is drawn up at a single point in time – the end of the financial period. As a result, the figures shown on the balance sheet represent the position at that single point in time and may not be representative of the position during the period. Wherever possible, average figures (perhaps based on monthly figures) should be used. However, an external user may only have access to the opening and closing balance sheets for the year and so a simple average based on these figures may be all that it is possible to calculate. Where a business is seasonal in nature or is subject to cyclical changes, this simple averaging may not be sufficient.

3.3   In view of the fact that *Z* scores are derived from information that is published by the businesses themselves, it is difficult to say that *Z* scores should not be made publicly available. Indeed, many of those connected with a business – shareholders, lenders, employees, and so on – may find this information extremely valuable in their decision making. However, there is a risk that a poor *Z* score will lead to a loss of confidence in the business among investors and suppliers, which will, in turn, prevent the business from taking corrective action as lines of credit and investment will be withdrawn.

3.4   The P/E ratio may vary between businesses within the same industry for the following reasons:

● *Accounting conventions.*   Differences in the methods used to compute profit (for example, stock valuation, depreciation, and so on) can lead to different profit figures and, therefore, different P/E ratios.
● *Different prospects.*   One business may be regarded as having a much brighter future owing to factors such as the quality of management, the quality of products, location and so on. This will affect the market price that investors are prepared to pay for the share and, hence, the P/E ratio.
● *Different asset structure.*   The underlying asset base of one business may be much higher and this may affect the market price of the shares.

Chapter 4

4.1   NPV is usually considered the best method of assessing investment opportunities because it takes account of:

● *The timing of the cash flows.*   By discounting the various cash flows associated with each project according to when it is expected to arise, it recognises the fact that cash flows do not all occur simultaneously. Associated with this is the fact that, by discounting, using the opportunity cost of finance (that is, the return that the next best alternative opportunity would generate), the net benefit after financing costs have been met is identified (as the NPV).
● *The whole of the relevant cash flows.*   NPV includes all of the relevant cash flows irrespective of when they are expected to occur. It treats them differently according to their date of occurrence, but they are all taken account of in the NPV and they all have, or can have, an influence on the decision.
● *The objectives of the business.*   NPV is the only method of appraisal where the output of the analysis has a direct bearing on the wealth of the business. (Positive NPVs enhance wealth, negative ones reduce it.) Since most private sector businesses seek to increase their value and wealth, NPV clearly is the best approach to use, at least out of the methods we have considered so far.

NPV provides clear decision rules concerning acceptance/rejection of projects and the ranking of projects. It is fairly simple to use, particularly with the availability of modern computer software, which takes away the need for routine calculations to be done manually.

4.2 The payback method, in its original form, does not take account of the time value of money. However, it would be possible to modify the payback method to accommodate this requirement. Cash flows arising from a project could be discounted, using the cost of finance as the appropriate discount rate, in the same way as the NPV and IRR methods. The discounted payback approach is used by some businesses and represents an improvement on the original approach described in the chapter. However, it still shows the other flaws of the original payback approach that were discussed: for example, it ignores relevant data after the payback period. Thus, even in its modified form, the PP method cannot be regarded as superior to NPV.

4.3 The IRR method does appear to be preferred to the NPV method among practising managers. The main reasons for this appear to be as follows:

- A preference for a percentage return ratio rather than an absolute figure as a means of expressing the outcome of a project. This preference for a ratio may reflect the fact that other financial goals of the business are often set in terms of ratios: for example, return on capital employed.
- A preference for ranking projects in terms of their percentage return. Managers feel it is easier to rank projects on the basis of percentage returns (although NPV outcomes should be just as easy for them). We saw in the chapter that the IRR method could provide misleading advice on the ranking of projects and the NPV method was preferable for this purpose.

4.4 Cash flows are preferred to profit flows because cash is the ultimate measure of economic wealth. Cash is used to acquire resources and for distribution to shareholders. When cash is invested in an investment project an opportunity cost is incurred as the cash cannot be used in other investment projects. Similarly, when positive cash flows are generated by the project they can be used to reinvest in other investment projects.

Profit, on the other hand, is relevant to reporting the productive effort for a period. This measure of effort may have only a tenuous relationship to cash flows for a period. The conventions of accounting may lead to the recognition of gains and losses in one period and the relevant cash inflows and outflows occurring in another period.

Chapter 5

5.1 Although inflation rates have been quite low in recent years, the effect of inflation on investments should be taken into account. Investments are often made over a long time period and even quite low rates of inflation can have a significant effect on cash flows over time. (a) The effect of discounting nominal cash flows at real discount rates will be to overstate the NPV calculations, as the cash flows will be increased in line with inflation whereas the discount rate will not. (b) The effect of discounting real cash flows at a nominal discount rate will be to understate the NPV as the discount rate will be increased in line with inflation whereas the cash flows will not.

5.2 According to one writer, risk is where more things can happen than will happen. In other words, the future is unclear and there is a chance that estimates made concerning the future may not necessarily occur. Risk is important in the context of investment decisions for two reasons:

- Investment projects often have long timescales and so there is a greater opportunity for things to go wrong.
- If things go wrong, there can be serious consequences because of the size of the investment.

5.3   The risk-adjusted discount rate suffers from three major problems:

- Subjective judgement is required in assigning projects to particular risk categories.
- The risk premium will reflect the views of the managers rather than the investors. Any difference between the attitudes of investors and the interpretation of these attitudes by managers can have an effect on the accept/reject decision.
- It assumes that risk increases over time. The further into the future the cash flows arise, the more heavily they are discounted. However, risk may not necessarily increase with time. It will be determined by the nature of the product or service being offered, and so on.

5.4   Risk arises when there is more than one possible outcome for a project. The standard deviation measures the variability of returns and can provide a useful measure of risk. Generally speaking, the higher the standard deviation, the higher the level of risk associated with a project. However, when the distribution of possible outcomes is skewed, the standard deviation may not provide a reliable measure of risk as it fails to distinguish between 'downside' risk and 'upside' risk.

Chapter 6

6.1   Share warrants may be particularly useful for young, expanding businesses wishing to attract new investors. They can help provide a sweetener for the issue of debentures. By attaching warrants it may be possible to agree a lower rate of interest or less restrictive loan covenants. If the business is successful, the warrants will provide a further source of finance. Investors will exercise their option to acquire shares if the market price of the shares exceeds the exercise price of the warrant. However, this will have the effect of diluting the control of existing shareholders.

6.2   A convertible loan gives an investor the right to convert a loan into ordinary shares at a given future date and at a specified price. The investor is not obliged to convert the loan or debenture to ordinary shares. This will be done only if the market price of the shares at the conversion date exceeds the agreed conversion price. The conversion price is usually higher than the market price at the time the convertible loans are issued and so the market price of the shares will usually have to rise over time in order for the lender to exercise the option to convert. During a period of stagnant or falling market prices, the lender is unlikely to exercise the option and so no conversion will take place. Hence, it cannot be assumed that there is an automatic conversion from loan capital to ordinary (equity) share capital.

6.3   A swap agreement can be a useful hedging device where there are different views concerning future movements in interest rates. For example, a business with a floating rate agreement may believe that interest rates are going to rise, whereas a business with a fixed rate agreement may believe that interest rates are going to fall. However, swap agreements may also be used to exploit imperfections in the capital markets. It is sometimes the case that one business has an advantage over another when negotiating interest rates for a fixed loan agreement, but would prefer a floating loan agreement, whereas the other business is in the opposite position. When this occurs, both businesses can benefit from a swap agreement.

   An interest rate swap involves two businesses agreeing to assume responsibility for the other's interest payments (although, in some cases, a bank may act as a counterparty to a swap agreement). Typically, it involves a business with a floating interest rate loan swapping interest payment obligations with a business with a fixed interest rate loan. A swap agreement can be undertaken through direct negotiations with another business, but it is usually easier to negotiate through a bank or other financial intermediary. Although there is an agreement to swap interest payments, the legal responsibility for these payments will still rest with the business that entered into the original loan agreement. Thus, the borrowing business may continue to make interest payments to the lender in line with the loan agreement. However, at the end of an agreed period, the two parties to the swap agreement will make a compensating cash adjustment between themselves.

6.4 Invoice discounting is a service offered to businesses by a financial institution whereby the institution is prepared to advance a sum equivalent to 80 per cent (or perhaps more) of outstanding debtors. The amount advanced is usually payable within 60 to 90 days. The business will retain responsibility for collecting the amounts owing from customers and the advance must be repaid irrespective of whether or not the debts have been collected. Factoring is a service that is also offered to businesses by financial institutions. In this case, the factor will take over the sales ledger of the business and will undertake to collect debts on behalf of the client business. The factor will also be prepared to make an advance of 80 per cent of approved debts, which is repayable from the amounts received from customers. The service charge for invoice discounting is often around 0.5 per cent of turnover, whereas the service charge for factoring is often around 3 per cent of turnover. This difference explains, in part, why businesses have shown a preference for invoice discounting rather than factoring in recent years (and why the financial institutions prefer to factor).

Chapter 7

7.1 Various reasons have been put forward to explain the difference in the proportion of total investment made in business start-ups by UK and US venture capitalists. These include:

- UK venture capitalists are more cautious than their US counterparts. Start-ups are more risky and UK venture capitalists may be less willing to take on these risks.
- UK venture capitalists have a shorter-term investment perspective that makes them prefer financing existing businesses.
- There is greater competition among US venture capitalists for good investment opportunities, which leads them to invest in business start-ups to achieve the required returns.

7.2 A listed business may wish to revert to unlisted status for a number of possible reasons. These include:

- *Cost.* A stock exchange listing can be costly as the business must adhere to certain administrative regulations and financial disclosures.
- *Scrutiny.* Listed businesses are subject to close scrutiny by analysts and this may not be welcome if the business is engaged in sensitive negotiations or controversial activities.
- *Takeover risk.* The shares of the business may be purchased by an unwelcome bidder and this may result in a takeover.
- *Investor profile.* If the business is dominated by a few investors who wish to retain their interest in the business and do not wish to raise further capital by public issues, the benefits of a listing are few.

7.3 An offer for sale involves an issuing house buying the shares in the business and then, in turn, selling the shares to the public. The issue will be advertised by the publication of a prospectus that will set out details of the business and the issue price of the shares (or reserve price if a tender issue is being made). The shares issued by the issuing house may be either new shares or shares that have been purchased from existing shareholders.

A public issue is where the business undertakes direct responsibility for issuing shares to the public. If an issuing house is employed it will usually be in the role of adviser and administrator of the issue. However, the issuing house may also underwrite the issue.

A public issue runs the risk that the shares will not be taken up and is a less popular form of issue for businesses.

7.4 A business should have owners who are:

- committed to realising the growth potential of the business
- prepared to sell some of the ordinary shares in the business
- comfortable with the financing arrangements that venture capitalists usually employ.

A business should have a management team that is:

- ambitious
- experienced
- capable
- well balanced.

Chapter 8

8.1 To find out whether or not a planned level of gearing is likely to be acceptable to investors, the managers of a business could look at the levels of gearing in similar businesses operating within the same industry. If the business adopts a much higher level of gearing than these businesses, there may be problems in raising long-term funds. The managers could also discuss the proposed level of gearing with prospective investors such as banks and financial institutions to see whether they regard the level of gearing as being acceptable.

8.2 The lender may consider the following factors:

- The security for the loan.
- The performance record of the business.
- Likely future prospects of the business and the industry.
- The existing level of gearing for the business.
- Likely interest cover for the loan.
- The purpose of the loan.
- The expected level of return compared with other investment opportunities of the same level of risk.
- Restrictive loan covenants in place from existing lenders.

8.3 It would not be appropriate to employ the specific cost of raising capital for an investment project as the appropriate discount rate. The use of such an approach could result in bizarre decisions being made. Projects with an identical return may be treated differently according to the particular cost of raising finance for each project. It is better to view the individual elements of capital as entering a pool of funds and thereby losing their separate identity. The cost of capital used for investment decisions will represent the average cost of the pool of funds. It should also be remembered that individual elements of capital are interrelated. It would not be possible, for example, to raise debt unless the business had a reasonable level of ordinary share capital. To treat each source of capital as being quite separate is therefore incorrect.

8.4 An important implication of (a), the traditional approach, is that financial managers should try to establish that mix of loan/share finance that will minimise the overall cost of capital. At this point, the business will be said to achieve an *optimal capital structure*. By minimising the overall cost of capital in this way, the value of the business will be maximised. An important implication of (b), the MM (excluding tax effects) approach, is that the financing decision is not really important. As the overall cost of capital remains constant, a business does not have an optimal capital structure as suggested by the traditionalists. This means that one particular capital structure is no better or worse than any other and so managers should not spend time evaluating different forms of financing the business. Instead, they should concentrate their efforts on evaluating and managing the investments of the business. However, (c), the MM (including tax effects) approach, recognises that the tax shield on loan capital benefits the ordinary shareholders and the higher the level of interest payments, the greater the benefits. The implications of this approach are that there is an optimal capital structure (and in that sense it is similar to the traditional approach), and that the optimal structure is a gearing ratio of 100 per cent.

Chapter 9

9.1 A business may decide to repurchase shares in order to:

● return surplus cash to shareholders
● get rid of unwelcome shareholders
● adjust its capital structure.

9.2 The residual theory of dividends states that dividends can be regarded as a residual amount arising when the business does not have enough profitable opportunities in which to invest. The argument assumes that shareholders will prefer the business to reinvest earnings rather than pay dividends, as long as the returns earned by the business exceed the returns that could be achieved by shareholders investing in similar projects. However, when all the profitable projects that meet this criterion have been taken up, any surplus remaining should be distributed to shareholders. Thus, dividends will be, in effect, a by-product of the investment decision as stated.

9.3 The type of distribution policy adopted may not be critical because of the clientele effect. The particular distribution policy will attract a certain type of investor depending on his or her cash needs and taxation position. Thus, investors who rely on dividend income to meet living expenses may prefer a high payout policy whereas investors with high marginal tax rates may prefer a low (or zero) payout policy.

9.4 Agency theory is based on the idea that the business is a coalition of interest groups, with each group seeking to maximise its own welfare. This behaviour is often at the expense of the other groups, and so 'agency costs' arise. In order to minimise these agency costs, the particular group bearing the costs may seek to restrain the actions of others through contractual or other arrangements. Thus, in order to prevent managers from awarding themselves various perks, the shareholders may insist that all surplus cash is returned to them in the form of a dividend. Similarly, in order to prevent shareholders from withdrawing their investment in the business and allowing lenders to bear all, or the majority of, the risks of the business, the lenders may seek to limit the amount that can be declared in the form of a dividend.

Chapter 10

10.1 Although the credit manager is responsible for ensuring that debtors pay on time, Tariq may be right in denying blame. Various factors may be responsible for the situation described which are beyond the control of the credit manager. These include:

● a downturn in the economy leading to financial difficulties among trade debtors;
● decisions by other managers within the business to liberalise credit policy in order to stimulate sales;

- an increase in competition among suppliers offering credit, which is being exploited by customers;
- disputes with customers over the quality of goods or services supplied;
- problems in the delivery of goods leading to delays.

You may have thought of others.

10.2 The level of stocks held will be affected in the following ways.

(a) An increase in production bottlenecks is likely to result in an increase in raw materials and work in progress being processed within the plant. Therefore, stock levels should rise.
(b) A rise in interest rates will make holding stocks more expensive (if they are financed by debt). This may, in turn, lead to a decision to reduce stock levels.
(c) The decision to reduce the range of products should result in fewer stocks being held. It would no longer be necessary to stock certain items in order to meet customer demand.
(d) Switching to a local supplier may reduce the lead time between ordering an item and receiving it. This should, in turn, reduce the need to carry such high levels of the particular item.
(e) A deterioration in the quality of bought-in items may result in the purchase of higher quantities of stocks in order to take account of the defective element in stocks acquired and, perhaps, an increase in the inspection time for items received. This would lead to a rise in stock levels.

10.3 Stocks are held to meet customer demand, to avoid the problems of running out of stock and to take advantage of profitable opportunities (for example, buying a product that is expected to rise steeply in price in the future). These reasons are similar to the transactionary, precautionary and speculative motives that were used to explain why cash is held by a business.

10.4 (a) The costs of holding too little cash are:

- failure to meet obligations when they fall due which can damage the reputation of the business and may, in the extreme, lead to the business being wound up;
- having to borrow and thereby incur interest charges;
- an inability to take advantage of profitable opportunities.

(b) The costs of holding too much cash are:

- failure to use the funds available for more profitable purposes;
- loss of value during a period of inflation.

Chapter 11

11.1 Some believe that it is difficult for these different approaches to coexist. It has been suggested, for example, that in the USA the stakeholder approach has been seriously affected by the pursuit of shareholder value. The application of various techniques to improve shareholder value, such as hostile takeovers, cost cutting and large management incentive bonuses, have badly damaged the interests of certain stakeholders such as employees and local communities. However, others argue that the shareholder value approach must consider the interests of other stakeholders in order to achieve its objectives.

11.2 Two problems were identified in the text. First, MVA depends on establishing a market price for shares and so only businesses listed on the Stock Exchange can use this technique. Secondly, MVA cannot be used to evaluate the performance of strategic business units as there is no market share price for each unit. However, there is also a third reason why it is inappropriate for management purposes. Share prices may fluctuate significantly over the short-term and this could obscure the performance of managers.

11.3 The problem with taking changes in the market value of the shares is that it does not take account of capital required to generate that market value.

Let us assume there are two companies, A and B, which each start with £100 million capital invested. After two years, let us assume that the market value of A is £250 million and the market value of B is £300 million. However, B raised £80 million in additional capital to finance the business. Although B has a higher market value after two years, it has been achieved through a much higher level of capital invested. MVA takes the difference between the market value and the capital invested and so avoids this problem.

11.4 If businesses are overcapitalised it is probably because insufficient attention is given to the amount of capital that is required. Management incentive schemes that are geared towards generating a particular level of profits or achieving a particular market share without specifying the level of capital invested can help create such a problem. EVA can help avoid the problem by focusing on the need to obtain a profitable return on capital invested.

Chapter 12

12.1 A merger involves a combination of two (or more) businesses of roughly equal size. The combination involves the creation of a new business and does not involve the purchase of the shares of one of the existing businesses by the other business. The merger is undertaken with the agreement of the managers and shareholders of each business and there is continuity of ownership of the resources. A takeover involves one business acquiring the shares of another business in order to gain control of the resources of that business. This may lead to a change of ownership and the takeover may be resisted by the managers of the target business. The significance of the distinction concerns the way in which the combination is reported in financial terms.

12.2 Reasons for divestment may include the following:

- A business may decide to focus on its core activities. Any activities that are not regarded as core activities may be sold following such a review. In recent years, a number of businesses have decided, often as a result of bitter experience, that it is better for them to 'stick to their knitting'.
- A business may receive an unwelcome takeover bid because it has particular operations that are of interest to the predator business. The target business may, therefore, try to sell off these operations in order to protect the rest of its operations from takeover.
- A business may decide that in order to improve its overall profitability, poorly performing operations should be sold. The business may not feel it is worth investing time and resources in trying to improve the level of performance achieved by these poorly performing operations.
- A business may require funds for investment purposes or to deal with cash flow problems. The disposal of certain business operations may be the most feasible solution to these problems.

12.3 Four reasons are:

- To exploit underutilised resources.
- To acquire complementary resources.
- To achieve benefits of scale.
- To eliminate competition and increase market share.

12.4 Four methods of resisting a takeover bid are:

- Find a white knight to take over the business instead.
- Refer the bid to the Competition Commission in the hope that this will result in a bid withdrawal.
- Become less attractive to the predator business by selling valuable assets.
- Issue information to shareholders indicating that it is not in their long-term interest to support the takeover.

Other reasons could have been cited.

Chapter 2

2.1 Choice Designs

(a) The projected profit and loss account for the year to 31 May 2006 is:

	£000	£000
Sales		1,400
Cost of sales (70%)		980
Gross profit (30%)		420
Admin. expenses	225	
Selling expenses	85	310
Net profit before tax		110
Taxation		34
Net profit after tax		76
Dividends (6.0p × 500)		30
Profit retained		46

(b) The projected balance sheet as at 31 May 2006 is:

	£000	£000	£000
Non-current assets			
Freehold premises at cost		600	
Less Depreciation		112	488
Fixtures and fittings at cost		140	
Less Depreciation		118	22
Motor vehicles at cost		40	
Less Depreciation		10	30
			540
Current assets			
Stock [240 + (25% × 240)]		300	
Trade debtors [8/52 × (80% × 1,400)]		172	
Bank (balancing figure)		42	
		514	
Current liabilities			
Trade creditors [12/52 × 1,040*]	240		
Corporation tax due (50% × 34)	17	257	257
			797
Equity			
Ordinary £1 shares			500
Retained profit			297
			797

* Purchases = Cost of sales + Closing stock − Opening stock
$$= 980 + 300 - 240$$
$$= 1,040$$

2.2   Prolog Ltd

(a) The cash projection for the six months to 30 June Year 6 is:

	Jan £000	Feb £000	Mar £000	Apr £000	May £000	June £000
Receipts						
Credit sales	100	100	140	180	220	260
Payments						
Trade creditors	112	144	176	208	240	272
Operating expenses	4	6	8	10	10	10
Shelving				12		
Taxation			25			
	116	150	209	230	250	282
Cash flow	(16)	(50)	(69)	(50)	(30)	(22)
Opening balance	(68)	(84)	(134)	(203)	(253)	(283)
Closing balance	(84)	(134)	(203)	(253)	(283)	(305)

(b) A banker may require various pieces of information before granting additional overdraft facilities. These may include the following:

- Security available for the loan.
- Details of past profit performance.
- Profit projections for the next 12 months.
- Cash projections beyond the next six months to help assess the prospects of repayment.
- Details of the assumptions underlying projected figures supplied.
- Details of contractual commitment between Prolog Ltd and its supplier.
- Details of management expertise. Can they manage the expansion programme?
- Details of the new machine and its performance in relation to competing models.
- Details of funds available from owners to finance the expansion.

2.5   Kwaysar Ltd

(a) The forecast profit and loss account for the six months to 30 November 2005 is as follows:

	£000	£000
Sales revenue		
Retailers [(£90 × 3,000) + (£90 × 3,600)]	594.0	
Public [(£90 × 900) + (£90 × 1,200)]	189.0	783.0
Opening stock	44.0	
Purchases [(£50 × 6,600) + (2,100 × £50)]	435.0	
	479.0	
Less Closing stock	44.0	435.0
Gross profit		348.0
Less Overheads		
Wages	108.0	
Advertising expenses	72.0	
Discount allowed [($\frac{1}{2}$ × 594) × 2%]	5.9	
Depreciation		
Freehold property	3.5	
Fixtures	6.0	
Motor vehicles	12.0	
Misc. overheads	84.0	291.4
Net profit for the period		56.6

(b) The forecast cash flow statement for the six months to 30 November 2005 is as follows:

Cash receipts	£000	£000
Sales		
Retailers – 1 month		290.1
– 3 months		135.0
Public		189.0
		614.1
Cash payments		
Trade creditors	387.0	
Advertising costs	72.0	
Motor vehicles	80.0	
Loan repaid	48.0	
Wages	108.0	
Misc. overheads	82.0	777.0
Cash deficit		(162.9)
Opening balance		120.0
Closing balance		(42.9)

(c) We can see from the forecast profit and loss account for the six-month period a 9 per cent decline in net profit as compared to the previous six-month period. The net profit per £1 of sales generated has declined from 11.9p in the previous period to 7.2p in the forecast period.

Implementing the new marketing strategy will mean that there will be additional expenditure on such items as motor vehicles and marketing costs, and receipts from customers will be slower. These factors will combine to produce a cash deficit for the six-month period which will have to be financed in some way.

The decline in profitability and liquidity in return for an increase in market share indicates that the new strategy has little to commend it – at least in the short term. However, it is possible that over the longer term a large market share will allow the business to increase profits and improve its cash flows to compensate for the short-term problems.

Chapter 3

3.1   Three businesses

A plc operates a supermarket chain. The grocery business is highly competitive and to generate high sales volumes it is usually necessary to accept low net profit margins. Thus, we can see that the net profit margin of A plc is the lowest of the three businesses. The stock turnover periods of supermarket chains also tend to be quite low. They are often efficient in managing stock and most supermarket chains have invested heavily in stock control and logistical systems over the years. The average collection period for debtors is very low as most sales are for cash: although where a customer pays by credit card, there is usually a small delay before the supermarket receives the amount due. A low stock turnover period and average collection period for debtors usually means that the investment in current assets is low. Hence, the current ratio (current assets/current liabilities) is also low.

B plc is the holiday tour operator. We can see that the sales to capital employed ratio is the highest of the three businesses. This is because tour operators do not usually require a large investment of capital: they do not need a large asset base in order to conduct their operations. The stock turnover period ratio does not apply to B plc. It is a service business, which does not hold stocks for resale. We can see that the average collection period for debtors is low. This may be because customers are invoiced near to the holiday date for any amounts outstanding and must pay before going on holiday. The lack of stocks held and low average collection period for debtors leads to a very low current ratio.

C plc is the food manufacturing business. We can see that the sales to capital employed ratio is the lowest of the three businesses. This is because manufacturers tend to invest heavily in both current and non-current assets. The stock turnover period is the highest of the three businesses. Three different kinds of stocks – raw materials, work in progress and finished goods – are held by manufacturers. The average debtors' collection period is also the highest of the three businesses. Manufacturers tend to sell to other businesses rather than to the public and their customers will normally demand credit. A one-month credit period for customers is fairly common for manufacturing businesses, although customers may receive a discount for prompt payment. The relatively high investment in stocks and debtors usually results in a high current ratio.

3.2 Amsterdam Ltd and Berlin Ltd

The ratios for Amsterdam Ltd and Berlin Ltd reveal that the average settlement period for Amsterdam Ltd is three times that for Berlin Ltd. Berlin Ltd is therefore much quicker in collecting amounts outstanding from customers. On the other hand, there is not much difference between the two businesses in the time taken to pay trade creditors.

It is interesting to compare the difference in the debtor and creditor collection periods for each business. As Amsterdam Ltd allows an average of 63 days' credit to its customers, yet pays creditors within 50 days, it will require greater investment in working capital than Berlin Ltd, which allows an average of only 21 days to its debtors but takes 45 days to pay its creditors.

Amsterdam Ltd has a much higher gross profit percentage than Berlin Ltd. However, the net profit percentage for the two businesses is identical. This suggests that Amsterdam Ltd has much higher overheads (as a percentage of sales revenue) than Berlin Ltd. The stock turnover period for Amsterdam Ltd is more than twice that of Berlin Ltd. This may be due to the fact that Amsterdam Ltd maintains a wider range of goods in stock in an attempt to meet customer requirements. The evidence therefore suggests that Amsterdam Ltd is the one that prides itself on personal service. The higher average settlement period for debtors is consistent with a more relaxed attitude to credit collection (thereby maintaining customer goodwill), and the high overheads are consistent with incurring the additional costs of satisfying customers' requirements. Amsterdam Ltd's high stock levels are consistent with maintaining a wide range of stock, with the aim of satisfying a range of customer needs.

Berlin Ltd has the characteristics of a more price-competitive business. Its gross profit percentage is much lower than that of Amsterdam Ltd, that is, a much lower gross profit for each £1 of sales revenue. However, overheads have been kept low, the effect being that the net profit percentage is the same as Amsterdam Ltd's. The low stock turnover period and average collection period for debtors are consistent with a business that wishes to minimise investment in current assets, thereby reducing costs.

3.6 Harridges Limited

(a)

	2005	2006
ROCE	$\frac{310}{1,600} = 19.4\%$	$\frac{350}{1,700} = 20.6\%$
ROSF	$\frac{155}{1,100} = 14.1\%$	$\frac{175}{1,200} = 14.6\%$
Gross profit margin	$\frac{1,040}{2,600} = 40\%$	$\frac{1,150}{3,500} = 32.9\%$
Net profit margin	$\frac{310}{2,600} = 11.9\%$	$\frac{350}{3,500} = 10\%$

	2005	*2006*
Current ratio	$\dfrac{735}{400} = 1.8$	$\dfrac{660}{485} = 1.4$
Acid test ratio	$\dfrac{485}{400} = 1.2$	$\dfrac{260}{485} = 0.5$
Days debtors	$\dfrac{105}{2,600} \times 365 = 15$ days	$\dfrac{145}{3,500} \times 365 = 15$ days
Days creditors	$\dfrac{235}{1,560} \times 365 = 55$ days	$\dfrac{300}{2,350^*} \times 365 = 47$ days
Stock turnover period	$\dfrac{250}{1,560} \times 365 = 58$ days	$\dfrac{400}{2,350} \times 365 = 62$ days
Gearing ratio	$\dfrac{500}{1,600} = 31.3\%$	$\dfrac{500}{1,700} = 29.4\%$
EPS	$\dfrac{155}{490} = 31.6\text{p}$	$\dfrac{175}{490} = 35.7\text{p}$

* Used because the credit purchases figure is not available.

(b) There has been a considerable decline in the gross profit margin during 2006. This fact, combined with the increase in sales revenue by more than one-third, suggests that a price-cutting policy has been adopted in an attempt to stimulate sales. The resulting increase in sales revenue, however, has led to only a small improvement in ROCE and ROSF. Similarly, there has only been a small improvement in EPS.

Despite a large cut in the gross profit margin, the net profit margin has fallen by less than 2 per cent. This suggests that overheads have been tightly controlled during 2006. Certainly, overheads have not risen in proportion to sales revenue.

The current ratio has fallen and the acid test ratio has fallen by more than half. Even though liquidity ratios are lower in retailing than in manufacturing, the liquidity of the business should now be a cause for concern. However, this may be a passing problem. The business is investing heavily in non-current assets and is relying on internal funds to finance this growth. When this investment ends, the liquidity position may improve quickly.

The debtors period has remained unchanged over the two years, and there has been no significant change in the stock turnover period in 2006. The gearing ratio is quite low and provides no cause for concern given the profitability of the business.

Overall, the business appears to be financially sound. Although there has been rapid growth during 2006, there is no real cause for alarm provided that the liquidity of the business can be improved in the near future. In the absence of information concerning share price, it is not possible to say whether or not an investment should be made.

Chapter 4

4.1 Mylo Ltd

(a) The annual depreciation of the two projects is:

$$\text{Project 1:} \quad \frac{(£100,000 - £7,000)}{3} = £31,000$$

$$\text{Project 2:} \quad \frac{(£60,000 - £6,000)}{3} = £18,000$$

Project 1

(i)

	Year 0 £000	Year 1 £000	Year 2 £000	Year 3 £000
Net profit (loss)		29	(1)	2
Depreciation		31	31	31
Capital cost	(100)			
Residual value				7
Net cash flows	(100)	60	30	40
10% discount factor	1.000	0.909	0.826	0.751
Present value	(100.00)	54.54	24.78	30.04
	NPV 9.36			

(ii) Clearly the IRR lies above 10 per cent; try 15 per cent:

15% discount factor	1.000	0.870	0.756	0.658
Present value	(100.00)	52.20	22.68	26.32
	NPV 1.20			

Thus the IRR lies a little above 15 per cent, perhaps around 16 per cent.

(iii) To find the payback period, the cumulative cash flows are calculated:

Cumulative cash flows	(100)	(40)	(10)	30

Thus the payback will occur after about 2 years 3 months (assuming that the cash flows accrue equally over the year), or 3 years if we assume year-end cash flows.

Project 2

(i)

	Year 0 £000	Year 1 £000	Year 2 £000	Year 3 £000
Net profit (loss)		18	(2)	4
Depreciation		18	18	18
Capital cost	(60)			
Residual value				6
Net cash flows	(60)	36	16	28
10% discount factor	1.000	0.909	0.826	0.751
Present value	(60.00)	32.72	13.22	21.03
	NPV 6.97			

(ii) Clearly the IRR lies above 10 per cent; try 15 per cent:

15% discount factor	1.000	0.870	0.756	0.658
Present value	(60.00)	31.32	12.10	18.42
	NPV 1.84			

Thus the IRR lies a little above 15 per cent; perhaps around 17 per cent.

(iii) The cumulative cash flows are:

Cumulative cash flows	(60)	(24)	(8)	20

Thus, the payback will occur after about 2 years 3 months (assuming that the cash flows accrue equally over the year) or 3 years (assuming year-end cash flows).

(b) Presuming that Mylo Ltd is pursuing a wealth-maximisation objective, project 1 is preferable since it has the higher NPV. The difference between the two NPVs is not significant, however.

(c) NPV is the preferred method of assessing investment opportunities because it fully addresses each of the following:

● *The timing of the cash flows.* Discounting the various cash flows associated with each project, according to when they are expected to arise, takes account of the fact that cash flows do not all occur simultaneously. Associated with this is the fact that by discounting, using the opportunity cost of finance (namely the return that the next-best alternative opportunity would generate), the net benefit, after financing costs have been met, is identified (as the NPV).

● *The whole of the relevant cash flows.* NPV includes all of the relevant cash flows irrespective of when they are expected to occur. It treats them differently according to their date of occurrence, but they are all taken into account in the calculation of the NPV and they all have, or can have, an influence on the decision.

● *The objectives of the business.* NPV is the only method of appraisal where the output of the analysis has a direct bearing on the wealth of the business. (Positive NPVs enhance wealth, negative NPVs reduce it.) Since most private sector businesses seek to increase their value and wealth, NPV clearly is the best approach to use.

4.5 Newton Electronics Ltd

(a) **Option 1**

	Year 0 £m	Year 1 £m	Year 2 £m	Year 3 £m	Year 4 £m	Year 5 £m
Plant and equipment	(9.0)					1.0
Sales		24.0	30.8	39.6	26.4	10.0
Variable costs		(11.2)	(19.6)	(25.2)	(16.8)	(7.0)
Fixed costs (exc. depr'n)		(0.8)	(0.8)	(0.8)	(0.8)	(0.8)
Working capital	(3.0)					3.0
Marketing costs		(2.0)	(2.0)	(2.0)	(2.0)	(2.0)
Opportunity costs		(0.1)	(0.1)	(0.1)	(0.1)	(0.1)
	(12.0)	9.9	8.3	11.5	6.7	4.1
Discount factor 10%	1.000	0.909	0.826	0.751	0.683	0.621
Present value	(12.0)	9.0	6.9	8.6	4.6	2.5
NPV 19.6						

Option 2

	Year 0 £m	Year 1 £m	Year 2 £m	Year 3 £m	Year 4 £m	Year 5 £m
Royalties	–	4.4	7.7	9.9	6.6	2.8
Discount factor 10%	1.000	0.909	0.826	0.751	0.683	0.621
Present value	–	4.0	6.4	7.4	4.5	1.7
NPV 24.0						

Option 3

	Year 0	Year 2
Instalments	12.0	12.0
Discount factor 10%	1.000	0.826
Present value	12.0	10.0
NPV 22.0		

(b) Before making a final decision, the board should consider the following factors:

● The long-term competitiveness of the business may be affected by the sale of the patents.

● At present, the business is not involved in manufacturing and marketing products. Would a change in direction be desirable?

● The business will probably have to buy in the skills necessary to produce the product itself. This will involve costs, and problems will be incurred. Has this been taken into account?

● How accurate are the forecasts made and how valid are the assumptions on which they are based?

(c) Option 2 has the highest NPV and is therefore the most attractive to shareholders. However, the accuracy of the forecasts should be checked before a final decision is made.

4.6   Chesterfield Wanderers

(a) and (b)

Player option

	0	1	2	3	4	5
	£000	£000	£000	£000	£000	£000
Sale of player	2,200					1,000
Purchase of Bazza	(10,000)					
Sponsorship and so on		1,200	1,200	1,200	1,200	1,200
Gate receipts		2,500	1,300	1,300	1,300	1,300
Salaries paid		(800)	(800)	(800)	(800)	(1,200)
Salaries saved		400	400	400	400	600
Net cash received (paid)	(7,800)	3,300	2,100	2,100	2,100	2,900
Discount factor 10%	1.000	0.909	0.826	0.751	0.683	0.621
Present values	(7,800)	3,000	1,735	1,577	1,434	1,801
NPV	1,747					

Ground improvement option

	1	2	3	4	5
	£000	£000	£000	£000	£000
Ground improvements	(10,000)				
Increased gate receipts	(1,800)	4,400	4,400	4,400	4,400
	(11,800)	4,400	4,400	4,400	4,400
Discount factor 10%	0.909	0.826	0.751	0.683	0.621
Present values	(10,726)	3,634	3,304	3,005	2,732
NPV	1,949				

(c) The ground improvement option provides the higher NPV and is therefore the preferable option, based on the objective of shareholder wealth maximisation.

(d) A professional football club may not wish to pursue an objective of shareholder wealth maximisation. It may prefer to invest in quality players in an attempt to enjoy future sporting success. If this is the case, the NPV approach will be less appropriate because the club is not pursuing a strict wealth maximisation objective.

Chapter 5

5.1   Lee Caterers Ltd

The first step is to establish the NPV for each project:

Cook/chill project

	Cash flows	Discount rate	Present value
	£000	10%	£000
Initial outlay	(200)	1.00	(200)
1 year's time	85	0.91	77.4
2 years' time	94	0.83	78.0
3 years' time	86	0.75	64.5
4 years' time	62	0.68	42.2
		NPV	62.1

Cook/freeze project

	Cash flows £000	Discount rate 10%	Present value £000
Initial outlay	(390)	1.00	(390)
1 year's time	88	0.91	80.1
2 years' time	102	0.83	84.7
3 years' time	110	0.75	82.5
4 years' time	110	0.68	74.8
5 years' time	110	0.62	68.2
6 years' time	90	0.56	50.4
7 years' time	85	0.51	43.4
8 years' time	60	0.47	28.2
		NPV	122.3

Eight years is the minimum period over which the two projects can be compared. The cook/chill will provide the following NPV over this period:

$$NPV = £62.1 + \frac{£62.1}{(1 + 0.1)^4}$$

$$= £104.5$$

This NPV of £104,500 is lower than the NPV for the cook/freeze project of £122,300 (see above). Hence, the cook/freeze project should be accepted.

Using the equivalent-annual-annuity approach we derive the following:

Cook/chill: £62.1 × 0.3155 = £19.59

Cook/freeze: £122.3 × 0.1874 = £22.92

This approach leads to the same conclusion as the earlier approach.

5.3 Simonson Engineers plc

(a) The steps in calculating the expected net present value of the proposed plant are as follows:

	(a) Estimated cash flows £m	(b) Probability of occurrence	(a) × (b) Expected value £m
Year 2	2.0	0.2	0.4
	3.5	0.6	2.1
	4.0	0.2	0.8
			3.3
Year 3	2.5	0.2	0.5
	3.0	0.4	1.2
	5.0	0.4	2.0
			3.7
Year 4	3.0	0.2	0.6
	4.0	0.7	2.8
	5.0	0.1	0.5
			3.9
Year 5	2.5	0.2	0.5
	3.0	0.5	1.5
	6.0	0.3	1.8
			3.8

Taking the expected cash flows for each year into account:

	Year 1	Year 2	Year 3	Year 4	Year 5
	£m	£m	£m	£m	£m
Expected cash flows	(9.0)	3.3	3.7	3.9	3.8
Discount factor	0.909	0.826	0.751	0.683	0.621
Expected present values	(8.18)	2.73	2.78	2.66	2.36
ENPV 2.35					

The expected net present value is £2.35 million.

(b) To find the NPV of the worst possible outcome and the probability of its occurrence:

	Year 1	Year 2	Year 3	Year 4	Year 5
	£m	£m	£m	£m	£m
Cash flows	(9.0)	2.0	2.5	3.0	2.5
Discount factor	0.909	0.826	0.751	0.683	0.621
Present values	(8.18)	1.65	1.88	2.05	1.55
NPV (1.05)					

Probability of occurrence $0.2 \times 0.2 \times 0.2 \times 0.2 = \underline{0.0016}$

(c) The ENPV of the project is positive and so acceptance will increase the wealth of shareholders.

5.4 Helena Chocolate Products Ltd

(a) The first step is to calculate expected sales (units) for each year:

	Sales (units)	Probability	Expected sales
Year 1	100,000	0.2	20,000
	120,000	0.4	48,000
	125,000	0.3	37,500
	130,000	0.1	13,000
			118,500
Year 2	140,000	0.3	42,000
	150,000	0.3	45,000
	160,000	0.2	32,000
	200,000	0.2	40,000
			159,000
Year 3	180,000	0.5	90,000
	160,000	0.3	48,000
	120,000	0.1	12,000
	100,000	0.1	10,000
			160,000

Then the expected net present value can be arrived at:

Expected demand (units)	Incremental cash flow per unit	Total cash flow	Discount rate 10%	ENPV
	£	£		£
118,500	0.38	45,030	0.909	40,932
159,000	0.38	60,420	0.826	49,907
160,000	0.38	60,800	0.751	45,661
				136,500

Less	
Initial outlay	(30,000)
Opportunity costs	(100,000)
ENPV	6,500

The expected net present value is £6,500.

Note: Interest charges should be ignored as the cost of capital is reflected in the discount factor.

(b) As the ENPV is positive, the wealth of shareholders should be increased as a result of taking on the project. However, the ENPV is quite small and so careful checking of the underlying figures and assumptions is essential. The business has the option to sell the new product for an amount that is certain, but this option may have associated risks. The effect of selling the product on the long-term competitiveness of the business must be carefully considered.

Chapter 6

6.1 (a) This topic is dealt with in the chapter. Refer as necessary.
(b) This topic is also dealt with in the chapter. Refer as necessary.
(c) A business may decide to repay a loan earlier than required for various reasons including:

- A fall in interest rates may make the existing loan interest rates higher than current loan interest rates. Thus, the business may decide to repay the existing loan using finance from a cheaper loan.
- A rise in interest rates or changes in taxation policy may make loan financing more expensive than other forms of financing. This may make the business decide to repay the loan using another form of finance.
- The business may have surplus cash and may have no other profitable uses for the cash.
- The business may wish to reduce the level of financial risk by reducing the level of gearing.

6.5 **Cybele Technology Ltd**

(a) **Cost of current policies**

	£
Cost of financing debtors (60/365 × £4m × 14%)	92,055
Bad debts	20,000
	112,055
Cost of using a factor	
Factor service charge (2% × £4m)	80,000
Finance charges [40/365 × (85% × £4m) × 12%]	44,712
Bank overdraft charges [40/365 × (15% × £4m) × 14%]	9,205
	133,917
Less Administration cost savings	(26,000)
	107,917

The expected increase in profits arising from using a factor is:

$$£112,055 - £107,917 = \underline{£4,138}$$

Thus it would be more profitable to employ a factor. However, the difference between the two options is fairly small and other considerations, such as the need to control all aspects of customer relationships, may have a decisive influence on the final outcome.

(b) This topic is dealt with in the chapter. Refer as necessary.

6.6   Telford Engineers plc

(a)

Projected profit and loss account (income statement)
for the year ending 31 December Year 10

	Debt £m		Shares £m
Profit before interest and tax	21.00		21.00
Interest payable	(7.80)	[(20m × 14%) + 5m]	(5.00)
Profit before taxation	13.20		16.00
Corporation tax (30%)	(3.96)		(4.80)
Profit after tax	9.24		11.20
Dividends payable	(4.00)		(5.00)
Retained profit	5.24		6.20

	Debt £m	Shares £m	
Equity			
Share capital 25p shares	20.00	25.00	[(20m × 0.25) + 20m]
Share premium	–	15.00	[20 × (1.00 – 0.25)]
Reserves*	48.24	49.20	
	68.24	89.20	
Loans	50.00	30.00	
	118.24	119.20	

* The reserves figures are the Year 9 reserves *plus* the Year 10 retained profit. The Year 9 figure for equity was 63, of which 20 (that is, 80 × 0.25) was share capital, leaving 43 as reserves. Add to that the retained profit for Year 10 (that is, 5.24 (debt) or 6.20 (shares)).

(b)

Earnings per share

Debt (9.24/80)	11.55p	
Shares (11.20/100)		11.20p

(c) The debt alternative will raise the gearing ratio and lower the interest cover of the business. This should not provide any real problems for the business as long as profits reach the expected level for Year 9 and remain at that level. However, there is an increased financial risk as a result of higher gearing, and shareholders must carefully consider the adequacy of the additional returns to compensate for this higher risk. This appears to be a particular problem since profit levels seem to have been variable over recent years. The figures above suggest only a marginal increase in EPS compared with the equity alternative at the expected level of profit for Year 9.

The share alternative will have the effect of reducing the gearing ratio and is less risky. However, there may be a danger of dilution of control by existing shareholders under this alternative and it may, therefore, prove unacceptable to them. An issue of equity shares may, however, provide greater opportunity for flexibility in financing future projects.

Information concerning current loan repayment terms and the attitude of shareholders and existing lenders towards the alternative financing methods would be useful.

Chapter 7

7.1   The answer to this question is covered in the chapter. Refer as necessary.

7.2   The answer to this question is covered in the chapter. Refer as necessary.

7.7   Carpets Direct plc

(a) The stages in calculating the theoretical ex-rights price of an ordinary share are as follows:

Earnings per share

$$\frac{\text{Profit after taxation}}{\text{No. of ordinary shares}} = \frac{£4.5m}{120m} = \underline{£0.0375}$$

Market value per share

$$\text{Earnings per share} \times \text{P/E ratio} = £0.0375 \times 22 = \underline{£0.825}$$

For the theoretical ex-rights price:

	£
Original shares (4 × £0.825)	3.30
Rights share (1 × £0.66)	0.66
Value of five shares following rights issue	3.96
	£3.96
Value of one share following the rights issue	———
	5
Theoretical ex-rights price	= 79.2p

(b) The price at which the rights are likely to be traded is derived as below:

Value of one share after rights issue	79.2p
Less Cost of a rights share	66.0p
Value of rights to shareholder	13.2p

(c) Comparing the three options open to the investor:

Option 1: Taking up rights issue

	£
Shareholding following rights issue [(4,000 + 1,000) × 79.2p]	3,960
Less Cost of rights shares (1,000 × 66p)	660
Shareholder wealth	3,300

Option 2: Selling the rights

Shareholding following rights issue (4,000 × 79.2p)	3,168
Add Proceeds from sale of rights (1,000 × 13.2p)	132
Shareholder wealth	3,300

Option 3: Doing nothing

As the rights are neither purchased nor sold, the shareholder wealth following the rights issue will be:

Shareholding (4,000 × 79.2p)	3,168

We can see that the investor will have the same wealth under the first two options. However, by doing nothing the rights issue will lapse and so the investor will lose the value of the rights and will be worse off.

Chapter 8

8.2 Celtor plc

(a) The cost of capital is important in the appraisal of investment projects as it represents the return required by investors. Incorrect calculation of the cost of capital can lead to incorrect investment decisions. Too high a cost of capital figure may lead to the rejection of profitable opportunities whereas too low a figure may lead to the acceptance of unprofitable opportunities.

(b) The first step in calculating the weighted average cost of capital is to arrive at the cost of ordinary shares:

$$K_0 = \frac{d_1}{P_0} + g$$

$$= \frac{(20 \times 1.04)}{390} + 0.04$$

$$= 9.3\%$$

Then the cost of loan capital:

$$K_d = \frac{I}{P_d}$$

$$= \frac{9(1 - 0.25)}{80} \times 100$$

$$= 8.4\%$$

The WACC can now be calculated:

	Cost	Target structure (weights)	Proportion	Contribution to WACC
	%		%	%
Cost of ordinary shares	9.3	100	58.8	5.5
Cost of loan capital	8.4	70	41.2	3.5
WACC				9.0

The weighted average cost of capital to use for future investment decisions is 9 per cent.

8.3 Grenache plc

(a) (i) **Loan issue**

Forecast profit and loss account (income statement)
for the year ended 30 April Year 8

	Optimistic £m	Most likely £m	Pessimistic £m
Profit before interest and taxation	22.0	18.1	11.8
Interest payable (£55m × 10%)	5.5	5.5	5.5
Profit before taxation	16.5	12.6	6.3
Corporation tax (25%)	4.1	3.2	1.6
Profit after taxation	12.4	9.4	4.7
Dividends proposed	5.7	5.7	4.2
Retained profit for the year	6.7	3.7	0.5

(ii) **Rights issue**

**Forecast profit and loss account (income statement)
for the year ended 30 April Year 8**

	Optimistic £m	Most likely £m	Pessimistic £m
Profit before interest and taxation	22.0	18.1	11.8
Interest payable (10% × £25m)	2.5	2.5	2.5
Profit before tax	19.5	15.6	9.3
Corporation tax (25%)	4.9	3.9	2.3
Profit after tax	14.6	11.7	7.0
Dividends for the year	6.9	6.9	5.0
Retained profit	7.7	4.8	2.0

(b) (i)   **Earnings per share (EPS) – loan option**

$$\text{EPS} = \frac{\text{Profit available for ordinary shareholders}}{\text{No. of ordinary shares in issue}}$$

		Optimistic	Most likely	Pessimistic
EPS	=	$\dfrac{£12.4m}{25m}$	$\dfrac{£9.4m}{25m}$	$\dfrac{£4.7m}{25m}$
	=	£0.50	£0.38	£0.19

Earnings per share – rights option

		Optimistic	Most likely	Pessimistic
EPS	=	$\dfrac{£14.6m}{30m}$	$\dfrac{£11.7m}{30m}$	$\dfrac{£7.0m}{30m}$
	=	£0.49	£0.39	£0.23

(ii) **Gearing ratio – loan option**

$$\text{Gearing ratio} = \frac{\text{Loan capital}}{\text{Ordinary share capital} + \text{Reserves} + \text{Loan}}$$

Optimistic	Most likely	Pessimistic
$= \dfrac{£55m}{£(55.0 + 43.6 + 6.7)m} \times 100\%$	$\dfrac{£55m}{£(55.0 + 43.6 + 3.7)m} \times 100\%$	$\dfrac{£55m}{£(55.0 + 43.6 + 0.5)m} \times 100\%$
$= 52.2\%$	53.8%	55.5%

Gearing ratio – rights option

Optimistic	Most likely	Pessimistic
$= \dfrac{£25m}{£(25.0 + 43.6 + 30.0 + 7.7)m} \times 100\%$	$\dfrac{£25m}{£(25.0 + 43.6 + 30.0 + 4.8)m} \times 100\%$	$\dfrac{£25m}{£(25.0 + 43.6 + 30.0 + 2.0)m} \times 100\%$
$= 23.5\%$	24.2%	24.9%

(c) The above calculations do not reveal any major differences in EPS between the two financing options. The optimistic and most likely options are almost identical. The pessimistic option favours the rights issue. The differences in the gearing ratios, however, are much more pronounced. Under each scenario the gearing ratio for the loan option is more than double that under the rights option. The loan option involves a significant increase in the level of financial risk for the business as the existing gearing ratio is 36.4 per cent (£25m/£68.6m).

The existing EPS is £0.40 (£9.9m/25m) and so the returns offered under the most likely and pessimistic scenarios do not compare favourably. This may make it difficult to persuade ordinary share investors that additional ordinary share finance should be provided. It may also mean that existing shareholders would resist any increase in gearing in order to finance the venture.

In order to produce a more considered assessment, it would be useful to attach probabilities to each of the three scenarios. An assessment of the likely implications of not undertaking a proposed change should also be provided. Finally, all investments undertaken by the business should be subject to proper investment appraisal using NPV analysis.

8.5   Ashcroft plc

(a) The earnings per share for Year 4 for the debenture and ordinary share alternatives are computed as follows:

	Debentures £m	Shares £m
Profit before interest and taxation	1.80	1.80
Interest payable	0.30	–
Profit before tax	1.50	1.80
Less Corporation tax	0.75	0.90
Profit available to ordinary shareholders	0.75	0.90
Shares issues	4.0m	5.3m
EPS	18.75p	17.0p

(b) Let X = the profit before interest and taxation at which the two schemes have equal EPS.

$$\text{Debentures} \qquad\qquad \text{Shares}$$

$$\frac{(X - £0.3m)(1 - 0.5)}{4.0m} = \frac{X(1 - 0.5)}{5.3m}$$

$$(5.3m\ X - £1.59m)(1 - 0.5) = 4.0m\ X\ (1 - 0.5)$$
$$0.65m\ X = £0.795m$$
$$X = £1.223m$$

This could also be solved graphically as described in the chapter.
(c) The following factors should be taken into account:

● stability of sales and profits
● stability of cash flows
● interest cover and gearing levels
● ordinary share investors' attitude towards risk
● dilution of control caused by new share issue
● security available to offer lenders
● effect on earnings per share and future cash flows.

Chapter 9

9.2   These factors are discussed in the chapter. Review as necessary.

9.4   Fellingham plc

The dividends over the period indicate a 9 per cent compound growth rate and so the chairman has kept to his commitment made in Year 1. This has meant that there has been a predictable stream of income for shareholders. However, during the period, inflation reached quite high levels and in order to maintain purchasing power the shareholders would have had to receive dividends adjusted in line with the general price index. These dividends would be as follows:

Year 2	10.00 × 1.11 = 11.10p
Year 3	11.10 × 1.10 = 12.21p
Year 4	12.21 × 1.08 = 13.19p

We can see the actual dividends (Year 2, 10.90p; Year 3, 11.88p; Year 4, 12.95p) have fallen below these figures and so there has been a decline in real terms in the dividend income received by shareholders. Clearly, the 9 per cent growth rate did not achieve the anticipated maintenance of purchasing power plus a growth in real income which was anticipated.

However, the 9 per cent dividend growth rate is already high in relation to the earnings of the business, and a higher level of dividend to reflect changes in the general price index may have been impossible to achieve. The dividend coverage ratios for each of the years is:

Dividend coverage (EPS/DPS)	
Year 1	1.1
Year 2	1.1
Year 3	0.9
Year 4	1.3

We can see that the earnings barely cover the dividend in the first two years and, in the third year, earnings fail to cover the dividend. The existing policy seems to be causing some difficulties for the business and can only be maintained if earnings grow at a satisfactory rate.

9.6 Traminer plc

(a) This part is dealt with in the chapter. Review as necessary.
(b) This part is also dealt with in the chapter. Review as necessary.
(c) The dividend payout ratio and dividend per share of the business over the past five years are:

Year	Dividend payout %	Dividend per share £
2001	50.0	0.84
2002	48.7	1.16
2003	23.9	0.43
2004	23.2	0.45
2005	37.9	0.97

We can see from this table that there is no stable dividend policy. The payout ratio fluctuated between 50 per cent and 23.2 per cent. The dividend per share has also fluctuated significantly over the period. This suggests that dividends are viewed simply as a residual, that is, dividends will only be paid when the business has no profitable opportunities in which to invest its earnings.

A fluctuating dividend policy is unlikely to be popular with shareholders. The evidence suggests that a policy that is predictable and contains no surprises is likely to be much more welcome. The signalling effect of dividends must also be borne in mind. Sudden changes in payout ratios may result in the market interpreting these changes incorrectly.

Thus, the chairman is probably wrong to suggest that the dividend policy need not be changed, and the view of the managing director seems more sensible.

Chapter 10

10.1 Hercules Wholesalers Ltd

(a) The liquidity ratios of the business seem low. The current ratio is only 1.1 (that is, 306/285) and its acid test ratio is 0.6 (that is, 163/285). This latter ratio suggests that the business has insufficient liquid assets to pay its short-term obligations. A cash flow projection for the next period would provide a better insight to the liquidity position of the business. The bank overdraft seems high and it would be useful to know whether the bank is pressing for a reduction and what overdraft limit has been established for the business.

(b) The operating cash cycle can be calculated as follows:

No. of days

Average stockholding period:

$$\frac{[(\text{Opening stock} + \text{Closing stock})/2] \times 360}{\text{Cost of sales}} = \frac{[(125 + 143)/2] \times 360}{323} = \underline{149}$$

Add Average settlement period for debtors:

$$\frac{\text{Trade debtors} \times 360}{\text{Credit sales}} = \frac{163}{452} \times 360 = \underline{130}$$

$$= 279$$

Less Average settlement period for creditors:

$$\frac{\text{Trade creditors} \times 360}{\text{Credit purchases}} = \frac{145}{341} \times 360 = \underline{153}$$

OCC $\underline{126}$

(c) The business can reduce the operating cash cycle in a number of ways. The average stockholding period seems quite long: at present, average stocks held represent almost five months' sales revenue. This period can be reduced by reducing the level of stocks held. Similarly, the average settlement period for debtors seems long at more than four months' sales revenue. This may be reduced by imposing tighter credit control, offering discounts, charging interest on overdue accounts, and so on. However, any policy decisions concerning stocks and debtors must take account of current trading conditions.

   The operating cash cycle would also be reduced by extending the period of credit taken to pay suppliers. However, for the reasons mentioned in the chapter, this option must be given careful consideration.

10.5 Mayo Computers Ltd

New proposals from credit control department

	£000	£000
Current level of investment in debtors (receivables)		
(£20m × (60/365))		3,288
Proposed level of investment in debtors		
[(£20m × 60%) × (30/365)]	(986)	
[(£20m × 40%) × (50/365)]	(1,096)	(2,082)
Reduction in level of investment		1,206

The reduction in overdraft interest as a result of the reduction in the level of investment will be £1,206,000 × 14% = £169,000 (to the nearest £000).

	£000	£000
Cost of cash discounts offered (£20m × 60% × $2\frac{1}{2}$%)		300
Additional cost of credit administration		20
		320
Bad debt savings	(100)	
Interest charge savings (see above)	(169)	(269)
Net cost of policy each year		51

These calculations show that the business would incur additional annual costs if it implemented this proposal. It would therefore be cheaper to stay with the existing credit policy.

10.6 Boswell Enterprises Ltd

(a)

	Current policy		New policy	
	£000	£000	£000	£000
Debtors				
[(£3m × 1/12 × 30%) + (£3m × 2/12 × 70%)]		425.0		
[(£3.15m × 1/12 × 60%) + (£3.15m × 2/12 × 40%)]				367.5
Stocks				
[£3m − (£3m × 20%)] × 3/12		600.0		
{[£3.15m − (£3.15m × 20%)] × 3/12}				630.0
Cash (fixed)		140.0		140.0
		1,165.0		1,137.5
Creditors				
[£3m − (£3m × 20%)] × 2/12	(400.0)			
{[£3.15m − (£3.15m × 20%)] × 2/12}			(420.0)	
Accrued variable expenses				
(£3m × 1/12 × 10%)	(25.0)			
(£3.15m × 1/12 × 10%)			(26.3)	
Accrued fixed expenses	(15.0)	(440.0)	(15.0)	(461.3)
Investment in working capital		725.0		676.2

(b) The forecast net profit for the year

	Current policy		New policy	
	£000	£000	£000	£000
Sales revenue		3,000.0		3,150.0
Cost of goods sold		(2,400.0)		(2,520.0)
Gross profit (20%)		600.0		630.0
Variable expenses (10%)	(300.0)		(315.0)	
Fixed expenses	(180.0)		(180.0)	
Discounts	–	(480.0)	(47.3)	(542.3)
Net profit		120.0		87.7

(c) Under the proposed policy we can see that the investment in working capital will be slightly lower than under the current policy. However, profits will be substantially lower as a result of offering discounts. The increase in sales revenue resulting from the discounts will not be sufficient to offset the additional costs of making the discounts to customers. It seems that the business should, therefore, stick with its current policy.

Chapter 11

11.1 Aquarius plc

There are a number of ways in which the accuracy of the predicted free cash flow figures may be checked. These include:

Internal
- *Past results.* These may be used to see whether the future projections are in line with past achievements.
- *Strategy.* The future free cash flows for the business should reflect the strategies that have been put in place over the planning period.
- *Capacity.* The ability of the business to generate the free cash flows from the resources available over the planning period should be considered.
- *Market research.* The evidence from any market research carried out by the business should be consistent with the estimates made.

External
- *Industry forecasts.* Forecasts for the industry as a whole may be examined to see whether the predicted sales and profits for the business are in line with industry forecasts.
- *External commentators.* Stockbrokers and financial journalists may have made predictions about the likely future performance of the business and so may provide an external (and perhaps more objective) view of likely future prospects.
- *Technology.* The likely impact of technological change on free cash flows may be assessed using technology forecasts.
- *Competitor analysis.* The performance of competitors may be used to help assess likely future market share.

This is not an exhaustive list. You may have thought of others.

11.3 Virgo plc

There is no single correct answer to this problem. The suggestions set out below are based on experiences that some businesses have had in implementing a management bonus system based on EVA® performance.

In order to get the divisional managers to think and act like the owners of the business, it is recommended that divisional performance, as measured by EVA®, should form a significant part of their total rewards. Thus, around 50 per cent of the total rewards paid to managers could be related to the EVA® that has been generated for a period. (In the case of very senior managers it could be more, and for junior managers less.)

The target for managers to achieve could be a particular level of improvement in EVA® for their division over a year. A target bonus can then be set for achievement of the target level of improvement. If this target level of improvement is achieved, 100 per cent of the bonus should be paid. If the target is not achieved, an agreed percentage (below 100 per cent) could be paid according to the amount of shortfall. If, on the other hand, the target is exceeded, an agreed percentage (with no upper limits) may be paid.

The timing of the payment of management bonuses is important. In the question it was mentioned that Virgo plc wishes to encourage a longer-term view among its managers. One approach is to use a 'bonus bank' system whereby the bonus for a period is placed in a bank and a certain proportion (usually one-third) can be drawn in the period in which it is earned. If the target for the following period is not met, there can be a charge against the bonus bank and so the total amount available for withdrawal is reduced. This will ensure that the managers try to maintain improvements in EVA® consistently over the years.

In some cases, the amount of bonus is determined by three factors: the performance of the business as a whole (as measured by EVA®), the performance of the division (as measured by EVA®) and the performance of the particular manager (using agreed indicators of performance). Performance for the business as a whole is often given the highest weighting and individual performance the lowest weighting. Thus, 50 per cent of the bonus may be for corporate performance, 30 per cent for divisional performance and 20 per cent for individual performance.

11.5   Pisces plc

Adjusted NOPAT

	£m	£m
Operating loss		(20.5)
EVA® adjustments		
Goodwill (Note 1)	10.0	
R&D costs [40 − (1/16 × 80)] (Note 2)	35.0	
Excess provision	6.5	51.5
Adjusted NOPAT		31.0

Adjusted net assets (or capital invested)

	£m	£m
Net assets per balance sheet		196.5
Add Goodwill adjustment (Note 1)	30.0	
R&D costs (Note 2)	70.0	
Provision for doubtful debts	6.5	
Restructuring costs (Note 3)	6.0	112.5
		309.0
Less Marketable investments		9.0
Adjusted net assets		300.0

Notes
1 The goodwill adjustment takes account of the fact that there was a £10 million write-off in Years 1, 2 and 3.
2 The R&D costs represent a writing back of £40 million and a writing off of 1/16 of the total cost of the R&D as the benefits are expected to last 16 years.
3 The restructuring costs are added back to the net assets as they provide benefits over an infinite period.

EVA® can be calculated as follows:

$$EVA® = NOPAT − (R × C)$$
$$= £31m − (8\% × £300m)$$
$$= £7.0m$$

Thus, the EVA® for the period is positive even though an operating loss was recorded. This means that shareholder wealth increased during the third year.

Chapter 12

12.2   Dawn Raider

(a)

		£m
(i)	The bid consideration is [(200m shares/2) × 198p]	198
	The market value of the shares in Sleepy Giant is (£100m × 2 × 72p)	144
	The bid premium is therefore	54

(ii)   Net assets per share are £446m/200m = £2.23

(iii) Dividends from Sleepy Giant before the takeover are $100 \times 7p = £7.00$
       Dividends from Dawn Raider after takeover are $50 \times 2p = £1.00$

(iv)   Earnings per share after takeover:

	£m
Expected post-tax profits of Dawn Raider	23
Current post-tax profits of Sleepy Giant	16
Post-tax savings	1
Improvements due to management	5
Total earnings	45
Expected EPS [£45m/(200m + 100m shares)]	15p

(v)   Expected share price following takeover will be calculated as follows: P/E ratio × expected EPS.

$$P/E \text{ ratio at 31 May Year 8} = \text{Share price/EPS}$$
$$= 198/9.0$$
$$= 22$$
$$\therefore \text{ Expected share price} = 22 \times 15p$$
$$= £3.30$$

(b) (i)   The net assets per share of the business is irrelevant. This represents a past investment that is irrelevant to future decisions. The key comparison is between the current market value of the shares of Sleepy Giant and the bid price.

  The dividend received from Dawn Raider will be substantially lower than those received from Sleepy Giant. However, the share value of Dawn Raider has grown much faster than that of Sleepy Giant. The investor must consider the total returns from the investment rather than simply the dividends received.

(ii)   We can see above that by accepting the bid, the shareholders of Sleepy Giant will make an immediate and substantial gain. The bid premium is more than 37 per cent higher than the current market value of the shares in Sleepy Giant. This could provide a sufficient incentive for the shareholders of Sleepy Giant to accept the offer. However, the shareholders of Dawn Raider must consider the bid carefully. Although the expected share price calculated above is much higher following the bid, it is based on the assumption that the P/E ratio of the business will not be affected by the takeover. However, this may not be the case. Sleepy Giant is a much larger business in terms of sales and net assets than Dawn Raider and has a much lower P/E ratio (nine times). The market would have to be convinced that Sleepy Giant's prospects will be substantially improved following the takeover.

12.4   Simat plc

(a) (i)   Calculating the value per share in the consideration of Stidwell Ltd on a net assets (liquidation) basis gives:

$$P_0 = \frac{\text{Total assets at realisable values} - \text{Total liabilities}}{\text{No. of shares in issue}}$$

$$= \frac{£347,000\,[(285 + 72 + 15 + 157) - (42 + 140)]}{300,000}$$

$$= £1.16$$

(ii) The dividend yield method gives:

$$P_0 = \frac{\text{Gross dividend per share}}{\text{Gross dividend yield}} \times 100$$

$$= \frac{(18{,}000/300{,}000) \times 100/90}{2.76} \times 100$$

$$= £2.42$$

(iii) The P/E ratio method gives:

$$P_0 = \frac{\text{P/E ratio} \times \text{Net profit}}{\text{No. of ordinary shares in issue}}$$

$$= \frac{11 \times £48{,}500}{300{,}000}$$

$$= £1.78$$

(b) This topic is covered in the chapter. Review as necessary.

12.6 **Larkin Conglomerates plc**

(a) The value of an ordinary share in Hughes Ltd according to the three methods is calculated as follows:

(i) Net assets (liquidation) basis:

$$P_0 = \frac{\text{Total assets at realisable values} - \text{Total liabilities}}{\text{No. of ordinary shares}}$$

$$= \frac{£(326 - 166)}{60}$$

$$= \frac{£160}{60}$$

$$= £2.67$$

(ii) Dividend yield method:

$$P_0 = \frac{(\text{Net dividend per share} \times 100/75)}{\text{Gross dividend yield}} \times 100$$

$$= \frac{(4.0/60.0) \times 100/75}{5} \times 100$$

$$= £1.78$$

(iii) Price/earnings ratio method:

$$P_0 = \frac{\text{P/E ratio} \times \text{Net profit}}{\text{No. of ordinary shares}}$$

$$= \frac{£16.4 \times 12}{60}$$

$$= £3.28$$

(b) Other information might include:

- Details of relations with suppliers, employees, the community and other stakeholders should be ascertained.
- The nature and condition of the assets owned by the target business should be examined. The suitability of the assets and their ability to perform the tasks required will be vitally important.
- Key personnel will need to be identified and their intentions with regard to the business following the takeover must be ascertained.
- Onerous commitments entered into by the business (for example, capital expenditure decisions, contracts with suppliers) must be identified and evaluated.
- Details of the state of the order book, the market share of the products or services provided by the business and the loyalty of its customers should be established.
- Examination of the budgets which set out expected performance levels, output levels and future financing needs would be useful.
- Information concerning the cost structure of the business would be useful.

Glossary of key terms

ABC system of stock control   A method of applying different levels of stock control based on the value of each category of stock. *p. 393*

Accounting rate of return (ARR)   The average profit from an investment, expressed as a percentage of the average investment made. *p. 115*

Acid test ratio   A liquidity ratio that relates the current assets (less stocks) to the current liabilities. *p. 79*

Ageing schedule of debtors   A report dividing debtors into categories, depending on the length of time outstanding. *p. 404*

Agency problem   The conflict of interest between shareholders (the principals) and the managers (agents) of a business which arises when the managers seek to maximise their own welfare. *p. 13*

Alternative Investment Market (AIM)   Second-tier market of the London Stock Exchange that specialises in the securities of smaller businesses. *p. 288*

Annuity   An investment that pays a constant sum each year over a period of time. *p. 166*

Arbitrage transactions   Transactions that exploit differences in price between similar shares (or other assets) and which involve selling the overpriced shares and purchasing the underpriced shares. *p. 340*

Asset-based finance   A form of finance where assets are used as security for cash advances to a business. Factoring and invoice discounting, where the security is trade debtors, are examples of asset-based finance. *p. 236*

Average settlement period for creditors   The average time taken by a business to pay its creditors. *p. 73, 416*

Average settlement period for debtors   The average time taken for debtors to pay the amounts owing. *p. 73, 403*

Average stock turnover period   An efficiency ratio that measures the average period for which stocks are held by a business. *p. 72*

Balance sheet (net book value) basis   A method of valuing the shares of a business by reference to the value of the net assets as shown in the balance sheet. *p. 491*

Bank overdraft   Amount owing to a bank that is repayable on demand. The amount borrowed and the rate of interest may fluctuate over time. *p. 231*

Behavioural finance   An approach to finance that rejects the notion that investors behave in a rational manner but make systematic errors when processing information. *p. 267*

Beta (coefficient)   A measure of the extent to which the returns on a particular share vary with the market as a whole. *p. 304*

Bill of exchange   A written agreement requiring one party to the agreement to pay a particular amount at some future date. *p. 232*

Bond   A long-term loan. *p. 216*

Bonus issue (scrip issue)   Transfer of reserves to share capital requiring the issue of new shares to shareholders in proportion to existing shareholdings. *p. 272*

Business angels   Wealthy individuals willing to invest in businesses at an early stage in their development. *p. 287*

Capital asset pricing model (CAPM)   A method of establishing the cost of share capital that identifies two forms of risk: diversifiable risk and non-diversifiable risk. *p. 303*

Capital markets   Financial markets for long-term loans, debentures and shares. *p. 5*

Capital rationing   Limiting the long-term funds available for investment during a period. Soft capital rationing is imposed by managers, and hard capital rationing is imposed by investors. *p. 144*

Cash discount   A reduction in the amount due for goods or services sold on credit in return for prompt payment. *p. 402*

Clientele effect   The phenomenon where investors seek out businesses whose dividend policies match their particular needs. *p. 365*

Coefficient of correlation   A statistical measure of association that can be used to measure the degree to which the returns from two separate projects are related. The measure ranges from +1 to –1. A measure of +1 indicates a perfect positive correlation and a measure of –1 indicates a perfect negative correlation. *p. 197*

Combined Code   A code of practice for companies listed on the London Stock Exchange which deals with corporate governance matters. *p. 15*

Competition Commission (formerly Monopolies and Mergers Commission)   A UK government regulatory body that seeks to prevent monopolies and mergers from occurring that are anti-competitive and not in the public interest. *p. 486*

Competitor profiling   Building a profile of the strengths and weaknesses of a major competitor in order to understand the threats posed. *p. 28*

Conglomerate merger   A merger between two businesses engaged in unrelated activities. *p. 466*

Convertible loan   Loan capital that can be converted into ordinary share capital at the option of the holders. *p. 217*

Corporate governance   Systems for directing and controlling a business. *p. 13*

Cost of capital   The rate of return required by investors in the business. The cost of capital is used as the criterion rate of return when evaluating investment proposals using the NPV and IRR methods of appraisal. *p. 130, 300*

Creative accounting   Adopting accounting policies to achieve a particular view of performance and position that preparers would like users to see rather than what is a true and fair view. *p. 98*

Crown jewels The most valued part of a business (which may be sold to fend off a hostile takeover bid). *p. 485*

Cum dividend A term used to describe the price of a share that includes the right to receive a forthcoming dividend. *p. 357*

Current ratio A liquidity ratio that relates the current assets of the business to the current liabilities. *p. 78*

Debenture A long-term loan evidenced by a trust deed. *p. 215*

Debt factoring *See* Factoring. *p. 232*

Deep discount bonds Redeemable bonds that are issued at a low or zero rate of interest and at a large discount to their redeemable value. *p. 217*

Degree of financial gearing A measure of the sensitivity of earnings per share to changes in profit before interest and taxation. *p. 322*

Demerger (spin off) The transfer of part of the assets in an existing business to a new business. Shareholders in the existing business will be given shares, usually on a pro rata basis, in the new business. *p. 488*

Discount factor The rate used when making investment decisions to discount future cash flows in order to arrive at their present value. *p. 128*

Discriminate function A boundary line, produced by multiple discriminate analysis, that identifies those businesses that are likely to suffer financial distress and those that are not. *p. 96*

Diversifiable risk That part of the total risk that is specific to an investment and which can be diversified away through combining the investment with other investments. *p. 199*

Diversification The process of reducing risk by investing in a variety of different projects or assets. *p. 196*

Divestment The selling off of part of the operations of a business. *p. 487*

Dividend A transfer of assets (usually cash) made by a business to its shareholders. *p. 356*

Dividend cover ratio The reciprocal of the dividend payout ratio (see below). *p. 83, 358*

Dividend payout ratio An investment ratio that divides the dividends announced for the period by the profit generated during the period and available for dividends. *p. 83*

Dividend per share An investment ratio that divides the dividends announced for a period by the number of shares in issue. *p. 84*

Dividend yield ratio An investment ratio that relates the cash return from a share to its current market value. *p. 84, 495*

Earnings per share An investment ratio that divides the earnings (profits) generated by a business, and available to ordinary shareholders, by the number of shares in issue. *p. 85*

Economic order quantity (EOQ) The quantity of stocks that should be purchased in order to minimise total stock costs. *p. 393*

Economic value added (EVA®)   The difference between the net operating profit after tax and the required returns from investors. *p. 438*

Efficient stock market   A stock market where new information is quickly and accurately absorbed by investors resulting in an appropriate share price adjustment. *p. 259*

Equivalent-annual-annuity approach   An approach to deciding among competing investment projects with unequal lives which involves converting the NPV of each project into an annual annuity stream over the project's expected life. *p. 166*

Eurobonds   Bearer bonds that are issued by listed businesses and other organisations in various countries with the finance being raised on an international basis. *p. 215*

Event tree diagram   A diagram that portrays the various events or outcomes associated with a particular course of action and the probabilities associated with each event or outcome. *p. 186*

Ex dividend   A term used to describe the price of a share that excludes any right to a forthcoming dividend. *p. 357*

Expected net present value (ENPV)   A method of dealing with risk that involves assigning a probability of occurrence to each possible outcome. The expected net present value of the project represents a weighted average of the possible NPVs where the probabilities are used as weights. *p. 184*

Expected value   A weighted average of a range of possible outcomes where the probabilities are used as weights. *p. 183*

Expected value–standard deviation rule   A decision rule that can be employed to discriminate among competing investments where the possible outcomes are known and are normally distributed. *p. 194*

Factoring   A method of raising short-term finance. A financial institution ('factor') will manage the sales ledger of the business and will be prepared to advance sums to the business based on the amount of trade debtors outstanding. *p. 232*

Finance lease   Agreement that gives the lessee the right to use a particular asset for substantially the whole of its useful life in return for regular fixed payments. It represents an alternative to outright purchase. *p. 227*

Financial derivative   Any form of financial instrument, based on share or loan capital, that can be used by investors either to increase their returns or to decrease their exposure to risk. *p. 224*

Financial gearing   The existence of fixed-payment-bearing securities (for example, loans) in the capital structure of a business. *p. 80*

Five Cs of credit   A checklist of factors to be taken into account when assessing the creditworthiness of a customer. *p. 398*

Fixed charge   Where a specific asset is offered as security for a loan or debenture. *p. 213*

Fixed costs   A cost that stays the same irrespective of the level of output. *p. 29*

Fixed interest rate   A rate of return payable to lenders that will remain unchanged with rises and falls in market interest rates. *p. 225*

Floating charge   Where the whole of the assets of the business is offered as security for a loan or debenture. The charge will 'crystallise' and fix on specific assets in the event of a default in loan obligations. *p. 213*

Floating interest rates   A rate of return payable to lenders that will rise and fall with market rates of interest. *p. 225*

Free cash flows   Cash flows available to long-term lenders and shareholders after any new investment in assets. *p. 432*

FTSE (Footsie) indices   Indices available to help monitor trends in overall share price movements of Stock Exchange listed businesses. *p. 254*

Future growth value (FGV®)   Value placed on the future growth potential of a business by investors. Equal to the market value of the business – capital invested + EVA®/r. *p. 455*

Gearing ratio   A ratio that relates the contribution of long-term lenders to the total long-term capital of the business. *p. 81*

Golden parachute   Substantial fee payable to a manager of a business in the event the business is taken over. *p. 485*

Gross profit margin   A profitability ratio relating the gross profit for the period to the sales for that period. *p. 70*

Hedging arrangement   An attempt to reduce or eliminate the risk associated with a particular action by taking some form of counteraction. *p. 225*

Horizontal merger   A merger between two businesses in the same industry and at the same point in the production/distribution chain. *p. 466*

Indifference point   The level of profit and interest before taxation at which two, or more, financing schemes provide the same level of return to ordinary shareholders. *p. 329*

Inflation   A rise in the general price level. *p. 125*

Information asymmetry   Where the availability of information differs between groups (such as managers and shareholders). *p. 366*

Information signalling   Conveying information to shareholders through management actions (for example, increasing dividends to convey management optimism concerning the future). *p. 366*

Interest cover ratio   A gearing ratio that divides the net profit before interest and taxation by the interest payable for a period. *p. 81*

Interest rate swap   An arrangement between two businesses whereby each business assumes responsibility for the other's interest payments. *p. 225*

Internal rate of return (IRR)   The discount rate for a project that has the effect of producing zero NPV. *p. 131*

Invoice discounting   A form of finance provided by a financial institution based on a proportion of the face value of the credit sales outstanding. *p. 234*

Junk (high yield) bonds   Loan capital with a relatively high level of investment risk for which investors are compensated by relatively high levels of return. *p. 219*

Just-in-time (JIT) stock management   A system of stock management that aims to have supplies delivered to production just in time for their required use. *p. 396*

Lead time   The time lag between placing an order for goods or services and their delivery. *p. 391*

Linear programming   A mathematical technique for rationing limited resources in such a way as to optimise the benefits. *p. 162*

Liquidation method   A method of valuing the shares of a business by reference to the net realisable values of its net assets. *p. 492*

Loan covenants   Conditions contained within a loan agreement that are designed to protect the lenders. *p. 214*

Market capitalisation   Total market value of the shares of a business. *p. 255*

Market value added (MVA)   The difference between the market value of the business and the total investment that has been made in it. *p. 447*

Materials requirement planning (MRP) system   A computer-based system of stock control that schedules the timing of deliveries of bought-in parts and materials to coincide with production requirements to meet demand. *p. 396*

Merger   When two or more businesses combine in order to form a single business. *p. 466*

Mission statement   A statement setting out the purpose for which a business exists. *p. 9*

Mortgage   A loan secured on property. *p. 215*

Multiple discriminate analysis   A statistical technique used to predict financial distress, which involves using an index based on a combination of financial ratios. *p. 94*

Net present value (NPV)   The net cash flows from a project that have been adjusted to take account of the time value of money. The NPV measure is used to evaluate investment projects. *p. 123*

Net profit margin   A profitability ratio relating the net profit for the period to the sales for that period. *p. 68*

Net realisable value   The selling price of an asset, less any costs incurred in selling the asset. *p. 492*

Non-diversifiable risk   That part of the total risk that is common to all investments and which cannot be diversified away by combining investments. *p. 199*

Normal distribution   The description applied to the distribution of a set of data which, when displayed graphically, forms a symmetrical bell-shaped curve. *p. 193*

Objective probabilities   Probabilities based on information gathered from past experience. *p. 194*

Offer for sale   Method of selling shares to the public through the use of an issuing house which acts as an intermediary. *p. 274*

Operating cash cycle   The time period between the outlay of cash to purchase goods supplied and the ultimate receipt of cash from the sale of the goods. *p. 411*

Operating lease   A short-term lease where the rewards and risks of ownership stay with the owner. *p. 227*

Opportunity cost   The value in monetary terms of being deprived of the next best opportunity in order to pursue the particular objective. *p. 137*

Optimal capital structure   The particular mix of long-term funds employed by a business that minimises the cost of capital. *p. 335*

Overtrading The situation arising when a business is operating at a level of activity that cannot be supported by the amount of finance which has been committed. *p. 91*

Pac-man defence A means of defending against a hostile takeover bid, which involves launching a bid for the bidding company. *p. 485*

Payback period (PP) The time taken for the initial investment in a project to be repaid from the net cash inflows of the project. *p. 120*

PBIT–EPS indifference chart A chart that plots the returns to shareholders at different levels of profit before interest and taxation for different financing schemes. *p. 328*

Per-cent-of-sales method A method of financial planning that first estimates the sales for the planning period and then estimates other financial variables as a percentage of the sales figure. *p. 41*

Placing An issue of shares to selected investors, such as financial institutions, rather than to the public. *p. 275*

Plug The particular form of finance used to fill a financing gap. *p. 42*

Poison pill A defensive measure taken by a business that is designed to make it unattractive to potential acquirers. *p. 485*

Post-completion audit A review of the performance of an investment project to see whether actual performance matched planned performance and whether any lessons can be drawn from the way in which the investment was carried out. *p. 148*

Price/earnings ratio An investment ratio that relates the market value of a share to the earnings per share. *p. 86*

Profitability index The present value of the future cash flows from a project divided by the present value of the outlay. *p. 161*

Projected financial statements Financial statements such as the cash flow statement, profit and loss account and balance sheet that have been prepared on the basis of estimates and which relate to the future. *p. 24*

Public issue Method of issuing shares that involves a direct invitation from the business to the public to subscribe for shares. *p. 274*

Record date A date that is set by the directors of a business to establish who is eligible to receive dividends. Those shareholders registered with the company on this date will receive any dividends announced for the period. *p. 357*

Relevant costs Costs that are relevant to a particular decision. *p. 136*

Replacement cost The cost of replacing an asset with an identical asset. *p. 492*

Residual theory of dividends A theory that states that managers should only make dividend distributions where the expected returns from investment opportunities are below the required rate of return for investors. *p. 370*

Return on capital employed (ROCE) A profitability ratio expressing the relationship between the net profit (before interest and taxation) and the long-term capital invested in the business. *p. 67*

Return on ordinary shareholders' funds (ROSF) A profitability ratio expressing the relationship between the profit available for ordinary shareholders during the period and the ordinary shareholders' funds invested in the business. *p. 66*

Rights issue An issue of shares to existing shareholders on the basis of the number of shares already held. *p. 269*

Risk The likelihood that what is estimated to occur will not actually occur. *p. 44, 124, 170*

Risk premium An extra amount of return from an investment, owing to a perceived level of risk: the greater the perceived level of risk, the larger the risk premium. *p. 125*

Risk-adjusted discount rate (RADR) A method of dealing with risk that involves adjusting the discount rate for projects according to the level of risk involved. The RADR will be the risk-free rate plus an appropriate risk premium. *p. 181*

Risk-averse investors Investors who select the investment with the lowest risk where the returns from different investments are equal. *p. 178*

Risk-neutral investors Investors who are indifferent to the level of risk associated with different investments. *p. 178*

Risk-seeking investors Investors who select the investment with the highest risk where the returns from different investments are equal. *p. 178*

Sale and leaseback An agreement to sell an asset (usually property) to another party and simultaneously lease the asset back in order to continue using the asset. *p. 229*

Sales revenue per employee An efficiency ratio that relates the sales generated during a period to the average number of employees of the business. *p. 75*

Sales revenue to capital employed An efficiency ratio that relates the sales generated during a period to the long-term capital employed. *p. 74*

Satisficing The idea that managers should try to provide each stakeholder group of the business with a satisfactory level of return. *p. 8*

Scenario analysis A method of dealing with risk that involves changing a number of variables simultaneously so as to provide a particular scenario for managers to consider. *p. 45, 176*

Scrip dividend A dividend to shareholders consisting of additional shares rather than cash. *p. 377*

Securitisation Bundling together illiquid financial or physical assets of the same type in order to provide backing for issuing interest-bearing securities, such as bonds. *p. 230*

Security An asset pledged or guarantee provided against a loan. *p. 213*

Semi-variable costs Costs that have an element of both fixed and variable costs. *p. 29*

Sensitivity analysis An examination of the key variables affecting a project to see how changes in each variable might influence the outcome. *p. 45, 170*

Share options A scheme that allows managers and employees to acquire shares in the business at some future date on favourable terms. *p. 14*

Shareholder wealth maximisation The idea that the main purpose of a business is to maximise the wealth of its owners (shareholders). This idea underpins modern financial management. *p. 5*

Shareholder value Putting the needs of shareholders at the heart of management decisions. *p. 428*

Shareholder value analysis (SVA)   Method of measuring and managing business value based on the long-term cash flows generated. *p. 431*

Shortest-common-period-of-time approach   A method of comparing the profitability of projects with unequal lives that establishes the shortest common period of time over which the projects can be compared. *p. 164*

Simulation   A method of dealing with risk that involves calculating probability distributions from a range of possible outcomes. *p. 46, 176*

Spin-off   *See* Demerger. *p. 488*

Standard deviation   A measure of spread that is based on deviations from the mean or expected value. *p. 190*

Stock Exchange   A primary and secondary market for business capital. *p. 252*

Subjective probabilities   Probabilities based on opinion rather than past data. *p. 195*

Subordinated loan   A loan that is ranked below other loan capital in order of interest payment and capital repayment. *p. 215*

Takeover   Normally used to describe a situation where a larger business acquires control of a smaller business, which is then absorbed by the larger business. *p. 466*

Tender issue   An issue of shares to investors that requires the investors to state the amount that they are prepared to pay for the shares. *p. 274*

Term loan   A loan, usually from a bank, which is tailored specifically to the needs of the borrower. The loan contract usually specifies the repayment date, interest rate and so on. *p. 215*

Total shareholder return (TSR)   The change in share value over a period plus any dividends paid during the period. *p. 451*

Univariate analysis   A method used to help predict financial distress, which involves the use of a single ratio as a predictor. *p. 94*

Utility function   A chart that portrays the level of satisfaction or pleasure obtained from receiving additional wealth at different levels of existing wealth. *p. 179*

Value drivers   Key variables that determine business performance. *p. 433*

Variable costs   A cost that varies according to the volume of activity. *p. 29*

Venture capital   Long-term capital provided by certain institutions to small and medium-sized businesses to exploit relatively high risk opportunities. *p. 277*

Vertical merger   A merger between a supplier of goods or services to its customer. *p. 466*

Warrant   A document giving the holder the right, but not the obligation, to acquire shares in a business at an agreed price at some future date. *p. 224*

Weighted average cost of capital (WACE)   A weighted average of the post-tax costs of the forms of long-term finance employed within a business where the market value of the particular forms of finance are used as weights. *p. 314*

White knight   A potential bidder for a business that is approached by the managers of that business to make a bid. The approach is made to defend the business against a hostile bid from another business. *p. 485*

White squire   A business that is approached by the managers of another business to purchase a large block of shares in that business with the object of rescuing the business from a hostile takeover. *p. 485*

Working capital   Current assets less current liabilities. *p. 386*

Zero coupon bonds   Loans that carry a zero rate of interest. *p. 217*

Index